Test and Analysis of Web Services

Luciano Baresi · Elisabetta Di Nitto (Eds.)

Test and Analysis of Web Services

With 140 Figures and 15 Tables

 Springer

Editors

Luciano Baresi

Politecnico di Milano
Dipto. Elettronica Informazione
Piazza Leonardo da Vinci 32
20133 Milano
Italy
baresi@elet.polimi.it

Elisabetta Di Nitto

Politecnico di Milano
Dipto. Elettronica Informazione
Piazza Leonardo da Vinci 32
20133 Milano
Italy
dinitto@elet.polimi.it

Library of Congress Control Number: 2007929741

ACM Computing Classification: H.4, D.2, C.2.4, C.4

ISBN 978-3-540-72911-2 Springer Berlin Heidelberg New York

Springer is a part of Springer Science+Business Media
springer.com
© Springer-Verlag Berlin Heidelberg 2007

Typesetting by the editors
Production: Integra Software Services Pvt. Ltd., Puducherry, India
Cover Design: KünkelLopka, Heidelberg

Printed on acid-free paper   45/3180/Integra   5 4 3 2 1 0

To the contributors of this monograph
and to our super heros

Preface

Web services provide a well-known and language-independent infrastructure for integrating heterogeneous components. Their neutral XML-based standards, along with supporting technology, help us federate components implemented using different programming languages and running on different platforms into a single, coherent system. Web services are a key breakthrough to support the openness, heterogeneity, and flexibility of modern software systems, but there is still a big gap between the underpinnings of the architectural style and its supporting technology. The architectural style embodies dynamism and flexibility, while supporting technologies are still static and rigid. If we concentrate on the main standards proposed to implement the service oriented paradigm, they tend to emphasize interoperability rather than the capability to accommodate seamless changes at runtime. In contrast, many research initiatives are pushing toward the runtime discovery of services and then their dynamic selection. These approaches assume that service discovery—maybe based on some ontologies—can happen while the application executes and thus any possible fault or need to change the intermediaries can be dealt with while the system evolves. These ideas move toward the concept of *self-healing* systems, but also pose new and challenging requirements for the validation of applications heavily based on Web services.

In this monograph, we thoroughly analyze this problem and we try to address its many facets. First of all, since Web service compositions are inherently distributed systems, their validation must not only consider the functional correctness of the different elements, but also tackle the usual problems behind distribution. The composition (of Web services) must not only be fast enough, to properly support users, but also be trustable, secure, and reliable. All these aspects, just to mention the most important ones, tend to widen the usual idea of validation where *functional* and *non-functional* quality dimensions have the same importance for the actual use of the application. Some problems, which were usually addressed before releasing the application, must now be considered while the application executes. The design-time validation of these applications in most cases can only provide some necessary conditions for the actual correctness of the application, while the sufficient conditions must in many cases be studied at runtime.

Given this wide spectrum, and also the relative novelty of the field (i.e., the testing and analysis of Web services), we have tried to conceive a monograph that addresses the different aspects of the field by presenting some state-of-the-art analyses and some interesting approaches proposed by significant research groups—both from industry and academia—worldwide. The different contributions are organized around three main dimensions: (1) static analysis, to acquire significant insights on how the system is supposed to behave, (2) conventional testing techniques, to sample the actual behavior of the system, (3) monitoring, to probe how the system behaves in operation and recovers from anomalous situations if needed. The final part emphasizes specifically the importance of non-functional cross-cutting aspects in the context of web service compositions.

We invite the reader to see this book as a first attempt to provide an organized presentation of what web service validation means in these days. We did our best to cover all the different dimensions, but we are also aware that the novelty and freshness of the field may have produced new and further approaches during the elaboration of this volume. We do hope, indeed, that this initial contribution will pave the road for a more complete and organic book on the subject.

Finally, we warmly thank all the contributors, whose work and ideas are the contents of this volume, the reviewers, who contributed to improve the quality of the different chapters by providing fundamental and constructive advices, and, last but not least, Springer, for their support to the project and for trusting us.

Milan,   *Luciano Baresi*
March 2007   *Elisabetta Di Nitto*

Contents

Part III Monitoring

Part IV Reliability, Security, and Trust

1

Introduction

Luciano Baresi and Elisabetta Di Nitto

Politecnico di Milano – Dipartimento di Elettronica e Informazione
Piazza L. da Vinci, 32 – I20133 Milano (Italy) `baresi|dinitto@elet.polimi.it`

The service-oriented approach is becoming more and more popular to integrate highly heterogeneous systems. Web services are the natural evolution of conventional middleware technologies to support web-based and enterprise-level integration, but the paradigm also serves as basis for other classes of systems such as ambient computing and automotive applications, which require high degree of flexibility and dynamism of configurations. In this scenario, complex applications can be obtained by *discovering* and *composing* existing services. The resulting composition can have the following characteristics:

- It assembles operations supplied by different services, which are owned by different providers.
- Since each provider is in charge of independently maintaining its services, service implementations can change "freely" outside the control of the composition and of its owner.
- Different executions of the same composition can *bind* to different service instances offering similar operations.

In the case the execution of a composition fails to work, the simple shutdown of the system is not a good solution, in general. The execution environment should be able to select new services and even to reorganize their composition if a perfect match does not exist.

The importance of non-functional requirements while setting the composition is another key feature of these systems. Bandwidth, availability, trustworthiness, and many other quality dimensions are as important as functional aspects. Such requirements require *Service Level Agreements* [3, 1] or *QoS contracts* to be negotiated, established, and enforced between service consumers and providers. This is to be true even in case a service does not have full control on the component services it exploits.

The aforementioned characteristics of service-oriented applications make their validation a *continuous process* that often runs in parallel with execution. In fact, it is not possible to clearly distinguish—as it happens for more traditional applications—between the pre-deployment validation of a system and its use, nor it is possible to guarantee that the checks passed at a certain time will be passed at a different time as well.

The required *continuous validation process* has to provide the following key features:

- It has to offer a methodology that embraces the different facets that are relevant for service-centric systems (e.g., functional, load, and stress testing, but also SLA and security checks).
- It has to provide *probes* as a part of the standard execution environment in order to continuously monitor the satisfaction of QoS parameters and to offer proper *test oracles*.
- It has to control the mechanisms to support dynamic binding and replanning of compositions to obtain the same functionality with a different set of services (e.g., two subsequent invocations might become a single call to a different service).

1.1 Aims and Goals

This monograph aims at becoming the starting point for both researchers and practitioners in the field of service-oriented architecture validation and verification approaches. Researchers will find a neat and comprehensive survey of existing approaches, while practitioners will find techniques and tools to improve their current practice and deliver quality service-oriented applications.

Specifically, the monograph aims at providing the following:

- A picture of what validating service-oriented applications means today.
- A comprehensive survey of existing approaches and tools for validating service-oriented applications.
- Detailed guidelines for the actual validation of service-oriented systems.
- References and scenarios for future research (and supporting tools) in the field.

In order to better understand the context in which validation and verification techniques for web services have to work, in Sect. 1.2 of this chapter we define the main concepts that are relevant to the service-oriented domain. In Sect. 1.3 we describe an application example that will be used to introduce the various issues tackled in the book. Finally, Sect. 1.4 discusses some challenges for verification and validation in the reference domain, and Sect. 1.5 presents the structure of the rest of the book.

1.2 Main Concepts Within the Service-Oriented Context

The area of service-oriented architectures is quite young and has attracted the interest of researchers and practitioners coming from different areas: web-based applications, middleware, software engineering, information systems, component-based systems, etc. In order to define the various concepts, we adopt a specific conceptualization that we are defining within the context of a European project called SeCSE [2].

Figure 1.1 shows the main concepts of the domain and the relationships between them. A *Service* is a *Resource* available on the network. It is implemented by a *Software System* and is able to execute some *Operations* through which it serves some *Service Requests*. Thus, while in general services could also be provided by non-software components (e.g., by human beings), we particularly focus our attention here on software services.

A Service can be characterized by one or more *Service Descriptions* usually stored in some *Service Registry*. The various Service Descriptions can provide different views on the same Service. This is useful when a *Service Provider* wants to offer to different *Service Consumers* some specialized view on the Service itself. Service Descriptions are usually composed of the specification (both syntactical and semantical) of the abilities of a service. This *Service Specification* is usually compiled by the same *Service Developer* implementing the Service. In addition, a Service Description can contain *Additional Information* on the Service that are collected while the Service is executing. This information usually concerns the behavior of the service as they are experienced during operation. This can be obtained through monitoring, as a result of a verification activity, or it can be simply inserted by the *Service Consumer* in terms of qualitative data about the efficacy of the Service. Verification, monitoring, or informal validation of a Service all aim at assessing if some *Service Properties* hold for the service and/or its Operations. The Additional Information can be used by consumers to assess if a Service actually behaves as expected based on its specifications.

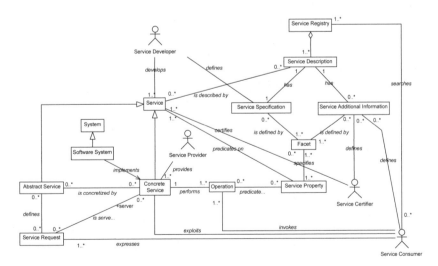

Fig. 1.1. Main concepts of service-oriented systems

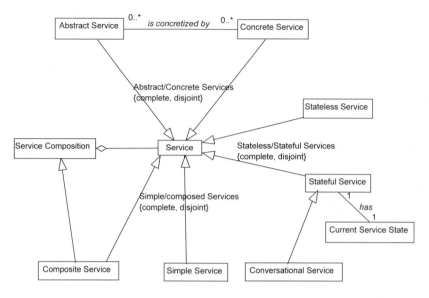

Fig. 1.2. Classification of services

A *Service Composition* is a special kind of Software System that is implemented by composing various Services. A *Composite Service* is, in turn, a Service Composition that behaves like a Service (it offers some Operations to its consumers, usually associated with some Service Descriptions and is able to serve some Service Requests). Services, either simple or composite, can also be orthogonally classified as *Stateful*, in case they keep a conversational state, or *Stateless* in the opposite case. Moreover, they can also be *Concrete* in case they are associated to an actual implementation or *Abstract* in case they simply represent an idea of service. Abstract Services, even if not executable, can still be very useful since they allow a service composition to be developed even if the binding to actual services is delayed to runtime. These classes of services are shown in Fig. 1.2.

1.3 Running Example

The proposal of a common scenario is intended to highlight the main issues we focus on in this monograph. To this end, the proposed scenario is general enough to accommodate the different facets embedded in modern applications based on web services, and to provide sufficient requirements for the applicability of approaches proposed in the subsequent chapters.

Next generation vehicles will be equipped with haptic devices to allow drivers interact with on-board services (e.g., the infotainment system), with the environment that surrounds the vehicle, and with the remote services associated with the user (e.g., the personal organizer).

In this context, John wants to plan a trip with his wife, to celebrate his new car. He starts planning the trip in his office with a laptop. He starts searching for a nice location: it must be close enough to where he lives (say, within 100 miles), by a lake and close to mountains. Moreover, John wants a nice and confortable hotel, where they can rest and enjoy the fitness center. After finding the place, he makes a reservation for a room for the weekend, but since he has to run home, he does not wait for the confirmation from the hotel.

The confirmation message from the hotel arrives on John's mobile while he is returning home. As soon as John acknowledges the reservation, the hotel withdraws the agreed amount of money from his credit card. At home, he describes the almost planned trip to his wife and they start searching for good restaurants and places to see close to the chosen location. Again, they reserve tickets for a couple of museums, and also reserve a table in a nice restaurant by the lake for lunch on Saturday.

The day after, while waiting for his wife, John starts downloading on the haptic device the plan he had created using his laptop and the reservations done at home. Before leaving, they also need a map and a good service to identify the best itinerary to reach the place. Thus, they decide to exploit a simple and cheap map service offering the resolution supported by the haptic device, and asks the itinerary planning service for the fastest way to reach the target.

After the first hour on the highway, the vehicles that move in the opposite direction report on a traffic jam that is ahead of them. If they keep following the planned itinerary, they would be jammed after a few miles. They have to leave the highway, but none of them knows the surroundings. To avoid getting lost, they ask the device to find an alternative path to reach the place. The device then needs to interact with a new (local) service to obtain a new contingency plan to bypass the traffic jam. Such a local service can provide as a result a map with different resolutions at different costs. Given the characteristics of the display, the device automatically negotiates the best resolution that can be displayed and asks the credit card company to pay for it. Since the lowest resolution offered by the service is still too high for the capabilities of the display, the device needs a further service to filter the map.

Everything works fine, and after the detour John and his wife can rejoin the highway and reach the hotel. All the highway fees are paid automatically through the toll system, which in turn interacts with the credit card company for the actual payments.

Before resting and enjoying the environment, John needs to find a parking lot. The hotel has no garage and he needs to find an alternative solution. Once more, John exploits the haptic device to solve the problem. The system highlights a garage not too far from the hotel and asks him if he wants to make a reservation. The garage offers different options and John negotiates the cheapest one. John parks the car and now he is ready to join his wife for the weekend.

1.4 Challenges

From the analysis of the example presented in the previous section various interesting issues arise. In particular, we notice that services can be contextual; for instance, John and his wife have used different map services in different locations. We also notice that some services are actually stateful and are able to maintain a conversational state that allow the user to interact with them through different steps. An example of this is the service that has allowed John to prepare a plan for his trip and to download it on its device the day after. Services are not necessarily for free. Some of them should to be paid (e.g., the map service). Of course in these cases, QoS Contracts, their negotiation (e.g., to select the right download resolution), and the consequent verification are of paramount importance.

Services can be composed together to obtain the desired result. Such a composition can be achieved both through a design level activity or at runtime, as in the case of the composition of the map service and the filter. Indeed, even when a service composition is defined at design time, still, the selection of the component services to be used and their consequent binding to the composition can happen either at deployment time or, dynamically, at runtime, and it can be modified over time depending on various circumstances. In fact, if for any reason a bound service is not anymore available, the simple shutdown of the system is not the solution, in general. The execution environment should be able to select new services and even to reorganize the Composition to find a solution that uses what is available, if a perfect match does not exist.

All the aforementioned aspects make services quite unique elements in the domain of software and introduce new challenges concerning their verification and validation. Indeed, *distributed ownership* of services makes these challenges even more difficult to achieve. This happens whenever a Service Provider decides to modify a component service *after* a Service Composition has been deployed. Changes in the Service Specification of this service component might make it become useless for the composition, or might require re-coding some parts of the composition to make up for the changes. Changes in its implementation, leaving Service Specifications untouched, might be regarded as either good or bad thing. For example, if a map service is improved by augmenting the resolution of the maps it provides, in general this will be regarded as an advantage, but it could turn out to be a problem in the context of portable clients, where the limited display would not allow the user to exploit the benefits of the higher resolution. This resolution, instead, would result even in more costs for the same service. Providers might also change the set of Services they offer, and the un-deployment of Services might leave "holes" in those Compositions that use them.

In general, if Services enter and leave the environment in an unpredictable fashion, this makes reasoning on a system in its entirety very difficult. It is not possible to clearly distinguish—as it happens for more traditional applications—between the pre-deployment validation of a system and its use. This is why continuous approaches to analysis, testing, and monitoring of service-oriented systems appear to be more and more relevant.

1.5 Structure of the Book

Consistently with the issues we have identified, the book is focused on presenting some relevant approaches within three different, but related aspects of verification. These aspects concern the following:

1. Analysis techniques applied to some formal model of a service or of a service composition (see Part I). As we will see, these techniques are exploited during the design phase but, as in the case of the work by van der Aalst and Pesic, they can also support the runtime monitoring part.
2. Testing techniques (see Part II). The ones that we will consider in the book focus on a variety of testing aspects ranging from unit testing of service compositions to regression testing of simple and composite services.
3. Monitoring techniques aiming at continuously checking the execution of a composition (see Part III). As we will see, monitoring can have various objectives (e.g., check if the functionality provided by a service offers a correct result vs check if the availability of the service fulfills the requirements defined in the established SLA) and can be achieved in many different ways. Also, the program used to monitor a composition can be automatically generated at design time.

Among the other aspects to be verified on a service-oriented system, there are some that result to be more critical than others and therefore deserve more attention. We cite here reliability, security, and trust that will be specifically addressed in the last part of the book (see Part IV).

References

1. Andrieux A. et al.: Web Services Agreement Specification. Global Grid Forum, May 2004, available from: http://www.gridforum.org/Meetings/GGF11/Documents/draft-ggf-graap-agreement.pdf
2. M. Di Penta D. Distante M. Zuccalà M. Colombo, E. Di Nitto. Speaking a Common Language: A Conceptual Model for Describing Service-Oriented Systems. In *Proceedings of the 3rd International Conference on Service Oriented Computing*, Amsterdam, The Netherlands, December 2005.
3. R. Kearney R. King A. Keller D. Kuebler H. Ludwig M. Polan M. Spreitzer A. Youssef A. Dan, D. Davis. Web services on demand: Wsla-driven automated management,. *IBM Systems Journal*, 43(1):136–158, March 2004. Special Issue on Utility Computing.

Part I

Analysis

Specifying and Monitoring Service Flows: Making Web Services Process-Aware

W.M.P. van der Aalst and M. Pesic

Department of Technology Management, Eindhoven University of Technology,
P.O.Box 513, NL-5600 MB, Eindhoven, The Netherlands
w.m.p.v.d.aalst@tm.tue.nl,m.pesic@tm.tue.nl

Abstract. BPEL has emerged as the de-facto standard for implementing processes based on web services while formal languages like Petri nets have been proposed as an "academic response" allowing for all kinds of analysis. Although languages such as BPEL and Petri nets can be used to describe service flows, they both tend to "overspecify" the process and this does not fit well with the autonomous nature of services. Therefore, we propose *DecSerFlow* as a *Declarative Service Flow Language*. By using a more declarative style, there is no need to overspecify service flows. The declarative style also makes DecSerFlow an ideal language for monitoring web services, i.e., using process mining techniques it is possible to check the conformance of service flows by comparing the DecSerFlow specification with reality. This can be used to expose services that do not follow the rules of the game. This is highly relevant given the autonomous nature of services.

2.1 Introduction

Web services, an emerging paradigm for architecting and implementing business collaborations within and across organizational boundaries, are currently of interest to both software vendors and scientists [4]. In this paradigm, the functionality provided by business applications is encapsulated within web services: software components described at a semantic level, which can be invoked by application programs or by other services through a stack of Internet standards including HTTP, XML, SOAP [23], WSDL [24], and UDDI [22]. Once deployed, web services provided by various organizations can be interconnected in order to implement business collaborations, leading to *composite web services*.

Today, workflow management systems are readily available [7, 58, 68] and workflow technology is hidden in many applications, e.g., ERP, CRM, and PDM systems. However, their application is still limited to specific industries such as banking and insurance. Since 2000, there has been a growing interest in web services. This resulted in a stack of Internet standards (HTTP,

XML, SOAP, WSDL, and UDDI) which needed to be complemented by a process layer. Several vendors proposed competing languages, e.g., IBM proposed WSFL (Web Services Flow Language) [57] building on FlowMark/MQSeries and Microsoft proposed XLANG (Web Services for Business Process Design) [84] building on Biztalk. BPEL [18] emerged as a compromise between both languages.

The *Business Process Execution Language for Web Services* (BPEL4WS, or BPEL for short) has become the de-facto standard for implementing processes based on web services [18]. Systems such as Oracle BPEL Process Manager, IBM WebSphere Application Server Enterprise, IBM WebSphere Studio Application Developer Integration Edition, and Microsoft BizTalk Server 2004 support BPEL, thus illustrating the practical relevance of this language. Although intended as a language for connecting web services, its application is not limited to cross-organizational processes. It is expected that in the near future a wide variety of process-aware information systems [30] will be realized using BPEL. Whilst being a powerful language, BPEL is difficult to use. Its XML representation is very verbose and readable only to the trained eye. It offers many constructs and typically things can be implemented in many ways, e.g., using links and the flow construct or using sequences and switches. As a result, only experienced users are able to select the right construct. Several vendors offer a graphical interface that generates BPEL code. However, the graphical representations are a direct reflection of the BPEL code and are not intuitive to end-users. Therefore, BPEL is closer to classical programming languages than, e.g., the more user-friendly workflow management systems available today.

In discussions, Petri nets [78] and Pi calculus [67] are often mentioned as two possible formal languages that could serve as a basis for languages such as BPEL. Some vendors claim that their systems are based on Petri nets or Pi calculus and other vendors suggest that they do not need a formal language to base their system on. In essence, there are three "camps" in these discussions: the "Petri net camp," the "Pi calculus" (or process algebra) camp, and the "Practitioners camp" (also known as the "No formalism camp"). This was the reason for starting the "Petri nets and Pi calculus for business processes" working group [76] in June 2004. More than two years later the debate is still ongoing and it seems unrealistic that consensus on a single language will be reached.

This chapter will *discuss the relation between Petri nets and BPEL and show that today it is possible to use formal methods in the presence of languages like BPEL*. However, this will *only be the starting point* for the results presented in this chapter. First of all, we introduce a new language *DecSer-Flow*. Second, we show that *process mining* techniques can be very useful when monitoring web services.

The language *DecSerFlow* is a *Declarative Service Flow Language*, i.e., it is intended to describe processes in the context of web services. The main motivation is that languages like BPEL and Petri nets are procedural by nature, i.e., rather than specifying "what" needs to happen these languages describe "how" things need to be done. For example, it is not easy to specify that anything is allowed as long as the receipt of a particular message is never followed by the sending of another message of a particular type. DecSerFlow allows for the specification of the "what" without having to state the "how." This is similar to the difference between a program and its specification. (For example, one can specify what an ordered sequence is without specifying an algorithm to do so.)

In a service-oriented architecture, a variety of events (e.g., messages being sent and received) are being logged [6, 73]. This information can be used for *process mining* purposes, i.e., based on some event log it is possible to *discover* processes or to *check conformance* [14, 13]. The goal of process discovery is to build models without a priori knowledge, i.e., based on sequences of events one can look for the presence or absence of certain patterns and deduce some process model from it. For conformance checking, there has to be an initial model. One can think of this model as a "contract" or "specification" and it is interesting to see whether the parties involved stick to this model. Using conformance checking it is possible to quantify the fit (fewer deviations result in a better fit) and to locate "problem areas" where a lot of deviations take place.

In this chapter we will show that there is a clear *link between more declarative languages such as DecSerFlow and process mining*. In order to do so, it is important to look at the roles that process specifications can play in the context of web services [94, 95]:

- DecSerFlow can be used as a *global model*, i.e., interactions are described from the viewpoint of an *external observer* who oversees all interactions between all services. Such a model is also called a *choreography model*. Note that such a global model does not need to be executable. However, the model is still valuable as it allows for conformance checking, i.e., by observing interactions it is possible to detect deviations from the agreed upon choreography model. Here DecSerFlow is competing with languages such as the *Web Services Choreography Description Language* (WS-CDL) [54].
- DecSerFlow can be used as a *local model*, i.e., the model that is used to specify, implement, or configure a particular service. Here DecSerFlow is competing with languages such as BPEL [18].

As discussed in [94, 95], it is interesting to link global and local models. Relating global models (that are produced by analysts to agree on interaction scenarios from a global perspective) to local models (that are produced during system design and handed on to implementers) is a powerful way of ensuring that services can work together. Although DecSerFlow can be used at both levels, we will argue that it is particularly useful at the global level. Moreover, we will show that global models can be used to check conformance using process mining techniques.

The remainder of this chapter is organized as follows. Section 2.2 describes the "classical approach" to processes in web services, i.e., Petri nets and BPEL are introduced and pointers are given to state-of-the-art mappings between them. Section 2.3 first discusses the need for a more declarative language and then introduces the DecSerFlow language. In Sect. 2.4 the focus shifts from languages to the monitoring of services. Finally, there is a section on related work (Sect. 2.5) and a conclusion (Sect. 2.6).

2.2 Classical Approaches: BPEL and Petri Nets

Before we introduce the DecSerFlow, we focus on two more traditional languages for the modeling of service flows, i.e., Petri nets and BPEL. Petri nets are more at the conceptual level and can serve only as a theoretical basis for the modeling and analysis of service flows. BPEL is emerging as the de-facto standard for implementing processes based on web services. In this section, we also discuss the link between Petri nets and BPEL and present two tools: one to map Petri nets onto BPEL and another to map BPEL onto Petri nets.

2.2.1 Petri Nets

Petri nets [78] were among the first formalisms to capture the notion of concurrency. They combine an intuitive graphical notation with formal semantics and a wide range of analysis techniques. In recent years, they have been applied in the context of process-aware information systems [30], workflow management [7, 9], and web services [64].

To illustrate the concept of Petri nets we use an example that will be used in the remainder of this chapter. This example is inspired by electronic bookstores such as Amazon and Barnes and Noble and taken from [16]. Figure 2.1 shows a Petri-net that will be partitioned over four partners: (1) the *customer*, (2) the *bookstore* (e.g., Amazon or Barnes and Noble), (3) the *publisher*, and (4) the *shipper*. As discussed in Sect. 2.1, Fig. 2.1 can be considered as a *global model*, i.e., interactions are described from the viewpoint of an external observer who oversees all interactions between all services.

The circles in Fig. 2.1 represent *places* and the squares represent *transitions*. Initially, there is one token in place *start* and all other places are empty (we consider one book order in isolation [7]). Transitions are *enabled* if there is a token on each of input places. Enabled transitions can *fire* by removing one token from each input place and producing one token for each output place. In Fig. 2.1, transition *place_c_order* is enabled. When it fires one token is consumed and two tokens are produced. In the subsequent state (also called marking) transition *handle_c_order* is enabled. Note that transitions *rec_acc* and *rec_decl* are not enabled because only one of their input places is marked with a token.

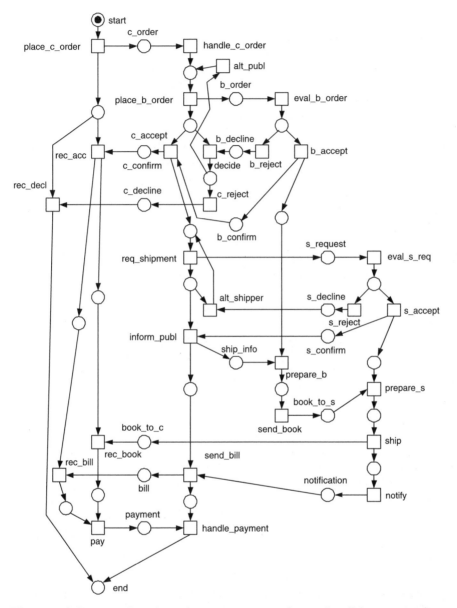

Fig. 2.1. A Petri net describing the process as agreed upon by all four parties (i.e., the global model)

Figure 2.1 represents an inter-organizational workflow that is initiated by a customer placing an order (activity *place_c_order*). This customer order is sent to and handled by the bookstore (activity *handle_c_order*). The electronic bookstore is a virtual company which has no books in stock. Therefore, the bookstore transfers the order of the desired book to a publisher (activity *place_b_order*). We will use the term "bookstore order" to refer to the transferred order. The bookstore order is evaluated by the publisher (activity *eval_b_order*) and either accepted (activity *b_accept*) or rejected (activity *b_reject*). In both cases an appropriate signal is sent to the bookstore. If the bookstore receives a negative answer, it decides (activity *decide*) to either search for an alternative publisher (activity *alt_publ*) or to reject the customer order (activity *c_reject*). If the bookstore searches for an alternative publisher, a new bookstore order is sent to another publisher, etc. If the customer receives a negative answer (activity *rec_decl*), then the workflow terminates. If the bookstore receives a positive answer (activity *c_accept*), the customer is informed (activity *rec_acc*) and the bookstore continues processing the customer order. The bookstore sends a request to a shipper (activity *req_shipment*), the shipper evaluates the request (activity *eval_s_req*) and either accepts (activity *s_accept*) or rejects (activity *b_reject*) the request. If the bookstore receives a negative answer, it searches for another shipper. This process is repeated until a shipper accepts. Note that, unlike the unavailability of the book, the unavailability of a shipper cannot lead to a cancellation of the order. After a shipper is found, the publisher is informed (activity *inform_publ*), the publisher prepares the book for shipment (activity *prepare_b*), and the book is sent from the publisher to the shipper (activity *send_book*). The shipper prepares the shipment to the customer (activity *prepare_s*) and actually ships the book to the customer (activity *ship*). The customer receives the book (activity *rec_book*) and the shipper notifies the bookstore (activity *notify*). The bookstore sends the bill to the customer (activity *send_bill*). After receiving both the book and the bill (activity *rec_bill*), the customer makes a payment (activity *pay*). Then the bookstore processes the payment (activity *handle_payment*) and the inter-organizational workflow terminates.

The Petri net shown in Fig. 2.1 is the so-called "WF-net" (WorkFlow-net) because it has one input place (*start*) and one output place (*end*) and all places' transitions are on a path from *start* to *end*. Using tools such as Woflan [88] or ProM [29], we can show that the process is *sound* [2, 7]. Figure 2.2 shows a screenshot of the Woflan plug-in of ProM. Soundness means that each process instance can terminate without any problems and that all parts of the net can potentially be activated. Given a state reachable from the marking with just a token in place *start*, it is always possible to reach the marking with one token place *end*. Moreover, from the initial state it is possible to enable any transition and to mark any place. Using ProM it is possible to prove that the Petri net shown in Fig. 2.1 is sound, cf. Fig. 2.2.

One can think of the Petri net shown in Fig. 2.1 as the contract between the customer, the bookstore, the publisher, and the shipper (i.e., global model). Clearly, there are many customers, publishers, and shippers. Therefore, the Petri net should be considered as the contract between all customers, publishers, and shippers. However, since we model the processing of an order for a single book, we can assume, without loss of generality, that only one customer, one publisher, and at most one shipper (at any time) are involved. Note that

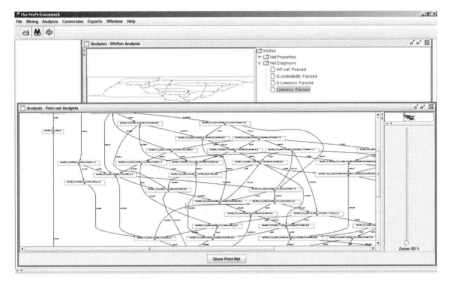

Fig. 2.2. Two analyses plug-in of ProM indicate that the Petri net shown in Fig. 2.1 is indeed sound. The top window shows some diagnostics related to soundness. The bottom window shows part of the state space

Fig. 2.1 abstracts from a lot of relevant things. However, given the purpose of this chapter, we do not add more details.

Figure 2.3 shows the same process but now all activities are partitioned over the four parties involved in the ordering of a book. It shows that each of the parties is responsible for a part of the process. In terms of web services, we can think of each of the four large-shaded rectangles as a service. The Petri-net fragments inside these rectangles can be seen as specifications of the corresponding services (i.e., local models).

It is interesting to point out that in principle multiple shippers could be involved, i.e., the first shipper may decline and then another shipper is contacted, etc. However, at any point in time, at most one shipper is involved in each process instance. Another interesting aspect is the *correlation* between the various processes of the partners. There may be many instances of the process shown in area labeled *bookstore* in Fig. 2.3. However, each instance is unique and messages passed over the places connecting the bookstore to the other partners refer to a particular process instance. In general, it is a non-trivial problem to correlate messages to process instances. See [6, 73] for a more detailed discussion on correlation.

We will refer to whole diagram shown in Fig. 2.3 as the *choreography* or *orchestration* model of the four services.

2.2.2 BPEL

BPEL [18] supports the modeling of two types of processes: executable and abstract processes. An *abstract* (not executable) *process* is a business protocol,

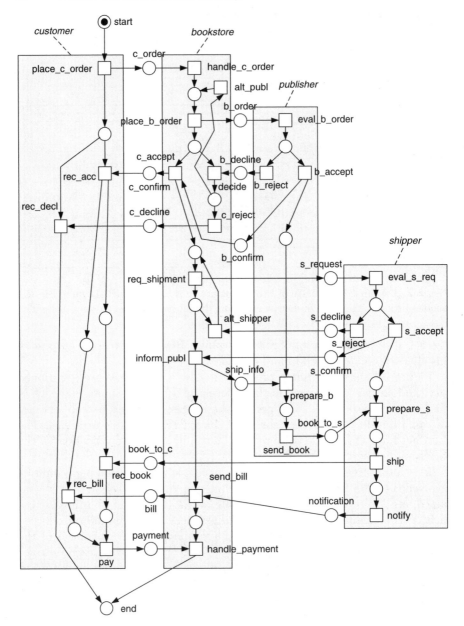

Fig. 2.3. The process as partitioned over (1) the *customer*, (2) the *bookstore*, (3) the *publisher*, and (4) the *shipper* (i.e., four local models and their interconnections)

specifying the message exchange behavior between different parties without revealing the internal behavior of any one of them. This abstract process views the outside world from the perspective of a single organization or (composite) service. An *executable process* views the world in a similar manner; however, things are specified in more detail such that the process becomes executable, i.e., an executable BPEL process specifies the execution order of a number of *activities* constituting the process, the *partners* involved in the process, the *messages* exchanged between these partners, and the *fault* and *exception handling* required in cases of errors and exceptions.

In terms of Fig. 2.3, we can think of *abstract BPEL* as the language to specify one service, i.e., describing the desired behavior of a single Petri-net fragment (e.g., *shipper*). *Executable BPEL* on the other hand can be used as the means to implement the desired behavior.

A BPEL process itself is a kind of flow-chart, where each element in the process is called an *activity*. An activity is either a primitive or a structured activity. The set of *primitive activities* contains *invoke*, invoking an operation on a web service; *receive*, waiting for a message from an external source; *reply*, replying to an external source; *wait*, pausing for a specified time; *assign*, copying data from one place to another; *throw*, indicating errors in the execution; *terminate*, terminating the entire service instance; and *empty*, doing nothing.

To enable the presentation of complex structures the following *structured activities* are defined: *sequence*, for defining an execution order; *switch*, for conditional routing; *while*, for looping; *pick*, for race conditions based on timing or external triggers; *flow*, for parallel routing; and *scope*, for grouping activities to be treated by the same fault-handler. Structured activities can be nested and combined in arbitrary ways. Within activities executed in parallel the execution order can further be controlled by the usage of *links* (sometimes also called control links, or guarded links), which allows the definition of directed graphs. The graphs too can be nested but must be acyclic.

As indicated in Sect. 2.1, BPEL builds on IBM's WSFL (Web Services Flow Language) [57] and Microsoft's XLANG (Web Services for Business Process Design) [84] and combines the features of a block-structured language inherited from XLANG with those for directed graphs originating from WSFL. As a result, simple things can be implemented in two ways. For example, a sequence can be realized using the *sequence* or *flow* elements (in the latter case links are used to enforce a particular order on the parallel elements), a choice based on certain data values can be realized using the *switch* or *flow* elements, etc. However, for certain constructs one is forced to use the block-structured part of the language, e.g., a *deferred choice* [8] can only be modeled using the *pick* construct. For other constructs one is forced to use links, i.e., the more graph-oriented part of the language, e.g., two parallel processes with a one-way synchronization require a *link* inside a *flow*. In addition, there are very subtle restrictions on the use of links: "A link MUST NOT cross the boundary of a while activity, a serializable scope, an event handler or a compensation handler... In addition, a link that crosses a fault-handler boundary MUST be outbound, i.e., it MUST have its source activity within the fault handler and its target activity within a scope that encloses the scope associated with the fault handler. Finally, a link MUST NOT create a control cycle, i.e., the source activity must not have the target activity as a logically preceding activity, where an activity A logically precedes an activity B if the initiation of B semantically requires the completion of A. Therefore, directed graphs created by links are always acyclic" (see p. 64 in [18]). All of this makes the language complex for end-users. A detailed or complete description of BPEL is beyond the scope of this chapter. For more details, the reader is referred to [18] and various web sites such as the web site of the OASIS technical committee on WS-BPEL [70].

2.2.3 BPEL2PN and PN2BPEL

As shown, both BPEL and Petri nets can be used to describe the process-aspect of web services. There are several process engines supporting Petri nets (e.g., COSA, YAWL, etc.) or BPEL (e.g., Oracle BPEL, IBM WebSphere, etc.). BPEL currently has strong industry support while Petri nets offer a graphical language and a wide variety of analysis tools (cf. Fig. 2.2). Therefore, it is interesting to look at the relation between the two. First of all, it is possible to map BPEL onto Petri nets for the purpose of analysis. Second, it is possible to generate BPEL on the basis of Petri nets, i.e., mapping a graphical, more conceptual, language onto a textual language for execution purposes.

Several tools have been developed to map BPEL onto Petri nets (see Sect. 2.5). As a example, we briefly describe the combination formed by BPEL2PNML and WofBPEL developed in close collaboration with QUT [72]. BPEL2PNML translates BPEL process definitions into Petri nets represented in the Petri Net Markup Language (PNML). WofBPEL, built using Woflan [88], applies static analysis and transformation techniques to the output produced by BPEL2PNML. WofBPEL can be used (1) to simplify the Petri net produced by BPEL2PNML by removing unnecessary silent transitions and (2) to convert the Petri net into the so-called "WorkFlow net" (WF-net) which has certain properties that simplify the analysis phase. Although primarily developed for verification purposes, BPEL2PNML and WofBPEL have also been used for conformance checking using abstract BPEL processes [6].

Few people have been working on the translation from Petri nets to BPEL. In fact, [9] is the only work we are aware of that tries to go from (colored) Petri nets to BPEL. Using our ProM tool [29] we can export a wide variety of languages to CPN Tools. For example, we can load Petri-net models coming from tools such as Protos, Yasper, and WoPeD, EPCs coming from tools such as ARIS, ARIS PPM, and EPC Tools, and workflow models coming from tools such as Staffware and YAWL, and automatically convert the control-flow in these models to Petri nets. Using our ProM tool this can then be exported to CPN Tools where it is possible to do further analysis (state space analysis, simulation, etc.). Moreover, WF-nets in CPN Tools can be converted into BPEL using *WorkflowNet2BPEL4WS* [9, 55]. To illustrate this, consider the

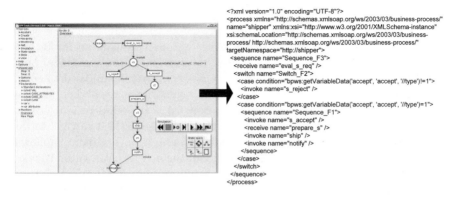

```
<?xml version="1.0" encoding="UTF-8"?>
<process xmlns="http://schemas.xmlsoap.org/ws/2003/03/business-process/"
name="shipper" xmlns:xsi="http://www.w3.org/2001/XMLSchema-instance"
xsi:schemaLocation="http://schemas.xmlsoap.org/ws/2003/03/business-
process/ http://schemas.xmlsoap.org/ws/2003/03/business-process/"
targetNamespace="http://shipper">
  <sequence name="Sequence_F3">
   <receive name="eval_s_req" />
   <switch name="Switch_F2">
    <case condition="bpws:getVariableData('accept', 'accept', '//type')!=1">
     <invoke name="s_reject" />
    </case>
    <case condition="bpws:getVariableData('accept', 'accept', '//type')=1">
     <sequence name="Sequence_F1">
      <invoke name="s_accept" />
      <receive name="prepare_s" />
      <invoke name="ship" />
      <invoke name="notify" />
     </sequence>
    </case>
   </switch>
  </sequence>
</process>
```

Fig. 2.4. The Petri net describing the service offered by the shipper is mapped onto BPEL code using WorkflowNet2BPEL4WS, a tool to automatically translate colored Petri nets into BPEL template code

shipper service shown in Fig. 2.3. The WF-net corresponding to the shipper process was modeled using the graphical editor of the COSA workflow management system. This was automatically converted by Woflan to ProM. Using ProM the process was automatically exported to CPN Tools. Then using WorkflowNet2BPEL4WS the annotated WF-net was translated into BPEL template code. Figure 2.4 shows both the annotated WF-net in CPN Tools (left) and the automatically generated BPEL template code (right).

The availability of the tools and systems mentioned in this section makes it possible to support *service flows*, i.e., the process-aspect of web services, at the design, analysis, and enactment levels. For many applications, BPEL, Petri nets, or a mixture of both provide a good basis for making web services "process-aware." However, as indicated in Sect. 2.1, the focus of this chapter is on DecSerFlow. Section 2.3 introduces DecSerFlow and shows that it is a truly declarative language which addresses the problem of overspecification typically resulting from the procedural languages described in this section. After introducing the language we focus on the monitoring of service flows (Sect. 2.4) specified in terms of DecSerFlow.

2.3 DecSerFlow

The goal of this section is to provide a "fresh view" on process support in the context of web services. We first argue why a more declarative approach is needed and then introduce a concrete language: DecSerFlow.

2.3.1 The Need for More Declarative Languages

Petri nets and BPEL have in common that they are highly procedural, i.e., after the execution of a given activity the next activities are scheduled.[1] Seen

---

[1] Note that both BPEL and Petri nets support the deferred choice pattern [8], i.e., it is possible to put the system in a state where several alternative activities are

from the viewpoint of an execution language the procedural nature of Petri nets and BPEL is not a problem. However, unlike the modules inside a classical system, web services tend to be rather autonomous and an important challenge is that all parties involved need to agree on an overall global process. Currently, terms like *choreography* and *orchestration* are used to refer to the problem of agreeing on a common process. Some researchers distinguish between choreography and orchestration, e.g., "In orchestration, there's someone—the conductor—who tells everybody in the orchestra what to do and makes sure they all play in sync. In choreography, every dancer follows a pre-defined plan—everyone independently of the others." We will not make this distinction and simply assume that *choreographies define collaborations between interacting parties*, i.e., the coordination process of interconnected web services all partners need to agree on. Note that Fig. 2.3 can be seen as an example of a choreography.

Within the Web Services Choreography Working Group of the W3C, a working draft defining version 1.0 of the *Web Services Choreography Description Language* (WS-CDL) has been developed [54]. The scope of WS-CDL is defined as follows: "Using the Web Services Choreography specification, a contract containing a global definition of the common ordering conditions and constraints under which messages are exchanged is produced that describes, from a global viewpoint, the common and complementary observable behavior of all the parties involved. Each party can then use the global definition to build and test solutions that conform to it. The global specification is in turn realized by a combination of the resulting local systems, on the basis of appropriate infrastructure support. The advantage of a contract based on a global viewpoint as opposed to any one endpoint is that it separates the overall global process being followed by an individual business or system within a domain of control (an endpoint) from the definition of the sequences in which each business or system exchanges information with others. This means that, as long as the observable sequences do not change, the rules and logic followed within a domain of control (endpoint) can change at will and interoperability is therefore guaranteed" [54]. This definition is consistent with the definition of choreography just given. Unfortunately, like most standards in the web services stack, CDL is verbose and complex. Somehow the essence as shown in Fig. 2.3 is lost. Moreover, the language again defines concepts such as "sequence," "choice," and "parallel" in some ad hoc notation with unclear semantics. This suggests that some parts of the language are an alternative to BPEL while they are not.

However, the main problem is that WS-CDL, like Petri nets and BPEL, is *not declarative*. A choreography should allow for the specification of the "what" without having to state the "how". This is similar to the difference

---

enabled but the selection is made by the environment (cf. the *pick* construct in BPEL). This allows for more flexibility. However, it does not change the fact that in essence both Petri nets and BPEL are procedural.

between the implementation of a program and its specification. For example, it is close to impossible to describe that within a choreography two messages exclude one another. Note that such an exclusion constraint is not the same as making a choice! To illustrate this, assume that there are two actions A and B. These actions can correspond to exchange of messages or some other type of activity which is relevant for the choreography. The constraint that "A and B exclude one another" is different from making a choice between A or B. First of all, A and B may be executed multiple times, e.g., the constraint is still satisfied if A is executed five times while B is not executed at all. Second, the moment of choice is irrelevant to the constraint. Note that the modeling of choices in a procedural language forces the designer to indicate explicit decision points which are evaluated at explicit decision times. Therefore, there is a tendency to overspecify things.

Therefore, we propose a more declarative approach based on *temporal logic* [61, 74] as described in the following subsection.

2.3.2 DecSerFlow: A Declarative Service Flow Language

Languages such as *Linear Temporal Logic* (LTL) [41, 45, 46] allow for more declarative style of modeling. These languages include temporal operators such as nexttime ($\bigcirc F$), eventually ($\Diamond F$), always ($\Box F$), and until ($F \sqcup G$), cf. Table 2.1. However, such languages are difficult to read. Therefore, we define a graphical syntax for the typical constraints encountered in service flows. The combination of this graphical language and the mapping of this graphical language to LTL forms the *Declarative Service Flow (DecSerFlow) Language*. We propose DecSerFlow for the *specification of a single service, simple service compositions, and more complex choreographies*.

Developing a model in DecSerFlow starts with creating activities. The notion of an activity is like in any other workflow-like language, i.e., an activity is atomic and corresponds to a logical unit of work. However, the nature of the *relations between activities* in DecSerFlow can be quite different than in

Table 2.1. Brief explanation of the basic LTL temporal operators

name	notation	explanation
nexttime	$\bigcirc F$	F has to hold at the next state, e.g., *[A,F,B,C,D,E]*, *[A,F,F,F,F,F,B,C,D,E]*, *[F,F,F,F,A,B,C,D,E]*, etc.
eventually	$\Diamond F$	F has to hold eventually, e.g., *[F,A,B,C,D,E]*, *[A,B,C,F,D,E]*, *[ABFCDFEF]*, etc.
always	$\Box F$	F has to always hold, e.g., *[F,F,F,F,F,F]*.
until	$F \sqcup G$	G holds at the current state or at some future state, and F has to hold until G holds. When G holds F does not have to hold any more. Examples are *[G,A,B,C,D,E]*, *[F,G,A,B,C,D,E]*, *[F,F,F,F,G,A,B,C,D,E]*, *[F,F,F,F,G,A,B,G,F,C,D,E,F,G]*, etc.

traditional procedural workflow languages (like Petri nets and BPEL). For example, places between activities in a Petri net describe causal dependencies and can be used to specify sequential, parallel, alternative, and iterative routing. By using such mechanisms, it is both possible and necessary to strictly define *how* the flow will be executed. We refer to the relations between activities in DecSerFlow as *constraints*. Each of the constraints represents a policy (or a business rule). At any point in time during the execution of a service, each constraint evaluates to *true* or *false*. This value can change during the execution. If a constraint has the value *true*, the referring policy is fulfilled. If a constraint has the value *false*, the policy is violated. The execution of a service is *correct* (according to the DecSerFlow model) at some point in time if all constraints (from the DecSerFlow model) evaluate to *true*. Similarly, a service has *completed correctly* if at the end of the execution all constraints evaluate to *true*. The goal of the execution of any DecSerFlow model is not to keep the values of all constraints *true* at all times during the execution. A constraint which has the value *false* during the execution is not considered an error. Consider, e.g., the LTL expression $\Box(A \longrightarrow \Diamond B)$ where A and B are activities, i.e., each execution of A is eventually followed by B. Initially (before any activity is executed), this LTL expression evaluates to *true*. After executing A the LTL expression evaluates to *false* and this value remains *false* until B is executed. This illustrates that a constraint may be temporarily violated. However, the goal is to end the service execution in a state where all constraints evaluate to *true*.

To create constraints in DecSerFlow, we use *constraint templates*. Each constraint template consists of a formula written in LTL and a graphical representation of the formula. An example is the "response constraint" which is denoted by a special arc connecting two activities A and B. The semantics of such an arc connecting A and B are given by the LTL expression $\Box(A \longrightarrow \Diamond B)$, i.e., any execution of A is eventually followed by B. We have developed a starting set of constraint templates and we will use these templates to create a DecSerFlow model for the electronic bookstore example. This set of templates is inspired by a collection of specification patterns for model checking and other finite-state verification tools [32]. Constraint templates define various types of dependencies between activities at an abstract level. Once defined, a template can be reused to specify constraints between activities in various DecSerFlow models. It is fairly easy to change, remove, and add templates, which makes DecSerFlow an "open language" that can evolve and be extended according to the demands from different domains. There are three groups of templates: (1) "existence," (2) "relation," and (3) "negation" templates. Because a template assigns a graphical representation to an LTL formula, we will refer to such a template as a formula.

Before giving an overview of the initial set of formulas and their notation, we give a small example explaining the basic idea. Figure 2.5 shows a DecSerFlow model consisting of four activities: A, B, C, and D. Each activity is tagged with a constraint describing the number of times the activity should

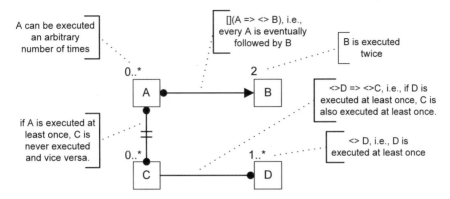

Fig. 2.5. A DecSerFlow model showing some example notations. (Note that the temporal operators ◇ and □ are denoted as <> and [ ])

be executed, these are the so-called "existence formulas." The arc between A and B is an example of a "relation formula" and corresponds to the LTL expression discussed before: $\Box(\ A \longrightarrow \Diamond B\ )$. The connection between C and D denotes another relation formula: $\Diamond D \longrightarrow \Diamond C$, i.e., if D is executed at least once, C is also executed at least once. The connection between A and C denotes a "negation formula" (the LTL expression $\Diamond(A) \Leftrightarrow \neg(\Diamond(B))$ is not shown in diagram but will be explained later). Note that it is not easy to provide a classical procedural model (e.g., a Petri net) that allows for all behavior modeled in Fig. 2.5.

Existence Formulas

Figure 2.6 shows the so-called "existence formulas". These formulas define the cardinality of an activity. For example, the first formula is called *existence* and its visualization is shown (i.e., the annotation "1..*" above the activity). This indicates that A is executed at least once. Formulas *existence2*, *existence3*, and *existence$_N$* all specify a lower bound for the number of occurrences of A. It is also possible to specify an upper bound for the number of occurrences of A. Formulas *absence*, *absence2*, *absence3*, and *absence$_N$* are also visualized by showing the range, e.g., "0...N" for the requirement *absence$_{N+1}$*. Similarly, it is possible to specify the exact number of occurrences as shown in Fig. 2.6, e.g., constraint *exactly$_N$*(A : *activity*) is denoted by an N above the activity and specifies that A should be executed exactly N times.

Table 2.2 provides the semantics for each of the notations shown in Fig. 2.6, i.e., each formula is expressed in terms of an LTL expression. Formula *existence*(A : *activity*) is defined as $\Diamond(A)$, i.e., A has to hold eventually which implies that in any full execution of the process A occurs at least once. Formula *existence$_N$*(A : *activity*) shows how it is possible to express a lower bound N for the number of occurrences of A in a recursive manner, i.e., *existence$_N$*(A) = $\Diamond(A \wedge \bigcirc(existence_{N-1}(A)))$. Formula *absence$_N$*($A$: *activity*) can be defined

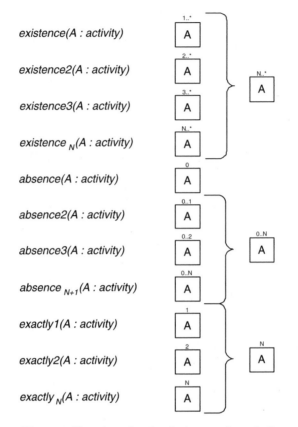

Fig. 2.6. Notations for the "existence formulas"

as the inverse of $existence_N(A)$. Together they can be combined to express that for any full execution, A should be executed a prespecified number N, i.e., $exactly_N(A) = existence_N(A) \wedge absence_{N+1}(A)$.

Relation Formulas

Figure 2.7 shows the so-called "relations formulas." While an "existence formula" describes the cardinality of one activity, a "relation formula" defines relation(s) (dependencies) between multiple activities. Figure 2.7 shows only binary relationships (i.e., between two activities); however, in DecSerFlow there are also notations involving generalizations to three or more activities, e.g., to model an OR-split. For simplicity, however, we first focus on the binary relationships shown in Fig. 2.7. All relation formulas have activities A and B as parameters and these activities are also shown in the graphical representation. The line between the two activities in the graphical representation is unique for the formula, and reflects the semantics of the relation. The *existence_response* formula specifies that if activity A is executed, activity

Table 2.2. Existence formulas

name of formula	LTL expression
$existence(A : activity)$	$\Diamond(A)$
$existence2(A : activity)$	$\Diamond(A \ \wedge \ \bigcirc(existence(A)))$
$existence3(A : activity)$	$\Diamond(A \ \wedge \ \bigcirc(existence2(A)))$
$\ldots$	$\ldots$
$existence_N(A : activity)$	$\Diamond(A \ \wedge \ \bigcirc(existence_{N-1}(A)))$
$absence(A : activity)$	$\Box(\neg A)$
$absence2(A : activity)$	$\neg existence2(A)$
$absence3(A : activity)$	$\neg existence3(A)$
$\ldots$	$\ldots$
$absence_N(A : activity)$	$\neg existence_N(A)$
$exactly1(A : activity)$	$existence(A) \ \wedge \ absence2(A)$
$exactly2(A : activity)$	$existence2(A) \ \wedge \ absence3(A)$
$\ldots$	$\ldots$
$exactly_N(A : activity)$	$existence_N(A) \ \wedge \ absence_{N+1}(A)$

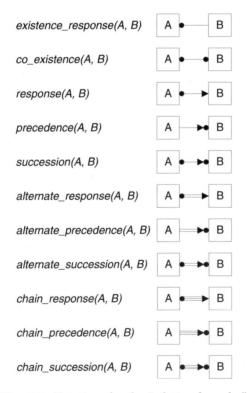

Fig. 2.7. Notations for the "relation formulas"

B also has to be executed (at any time, i.e., either before or after activity *A* is executed). According to the *co-existence* formula, if one of the activities *A* or *B* is executed, the other one has to be executed also. While the first two formulas do not consider the order of activities, formulas *response*, *precedence*, and *succession* do consider the ordering of activities. Formula *response* requires that every time activity *A* executes, activity *B* has to be executed after it. Note that this is a very relaxed relation of response, because *B* does not have to execute straight after *A*, and another *A* can be executed between the first *A* and the subsequent *B*. For example, the execution sequence *[B,A,A,A,C,B]* satisfies the formula *response*. The formula *precedence* requires that activity *B* is preceded by activity *A*, i.e., it specifies that if activity *B* was executed, it could not have been executed until activity *A* was executed. According to this formula, the execution sequence *[A,C,B,B,A]* is correct. The combination of the *response* and *precedence* formulas defines a bi-directional execution order of two activities and is called *succession*. In this formula, both *response* and *precedence* relations have to hold between the activities *A* and *B*. Thus, this formula specifies that every activity *A* has to be followed by an activity *B* and there has to be an activity *A* before every activity *B*. For example, the execution sequence *[A,C,A,B,B]* satisfies the *succession* formula.

Formulas *alternate_response*, *alternate_precedence*, and *alternate_succession* strengthen the *response*, *precedence*, and *succession* formulas, respectively. If activity *B* is *alternate response* of activity *A*, then after the execution of an activity *A* activity *B* has to be executed and between the execution of each two activities *A* at least one activity *B* has to be executed. In other words, after activity *A* there must be an activity *B*, and before that activity *B* there cannot be another activity *A*. The execution sequence *[B,A,C,B,A,B]* satisfies the *alternate response*. Similarly, in the *alternate precedence* every instance of activity *B* has to be preceded by an instance of activity *A* and the next instance of activity *B* cannot be executed before the next instance of activity *A* is executed. According to the *alternate_precedence*, the execution sequence *[A,C,B,A,B,A]* is correct. The *alternate_succession* is a combination of the *alternate_response* and *alternate_precedence* and the sequence *[A,C,B,A,B,A,B]* would satisfy this formula.

Even more strict ordering relations are specified by the last three constraints shown in Fig. 2.7: *chain_response*, *chain_precedence*, and *chain_succession*. These require that the executions of the two activities (*A* and *B*) are next to each other. According to the *chain_response* constraint the first activity after activity *A* has to be activity *B* and the execution *[B,A,B,C,A,B]* would be correct. The *chain_precedence* formula requires that the activity *A* is the activity directly preceding any *B* and, hence, the sequence *[A,B,C,A,B,A]* is correct. Since the *chain_succession* formula is the combination of the *chain_response* and *chain_precedence* formulas, it requires that activities *A* and *B* are always executed next to each other. The execution sequence *[A,B,C,A,B,A,B]* is correct with respect to this formula.

Table 2.3. Relation formulas

name of formula	LTL expression
$existence\_response(A : activity, B : activity)$	$\Diamond(A) \Rightarrow \Diamond(B)$
$co\_existence(A : activity, B : activity)$	$\Diamond(A) \Leftrightarrow \Diamond(B)$
$response(A : activity, B : activity)$	$\Box(A \Rightarrow \Diamond(B))$
$precedence(A : activity, B : activity)$	$\Diamond(B) \Rightarrow ((\neg B) \sqcup A)$
$succession(A : activity, B : activity)$	$response(A, B) \wedge precedence(A, B)$
$alternate\_response(A : activity, B : activity)$	$\Box(A \Rightarrow \bigcirc((\neg A) \sqcup B))$
$alternate\_precedence(A : activity, B : activity)$	$precedence(A, B) \wedge$ $\Box(B \Rightarrow \bigcirc(precedence(A, B)))$
$alternate\_succession(A : activity, B : activity)$	$alternate\_response(A, B) \wedge$ $alternate\_precedence(A, B)$
$chain\_response(A : activity, B : activity)$	$\Box(A \Rightarrow \bigcirc(B))$
$chain\_precedence(A : activity, B : activity)$	$\Box(\bigcirc(B) \Rightarrow A)$
$chain\_succession(A : activity, B : activity)$	$\Box(A \Leftrightarrow \bigcirc(B))$

Table 2.3 shows the formalization of the "relations formulas" depicted in Fig. 2.7. $existence\_response(A, B)$ is specified by $\Diamond(A) \Rightarrow \Diamond(B)$ indicating that some occurrence of A should always imply an occurrence of B either before or after A. $co\_existence(A, B)$ means that the existence of one implies the existence of the other and vice versa, i.e., $\Diamond(A) \Leftrightarrow \Diamond(B)$. $response(A, B)$ is defined as $\Box(A \Rightarrow \Diamond(B))$. This means that at any point in time where activity A occurs there should eventually be an occurrence of B. $precedence(A, B)$ is similar to response but now looking backward, i.e., if B occurs at all, then there should be no occurrence of B before the first occurrence of A. This is formalized as $\Diamond(B) \Rightarrow ((\neg B) \sqcup A)$. Note that we use the $\sqcup$ (until) operator here: $(\neg B) \sqcup A$ means that A holds (i.e., occurs) at the current state or at some future state, and $\neg B$ has to hold until A holds. When A holds $\neg B$ does not have to hold any more (i.e., B may occur). $succession(A, B)$ is defined by combining both into $response(A, B) \wedge precedence(A, B)$. $alternate\_response(A, B)$ is defined as $\Box(A \Rightarrow \bigcirc((\neg A) \sqcup B))$, i.e., any occurrence of A implies that in the next state and onward no A may occur until a B occurs. In other words, after activity A there must be an activity B, and before that activity B occurs there cannot be another activity A. $alternate\_precedence(A, B)$ is a bit more complicated: $\Box((B \wedge \bigcirc(\Diamond(B))) \Rightarrow \bigcirc(A \sqcup B))$. This implies that at any point in time where B occurs and at least one other occurrence of B follows, an A should occur before the second occurrence of B. $alternate\_succession(A, B)$ combines both into $alternate\_response(A, B) \wedge alternate\_precedence(A, B)$. $chain\_response(A, B)$ is defined as $\Box(A \Rightarrow \bigcirc(B))$ indicating that any occurrence of A should be directly followed by B. $chain\_precedence(A, B)$ is the logical counterpart: $\Box(\bigcirc(B) \Rightarrow A)$. $chain\_succession(A, B)$ is defined as $\Box(A \Leftrightarrow \bigcirc(B))$ and specifies that any occurrence of A should be directly followed by B and any occurrence of B should be directly preceded by A.

Negation Formulas

Figure 2.8 shows the "negation formulas," which are the negated versions of the "relation formulas." (Ignore the grouping of constraints on the right-hand side of Fig. 2.8 for the moment. Later, we will show that the eight constraints can be reduced to three equivalence classes.) The first two formulas negate the *existence_response* and *co_existence* formulas. The *neg_exist-ence_response* formula specifies that if activity *A* is executed activity then *B* must never be executed (not before nor after activity *A*). The *neg_co_existence* formula applies *neg_existence_response* from *A* to *B* and from *B* to *A*. It *is important to note that the term* "negation" *should not be interpreted as the* "logical negation," e.g., if activity *A* never occurs, then both *exis-tence_response(A,B)* and *neg_existence_response(A,B)* hold (i.e., one does not exclude the other). The *neg_response* formula specifies that after the execution of activity *A*, activity *B* cannot be executed any more. According to the formula *neg_precedence*, activity *B* cannot be preceded by activity *A*. The last three formulas are negations of formulas *chain_response*, *chain_precedence*, and *chain_succession*. *neg_chain_response* specifies that *A* should never be followed directly by *B*. *neg_chain_precedence* specifies that *B* should never be preceded directly by *A*. *neg_chain_succession* combines both *neg_chain_response* and *neg_chain_precedence*. Note that Fig. 2.8 does not show "negation formulas" for the alternating variants of response, precedence, and succession. The reason is that there is no straightforward and intuitive interpretation of the converse of an alternating response, precedence, or succession.

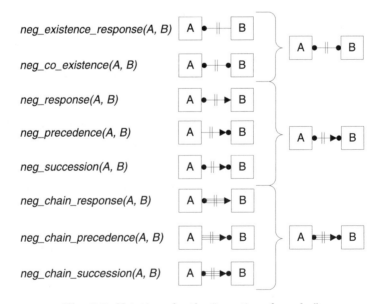

Fig. 2.8. Notations for the "negations formulas"

Table 2.4. Negation formulas (formulas grouped together are equivalent)

name of formula	LTL expression
$neg\_existence\_response(A : activity, B : activity)$	$\Diamond(A) \Rightarrow \neg(\Diamond(B))$
$neg\_co\_existence(A : activity, B : activity)$	$neg\_existence\_response(A, B) \wedge$ $neg\_existence\_response(B, A)$
$neg\_response(A : activity, B : activity)$	$\Box(A \Rightarrow \neg(\Diamond(B)))$
$neg\_precedence(A : activity, B : activity)$	$\Box(\Diamond(B) \Rightarrow (\neg A))$
$neg\_succession(A : activity, B : activity)$	$neg\_response(A, B) \wedge$ $neg\_precedence(A, B)$
$neg\_chain\_response(A : activity, B : activity)$	$\Box(A \Rightarrow \bigcirc(\neg(B)))$
$neg\_chain\_precedence(A : activity, B : activity)$	$\Box(\bigcirc(B) \Rightarrow \neg(A))$
$neg\_chain\_succession(A : activity, B : activity)$	$neg\_chain\_response(A, B) \wedge$ $neg\_chain\_precedence(A, B)$

Table 2.4 shows the LTL expressions of the notations shown in Fig. 2.8. Table 2.4 also shows that some of the notions are equivalent, i.e., *neg_co_existence* and *neg_existence_response* are equivalent and similarly the next two pairs of three formulas are equivalent. Note that a similar grouping is shown in Fig. 2.8 where a single representation for each group is suggested. *neg_existence_ response*(A, B) is defined as $\Diamond(A) \Rightarrow \neg(\Diamond(B))$. However, since the ordering does not matter, $neg\_existence\_response(A, B) = neg\_existence\_response(A, B)$ and hence coincides with $neg\_co\_existence(A, B)$. $neg\_response(A, B)$ is defined as $\Box(A \Rightarrow \neg(\Diamond(B)))$, i.e., after any occurrence of A, B may never happen (or formulated alternatively: any occurrence of B should take place before the first A). $neg\_precedence(A, B)$ is defined as $\Box(\Diamond(B) \Rightarrow (\neg A))$, i.e., if B occurs in some future state, then A cannot occur in the current state. It is easy to see that $neg\_precedence(A, B) = neg\_response(A, B)$ because both state that no B should take place after the first A (if any). Since $neg\_succession(A, B)$ combines both, also $neg\_succession(A, B) = neg\_response(A, B)$. The last three formulas are negations of formulas *chain_response*, *chain_precedence*, and *chain_succession*. It is easy to see that they are equivalent, $neg\_chain\_response(A, B) = neg\_chain\_precedence(A,B) = neg\_chain\_succession(A, B)$.

Figures 2.7 and 2.8 and the corresponding formalizations show only binary relationships. However, these can easily be extended to deal with more activities. Consider, e.g., the *response* relationship, i.e., $response(A, B) = \Box(A \Rightarrow \Diamond(B))$. This can easily be extended to $response(A, B, C) = \Box(A \Rightarrow (\Diamond(B) \vee \Diamond(C)))$, i.e., every occurrence of A is eventually followed by an occurrence of B or C. This can also be extended to a choice following A of N alternatives, i.e., $response(A, A_1, A_2, \ldots, A_N) = \Box(A \Rightarrow (\Diamond(A_1) \vee \Diamond(A_2) \vee \ldots \vee \Diamond(A_N)))$. Many of the other formulas can be generalized in a similar fashion and represented graphically in an intuitive manner. For example, $response(A, B, C)$, i.e., A is eventually followed by an occurrence of B or C, is depicted by multiple arcs that start from the same dot. Similarly, it is possible to have a precedence constraint where different arrows end in the same dot indicating that at least one of the preceding activities should occur before the subsequent activity is executed.

DecSerFlow is an extendible language, i.e., designers can add their own graphical notations and provide their semantics in terms of LTL. For example, one can add constraints similar to the control-flow dependencies in classical languages such as Petri nets, EPCs, etc. and draw diagrams similar to the diagrams provided by these languages. However, the aim is to have a relatively small set of intuitive notations. In this chapter we show only a core set. Figure 2.9 assists in reading diagrams using this core notation. When extending the language with new constraints, it is important to use a set of drawing conventions as shown in Fig. 2.9. For example, a dot connected to some activity A means that "A occurs" and is always associated to some kind of connection, a line without some arrow means "occurs at some point in time," an arrow implies some ordering relation, two short vertical lines depict a negation, etc. Note that Fig. 2.9 also shows the $response(A, A_1, A_2, \ldots, A_N)$ constraint described earlier, i.e., A is followed by at least one of its successors.

2.3.3 The amazon.com Example in DecSerFlow

In this subsection, we revisit the amazon.com example to show how DecSer-Flow language can be used to model services. For this purpose, we will model

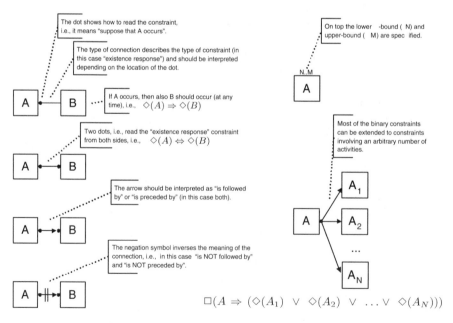

Fig. 2.9. Explanation of the graphical notation

the customer service using existence, relation, and negation formulas. In this way, we will use the defined templates for formulas, apply them to activities from our example and thus create real constraints in our DecSerFlow model. In addition to this model of a single service, we will also show how the communication between services can be presented with DecSerFlow by modeling the communication of the customer service with other services. We start by removing all arcs and places from the example model. This results in an initial DecSerFlow model populated only by unconnected activities. Next, we create necessary constraints for the *customer*. Adding constraints to the rest of the model is straightforward and easy but not necessary for illustrating the DecSerFlow language.

Figure 2.10 shows the new model with DecSerFlow constraints for the *customer*. We added *existence* constraints for all activities which can be seen as cardinality specifications above activities. Activity *place_c_order* has to be executed exactly one time. Activities *rec_acc* and *rec_decl* can be executed zero or one time, depending on the reply of the bookstore. Similarly, activities *rec_book*, *rec_bill*, and *pay* can be executed at most one time.

Every occurrence of *place_c_order* is eventually followed by at least one occurrence of *rec_acc* or *rec_decl*, as indicated by the non-binary relationship also shown in Fig. 2.9. However, it is possible that both activities are executed, and to prevent this we add the *neg_co_existence* constraint between activities *rec_acc* and *rec_decl*. So far, we have managed to make sure that after activity *place_c_order* one of the activities *rec_acc* and *rec_decl* will execute in the service. One problem remains to be solved – we have to specify that none of the activities *rec_acc* and *rec_decl* can be executed before activity *place_c_order*. We achieve this by creating two *precedence* constraints: (1) the one between the activities *place_c_order* and *rec_acc*, making sure that activity *rec_acc* can be executed only after activity *place_c_order* was executed and (2) the one between activities *place_c_order* and *rec_decl*, making sure that activity *rec_decl* can be executed only after activity *place_c_order* was executed. It is important to note that the constraints related to *place_c_order*, *rec_acc*, and *rec_decl* together form a "classical choice". It may seem rather clumsy that four constraints are needed to model a simple choice. However, (1) the four constraints can be merged into a single notation and LTL formula that can be re-used in other diagrams and (2) it is a nice illustration of how procedural languages like Petri nets and BPEL tend to overspecify things. In fact, in a classical language one would not only implicitly specify four elementary constraints but would typically need to specify the data conditions. In DecSerFlow one can add these conditions, but one does not need to do so, i.e., one can drop any of the four constraints involving *place_c_order*, *rec_acc*, and *rec_decl* and still interpret the resulting set of constraints in a meaningful way.

The next decision to be made is the dependency between the activities *rec_acc* and *rec_book*. In the old model, we had a clear sequence between these two activities. However, due to some problems or errors in the bookstore it might happen that, although the order was accepted (activity *rec_acc* is

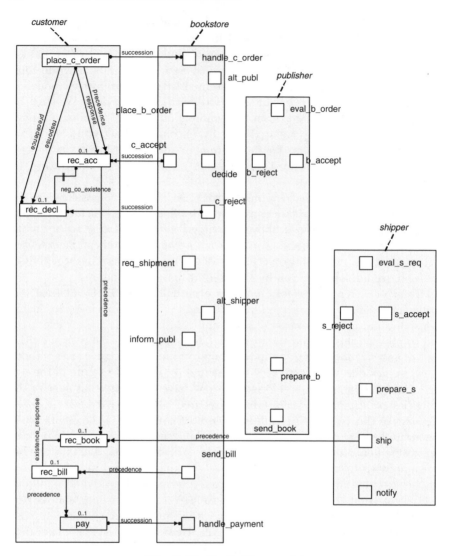

Fig. 2.10. DecSerFlow model

executed), the book does not arrive (activity *rec_book* is not executed). However, we assume that the book will not arrive before the order was accepted. The constraint *precedence* between the activities *rec_acc* and *rec_book* specifies that activity *rec_book* can be executed only after activity *rec_acc* is executed. The old model specified that the bill arrives after the book. This may not be always true. Since the bill and the book are shipped by different services through different channels, the order of their arrival might vary. For example, it might happen that the shipper who sends the book is closer to the location of the customer and the bookstore is on another continent, or the other way around. In the first scenario the book will arrive before the bill, and in the second one the bill will arrive before the book. Therefore, we choose not to create an *ordering* constraint between the activities *rec_book* and *rec_bill*. Even more, our DecSerFlow model accepts the error when the bill arrives even without the book being sent. This could happen in the case of an error in the *bookstore* when a declined order was archived as accepted, and the bill was sent without the shipment of the book. However, we assume that every bookstore that delivers a book, also sends a bill for the book. We specify this with the *existence_response* constraint between the *rec_book* activity and the *rec_bill* activity. This constraint forces that if activity *rec_book* is executed, then activity *rec_bill* must have been executed before or will be executed after activity *rec_book*. Thus, if the execution of activity *rec_book* exists, then the execution of activity *rec_bill* also exists. The constraint *precedence* between the activities *rec_bill* and *pay* means that the customer will pay only after the bill is received. However, after the bill is received the customer does not necessarily pay, like in the old model. It might happen that the received book was not the one that was ordered or it was damaged. In these cases, the customer can decide not to pay the bill.

Besides for the modeling of a single service, DecSerFlow language can as well be used to model the communication between services. In Fig. 2.10, we can see how constraints specify the communication of the customer with the bookstore and the shipper. First, the *succession* constraint between activities *place_c_order* and *handle_c_order* specifies that after activity *place_c_order* activity *handle_c_order* has to be executed, and that activity *handle_c_order* can be executed only after activity *place_c_order*. This means that every order of a customer will be handled in the bookstore, but the bookstore will handle the order only after it is placed. The same holds (constraint *succession*) for the pairs of activities (*c_accept*, *rec_acc*), (*c_reject*, *rec_decl*), and (*pay*, *handle_payment*). The relations between the pairs of activities (*ship*, *rec_book*) and (*send_bill*, *rec_bill*) are more *relaxed* than the previous relations. These two relations are not *succession*, but *precedence*. We can only specify that the book will be received after it is sent, but we cannot claim that the book that was sent will indeed be received. It might happen that the shipment is lost or destroyed before the customer receives the book. The same holds for the bill. Because of this, we create the two *precedence* constraints. The first precedence constraint is between activity *ship* and *rec_book* to specify that activity *rec_book* can be executed only after activity *ship* was executed. The second one is between the activities *send_bill* and *rec_bill*, according to which activity *rec_bill* can be executed only after activity *send_bill* is executed.

Figure 2.10 shows how DecSerFlow language can be used to specify services. While the old Petri-net model specified the strict sequential relations between activities, with DecSerFlow we were able to create many different relations between the activities in a more natural way. For the illustration, we developed constraints only for the *customer* service and its communication with other services, but developing of the rest of the model is as easy and straightforward.

2.3.4 Mapping DecSerFlow Onto Automata

DecSerFlow can be used in many different ways. Like abstract BPEL it can be used to specify services but now in a more declarative manner. However, like executable BPEL we can also use it as an execution language. The DecSerFlow language can be used as an execution language because it is based on LTL expressions. Every constraint in a DecSerFlow model has both a graphical representation and a corresponding parameterized LTL formula. The graphical notation enables a user-friendly interface and masks the underlying formula. The formula, written in LTL, captures the semantics of the constraint. The core of a DecSerFlow model consists of a set of activities and a number of LTL expressions that should all evaluate to *true* at the end of the model execution.

Every LTL formula can be translated into an automaton [26]. Algorithms for translating LTL expressions into automata are given in [40, 92]. The possibility to translate an LTL expression into an automaton and the algorithms to do so have been extensively used in the field of *model checking* [26]. Moreover, the initial purpose for developing such algorithms comes from the need to, given a model, check if certain properties hold in the model. The SPIN tool [50] can be used for the simulation and exhaustive formal verification of systems, and as a proof approximation system. SPIN uses an automata theoretic approach for the automatic verification of systems [86]. To use SPIN, the system first has to be specified in the verification modeling language Promela (PROcess MEta LAnguage) [50]. SPIN can verify the correctness of requirements, which are written as LTL formulas, in a Promela model using the algorithms presented in [40, 48, 49, 51, 52, 86, 77, 91]. When checking the correctness of an LTL formula, SPIN first creates an automaton for the *negation* of the formula. If the intersection of this automaton and the system model automaton is empty, the model is correct with respect to the requirement described in LTL. When the system model does not satisfy the LTL formula, the intersection of the model and the automaton for the negated formula will not be empty, i.e., this intersection is a *counterexample* that shows how the formula is violated. The approach based on the negation of the formula is quicker, because the SPIN runs verification until the first counterexample is found. In the case of the formula itself, the verifier would have to check all possible scenarios to prove that a counterexample does not exist.

Unlike SPIN, which generates an automaton for the negation of the formula, we can execute a DecSerFlow model by constructing an automaton for the *formula itself*. We will use a simple DecSerFlow model to show how processes can be executed by translating LTL formulas into automata. Figure 2.11 shows a DecSerFlow model with three activities: *curse*, *pray*, and *bless*. The only constraint in the model is the *response* constraint between activity *curse* and activity *pray*, i.e., $response(curse, pray) = \Box(curse \Rightarrow \Diamond(pray))$. This

Fig. 2.11. A simple model in DecSerFlow

constraint specifies that if a person curses, she/he should eventually pray after this. Note that there is no restriction on the execution of the activities *pray* and *bless*. There are no existence constraints in this model, because all three activities can be executed an arbitrary number of times.

Using the example depicted in Fig. 2.11, we briefly show the mapping of LTL formulas onto automata [40], which is used for execution of DecSerFlow models. Automata consists of states and transitions. By executing activities of DecSerFlow model, we fire transitions and thus change state of the related automaton. Automaton can be in an accepting or not-accepting state. If the automaton is in an accepting state after executing a certain trace (of DecSerFlow activities), the trace fulfills the related LTL formula. If the automaton is not in an accepting state after executing a certain trace, the trace violates the related LTL formula. Automata created by the algorithm presented in [40] deal with infinite traces and cannot be used for execution of finite traces like DecSerFlow traces. Therefore, a variation of this algorithm that enables work with finite traces is used [41]. A more detailed introduction to automata theory and the creation of Büchi automata from LTL formulas is out of scope of this article and we refer the interested reader to [26, 40, 41, 48].

Figure 2.12 shows a graph representation of the automaton which is generated for the *response* constraint [40].[2] Automaton states are represented as nodes, and transitions as edges. An initial state is represented by an incoming edge with no source node. An accepting state is represented as a node with a double-lined border. The automaton in Fig. 2.12 has two states: *p1* and *p2*. State *p1* is both the initial and accepting state. Note that such automaton can also be generated for a DecSerFlow model with multiple constraints, i.e., for more than one LTL formula, by constructing one *big* LTL formula as a *conjunction* of each of the constraints.

$$response(curse, pray) = \Box(curse \Rightarrow \Diamond(pray))$$

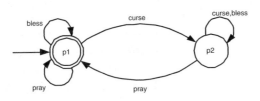

Fig. 2.12. Automaton for the formula response

---

[2] Note that the generated automaton is a non-deterministic automaton. For reasons of simplicity, we use a deterministic automaton with the same results.

Note that for illustration purposes, we only show a simplified automaton in Fig. 2.12. Any LTL expression is, actually, translated into a automaton, i.e, a *non-deterministic* automaton for *infinite words*. An automaton is deterministic if in each state there is exactly one transition for each possible input. In case of a deterministic automaton, we can simply change the state of the automata when executing an activity. To check the correctness of the execution, we check if the current state is an accepting one. In non-deterministic automata, there can be multiple transitions from a given state for a given possible input. In case of a DecSerFlow model, the fact that we are dealing with non-deterministic automata means that executing an activity might transfer an automaton to more that one next state—a *set* of possible states. To check the correctness of the execution, we need to check if the current *set* of possible states contains at least one accepting state. Another issue when executing automata for DecSerFlow models is the fact that we assume that every execution will be completed at some point of time, i.e., an execution of a DecSerFlow model is a *finite* one. The original algorithm for creating automata from LTL expressions generates automata for infinite words, i.e., for infinite executions [40]. That creates problems because the criteria for deciding which states are accepting are different for finite and infinite words. Therefore, we use a modified version of the original algorithm [41], which was constructed for verification of finite software traces. We use the Java PathExplorer (JPAX), a runtime verification tool, as a basis [41]. The algorithm in JPAX assumes that the system will start the execution, and does not consider empty traces. To allow an empty execution of a DecSerFlow model, we add an invisible activity *init* and a constraint *initiate* that specifies that activity *init* has to be executed as the first activity in the model. We automatically execute activity *init* at the beginning of the enactment of a DecSerFlow model. Another small complication is that in the JPAX implementation of [41], the $\bigcirc$ operator is slightly weaker (if there is no next step, $\bigcirc F$ evaluates to true by definition). This can be modified easily by redefining $\bigcirc F$ to $(\bigcirc F \wedge \Diamond F)$.

The mapping for LTL constraints onto automata allows for the guidance of people, e.g., it is possible to show whether a constraint is in an accepting state or not. Moreover, if the automaton of a constraint is not in an accepting state, indicate whether it is still possible to reach an accepting state. To do this, we can color the constraints *green* (in accepting state), *yellow* (accepting state can still be reached), or *red* (accepting state cannot be reached anymore). Using the automaton, some engine could even enforce a constraint, i.e., the automaton could be used to drive a classical workflow engine [7].

2.3.5 Using DecSerFlow to Relate Global and Local Models

In the first part of the chapter, we distinguished between *global* and *local* models. In the global model, interactions are described from the viewpoint of an external observer who oversees all interactions between all services. Local models are used to specify, implement, or configure particular services.

Clearly, both types of models can be represented using DecSerFlow. Moreover, as just shown, it is possible to construct an automaton to enact a DecSerFlow specification. This seems particularly relevant for local models. As we will see in the next section, both global and local models can be used for monitoring services. For example, given a DecSerFlow specification we can also check whether each party involved in a choreography actually sticks to the rules agreed upon. The ProM framework offers the so-called "LTL-checker" to support this (cf. Sect. 2.4.2). However, before focusing on the monitoring of service flows, we briefly discuss the relevance of DecSerFlow in relating global and local models.

Using DecSerFlow both global and local models can be mapped onto LTL expressions and automata. This allows for a wide range of model checking approaches. For example, it is possible to check if the constraints in the local model are satisfied by the global model and vice versa. Note that the set of activities in both models does not need to be the same. However, given the logical nature of DecSerFlow this is not a problem. Also, note that the different notions of inheritance of dynamic behavior can be used in this context [2] (e.g., map activities onto τ actions). The only constraints that seem problematic in this respect are chained relation formulas, i.e., *chain_response*, *chain_precedence*, and *chain_succession*. These use the "nexttime" ($\bigcirc F$) operator whose interpretation depends on the context, i.e., from a global perspective an activity in one service may be followed by an activity in another service thus violating some "nexttime" constraint. Nevertheless, it seems that the LTL foundation of DecSerFlow offers a solid basis for comparing global and local models and generating templates for local models from some partitioned global model.

2.4 Monitoring Service Flows

DecSerFlow can be used to create both local and global models. As shown in the previous section, these models can be used to specify a (part of some) service flow and to enact it. In this section, we show that DecSerFlow can also be used in the context of *monitoring service flows*.

In a service-oriented architecture, and also in classical enterprise systems, a variety of events (e.g., messages being sent and received) are being logged. This information can be used for *process mining* purposes, i.e., based on some event log some knowledge is extracted. In the context of service flows an obvious starting point is the interception of messages exchanged between the various services. For example, SOAP messages can be recorded using TCP Tunneling techniques [6] or, if middleware solutions such as IBM's Websphere are used, different events are logged in a structured manner [73]. Although possible, it is typically not easy to link events (e.g., SOAP messages) to process instances (cases) and activities. However, as pointed out by many researchers, the problem of correlating messages needs to be addressed anyway. Hence, in the remainder, we assume that it is possible to obtain an event log where each event can be linked to some process instance and some activity identifier.

2.4.1 Classification of Process Mining

Assuming that we are able to monitor activities and/or messages being exchanged, a wide range of process mining techniques comes into reach. Before we focus on the relation between DecSerFlow and process mining, we provide a basic classification of process mining approaches. This classification is based on whether there is an a priori model (e.g., a DecSerFlow specification) and, if so, how it is used.

- *Discovery*: There is no a priori model, i.e., based on an event log some model is constructed. For example, using the α algorithm [15] a process model can be discovered based on low-level events. There exist many techniques to automatically construct process models (e.g., in terms of a Petri net) based on some event log [15, 17, 27, 28, 89]. Recently, process mining research also started to target the other perspectives (e.g., data, resources, time, etc.). For example, the technique described in [11] can be used to construct a social network.

- *Conformance*: There is an a priori model. This model is compared with the event log, and discrepancies between the log and the model are analyzed. For example, there may be a process model indicating that purchase orders of more than €1 million require two checks. Another example is the checking of the so-called "four-eyes" principle. Conformance checking may be used to detect deviations, to locate and explain these deviations, and to measure the severity of these deviations. An example is the conformance checker described in [79] which compares the event log with some a priori process model expressed in terms of a Petri net.

- *Extension*: There is an a priori model. This model is extended with a new aspect or perspective, i.e., the goal is not to check conformance but to enrich the model. An example is the extension of a process model with performance data, i.e., some a priori process model is used to project the bottlenecks on. Another example is the decision miner described in [80] which takes an a priori process model and analyzes every choice in the process model. For each choice the event log is consulted to see which information is typically available the moment the choice is made. Then classical data mining techniques are used to see which data elements influence the choice. As a result, a decision tree is generated for each choice in the process.

Figure 2.13 illustrates the classification just given in the context of DecSerFlow. The figure shows different web services together realizing a service flow. A DecSerFlow can be used to specify the whole service flow (global model) or individual services (local models). As shown in Fig. 2.13, we assume that we are able to record events which are stored on some event log. Given such

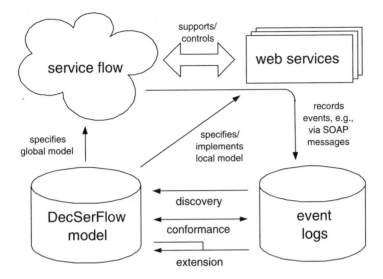

Fig. 2.13. Overview of the various process mining approaches related to DecSerFlow

an event log, the three types of process mining (discovery, conformance, and extension) become possible.

Discovery in the context of DecSerFlow would mean that, based on the event log, we discover a DecSerFlow model, i.e., by analyzing the log different constraints are discovered. For example, if an activity is always followed by another, this can be easily be deduced from the log. Currently, there exist many process discovery approaches [15, 17, 27, 28, 89]. Although none of them is tailored toward DecSerFlow, it is easy to modify these to yield a (partial) DecSerFlow model. Note that ordering relations discovered by the α algorithm [15] can easily be visualized in DecSerFlow.

Conformance checking requires an a priori DecSerFlow model, e.g., a global model showing the overall service flow. This model can easily be compared with the event logs, i.e., each constraint in the DecSerFlow specification is mapped onto an LTL expression and it is easy to check whether the LTL expression holds for a particular process instance. Hence it is possible to classify process instances into conforming or non-conforming for each constraint. This way it is possible to show where and how frequent deviations occur. Moreover, the (non-)conforming process instances can be investigated further using other process mining techniques, e.g., to discover the typical features of cases that deviate.

The third type of process mining also requires an a priori DecSerFlow model. However, now the model is extended with complementary information. For example, performance data are projected onto the DecSerFlow model or decision trees are generated for decision points in the process.

As suggested by Fig. 2.13, DecSerFlow can be used in combination with various process mining approaches. *It is important to note that the autonomous nature of services, the declarative style of modeling (avoiding any overspecification), and process mining fit well together.* The autonomous nature of services allows services to operate relatively independently. In many cases it is not possible to enforce control. At best one can agree on a way of working (the global model) and hope that the other parties involved will operate as promised. However, since it is often not possible to control other services, one can only observe, detect deviations, and monitor performance.

In the remainder of this section, we discuss some of the features of ProM [29]: a process mining framework offering plug-ins for discovery, conformance, and extension.

2.4.2 Linking DecSerFlow to the ProM LTL Checker

The ProM framework [29] is an open-source infrastructure for process mining techniques. ProM is available as open source software (under the Common Public License, CPL) and can be downloaded from [75]. It has been applied to various real-life processes, ranging from administrative processes and healthcare processes to the logs of complex machines and service processes. ProM is plug-able, i.e., people can plug-in new pieces of functionality. Some of the plug-ins are related to model transformations and various forms of model analysis (e.g., verification of soundness, analysis of deadlocks, invariants, reductions, etc.). Most of the plug-ins, however, focus on a particular process mining technique. Currently, there are more than 100 plug-ins of which about half are mining and analysis plug-ins.

Starting point for ProM are event logs in MXML format. The MXML format is system independent and using ProMimport it is possible to extract logs from a wide variety of systems, i.e., systems based on products such as SAP, Peoplesoft, Staffware, FLOWer, WebSphere, YAWL, ADEPT, ARIS PPM, Caramba, InConcert, Oracle BPEL, Outlook, etc. and tailor-made systems. It is also possible to load and/or save a variety of models, e.g., EPCs (i.e., event-driven process chains in different formats, e.g., ARIS, ARIS PPM, EPML, and Visio), BPEL (e.g., Oracle BPEL, Websphere), YAWL, Petri nets (using different formats, e.g., PNML, TPN, etc.), CPNs (i.e., colored Petri nets as supported by CPN Tools), and Protos.

One of the more than 100 plug-ins offered by ProM is the so-called "LTL checker" [3]. The LTL checker offers an environment to provide parameters for predefined parameterized LTL expressions and check these expressions with respect to some event log in MXML format. For each process instance, it is determined whether the LTL expression holds or not, i.e., given an LTL expression all process instances are partitioned into two classes: conforming and nonconforming. We have predefined 60 typical properties one may want to verify using the LTL checker (e.g., the 4-eyes principle) [3]. These can be used without any knowledge of the LTL language. In addition the user can define new sets of properties. These properties may be application specific and may refer to data. Each property is specified in terms of an LTL expression. Formulas may be parameterized, are reusable, and carry explanations in HTML format. This way both experts and novices may use the LTL checker.

Recall that each model element of the DecSerFlow is mapped onto an LTL expression. Therefore, it is possible to use the ProM LTL checker to assess the conformance of a DecSerFlow model in the context of a real log. All notations defined in Figs. 2.6, 2.7, and 2.8 map directly onto LTL expressions that can be stored and loaded into ProM. Currently, we do not yet provide a direct connection between the DecSerFlow editor and the ProM LTL checker. Hence, it is not yet possible to visualize violations on the DecSerFlow editor. However, it is clear that such integration is possible.

2.4.3 Other Process Mining Techniques in ProM

Clearly, the LTL checker is one of the most relevant plug-ins of ProM in the context of DecSerFlow. However, the LTL checker plug-in is only one of more than 100 plug-ins. In this subsection, we show some other plug-ins relevant to process mining of service flows. First, we show some plug-ins related to process discovery. Then, we show the ProM conformance checker that has been successfully used in the context of (BPEL) service flows.

The basic idea of process discovery is to derive a model from some event log. This model is typically a process model. However, there are also techniques to discover organization models, social networks, and more data-oriented models such as decision trees. To illustrate the idea of process mining consider the log shown in Table 2.5. Such a log could have been obtained by monitoring the SOAP messages the *shipper* service in Fig. 2.3 exchanges with it its environment. Note that we do not show the content of the message. Moreover, we do not show additional header information (e.g., information about sender and receiver).

Using process mining tools such as ProM, it is possible to discover a process model as shown in Fig. 2.14. The figure shows the result of three alternative process discovery algorithms: (1) the α miner shows the result in terms of a Petri net, (2) the multi-phase miner shows the result in terms of an EPC, and (3) the heuristics miner shows the result in terms of a heuristics net.[3] They are all able to discover the *shipper* service as specified in Fig. 2.3. Note that Fig. 2.14 shows the names of the messages rather than the activities because this is the information shown in Table 2.5. Note that the algorithms used in Fig. 2.14 can easily be modified to generate DecSerFlow models, i.e., constraints imposed by, e.g., a Petri net can be mapped onto DecSerFlow notations.

For process discovery, we do not assume that there is some a priori model, i.e., without any initial bias we try to find the actual process by analyzing some event log. However, in many applications there is some a priori model. For

---

[3] Note that ProM allows for the mapping from one format to the other if needed. Fig. 2.14 shows the native format of each of the three plug-ins.

Table 2.5. An event log

case identifier	activity identifier	time	data
order290166	s_request	2006-04-02T08:38:00	...
order090504	s_request	2006-04-03T12:33:00	...
order290166	s_confirm	2006-04-07T23:55:00	...
order261066	s_request	2006-04-15T06:43:00	...
order160598	s_request	2006-04-19T20:13:00	...
order290166	book_to_s	2006-05-10T07:31:00	...
order290166	book_to_c	2006-05-12T08:43:00	...
order160598	s_confirm	2006-05-20T07:01:00	...
order210201	s_request	2006-05-22T09:20:00	...
order261066	s_confirm	2006-06-08T10:29:00	...
order290166	notification	2006-06-13T14:44:00	...
order160598	book_to_s	2006-06-14T16:56:00	...
order261066	book_to_s	2006-07-08T18:01:00	...
order090504	s_decline	2006-07-12T09:00:00	...
order261066	book_to_c	2006-08-17T11:22:00	...
order210201	s_decline	2006-08-18T12:38:00	...
order160598	book_to_c	2006-08-25T20:42:00	...
order261066	notification	2006-09-27T09:51:00	...
order160598	notification	2006-09-30T10:09:00	...

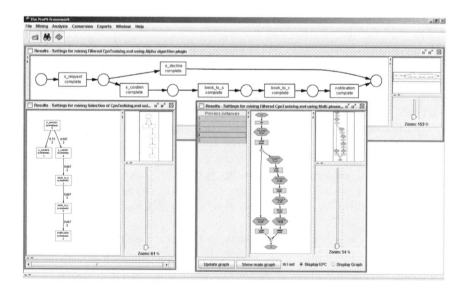

Fig. 2.14. The output of three process discovery algorithms supported by ProM when analyzing the event log shown in Table 2.5

example, we already showed that ProM's LTL checker can be used to check the conformance of a DecSerFlow model. However, ProM is not limited to DecSerFlow and can also be used to check the conformance of a specification in terms of abstract BPEL, EPC, or Petri nets. To illustrate this, assume that we add an additional process instance to Table 2.5 where the notification is sent before the book is shipped to the customer (i.e., in Fig. 2.3 activity *notify* takes place before activity *ship*).

If we assume there is some a priori model in terms of a Petri net, we can use the *conformance checker plug-in* of ProM. Figure 2.15 shows the result of this analysis (top-right corner). It shows that the *fitness* is 0.962 and also highlights the part of the model where the deviation occurs (the place connecting *ship/book_to_c* and *notify/notification*). An event log and Petri net "fit" if the Petri net can generate each trace in the log. In other words, the Petri net describing the choreography should be able to "parse" every event sequence observed by monitoring, e.g., SOAP messages. In [79] it is shown that it is possible to quantify fitness as a measure between 0 and 1. The intuitive meaning is that a fitness close to 1 means that all observed events can be explained by the model (in the example about 96 percent). However, the precise meaning is more involved since tokens can remain in the network and not all transactions in the model need to be logged [79].

Unfortunately, a good fitness does not only imply conformance, e.g., it is easy to construct Petri nets that are able to parse any event log (corresponding to a DecSerFlow model without any constraints, i.e., a model described by *true*). Although such Petri nets have a fitness of 1 they do

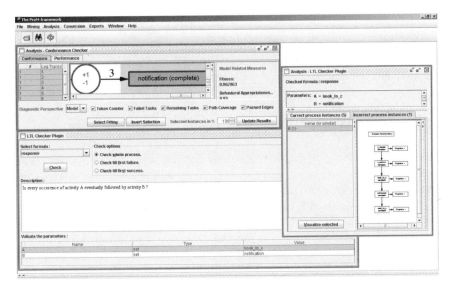

Fig. 2.15. Both the conformance checker plug-in and the LTL checker plug-in are able to detect the deviation

not provide meaningful information. Therefore, we use a second dimension: *appropriateness*. Appropriateness tries to capture the idea of *Occam's razor*, i.e., "one should not increase, beyond what is necessary, the number of entities required to explain anything." Appropriateness tries to answer the following question: "Does the model describe the observed process in a suitable way" and can it be evaluated from both a *structural* and a *behavioral* perspective? To explain the concept in more detail, it is important to note that there are two extreme models that have a fitness of 1. First of all, there is a model that starts with a choice and then has one path per process instance, i.e., the model simply enumerates all possibilities. This model is "overfitting" since it is simply another representation of the log, i.e., it does not allow for more sequences than those that were observed in the log. Therefore, it does not offer a better understanding than what can be obtained by just looking at the aggregated log. Secondly, there is the so-called "flower Petri net" [79] that can parse any log, i.e., there is one state in which all activities are enabled. This model is "underfitting" since it contains no information about the ordering of activities. In [79] it is shown that a "good" process model should somehow be minimal in structure to clearly reflect the described behavior, referred to as *structural appropriateness*, and minimal in behavior in order to represent as closely as possible what actually takes place, which will be called *behavioral appropriateness*. The ProM conformance checker supports both the notion of fitness and the various notions of appropriateness.

In [6] we have demonstrated that any (abstract) BPEL specification can automatically be mapped onto a Petri net that can be used for conformance checking using ProM's conformance checker.

Figure 2.15 also shows the LTL checker plug-in while checking the *response* property on *book_to_c* and *notification*. This check shows that indeed there is one process instance where activity *notify* takes place before activity *ship*. This example shows that it is possible to compare a DecSerFlow specification and an event log and to locate the deviations.

2.5 Related Work

Since the early 1990s, workflow technology has matured [39] and several textbooks have been published, e.g., [7, 30]. Most of the available systems use some proprietary process modeling language and, even if systems claim to support some "standard," there are often all kinds of system-specific extensions and limitations. Petri nets have been used not only for the modeling of workflows [7, 25, 30] but also for the orchestration of web services [65]. Like most proprietary languages and standards, Petri nets are highly procedural. This is the reason why we introduced the DecSerFlow language in this chapter.

Several attempts have been made to capture the behavior of BPEL [18] in some formal way. Some advocate the use of finite state machines [35], others process algebras [34], and yet others abstract state machines [33] or Petri nets [71, 62, 83, 87]. (See [71] for a more detailed literature review.) For a detailed analysis of BPEL based on the workflow patterns [8], we refer to [90]. Few researchers have explored the other direction, e.g., translating (Colored) Petri nets into BPEL [9].

The work presented in this chapter is also related to the choreography language "Let's Dance" [94, 95]. Let's Dance is a language for modeling service interactions and their flow dependencies. The focus of Let's Dance is not so much on the process perspective (although a process modeling notation is added); instead, it focuses on interaction patterns and mechanisms. Similar to DecSerFlow it is positioned as an alternative to the Web Services Choreography Description Language (WS-CDL) [54].

Clearly, this chapter builds on earlier work on process discovery, i.e., the extraction of knowledge from event logs (e.g., process models [15, 17, 27, 37, 38, 47] or social networks [12]). For example, the well-known α algorithm [15] can derive a Petri net from an event log. In [6] we used the conformance checking techniques described in [79] and implemented in our ProM framework [29] and applied this approach to SOAP messages generated from Oracle BPEL. The notion of conformance has also been discussed in the context of security [10], business alignment [1], and genetic mining [66].

It is impossible to give a complete overview of process mining here. Therefore, we refer to a special issue of Computers in Industry on process mining [14] and a survey paper [13]. Process mining can be seen in the broader context of Business (Process) Intelligence (BPI) and Business Activity Monitoring (BAM). In [43, 44, 81] a BPI toolset on top of HP's Process Manager is described. The BPI toolset includes the so-called "BPI Process Mining Engine." In [69] Zur Muehlen describes the PISA tool which can be used to extract performance metrics from workflow logs. Similar diagnostics are provided by the ARIS Process Performance Manager (PPM) [53]. The latter tool is commercially available and a customized version of PPM is the Staffware Process Monitor (SPM) [85] which is tailored toward mining Staffware logs.

The need for monitoring web services has been raised by other researchers. For example, several research groups have been experimenting with adding monitor facilities via SOAP monitors in Axis [19]. Reference [56] introduces an assertion language for expressing business rules and a framework to plan and monitor the execution of these rules. Reference [21] uses a monitoring approach based on BPEL. Monitors are defined as additional services and linked to the original service composition. Another framework for monitoring the compliance of systems composed of web-services is proposed in [60]. This approach uses event calculus to specify requirements. Reference [59] is an approach based on WS-Agreement defining the Crona framework for the creation and monitoring of agreements. In [42, 31], Dustdar et al. discuss the concept of web services mining and envision various levels (web service operations, interactions, and workflows) and approaches. Our approach fits in their framework and shows that web-services mining is indeed possible. In [73] a tool named the Web Service Navigator is presented to visualize the execution of web services based on SOAP messages. The authors use message sequence diagrams and graph-based representations of the system topology. Note that also in [5] we suggested to focus less on languages like BPEL and more on questions related to the monitoring of web services. In [6] we showed that it is possible to translate abstract BPEL into Petri nets and SOAP messages exchanged between services into event logs represented using the MXML format (i.e., the format used by our process mining tools). As a result, we could demonstrate that it is possible to compare the modeled behavior (in terms of a Petri net) and the observed behavior (in some event log). We used Oracle BPEL and demonstrated that it is possible to monitor SOAP messages using TCP Tunneling technique [6]. This comparison could be used for monitoring deviations and to analyze the most frequently used parts of the service/choreography.

This chapter discussed the idea of conformance checking by comparing the observed behavior recorded in logs with some predefined model. This could be termed "run-time conformance." However, it is also possible to address the issue of *design-time conformance*, i.e., comparing different process models before enactment. For example, one could compare a specification in abstract BPEL with an implementation using executable BPEL. Similarly, one could check at design-time the compatibility of different services. Here one can use the inheritance notions [2] explored in the context of workflow management and implemented in Woflan [88]. Axel Martens et al. [62, 63, 64, 82] have explored questions related to design-time conformance and compatibility using a Petri-net-based approach. For example, [63] focuses on the problem of consistency between executable and abstract processes and [64] presents an approach where for a given composite service the required other services are generated. Also related is [36] where Message Sequence Charts (MSCs) are compiled into the "Finite State Process" notation to describe and reason about web service compositions.

2.6 Conclusion

This chapter focused on *service flows* from the viewpoint of both specification/enactment and monitoring.

First, we discussed more traditional approaches based on Petri nets and BPEL. We showed that Petri nets provide a nice graphical representation and a wide variety of analysis techniques, and mentioned that BPEL has strong industry support making it a viable execution platform. We also showed that there are mappings from BPEL to Petri net for the purpose of analysis (cf. BPEL2PNML and WofBPEL [72]). Moreover, it is possible to translate graphical languages such a Petri nets to BPEL (cf. WorkflowNet2BPEL4WS [55]). Using such techniques, it is also possible to translate languages such as EPCs, BPMN, etc. to BPEL.

Although the first author has been involved in the development of these tools and these tools are mature enough to be applied in real-life applications, both Petri nets and BPEL are rather procedural and this does not fit well with the autonomous nature of services. Therefore, we proposed a new, more declarative language, *DecSerFlow*. Although DecSerFlow is graphical, it is grounded in temporal logic. It can be used for the *enactment* of processes, but it is particularly suited for the *specification* of a single service or a complete choreography. In the last part of this chapter, the focus shifted from languages to process mining. We showed that the combination of DecSerFlow and process mining (conformance checking in particular) is useful in the setting of web services. Moreover, we showed that DecSerFlow can be combined well with the conformance-checking techniques currently implemented in ProM (cf. the LTL checker plug-in).

DecSerFlow also seems to be an interesting proposal for linking global and local models. If both the global model (i.e., the view on the process as seen by some external observer) and one or more local models (i.e., the specification or implementation of a single service or service composition) are modeled in DecSerFlow, standard model checking techniques can be used to compare both.

To conclude, we would like to mention that all of the presented analysis and translation tools can be downloaded from various web sites: [75] (ProM), [20] (BPEL2PNML and WofBPEL), and [93] (WorkflowNet2BPEL4WS).

References

1. W.M.P. van der Aalst. Business Alignment: Using Process Mining as a Tool for Delta Analysis. In J. Grundspenkis and M. Kirikova, editors, *Proceedings of the 5th Workshop on Business Process Modeling, Development and Support (BPMDS'04)*, volume 2 of *Caise'04 Workshops*, pages 138–145. Riga Technical University, Latvia, 2004.
2. W.M.P. van der Aalst and T. Basten. Inheritance of Workflows: An Approach to Tackling Problems Related to Change. *Theoretical Computer Science*, 270 (1-2):125–203, 2002.
3. W.M.P. van der Aalst, H.T. de Beer, and B.F. van Dongen. Process Mining and Verification of Properties: An Approach based on Temporal Logic. In R. Meersman and Z. Tari et al., editors, *On the Move to Meaningful Internet Systems 2005: CoopIS, DOA, and ODBASE: OTM Confederated International Conferences, CoopIS, DOA, and ODBASE 2005*, volume 3760 of *Lecture Notes in Computer Science*, pages 130–147. Springer-Verlag, Berlin, 2005.
4. W.M.P. van der Aalst, M. Dumas, and A.H.M. ter Hofstede. Web Service Composition Languages: Old Wine in New Bottles? In G. Chroust and C. Hofer, editors, *Proceeding of the 29th EUROMICRO Conference: New Waves in System Architecture*, pages 298–305. IEEE Computer Society, Los Alamitos, CA, 2003.
5. W.M.P. van der Aalst, M. Dumas, A.H.M. ter Hofstede, N. Russell, H.M.W. Verbeek, and P. Wohed. Life After BPEL? In M. Bravetti, L. Kloul, and

G. Zavattaro, editors, *WS-FM 2005*, volume 3670 of *Lecture Notes in Computer Science*, pages 35–50. Springer-Verlag, Berlin, 2005.

6. W.M.P. van der Aalst, M. Dumas, C. Ouyang, A. Rozinat, and H.M.W. Verbeek. Choreography Conformance Checking: An Approach based on BPEL and Petri Nets (extended version). BPM Center Report BPM-05-25, BPMcenter.org, 2005.

7. W.M.P. van der Aalst and K.M. van Hee. *Workflow Management: Models, Methods, and Systems*. MIT press, Cambridge, MA, 2002.

8. W.M.P. van der Aalst, A.H.M. ter Hofstede, B. Kiepuszewski, and A.P. Barros. Workflow Patterns. *Distributed and Parallel Databases*, 14(1):5–51, 2003.

9. W.M.P. van der Aalst, J.B. Jørgensen, and K.B. Lassen. Let's Go All the Way: From Requirements via Colored Workflow Nets to a BPEL Implementation of a New Bank System Paper. In R. Meersman and Z. Tari et al., editors, *On the Move to Meaningful Internet Systems 2005: CoopIS, DOA, and ODBASE: OTM Confederated International Conferences, CoopIS, DOA, and ODBASE 2005*, volume 3760 of *Lecture Notes in Computer Science*, pages 22–39. Springer-Verlag, Berlin, 2005.

10. W.M.P. van der Aalst and A.K.A. de Medeiros. Process Mining and Security: Detecting Anomalous Process Executions and Checking Process Conformance. In N. Busi, R. Gorrieri, and F. Martinelli, editors, *Second International Workshop on Security Issues with Petri Nets and other Computational Models (WISP 2004)*, pages 69–84. STAR, Servizio Tipografico Area della Ricerca, CNR Pisa, Italy, 2004.

11. W.M.P. van der Aalst, H.A. Reijers, and M. Song. Discovering Social Networks from Event Logs. *Computer Supported Cooperative work*, 14(6):549–593, 2005.

12. W.M.P. van der Aalst and M. Song. Mining Social Networks: Uncovering Interaction Patterns in Business Processes. In J. Desel, B. Pernici, and M. Weske, editors, *International Conference on Business Process Management (BPM 2004)*, volume 3080 of *Lecture Notes in Computer Science*, pages 244–260. Springer-Verlag, Berlin, 2004.

13. W.M.P. van der Aalst, B.F. van Dongen, J. Herbst, L. Maruster, G. Schimm, and A.J.M.M. Weijters. Workflow Mining: A Survey of Issues and Approaches. *Data and Knowledge Engineering*, 47(2):237–267, 2003.

14. W.M.P. van der Aalst and A.J.M.M. Weijters, editors. *Process Mining*, Special Issue of Computers in Industry, Volume 53, Number 3. Elsevier Science Publishers, Amsterdam, 2004.

15. W.M.P. van der Aalst, A.J.M.M. Weijters, and L. Maruster. Workflow Mining: Discovering Process Models from Event Logs. *IEEE Transactions on Knowledge and Data Engineering*, 16(9):1128–1142, 2004.

16. W.M.P. van der Aalst and M. Weske. The P2P approach to Interorganizational Workflows. In K.R. Dittrich, A. Geppert, and M.C. Norrie, editors, *Proceedings of the 13th International Conference on Advanced Information Systems Engineering (CAiSE'01)*, volume 2068 of *Lecture Notes in Computer Science*, pages 140–156. Springer-Verlag, Berlin, 2001.

17. R. Agrawal, D. Gunopulos, and F. Leymann. Mining Process Models from Workflow Logs. In *Sixth International Conference on Extending Database Technology*, pages 469–483, 1998.

18. T. Andrews, F. Curbera, H. Dholakia, Y. Goland, J. Klein, F. Leymann, K. Liu, D. Roller, D. Smith, S. Thatte, I. Trickovic, and S. Weerawarana. Business

Process Execution Language for Web Services, Version 1.1. Standards proposal by BEA Systems, International Business Machines Corporation, and Microsoft Corporation, 2003.

19. Apache Axis, http://ws.apache.org/axis/.

20. BABEL, Expressiveness Comparison and Interchange Facilitation Between Business Process Execution Languages, http://www.bpm.fit.qut.edu.au/ projects/babel/tools/.

21. L. Baresi, C. Ghezzi, and S. Guinea. Smart Monitors for Composed Services. In *ICSOC '04: Proceedings of the 2nd International Conference on Service Oriented Computing*, pages 193–202, New York, NY, USA, 2004. ACM Press.

22. T. Belwood and et al. UDDI Version 3.0. http://uddi.org/pubs/uddi_v3. htm, 2000.

23. D. Box, D. Ehnebuske, G. Kakivaya, A. Layman, N. Mendelsohn, H. Nielsen, S. Thatte, and D. Winer. Simple Object Access Protocol (SOAP) 1.1. http://www.w3.org/TR/soap, 2000.

24. E. Christensen, F. Curbera, G. Meredith, and S. Weerawarana. Web Services Description Language (WSDL) 1.1. http://www.w3.org/TR/wsdl, 2001.

25. P. Chrzastowski-Wachtel. A Top-down Petri Net Based Approach for Dynamic Workflow Modeling. In W.M.P. van der Aalst, A.H.M. ter Hofstede, and M. Weske, editors, *International Conference on Business Process Management (BPM 2003)*, volume 2678 of *Lecture Notes in Computer Science*, pages 336–353. Springer-Verlag, Berlin, 2003.

26. E.M. Clarke, O. Grumberg, and D.A. Peled. *Model Checking*. The MIT Press, Cambridge, Massachusetts and London, UK, 1999.

27. J.E. Cook and A.L. Wolf. Discovering Models of Software Processes from Event-Based Data. *ACM Transactions on Software Engineering and Methodology*, 7(3):215–249, 1998.

28. A. Datta. Automating the Discovery of As-Is Business Process Models: Probabilistic and Algorithmic Approaches. *Information Systems Research*, 9(3): 275–301, 1998.

29. B.F. van Dongen, A.K. Alves de Medeiros, H.M.W. Verbeek, A.J.M.M. Weijters, and W.M.P. van der Aalst. The ProM framework: A New Era in Process Mining Tool Support. In G. Ciardo and P. Darondeau, editors, *Application and Theory of Petri Nets 2005*, volume 3536 of *Lecture Notes in Computer Science*, pages 444–454. Springer-Verlag, Berlin, 2005.

30. M. Dumas, W.M.P. van der Aalst, and A.H.M. ter Hofstede. *Process-Aware Information Systems: Bridging People and Software through Process Technology*. Wiley & Sons, 2005.

31. S. Dustdar, R. Gombotz, and K. Baina. Web Services Interaction Mining. Technical Report TUV-1841-2004-16, Information Systems Institute, Vienna University of Technology, Wien, Austria, 2004.

32. M.B. Dwyer, G.S. Avrunin, and J.C. Corbett. Patterns in Property Specifications for Finite-State Verification. In *ICSE '99: Proceedings of the 21st international conference on Software engineering*, pages 411–420, Los Alamitos, CA, USA, 1999. IEEE Computer Society Press.

33. D. Fahland and W. Reisig. ASM-based semantics for BPEL: The negative control flow. In D. Beauquier and E. Börger and A. Slissenko, editor, *Proc. 12th International Workshop on Abstract State Machines*, pages 131–151, Paris, France, March 2005.

34. A. Ferrara. Web services: A process algebra approach. In *Proceedings of the 2nd international conference on Service oriented computing*, pages 242–251, New York, NY, USA, 2004. ACM Press.

35. J.A. Fisteus, L.S. Fernández, and C.D. Kloos. Formal verification of BPEL4WS business collaborations. In K. Bauknecht, M. Bichler, and B. Proll, editors, *Proceedings of the 5th International Conference on Electronic Commerce and Web Technologies (EC-Web '04)*, volume 3182 of *Lecture Notes in Computer Science*, pages 79–94, Zaragoza, Spain, August 2004. Springer-Verlag, Berlin.

36. H. Foster, S. Uchitel, J. Magee, and J. Kramer. Model-based Verification of Web Service Composition. In *Proceedings of 18th IEEE International Conference on Automated Software Engineering (ASE)*, pages 152–161, Montreal, Canada, October 2003.

37. W. Gaaloul, S. Bhiri, and C. Godart. Discovering Workflow Transactional Behavior from Event-Based Log. In R. Meersman, Z. Tari, W.M.P. van der Aalst, C. Bussler, and A. Gal et al., editors, *On the Move to Meaningful Internet Systems 2004: CoopIS, DOA, and ODBASE: OTM Confederated International Conferences, CoopIS, DOA, and ODBASE 2004*, volume 3290 of *Lecture Notes in Computer Science*, pages 3–18, 2004.

38. W. Gaaloul and C. Godart. Mining Workflow Recovery from Event Based Logs. In W.M.P. van der Aalst, B. Benatallah, F. Casati, and F. Curbera, editors, *Business Process Management (BPM 2005)*, volume 3649, pages 169–185. Springer-Verlag, Berlin, 2005.

39. D. Georgakopoulos, M. Hornick, and A. Sheth. An Overview of Workflow Management: From Process Modeling to Workflow Automation Infrastructure. *Distributed and Parallel Databases*, 3:119–153, 1995.

40. R. Gerth, D. Peled, M.Y. Vardi, and P. Wolper. Simple On-The-Fly Automatic Verification of Linear Temporal Logic. In *Proceedings of the Fifteenth IFIP WG6.1 International Symposium on Protocol Specification, Testing and Verification XV*, pages 3–18, London, UK, 1996. Chapman & Hall, Ltd.

41. D. Giannakopoulou and K. Havelund. Automata-based verification of temporal properties on running programs. In *ASE '01: Proceedings of the 16th IEEE international conference on Automated software engineering*, page 412, Washington, DC, USA, 2001. IEEE Computer Society.

42. R. Gombotz and S. Dustdar. On Web Services Mining. In M. Castellanos and T. Weijters, editors, *First International Workshop on Business Process Intelligence (BPI'05)*, pages 58–70, Nancy, France, September 2005.

43. D. Grigori, F. Casati, M. Castellanos, U. Dayal, M. Sayal, and M.C. Shan. Business Process Intelligence. *Computers in Industry*, 53(3):321–343, 2004.

44. D. Grigori, F. Casati, U. Dayal, and M.C. Shan. Improving Business Process Quality through Exception Understanding, Prediction, and Prevention. In P. Apers, P. Atzeni, S. Ceri, S. Paraboschi, K. Ramamohanarao, and R. Snodgrass, editors, *Proceedings of 27th International Conference on Very Large Data Bases (VLDB'01)*, pages 159–168. Morgan Kaufmann, 2001.

45. K. Havelund and G. Rosu. Monitoring Programs Using Rewriting. In *Proceedings of the 16th IEEE International Conference on Automated Software Engineering (ASE'01)*, pages 135–143. IEEE Computer Society Press, Providence, 2001.

46. K. Havelund and G. Rosu. Synthesizing Monitors for Safety Properties. In *Proceedings of the 8th International Conference on Tools and Algorithms for the*

Construction and Analysis of Systems (TACAS 2002), volume 2280 of *Lecture Notes in Computer Science*, pages 342–356. Springer-Verlag, Berlin, 2002.

47. J. Herbst. A Machine Learning Approach to Workflow Management. In *Proceedings 11th European Conference on Machine Learning*, volume 1810 of *Lecture Notes in Computer Science*, pages 183–194. Springer-Verlag, Berlin, 2000.

48. G.J. Holzmann. The Model Checker SPIN. *IEEE Trans. Softw. Eng.*, 23(5): 279–295, 1997.

49. G.J. Holzmann. An Analysis of Bitstate Hashing. *Form. Methods Syst. Des.*, 13(3):289–307, 1998.

50. G.J. Holzmann. *The SPIN Model Checker: Primer and Reference Manual.* Addison-Wesley, Boston, Massachusetts, USA, 2003.

51. G.J. Holzmann and D. Peled. An Improvement in Formal Verification. In *FORTE 1994 Conference*, Bern, Switzerland, 1994.

52. G.J. Holzmann, D. Peled, and M. Yannakakis. On nested depth-first search. In *The Spin Verification System, Proceedings of the 2nd Spin Workshop.)*, pages 23–32. American Mathematical Society, 1996.

53. IDS Scheer. ARIS Process Performance Manager (ARIS PPM): Measure, Analyze and Optimize Your Business Process Performance (whitepaper). IDS Scheer, Saarbruecken, Gemany, http://www.ids-scheer.com, 2002.

54. N. Kavantzas, D. Burdett, G. Ritzinger, T. Fletcher, and Y. Lafon. Web Services Choreography Description Language, Version 1.0. W3C Working Draft 17-12-04, 2004.

55. K.B. Lassen and W.M.P. van der Aalst. WorkflowNet2BPEL4WS: A Tool for Translating Unstructured Workflow Processes to Readable BPEL. BETA Working Paper Series, WP 167, Eindhoven University of Technology, Eindhoven, 2006.

56. A. Lazovik, M. Aiello, and M. Papazoglou. Associating Assertions with Business Processes and Monitoring their Execution. In *ICSOC '04: Proceedings of the 2nd International Conference on Service Oriented Computing*, pages 94–104, New York, NY, USA, 2004. ACM Press.

57. F. Leymann. Web Services Flow Language, Version 1.0, 2001.

58. F. Leymann and D. Roller. *Production Workflow: Concepts and Techniques.* Prentice-Hall PTR, Upper Saddle River, New Jersey, USA, 1999.

59. H. Ludwig, A. Dan, and R. Kearney. Crona: An Architecture and Library for Creation and Monitoring of WS-agreements. In *ICSOC '04: Proceedings of the 2nd International Conference on Service Oriented Computing*, pages 65–74, New York, NY, USA, 2004. ACM Press.

60. K. Mahbub and G. Spanoudakis. A Framework for Requirents Monitoring of Service Based Systems. In *ICSOC '04: Proceedings of the 2nd International Conference on Service Oriented Computing*, pages 84–93, New York, NY, USA, 2004. ACM Press.

61. Z. Manna and A. Pnueli. *The Temporal Logic of Reactive and Concurrent Systems: Specification.* Springer-Verlag, New York, 1991.

62. A. Martens. Analyzing Web Service Based Business Processes. In M. Cerioli, editor, *Proceedings of the 8th International Conference on Fundamental Approaches to Software Engineering (FASE 2005)*, volume 3442 of *Lecture Notes in Computer Science*, pages 19–33. Springer-Verlag, Berlin, 2005.

63. A. Martens. Consistency between executable and abstract processes. In *Proceedings of International IEEE Conference on e-Technology, e-Commerce, and e-Services (EEE'05)*, pages 60–67. IEEE Computer Society Press, 2005.

64. P. Massuthe, W. Reisig, and K. Schmidt. An Operating Guideline Approach to the SOA. In *Proceedings of the 2nd South-East European Workshop on Formal Methods 2005 (SEEFM05)*, Ohrid, Republic of Macedonia, 2005.

65. M. Mecella, F. Parisi-Presicce, and B. Pernici. Modeling E-service Orchestration through Petri Nets. In *Proceedings of the Third International Workshop on Technologies for E-Services*, volume 2644 of *Lecture Notes in Computer Science*, pages 38–47. Springer-Verlag, Berlin, 2002.

66. A.K.A. de Medeiros, A.J.M.M. Weijters, and W.M.P. van der Aalst. Using Genetic Algorithms to Mine Process Models: Representation, Operators and Results. BETA Working Paper Series, WP 124, Eindhoven University of Technology, Eindhoven, 2004.

67. R. Milner. *Communicating and Mobile Systems: The Pi-Calculus.* Cambridge University Press, Cambridge, UK, 1999.

68. M. zur Muehlen. *Workflow-based Process Controlling: Foundation, Design and Application of workflow-driven Process Information Systems.* Logos, Berlin, 2004.

69. M. zur Mühlen and M. Rosemann. Workflow-based Process Monitoring and Controlling - Technical and Organizational Issues. In R. Sprague, editor, *Proceedings of the 33rd Hawaii International Conference on System Science (HICSS-33)*, pages 1–10. IEEE Computer Society Press, Los Alamitos, California, 2000.

70. OASIS Web Services Business Process Execution Language (WSBPEL) TC, http://www.oasis-open.org/committees/tc_home.php?wg_abbrev=wsbpel.

71. C. Ouyang, W.M.P. van der Aalst, S. Breutel, M. Dumas, A.H.M. ter Hofstede, and H.M.W. Verbeek. Formal Semantics and Analysis of Control Flow in WS-BPEL. BPM Center Report BPM-05-15, BPMcenter.org, 2005.

72. C. Ouyang, E. Verbeek, W.M.P. van der Aalst, S. Breutel, M. Dumas, and A.H.M. ter Hofstede. WofBPEL: A Tool for Automated Analysis of BPEL Processes. In B. Benatallah, F. Casati, and P. Traverso, editors, *Proceedings of Service-Oriented Computing (ICSOC 2005)*, volume 3826 of *Lecture Notes in Computer Science*, pages 484–489. Springer-Verlag, Berlin, 2005.

73. W. De Pauw, M. Lei, E. Pring, L. Villard, M. Arnold, and J.F. Morar. Web Services Navigator: Visualizing the Execution of Web Services. *IBM Systems Journal*, 44(4):821–845, 2005.

74. A. Pnueli. The Temporal Logic of Programs. In *Proceedings of the 18th IEEE Annual Symposium on the Foundations of Computer Science*, pages 46–57. IEEE Computer Society Press, Providence, 1977.

75. Process Mining Home Page, http://www.processmining.org.

76. Process Modelling Group, http://process-modelling-group.org.

77. A. Puri and G.J. Holzmann. A Minimized automaton representation of reachable states. In *Software Tools for Technology Transfer*, volume 3. Springer-Verlag, Berlin, 1993.

78. W. Reisig and G. Rozenberg, editors. *Lectures on Petri Nets I: Basic Models*, volume 1491 of *Lecture Notes in Computer Science*. Springer-Verlag, Berlin, 1998.

79. A. Rozinat and W.M.P. van der Aalst. Conformance Testing: Measuring the Fit and Appropriateness of Event Logs and Process Models. In C. Bussler et al., editor, *BPM 2005 Workshops (Workshop on Business Process Intelligence)*,

volume 3812 of *Lecture Notes in Computer Science*, pages 163–176. Springer-Verlag, Berlin, 2006.

80. A. Rozinat and W.M.P. van der Aalst. Decision Mining in ProM. In S. Dustdar, J.L. Faideiro, and A. Sheth, editors, *International Conference on Business Process Management (BPM 2006)*, volume 4102 of *Lecture Notes in Computer Science*, pages 420–425. Springer-Verlag, Berlin, 2006.

81. M. Sayal, F. Casati, U. Dayal, and M.C. Shan. Business Process Cockpit. In *Proceedings of 28th International Conference on Very Large Data Bases (VLDB'02)*, pages 880–883. Morgan Kaufmann, 2002.

82. B.H. Schlingloff, A. Martens, and K. Schmidt. Modeling and model checking web services. *Electronic Notes in Theoretical Computer Science: Issue on Logic and Communication in Multi-Agent Systems*, 126:3–26, mar 2005.

83. C. Stahl. Transformation von BPEL4WS in Petrinetze (In German). Master's thesis, Humboldt University, Berlin, Germany, 2004.

84. S. Thatte. XLANG Web Services for Business Process Design, 2001.

85. TIBCO. TIBCO Staffware Process Monitor (SPM). http://www.tibco.com, 2005.

86. M.Y. Vardi and P. Wolper. An automata-theoretic approach to automatic program verification. In *In Proceedings of the 1st Symposium on Logic in Computer Science*, pages 322–331, Cambridge, Massachusetts, USA, 1986.

87. H.M.W. Verbeek and W.M.P. van der Aalst. Analyzing BPEL Processes using Petri Nets. In D. Marinescu, editor, *Proceedings of the Second International Workshop on Applications of Petri Nets to Coordination, Workflow and Business Process Management*, pages 59–78. Florida International University, Miami, Florida, USA, 2005.

88. H.M.W. Verbeek, T. Basten, and W.M.P. van der Aalst. Diagnosing Workflow Processes using Woflan. *The Computer Journal*, 44(4):246–279, 2001.

89. A.J.M.M. Weijters and W.M.P. van der Aalst. Rediscovering Workflow Models from Event-Based Data using Little Thumb. *Integrated Computer-Aided Engineering*, 10(2):151–162, 2003.

90. P. Wohed, W.M.P. van der Aalst, M. Dumas, and A.H.M. ter Hofstede. Analysis of Web Services Composition Languages: The Case of BPEL4WS. In I.Y. Song, S.W. Liddle, T.W. Ling, and P. Scheuermann, editors, *22nd International Conference on Conceptual Modeling (ER 2003)*, volume 2813 of *Lecture Notes in Computer Science*, pages 200–215. Springer-Verlag, Berlin, 2003.

91. P. Wolper and D. Leroy. Reliable hashing without collision detection. In *Proc. 5th Int. Conference on Computer Aided Verification*, pages 59–70, 1993.

92. P. Wolper, M.Y. Vardi, and A.P. Sistla. Reasoning about Infinite Computation Paths. In *Proceedings of the 24th IEEE symposium on foundation of cumputer science*, pages 185–194, Tucson, Arizona, November 1983.

93. WorkflowNet2BPEL4WS,   http://www.daimi.au.dk/~krell/WorkflowNet2BPEL4WS/.

94. J.M. Zaha, A. Barros, M. Dumas, and A.H.M. ter Hofstede. Let's Dance: A Language for Service Behavior Modeling. QUT ePrints 4468, Faculty of Information Technology, Queensland University of Technology, 2006.

95. J.M. Zaha, M. Dumas, A.H.M. ter Hofstede, A. Barros, and G. Dekker. Service Interaction Modeling: Bridging Global and Local Views. QUT ePrints 4032, Faculty of Information Technology, Queensland University of Technology, 2006.

3

Analyzing Conversations: Realizability, Synchronizability, and Verification

Tevfik Bultan[1], Xiang Fu[2], and Jianwen Su[1]

[1] Department of Computer Science, University of California, Santa Barbara, CA 93101, USA {bultan,su}@cs.ucsb.edu
[2] School of Computer and Information Science, Georgia Southwestern State University, 800 Wheatley Street, Americus, GA 31709, USA xfu@canes.gsw.edu

Abstract. Conversations provide an intuitive and simple model for analyzing interactions among composite web services. A conversation is the global sequence of messages exchanged among the peers participating in a composite web service. Interactions in a composite web service can be analyzed by investigating the temporal properties of its conversations. Conversations can be specified in a top-down or bottom-up manner. In a top-down conversation specification, the set of conversations is specified first, without specifying the individual behaviors of the peers. In a bottom-up conversation specification, on the other hand, behavior of each peer is specified separately and the conversation set is defined implicitly as the set of conversations generated by these peers. For both top-down and bottom-up specification approaches we are interested in the following: (1) Automatically verifying properties of conversations and (2) investigating the effect of asynchronous communication on the conversation behavior. These two issues are closely related since asynchronous communication with unbounded queues increases the difficulty of automated verification significantly.

In this chapter, we give an overview of our earlier results on analysis and verification of conversations. We discuss two analysis techniques for identifying bottom-up and top-down conversation specifications that can be automatically verified. Synchronizability analysis identifies bottom-up conversation specifications for which the conversation set remains the same for asynchronous and synchronous communication. Realizability analysis, on the other hand, identifies top-down conversation specifications which can be implemented by a set of finite state peers interacting with asynchronous communication. We discuss sufficient conditions for synchronizability and realizability analyses which are implemented in our Web Service Analysis Tool (WSAT). WSAT can be used for verification of LTL properties of both top-down and bottom-up conversation specifications.

3.1 Introduction

Web services provide a promising framework for development, integration, and interoperability of distributed software applications. Wide-scale adoption of the web services technology in critical business applications will depend on the feasibility of building highly dependable services. Web services technology enables interaction of software components across organizational boundaries. In such a distributed environment, it is critical to eliminate errors at the design stage, before the services are deployed.

One of the important challenges in static analysis and verification of web services is dealing with asynchronous communication. Asynchronous communication makes most analysis and verification problems undecidable, even when the behaviors of web services are modeled as finite state machines. In this chapter, we give an overview of our earlier results on analysis and verification of interactions among web services in the presence of asynchronous communication.

In our formal model, we assume that a composite web service consists of a set of individual services (peers) which interact with each other using asynchronous communication. In asynchronous communication, the sender and the receiver of a message do not synchronize their send and receive actions. The sender can send a message even when the receiver is not ready to receive that message. When a message arrives, it is stored in the receiver's message buffer. Message buffers are typically implemented as FIFO queues, i.e., messages in a message buffer are processed in the order they arrive. A message will wait in the message buffer without being processed until it moves to the head of the message buffer and the receiver becomes available to consume it by executing a receive action.

Asynchronous communication is important for building robust web services [5]. Since asynchronous communication does not require the sender and the receiver to synchronize during message exchange, temporary pauses in availability of the services and delays in the delivery of the messages can be tolerated. In practice, asynchronous messaging is supported by message delivery platforms such as Java Message Service (JMS) [26] and Microsoft Message Queuing Service (MSMQ) [32].

Although asynchronous communication improves the robustness of web services, it also increases the complexity of design and verification of web service compositions as demonstrated by the two examples below.

Example 1 Consider a small portion of the example from Chap. 1, where the GPS device of the traveler automatically negotiates a purchase agreement with two existing map service providers. Fig. 3.1a provides a *top-down* specification of this composition. There are three peers, the traveler (T), map provider 1 (M_1), and map provider 2 (M_2). Assume that before the composition starts, a "call for bid" message has been broadcast to both map providers. The finite state machine in Fig. 3.1 describes the bidding process. Intuitively, the protocol specifies that the first bidder will win the contract. Fig. 3.1b demonstrates a sample implementation for all peers involved in the composition. For each peer the sample implementation is generated by a *projection* operation. Given a protocol (represented as a finite state machine) and a peer to project

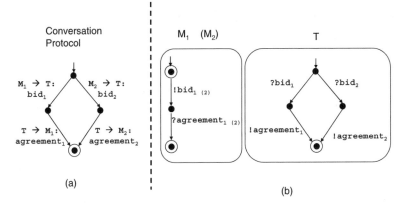

Fig. 3.1. An unrealizable design due to asynchronous communication

to, the projection operation replaces the transitions that are labeled with a message that is neither sent nor received by the given peer by ϵ edges, and then minimizes the resulting automaton.

Now, let us consider whether this protocol is *realizable*, i.e., if there are implementations for all peers, whose composition can generate exactly the same set of global behaviors as specified by the protocol automaton in Fig. 3.1a. If *synchronous communication* is used, the protocol can be executed without any problem. Synchronous communication is similar to communicating with telephone calls, but without answering machines. For a message exchange to occur, the sender and the receiver both have to be on the phone at the same time. With synchronous communication, the peer implementations shown in Fig. 3.1b can generate exactly the conversation set as specified by Fig. 3.1a. Notice that according to these implementations, at the beginning stage, both map service providers call the traveler to bid. When the first bidder successfully makes the call, the traveler, according to the protocol, will not answer any other calls. Hence the call by the second bidder will not go through and the winner is decided. The second bidder will just stay in its initial state, which is also one of its final states.

If we continue with the telephone analogy, *asynchronous communication* is similar to communicating with answering machines where each phone call results in a message that is recorded to the answering machine of the callee. The callee retrieves the messages from the answering machine in the order they are received. If the peer implementations shown in Fig. 3.1b interact with asynchronous communication, then the map service providers do not have to synchronize their send actions with the traveler's receive actions. For example, if asynchronous communication is used, at the initial state, both map service providers can send out the *bid* messages. However, in such a scenario only one of them will successfully complete the transaction, and the other will be stuck waiting for an answer and it will never reach a final state. To put it another way, if asynchronous communication is used then the composition of these three peers can generate a global behavior that is not described in the protocol given in Fig. 3.1a. One such undesired behavior can be described using the following sequence of messages:

$$M_1 \rightarrow T : bid_1; \ M_2 \rightarrow T : bid_2; \ T \rightarrow M_1 : agreement.$$

This behavior results with the map service provider 2 being stuck because the traveler will never respond to his request. Again using the telephone analogy, in this scenario, both map providers call the traveler and leave a bid message in the traveler's answering machine. However, based on its state machine (shown on the right side of Fig. 3.1b) the traveler listens to only the first bid message in its answering machine and calls back the map provider that left the first message. The other map provider never hears back from the traveler and is stuck at an intermediate state waiting for a call.

A conversation protocol specified as a finite state machine is realizable if and only if it is realized by its projections to all peers [16]. Hence, the protocol in Fig. 3.1 is not realizable.

Figure 3.1 is an example of how asynchronous communication complicates the design of composite web services. In the next example given below, we discuss how asynchronous communication affects the complexity of verification. This time we consider bottom-up specification of web services.

Example 2 Assume that the GPS device of the traveler needs to invoke the service of the map service provider for a new map whenever the vehicle moves one mile away from its old position. Fig. 3.2 presents two different sets of implementations for the GPS device and the map service provider. Note that we are assuming that the interaction mechanism is asynchronous communication.

The map provider replies to each request message (req) that the client sends with a map data message (map); the interaction terminates when the GPS device sends an end message. In Fig. 3.2a, the GPS device does not wait for a map message from the provider after it sends a req message. In the resulting global behavior, the req and map messages can be interleaved arbitrarily, except that at any moment the number of req messages is greater than or equal to the number of map messages. In Fig. 3.2b, the GPS device waits for a map message before it sends the next req message. Now the question is, which composition is *easier* to verify?

We can show that Fig. 3.2b is easier to verify because it falls into a category of compositions called *synchronizable* web service compositions. A synchronizable composition produces the same set of conversations under both synchronous and asynchronous communication semantics. When all the peers involved in a composition are finite state machines, their composition using synchronous communication semantics is also a finite state machine. Hence,

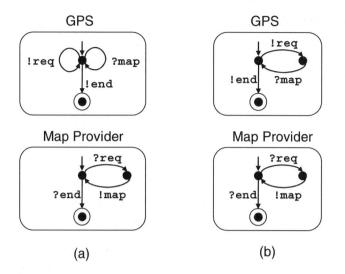

Fig. 3.2. An unsynchronizable (**a**) and a synchronizable (**b**) design

the problem becomes a finite state verification problem and can be solved using existing finite state model checking techniques and tools. On the other hand, it is impossible to characterize the conversation set of the composition in Fig. 3.2a using a finite-state machine because a finite-state machine cannot keep track of the number of unacknowledged req messages, which can be arbitrarily large.

In the rest of this chapter, we will present a survey of our earlier results on realizability and synchronizability of web services that can be used for identifying realizable top-down web service specifications and synchronizable bottom-up web service specifications, respectively. The technical details and proofs of these results can be found in our earlier publications [8, 9, 14, 15, 16, 18, 20, 21]. Our goal in this chapter is to provide an overview of our earlier results and explain how they can be applied to the example discussed in Chap. 1. We will also briefly discuss how we integrated these analysis techniques into an automated verification tool for web services [19, 39].

The rest of the chapter is organized as follows. Section 3.2 presents our conversation model which was originally proposed in [8]. Section 3.3 discusses the synchronizability analysis presented in [15, 21]. Section 3.4 discusses the realizability analysis from [14, 16]. Section 3.5 discusses the extensions of the synchronizability and realizability analyses to protocols in which message contents influence the control flow [18, 20]. Section 3.6 briefly describes the Web Service Analysis Tool [39, 19]. Section 3.7 discusses the related work and Sect. 3.8 lists our conclusions.

3.2 A Conversation-Oriented Model

In this section, we present a formal model for interacting web services [8, 15, 16, 21]. We concentrate our discussion on *static* web service compositions, where the composition structure is statically determined prior to the execution of the composition and we assume that interacting web services do not dynamically create communication channels or instantiate new business processes.

We assume that a *web service composition* is a closed system where a finite set of interacting (individual) web services, called *peers*, communicate with each other via asynchronous messaging. In this section, we consider the problem of how to characterize the interactions among peers. We use the sequence of send events to characterize a global behavior generated by the composition of a set of peers. Based on this conversation model, Linear Temporal Logic (LTL) can be used to express the desired properties of the system.

We will first introduce the notion of a composition schema, which specifies the static interconnection pattern of a web service composition. Then we discuss the specification of each peer, i.e., each participant of a web service composition. Next we discuss how to characterize the interactions among the peers, and introduce the notion of a conversation. Then we present some observations on conversation sets, which motivate the synchronizability analysis presented in the next section.

3.2.1 Composition Architecture

There are two basic approaches for specifying a web service composition, namely the *top-down* and *bottom-up* specification approaches. In the top-down approach, the desired message exchange sequences among multiple peers are specified, e.g., the IBM Conversation Support Framework for Business Process Integration [22] and the Web Service Choreography Description Language (WS-CDL) [40]. The bottom-up approach specifies the logic of individual peers and then peers are composed and their global behaviors are analyzed. Many industry standards, e.g., WSDL [41] and BPEL4WS [6], use this approach. In our formalization, the bottom-up and top-down specification approaches have different expressive power. Bottom-up approach is more expressive and can be used to specify more complex interactions.

In order to explain our formal model, we will use an example derived from the one discussed in Chap. 1 as our running example in this section.

Example 3 In this example there are three peers interacting with each other: John, Agent, and Hotel. John wants to take a vacation. He has certain constraints about where he wants to go for vacation, so he sends a query to his Agent stating his constraints and asking for advice. The Agent responds to John's query by sending him a suggestion. If John is not happy with the Agent's suggestion he sends another query requesting another suggestion. Eventually, John makes up his mind and sends a reservation request to

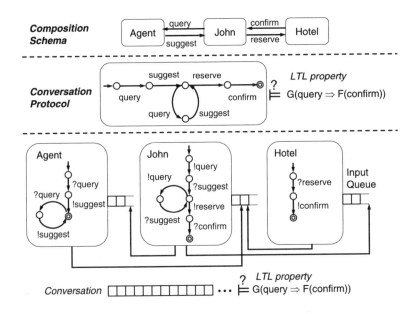

Fig. 3.3. An example demonstrating our model

the hotel he picks. The hotel responds to John's reservation request with a confirmation message. Figure 3.3 shows both top-down and bottom-up specifications of this example in our framework. Top part of Fig. 3.3 shows the set of peers participating in this composition and the messages exchanged among them. Middle part of Fig. 3.3 gives a top-down specification of the possible interactions among these peers. Note that in this top-down specification the behaviors of the individual peers are not given. Bottom part of Fig. 3.3, on the other hand, is a bottom-up specification which gives behavioral descriptions of all the peers participating in the composition. The interaction behavior is implicitly defined as the set of interactions generated by these peers. In either approach, we are interested in verifying LTL properties of interactions and we model the interactions as conversations. Below we will use this example to explain different components of our framework.

A composition schema specifies the set of peers and the set of messages exchanged among peers [8, 21].

Definition 1 *A composition schema is a tuple (P, M) where $P = \{p_1, \ldots, p_n\}$ is the set of peer prototypes, and M is the set of messages. Each peer prototype $p_i = (M_i^{in}, M_i^{out})$ is a pair of disjoint sets of messages $(M_i^{in} \cap M_i^{out} = \emptyset)$, where M_i^{in} is the set of incoming messages, M_i^{out} is the set of outgoing messages, and $M_i = M_i^{in} \cup M_i^{out}$ is the set of messages of peer p_i where $\bigcup_{i \in [1..n]} M_i^{in} = \bigcup_{i \in [1..n]} M_i^{out} = M$. We assume that each message has a* *unique sender and a unique receiver, and a peer cannot send a message back to itself.*

For example, top part of Fig. 3.3 shows a composition schema where the set of peer prototypes are $P = \{\mathsf{Agent}, \mathsf{John}, \mathsf{Hotel}\}$, and the set of messages are $M = \{\mathsf{query}, \mathsf{suggest}, \mathsf{confirm}, \mathsf{reserve}\}$. The input and output messages for peer prototypes are defined as $M^{in}_{\mathsf{Agent}} = \{\mathsf{query}\}$, $M^{out}_{\mathsf{Agent}} = \{\mathsf{suggest}\}$, $M^{in}_{\mathsf{John}} = \{\mathsf{suggest}, \mathsf{confirm}\}$, $M^{out}_{\mathsf{John}} = \{\mathsf{query}, \mathsf{reserve}\}$, $M^{in}_{\mathsf{Hotel}} = \{\mathsf{reserve}\}$, and $M^{out}_{\mathsf{Hotel}} = \{\mathsf{confirm}\}$.

3.2.2 Top-Down vs Bottom-Up Specification

Conversation protocols correspond to top-down specification of interactions among web services. Middle part of Fig. 3.3 (labeled conversation protocol) shows a top-down specification for the interactions among a set of peers. We define a conversation protocol as a finite state machine as follows.

Definition 2 *Let $S = (P, M)$ be a composition schema. A conversation protocol over S is a tuple $\mathcal{R} = \langle (P, M), \mathcal{A} \rangle$ where $\mathcal{A}$ is a finite state automaton with alphabet M. We let $L(\mathcal{R}) = L(\mathcal{A})$, i.e., the language recognized by $\mathcal{A}$.*

The conversation protocol in Fig. 3.3 corresponds to a finite state automaton with the set of states $\{s_0, s_1, s_2, s_3, s_4, s_5\}$, the initial state s_0, the set of final states $\{s_5\}$, the alphabet $\{\mathsf{query}, \mathsf{suggest}, \mathsf{confirm}, \mathsf{reserve}\}$, and the set of transitions $\{(s_0, \mathsf{query}, s_1), (s_1, \mathsf{suggest}, s_2), (s_2, \mathsf{query}, s_3), (s_3, \mathsf{suggest}, s_2), (s_2, \mathsf{reserve}, s_4),$ and $(s_4, \mathsf{confirm}, s_5)\}$.

Note that the language recognized by the conversation protocol in Fig. 3.3 can be characterized by the following regular expression:

$$\mathsf{query}\ \mathsf{suggest}\ (\mathsf{query}\ \mathsf{suggest})^*\ \mathsf{reserve}\ \mathsf{confirm}$$

A bottom-up specification consists of a set of finite state peers. Bottom part of Fig. 3.3 shows the bottom-up specification of the same web service composition. We call a bottom-up specification a *web service composition* which is defined as follows.

Definition 3 *A web service composition is a tuple $\mathcal{W} = \langle (P, M), \mathcal{A}_1, \ldots, \mathcal{A}_n \rangle$, where (P, M) is a composition schema, $n = |P|$, and $\mathcal{A}_i$ is the peer implementation for the peer prototype $p_i = (M^{in}_i, M^{out}_i) \in P$.*

We assume that each peer implementation is given as a finite state machine. Each peer implementation describes the control flow of a peer. Since peers communicate with asynchronous messages, each peer is equipped with a FIFO queue to store incoming messages. Formally, a peer implementation is defined as follows.

Definition 4 *Let* $S = (P, M)$ *be a composition schema and* $p_i = (M_i^{in}, M_i^{out}) \in$ *P be a peer prototype. A* peer implementation $\mathcal{A}_i$ *for a peer prototype* p_i *is a finite state machine with an input queue. Its message set is* $M_i = M_i^{in} \cup M_i^{out}$. *A transition between two states* t_1 *and* t_2 *in* $\mathcal{A}_i$ *can be one of the following three types:*

1. *A* send-transition *of the form* $(t_1, !m_1, t_2)$ *which sends out a message* $m_1 \in M_i^{out}$ *(i.e., inserts the message to the input queue of the receiver).*
2. *A* receive-transition *of the form* $(t_1, ?m_2, t_2)$ *which consumes a message* $m_2 \in M_i^{in}$ *from the input queue of* $\mathcal{A}_i$.
3. *An* ϵ-transition *of the form* (t_1, ϵ, t_2).

Bottom part of Fig. 3.3 presents the peer implementations for the peer prototypes shown at the top. For example, the peer implementation for the peer Agent corresponds to a finite state machine with the set of states $\{q_0, q_1, q_2, q_3\}$, the initial state q_0, the set of final states $\{q_2\}$, the message set $\{\text{query}, \text{suggest}\}$, and the set of transitions $\{(q_0, ?\text{query}, q_1), (q_1, !\text{suggest}, q_2), (q_2, ?\text{query}, q_3), \text{and } (q_3, !\text{suggest}, q_2)\}$. Similarly, the peer John corresponds to a finite state machine with the set of states $\{t_0, t_1, t_2, t_3, t_4, t_5\}$, the initial state t_0, the set of final states $\{t_5\}$, the message set $\{\text{query}, \text{suggest}, \text{confirm}, \text{reserve}\}$, and the set of transitions $\{(t_0, !\text{query}, t_1), (t_1, ?\text{suggest}, t_2), (t_2, !\text{query}, t_3), (t_3, ?\text{suggest}, t_2), (t_2, !\text{reserve}, t_4), \text{and } (t_4, ?\text{confirm}, t_5)\}$. And finally, the peer Hotel corresponds to a finite state machine with the set of states $\{r_0, r_1, r_2\}$, the initial state r_0, the set of final states $\{r_2\}$, the message set $\{\text{reserve}, \text{confirm}\}$, and the set of transitions $\{(r_0, ?\text{reserve}, r_1) \text{ and } (r_1, !\text{confirm}, r_2)\}$. We will use these peer implementations for our running example for the rest of this section.

3.2.3 Conversations

A conversation is the sequence of messages exchanged among the peers during an execution, recorded in the order they are sent. In order to formalize the notion of conversations, we first need to define the configurations of a composite web service and the derivation relation which specifies how the system evolves from one configuration to another [8, 16, 21].

Definition 5 *Let* $\mathcal{W} = \langle (P, M), \mathcal{A}_1, \ldots, \mathcal{A}_n \rangle$ *be a web service composition. A* configuration *of* $\mathcal{W}$ *is a* $(2n)$-tuple *of the form*

$$(Q_1, t_1, ..., Q_n, t_n),$$

where for each $j \in [1..n]$, $Q_j \in (M_j^{in})^*$, *and* $t_j \in T_j$. *Here* t_j *and* Q_j *denote the local state and the queue contents of* $\mathcal{A}_j$, *respectively.*

Intuitively, a configuration records a snap-shot during the execution of a web service composition by recording the local state and the FIFO queue contents of each peer. For example, the initial configuration of our running example is $(\epsilon, q_0, \epsilon, t_0, \epsilon, r_0)$ where all the peers are in their initial states and all the queues are empty. When the peer John takes the transition $(t_0, !query, t_1)$, the next configuration is $(query, q_0, \epsilon, t_1, \epsilon, r_0)$, i.e., in the next configuration the message query is in the input queue of the peer Agent and the peer John is in state t_1. Then, the peer Agent can receive the query message by taking the $(q_0, ?query, q_1)$ transition which would lead to the following configuration: $(\epsilon, q_1, \epsilon, t_1, \epsilon, r_0)$, i.e., the message query is removed from the input queue of the peer Agent and the peer Agent is now in state q_1.

We can formalize this kind of evolution of the system from one configuration to another as a derivation relation using the transitions of the peer implementations. A derivation step is an atomic and minimal step in a global behavior generated by a web service composition. Given two configurations c and c', we say that c *derives* c', written as $c \to c'$, if it is possible to go from configuration c to configuration c' by one of the following three types of derivation steps:

1. *send action*, where one peer sends out a message m to another peer (denoted as $c \xrightarrow{!m} c'$). The send action results in the state transition of the sender, and the transmitted message is placed in the input queue of the receiver.
2. *receive action*, where one peer consumes the message m that is at the head of its input message queue (denoted as $c \xrightarrow{?m} c'$). The receive action results in the state transition of the receiver and the removal of the consumed message from the head of the receiver's input queue.
3. ϵ *action*, where one peer takes an ϵ transition (denoted as $c \xrightarrow{\epsilon} c'$). This action results in the state transition of that peer; however, it does not affect any of the message queues.

For our running example, two example derivations we discussed above can be written as $(\epsilon, q_0, \epsilon, t_0, \epsilon, r_0) \xrightarrow{!query} (query, q_0, \epsilon, t_1, \epsilon, r_0)$ and $(query, q_0, \epsilon, t_1, \epsilon, r_0) \xrightarrow{?query} (\epsilon, q_1, \epsilon, t_1, \epsilon, r_0)$.

Now we can define a run of a web service composition as follows.

Definition 6 *Let* $\mathcal{W} = \langle (P, M), \mathcal{A}_1, \ldots, \mathcal{A}_n \rangle$ *be a web service composition, a sequence of configurations* $\gamma = c_0 c_1 \ldots c_k$ *is a run of* $\mathcal{W}$ *if it satisfies the following conditions:*

1. *The configuration* $c_0 = (\epsilon, s_1, \ldots, \epsilon, s_n)$ *is the initial configuration where* s_i *is the initial state of* $\mathcal{A}_i$ *for each* $i \in [1..n]$, *and* ϵ *is the empty word.*
2. *For each* $j \in [0..k-1]$, $c_j \to c_{j+1}$.
3. *The configuration* $c_k = (\epsilon, t_1, \ldots, \epsilon, t_n)$ *is a final configuration where* t_i *is a final state of* $\mathcal{A}_i$ *for each* $i \in [1..n]$.

We define the *send sequence* generated by γ, denoted by $ss(\gamma)$, as the sequence of messages containing one message for each send action (i.e., $c \xrightarrow{!m} c'$) in γ, where the messages in $ss(\gamma)$ are recorded in the order they are sent.

For example, a run of our running example would be 9

$$(\epsilon, q_0, \epsilon, t_0, \epsilon, r_0) \overset{!\text{query}}{\rightarrow} (\text{query}, q_0, \epsilon, t_1, \epsilon, r_0) \overset{?\text{query}}{\rightarrow} (\epsilon, q_1, \epsilon, t_1, \epsilon, r_0) \overset{!\text{suggest}}{\rightarrow}$$

$$(\epsilon, q_2, \text{suggest}, t_1, \epsilon, r_0) \overset{?\text{suggest}}{\rightarrow} (\epsilon, q_2, \epsilon, t_2, \epsilon, r_0) \overset{!\text{reserve}}{\rightarrow} (\epsilon, q_2, \epsilon, t_4, \text{reserve}, r_0)$$
$$\overset{?\text{reserve}}{\rightarrow}$$

$$(\epsilon, q_2, \epsilon, t_4, \epsilon, r_1) \overset{!\text{confirm}}{\rightarrow} (\epsilon, q_2, \text{confirm}, t_4, \epsilon, r_2) \overset{?\text{confirm}}{\rightarrow} (\epsilon, q_2, \epsilon, t_5, \epsilon, r_2).$$

The send sequence generated by this run is query suggest reserve confirm. Finally, we define the conversations as follows.

Definition 7 *A word w over M ($w \in M^*$) is a* conversation *of web service composition $\mathcal{W}$ if there exists a run γ such that $w = ss(\gamma)$, i.e., a conversation is the send sequence generated by a run. The* conversation set *of a web service composition $\mathcal{W}$, written as $\mathcal{C}(\mathcal{W})$, is the set of all conversations for $\mathcal{W}$.*

For example, the conversation set of our running example, the web service composition at the bottom of Fig. 3.3, can be captured by the regular expression:

$$\text{query suggest (query suggest)}^* \text{ reserve confirm}$$

.

Linear Temporal Logic can be used to characterize the properties of conversation sets in order to specify the desired system properties. The semantics of LTL formulas can be adapted to conversations by defining the set of atomic propositions as the power set of messages. For example, the composition in Fig. 3.3 satisfies the LTL property: $\mathbf{G}(\text{query} \Rightarrow \mathbf{F}(\text{confirm}))$, where $\mathbf{G}$ and $\mathbf{F}$ are temporal operators which mean "globally" and "eventually," respectively.

Standard LTL semantics is defined on infinite sequences [11], whereas in our definitions above we used finite conversations. It is possible to extend the definitions above to infinite conversations and then use the standard LTL semantics as in [14, 16]. We can also adapt the standard LTL semantics to finite conversations by extending each conversation to an infinite string by adding an infinite suffix which is the repetition of a special termination symbol.

Unfortunately, due to the asynchronous communication of web services, LTL verification of conversations of web service compositions is undecidable [16].

Theorem 1 *Given a web service composition $\mathcal{W}$ and an LTL property ϕ, determining if all the conversations of $\mathcal{W}$ satisfy ϕ is undecidable.*

The proof is based on an earlier result on Communicating Finite State Machines (CFSMs) [7]. We can show that a web service composition is essentially a system of CFSMs. It is known that CFSMs can simulate Turing Machines [7]. Similarly, one can show that, given a Turing Machine TM it is possible to construct a web service composition $\mathcal{W}$ that simulates TM and exchanges a special message (say m_t) once TM terminates. Thus, TM terminates if and only if the conversations of $\mathcal{W}$ satisfy the LTL formula $\mathbf{F}(m_t)$, which means that "eventually message m_t will be sent." Hence, undecidability of the halting problem implies that verification of LTL properties of conversations of a web service composition is an undecidable problem.

3.3 Synchronizability

Asynchronous communication among web services leads to the undecidability of the LTL verification problem. If synchronous communication is used instead of asynchronous communication, the set of configurations of a web service composition would be a finite set, and it is well known that LTL model checking is decidable for finite state systems. In this section, we discuss the *synchronizability analysis* [15, 21] which identifies bottom-up web service specifications which generate the same conversation set with synchronous and asynchronous communication semantics. We call such web service compositions *synchronizable*. We can verify synchronizable web service compositions using the synchronous communication semantics, and the verification results we obtain are guaranteed to hold for the asynchronous communication semantics.

3.3.1 Synchronous Communication

To define synchronizability, we first have to define synchronous communication. Intuitively, synchronous communication requires that the sender and the receiver of a message should take the send and the receive actions simultaneously to complete the message transmission. In other words, the send and the receive actions of a message transmission form an atomic and non-interruptible step. In the following, we define the synchronous global configuration and synchronous communication semantics.

Given a web service composition $\mathcal{W} = \langle (P, M), \mathcal{A}_1, ..., \mathcal{A}_n \rangle$ where each automaton $\mathcal{A}_i$ describes the behavior of a peer, the configuration of a web service composition with respect to the *synchronous semantics*, called the *syn-configuration*, is a tuple $(t_1, ..., t_n)$, where for each $j \in [1..n]$, $t_j \in T_j$ is the local state of peer $\mathcal{A}_j$. Notice that in a syn-configuration only the local automata state of each peer is recorded—peers do not need message buffers to store the incoming messages due to the synchronous communication semantics.

For two syn-configurations c and c', we say that c *synchronously derives* c', written as $c \rightarrow_{syn} c'$, if c' is the result of simultaneous execution of the send and the receive actions for the same message by two peers, or the execution of an ϵ action by a single peer.

The definition of the derivation relation between two syn-configurations is different than the asynchronous case. In the synchronous case a send action can only be executed concurrently with a matching receive action, i.e., sending and receiving of a message occur synchronously. We call this semantics the *synchronous semantics* of a web service composition and the semantics defined in Sect. 3.2 is called the *asynchronous semantics*.

The definitions of a run, a send sequence, and a conversation for synchronous semantics is similar to those of the asynchronous semantics given in Sect. 3.2 (we will use "syn" as a prefix to distinguish between the synchronous and asynchronous versions of these definitions when it is not clear from the context). Given a web service composition W, let $C_{\text{syn}}(W)$ denote the conversation set under the synchronous semantics. Then synchronizability is defined as follows.

Definition 8 *A web service composition W is* synchronizable *if its conversation set remains the same when the synchronous semantics is used instead of the asynchronous semantics, i.e., $C(W) = C_{\text{syn}}(W)$.*

Clearly, if a web service composition is synchronizable, then we can verify its interaction behavior using synchronous semantics (without any input queues) and the results of the verification will hold for the behaviors of the web service composition in the presence of asynchronous communication with unbounded queues.

Given a web service composition W, its conversation set with respect to synchronous semantics is always a subset of its conversation set with respect to asynchronous semantics, i.e., $C_{\text{syn}}(W) \subseteq C(W)$ [21]. In some cases the containment relationship can be strict, i.e., there are web service compositions that are not synchronizable. The following is an example.

Example 4 Consider a web service composition W in Fig. 3.4. Two peers A and B can exchange two messages a (from A to B) and b (from B to A). The peer implementation of A sends out a and then waits for and consumes message b from its input queue. Peer b sends out b first then receives a. Obviously, if asynchronous semantics is used then there exists a run which generates the conversation ab. However, note that, when synchronous semantics is used there is no run which generates the same conversation, because at the initial state both peers are trying to send out a message and neither of them can get the co-operation of the other peer to complete the send operation. Based on the definitions of the conversation sets, we have $C(W) = \{ab, ba\}$ and $C_{\text{syn}}(W) = \emptyset$. Hence, W is not synchronizable.

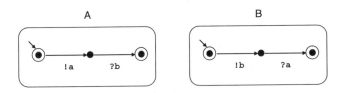

Fig. 3.4. An example specification that is not synchronizable

3.3.2 Synchronizability Analysis

We now present two conditions for identifying synchronizable web service compositions. Together these conditions guarantee synchronizability, i.e., they form a sufficient condition for synchronizability.

Synchronous compatible condition: If we construct the synchronous composition of a set of peers, the synchronous compatible condition requires that for each syn-configuration c that is reachable from the initial configuration, if there is a peer which has a send transition for a message m from its local state in c, then the receiver of m should have a receive transition for m either from its local state in c or from a configuration reachable from c via ϵ-actions.

Note that the composition of A and B in Fig. 3.4 does not satisfy the synchronous compatible condition. The initial syn-configuration c_0 of the composition can be represented as a tuple (s_1^A, s_1^B), where s_1^A and s_1^B are the local initial states of A and B respectively. Obviously, at c_0 peer A can send out a; however, it is not able to because B is not in a state where it can receive the message.

An algorithm for checking the synchronous compatible condition is given in [21]. The basic idea in the algorithm is to construct a finite state machine that is the product (i.e., the synchronous composition) of all peers. Each state (i.e., syn-configuration) of the product machine is a vector of local states of all peers. During the construction, if we find a peer ready to send a message but the corresponding receiver is not ready to receive it (either immediately or after executing several ϵ-actions), the composition is identified as not synchronous compatible. If all states of the product machine are examined without finding a violation of the synchronous compatible condition, then the algorithm returns true. The worst case complexity of the algorithm is quadratic on the size of the product and the size of the product is exponential in the number of peers.

Autonomous condition: A web service composition is autonomous if each peer, at any moment, can do only one of the following: (1) terminate, (2) send a message, or (3) receive a message.

To check the autonomous condition, we determinize each peer implementation and check that outgoing transitions for each non-final state are either all send transitions or all receive transitions [21]. We also check that final states have no outgoing transitions. The complexity of the algorithm can be exponential in the size of the peers in the worst case due to the determinization step.

In Fig. 3.1b, neither of the peer implementations of the map service providers (M_1 and M_2) are autonomous because there is a transition originating from the initial state which is also a final state. However, the implementation of traveler (T) is autonomous.

In Fig. 3.2a the implementation of GPS is not autonomous, because at the initial state the peer can send message `req` and receive message `map`.

We now present the key result concerning the synchronizability analysis. The proof for the following results can be found in [21].

Theorem 2 *Let* $\mathcal{W} = \langle (P, M), \mathcal{A}_1, \ldots, \mathcal{A}_n \rangle$ *be a web service composition. If* $\mathcal{W}$ *is synchronous compatible and autonomous, then for any conversation generated by* $\mathcal{W}$ *there exists a run which generates the same conversation in which every send action is immediately followed by the corresponding receive action.*

When the synchronous compatibility and autonomy conditions are satisfied by a web service composition, then for each conversation generated by that composition, there is always a run which generates the same conversation where each send action is immediately followed by the corresponding receive action. By collapsing the pairs of send/receive actions for the same message, we get a synchronous run which generates the same conversation. Then based on Theorem 2 we get the following result.

Theorem 3 *Let* $\mathcal{W} = \langle (P, M), \mathcal{A}_1, \ldots, \mathcal{A}_n \rangle$ *be a web service composition. If* $\mathcal{W}$ *is synchronous compatible and autonomous, then* $\mathcal{W}$ *is synchronizable.*

Theorem 3 implies that web service compositions that satisfy the two synchronizability conditions can be analyzed using the synchronous communication semantics and the verification results hold for asynchronous semantics.

Notice that synchronizability does not imply deadlock freedom. Think about the following composition of two peers A and B, which exchange messages m_1 (from A to B) and m_2 (from B to A). If A accepts one word $?m_2$, and B accepts one word $?m_1$, it is not hard to verify that the composition of A and B is synchronizable; however, they are involved in a deadlock right at the initial state since both peers are waiting for each other. Hence, before the LTL verification of a web service composition, designers may have to check the composition for deadlocks. However, for synchronizable web service compositions the deadlock check can be done using the synchronous semantics (instead of the asynchronous semantics), since it is possible to show that [13] a synchronizable web service composition has a run (with asynchronous semantics) that leads to a deadlock if and only if it has a syn-run (with synchronous semantics) that leads to a deadlock.

3.4 Realizability of Conversation Protocols

In this section, we discuss the realizability problem for top-down web service specifications, i.e., conversation protocols [8, 16]. We also discuss the relationship between synchronizability and realizability analyses.

Intuitively, realizability means that given a conversation protocol it can be realized by some web service composition, i.e., the conversation set generated by the web service composition is exactly the same as the language accepted by the conversation protocol.

Definition 9 *Let* $S = (P, M)$ *be a composition schema, and let the conversation protocol* $\mathcal{R}$ *and the web service composition* $\mathcal{W}$ *both share the same schema* S. *We say that* $\mathcal{W}$ *realizes* $\mathcal{R}$ *if* $\mathcal{C}(\mathcal{W}) = L(\mathcal{R})$. *A conversation protocol* $\mathcal{R}$ *is realizable if there exists a web service composition that realizes* $\mathcal{R}$.

Let us first consider the following question: Are all conversation protocols realizable? The answer is negative as we show below.

Example 5 Figure 3.5 shows a conversation protocol over four peers A, B, C, and D. The message alphabet consists of two messages: a (from A to B) and c (from C to D). The protocol specifies a conversation set which consists of one conversation only ($\{ac\}$). It is not hard to see that any peer implementation which can generate the conversation ac can generate ca too, because there is no way for peers A and C to coordinate their actions. Hence, the conversation protocol shown in Fig. 3.5 is not realizable.

Notice that the problem of realizability is also an issue for synchronous communication semantics. For example, the protocol in Fig. 3.5 is not realizable using synchronous semantics either. However, the asynchronous semantics does introduce new complexities into this problem as discussed in [16, 21].

Below we will argue that realizability of conversation protocols can be solved by extending the synchronizability analysis. First we need to introduce notions of projection and join for peer implementations and conversation protocols.

For a composition schema (P, M), the projection of a word w to the alphabet M_i of the peer prototype p_i, denoted by $\pi_i(w)$, is a subsequence of w obtained by removing all the messages which are not in M_i. When the projection operation is applied to a set of words the result is the set of words generated by application of the projection operator to each word in the set.

For composition schema (P, M), let $n = |P|$ and let $L_1 \subseteq M_1^*, \ldots, L_n \subseteq M_n^*$, the join operator is defined as follows:

$$\text{JOIN}(L_1, \ldots, L_n) = \{w \mid w \in M^*, \forall i \in [1..n] : \pi_i(w) \in L_i\}.$$

Let $L = \{ac\}$ be the conversation set specified by the conversation protocol in Fig. 3.5. $\pi_A(L) = \{a\}$, $\pi_B(L) = \{a\}$, $\pi_C(L) = \{c\}$, and $\pi_D(L) = \{c\}$. The

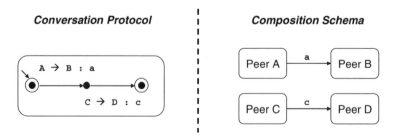

Fig. 3.5. A non-realizable protocol in both synchronous and asynchronous semantics

join of all these peer projections will produce a larger conversation set:

$$\text{JOIN}(\pi_A(L), \pi_B(L), \pi_C(L), \pi_D(L)) = \{ac, ca\}$$

We now introduce a third condition used in the realizability analysis.

Lossless join condition: A conversation protocol $\mathcal{R}$ is *lossless join* if $L(\mathcal{R}) = \text{JOIN}(\pi_1(L(\mathcal{R})), \ldots, \pi_n(L(\mathcal{R})))$, where n is the number of peers involved in the protocol.

The lossless join condition requires that a conversation protocol should include all words in the join of its projections to all peers. An algorithm for checking the lossless join property is given in [21]. Intuitively, the lossless join property requires that the protocol should be realizable under synchronous communication semantics. The algorithm simply projects the conversation protocol to each peer prototype, and then constructs the product of all projections. If the resulting product is equivalent to the protocol, then the algorithm reports that the lossless join property is satisfied. The algorithm can be exponential in the size of the conversation protocol in the worst case due to the equivalence check on two non-deterministic finite state machines.

The lossless join property is a necessary condition for the realizability of conversation protocols. If synchronous semantics is used, it is the necessary and sufficient condition. The following result connects the synchronizability analysis and the realizability analysis.

Theorem 4 *Given a conversation protocol $\mathcal{R} = \langle (P, M), \mathcal{A} \rangle$ where $n = |P|$, let $\mathcal{W} = \langle (P, M), \mathcal{A}_1, \ldots, \mathcal{A}_n \rangle$ be a web service composition s.t. for each $i \in [1..n]$, $\mathcal{A}_i$ is the minimal deterministic FSA such that $L(\mathcal{A}_i) = \pi_i(L(\mathcal{R}))$. If $\mathcal{W}$ is synchronizable, and $\mathcal{R}$ is lossless join, then $\mathcal{R}$ is realized by $\mathcal{W}$.*

The proof of this property follows directly from Theorem 3 and the fact that the synchronous composition of a set of peers accepts the join of their languages. Theorem 4 demonstrates an interesting relationship between the synchronizability analysis introduced in [21] and the realizability analysis introduced in [16].

3.5 Message Contents

In the previous sections, we assumed that the contents of the messages were abstracted away, i.e., in our formal model messages did not have any content. This type of abstraction would be fine as long as the contents of the messages do not influence the control flow of the peers. In practice, this assumption may be too restrictive, i.e., contents of a message received by a peer may influence the control flow of that peer. One natural question is, is it possible to extend the analyses introduced in the earlier sections to an extended web service model where messages have contents?

To facilitate the technical discussions, let us extend the web service specification framework as follows. Assume that each peer in a web service composition is a *guarded automaton* instead of a standard finite state automaton. In the guarded automata model, messages have contents. A message class defines the structure of a message and a message is an instance of a message class. Each transition is labeled with a message class and a guard. A guard is a relational expression which evaluates to a boolean value. The building elements of a guard are the attributes of messages. Only when the guard evaluates to true, can the transition be fired (if the automaton is in its source state).

Example 6 Figure 3.6 presents a modified version of the example given in Fig. 3.3 by extending the messages with contents and the transitions with guards. In Fig. 3.6 message classes req and map have an integer attribute id. The guard of each transition is a boolean expression enclosed in a pair of square brackets. For example, the send transition !req has a guard "id$'$ = id + 1." This means that whenever a new req message is sent, its id attribute is incremented by 1. Note that here the primed-variable id$'$ represents the "next value" of the attribute id. The receive transition ?req in the map provider service requires that the ids of the incoming req messages must monotonically increase. Obviously, the implementation of GPS satisfies this requirement. Similarly, the guard of the send transition !map guarantees that the id attribute of a map message must match that of the most recent req message.

We call a web service composition a "guarded composition" if its peers are specified using guarded automata. Similarly, we define the "guarded peer," "guarded protocol", etc. Given a guarded automaton, if we remove the contents of the messages and the guards of the transitions then we get a standard finite state automaton. We call this resulting automaton the *skeleton automaton*. Similarly, we use the name "skeleton peer," "skeleton composition," and "skeleton protocol" to refer the skeleton of a guarded peer, guarded composition, and guarded protocol, respectively.

One natural conjecture is the following: Does the synchronizability of a skeleton composition imply the synchronizability of the corresponding

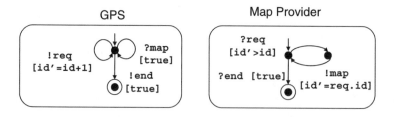

Fig. 3.6. An example with message contents

guarded composition? The answer is negative as demonstrated by the following example.

Example 7 Figure 3.7 presents an example guarded composition that shows that the above conjecture is false. The composition consists of two peers A and B. Peer A can send a message a to B, and B can send a message b to A. Both messages a and b have an integer attribute id which varies between 1 and 2. In the following, we use the notation $a(1)$ to represent a message a whose attribute id is 1. The composition produces two conversations $a(1)b(2)$ and $b(2)a(1)$. In addition, to produce these two conversations, asynchronous semantics has to be used. For example, to produce $a(1)b(2)$, the message $a(1)$ has to stay in the input queue of peer B when b is sent out. Such a conversation cannot be generated by synchronous composition of these two peers.

On the other hand, if we drop the message contents and guards of the guarded automata in Fig. 3.7, we get two standard finite state automata, which accept conversations {!a?b, ?b!a} and {!b?a, ?a!b}, respectively. The composition of these two finite state automata peers are synchronizable.

Example 7 demonstrates that the synchronizability of the skeleton composition does not imply the synchronizability of the guarded composition. Interestingly, if the skeleton composition is not synchronizable, it does not imply that the guarded composition is not synchronizable either. Similar observations hold for conversation protocols. It is not possible to tell if a guarded conversation protocol is realizable or not based on the realizability of its skeleton protocol. Examples and arguments for the above conclusions can be found in [13, 18, 20].

Skeleton of a guarded composition, however, can still be used for synchronizability analysis. The following theorem forms the basis of a skeleton analysis for synchronizability of guarded compositions.

Theorem 5 *A guarded web service composition is synchronizable if its skeleton satisfies the autonomous and synchronous compatible conditions.*

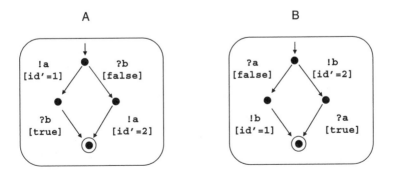

Fig. 3.7. A counter-example for the conjecture on skeleton synchronizability

Theorem 5 implies that if the skeletons of a guarded composition satisfies the two sufficient synchronizability conditions, then the guarded composition is guaranteed to be synchronizable. The proof of Theorem 5 is based on the following observation. For any run of a guarded composition, we can find a corresponding run of its skeleton composition, which traverses through the same path (states and transitions) and has the same input queue contents (disregarding message contents) at each peer. Since the skeleton composition satisfies autonomous and synchronous compatible conditions, there exists an equivalent execution of the skeleton composition in which each message is consumed immediately after it is sent. From this execution of the skeleton composition we can construct an execution for the guarded composition in which each message is consumed immediately after it is sent. This leads to the synchronizability of the guarded composition as shown in [13].

A similar skeleton analysis can be developed for guarded conversation protocols. A guarded conversation protocol is realizable if its skeleton satisfies the autonomous, synchronous compatible, lossless join conditions, and a fourth condition called "deterministic guards condition." Intuitively, the deterministic guards condition requires that for each peer, according to the guarded conversation protocol, when it is about to send out a message, the guard that is used to compute the contents of the message is uniquely decided by the sequence of message classes (note, not messages) exchanged by the peer in the past. The details of this analysis can be found in [20].

Skeleton analysis sometimes can be inaccurate. Below we will discuss this inaccuracy and techniques that can be used to refine the skeleton analysis.

Example 8 Consider the modified composition of GPS and Map Provider in Fig. 3.8. The composition is actually synchronizable. In GPS implementation, the guard id = map.id in transition !req enforces that the sending of next req message must wait for the last req message being matched by a corresponding map message. Thus, the interaction of two services runs in lock-step fashion, where the id attribute of req messages alternates between 0 and 1. However, the skeleton analysis cannot reach the conclusion that the guarded composition is synchronous, because the skeleton of GPS does not satisfy the autonomous condition.

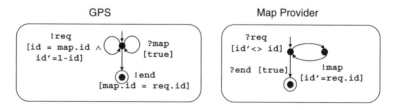

Fig. 3.8. An example on inaccuracy of skeleton analysis

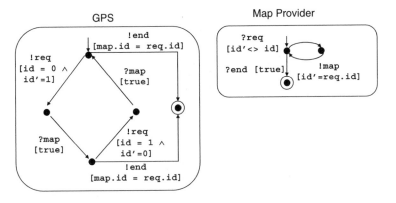

Fig. 3.9. A refined version of the guarded composition in Fig. 3.8

The inaccuracy of skeleton analysis can be fixed by a refined symbolic analysis of guarded compositions. The basic idea is to symbolically explore the configuration space of a guarded automaton, and split its states and remove redundant transitions if necessary. The result is another guarded automaton which generates the same set of conversations, but has more states.

Example 9 For example, after applying the iterative symbolic analysis on the GPS service in Fig. 3.8, we obtain the refined guarded automaton in Fig. 3.9. The refined automaton splits the initial state to four different states. If we examine the four non-final states (starting from the initial state and walking anti-clockwise), these states represent four different system configurations where the id attributes of the latest copies of req and map messages are $(0, 0)$, $(1, 0)$, $(1, 1)$, and $(0, 1)$, respectively. The refined automaton is equivalent to the original GPS implementation in Fig. 3.8. If we apply the skeleton analysis on Fig. 3.9, we can now reach the conclusion that the composition is synchronizable.

The algorithm for the iterative symbolic analysis can be found in [20].

3.6 Web Service Analysis Tool

The synchronizability and realizability analyses are implemented and integrated to the Web Service Analysis Tool (WSAT) [19, 39]. WSAT accepts web service specifications in popular web service description languages (such as WSDL and BPEL4WS), system properties specified in LTL, and verifies if the conversations generated conform to the LTL property.

Figure 3.10 shows the architecture of WSAT. WSAT uses Guarded Automata (GA) as an intermediate representation. A GA is a finite state machine which sends and receives XML messages and has a finite number of XML variables. The types of XML messages and variables are defined using XML

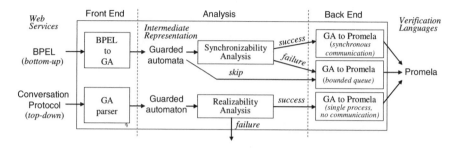

Fig. 3.10. WSAT architecture

schema. In the GA representation used by WSAT, all the variable and message types are bounded. Each send transition can have a guard, which is essentially an assignment that determines the contents of the message being sent. Each receive transition can also have a guard—if the message being received does not satisfy the guard, the receive action is blocked. The GA representation is capable of capturing both the control flow and data manipulation semantics of web services. WSAT includes a translator from BPEL to GA that supports bottom-up specification of web service compositions. It also includes a translator from top-down conversation protocol specifications to GA. Support for other languages can be added to WSAT by integrating new translators to its front end without changing the analysis and the verification modules.

Synchronizability and realizability analyses are implemented in WSAT. When the analysis succeeds, LTL verification can be performed using the synchronous communication semantics instead of asynchronous communication semantics. When the analysis is not successful on the web service input, asynchronous semantics is used and a partial verification is conducted for bounded communication channels. WSAT also implements extensions to the synchronizability and realizability analyses to handle the guards of the transitions in the GA model [18]. Algorithms for translating XPath expressions to Promela code are presented in [17] where model checker SPIN [24] is used at the back-end of WSAT to check LTL properties.

We applied WSAT to a range of examples, including six conversation protocols converted from the IBM Conversation Support Project [25], five BPEL services from BPEL standard and Collaxa.com, and the SAS example from [17]. We applied the synchronizability or the realizability analysis to each example, depending on whether the specification is bottom-up or top-down. As reported in [21], only 2 of the 12 examples violate the conditions discussed in this chapter (both violate the autonomous condition). This demonstrates that the sufficient conditions used in the synchronizability and realizability analyses are not too restrictive and that they are able to show the synchronizability and realizability of practical web service applications.

3.7 Related Work and Discussion

This section presents a survey of related work on modeling and analyzing web services. Particularly, we are interested in the following four topics: (1) modeling approaches for distributed systems, (2) description of global behaviors in distributed systems, (3) realizability analysis, and (4) automated analysis and verification of web services. At the end of this section we also present a discussion about our approach, identifying its limitations and possible extensions.

3.7.1 Modeling Approaches and Communication Semantics

Since the web service technology can be regarded as essentially a branch of distributed systems, we include a discussion of earlier models for describing interaction and composition of distributed systems. Traditionally, many modeling approaches use synchronous communication semantics, where sender and receiver of a message transmission have to complete the send and the receive actions simultaneously. The typical examples include (but not limited to) CSP [23], I/O automata [29], and interface automata [2].

In the models which use asynchronous communication semantics, FIFO queue is the most commonly used message buffer. Communicating Finite State Machines (CFSM) were proposed in early 1980s as a simple model with asynchronous communication semantics [7]. Brand et al. showed that CFSM can simulate Turing Machines [7]. Other related modeling approaches for distributed systems include Codesign Finite State Machine model [10], Kahn Process Networks [27], π-Calculus [30], and Microsoft Behave! Project [37]. Most of them, e.g., π-Calculus and Behave! Project, use or support simulation of asynchronous communication semantics.

3.7.2 Modeling Global Behaviors

In the conversation model, a global behavior is modeled as a sequence of send events. In many other modeling approaches, e.g., Message Sequence Charts (MSCs) [31], both send and receive events are captured. Such different modeling perspectives can lead to differences in the expressive power and in the difficulty of analysis and verification problems. We now briefly compare the conversation model and the MSC model [4]. This section is a summary of the more detailed discussion given in [21].

MSC model [31] is a widely used specification approach for distributed systems. A comparison with the basic MSC model would not be fair since using the MSC model one can specify only a fixed number of message traces. Instead, we compare our model with the more expressive MSC graphs [4], which are finite state automata that are constructed by composing basic MSCs. MSC graphs use asynchronous communication semantics. There are other MSC extensions such as the high-level MSC (hMSC) [38]. However, hMSC is mainly used for studying infinite traces and the composition model used in [38] is synchronous. Therefore, the MSC graph is a more suitable model for comparison.

An MSC consists of a finite set of peers, where each peer has a single sequence of send/receive events. We call that sequence the *event order* of that peer. There is a bijective mapping that matches each pair of send and receive events. Given an MSC M, its language $L(M)$ is the set of *linearizations* of all events that follow the event order of each peer. Essentially, $L(M)$ captures the "join" of local views from each peer. A formal definition of MSC can be found in [4].

An MSC graph [4] is a finite state automaton where each node of the graph (i.e., each state of the automaton) is associated with an MSC. Given an MSC graph G, a word w is accepted by G, if and only if there exists an accepting path in G where w is a linearization of the MSC that is the result of concatenating the MSCs along that path.

The main difference between the MSC graph framework and the conversation-oriented framework is the fact that the MSC model specifies the ordering of the receive events whereas the conversation model does not. In the conversation model the timing of a receive event is considered to be a local decision of the receiving peer and is not taken into account during the analysis of interactions among multiple peers.

Conversation protocols and MSC graphs are incomparable in terms of their expressive power [21]. For example, it is possible to construct two MSC graphs with different languages but identical conversation sets. This implies that there are interactions that can be differentiated using MSC graphs but not using conversation protocols. On the other hand, there are interactions which can be specified using a conversation protocol but cannot be specified with any MSC graph. Hence, expressiveness of MSC graphs and conversation protocols are incomparable. It is also possible to show that the expressive power of the MSC graphs and the bottom-up specified web service compositions are incomparable [21].

One natural question is, which approach is better? Both approaches have pros and cons. In the conversation model the ordering of receive events is like a "don't care" condition which can simplify the specification of interactions. On the other hand, realizability problem in the conversation model can be more severe since we focus on global ordering of send events. For example, the non-realizable conversation protocol $\{a_{A \to B} \; b_{C \to A}\}$ cannot be specified using MSCs.

The different modeling perspectives on global behaviors leads to different realizability analysis techniques. Alur et al. investigated the weak and safe realizability problems for sets of MSCs and the MSC graphs [3, 4]. They showed that determining realizability of a set of MSCs is decidable; however, it is not decidable for MSC graphs. They gave one sufficient and necessary condition for realizability of MSC graphs. The sufficient and necessary condition looks very similar to the *lossless join* condition in the realizability analysis on the conversation model. However, there are key differences: (1) In the MSC model, the condition is both sufficient and necessary whereas in the conversation model lossless join is a sufficient condition only and (2) it is undecidable to check the condition for MSC graphs. Alur et al. introduced another condition called *boundedness* condition, which ensures that during the composition of peers the queue length will not exceed a certain preset bound (on the size of the MSC graph). This condition excludes some of the realizable designs. Note that the realizability conditions in the conversation model do not require queue length to be bounded. However, notice that the realizability analysis on conversation model does not subsume the realizability analysis on MSC graphs. There are examples which can pass the realizability analysis on MSC graphs but are excluded by the realizability analysis we presented for the conversation model.

3.7.3 Realizability and Synchronizability

Interest in the realizability problem dates back to 1980s (see [1, 35, 36]). However, the realizability problem means different things in different contexts. For example, in [1, 35, 36], realizability problem is defined as whether a peer has a strategy to cope with the environment no matter how the environment decides to move. The concept of realizability studied in this chapter is rather different. We are investigating realizability in a closed system that consists of multiple peers interacting with each other. Our definition of realizability requires that the implementation generates exactly the same set of global behaviors as specified by the protocol. A closer notion to the realizability problem in this chapter is the "weak realizability" of MSC graphs studied in [4]. Different communication assumptions can lead to different realizability analysis. For example, realizability problem for high-level MSC is studied in [38].

To the best of our knowledge, synchronizability analysis was first proposed in [15]. The relationship between synchronizability (for bottom-up specifications) and realizability (for top-down specifications) was discussed in [21].

3.7.4 Verification of Web Services

Application of automated verification techniques to web services has been an active area. Narayanan et al. [34] modeled web services as Petri Nets and investigated the simulation, verification, and composition of web services using the Petri-net model. Foster et al. [12] used LTSA (Labeled Transition System Analyzer) to verify BPEL web services using synchronous communication semantics and MSC model. Nakajima [33] proposed an approach in which a given web service flow specified in WSFL was verified using the model checker SPIN. The approach presented by Kazhamiakin et al. [28] determined the simplest communication mechanism necessary to verify a web service composition, and then verifies the composition using that communication mechanism. Hence, if a web service is not synchronizable it is analyzed using asynchronous communication semantics.

3.7.5 Discussion

We conclude this section with a discussion of possible limitations of the presented framework and possible extensions.

We believe that an important limitation of the presented analyses techniques is the fact that they do not handle dynamic service creation or establishment of dynamic connections among different services. In the model discussed here we assume that interacting web services do not dynamically create communication channels or instantiate new business processes. Since dynamic service discovery is an important component of service oriented computing, in order to make the approach presented in this chapter applicable to a wider class of systems, it is necessary to handle dynamic instantiation of peers and communication channels. Extending synchronizability and realizability analyses to such specifications is a promising research direction.

So far we have only applied the presented analysis techniques to protocols with a modest number of states. This is due to the fact that most web service composition examples we have found do not have a large number of control states. In the future, it would be interesting to investigate the scalability of the presented techniques for specifications with large number of states. Generally, we believe that the presented techniques will be scalable as long as the specifications are deterministic, and, therefore, the cost of determinization can be avoided.

Currently, we do not have an implementation of symbolic synchronizability and realizability analyses for handling specifications in which message contents influence the control flow. At this point, the WSAT tool only performs skeleton analyses for the guarded automata specifications. This makes the synchronizability and realizability analyses conditions quite restrictive, and using symbolic techniques can relax these conditions. However, it is necessary to find a symbolic representation for XML data in order to implement symbolic analyses, which could be a difficult task. If successful, such a symbolic representation can also be used for symbolic verification of web services as opposed to the explicit state model checking approach we are currently using.

Finally, the synchronizability and realizability conditions presented in this chapter are sufficient conditions and it could be possible to relax them. Finding necessary and sufficient conditions for synchronizability and realizability of conversations is an open problem.

3.8 Conclusions

Conversations are a useful model for specification of interactions among web services. By analyzing conversations of web services one can investigate properties of the interactions among them. However, asynchronous communication semantics makes verification and analysis of conversations difficult. We discussed two techniques that can be used to overcome the difficulties that arise in verification due to asynchronous communication. Synchronizability analysis identifies web service compositions for which the conversation behavior does not change when different communication mechanisms are used. Using the synchronizability analysis one can verify properties of conversations using the simpler synchronous communication semantics without giving up the benefits of asynchronous communication. Realizability analysis is used to make sure that for top-down web service specifications asynchronous communication does not create unintended behaviors. Realizable conversation protocols enable analysis and verification of conversation properties at a higher level of abstraction without considering the asynchronous communication semantics. As we discussed, it is also possible to extend synchronizability and realizability analyses to specifications in which message contents influence the control flow.

References

1. M. Abadi, L. Lamport, and P. Wolper. Realizable and unrealizable specifications of reactive systems. In *Proc. of 16th Int. Colloq. on Automata, Languages and Programming*, volume 372 of *LNCS*, pages 1–17. Springer Verlag, 1989.
2. L. D. Alfaro and T. A. Henzinger. Interface automata. In *Proc. 9th Annual Symp. on Foundations of Software Engineering*, pages 109–120, 2001.
3. R. Alur, K. Etessami, and M. Yannakakis. Inference of message sequence charts. In *Proc. 22nd Int. Conf. on Software Engineering*, pages 304–313, 2000.
4. R. Alur, K. Etessami, and M. Yannakakis. Realizability and verification of MSC graphs. In *Proc. 28th Int. Colloq. on Automata, Languages, and Programming*, pages 797–808, 2001.
5. Adam Bosworth. Loosely speaking. *XML & Web Services Magazine*, 3(4), April 2002.
6. Business Process Execution Language for Web Services (Version 1.0). `http://www.ibm.com/developerworks/library/ws-bpel`, 2002.
7. D. Brand and P. Zafiropulo. On communicating finite-state machines. *Journal of the ACM*, 30(2):323–342, 1983.
8. T. Bultan, X. Fu, R. Hull, and J. Su. Conversation specification: A new approach to design and analysis of e-service composition. In *Proc. 12th Int. World Wide Web Conf.*, pages 403–410, May 2003.
9. T. Bultan, X. Fu, and J. Su. Analyzing conversations of web services. *IEEE Internet Computing*, 10(1):18–25, 2006.
10. M. Chiodo, P. Giusto, A. Jurecska, L. Lavagno, H. Hsieh, and A. San giovanni Vincentelli. A formal specification model for hardware/software codesign. In *Proc. Intl. Workshop on Hardware-Software Codesign*, October 1993.
11. E.M. Clarke, O. Grumberg, and D. A. Peled. *Model Checking*. The MIT Press, Cambridge, Massachusetts, 1999.
12. H. Foster, S. Uchitel, J. Magee, and J. Kramer. Model-based verification of web service compositions. In *Proc. 18th IEEE Int. Conf. on Automated Software Engineering Conference*, pages 152–163, 2003.
13. X. Fu. *Formal Specification and Verification of Asynchronously Communicating Web Services*. PhD thesis, University of California, Santa Barbara, 2004.

14. X. Fu, T. Bultan, and J. Su. Conversation protocols: A formalism for specification and verification of reactive electronic services. In *Proc. 8th Int. Conf. on Implementation and Application of Automata*, volume 2759 of *LNCS*, pages 188–200, 2003.

15. X. Fu, T. Bultan, and J. Su. Analysis of interacting web services. In *Proc. 13th Int. World Wide Web Conf.*, pages 621 – 630, New York, May 2004.

16. X. Fu, T. Bultan, and J. Su. Conversation protocols: A formalism for specification and analysis of reactive electronic services. *Theoretical Computer Science*, 328(1-2):19–37, November 2004.

17. X. Fu, T. Bultan, and J. Su. Model checking XML manipulating software. In *Proc. 2004 ACM/SIGSOFT Int. Symp. on Software Testing and Analysis*, pages 252–262, July 2004.

18. X. Fu, T. Bultan, and J. Su. Realizability of conversation protocols with message contents. In *Proc. 2004 IEEE Int. Conf. on Web Services*, pages 96–203, July 2004.

19. X. Fu, T. Bultan, and J. Su. WSAT: A tool for formal analysis of web service compositions. In *Proc. 16th Int. Conf. on Computer Aided Verification*, volume 3114 of *LNCS*, pages 510–514, July 2004.

20. X. Fu, T. Bultan, and J. Su. Realizability of conversation protocols with message contents. *International Journal of Web Services Research (JWSR)*, 2(4): 68–93, 2005.

21. X. Fu, T. Bultan, and J. Su. Synchronizability of conversations among web services. *IEEE Transactions on Software Engineering*, 31(12):1042–1055, December 2005.

22. J. E. Hanson, P. Nandi, and S. Kumaran. Conversation support for business process integration. In *Proc. of 6th IEEE Int. Enterprise Distributed Object Computing Conference*, 2002.

23. C. A. R. Hoare. Communicating sequential processes. *Communications of the ACM*, 21(8):666–677, 1978.

24. G. J. Holzmann. *The SPIN Model Checker: Primer and Reference Manual*. Addison-Wesley, Boston, Massachusetts, 2003.

25. IBM. Conversation Support Project. http://www.research.ibm.com/ convsupport/.

26. Java Message Service. http://java.sun.com/products/jms/.

27. G. Kahn. The semantics of a simple language for parallel programming. In *Proc. IFIP 74*, pages 471–475. North-Holland, 1974.

28. Raman Kazhamiakin, Marco Pistore, and Luca Santuari. Analysis of communication models in web service compositions. In *Proc. of 15th World Wide Web Conference (WWW)*, pages 267–276, 2006.

29. N. Lynch and M. Tuttle. Hierarchical correctness proofs for distributed algorithms. In *Proc. 6th ACM Symp. Principles of Distributed Computing*, pages 137–151, 1987.

30. R. Milner. *Communicating and Mobile Systems: the π-Calculus*. Cambridge University Press, 1999.

31. Message Sequence Chart (MSC). ITU-T, Geneva Recommendation Z.120, 1994.

32. Microsoft Message Queuing Service. http://www.microsoft.com/ windows2000/technologies/communications/msmq/default.mspx.

33. Shin Nakajima. Model checking verification for reliable web service. In *Proc. of the 1st International Symposium on Cyber Worlds (CW 2002)*, pages 378–385, November 2002.

34. S. Narayanan and S. McIlraith. Simulation, verification and automated composition of web services. In *Proc. International World Wide Web Conference (WWW)*, 2002.
35. A. Pnueli and R. Rosner. On the synthesis of a reactive module. In *Proc. 16th ACM Symp. Principles of Programming Languages*, pages 179–190, 1989.
36. A. Pnueli and R. Rosner. On the synthesis of an asynchronous reactive module. In *Proc. 16th Int. Colloq. on Automata, Languages, and Programs*, volume 372 of *LNCS*, pages 652–671, 1989.
37. S. K. Rajamani and J. Rehof. A behavioral module system for the pi-calculus. In *Proc. 8th Static Analysis Symposium*, pages 375–394, July 2001.
38. S. Uchitel, J. Kramer, and J. Magee. Incremental elaboration of scenario-based specifications and behavior models using implied scenarios. *ACM Transactions on Software Engineering and Methodology*, 13(1):37–85, 2004.
39. Web Service Analysis Tool (WSAT). http://www.cs.ucsb.edu/~su/WSAT.
40. Web Service Choreography Description Language (WS-CDL). http://www.w3.org/TR/ws-cdl-10/, 2005.
41. Web Services Description Language (WSDL) 1.1. http://www.w3.org/TR/wsdl, March 2001.

4

WS-Engineer: A Model-Based Approach to Engineering Web Service Compositions and Choreography

Howard Foster, Sebastian Uchitel, Jeff Magee and Jeff Kramer

Distributed Software Engineering Group, Department of Computing,
Imperial College London, 180 Queen's Gate, London, United Kingdom
{h.foster,s.uchitel,j.magee,j.kramer}@imperial.ac.uk

Abstract. In this chapter, we describe a model-based approach to the analysis of service interactions for web service choreography and their coordinated compositions. The move towards implementing web service choreography requires both design time verification and execution time validation of these service interactions to ensure that service implementations fulfil requirements of multiple interested partners before such compositions and choreographies are deployed for use. The approach employs several formal analysis techniques and perspectives, and applies these to the domain of web service choreographies and the compositional implementations that each role in these choreographies must satisfy. Our approach models the service interaction designs of choreographies (in the form of Message Sequence Charts), the service choreography descriptions (in WS-CDL – the Web Service Choreography Description Language) and the service composition processes (in BPEL4WS – the Business Process Language for Web Services). We translate models between UML and Web service specifications using the Finite State Process algebra notation. Where interactions deviate from choreography rules, the interaction sequences can be shown back to the user of the approach in an easy and accessible way, in the UML form. The described approach is supported by a suite of cooperating tools, formal modelling, simulation, animation and providing verification results from choreographed web service interactions. The tool suite and related papers are available for download at **http://www.doc.ic.ac.uk/ltsa/eclipse/wsengineer**.

4.1 Introduction

Distributed software systems, and the interactions between components within these systems, can exhibit a high level of complexity and lead to difficulty in the assessment of what system behaviour is possible in multiple scenarios [18]. Constraining such a system requires us to fully understand the behaviour of the system and place controls on which sets of activities a system can perform. A distributed software system also encourages system evolution, by offering reusable services so that other systems may also include components from each other without fully reengineering solutions. Web services (components interfaced using XML and standard Internet protocols) are one such software architecture to exhibit this need for control, combining the flexibility and reach of the Internet, the principles of reusability, with that of conventional distributed systems engineering practices. Recent attempts to standardise descriptions of web service interactions in a Web Services Architecture (WS-A) [2] appear to concentrate only on the vocabulary, whilst the emerging overall process is difficult to assess or verify. Some of the current common standards for these descriptions are illustrated in Fig. 4.1, with the related WS-A layer element and with a connection to a related Software Process Analysis (SPA) [5] area. We believe the complexity in designing web service compositions to satisfy choreography policies can be eased by modelling the required composition processes in an accessible and concise notation which can then be used to verify and validate, not only web service workflows but expected behaviour over cross-domain services (to form the choreography).

In this chapter, we describe an approach, known simply as "WS-Engineer", which specifically addresses adding semantic representation to web service compositions and choreography elements of the standards stack illustrated above, and extends a tool to support a mechanical aid for verification and validation of these processes. Whilst standards evolve, and debate grows around where standards fit in service architecture, we see the Business Execution Language for Web services (BPEL4WS) [1] and the Web Services Choreography Description Language (WS-CDL) [21] complementing each other in service composition development with one as a local service interaction process and the other as a global cross-enterprise service interaction policy. We translate service design and implementation models between UML and web service specifications using the Finite State Process [28, 29] algebra notation. Where interactions deviate from choreography rules, the interaction sequences can be shown back to the user of the approach in an easy and accessible way, again using the UML form. We discuss the issues with a software engineering perspective, describe how our approach to tackle these issues can be undertaken

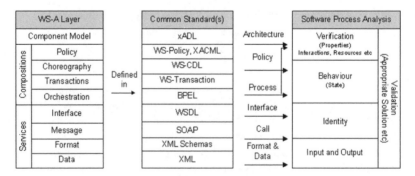

Fig. 4.1. Web Service Architecture, Standards and Software Process Analysis Links

in testing web service in various scenarios and describe the assumptions and limitations which forms our continued work.

4.2 Background

Web service compositions and choreography provide additional layers above basic service invocation whereby collaborative client scenarios enables the differing uses of these services in a wider cross-enterprise domain. This is seen as an important element of making web services viable for wide spread use, and to provide a closer representation of business transactions in cross-domain enterprises. The effect of using earlier architecture styles has been prone to issues of semantic failure and difficulties in providing the necessary compensation handling sequences [3]. This has been attributed to the strict binding of services with specific technologies. Where previously designers of a workflow had to work very closely with the developers of the technical solution, we now have a mechanism to support technology-independent workflow service invocation. This provides an opportunity for the designers to concentrate on exactly what is required from a workflow without hindrance from technical limitations and implementation effort. One key part of the verification in this context is to check the trace equivalence with reference to the actions of the design specification, and specifically how sequencing multiple service conversations is achieved. Whilst there have been other attempts to use model-checking techniques for reliable web service verification, such as in [13, 31, 32], there has been little published on the process of using Message Sequence Charts (MSCs) [19] for service composition specifications and combining these with composition implementations to verify and validate service behaviour against those specified in the requirements. In our previous work [9, 12, 10], we have discussed how to model web service compositions, built using the standard of BPEL4WS, and more recently the translation of WS-CDL.

4.2.1 Web Service Behaviour Analysis

Web service behaviour analysis consists of analysing two aspects of the web service architecture style. A web service formally exhibits its identity and permissible interactions through an interface definition in the form of the Web Service Description Language (WSDL) [4]. Within the implementation for a web service, however, the actual behaviour of its interactions is defined (i.e. the sequence and occurrence). The coordination of a service's behaviour is formed from the basic operations of requesting, receiving a new request, replying to a partner or receiving the reply from a request and this forms the basis for service conversations as part of its behaviour towards an overall goal. Standards elaborate the specification of how, what and when these interactions can occur. The layers above a basic service are described with service compositions, choreography, transactions and policies. Behaviour analysis of the service interactions described using these standards aims to provide a tool to expose potential problems or inconsistencies using properties of interest (such as service process deadlocks, process liveness and interaction compatibility).

4.2.2 Related Work

To date, web service behaviour analysis has largely focused on the interactions between services from the viewpoint that service logic is checked for completeness using safety and liveness properties (e.g. absence of deadlock) and that interaction cycles are completed between partners (a form of interaction compatibility). One of the earlier proposals for formal analysis of composition implementations was given in [31] for the DAML-S "semantic web" ontology to provide a mark-up language for content and capabilities of web services. They extend semantics to evaluate web service compositions described in DAML-S. Whilst their technique is useful to reference particular properties of compositions in verification, the practical nature of this work does not relate directly to those standards defined in Sect. 4.2.1. The author of this work has also provided analysis of compositions in terms of those implemented in the Web Service Flow Language (WSFL) [26] and implements a mapping between WSFL and Promela (the language of the SPIN tool) [31]. The work is a good example of translating service composition descriptions as the technique can be undertaken against more recent service specifications; however, the work is not complete enough to give a thorough covering of analysis topics in service composition analysis as the range of properties analysed is limited. More recently, analysis of web service composition specifications has increased the use of modelling techniques for formal verification, including that of BPEL to Petri Nets [34], for control logic checking of BPEL and describes addition analysis for isolating "redundant messages" that are not necessary if a certain activity has been performed. This appears to be an advantage for efficiency in composition processing although the level of benefit of this ability is difficult to measure. Alternatively, [16] uses Petri net-based models to represent web service composition flows independently of a particular specification. In this work the authors define a "web service algebra" (in BNF-like notation). However, there is a little coverage of how this maps to current standard web service composition languages (such as BPEL4WS or WS-CDL). In [35] web service compositions are described in the Language of Temporal Ordering Specifications (LOTOS). The authors extend a mapping between the algebra and the BPEL4WS by providing rules for partial two-way process, but again there is no easily accessible mechanism for web service engineers to perform this analysis. Fu [13] provides an analysis tool based upon translation of BPEL4WS descriptions to Promela and analysed using the SPIN tool. They also apply limited XPath expressions for state variable access analysis. We summarise the comparison of related work in Table 4.1. We illustrate the coverage of verification with properties defined in process (traditional properties for process models) and those properties

Table 4.1. Comparison of related work with analysis techniques and tools

	Web Service Specifications	Languages and Tools	Properties (Process & Service)
Nakajima [31]	WSFL	SPIN, Promela	Process: Reachability, deadlock freedom.
Ouyang [34]	BPEL4WS	Petri-Net, PNML, WofBPEL	Process: Reachability, deadlock freedom. Service: Message redundancy checking
Salaün [35]	BPEL4WS	LOTOS	Process: Reachability, deadlock freedom. Service: Equivalence by observation of external behaviour.
Fu [13]	BPEL4WS	"WSAT" as SPIN & Promela	Process: Reachability, deadlock freedom. Synchronous and Asynchronous interaction simulation, Data analysis through XPath models. Service: LTSA, Message Sequence Charts
Foster [11]	WSDL, BPEL4WS, WS-CDL, Interaction Logs	Finite State Process	Process: Capabilities of LTSA (safety, progress, fluents). Service: Compatibility, obligations, runtime analysis of Composition Interaction logs

aimed specifically at addressing the service oriented aspects of compositions (including interactions, their compatibility and choreography).

In comparison to these related works, the strength of our approach is to consolidate the use and analysis of specifications for web service compositions, and in particular those from *interface* through to *policy* specifications (refer to Fig. 4.1) and allow the engineers to verify that designs and implementations exhibit the appropriate safety and liveness in all use cases using an accessible method by way of describing Message Sequence Charts (for interactions). Substantial work has been carried out in the area of behaviour model synthesis from scenario-based specifications. Variants to the scenario language presented above have been studied, of particular interest are those that are more expressive such as [7, 24]. In addition, various synthesis algorithms that include different assumptions than those described above have been studied, e.g. [22, 6]. Surveys of the area can be found in [23, 38].

As our approach is built on proven and widely used tools (such as LTSA) we are also able to leverage additional analysis in the form of Fluents (time-varying properties of the world) [39] which are true at particular time-points if they have been initiated by an event occurrence at some earlier time point, and not terminated by another event occurrence in the meantime. We believe that this, along with the work described in this chapter, greatly facilitates those in the role of web service engineers to construct appropriate and correct compositions, whilst upholding choreography obligations through defining the necessary interactions prior to deployment in the service environment.

4.3 The WS-Engineer Approach

Our approach (illustrated in Fig. 4.2) considers analysis of a web service composition process from two viewpoints. Firstly, process model verification can be used to identify parts of the service behaviour that have been implemented incorrectly, or can exhibit unexpected behaviour results. Secondly, validation can be used to determine whether the engineered solution is suitable for specified requirements. The approach is undertaken as follows: A designer, given a set of web service requirements, specifies a series of MSCs or WS-CDL documents to describe how the services will be used and to model how each service requests or receives a reply in a series of service scenarios. The resulting set of scenarios is synthesised to generate a behavioural model, in the form of a state transition system. The service implementation is undertaken by a BPEL4WS engineer, who builds the BPEL4WS process from either specification or requirements. The BPEL4WS specification is used to generate a second behavioural model (transition system) by a process of abstracting the BPEL4WS, with respect to data, to yield a model of interaction. Validation and verification consists of comparing and observing states of these two transition systems.

The approach can assist in determining whether the implementation contains all the specified scenarios and whether any additional scenarios implied by the implementation are acceptable to the end-user. In addition, checks can be made on the models with respect to desirable general global properties such as absence of deadlock and liveness (using model-checking). Feedback to the user is in the form of UML style MSCs. The aim is to hide the underlying Labelled Transition System (LTS) representations and let the user view only the BPLE4WS implementations and the MSCs as a simple intuitive and visual

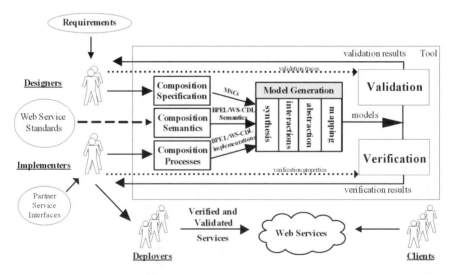

Fig. 4.2. Engineering web service compositions in the WS-Engineer approach

formalism accessible to most engineers [37]. The verification approach is from an abstract behavioural specification using the MSC notation and WS-CDL definitions. The approach uses the UML [33] style design of these sequences away from a technical implementation, and evaluates their transitional state and behaviour locally before deploying any parts of the workflow, and realising the true effect of the process flow. The verification side, of the approach aims to provide a mechanism to support such questions as, can the implementation (such as defined in the BPEL4WS standard) fulfil the interaction requirements and did we build the *process interactions correctly*? The second viewpoint is from that of validation. The focus of validation is clarifying the understanding of requirements against that of the web service composition implementation. Some questions help us identify the validation areas that the approach can assist with in this. For example, has the implementer understood the needs of all expected clients, their intended use of the process and in all possible contexts? Ultimately, the result of validation is to ensure that the *right process was built*. Validation allows the designers and also prospective users of the process to step through the model and determine whether the design is fit for their requirements. Validation of web service composition specification models are a useful step prior to verification of implemented web service compositions, such that designers and users can evaluate a modal as representing an equal view of their requirements.

MSCs form the service interaction design specifications, whilst WS-CDL describes the global service obligations policy. In a similar way to traditional obligation policies, which specify those activities a subject must or must not do to a set of target objects [27], a service obligation policy describes the service interactions which are permissible between partners for one or more given collaboration goals. In the domain of web services, the objects are services, providers and clients that interact with sequence or with a concurrent communication protocol. Note that both WS-CDL and MSC are illustrated as composition and choreography specifications, as they can be used to describe both partial local and full global service interaction policies. In essence, the WS-CDL and MSC specifications can be used as a design specification for service interactions, for which BPEL4WS or other implementation specifications can be used to implement service processes. Collectively, our analysis approach offers reasoning techniques for the following service-oriented verification properties:

- Safety of workflow processes in service composition processes.
- Complete cycles of interactions between service partners.
- Compatibility of interactions between service partners.
- Obligations analysis of partner compositions in service choreography.

4.3.1 FSP, LTS and Behaviour Models

Our approach uses an intermediate representation to undertake analysis of web service compositions and choreography. The FSP notation [28, 29] is designed to be easily machine readable, and thus provides a preferred language to specify abstract workflows. FSP is a textual notation (technically a process calculus) for concisely describing and reasoning about concurrent programs. The constructed FSP can be used to model the exact transition of workflow processes through a modelling tool such as the Labelled Transition System Analyzer (LTSA) [23], which provides a compilation of an FSP into a state machine and provides a resulting Labelled Transition System (LTS). State transition systems with a finite number of states and transitions can be represented as directed graphs. There are at least two basic types of state transition systems: labelled or unlabelled. An LTS is a directed graph with labels attached to each state transition to represent a semantic progress in a process behaviour model. LTSA is a tool which provides a means to construct and analyse complex LTS models of finite state process specifications. This tool, which is fully explained in [28], provides us with an opportunity to model workflows prior to implementation and deployment testing, and with an MSC editor and synthesis extensions [37] to easily model a scenario-based design specification, which can increase the expectation that process composition will provide the necessary path of invocation in all states specified (e.g. reliably by eliminating deadlock situations). With process animator extensions, the tool can also provide a facilitator in simulating workflow specifications for validation.

Each FSP expression E can be mapped onto a finite LTS using a series of operators. FSP has two keywords that are used just before the definition of a process and that force LTSA to perform a complex operation on the process. The first keyword, minimal, makes LTSA construct the minimal LTS with respect to strong semantic equivalence. The second, deterministic, makes LTSA construct the minimal LTS with respect to trace equivalence. If there are no traces leading to END states that are proper prefixes of other traces, then deterministic preserves END states. This means that a trace in the original process leads to an END state if and only if the trace leads to an END state in the determinised process. Throughout the chapter we compare different LTSs to see if the behaviour they model is the same. Various notions of equivalence can be used to compare LTSs, including strong and weak equivalence [30] and trace and failures-divergence equivalence [17]. In the context of this chapter, we use two different equivalences. The first is trace equivalence, where two LTSs are considered equivalent if they are capable of producing the same set of traces. We use this to compare different LTSs that provide the behaviour specified in a MSC specification. Note that the fact that a state is an error or end states is not relevant in the definitions of these equivalences. The second equivalence (strong) is used in the context of some of the proofs in the verification parts. It is a much stronger equivalence relation than that of trace equivalence and, as such, it preserves many behavioural properties [30].

A summary of the operators for FSP is given as follows.

- **Action prefix** "$->$": $(x -> P)$ describes a process that initially engages in the action x and then behaves as described by the auxiliary process P.

- **Choice** "|": $(x-> P|y-> Q)$ describes a process which initially engages in either x or y, and whose subsequent behaviour is described by auxiliary processes P or Q, respectively.
- **Recursion**: the behaviour of a process may be defined in terms of itself, in order to express repetition.
- **End state** "END": describes a process that has terminated successfully and cannot perform any more actions.
- **Sequential composition** ";": $(P;Q)$ where P is a process with an END state, describes a process that behaves as P and when it reaches the END state of P starts behaving as the auxiliary process Q.
- **Parallel composition** "||": $(P||Q)$ describes the parallel composition of processes P and Q.
- **Trace equivalence minimisation** "*deterministic*": deterministic P describes the minimal trace equivalent process to P. If no terminating traces are proper prefixes of other traces, then it also preserves END states.
- **Strong semantic equivalence minimisation** "*minimal*": minimal P describes the minimal strong semantic equivalent process to P.

4.4 A Vacation Planning Example

The vacation planning example is based upon the scenario set out as an introduction to this monograph, in Chap. 1. John, the main partner in this collaboration, can be seen as a partner of the wider service-oriented architecture. Although service-oriented architectures (SOA) are much more than the services they encompass (with change management, security and monitoring being a few examples of other factors in an SOA) the scenario suggests a series of services interacting to fulfil all of John's trip requirements. In this case, we highlight the need for *Hotel* services (finding by location and characteristics), *Route* services (route planning services providing, e.g., the quickest route avoiding current traffic problems), and *Site* services, locating interest and historical sites given a location, route or specific range of interests. Figure 4.3 illustrates a partial SOA view for these interacting services to fulfil John's requests. We consider the problem of engineering the interactions between services as part of a growing problem domain, which is practically constrained through processes and descriptions of interaction policies.

In Fig. 4.3, the problem domain (1) consists of choreography policies (2) and key composition services (3) fulfilling obligations as part of the service interactions. Other partner services (4) facilitate the composition services to achieve the detailed functional requirements needed. John is fortunate to have access to a vacation planning service (one of the key composition services) which aids the number of requests he has to make. In testing, a major issue is how we provide such key compositions and service interaction policies such that John and other partners with possibly differing scenarios are provided with sufficient interaction sequences to accomplish the problem

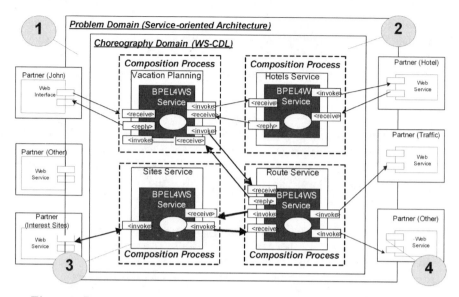

Fig. 4.3. Partial service-oriented architecture for vacation planning services

requiring a solution. We now consider the design, implementation and analysis steps to consider the issues based around the example.

4.5 Modelling Service Compositions and Choreography

4.5.1 Service Design Specifications

The scenario-based design approach has been a popular technique to capture user requirements by way of storytelling [20]. This method provides a concise yet simple tool for *painting a picture* of how actors (clients), components and messages are composed together to complete one or more system goals. It has commonly been used in the past for actual interactions by system users [14], the actors can also represent any agent or service that interacts with the system being described by way of activities. The messages and their sequences that pass between components in a process can be described by way of a MSC or similar Sequence Chart notation in the Unified Modelling Language (UML) [33]. MSCs are part of building a set of scenarios of partial system behaviour [38]. As an example, we illustrate a scenario in Fig. 4.4 for the activities required by a client (John) who requires a composition of service calls to resolve particular vacation planning needs. A higher-level sequence chart (hMSC) can be used to sequence basic sequence charts (bMSC) together (as a choice or sequence).

A web service composition design can be seen as a composed process consisting of various scenarios which when combined together provides a complete

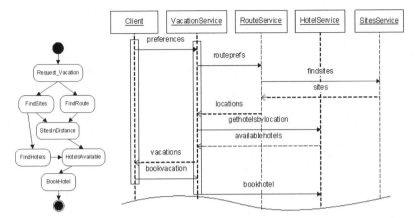

Fig. 4.4. Composition and choreography design as high-level **(left)** and basic **(right)** sequence charts

set of sequence paths describing all possible paths through a service composition design. We relate the concepts of scenarios to web service compositions using a mapping between the elements of message sequence charts and those in building a standards-based web service composition in Table 4.2. Each of the elements of the MSC (defined by ITU) is described in relation to elements of web service compositions and web service choreography (defined by OASIS for BPEL4WS and W3C for WS-CDL respectively).

MSCs are visual aids to design requirements specifications for web service compositions, yet their combined behaviour (as a set of partial stories in a complete composition behaviour model) is still difficult to analyse by human observation alone. The process of synthesising these MSC scenarios to a Labelled Transition System (LTS), which are state transition systems (consisting of states and labels) used in the study of computation, provides a way to computationally and mechanically analyse these scenarios to determine whether the behaviour specified is desirable given a complete system behaviour model. A formal syntax and semantics for MSCs is described in [38, 37] using the FSP notation, whilst a corresponding algorithm to synthesise MSCs to a LTS based upon these definitions is described in [36]. For the sequence chart illustrated previously in Fig. 4.4, a representative LTS is illustrated in Fig. 4.5. Note that full service interaction labels have been reduced for clarity of label reading where "cli" is for Client, "rou" is for Route Service, "hot" is for Hotel Service, "sit... " is for Sites Service and "Vac... " is for the Vacation Planning service.

4.5.2 Assumptions and Limitations

We have made some assumptions here about the example. For instance, the use of a central "vacation planning service" is a key process to the model of scenarios. However, it is likely that individual services may also be called

Table 4.2. A sub-set of web service compositions and choreography as MSC elements

MSC Element	ITU Definition	Web Service Compositions	Web Service Choreography
Higher Level MSC (hMsc)	Describes high level sequence of partial interaction behaviour	Links several compositions or episodes together to form complete system behaviour	Defines a sequence of process compositions and overall choreography behaviour in wider context
Basic MSC (bMSC)	Describes a partial behaviour of a system between instances	A composition MSC is used to describe a single participant view of the overall message exchanges	A choreography MSC is used to describe a single scenario of the overall web service collaboration and participant message exchanges
Instance	Names blocks, processes or services of a system	Relates to partners in a composition, as seen from a local process perspective. Specific process name may also be included in the instance title	Partners in choreography. Local partner services or compositions are created upon a signified request
Messages	A relation between an instance output and input. The message exchange can be split into two messages for input and output events.	Communication between composition partners or internal process components. Messages are mapped to activities in the local composition	Communication between all partners in choreography. Messages are related directly to an abstract process of web service calls between services and the compositions (as services)

by the client, away from the central composition. This broadens the scope of interactions between services and the possible alternative paths through a series of service calls, particularly where calls are made concurrently in which alternative invocations and replies will increase the complexity of paths through the possible service call sequences. Related to this, there is also the limitation of the "state space explosion" problem [40], where the size of the state machines generated grows exponentially with the number of states and transitions produced (i.e. the number of request and reply combinations modelled for each interaction in the service context). Advances in computing and model-checking technology, however, may provide ease to this resource issue. The scenario illustrated represents one such basic scenario in a composition and choreography of service calls, yet there is the possibility of many others, and indeed there are also *implied* scenarios (which can be exhibited from all possible traces of alternative scenarios).

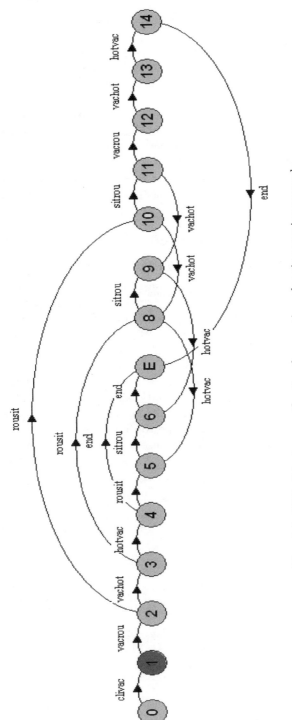

Fig. 4.5. LTS of design specification for vacation planning service example

4.6 Implementations of Service Compositions

Let us suppose we take each of the actors in the design specifications constructed in Sect. 4.5.1, and we are required to build these in such a way that the interactions are fulfilled for all the varying service usage scenarios desired. In a similar way to analysing these interactions as part of a design, building them can be equally as complex. Later in this chapter, we will describe how our approach provides a suitable mechanism to analyse compositions, built in the standard of BPEL4WS to support verification of these built processes against service interaction design specifications. We begin by providing a series of examples in BPEL4WS related to the vacation planning example used previously and to describe how these are modelled in the preparation for analysis.

4.6.1 The BPEL4WS Specification

The structure of a BPEL4WS process specification is illustrated in Fig. 4.6. BPEL4WS is an XML schema with constructs for basic interaction actions, structured process flow, and fault and compensation handling. State of messages (and other data) can be held in local variables and used to build other messages, or to determine a path of action through the process. To define complete business interactions, a formal description of the message exchange protocols used by business processes in their interactions can be implemented for BPEL4WS as a private process with a public interaction summary added to the service WSDL document. The definition of such public *business protocols* involves precisely specifying the mutually visible message exchange behaviour of each of the parties involved in the protocol, without revealing their internal implementation. There are two good reasons to separate the public aspects of

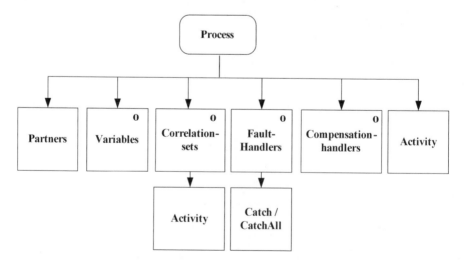

Fig. 4.6. Basic BPEL4WS process structure and activity groups

business process behaviour from internal or private aspects. One is that businesses may not wish to reveal all their internal decision-making and data management to their business partners. The other is that, even where this is not the case, separating public from private process provides the freedom to change private aspects of the process implementation without affecting the public business protocol. The viewpoint of interaction analysis in this work, however, is aimed at the designers and the implementers of the compositions and it is therefore necessary to analyse the private process and how its logical parts define the behaviour of what the composition execution may actually perform.

A private process is implemented in BPEL4WS using a series of XML constructs (described later in this section) for basic logic, structural and concurrent activities in a separate document. This document forms the executable process which we use as source for private process modelling. In the later stages of analysis in our work, both public and private processes are collated to support a complete interaction analysis. In our previously reported work [9, 12, 10], we have discussed modelling a service process as defined by a service composition, implemented in the standard of BPEL4WS. A process consists of a series of BPEL4WS activity statements, specifying the interactions between services and local logic to manipulate message data for these interactions. Let us first consider the *vacation planning service* as described in Sect. 4.4. An example BPEL4WS process for coordinating the route and hotel services as part of John's preferences is illustrated in Fig. 4.7. The (xml tree) structure forms a concurrent sequence of interactions between route and hotel services.

The *receive* construct initiates the planning process by accepting a new request from a partner (in the example this is John's vacation request). Concurrently, marked as a *flow* construct, the service composition *invokes* a route planning service and a hotel locator service. When all replies are received back from the partnered services, the process replies to the original request. The remaining composition service interactions are built in a similar way.

4.6.2 BPEL4WS to Finite State Process Models

The BPEL4WS service compositions are then translated into the FSP notation, where the semantics of BPEL4WS specifications are given equivalent

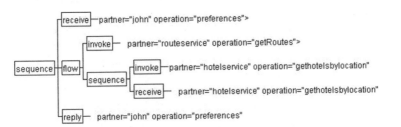

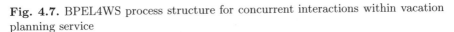

Fig. 4.7. BPEL4WS process structure for concurrent interactions within vacation planning service

```
// BPEL4WS translation to FSP
// Sequences ———
RECEIVEJOHN = (john_vs_rec_preferences- >END).
REPLYJOHN = (vs_john_rep_preferences- >END).
ROUTE_REQ = (vs_rs_inv_getroutes- >END).
ROUTE_REP = (rs_vs_rec_getroutes- >END).
ROUTE_SEQ = ROUTE_REQ; ROUTE_REP; END.
HOTELS_REQ = (vs_hs_inv_gethotelsbylocation- >END).
HOTELS_REP = (hs_vs_rec_gethotelsbylocation- >END).
HOTELS_SEQ = HOTELS_REQ; HOTELS_REP; END.
|| VPLANFLOW = (ROUTE_SEQ || HOTELS_SEQ).
VPLANSEQ = RECEIVEJOHN ; VPLANFLOW ; REPLYJOHN; END.
// Parallel composition process ————
|| VS_BPELModel = (VPLANSEQ).
```

Fig. 4.8. LTS of vacation planning service composition

representation as processes in FSP (Fig. 4.8). In FSP, processes are defined using the $->$ operator, sequences are represented using the sequence operator of ; and concurrent processes are defined using the parallel composition operator $||$. The abstraction from the BPEL4WS is based upon modelling the sequence of interactions in the process, and enumerating the conditional elements which affect the possible paths of execution depending on values within messages. A full guide of mapping BPEL4WS to FSP is given in [8]. A graphical LTS for the FSP is illustrated in Fig. 4.9.

4.6.3 Synchronisation Models of Composition Interactions

Note that the BPEL examples given previously involved several "partnered" service interaction cycles (*invoke, invoke/receive* and *reply*). A secondary step is required to build a synchronisation model between interactions of the compositions. In this way, we are examining the pattern of invoking a partner process, the receiving activity of the partner process and the reply message back to the requestor process. To achieve this, we add a port connector process between the compositions by analysing how they interact, from the viewpoint of each individual composition. The synchronised interactions can be represented in FSP by using the notion of a *connector*, which encapsulates the interaction between the components of the architecture. In [28] this is implemented in FSP as a *monitor*, allowing us to combine the concepts of information hiding and synchronisation. Transition semantics are labelled using the service interaction invoker and receiver *partner* names, the compositional construct name (i.e. "invoke" or "receive"), and by the *operation* being requested. These provide us with a set of labelled process transitions, such as "*vacationservice_hotelservice_invoke_gethotelsbylocation*". If there is more than one invoke in the sender process, then this can be sequentially numbered. The labelled transitions can then be synchronised together by

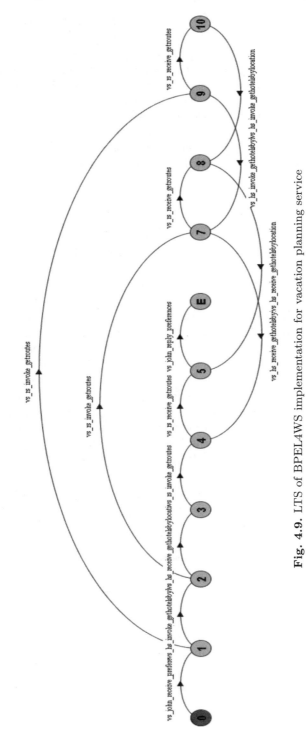

Fig. 4.9. LTS of BPEL4WS implementation for vacation planning service

searching for the relevant receive activity given an invoke transition. With further analysis we can align the invoke operation with the receive operation defined, through a search of related partner interface definitions (defined in the WSDL specification). The result of modelling these compositions, and applying port connector models between compositions, is that we have a complete model representing the implementation of services carrying out one or many roles within the specification given earlier. This model represents the source for analysing the behaviour of the implementations against the choreography design and implementations which we discuss in Sect. 4.8.4. Figure 4.10 illustrates synchronised compositions between vacation and hotel services.

4.6.4 Assumptions and Limitations

Amongst the assumptions in our semantic mappings of BPEL4WS to FSP, we have considered that a process lifecycle begins at the first receive activity specified in the process document. The possibility of multiple start points as part of a series of receive activities (discussed earlier) would affect the order in which activities are executed. We anticipate the mapping would be evolved to consider this in our future work. Our mapping is also currently limited in the translation of variables, in that we are mapping on the basis of a static representation (to values enumerated based upon occurrence of conditional variable comparisons). To provide some flexibility in determining how the values of variables affect the process execution path, we add further mapping to enumerate static values within the process. The mapping does not consider translating event handling, as part of an activity scope. Such a mapping would, however, take a form similar to the fault and compensation handling although the semantics behind event handling are much more towards a time-based simulation basis. We are seeking to evolve the methods described here to ease these limitations and provide a closer representation of a BPEL process model.

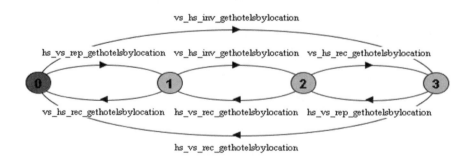

Fig. 4.10. LTS of vacation and hotel service synchronised port interactions

4.7 Descriptions of Service Choreography

The choreography rules of the service interactions can be implemented in the WS-CDL specification language, and then potentially executed on a choreography engine. As part of this specification, the engineer can build the necessary interactions as control flows (resembling traditional structured control), work units (scoped repeatable activity sets) or basic activities (an interaction or a call to perform another choreography set for example). The interactions specified must be part of agreed "cross-service" scenarios. Whilst the implementation of service compositions (implemented as an example in BPEL4WS in the previous section) could be developed with local logic and carried out by individual development teams, the specification must be agreed concisely between groups, and the behaviour specified between services must not only be compatible but also adhere to the choreography rules set. We examine here how the specifications, in WS-CDL form, are translated and modelled as a set of processes.

4.7.1 The WS-CDL Specification

WS-CDL provides a specification and language for defining rules of choreographed web service interactions. WS-CDL provides a layer above BPEL4WS coordinating partner interactions. A choreography *package* is created for each specification instance that is attributed to one or more logical scenarios. Within this package, the partners, roles and relationships (in terms of relationship types – such as "buyer or seller" roles) are specified for all exchanges between services participating in the interaction scenarios. A *choreography* subsection of the specification then details a group of physical interactions between partners and data exchanges as messages are sent or received. The structure of a WS-CDL package is illustrated in Fig. 4.11. The interaction construct is the key activity to expressing that an exchange of messages between two partners should occur. This interaction can be expressed as a request (to a partner of the choreography), a response (from a partner in the choreography) and a request–response (expecting a reply from a request between two partners). Although an information variable is defined as part of the exchange, WS-CDL also provides *channels* to describe a shareable variable storage in which partner requests or responses may be passed along. The control-flow aspects of the specification are represented by the three constructs of *sequence, parallel* and *choice*. These subsequently represent a sequential process and parallel composition of processes or a selective guarded process on one or more conditional elements respectively.

Although these constructs are also represented in BPEL4WS, in WS-CDL the basis for *choice* is dependent on the guard in question and whether that guard is data-driven (evaluation is based upon data values) or event-driven

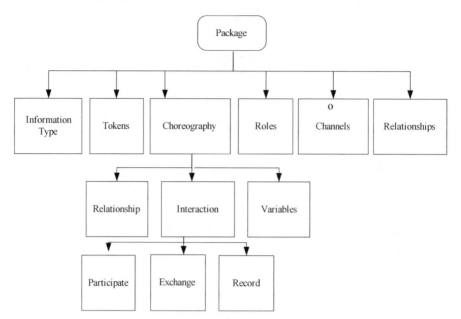

Fig. 4.11. WS-CDL specification structure

(that some event has occurred during the choreography). In addition, a work-unit represents a scoped block of activities which can be repeated and expressed as non-blocking or blocking (depending on whether the work-unit should wait for certain variables to become available). A guard encompasses the work-unit and when evaluated to true, the work-unit process is undertaken. Fault and exception handling is also provided in the form of designated work-units. These can be activated if a particular exception is discovered (such as an interaction failure in which the sending of a message did not succeed or an application failure in the result of receiving a message which raises some application level exception). Under normal choreography running, a finaliser work-unit can be defined to perform some "end of choreography" activities (e.g. a final interaction which can be undertaken only when a choreography group has been completed). Referring back to the vacation planning example, we can see that a policy is needed as to when and how the services can interact to provide a solution for John. In this case an example is when he has to pay the highway fees through the toll system. There is a need to coordinate the interactions between vehicle, John's credit card company and Highway Toll services. For example, John may only be allowed to proceed if the payment has been debited from John's credit card account successfully and that he is in the appropriately registered vehicle for the toll system. A choreography policy would define the interactions between John (as the client), the toll system and John's credit card company. A scenario for this choreography is illustrated (in part) as WS-CDL in Fig. 4.12.

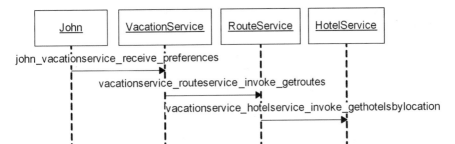

Fig. 4.12. WS-CDL description for partial toll system interactions

Further scenarios would introduce a choice of responses; e.g., to respond with a non-authorised vehicle requesting use of the highway. One or many WS-CDL choreography descriptions can be built to represent different aspects of the service-oriented interaction goals. For example, the partial toll system interactions described above can be included in the wider transaction policy for tracking the movements of vehicles using the highways.

4.7.2 WS-CDL to Finite State Process Models

As with the translation from BPEL4WS to FSP, we provide a translation between WS-CDL and FSP processes by way of abstracting the choreography sets and interactions contained within these sets. The process considers each construct in the choreography tree and maps the construct with associated actions to represent the information contained within the construct's children. The process is iterative for each child in each tree of the choreography specification. For example, the choreography policy defined previously is translated into a set of processes to define each of the interactions as a set of invoke, receive, reply and synchronised invoke_reply (invrep) processes. This is sequenced in FSP to represent the ordering of an invocation and replying to an exchange. In Fig. 4.13 we have also listed the FSP for this translation. Note that each interaction in a choreography group is built on the basis of a synchronised service connection. The sequence construct in WS-CDL is translated to a parallel composition in FSP using its —— operator, whereby the CHOREOGRAPHY1_SEQ process composes the sequences of interaction 1 and 2. Finally, another composition forms the group for the choreography (CDLArchitectureModel). Compiling this FSP into an LTS provides us with a model of the concurrent interaction rules for this choreography. With conditional choreography interaction rules, based upon the *choice* construct in WS-CDL, the FSP guarded variable operators provide a mechanism to represent alternative choices possible in the choreography model. This is similar to the representation for the *switch..case* construct in BPEL4WS.

```
// CDL Interaction Process
// Sequences ——
REQVETVA = (vehicle_tollvehauth_request_authorisation– >END).
REQTSCB = (tollvehauth_centralbank_request_reqpayment– >END).
RESVETVA = (tollvehauth_respond_authorisation– >END).
CHOREOGRAPHY1_SEQ = REQVETVA; REQTSCB; RESVETVA; END.
// CDL Choreography Process ——
|| CDLArchitectureModel = (CHOREOGRAPHY1_SEQ).
```

Fig. 4.13. Sample FSP process model for concurrent interactions of vacation planning service composition

4.7.3 Assumptions and Limitations

We currently consider modelling the choreography only from a perspective of abstracting the behaviour defined based upon the interaction blocks in the specification. The choreography specification contains a far greater depth to define when and how events should occur, and if they influence a change in interaction behaviour. Our approach uses a simple model of general interaction paths which, in the case of the example given previously, is suitable to provide early yet partial verification results to the engineers.

4.8 Analysis Through Verification and Validation

In analysis, we consider two views of analysis using verification and validation techniques. Verification is achieved through the use of formal software process model checking techniques, but we evaluate specific topics of our approach for web service compositions by wrapping and applying these techniques under the notions of deadlock freedom and safety and progress property analysis. We can check the behaviour of a composition or choreography is *deadlock free* (i.e. that there are no states with no outgoing transitions). In a finite state model (such as the models we produced from design specification and implementations in Sects. 4.6.2 and 4.7.2), a deadlock state is a state with no outgoing transitions in these models. A process in such a state can engage in no further actions. The deadlock states we are interested in are those that arise from a parallel composition of concurrent activities in a single BPEL4WS composition, a number of interacting BPEL4WS compositions and one or many compositions against that of their MSC design specifications or WS-CDL policy obligations.

Whilst the models synthesised from the MSC design of a web service composition are focused on service interactions, the implementation may also include additional representation in the form of conditions and constraints (also known as *links* in BPEL4WS). The naming scheme of the MSC message interactions is also likely to be differing to that of the implementation specification naming standards for interaction activities. It is necessary to abstract these additional representations away from the implementation by hiding or mapping them in the model composition. The common elements of the models produced for both the design and the implementation of web service compositions are the interaction activities. In essence, our preparation focuses on abstraction of interaction processes, applying a concise labelling scheme to the implementation specification, hiding implementation specific activities which are not based upon direct interaction messages and identifying a mapping between activities specified in the implementation and the design. We highlight some of the core verification opportunities in our approach as the following topics.

- Design and implementation equivalence – between MSC, WS-CDL and BPEL4WS.
- Composition process analysis – between multiple BPEL4WS processes.
- Process interaction compatibility – interface and interactions compatibility between partners in a service-oriented architecture.
- Partner obligations analysis – checking roles of services against specifications.

4.8.1 Design and Implementation Equivalence

The essence of this verification is to prove that a property exists in the composition modelling of combined implementation and design models. This combined model is used as source for the trace equivalence verification. Furthermore, any additional behaviour can be fed back to the implementer as counter examples. It is also the case that by definition of trace equivalence, the MSC design can be checked against that of the implementation. However, this may appear less useful in the design approach of web service compositions, but essentially this also provides a technique for future re-engineering and checking against existing compositions where the implementation is the initial requirements in focus. In summary, the equivalence verification may also be used to check that a MSC design specification exhibits the behaviour of a BPEL4WS implementation. We continue to use the Vacation Planning service composition example for ease of following the approach steps, and to illustrate how this verification is undertaken with the composition models.

We begin with the synthesised models of the MSC design and the BPEL4WS compositions (as illustrated in Sects. 4.5.1 and 4.6.2 respectively). The models are then combined using an architecture composition, with a mapping between models based upon service partner names, the activity construct (invoke, receive, etc.) and the *from* and *to* roles – where *from* is the sending partner and *to* is the receiving partner. In Fig. 4.14 the MSC and BPEL models are combined (CheckBPEL) and a property is declared as that of the deterministic MSC process.

Although we have built models of both MSC and BPEL4WS activities, we are interested in the minimal trace equivalence in both these models. To specify this in FSP, we use the *deterministic* operation on the given MSC model and include abstracting the *endAction* transition as it is not included

```
// FSP Code for equivalence checking of MSC specification and BPEL4WS
// compositions with property that BPEL4WS implementation should uphold
// activities of MSC design —
// CDL Interaction Process
MSC_ArchitectureModel = MSC model FSP
BPEL_ArchitectureModel = BPEL model FSP + mappings ...
deterministic || DetMSC = MSC_ArchitectureModel.
property || Bis_MSCBPEL = DetMSC.
|| CheckBPEL = (Bis_MSCBPEL || BPEL_ArchitectureModel).
```

Fig. 4.14. FSP code for equivalence verification of BPEL4WS against MSC models

in the BPEL4WS model. If we pass this model through an LTS analyzer, the analysis of the combined model results in a property violation as illustrated in Fig. 4.15.

The reason for this violation is that the BPEL4WS service composition for the vacation planning service permits the concurrent execution of both *getroutes* of the routeservice and *gethotelsbylocation* of the hotelservice. The MSC design does not specify that this is an expected scenario. The service engineer and designer may need to consider whether this is applicable to their composition offered. To correct this violation, either the BPEL4WS composition or MSC design is updated to reflect the actual requirements needed

4.8.2 Composition Process Analysis

By specifying particular properties of interest, engineers can check whether a web service composition can reach a particular state in terms of its *obligations* in more general cases (over that of individual scenarios used in Sect. 4.7). This assists in building reusable service-oriented architectures, for which a policy states obligations in which web service choreography may be undertaken. We describe the model checking techniques for general properties of the composition models under two different types in our approach, categorised as follows:

1. Safety – providing assurance that the composition is checked for partial correctness of transitions for a given property within the model, e.g. that a partner service invocation is always logged following an failure.

```
// Trace run example of MSC over BPEL4WS equivalence
Trace to property violation in Bis_MSCBPEL:
john_vacationservice_receive_preferences
vacationservice_routeservice_invoke_getroutes
vacationservice_hotelservice_invoke_gethotelsbylocation
```

Fig. 4.15. Trace run example of trace equivalence of MSC and BPEL4WS models

2. Progress – providing assurance against starvation of progress in the composition, such that, whatever state the composition is in, an activity will always be executed, e.g., that a reply is always sent back to the original requester.

For both property types, we can reuse the model building steps described for trace equivalence (Sect. 4.8.1) but excluding the design specification requirement. The building step requirements for including one or many processes is dependent on the source in question or, in other words, whether it is that the property must be tested on one composition or over a choreographed domain of processes. In this section, we simplify the examples by concentrating on one composition to illustrate how each of the property checks is carried out in analysis. In *safety analysis* of the compositions, we are seeking to assist the engineer to specify properties (or activities in the composition) that should be upheld in the composition. For example, the engineer may want to revisit the requirements for the service to be provided and note a series of conditional processing dependent on a sequence of activities having been carried out. To model check this and perform a safety analysis, we can use the FSP syntax of **property** to describe the safety property of interest in our model. A safety property defines *a deterministic process that asserts that any trace including actions in the alphabet of the process P is accepted by P*. The property syntax for a check that "John can receive route information before hotels... " is listed in Fig. 4.16. Performing an analysis on the process "BPEL_PropertyCheck" will highlight a trace to property violation, where this property cannot be upheld in the current version of the composition.

Progress analysis is similarly specified by activity properties, but the focus is on those properties which will eventually happen (such as the example given previously that a reply will always be given back to a client from a service). In FSP, the syntax for defining progress properties uses the **progress** keyword. A progress $P = a_1, a_2 \ldots a_n$ defines a progress property P which asserts that in an infinite execution of a target system, at least one of the actions $a_1, a_2 \ldots .a_n$ will be executed infinitely often. This definition allows us to specify a range of progress properties, with the condition that at least one must be upheld in a service composition. By way of example, we use the vacation planning service model to check whether a route is always located for a client's request, as illustrated in Fig. 4.17.

// Property to safety check that Client can receive partial
//(route) planning information before hotel information —
property ROUTEREPLY = (vacationservice_routeservice_invoke_getroutes− >
vacationservice_john_reply_preferences − >
vacationservice_hotelservice_invoke_gethotelsbylocation− >END)
// Compose composition architecture model with property —
|| **BPEL_PropertyCheck = (BPEL_VacationService —— ROUTEREPLY).**

Fig. 4.16. FSP for Safety Check of Client Receive Route Planning Information

// Property to safety check that the Client can always
// receive a reply from the vacation planning service —
progress ALWAYSREPLY = (vacationservice_john_reply_preferences— >END)
// Compose composition architecture model with property —
|| **BPEL_PropertyCheck = (BPEL_VacationService** || **ALWAYSREPLY).**

Fig. 4.17. FSP code for progress property that a reply to a client is always made

4.8.3 Process Interaction Compatibility

Compatibility verification is an important aspect of behaviour requirements between different clients of compositions. Clients will likely anticipate different behaviour depending on their individual requests and therefore the composition must be tested against various scenarios to reflect these different sequences of activities. There is also an assumption that a web service composition will work in any process environment (not just the original development domain). A greater level of *assurance in compatibility* can be given if interacting services are checked whether a composition exhibits the correct behaviour for its own use. Web service compositions can also be seen as the implementation layer of a multi-stakeholder distributed system (MSDS) [15]. An MSDS is defined as "a distributed system in which subsets of the nodes are designed, owned, or operated by distinct stakeholders. The nodes of the system may, therefore, be designed or operated in ignorance of one another, or with different, possibly conflicting goals." The focus is on interaction with multiple parties and the behaviour could be somewhat ad hoc depending on the requirements of the partner services. However, three basic levels of compatibility for component compositions have been previously reported in [25]. These are defined as *interface, behaviour* and *input–output (data)* compatibility. Whilst input–output data compatibility is of interest, it is not the main focus of this verification work. We would, however, expect a related growth of data analysis work to monitor and analyse service messages. We now apply the first two of the concepts discussed for compatibility, and describe *interface compatibility* specifically for web service compositions as the activity of correlating invocations against receiving and message replies between partner processes, such that invoke, receive and reply activities are synchronised. Given a series of service implementations (in the form of BPEL4WS processes), the approach elaborates on the interaction mappings between processes and further inputs from port connectors between interaction activities in these processes. In Fig. 4.18 two such interaction connector models are illustrated for the *Client_VactionService* and *VacationService_RouteService* interaction cycles.

To check that interactions are compatible with those specified in the BPEL4WS compositions, we compose the port connector and BPEL4WS models and map the interactions from composition to port connector (as illustrated in Fig. 4.19).

Compiling "CompatibilityModel" and performing an analysis of the process provides a trace to a property violation as illustrated in Fig. 4.20. The

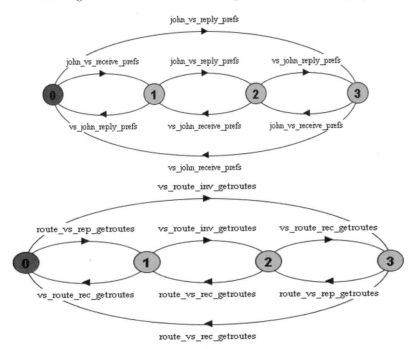

Fig. 4.18. Port connectors for service interactions between client with vacation services (**top**) and vacation with route services (**bottom**)

// FSP code for parallel composition of BPEL4WS service and interaction
// port connectors —
——CompatibilityModel = (CLIENT_BPELModel || CLIENT_VS_PORT_MAPPING || VS_BPELModel || VS_ROUTESERVICE_PORT_MAPPING || ROUTESER-VICE_BPELModel).

Fig. 4.19. FSP code for parallel composition of BPEL4WS services and port connectors

// Trace run example from Compatibility Verification of Client,
// Vacation Planning and Route Service Compositions —
Trace to property violation in CompatibilityModel:
john_vacationservice_receive_preferences
vacationservice_routeservice_invoke_getroutes
routeservice_vacationservice_reply_getroutes

Fig. 4.20. Trace run example of compatibility in service interaction models

reason for this trace is that a violation was located at the point in which the *routeservice* is supposed to reply to the vacation planning service. The engineer can check the composition to ensure that a reply is indeed given in all cases (and, in particular, within the scope to fulfil this scenario).

4.8.4 Partner Obligations Analysis

Service obligation verification provides a service engineer and any partnered services to check the suitability of service conversations in composition implementations against that of the obligations policy. This obligations check discovers if the conversations between compositions fulfils the rules set in the choreography specification. To compose a model for checking a series of interacting service compositions requires that the "interaction verification" (discussed in Sect. 4.8.3) has been successful. An example undertakes these two steps to illustrate how the models are built and analysed. The steps to check for obligations verification is for checking composition interactions against those specified in the WS-CDL implementation. Given a series of interacting models formed from BPEL4WS implementations (such as that used previously for service interaction compatibility analysis), the approach can be used to check that the possible interactions exhibited by these compositions fulfils the rules specified in the choreography sets. An example of the vacation trip services is as follows. Given three models of interacting services, in this case the Client (John), Client's Vehicle and Toll services, a composed model of interactions is compiled. This composed model is then used as a *property* against the choreography policy. A *property* check can reveal whether the service composition interactions comply with the rules set out in the choreography by equivalent interaction traces. Furthermore, any additional interactions which are exhibited between the partners in the compositions are highlighted back to the engineer. In Fig. 4.21, we have given the FSP for building a deterministic model of the WS-CDL model and then specified this as the property for analysis against the BPEL4WS models.

The other interactions in the TollService are "silent" to the obligations checking. Interestingly, we can also reverse this approach to check which other traces are permissible given the composition model as a property to check against the WS-CDL.

// Trace run example of compatibility in service interaction models —
// WS-CDL property against BPEL4WS models —
|| WSBPEL_Arch = (BPEL_John || BPEL_VehicleService || BPEL_TollServices).
|| WSCDL_Arch = CDLArchitectureModel.
deterministic || DetModel = WSCDL_Arch.
property || P_DetCDL = DetModel.
|| CheckObligations = (P_DetCDL —— WSBPEL_Arch).

Fig. 4.21. Trace run example of compatibility in service interaction models

4.9 Summary of Results

Using the WS-Engineer approach, we have examined a series of web service compositions for a vacation planning SoA example and compared them against service choreography rules as outlined in either MSCs or WS-CDL descriptions. In the SOA example for the Vacation Planning services, we examined the processes that may be constructed to assist in service interactions, and how these can exhibit properties which may lead to a lesser quality of service when used by service clients. Although the elements of service-oriented architectures are much more than simply the interactions (security, service configuration management being some others), we have used model checking to exhibit early warnings in the design and implementation phases of service components. For example, this particularly highlighted design decisions lead to a breach of conformance to service choreographies. The verification approach for specifying obligation policies, building web service compositions and implementing policies in WS-CDL has been built into a tool which is described in Sect. 4.10.

4.10 Tool Support

The tool we have developed (Fig. 4.22) to complement this approach is built to extend the existing LTSA tool suite [28] written by Jeff Magee of Imperial College London. LTSA uses the FSP to specify behaviour models. From the FSP description, the tool generates a LTS model. The user can animate the LTS by stepping through the sequences of actions it models, and model-check the LTS for various properties, including deadlock freedom, safety and progress properties. The MSC extension builds on this introducing a graphical editor for MSCs and by generating an FSP specification from a scenario description [37]. FSP code is generated for the architecture, trace and constraint models described previously. LTSA model checking capabilities (for safety and liveness checks) are then used to detect implied scenarios. The tool is available for download from http://www.ws-engineer.net

4.11 Conclusions and Future Work

Our main contribution in our work is to provide an approach which, when implemented within the tool, provides a mechanical verification of properties of interest to both designers and implementers of web service compositions. The use of a formal, well-defined, process algebra (in this case FSP) provided a semantic mapping between the composition implementation (in the BPEL4WS specification for web service compositions and WS-CDL for service choreography policies), and we were fortunate to leverage some work previously

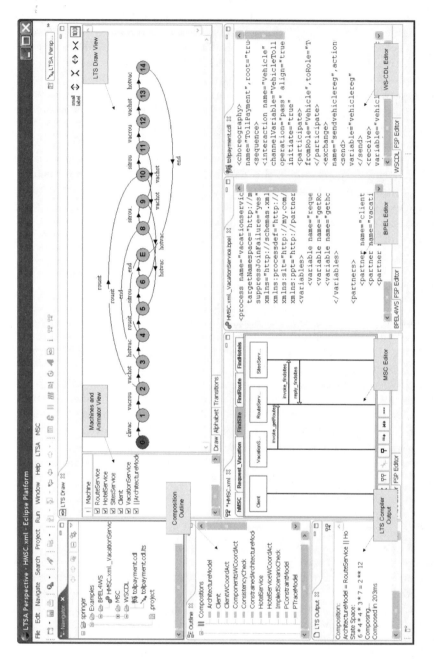

Fig. 4.22. The WS-Engineer tool with supporting web service composition editors and views

reported in [38] for the synthesis of design specifications, in the form of message sequence charts, to the same process algebra. These two representations as models form the basis to provide rich model-based verification. We plan to expand the approach to consider dynamic analysis of policies for service interactions in service choreography and also the analysis of service composition deployments on distributed architectures. In this chapter, we presented an approach towards our goals in the form of a static analysis tool to test service designs (in the form of MSCs), service composition implementations (for equal requirements in BPEL4WS) and service choreography policies (for service partner obligations analysis). The approach provides an extendable framework in which further properties can be defined and implemented to assist in an efficient, mechanical service testing and analysis tool set.

References

1. Tony Andrews, Francisco Curbera, Hitesh Dholakia, Yaron Goland, Johannes Klein, Frank Leymann, Kevin Liu, Dieter Roller, Doug Smith, Satish Thatte, Ivana Trickovic, and Sanjiva Weerawarana. Business process execution language for web services version 1.1, 2004.
2. David Booth, Hugo Haas, Francis McCabe, Eric Newcomer, Michael Champion, Chris Ferris, and David Orchard. Web services architecture (ws-a) - w3c working group note 11 february 2004, 2004.
3. O. Bukhres and C.J. Crawley. Failure handling in transactional workflows utilizing corba 2.0. In *10th ERCIM Database Research Group Workshop on Heterogeneous Information Management*, Prague, 1996.
4. Erik Christensen, Francisco Curbera, Greg Meredith, and Sanjiva Weerawarana. Web services description language (wsdl) 1.2, 2003.
5. Jonathan E. Cook. Software process analysis: integrating models and data. *SIGSOFT Softw. Eng. Notes*, 25(1):44, 2000.
6. Christophe Damas, Bernard Lambeau, Pierre Dupont, and Axel van Lamsweerde. Generating annotated behavior models from end-user scenarios. *IEEE Trans. Software Eng.*, 31(12):1056–1073, 2005.
7. W. Damm and D. Harel. "LSCs: Breathing Life into Message Sequence Charts.". *FMSD*, 19(1):45–80, 2001.
8. Howard Foster. *A Rigorous Approach to Engineering Web Service Compositions*. PhD thesis, Univeristy of London, Imperial College London, UK, Jan 2006.
9. Howard Foster, Sebastian Uchitel, Jeff Magee, and Jeff Kramer. Compatibility for web service choreography. In *3rd IEEE International Conference on Web Services (ICWS)*, San Diego, CA, 2004a. IEEE.
10. Howard Foster, Sebastian Uchitel, Jeff Magee, and Jeff Kramer. Tool support for model-based engineering of web service compositions. In *3rd IEEE International Conference on Web Services (ICWS2005)*, Orlando, FL, 2005. IEEE.
11. Howard Foster, Sebastian Uchitel, Jeff Magee, and Jeff Kramer. Ws-engineer:tool support for model-based engineering of web service compositions

and choreography. In *IEEE International Conference on Software Engineering (ICSE2006)*, Shanghai, China, 2006. IEEE.

12. Howard Foster, Sebastian Uchitel, Jeff Magee, Jeff Kramer, and Michael Hu. Using a rigorous approach for engineering web service compositions: A case study. In *2nd IEEE International Conference on Services Computing (SCC2005)*, Orlando, FL, 2005. IEEE.

13. Xiang Fu, Tevfik Bultan, and Jianswen Su. Wsat: A tool for formal analysis of web services. In *16th International Conference on Computer Aided Verification (CAV)*, Boston, MA, 2004.

14. Peter Graubmann. Describing interactions between msc components: the msc connectors. *The International Journal of Computer and Telecommunications Networking*, 42(3):323–342, 2003.

15. Robert J. Hall. Open modeling in multi-stakeholder distributed systems: Model-based requirements engineering for the 21st century. In *Proc. First Workshop on the State of the Art in Automated Software Engineering,*, U.C. Irvine Institute for Software Research, 2003.

16. Rachid Hamadi and Boualem Benatallah. A petri net-based model for web services composition. In *3rd IEEE International Conference On Web Services (ICWS)*, San Diego, CA, 2004.

17. C.A.R. Hoare. *Communicating Sequential Processes*. Prentice-Hall, Englewood Cliffs, New Jersey, 1985.

18. Tad Hogg and Bernardo A. Huberman. Controlling chaos in distributed systems. *IEEE Transactions on Systems Management and Cybernetics*, 21: 1325–1332, 1991.

19. ITU. Message sequence charts. Technical report, Recommendation Z.120, International Telecommunications Union. Telecommunication Standardisation Sector, 1996.

20. I Jacobson, J Rumbaugh, and G Booch. *The Unified Software Development Process*. Addison-Wesley, Harlow, UK, 1999.

21. Nickolas Kavantzas, David Burdett, Gregory Ritzinger, Tony Fletcher, and Yves Lafon. Web services choreography description language version 1.0 - w3c working draft 17 december 2004, 2004.

22. Kai Koskimies and Erkki Mäkinen. Automatic synthesis of state machines from trace diagrams. *Software Practice and Experience*, 24(7):643–658, 1994.

23. I Krüger. *Distributed system design with message sequence charts*. PhD thesis, Technische Universität, 2000.

24. Ingolf Krüger. Capturing overlapping, triggered, and preemptive collaborations using mscs. In Mauro Pezzè, editor, *FASE*, volume 2621 of *Lecture Notes in Computer Science*, pages 387–402. Springer, 2003.

25. A. Larrson and I. Crnkovic. New challenges for configuration management. In *Software Configuration Management Workshop*, Toulouse, France, 1999.

26. Frank Leymann. Web services flow language (wsfl 1.0). Technical report, IBM Academy Of Technology, 2001.

27. E. C. Lupu and M. S. Sloman. Conflict analysis for management policies. In *Proceedings of the 5th IFIP/IEEE International Symposium on Integrated Network management IM'97, San Diego, CA*, 1997.

28. J. Magee and J. Kramer. *Concurrency - State Models and Java Programs*. John Wiley, 1999.

29. Jeff Magee, Jeff Kramer, and D. Giannakopoulou. Analysing the behaviour of distributed software architectures: a case study. In *5th IEEE Workshop on Future Trends of Distributed Computing Systems*, Tunisia, 1997.
30. R. Milner. *Communication and Concurrency*. Prentice-Hall, London, 1989.
31. Shin Nakajima. Model-checking verification for reliable web service. In *OOP-SLA 2002 Workshop on Object-Oriented Web Services*, Seattle, Washington, 2002.
32. Srini Narayanan and Shela A. McIlraith. Simulation, verification and automated composition of web services. In *Eleventh International World Wide Web Conference (WWW-11)*, Honolulu, Hawaii, 2002.
33. OMG. Unified modelling language. Technical report, Object Modelling Group, 2002.
34. C. Ouyang, W.v.d Aalst, S. Breutel, M. Dumas, A.t. Hofstede, and H. Verbeek. Formal semantics and analysis of control flow in ws-bpel (revised version) bpm-05-15. Technical report, BPMcenter. org, 2005.
35. G. Salalün, L. Bordeaux, and M. Schaerf. Describing and reasoning on web servicesusing process algebra. In *3rd IEEE International Conference On Web Services (ICWS)*, San Diego, CA, 2004.
36. S Uchitel, J.Magee, and J.Kramer. Detecting implied scenarios in message sequence chart specifications. In *9th European Software Engineering Conferece and 9th ACM SIGSOFT International Symposium on the Foundations of Software Engineering (ESEC/FSE'01)*, Vienna, Austria, 2001.
37. S. Uchitel and J. Kramer. A workbench for synthesising behaviour models from scenarios. In *the 23rd IEEE International Conference on Software Engineering (ICSE'01)*, Toronto, Canada, 2001.
38. S. Uchitel, J. Kramer, and J. Magee. "Incremental Elaboration of Scenario-Based Specifications and Behaviour Models using Implied Scenarios". *ACM TOSEM*, 13(1), 2004.
39. Sebastian Uchitel, Robert Chatley, Jeff Kramer, and Jeff Magee. Fluent-based animation: exploiting the relation between goals and scenarios for requirements validation. *Requirements Engineering Journal*, 10(4), 2005.
40. A Valmari. The state explosion problem. In *Lectures on Petri nets: advances in Petri nets*, volume 6, Berlin,Heidelberg, 1998. Springer-Verlang.

5

Model Checking with Abstraction for Web Services

Natasha Sharygina[1] and Daniel Kröning[2]

[1] University of Lugano, Informatics Department, Lugano, Switzerland and
  Carnegie Mellon University, School of Computer Science, Pittsburgh, USA
[2] ETH Zürich, Computer Systems Institute, Switzerland

Abstract. Web services are highly distributed programs and, thus, are prone to concurrency-related errors. Model checking is a powerful technique to identify flaws in concurrent systems. However, the existing model checkers have only very limited support for the programming languages and communication mechanisms used by typical implementations of web services. This chapter presents a formalization of communication semantics geared for web services, and an automated way to extract formal models from programs implementing web services for automatic formal analysis. The formal models are analyzed by means of a symbolic model checker that implements automatic abstraction refinement. Our implementation takes one or more PHP5 programs as input, and is able to verify joint properties of these programs running concurrently.

5.1 Introduction

Web services are instantiations of service-oriented architectures, where a service is a function that is well defined, self-contained and does not depend on the context or state of other services [1]. They are designed to be published, accessed and used via intranet or Internet. The elements of the design are (1) a service provider, which offers some service; (2) a service broker who maintains a catalog of available services; and (3) service requesters which seek for a service from the service broker, and then attach to the service provider by composing the offered services with its own components. A web service offers an arbitrary complex functionality, which is described in a global system structure. Examples of web services include information systems such as map or travel services, e-commerce systems such as web shops, travel agencies, stock brokers, etc. Clearly, it is essential to enforce security and safety requirements in the development of such systems.

Web services are typically implemented in a very distributed manner and, thus, are prone to errors caused by the distribution. They often involve multiple parties. As an example, consider an online shop that accepts charges to a credit card as form of payment. The parties involved are the users or customers, the vendor itself, and back-office service providers, e.g., the payment clearing service. The authorization of the payment is given by a service company for credit card transactions, whereas the "shopping basket" and warehousing are implemented by the vendor. It is easy to imagine another party involved in a transaction, e.g., a company that performs the actual shipment.

Each party typically employs a large set of machines for the purpose of load sharing. The safety and security requirements are often global, i.e., require reasoning about multiple parties and may involve more than one server at each party.

A typical scenario is depicted in Fig. 5.1. A merchant is operating three hosts (e.g., for redundancy or load-balancing reasons). Two of these hosts ('Host 1' and 'Host 2') are used to run a web server, e.g., Apache. The web server itself is split up into multiple processes, $T_1, \ldots, T_4$. The web server processes have joint access to a shared database, e.g., using the SQL protocol. This database is assumed to be the only form of communication between the server processes. The server processes may contact a third party, e.g., to authorize a payment. Incoming client requests are modeled by means of processes T_5 and T_6.

Analyzing software that implements such services, therefore, requires reasoning about many programs running in parallel. Concurrent software is notoriously error-prone. Approaches based on testing often fail to find important concurrency bugs.

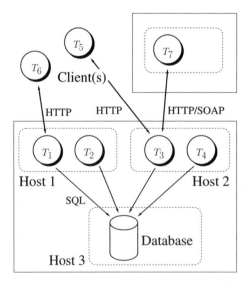

Fig. 5.1. A typical scenario—A merchant operating multiple machines offering a service to multiple clients, and communicating with a third party

Model checking [2, 3] is a formal verification technique. It has been shown to be especially useful for verifying concurrency-related properties, and identifying bugs related to process schedules. In the context of web services, there are manifold properties that model checking can be used to verify:

- Safety properties, e.g., that no exceptions are thrown by the code, that the code is free of data races, or that certain security properties hold.
- Liveness properties, e.g., that the code does not get into a state in which it deadlocks or livelocks.

However, model checking suffers from the *state explosion problem*. In case of BDD-based symbolic model checking, this problem manifests itself in the form of unmanageably large BDDs [4]. In case of concurrent software, the state–space explosion problem comes from two sources: (1) The model checker has to consider manifold interleavings between the threads, and (2) software usually operates on a very large set of data variables.

The principal technique to address the first problem is partial order reduction [5]. The principal method for addressing the large amount of data is *abstraction*. Abstraction techniques reduce the state space by mapping the set of states of the actual, concrete system to an abstract and smaller set of states in a way that preserves the relevant behaviors of the system. The use of abstraction on transition systems is formalized by the abstract interpretation framework [6].

Predicate abstraction [7, 8] is one of the most popular and widely applied methods for systematic abstraction of programs. It abstracts data by only keeping track of certain predicates on the data. Each predicate is represented by a Boolean variable in the abstract program, while the original data variables are eliminated. Verification of a software system with predicate abstraction consists of constructing and evaluating a finite-state system that is an abstraction of the original system with respect to a set of predicates.

Typically, this abstract program is created using *Existential Abstraction* [9]. This method defines the instructions in the abstract program so that it is guaranteed to be a *conservative* over-approximation of the original program for reachability properties. Thus, in order to show that no erroneous state is reachable, it is sufficient to show that the abstract model does not contain it.

The drawback of such a conservative abstraction is that when model checking of the abstract program fails, it may produce a counterexample that does not correspond to any counterexample of the original program. This is usually called a *spurious counterexample*. When a spurious counterexample is encountered, *refinement* is performed by adjusting the set of predicates in a way that eliminates this counterexample from the abstract program. This process is iterated until either a counterexample is found, or the property is shown. The actual steps of the loop follow the *counterexample guided abstraction refinement* (CEGAR) framework.

The CEGAR framework has been implemented in most software model checking tools (e.g., SLAM [10, 11], MAGIC [12], BLAST [13], SATABS [14]). The existing software Model Checkers, however, are not readily applicable for most programs implementing web services. This is due to the fact that the existing tools lack support for the programming languages and the communication primitives used for web services.

A number of programming languages has been designed specifically for implementing web services. The commonly used programming languages for web-applications are WSDL, BPEL, PHP [15], and ASP [16]. While in general their goal is to provide the programming constructs for the implementation of web services, they differ in the level at which they address the web service operations. For example, BPEL [17] has been developed to specify interaction protocols (synchronous and asynchronous) between web services. BPEL is also a high-level language for implementing web service applications, and is supported by the most industrial players in the field (IBM, Oracle, BEA). It is designed for specifying the communication among service participants and its users. Its disadvantage is that it does not support the low-level implementation details of the service functionality.

Among the programming languages that support low-level details of web service implementations are ASP and PHP. ASP (Active Server Pages) is based on either Visual Basic Script or JScript. ASP is a proprietary system that is natively implemented only on Microsoft Internet Information Server (IIS). There are attempts of implementations of ASP on other architectures, e.g., InstantASP from Halcyon and Chili!Soft ASP. Formal models of ASP scripts are difficult to generate as ASP permits full access to the WIN32 API, which offers an enormous amount of functions.

The other commonly used programming language for web applications is PHP, a scripting language specialized for the generation of HTML, server-side JAVA, Microsoft's ASPx, and more recently, C# as part of .NET. PHP is an interpreted programming language that has a C-like syntax. The most commonly used platform for PHP is the Apache web server, but there are implementations for IIS-based servers as well.

A large number of tools and techniques for modeling and model checking BPEL processes have been developed (see e.g., [18, 19, 20, 21, 22, 23, 24, 25]). They focus on analyzing the interaction protocols, the orchestration, and the composition of web services. They are not applicable, however, to verifying the actual applications that implement the web services due to the restrictions of the BPEL notation. As far as the verification of the actual implementations of web services, there are no tools available yet. Moreover, to the best of our knowledge there are no implementations of the abstraction-refinement framework available for any of the languages that are typically used for implementations of web services.

While there are model checkers for concurrent Java, the concurrency is assumed to be implemented using the Java thread interface. Communication between the processes is assumed to be implemented by means of shared data. In contrast to that, programs implementing web services are usually *single threaded*. The concurrency arises from the fact that there are multiple instances of the same single-threaded program running. Communication between the processes is typically implemented by either

1. TCP sockets using protocols such as HTML or XML, or
2. shared databases using query languages such as SQL.

Note that the two communication primitives above have different semantics: in the context of web services, communication through a TCP socket is usually done in a *synchronous*, blocking way i.e., after sending data, the sending process usually waits for an acknowledgment by the receiver and, thus, is blocked until the receiving process accepts and processes the message.

In contrast to that, database accesses are usually performed independently by each process. Blocking is avoided in order to obtain scalability in the number of database clients. While the SQL protocol itself is blocking, the communication between processes through a shared database has *asynchronous* semantics. Thus, the interleavings of competing accesses to the database become relevant.

Returning to the scenario described above (Fig. 5.1), shared databases are usually only accessible within the realm of a single party. Links to external parties (clients, third-party service providers) are typically implemented using synchronizing protocols such as SOAP.

Formal reasoning about global properties of web services requires identification and modeling of *both* of these communication primitives. In particular, support is needed for both synchronions and asynchronous inter-process communication. None of the existing software model checkers provides such support.

We propose to use *Labeled Kripke Structures* (LKS) as means of modeling web services: LKSs are directed graphs in which states are labeled with atomic propositions and transitions are labeled with actions. The synchronization semantics is derived from CSP (Communicating Sequential Processes), i.e., processes synchronize on shared events and proceed independently on local ones. The formalism supports shared variables. Once the formal model is extracted from the implementation, the web service becomes amenable to formal analysis by means of model checking [26].

5.1.1 Contribution

This chapter addresses a problem of verifying the applications that implement the web services and develops techniques for modeling and verification of low-level languages used for the implementation of web services.

We formalize the semantics of a PHP-like programming language for web services by means of labeled Kripke structures. We use a computational model that allows both synchronizing and interleaving communication. Previous models are limited to either synchronous or asynchronous inter-process communication. Once the model is obtained, automatic predicate abstraction is applied to formally analyze the web services. Manual and, thus error-prone generation of models is no longer needed.

We implement the technique described above in a tool called SATABS. It is able to check safety properties of a combination of multiple PHP scripts. It uses the Zend 2 engine as a front-end for PHP. The abstract model is computed using SAT, and analyzed using a symbolic model checker that features partial order reduction.

5.1.2 Related Work

Formal models for synchronization mechanisms have been thoroughly explored. For example, CSP [30] and the calculus of communicating systems (CCS for short) [31] were introduced in the same years and influenced one another throughout their development. CSP and CCS allow the description of systems in terms of component processes that operate independently, and interact with each other solely through different synchronization mechanisms. In CSP, two processes must synchronize on any identically named action (i.e., by means of shared actions) that both are potentially capable of performing. Moreover, any number of processes may interact on a single shared action. In CCS, processes may interact on two complementary actions (e.g., a and $\bar{a}$, respectively input and output action over a shared channel named a), and only bi-party interaction is supported.

Both CSP and CCS do not provide a way to directly represent and reason about dynamic communications topologies and migrating computational agents, which are an important aspect of many modern systems. Some people see this as a major drawback of their theory. The pi-calculus [32] arose as a generalization of CCS [31]. In the pi-calculus, processes not only synchronize on two input/output actions over a shared channel, lent also send data along those channels.

This chapter builds on work described in [26], where SAT-based predicate abstraction is applied to a SystemC design. SystemC is a description language based on C++ that is used to model both hardware and software components of embedded designs. The concurrency primitives of SystemC are modeled using the state/event-based notation introduced in [33]. As in this work, the modeling framework consists of labeled Kripke structures.

The combined state-based and event-based notation has been explored by a number of researchers. De Nicola and Vaandrager [34], for instance, introduced 'doubly labeled transition systems', which are very similar to our LKSs. Kindler and Vesper [35] used a state/event-based temporal logic for Petri nets. Abstraction-based model checking is not reported for these formalizations. Huth *et al.* [36] also proposed a state/event framework, and defined rich notions of abstraction and refinement. In addition, they provided 'may' and 'must' modalities for transitions, and showed how to perform efficient three-valued verification on such structures.

Most of the related work on formal analysis of web services consists of verifying a formal description of the web service using a model checker. For example, in [27] the authors propose translating models described in BPEL into Promela and check the web service flow with the SPIN model-checker. Another example of modeling and model checking of BPEL protocols is [18]. It uses Petri-nets for modeling and verification of coordination of the BPEL processes.

In [28], a similar approach uses NuSMV. The verification of Linear Temporal First-Order properties of asynchronously communicating web services is studied in [29]. The peers receive input from their users and asynchronous messages from other peers. The authors developed a special purpose model checker [29] that allows verification of Web applications specified in WebML.

Among other major techniques for analyzing web services there are works of Bultan and others. This group developed a formal model for interactions of composite web services supported by techniques for analysis of such interactions [25, 24, 23, 39, 22]. Kramer et al. [40] defined a model-based approach to verifying process interactions for coordinated web service compositions. The approach uses finite state machine representations of web service orchestrations and assigns semantics to the distributed process interactions. Pistore et al. proposed techniques for the automated synthesis of composite web services from abstract BPEL components [20], and verification of Web service compositions defined by sets of BPEL processes [19]. The modeling techniques are adopted for representing the communications among the services participating in the composition. Indeed, these communications are asynchronous and buffered in the existing execution frameworks, while most verification approaches assume a synchronous communication model for efficiency reasons.

In [37] at least the interface specification is verified at the source code level using Java PathFinder. The SPIN model-checker is used for the behavior verification of the asynchronously communicating peers (bounded message queues). A language for specifying web service interfaces is presented in [38]. None of the above techniques uses automated abstraction-based verification and, thus, are less competitive in verification of large-scale web systems.

5.1.3 Outline

We provide background information on PHP and related languages and predicate abstraction in Sect. 5.2. We explain the computational model in Sect. 5.3 and formalize the semantics of the subset of PHP we handle. Section 5.4 provides details on how to abstract the generated model and how to verify it.

5.2 Background

5.2.1 Implementations of Web Services

A web service is a system that provides an interface defined in terms of XML messages and that can be accessed over the Internet [41]. It is intended for machine-to-machine interaction.

Such a service is usually embedded in an application server. The application server is a program that runs in an infinite loop and waits until a client connects via a socket (by means of bidirectional communication over the Internet) to a specified port. In order to process several requests simultaneously, each incoming request is handled by a new thread from a thread pool. Thus, there might be multiple instances of the same code running concurrently.

There are three main XML-based standards that define the web services architecture: the Universal Description, Discovery and Integration (UDDI) protocol is used to publish and discover web services, which are specified in the Web Service Description Language (WSDL). The communication between web services is defined by the Simple Object Access Protocol (SOAP).

There are three major roles within the web service architecture (Fig. 5.2):

1. *Service provider*—The service provider implements the service and makes it available on the Internet.
2. *Service requester*—The client that connects to the web service.
3. *Service broker*—This is a logically centralized directory of services where service providers can publish their services together with a service description. The service requester can search for services in this directory.

We restrict the presentation to service providers and requesters, i.e., we assume that services are addressed statically by the requesters. Since there are XML tools for nearly every operating system and every programming language, web services are independent from the machine architecture, the operating system, and the programming language. We use PHP syntax to present our formalism. The formalism is applicable to similar languages for web services as well with minor modifications specific to the syntax of those languages.

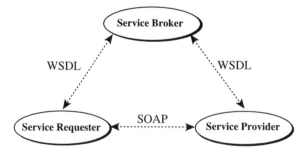

Fig. 5.2. Web service actors and protocols

5.2.2 Synchronous Communication

Synchronous communication within web services is characterized by the client being blocked until the service request has been processed.

Example 1 An example of synchronous communication is a credit card service used in an e-commerce application: when the customer checks out his shopping cart, the credit card service is invoked and the application then *waits* for the approval or denial of the credit card transaction (Fig. 5.3). Figures 5.4 and 5.5 show an example of how a client and a server might be implemented, respectively.

5.2.3 Asynchronous Communication

Asynchronous communication is used when the program cannot wait for the receiver to acknowledge that the data was received. As an example, consider the part of the e-commerce application that maintains a shopping basket. This shopping basked is typically stored in persistent memory, e.g., a database. The information is typically accessed by multiple processes over the lifetime of the interaction with the client and, in a sense, communicated from one instance of the server process to the next.

The time that passes between the accesses to the basket are arbitrary. Synchronization between the time the data is sent (stored) and received (read) is not desired. Also, note that the order of operations becomes important: as an example, assume that a customer simultaneously issues a request to add an item of a particular type to the basket and, independently, another request to remove all items of that same type. The final result (none or one item of that type) depends on the order in which the database transactions are processed.[3]

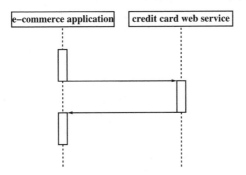

Fig. 5.3. Synchronous communication

---

[3] Synchronous communication, as described above, may in principle be implemented by means of a database. However, the resulting implementation would need to rely on polling and, thus, is very unlikely to scale.

```
1   $client = new
2   SoapClient ( ' ' http :// example . net / soap / urn : creditcard . wsdl " );
3   if ( $client ->debit ( $cardnumber , $amount ) ) {
4   // transaction approved
5   // ...
6 } else {
7   // transaction failed
8   // ...
9 }
```

Fig. 5.4. Example of SOAP client code

We assume that a shared database is the only means to exchange data among the processes in a non-synchronizing way, i.e., we do not model local, shared files that can be written into, or the like. The database is expected to guarantee a specific level of atomicity in the form of transactions. The different transactions from the various processes accessing the database are assumed to interleave arbitrarily. The issue of ordering is captured by the concept of *races*. The shopping-basked described above is an instance of such a race. Such races often represent erroneous behavior. Bugs caused by race conditions are a well-known problem of any system with asynchronous concurrency and are very difficult to detect by means of testing.

5.2.4 Predicate Abstraction

The abstraction refinement process using predicate abstraction has been promoted by the success of the SLAM project at Microsoft Research, which aims at verifying partial correctness of Windows device drivers [10]. The algorithm starts with a coarse abstraction, and if it is found that an error-trace reported by the model checker is not realistic, the error trace is used to refine the abstract program, and the process proceeds until no spurious error traces can

```
1  class  CreditCardTransaction {
2    function debit ( $cardnumber , $amount) {
3      // debit money from credit card and return error code
4      // ...
5      return $success ;
6    }
7 }
8
9  $server = new  SoapServer (" creditcard . wsdl " );
10 $server ->setClass (" CreditCardTransaction " );
11 $server ->handle ();
```

Fig. 5.5. Example of SOAP server code

be found. The actual steps of the loop follow the *counterexample guided abstraction refinement* (CEGAR) paradigm and depend on the abstraction and refinement techniques used. Assume that a program M consists of components $M_1, \ldots, M_n$ executing concurrently. The verification procedure checks if a property φ holds for M by using the following three-step iterative process:

1. Abstract: Create an abstraction $\widehat{M}$ such that if M has a bug, then so does $\widehat{M}$. This can be done component-wise without constructing the full state space of M.
2. Verify: Check if a property φ holds for $\widehat{M}$. If yes, report success and exit. Otherwise, let $\widehat{C}$ be a counterexample that indicates where φ fails in $\widehat{M}$.
3. Refine: Check if $\widehat{C}$ is a valid counterexample with respect to M. This step is called *simulation*. Again, this can be done component-wise. If $\widehat{C}$ corresponds to a real behavior then the algorithm reports the flaw and a fragment of each M_i that shows why the property is not satisfied ($M \not\models \varphi$). Otherwise, $\widehat{C}$ is spurious, and $\widehat{M}$ is refined using $\widehat{C}$ to obtain a more precise abstraction. The algorithm continues with Step 1.

Existential Abstraction

The goal of *abstraction* is to compute an abstract model $\hat{M}$ from the concrete model M such that the size of the state-space is reduced and the property of interest is preserved. We denote the set of abstract states by $\hat{S}$. A concrete state is mapped to an abstract state by means of an *abstraction function*, which we denote by $\alpha : S \longrightarrow \hat{S}$. We also extend the definition of α to sets of states: Given a set $S' \subseteq S$, we denote $\{\hat{s} \in \hat{S} \mid \exists s \in S'.\alpha(s) = \hat{s}\}$ by $\alpha(S')$.

We restrict the presentation to *reachability properties*. The goal, therefore, is to compute an abstraction that preserves reachability: any program location that is reachable in M must be reachable in $\hat{M}$. *Existential abstraction* is a form of abstraction that preserves reachability [9].

Definition 1 (Existential Abstraction [9]) *Given an abstraction function* $\alpha : S \longrightarrow \hat{S}$, *a model* $\hat{M} = (\hat{S}, \hat{S}_0, \hat{R})$ *is called an* Existential Abstraction *of* $M = (S, S_0, R)$ *(here* $\hat{S}_0, S_0, \hat{R}, R$ *are the initial states and transitions functions of* $\hat{M}$ *and* M *respectively) iff the following conditions hold:*

1. *The abstract model can make a transition from an abstract state* $\hat{s}$ *to* $\hat{s}'$ *iff there is a transition from* s *to* s' *in the concrete model and* s *is abstracted to* $\hat{s}$ *and* s' *is abstracted to* $\hat{s}'$:

$$\forall \hat{s}, \hat{s}' \in (\hat{S} \times \hat{S}).(\hat{R}(\hat{s}, \hat{s}') \iff$$
$$(\exists s, s' \in (S \times S).R(s, s') \wedge \qquad (5.1)$$
$$\alpha(s) = \hat{s} \wedge \alpha(s') = \hat{s}'))$$

2. *An abstract state* $\hat{s} \in \hat{S}$ *is an initial state iff there exists an initial state* s *of* M *that is abstracted to* $\hat{s}$:

$$\forall \hat{s} \in \hat{S}.(\hat{s} \in \hat{S}_0 \iff \exists s \in S_0.\alpha(s) = \hat{s}) \qquad (5.2)$$

Existential abstraction is a conservative abstraction with respect to reachability properties, which is formalized as follows.

Theorem 1 *Let $\hat{M}$ denote an existential abstraction of M, and let ϕ denote a reachability property. If ϕ holds on $\hat{M}$, it also holds on M:*

$$\hat{M} \models \phi \Longrightarrow M \models \phi$$

Thus, for an existential abstraction $\hat{M}$ and any program location l that is not reachable in the abstract model $\hat{M}$, we may safely conclude that it is also unreachable in the concrete model M. Note that the converse does not hold, i.e., there may be locations that are reachable in $\hat{M}$ but not in M.

Notation

We denote the set of program locations by L. In program verification, the abstract transition relation $\hat{R}$ is typically represented using a partitioning, similarly to the concrete transition relation R. The abstract transition relation for program location $l \in L$ is denoted by $\hat{R}_l(\hat{s}, \hat{s}')$, and the program location of an abstract state $\hat{s}$ by $\hat{s}.\ell$.

$$\hat{R}(\hat{s}, \hat{s}') \iff \bigwedge_{l \in L} (s.\ell = l \longrightarrow \hat{R}_l(\hat{s}, \hat{s}')) \qquad (5.3)$$

The computation of $\hat{R}$ follows the structure of the partitioning according to the program locations, i.e., $\hat{R}$ is generated by computing $\hat{R}_l$ from R_l for each location $l \in L$ separately. The following sections describe algorithms for computing $\hat{R}_l$.

Predicate Abstraction

There are various possible choices for an abstraction function α. *Predicate abstraction* is one possible choice. It is one of the most popular and widely applied methods for systematic abstraction of programs and was introduced by Graf and Saïdi [7]. An automated procedure to generate predicate abstractions was introduced by Colón and Uribe [8]. Predicate abstraction abstracts data by keeping track only of certain predicates on the data. The predicates are typically defined by Boolean expressions over the concrete program variables. Each predicate is then represented by a Boolean variable in the abstract program, while the original data variables are eliminated. Verification of a software system by means of predicate abstraction entails the construction and evaluation of a system that is an abstraction of the original system with respect to a set of predicates.

We denote the set of Boolean values by $\mathbb{B} := \{\mathsf{T}, \mathsf{F}\}$. Let $P := \{\pi_1, \ldots, \pi_n\}$ denote the set of predicates. An abstract state $\hat{s} \in \hat{S}$ consists of the program location and a valuation of the predicates, i.e., $\hat{S} = L \times \mathbb{B}^n$. We denote the vector of predicates by $\hat{s}.\pi$. We denote the value of predicate i by $\hat{s}.\pi_i$. The abstraction function $\alpha(s)$ maps a concrete state $s \in S$ to an abstract state $\hat{s} \in \hat{S}$:

$$\alpha(s) := \langle s.\ell, \pi_1(s), \ldots, \pi_n(s) \rangle \tag{5.4}$$

Example 2 As an example, consider the following program statement, where i denotes an integer variable:

```
i++;
```

This statement translates to the following concrete transition relation $R_l(s, s')$:

$$R_l(s, s') \iff s'.i = s.i + 1$$

Assume that the set of predicates consists of $\pi_1 \iff i = 0$ and $\pi_2 \iff even(i)$, where $even(i)$ holds iff i is an even number. With $n = 2$ predicates, there are $(2^n)^2 = 16$ potential abstract transitions. A naïve way of computing $\hat{R}$ is to enumerate the pairs $\hat{s}$ and $\hat{s}'$ and to check (5.1) for each pair separately. As an example, the transition from $\hat{s} = (l, \mathsf{F}, \mathsf{F})$ to $\hat{s}' = (l, \mathsf{F}, \mathsf{F})$ corresponds to the following formula over concrete states:

$$\begin{aligned} \exists s, s'. \ \neg s.i = 0 \wedge \neg even(s.i) \quad \wedge \\ s'.i = s.i + 1 \quad \wedge \\ \neg s'.i = 0 \wedge \neg even(s'.i) \end{aligned} \tag{5.5}$$

This formula can be checked by means of a decision procedure. For instance, an automatic theorem prover such as Simplify [42] can be used if a definition of $even(i)$ is provided together with (5.5). Since (5.5) does not have any solution, this abstract transition is not in $\hat{R}_l$. Figure 5.6 shows the abstract transitions for the program statement above, and one corresponding concrete transition (i.e., a satisfying assignment to (5.1)) for each possible abstract transition.

Abstract Transition				Concrete Transition	
$\hat{s}.\pi_1$	$\hat{s}.\pi_2$	$\hat{s}'.\pi_1$	$\hat{s}'.\pi_2$	s	s'
F	F	F	T	$s.i = 1$	$s'.i = 2$
F	F	T	T	$s.i = -1$	$s'.i = 0$
F	T	F	F	$s.i = 2$	$s'.i = 3$
T	T	F	F	$s.i = 0$	$s'.i = 1$

Fig. 5.6. Example for existential abstraction: Let the concrete transition relation $R_l(s, s')$ be $s'.i = s.i + 1$ and let $\pi_1 \iff i = 0$ and $\pi_2 \iff even(i)$. The table lists the transitions in $\hat{R}_l$ and an example for a corresponding concrete transition

5.3 Extracting Formal Models of Web Services

5.3.1 Computational Model

A labeled Kripke structure [33] (LKS for short) is a 7-tuple $(S, Init, P, \mathcal{L}, T, \Sigma, \mathcal{E})$ with S a finite set of *states*, $Init \subseteq S$ a set of initial states, P a finite set of *atomic state propositions*, $\mathcal{L} : S \to 2^P$ a *state-labeling function*, $T \subseteq S \times S$ a transition relation, Σ a finite set (*alphabet*) of *events* (or *actions*), and $\mathcal{E} : T \to (2^{\Sigma} \setminus \{\emptyset\})$ a *transition-labeling function*. We write $s \xrightarrow{A} s'$ to mean that $(s, s') \in T$ and $A \subseteq \mathcal{E}(s, s')$.[4] In case A is a singleton set $\{a\}$, we write $s \xrightarrow{a} s'$ rather than $s \xrightarrow{\{a\}} s'$. Note that both states and transitions are 'labeled', the former with sets of atomic propositions, and the latter with non-empty sets of actions.

A *path* $\pi = \langle s_1, a_1, s_2, a_2, \ldots \rangle$ of an LKS is an alternating infinite sequence of states and actions subject to the following: for each $i \geqslant 1$, $s_i \in S$, $a_i \in \Sigma$, and $s_i \xrightarrow{a_i} s_{i+1}$.

The *language* of an LKS M, denoted $L(M)$, consists of the set of maximal paths of M whose first state lies in the set *Init* of initial states of M.

5.3.2 Abstraction

Let $M = (S, Init, P, \mathcal{L}, T, \Sigma, \mathcal{E})$ and $\hat{M} = (S_{\hat{M}}, Init_{\hat{M}}, P_{\hat{M}}, \mathcal{L}_{\hat{M}}, T_{\hat{M}}, \Sigma_{\hat{M}}, \mathcal{E}_{\hat{M}})$ be two LKSs. We say that $\hat{M}$ is an *abstraction* of M, written $M \sqsubseteq \hat{M}$, iff

1. $P_{\hat{M}} \subseteq P$.
2. $\Sigma_{\hat{M}} = \Sigma$.
3. For every path $\pi = \langle s_1, a_1, \ldots \rangle \in L(M)$ there exists a path $\pi' = \langle s'_1, a'_1, \ldots \rangle \in L(\hat{M})$ such that, for each $i \geqslant 1$, $a'_i = a_i$ and $\mathcal{L}_{\hat{M}}(s'_i) = \mathcal{L}(s_i) \cap P_{\hat{M}}$.

In other words, $\hat{M}$ is an abstraction of M if the 'propositional' language accepted by $\hat{M}$ contains the 'propositional' language of M, when restricted to the atomic propositions of $\hat{M}$. This is similar to the well-known notion of 'existential abstraction' for Kripke structures in which certain variables are hidden [43].

Two-way abstraction defines an equivalence relation $\sim$ on LKSs: $M \sim M'$ iff $M \sqsubseteq M'$ and $M' \sqsubseteq M$. We shall be interested in LKSs only up to $\sim$-equivalence.

5.3.3 Parallel Composition

Many properties of web services can only be verified in the context of multiple processes. We expect that large amounts of data have to be passed between those processes. We, therefore, modify the notion of parallel composition

---

[4] By keeping with standard mathematical practice, we write $\mathcal{E}(s, s')$ rather than the more cumbersome $\mathcal{E}((s, s'))$.

in [33] to allow communication through shared variables. The shared variables are used to model both communication through a database and the data that is passed over sockets.

Let $M_1 = (S_1, Init_1, P_1, \mathcal{L}_1, T_1, \Sigma_1, \mathcal{E}_1)$ and $M_2 = (S_2, Init_2, P_2, \mathcal{L}_2, T_2, \Sigma_2, \mathcal{E}_2)$ be two LKSs. We assume M_1 and M_2 share the same state space, i.e., $S = S_1 = S_2$, $P = P_1 = P_2$, and $\mathcal{L} = \mathcal{L}_1 = \mathcal{L}_2$. We denote by $s \xrightarrow{A}_i s'$ the fact that M_i can make a transition from s to s'.

The parallel composition of M_1 and M_2 is given by $M_1 \parallel M_2 = (S, Init_1 \cap Init_2, P, \mathcal{L}, T, \Sigma_1 \cup \Sigma_2, \mathcal{E})$, where T and $\mathcal{E}$ are such that $s \xrightarrow{A} s'$ iff $A \neq \emptyset$ and one of the following holds:

1. $A \subseteq \Sigma_1 \setminus \Sigma_2$ and $s \xrightarrow{A}_1 s'$,
2. $A \subseteq \Sigma_2 \setminus \Sigma_1$ and $s \xrightarrow{A}_2 s'$, or
3. $A \subseteq \Sigma_1 \cap \Sigma_2$ and $s \xrightarrow{A}_1 s'$ and $s \xrightarrow{A}_2 s'$.

In other words, components must synchronize on shared actions and proceed independently on local actions. This notion of parallel composition is similar to the definition used for CSP; see also [44].

5.3.4 Transforming PHP into an LKS

We assume that there is a set of services Σ, each with its own implementation. The programs are assumed not to have explicitly generated threads. Instead, we assume that n^σ identical copies of the service $\sigma \in \Sigma$ are running in parallel.

For the verification of the web service, we first construct a formal model for it. We use LKSs for modeling the processes involved in the service. If the source code of a component is not available, e.g., in the case of a third-party service, we assume that an LKS summarizing the interface of the service is written manually, using a (possibly informal) specification of the service as a guide.

If the source code of the component is available, we compute a formal model of the program automatically. The first step is to parse and type-check the PHP program. Our scanner and parser is based on the scanner and parser of the Zend Engine, version 2.0.[5] The Zend engine is also used by most execution environments for PHP.

The type-checking phase is complicated by the fact that the PHP language is typically interpreted and, thus, variables in PHP scripts may have multiple types, to be determined at run-time. We address this problem by introducing multiple 'versions' of each variable, one for each type that the variable might have. A new variable is added that stores the actual type that the program variable has at a given point in time.

---

[5] The Zend engine is available freely at http://www.zend.com/

The next step is to further pre-process the program. Object construction and destruction is replaced by corresponding calls to the construction and destruction methods, respectively.[6] Side effects are removed by syntactic transformations, and the control flow statements (if, while, etc.) are transformed into guarded goto statements. As PHP permits method overloading, we perform a standard value-set analysis in order to obtain the set of methods that a method call may resolve to. This is identical to the way function pointers are handled in a programming language such as ANSI-C. The guarded goto-program is essentially an annotated control flow graph (CFG). The CFG is then transformed into an LKS, which is straightforward.

We formalize the semantics of a fragment of PHP using an LKS M^σ for each service $\sigma \in \Sigma$. The behavior of the whole system is given by the parallel composition $M_1^\sigma \| \ldots \| M_{n^\sigma}^\sigma$ for all services σ, i.e., all copies of all services are composed.

The only point of synchronization of processes is assumed to be a call using SOAP or the like. For each thread i of service σ, we define a synchronization event ω_i^σ. We also define local actions τ_i^σ for all $\sigma \in \Sigma$ and $i \in \{1, \ldots, n^\sigma\}$. The τ_i^σ events are used exclusively by thread i of service σ. If the thread is clear from the context, we simply write $s \xrightarrow{\tau} s'$ for a local transition of the tread.

Notation

The global state space $S = S_1 = \ldots = S_n$ is spanned by the data and variables for all services and a program counter PC_i^σ for each thread. Thus, a state $s \in S$ is a pair $(\overline{V}, \overline{PC})$ consisting of a vector $\overline{V}$ for the program variables and a vector $\overline{PC}$ for the PCs. Given a state $s \in S$, we denote the projection of the value of PC_i from s as $s.PC_i$.

The execution of a statement by thread i increases the PC of thread i, while the other PCs remain unchanged. Let $\nu_i(\overline{\sigma})$ be a shorthand for $\overline{PC}'$ with $PC_i' = PC_i + 1$ and $PC_j' = PC_j$ for all $j \neq i$.

Initialization

We define the set of initial states *Init* as the set of states $s \in S$ such that the PCs are set to the start of each thread. The initialization of the variables is assumed to be performed as part of the program.

Transition Relation

The transition relation of LKS M_i is defined by a case split on the instruction that is to be executed. There are four different statements: assignments, guarded gotos, requests, and acknowledgments. Assignments are used to model reading and writing of program variables and transactions on data in

---

[6] In the case of PHP, only a very limited form of destruction is performed.

the database. The guarded gotos model the control flow of the program. The synchronizing calls to other web services, e.g., by means of SOAP as described above, are modeled by means of two sync statements: the first sync statement is used for the synchronization of the request, and the second sync statement is used for the synchronization of the acknowledgment. The semantics of both statements is identical.

Formally, let $\mathcal{P}_t(PC)$ denote the instruction pointed to by PC in thread t. Let I be a shorthand for $\mathcal{P}_t(s.PC_t)$.

- If I is a $\texttt{sync}(\sigma)$ statement, the thread t non-deterministically chooses a server thread $i \in \{1, \ldots, n^\sigma\}$ and makes a ω_i^σ-transition. No synchronization with other threads is performed. Formally,

$$I = \texttt{sync}(\sigma); \Longrightarrow s \xrightarrow{\omega_i^\sigma}_t s'$$

  with $s'.\overline{V} = s.\overline{V}$, $s'.\overline{PC} = \nu_i(s.\overline{PC})$.

- If I is a statement that assigns the value of the expression e to the variable x, the thread i makes a τ-transition and changes the global state accordingly. Let $s(e)$ denote the value of the expression e evaluated in state s.

$$I = \texttt{x=e}; \Longrightarrow s \xrightarrow{\tau}_i s'$$

  with $s'.x = s(e)$, $s'.y = s.y$ for $y \neq x$, $s'.\overline{PC} = \nu_i(s.\overline{PC})$. If the modification of x triggers events that other threads are sensitive to, this can be realized by an implicit $\texttt{notify}$ statement after the assignment.

- If I is a guarded $\texttt{goto}$ statement with guard g and target t, the thread i makes a τ-transition and changes its PC accordingly:

$$I = \texttt{if(g) goto t}; \Longrightarrow s \xrightarrow{\tau}_i s'$$

with $s'.\overline{V} = s.\overline{V}$, and

$$s'.PC_j = \begin{cases} t & : i = j \wedge s(g) \\ PC_j + 1 & : \text{otherwise} \end{cases}$$

5.4 Model Checking with Abstraction for Web Services

5.4.1 Existential Abstraction of Transition Systems with Events

For the verification of the web service, we first construct an abstract, formal model for it. We assume that we have generated or written concrete LKSs as described in Sect. 5.3.4. The concrete LKSs are then abstracted into abstract LKSs. The labels on the states of the abstract LKSs correspond to predicates that are used for predicate abstraction. As done in [45], we use SAT in order to compute the abstraction of the instructions in the PHP programs. This section provides a short overview of the algorithm. For more information on the algorithm, we refer the reader to [46, 45].

Recall that S denotes the (global) set of concrete states. Let $\alpha(s)$ with $s \in S$ denote the abstraction function. The abstract model makes an A-transition from an abstract state $\hat{s}$ to $\hat{s}'$ iff there is an A-transition from s to s' in the concrete model and s is abstracted to $\hat{s}$ and s' is abstracted to $\hat{s}'$. Let $\hat{T}$ denote this abstract transition relation. Formally,

$$\hat{s} \xrightarrow{A} \hat{s}' : \Longleftrightarrow \exists s, s' \in S : s \xrightarrow{A} s' \wedge \\ \alpha(s) = \hat{s} \wedge \alpha(s') = \hat{s}' \tag{5.6}$$

This formula is transformed into conjunctive normal form (CNF) by replacing the bit-vector arithmetic operators by arithmetic circuits. Due to the quantification over the abstract states this corresponds to an all-SAT instance. For efficiency, one over-approximates $\hat{T}$ by partitioning the predicates into clusters [47]. The use of SAT for this kind of abstraction was first proposed in [48]. We use Boolean programs [10] to represent the abstract models. In order to represent the synchronizing events, a special `sync` instruction is added to the language.

5.4.2 Thread-Modular Abstraction

The abstract models are built separately for each LKS corresponding to an individual PHP program, or thread of execution. The advantage of this approach is that the individual programs are much smaller than the overall system description, which usually consists of multiple PHP scripts. After abstracting the threads separately, we form the parallel composition of the abstract LKSs, which can then be verified. The following formalizes our modular abstraction approach.

Let M_1 and M_2 be two LKSs, and let $\pi = \langle s_1, a_1, \ldots \rangle$ be an alternating infinite sequence of states and actions of $M_1 \parallel M_2$. The *projection* $\pi \restriction M_i$ of π on M_i consists of the (possibly finite) subsequence of $\langle s_1, a_1, \ldots \rangle$ obtained by simply removing all pairs $\langle a_j, s_{j+1} \rangle$ for which $a_j \notin \Sigma_i$. In other words, we keep from π only those states that belong to M_i, and excise any transition labeled with an action not in M_i's alphabet.

We now record the following claim, which extends similar standard results for the process algebra CSP [49] and LKSs [33].

Claim

1. Parallel composition is (well-defined and) associative and commutative up to $\sim$-equivalence. Thus, in particular, no bracketing is required when combining more than two LKSs.

2. Let $\hat{M}_i$ denote the abstraction of M_i, and let $\hat{M}_{\parallel}$ denote the abstraction of the parallel composition of $M_1, \ldots, M_n$. Then $\hat{M}_1 \parallel \ldots \parallel \hat{M}_n \sim \hat{M}_{\parallel}$. In other words, the composition of the abstract machines $(\hat{M}_1, \ldots, \hat{M}_n)$ is an abstraction of the composition of the concrete machines $(M_1, \ldots, M_n)$.

For detailed related proofs of the compositional approach, we refer the reader to [49, Chapter 2].

Claim 1 formalizes our thread-modular approach to abstraction. Simulation and refinement can also be performed without building the transition relation of the product machine. This is justified by the fact that the program visible state variables ($\overline{V}$ and $\overline{PC}$) are only changed by one thread on shared transitions. Thus, abstraction, counterexample validation, and abstraction refinement can be conducted one thread at a time.

5.4.3 Abstraction-Refinement Loop

Once the abstract model is constructed, it is passed to the model checker for the consistency check against the properties. We use the SATABS model checker [14], which implements the SAT-based predicate abstraction approach for verification of ANSI-C programs. It employs a full counterexample-guided abstraction refinement verification approach. Following the abstraction-refinement loop, we iteratively refine the abstract model of the PHP program if it is detected that the counterexample produced by the model checker cannot be simulated on the original program. Since spurious counterexamples are caused by existential abstraction and since SAT solvers are used to construct the abstract models, we also use SAT for the simulation of the counterexamples. Our verification tool forms a SAT instance for each transition in the abstract error trace. If it is found to be unsatisfiable, it is concluded that the transition is spurious. As described in [50], the tool then uses the unsatisfiable core of the SAT instance for efficient refinement of the abstract model.

Clearly, the absence of individual spurious transitions does not guarantee that the error trace is real. Thus, our model checker forms another SAT instance. It corresponds to Bounded Model Checking (BMC) [51] on the original PHP program following the control flow and thread schedule given by the abstract error trace. If satisfiable, our tool builds an error trace from the satisfying assignment, which shows the path to the error. A similar approach is used in [52] for DSP software. The counterexample is mapped back to the program locations and syntax of the original PHP program in order to provide a useful basis for error diagnosis. In particular, the counterexample trace includes values for all concrete variables that are assigned on the path. If unsatisfiable, the abstract model is refined by adding predicates using weakest preconditions. Again, we use the unsatisfiable core in order to select appropriate predicates.

5.4.4 Object References and Dynamic Memory Allocation

The PHP language is based on C and C++ and, thus, makes frequent use of dynamically allocated objects using the **new** operator. Also, it permits to take the address of variables for building references. We support such constructs by the following means:

- We allow references and the (implicit) dereferencing operators within the predicates.
- For each variable that may be assigned a reference, we have special predicates that keep track of the size and a valid bit to track whether the reference is NULL. It is set or cleared upon assignment. Each time the pointer is dereferenced, we assert that the valid predicate holds. We denote the predicate by $\zeta(o)$, for any object o.
- During the construction of (5.6), we employ a standard, but control flow-sensitive points-to analysis in order to obtain the set of variables a pointer may point to. This is used to perform a case-split in order to replace the pointer dereferencing operators. Dynamic objects are handled as follows: we generate exactly as many instances as there are different points that may alias to the same dynamic object.

This approach not only allows handing references within PHP programs, but also efficiently manages the size of the generated CNF equations since it avoids handling data that pointers do not point to.

Note that concurrency issues can be ignored during the alias analysis, as references cannot be shared (practically) among processes. Thus, we can use efficient and precise alias analysis algorithms for sequential programs.

Example

Figure 5.7 shows an example of predicate abstraction in the presence of dynamically allocated objects. The left-hand side shows the code to be abstracted, the right-hand side shows the predicates that hold after the execution of the code. In order to show the last predicate, the equality of the two integer fields is built, the following formula, where D_1 and D_2 denote the two dynamic objects, and b_3 denotes the Boolean variable corresponding to the predicate $p\text{->}n\text{->}i = p\text{->}i + 1$:

$$p = \&D_1 \wedge D_1.n = \&D_2 \wedge$$
$$D_2'.p = D_2.p \wedge D_2'.i = D_1.i \wedge$$
$$(b_3 \iff (D_2'.i = D_1.i + 1))$$

This formula is only valid for $b_3 = \textbf{true}$, which shows the predicate.

```
class s {
        var $n;
        var $i;
}
...
$p=new s;          ζ(*p)
$p->n=new s;       ζ(*p), ζ(*(p->n))
$p->n->i=$p->i+1;  p->n->i = p->i + 1
```

Fig. 5.7. Example of abstraction in presence of dynamic objects

5.4.5 Case Study

We have experimented with a set of PHP scripts in order to quantify the performance of predicate abstraction on programs written in a scripting language. Two different scripts implement the two parts of the service:

1. A front-end script handles client connections and interacts with them by means of HTML forms. It maintains the user sessions and uses SOAP to communicate with the back-end script.
2. The back-end script receives commands from the front-end script via SOAP and stores transactions in a MySQL database.

The front-end and back-end scripts have about 4000 and 3000 lines of code, respectively, not including in-line HTML. The property we check is an assertion on the transaction records generated. It is enforced by the front-end script (input data not compliant is rejected). For the purpose of verification, we add an assertion that checks it in the back-end as well. We verify this property for an unbounded number of client and front-end processes, and one back-end process.

The main challenge when applying formal methods to scripting languages such as PHP is to model the extensive library (as implemented by the PHP execution environment). We have only completed that task to the point that was required for the property described above to pass; a verification tool of industrial relevance has to include an almost complete set of models for all functions offered by the execution environment. Similar issues exist for languages such as JAVA and C# as well, however. In particular, the direct access to the SQL databases permitted by the PHP scripting language actually requires statically analyzing SQL commands. Unfortunately, PHP does not provide a suitable abstraction layer and, thus, the commands used to access databases even depend on the vendor.

Our verification engine has been applied in the past to ANSI-C programs of much larger size and higher complexity and, thus, typical scripts do not pose a capacity challenge. The verification requires only five refinement iterations, generating 120 predicates, and terminates within 51 seconds on a modern machine with 3.0 GHz. Most components of the abstraction-refinement loop have linear run-time in the size of the programs. The only exception is the verification of the abstract model, which may be exponential in practice. However, in the case of PHP, this is rarely observed: as there is very little interaction between the processes (when compared with C programs that use shared-variable concurrency), the partial order reduction that our model checker implements eliminates almost all interleavings between the threads, and the complexity of verifying the abstract models becomes comparable to that of checking sequential programs.

5.5 Conclusion

This chapter formalizes the semantics of a PHP-like language for implementing web services by means of labeled Kripke structures. The LKS notation permits both synchronizing and non-synchronizing (interleaving) communication in the model. Both forms of communication are typical for web services. While each form of communication can be replaced by the other one, doing so typically results in a blowup of the model. The LKSs of the threads can be analyzed formally by means of automatic predicate abstraction. These results enable the verification of the applications that implement web services.

We have implemented these techniques in a tool called SATABS. While our implementation is currently limited to the verification of PHP5 scripts, the method is also applicable to other programming languages used in this context. It could be extended to handle systems that use multiple programming languages, e.g., both PHP5 and JAVA, or PHP5 and C#.

Our implementation is able to show safety properties of a combination of multiple PHP scripts running in parallel. Most steps of the analysis loop are done in a thread-modular manner and, thus, the analysis scales in the number of threads. The verification of the abstract (Boolean) model is the only part of the analysis that examines the entire system.

Our implementation currently lacks support for liveness properties, despite the fact that liveness is a property of high importance in the context of web services. While predicate abstraction is in general suitable to prove liveness properties, it has to be augmented with a generator for ranking functions in order to prove termination of most loops [53]. Another future direction of research is to extend the implementation to prove concealment properties, e.g., that session IDs do not leak out.

Model checking for PHP or similar scripting languages possibly has applications beyond property checking. For example, the information obtained about the reachable state-space could be exploited to efficiently compile a PHP program (which is usually interpreted) into machine code.

References

1. Douglas K. Barry. Web services and service-oriented architectures. *Morgan Kaufmann*, 2003.
2. Edmund M. Clarke, Orna Grumberg, and Doron Peled. *Model Checking*. MIT Press, December 1999.
3. Edmund M. Clarke and E. Allen Emerson. Synthesis of synchronization skeletons for branching time temporal logic. In *Logic of Programs: Workshop*, volume 131 of *Lecture Notes in Computer Science*. Springer, 1981.
4. Jerry R. Burch, Edmund M.Clarke, Kenneth L. McMillan, David L. Dill, and L. J. Hwang. Symbolic model checking: 10^{20} states and beyond. *Information and Computation*, 98(2):142–170, 1992.

5. Gerard J. Holzmann and Doron Peled. An improvement in formal verification. In Dieter Hogrefe and Stefan Leue, editors, *Formal Description Techniques VII, Proceedings of the 7th IFIP WG6.1 International Conference on Formal Description Techniques, Berne, Switzerland, 1994*, volume 6 of *IFIP Conference Proceedings*, pages 197–211. Chapman & Hall, 1995.

6. Patrik Cousot. Abstract interpretation. *Symposium on Models of Programming Languages and Computation, ACM Computing Surveys*, 28(2):324–328, June 1996.

7. Susanne Graf and Hassen Saïdi. Construction of abstract state graphs with PVS. In O. Grumberg, editor, *Proc. 9th International Conference on Computer Aided Verification (CAV'97)*, volume 1254, pages 72–83. Springer, 1997.

8. Michael Colón and Thomás E. Uribe. Generating finite-state abstractions of reactive systems using decision procedures. In *Computer Aided Verification (CAV)*, volume 1427 of *Lecture Notes in Computer Science*, pages 293–304. Springer, 1998.

9. Edmund M. Clarke, Orna Grumberg, and David E. Long. Model checking and abstraction. In *POPL*, 1992.

10. Thomas Ball and Sriram K. Rajamani. Boolean programs: A model and process for software analysis. Technical Report 2000-14, Microsoft Research, February 2000.

11. Thomas Ball, Rupak Majumdar, Todd D. Millstein, and Sriram K. Rajamani. Automatic predicate abstraction of C programs. In *PLDI 01: Programming Language Design and Implementation*, pages 203–213. ACM, 2001.

12. Sagar Chaki, Edmund M. Clarke, Alex Groce, Somesh Jha, and Helmut Veith. Modular verification of software components in C. In *ICSE*, pages 385–395. IEEE Computer Society, 2003.

13. Thomas A. Henzinger, Ranjit Jhala, Rupak Majumdar, and Grégoire Sutre. Software verification with BLAST. In Thomas Ball and Sriram K. Rajamani, editors, *SPIN*, volume 2648 of *Lecture Notes in Computer Science*, pages 235–239. Springer, 2003.

14. Edmund M. Clarke, Daniel Kroening, Natasha Sharygina, and Karen Yorav. SATABS: SAT-based predicated abstraction for ANSI-C. In *Tools and Algorithms for the Construction and Analysis of Systems, 11th International Conference (TACAS)*, volume 3440 of *Lecture Notes in Computer Science*, pages 570–574. Springer, 2005.

15. PHP: Hypertext preprocessor. http://www.php.net/.

16. http://www.asp.net/.

17. http://www.ibm.com/developerworks/library/specification/ws-bpel/.

18. Bernd-Holger Schlingloff, Axel Martens, and Karsten Schmidt. Modeling and model checking web services. *Electr. Notes Theor. Comput. Sci.*, 126:3–26, 2005.

19. Raman Kazhamiakin, Marco Pistore, and Luca Santuari. Analysis of communication models in web service compositions. In *WWW '06: Proceedings of the 15th international conference on World Wide Web*, pages 267–276, New York, NY, USA, 2006. ACM Press.

20. Marco Pistore, Paolo Traverso, Piergiorgio Bertoli, and Annapaola Marconi. Automated synthesis of executable web service compositions from BPEL4WS processes. In Ellis and Hagino [21], pages 1186–1187.

21. Allan Ellis and Tatsuya Hagino, editors. *Proceedings of the 14th international conference on World Wide Web, WWW 2005, Chiba, Japan, May 10-14, 2005 - Special interest tracks and posters*. ACM, 2005.

22. Tuba Yavuz-Kahveci, Constantinos Bartzis, and Tevfik Bultan. Action language verifier, extended. In Kousha Etessami and Sriram K. Rajamani, editors, *CAV*, volume 3576 of *Lecture Notes in Computer Science*, pages 413–417. Springer, 2005.

23. Xiang Fu, Tevfik Bultan, and Jianwen Su. Analysis of interacting BPEL web services. In Stuart I. Feldman, Mike Uretsky, Marc Najork, and Craig E. Wills, editors, *WWW*, pages 621–630. ACM, 2004.

24. Xiang Fu, Tevfik Bultan, and Jianwen Su. Model checking XML manipulating software. In George S. Avrunin and Gregg Rothermel, editors, *ISSTA*, pages 252–262. ACM, 2004.

25. Tevfik Bultan, Xiang Fu, Richard Hull, and Jianwen Su. Conversation specification: a new approach to design and analysis of e-service composition. In *WWW*, pages 403–410, 2003.

26. Daniel Kroening and Natasha Sharygina. Formal verification of SystemC by automatic hardware/software partitioning. In *Proceedings of MEMOCODE 2005*, pages 101–110. IEEE, 2005.

27. Shin Nakajima. Model-checking of safety and security aspects in web service flows. In Nora Koch, Piero Fraternali, and Martin Wirsing, editors, *Web Engineering - 4th International Conference, ICWE 2004, Munich, Germany, July 26-30, 2004, Proceedings*, volume 3140 of *Lecture Notes in Computer Science*, pages 488–501. Springer, 2004.

28. Marco Pistore, Marco Roveri, and Paolo Busetta. Requirements-driven verification of web services. *Electr. Notes Theor. Comput. Sci.*, 105:95–108, 2004.

29. Alin Deutsch, Monica Marcus, Liying Sui, Victor Vianu, and Dayou Zhou. A verifier for interactive, data-driven web applications. In Fatma Ozcan, editor, *Proceedings of the ACM SIGMOD International Conference on Management of Data, Baltimore, Maryland, USA, June 14-16, 2005*, pages 539–550. ACM, 2005.

30. A. William Roscoe. *The Theory and Practice of Concurrency*. Prentice-Hall, 1998.

31. Robin Milner. *Communication and Concurrency*. Prentice-Hall, 1989.

32. Robin Milner, Joachim Parrow, and David Walker. A Calculus of Mobile Processes, I and II. *Information and Computation*, 100(1):1–40,41–77, September 1992.

33. Edmund M. Clarke, Sagar Chaki, Natasha Sharygina, Joel Ouaknine, and Nishant Sinha. State/event-based software model checking. In *Proceedings of the International Conf. on Integrated Formal Methods*, volume 2999 of *Lecture Notes in Computer Science*. Springer, 2004.

34. Rocco De Nicola and Frits W. Vaandrager. Three logics for branching bisimulation. *Journal of the ACM (JACM)*, 42(2):458–487, 1995.

35. Ekkart Kindler and Tobias Vesper. ESTL: A temporal logic for events and states. In *Application and Theory of Petri Nets 1998, 19th International Conference (ICATPN'98)*, volume 1420 of *Lecture Notes in Computer Science*, pages 365–383. Springer, 1998.

36. Michael Huth, Radha Jagadeesan, and David A. Schmidt. Modal transition systems: A foundation for three-valued program analysis. In *Lecture Notes in Computer Science*, volume 2028, page 155. Springer, 2001.

37. Aysu Betin-Can, Tevfik Bultan, and Xiang Fu. Design for verification for asynchronously communicating web services. In *WWW '05: Proceedings of the 14th*

international conference on World Wide Web, pages 750–759, New York, NY, USA, 2005. ACM Press.

38. Dirk Beyer, Arindam Chakrabarti, and Thomas A. Henzinger. Web service interfaces. In *WWW '05: Proceedings of the 14th international conference on World Wide Web*, pages 148–159, New York, NY, USA, 2005. ACM Press.

39. Xiang Fu, Tevfik Bultan, and Jianwen Su. Realizability of conversation protocols with message contents. In *ICWS*, pages 96–. IEEE Computer Society, 2004.

40. Howard Foster, Sebastián Uchitel, Jeff Magee, and Jeff Kramer. Compatibility verification for web service choreography. In *ICWS*, pages 738–741. IEEE Computer Society, 2004.

41. David Booth, Hugo Haas, Francis McCabe, Eric Newcomer, Mike Champion, Christopher Ferris, and David Orchard. Web services architecture. World-Wide-Web Consortium (W3C). Available from http://www.w3.org/TR/ws-arch/, 2003.

42. David Detlefs, Greg Nelson, and James B. Saxe. Simplify: A theorem prover for program checking. Technical Report HPL-2003-148, HP Labs, January 2003.

43. Edmund M.Clarke, O. Grumberg, S. Jha, Y. Lu, and H. Veith. Counterexample-guided abstraction refinement. In *Computer Aided Verification*, volume 1855 of *Lecture Notes in Computer Science*, pages 154–169. Springer, 2000.

44. Thomas S. Anantharaman, Edmund M. Clarke, Michael J. Foster, and Bud Mishra. Compiling path expressions into VLSI circuits. In *Proceedings of POPL*, pages 191–204, 1985.

45. Himanshu Jain, Edmund M. Clarke, and Daniel Kroening. Verification of SpecC and Verilog using predicate abstraction. In *Proceedings of MEMOCODE 2004*, pages 7–16. IEEE, 2004.

46. Edmund M. Clarke, Daniel Kroening, Natasha Sharygina, and Karen Yorav. Predicate abstraction of ANSI–C programs using SAT. *Formal Methods in System Design*, 25:105–127, September–November 2004.

47. Himanshu Jain, Daniel Kroening, Natasha Sharygina, and Edmund Clarke. Word level predicate abstraction and refinement for verifying RTL Verilog. In *Proceedings of DAC 2005*, pages 445–450. ACM, 2005.

48. Edmund Clarke, Orna Grumberg, Muralidhar Talupur, and Dong Wang. High level verification of control intensive systems using predicate abstraction. In *First ACM and IEEE International Conference on Formal Methods and Models for Co-Design (MEMOCODE'03)*, pages 55–64. IEEE, 2003.

49. A. William Roscoe. *The Theory and Practice of Concurrency*. Prentice-Hall International, London, 1997.

50. Edmund M. Clarke, Himanshu Jain, and Daniel Kroening. Predicate Abstraction and Refinement Techniques for Verifying Verilog. Technical Report CMU-CS-04-139, 2004.

51. Armin Biere, Alessandro Cimatti, Edmund M. Clarke, and Yunshan Yhu. Symbolic model checking without BDDs. In *TACAS*, volume 1579 of *Lecture Notes in Computer Science*, pages 193–207. Springer, 1999.

52. David W. Currie, Alan J. Hu, and Sreeranga Rajan. Automatic formal verification of DSP software. In *Proceedings of DAC 2000*, pages 130–135. ACM Press, 2000.

53. Byron Cook, Andreas Podelski, and Andrey Rybalchenko. Terminator: Beyond safety. In *Computer Aided Verification, 18th International Conference, (CAV)*, volume 4144 of *Lecture Notes in Computer Science*, pages 415–418. Springer, 2006.

Part II

Testing

6

Unit Testing BPEL Compositions

Daniel Lübke

Leibniz Universität Hannover, FG Software Engineering, Germany
daniel.luebke@inf.uni-hannover.de

Abstract. Service-Oriented Architecture is a new emerging architectural style for developing distributed business applications. Those applications are often realized using Web services. These services are grouped into BPEL compositions.

However, these applications need to be tested. For achieving better software quality, testing has to be done along the whole development process. Within this chapter a unit testing framework for BPEL named BPELUnit is presented. BPELUnit allows unit and integration tests of BPEL compositions. The tester is supported as much as possible: The used Web services can be replaced during test execution. This allows to really isolate the BPEL composition as a unit and guarantees repeatable tests.

6.1 Introduction

Service-Oriented Architecture (SOA) has become an accepted architectural style for building business applications. The application's logic is decomposed into fine-grained services which are composed into executable business processes. Services in SOA are loosely coupled software components, which most often offer functionality in a platform-independent and network-accessible way. Therefore, SOA is a *functional* decomposition of a system.

SOA aims to better align business processes and their supporting IT systems. Thus, changes within the processes should easily be incorporated into the IT infrastructure. Using fine-grained services, compositions can be updated easily by rearranging said services – hopefully without the need to change the services themselves. In this scenario, services can be offered by internal IT systems or can be bought from external service providers or partner organizations. This way, it is possible to integrate IT systems from different enterprises, e.g. in order to optimize supply chains or building virtual organizations.

While SOA as an architectural style is not dependent on any technology, the dominant implementation strategy is to use Web service standards. Supported by all major software companies, Web services and their related technologies, like the Business Process Execution Language (BPEL), have relatively good development support despite being a new technique.

BPEL is used for composing Web services into complex business processes. It supports rather complex programming constructs. These are the same as in normal programming languages, e.g. conditions, loops and fault handling. Therefore, BPEL compositions are software artefacts as well, possibly containing complex logic which is error-prone.

Being aware that BPEL compositions are subject to the same problems as normal software, it is necessary to test them in order to find as many defects as possible. This is especially necessary since BPEL compositions are normally deployed at high-risk positions within a company. However, testing BPEL is problematic due to its nature: BPEL compositions have many external dependencies, namely the Web services it accesses.

While non-functional testing has attracted much attention within the research community, functional testing of service compositions can be problematic as shown in this chapter. To address this issue, this chapter presents a unit testing framework for BPEL processes called BPELUnit. The framework was developed to ease the burden of testers and programmers in BPEL-related projects by allowing Web services to be mocked at run-time.

The next section of this chapter will shortly categorize services before some problems special to testing service compositions are presented in Sect. 6.3. Afterwards, different test types, which developers and testers will face in SOA projects, are described in Sect. 6.4. Section 6.5 describes a generic layered architecture for test tools, especially unit testing frameworks. This architecture has been used to develop BPELUnit – a unit testing framework for BPEL compositions – which is presented afterwards. The last section illustrates the difficulties in testing compositions presented during this chapter by giving a short example.

6.2 Service Classification

Web services are categorized within this chapter by two dimensions: The organizational dimension and the composition dimension as shown in Fig. 6.1.

A service can be developed and deployed by the organization itself or can be offered by an external party. Examples for internally developed services are wrappers around legacy systems and custom created services. Source code for

	Atomic Service	**Composed Service**
Internal	Legacy Wrapper Custom Services	BPEL Orchestrations
External	Network-accessible Service hosted outside the organization	

Fig. 6.1. Categorization for services

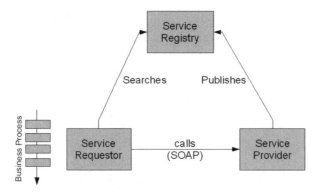

Fig. 6.2. Distributed roles in SOA make testing more difficult

such services is available and generally they can be replicated in a testing environment. In contrast, many services are available in the Internet, which can be used by applications without knowing how the services work. Consequently, such services cannot be replicated within a testing environment.

The organizational dimension can be seen in the SOA triangle as illustrated in Fig. 6.2: SOA systems span multiple roles, most important the service provider and the service requester.

The other dimension is (visible) service composition: Services can either be atomic, i.e. provided as such, or put together by composing other services. The former ones are either implemented in traditional programming languages like Java or are provided as is without access to the services' logic. The latter are processes composed in-house using composition languages like the Business Process Execution Language (BPEL).

It is notable that there is no composed, external service from an organization's point of view: Since the service is external, it cannot be accessed, modified nor installed locally. It is a black box and therefore it is irrelevant for the tester in which way the service is implemented. Such external services are an obstacle in testing: Normally, they cannot be used intensively for testing, because they need to be paid for or no test account is available. However, integration and system tests – as described in Sects. 6.4.3 and 6.4.4 – are only possible if the original services can be used.

In contrast, when unit testing BPEL compositions, all atomic services can be mocked, i.e. replaced by dummy services. This allows the composed services to be tested in isolation and without the need for external dependencies.

6.3 Challenges in BPEL Testing

Testing software is a time-consuming and often neglected task. Testing BPEL compositions is even harder due to the following reasons:

- Test performance: BPEL compositions depend on calling Web services. SOAP calls are extremely costly due to intense XML parsing and often associated XSL transformations, as well as network overhead. Example measures are, e.g., given by [9].

- Error conditions: Due to the distributed nature, many errors must be expected and handled by the system. For example, networking errors and temporarily not reachable services need careful error handling which needs to be tested too.
- Dependencies: Web services represent external dependencies for the BPEL composition. The composition relies on the correct behaviour of the services in order to fulfil its tasks.
- Deployment: BPEL compositions need to be transferred on a BPEL server and be made ready for execution. This process, called deployment, requires time-consuming preparation before testing can start.
- Complexity: BPEL compositions normally contain many elements, like assigns and Web service calls. Especially, the use of complex XPath queries and XSL transformations lead to many cases which need to be tested.
- Organizational borders: As already outlined, SOA systems can span multiple organizations, which do not share their service implementations. This hinders setting up a test environment as outlined in Sect. 6.2.

Because BPEL is a relatively new technique, testers and developers do not have much experience in which areas defects are likely to occur. This reduces test efficiency until testers are able to get a "feeling" in which areas they are likely able to find defects.

All these factors require intensive research into testing habits and test support for service compositions in general and for BPEL in particular.

6.4 Test Types for Compositions

6.4.1 Test Levels

Software testing is a widely used quality-improvement activity, supported by both academic research and commercial experience. In his timeless classic, *The Art of Software Testing*, Myers offers a definition of software testing: "Testing is the process of executing a program with the intent of finding errors" ([15]).

While newer definitions are available, this simple but precise definition hints at the attitude a software tester should have: He or she should not try to prove that a software works correctly (i.e. has no defects), but rather to find cases in which it does not work (i.e. has defects). The former is impossible anyway – as pointed out by [3]: Testing can only show the presence of errors, but not their absence.

There are many different forms of software testing, each on a different level addressing different error types (see also [14]):

- Unit testing: A unit test is used to test a single class, routine, or more generally, component, in isolation from the rest of the system it belongs to. This type of tests try to detect errors inherent to one unit, like wrong logic etc.

- Integration testing: An integration test is used to test combined, or integrated, components of a software system. Such tests try to spot errors which are introduced by the combination of different components, e.g. differently interpreted interfaces etc.
- System testing: System testing is the process of testing the complete, final system, which includes interactions with other systems and all components. Such tests are typically done at the end of an iteration. Using this kind of tests, projects try to find any fatal errors before delivering the software.

All types of tests can be automated. Automated test are often used in regression testing, which can therefore be repeated easily and cheaply. Regression testing intends to find bugs in updated software which previously has already passed the tests.

An extreme form of automated testing is Test-First. Test-First has established itself as a new way of creating test cases before code is written. Especially successful in Agile Methods, like Extreme Programming ([2]), it has shown its ability to increase the quality of the tests, e.g. in ([5, 4]).

In the following course of this section, the different kinds of tests are described more precisely. This includes special problems service compositions raise in these corresponding contexts.

6.4.2 Unit Tests

As pointed out above, unit testing is the process of testing a single component, named a unit, of a program in isolation. It has been wholly embraced by the Extreme Programming community ([2]) and in the area of Test-Driven Development.

In the context of service compositions and BPEL, unit testing implies that all Web services, as they represent external dependencies, need to be replaced by mocks. However, those mocks need to be implemented and deployed which can be a rather time-consuming task. Furthermore, in order to develop Web services (e.g. in Java and .Net), programming skills are needed which are not necessarily available in a testing team.

The problem of mocking external services is one of the most important drivers for tool automation for unit tests. Even in other languages like Java there are mocking facilities available ([7]). However, in the world of Web services, tool support is more critical due to the mentioned reasons. Because of this, mocking support has been incorporated into the unit testing framework itself rather than being an independent component.

While other languages have support for unit tests by special frameworks, like JUnit for Java ([8]), BPEL lacks such support. Therefore, one of our research goals was to develop unit test support for BPEL, which is described in Sect. 6.6.

6.4.3 Integration Tests

Integration testing concerns two or more components. Ideally, these components are tested using unit tests, so that the functionality can be anticipated to work (mostly) correctly.

Integration testing tries to verify the interaction between several components. The tests try to trigger all communication and calls between the components.

Integration testing in service composition is mostly an organizational challenge: For testing compositions all services need to be available. Normally, a testing environment is set-up, in which services, databases etc. are replicated and can be used and their contents changed. However, when using an externally provided service, like a payment service, it is impossible to install the same service on-site. Instead, there are essentially two possibilities during integration testing, whenever a test environment is not available:

1. Mocking of external, atomic services: External services are mocked as they are in unit tests. This has the advantage that communication between all self-developed components can be done at all times during the development process. However, the interaction between the self-developed parts and external services cannot be tested this way. This option is only applicable for testing two compositions depending on each other, so that their combination can be tested without the need of the respective dependent services.
2. Test accounts: The service provider may offer test accounts, e.g. a dummy environment for a CRM system may be offered. This environment can be used for testing purposes by the testers.

It is notable, however, that this problem only arises when services store data. Whenever a service only calculates data or returns values, like search engines, the original service can normally be used without any problems.

In case of non-free services, for which the consumer has to pay, integration tests should be optimized for using as few calls to services as possible. Mocking service calls in non-essential situations may be an option too.

Integration testing is especially important in Web service–based projects, since WSDL descriptions of Web services only define the syntax of the services but neglect semantic aspects like meaning of parameters, fault behaviour etc.

6.4.4 System Tests

At the end of an iteration or the project, the system is tested in its entirety. Therefore, the whole system is normally installed in a test environment, replicating the real environment in which the application will run later on. This will include the composition engine, e.g. the BPEL server, and the developed services. As with integration tests, the problem during system test is the replication of external services. However, during system test it is unacceptable to mock certain services. If services cannot be replicated internally, a test account must be created by the service provider or the test team needs to utilize the final configuration.

Dynamic discovery of services poses a significant problem for system testing: If a service is not bound statically to the composition, the composition engine tries to discover, e.g. by using UDDI, a matching service. The selected service can change over time. However, the new service has not been part of the system test, possibly rendering its results worthless.

6.4.5 Test-First

Test-First is not directly a class of testing as unit integration and system tests are. Instead, it describes a philosophy of development: Tests are written in small chunks before actual code is written. Test-First is an inherent practice in Extreme Programming and Test-Driven Development. For service compositions, this means that a part of the process is specified before development as a test case. Afterwards, the composition is written, e.g. one service is called and the correspondent variable assignments are made. Finally, the tests are complemented with tests for error handling and new functionality and the composition is updated to fulfil the tests. Hereby, all external dependencies are excluded and mocked as well. These steps continue until all requirements and error handling routines have been developed.

Especially with composition projects, in which not all services are initially available to the development organization, Test-First is a good option to start development: All external references to unavailable services can be replaced by dummy services called mocks. The missing services can be integrated later and are immediately ready for integration testing, which will try to detect misunderstood interfaces.

For Test-First, test automation is very important. Since tests are run after every little implementation step, manual testing is too cumbersome and time-consuming. Therefore, unit testing frameworks are a necessity in test-driven projects.

6.4.6 Remarks

Testing service compositions is comparable to testing "normal" software systems. The same types of tests can be integrated into the development process. However, their relevance changes: Unit testing compositions is easier than in traditional programming languages, since all parts of the system are already loosely coupled and can be replaced by mocks. Mocks play a special role in testing compositions since they can replace external services in all types of tests whenever the use of original services is impossible or at least too costly. This hints at the major problem: Replicating the system in a test environment is often impossible whenever services are hosted externally. The testing team should try to mitigate these problems early and try to replace the services or have special accounts not interfering with the production environment.

Because of the special role of using mocks and trying to isolate parts of the system over which the development organization has control, tool support is necessary. Only by using adequate tools, compositions can be easily and efficiently isolated and mocks created accordingly.

Furthermore, since service compositions, especially BPEL, are normally geared towards machine-to-machine communication, automation is a desirable goal: Repeated tests using manually entered XML-data are enormously expensive and time-consuming. Additionally, all XML artefacts need to be managed. Accordingly, tools should be able to handle and store the large and, for humans, often unreadable XML data.

One available tool for generating stubs is WSUnit ([6]). However, it lacks integration into the other test tools: WSUnit needs to be deployed in a J2EE web container before it is used and cannot detect whether the values passed to it are correct and consequently abort the test run. The deployment has to be done before the tests are run and therefore needs to be integrated into an automated test run.

6.5 Testing Architectures

In this section, a generic, layer-based approach for creating BPEL testing frameworks is presented, which is later used for the design of the BPELUnit framework [13]. As a side effect, this layer-based model can be used for classifying existing frameworks or implementations of other frameworks.

Testing tools can be geared towards different roles in development projects which consequently have different requirements, usage models and technical backgrounds. For example, the "test infected developer" doing Test-First on his BPEL composition is a technical savvy person, understanding XML data and has knowledge in SOAP. He or she wants to write tests efficiently and run them every five minutes. However, a pure tester does not want to deal with technical details. He or she most likely does not need mocking support but wants to organize a large number of test-cases. Therefore, design decisions must differ for the intended target group, but the layered architecture can be the same for all.

The proposed architecture consists of several layers which build upon one another, as outlined in Fig. 6.3. The functionality of each layer can be implemented in various ways, which are shortly pointed out in the subsequent sections.

The first (bottom) layer is concerned with the test specification – i.e. how the test data and behaviour are formulated. Building on this, the tests must be organized into test suites, which is the responsibility of the test organization layer. A test – and therefore also the process under test – must be executed. This task is performed by the test execution layer. During the test

Test Results
result types & acquisition

Test Execution
execution type & support

Test Organization
organization form & technical realization

Test Specification
specification language & expressiveness

Fig. 6.3. Layers for unit testing frameworks

run, results must be gathered and presented to the user, which is done in the test results layer.

6.5.1 Test Specification

Testing a process means sending data to and receiving data from its endpoints, according to the business protocol imposed by the process under test (PUT) and its partner processes.

BPEL interfaces are described using WSDL port types and operations. However, the WSDL syntax lacks a description of the actual protocol of a Web service, i.e. which operation must be invoked after or before another operation (for a discussion, see [1, pp. 137]). This is particularly relevant for asynchronous operations. A testing framework must provide a way for the tester to specify such a protocol and check whether it has been followed or not.

As for the information flow between the BPEL composition and its partner processes, the data can be differentiated between incoming and outgoing data from the perspective of the test.

The test specification must be concrete enough to validate the correctness of incoming data as well for creating outgoing data. As pointed out by [11], incoming data errors can be classified into three types:

1. incorrect content
2. no message at all, when one is expected
3. an incorrect number of messages (too few or too many).

There are several ways of formulating the test specification to achieve these goals. The following two examples are the most extreme:

1. Data-centred approach (e.g. using fixed SOAP data, augmented with simple rules): Incoming data from the process is compared against a predefined SOAP message (which, e.g., resides in some file on disk). Outgoing data is predefined, too, read from a file and sent to the process. A simple set of rules determines if messages are expected at all and defines which replies to send. This approach is not only very simple, but also least expressive to implement tests in.
2. Logic-centred approach (e.g. using a fully-fledged programming language for expressing the test logic): A program is invoked on each incoming transmission which may take arbitrary steps to test the incoming data. The outgoing data is also created by a program. This approach is very flexible and expressive, but requires a lot more work by the test developer and is therefore more expensive to implement.

Of course, there are several approaches in-between. A data-centred approach could use a simple XML specification language to allow testers to specify test data at the level of BPEL, i.e. XML-typed data records instead of SOAP messages. A logic-centred approach could use a simple language for expressing basic conditional statements ("if the input data is such-and-such, send package from file A, otherwise from file B").

The choices made here have significant influence on the complexity of the test framework and the ease of use for the test developer. In most cases, the complexity of the framework reduces work for the test developer, and vice versa.

Beside the questions of expressiveness of the logic and simplicity for the tester, two additional requirements must be considered:

1. Automation: The ultimate goal of a BPEL testing framework is repeatable automated testing. This means the test must be executable as a whole. In turn, this indicates that the test must be specified in an unambiguous, machine-readable and executable form. The more sophisticated the test logic, the more complex the test execution will be.
2. Tool support: It should be possible to automate at least some of the steps a test developer must do for creating the test specification. The effort needed to automate a test can become quite high. Consequently, it is necessary to relieve the test developer of the more tedious tasks and let him focus on the actual problem.

Regardless of how the test specification is implemented, it will be used by the test developer for describing BPEL test cases. A BPEL test case contains all relevant data for executing a BPEL composition to test a certain path.

6.5.2 Test Organization

As pointed out before, the test specification allows users to define test cases. While a test case contains all necessary information for testing a certain path of a BPEL composition, it is not yet bound to a specific BPEL composition, which may be identified by an URL, a set of files, or something completely different. The test organization must provide a way to link the test cases to a concrete BPEL composition for testing. Additionally, it is beneficial to allow testers to organize their test cases into groups, which are called test suites in existing frameworks.

For these two purposes, the test suite concept of conventional xUnit approaches is extended as follows:

- A BPEL test case will always be executed as part of a test suite.
- The test suite provides the test fixture for all enclosed test cases. This fixture contains the link to the BPEL composition under test.

By using this approach, the fixture is globally specified in the suite and applicable to all test cases, which do not need to specify the BPEL composition binding again. This reduces the work done by the tester, because such bindings can become very complex.

There are two basic approaches to test organization:

1. Integrated test suite logic: The first approach is to integrate test organization with the test specification. This is possible only when a sophisticated test specification method is in place (e.g. when using a high-level language). This approach has the benefit of being very flexible for the test developer.
2. Separate test suite specification: The second approach is to allow formulation of separate test organization artefacts. These artefacts could include links to the actual test cases and the test fixture.

As in the previous section about test specification, it is also important to stress the importance of automation and tool support for test organization, as the organization artefacts are the natural wrappers for the test specification.

6.5.3 Test Execution

For normal execution, BPEL compositions are usually deployed into a BPEL engine, instantiated and run upon receipt of a message triggering instance creation. However, for testing a BPEL composition there are other possibilities too.

BPEL testing means executing a BPEL composition with a test environment, the so-called "harness", around it handling input and output data according to the test specification. This can be done in several ways. The following two approaches are the most obvious ones:

1. Simulated testing: Simulated testing, as defined here, means the BPEL composition is not actually deployed onto a server and invoked afterwards by Web service invocations. Instead, the engine is contacted directly via some sort of debug API and instructed to run the PUT. Through the debug API, the test framework closely controls the execution of the

PUT. It is, therefore, possible to intercept calls to other Web services and handle them locally; it is also possible to inject data back into the PUT. This approach is taken by some editors currently available for manual testing and debugging. Simulated BPEL execution works only if the engine supports debugging, i.e. it has a rich API for controlling the execution of a BPEL instance. While most engines do support such features, unfortunately they are in no way standardized. To avoid vendor lock-in, a test framework must therefore factor out this part and create adapters for each BPEL engine to be supported, which may get rather tedious.

2. Real-life testing: Real-life testing, as defined here, means actually deploying the PUT into an engine and invoking it using Web service calls. Note that this means that all partner Web services must be replaced by mock Web services in a similar way, i.e. they must be available by Web service invocation and be able to make Web service calls themselves. The PUT must be deployed such that all partner Web service URIs are replaced by URIs to the test mocks. Real-life BPEL execution requires the process to be deployed first, binding the PUT to custom (test) URIs for the test partner processes. However, most engines rely on custom, vendor-specific deployment descriptors, which the test framework must provide, and which are not standardized as well. Furthermore, the BPEL specification allows dynamic discovery of partner Web services. Although frequent use of such features is doubted ([1]), a framework relying on real-life test execution will have no way to counter such URI replacements.

There are certain correlations between the two approaches discussed in Sect. 6.5.1 and the two execution types. For example, the test framework can directly use predefined SOAP messages in the case of simulated testing; real-life execution requires Web service mocks, which can be formulated in a higher-level programming language.

However, other combinations are also possible and depend on the amount of work done by the framework. It is relatively easy to create simple Web services out of test data, and simulating BPEL inside an engine does not mean the test framework cannot forward requests to other Web services or sophisticated programs calculating a return value.

As in the xUnit family, the part of the framework responsible for executing the test is called the test runner. There may be several test runners for one framework, depending on the execution environment.

6.5.4 Test Results

Execution of the tests yields results and statistics, which are to be presented to the user at a later point in time. Many metrics have been defined for testing (a good overview is given by [18]), and a testing framework must choose which ones – if any – to calculate and how to do this.

The most basic of all unit test results is the boolean test execution result which all test frameworks provide: A test succeeds, or it fails. Failures can additionally be split into two categories, as is done in the xUnit family: an actual failure (meaning the program took a wrong turn) or an error (meaning an abnormal program termination). Furthermore, test metrics, like test coverage, can be calculated.

The more sophisticated the metrics, the more information is usually required about the program run. This is an important aspect to discuss because control over the execution of a BPEL composition is not standardized as pointed out in the last section. For example, it is rather easy to derive numbers on test case failures, but activity coverage analysis requires knowledge about which BPEL activities have actually been executed. There are several ways of gathering this information:

- During BPEL simulation or debugging: APIs may be used to query the activity which is currently active. However, these APIs, if they exist, are vendor specific.
- During execution using instrumentation: Tools for other programming languages, like Cobertura for Java, are instrumenting the source code or binary files in order to being informed which statements are executed ([16]). Since the BPEL engine's only capability to communicate to the outside world are Web service calls, the notification need to be done this way. However, this approach imposes a high-performance penalty due to frequent Web service calls.
- During execution by observing external behaviour: The invoked mock partner processes are able to log their interactions with the PUT. It is thus possible to detect execution of some PUT activities (i.e. all activities which deal with outside Web services). However, this requires additional logic inside the mock partner processes which will complicate the test logic. Conclusions about path coverage may also be drawn from this information, but they will not be complete as not all paths must invoke external services.
- As a follow-up: It has been suggested ([11]) to use log files produced by BPEL engines to extract information about the execution of a particular instance, and to use this information to calculate test coverage. Such logs, if they exist, are of course again vendor specific.

The calculated test results must also be presented to the user. A BPEL test framework should make no assumptions about its environment, i.e., whether it runs in a graphical UI, or headless on a server. For all these cases, the test runners should be able to provide adequately formatted test results; e.g., a graphical UI for the user, or a detailed test result log in case of headless testing.

With this explanation of the test result layer, the description of the four-layer BPEL testing framework architecture is complete. In the next section, our design decisions for the BPELUnit framework are given.

6.6 BPELUnit

As part of our research, BPELUnit ([12]) has been developed. BPELUnit is the first step for addressing the difficulties encountered in unit testing BPEL compositions and is based on the layered architecture described in Sect. 6.5. Because its main focus is unit testing, the natural user group for BPELUnit are developers. Therefore, all technical details are readily accessible during and after test-runs, and XML is used intensively to define test cases, test parameters etc. BPELUnit is available under an open source license at http://www.bpelunit.org.

BPELUnit is implemented in Java. The core itself is not dependent on any presentation layer technique and therefore can be used from any build and development environment. Part of BPELUnit are

- a command-line client
- integration into ant for automatic builds
- an Eclipse plug-in for supporting development using various BPEL editors based on the Eclipse platform (Fig. 6.4).

The integration into development environments like Eclipse is important especially for developers, because switching between testing and developing is easier and quicker to do. Furthermore, assistants in the development environment can be used to quickly create tests, prepare values, generate XML fragments etc.

Various BPEL engines are supported, and new engines can be integrated by writing matching adapters. BPEL engines only need to support automatic

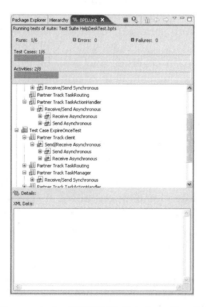

Fig. 6.4. Screenshot of BPELUnit integration into Eclipse

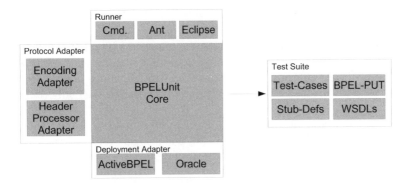

Fig. 6.5. BPELUnit architecture and test suite

deployment and undeployment of BPEL compositions. The general software architecture can be see in Fig. 6.5.

6.6.1 Architectural Layers

BPELUnit's design is aligned to the layers presented above. In the following, the design choices in each layer are described to give an overview about BPELUnit's principal architecture.

Test Specification

Tests in BPELUnit are specified in XML. The data is specified in XML, i.e. as it is in SOAP itself. Therefore, the developer has maximal control over the data sent to the BPEL composition.

The description of interactions of the BPEL composition can be verified by using XPath statements applied to the returned data. XPath is the natural choice for selecting data from XML documents. Furthermore, the interaction style between partners and composition can be stored in the specification: So far one-way (receive-only and send-only), two-way synchronous (send-receive and receive-send), and two-way asynchronous (send-receive and receive-send) are supported.

Test Organization

The test specification is organized as a set of parallel interaction threads. Each thread describes expected communication to and from one partner of the BPEL composition. These tests can be grouped into test suites. A test suite references all necessary elements for its corresponding tests: The WSDL descriptions of services, XML schemata etc. Furthermore, the suite defines the test environment, as it contains all set-up information like the server and URLs.

In order to ease the creation of tests, test cases can be inherited: Common interaction sequences can be defined once and inherited into another test case. The new test case can add new partners and input values. This way, much effort can be saved since tests for the same compositions normally differ only slightly.

The test suites containing test cases are stored using XML. Their files normally end in .bpts (BPel Test Suite). The schema contains the following components (as illustrated in Fig. 6.6):

- A **name** used for identifying the test suite.
- The **base URL** under which the mocks should be accessible.
- Within the **deployment section** the BPEL process and all partner WSDL descriptions are referenced. The partner descriptions are used for creating the mocks.
- The **Test Cases** contain the client track responsible for feeding input to the BPEL process and the partner definitions. Those partner definitions are used to create the stubs' logic: Expected values and data to send back to the process are defined within the partner definitions.

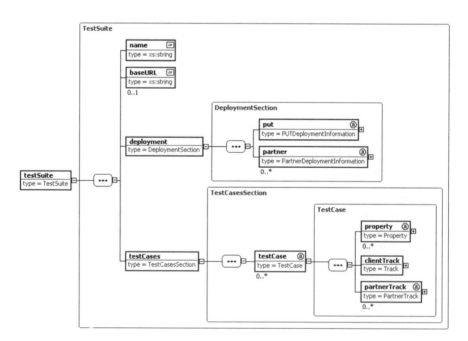

Fig. 6.6. XML schema of test Suite specifications

Test Execution

The aim of BPELUnit's execution layer is to take most of the burden from the developer. Test execution in BPELUnit can automatically deploy and undeploy compositions on servers, and offers a stub engine which resembles the behaviour specified in the parallel execution threads.

Especially, the mock engine – as it simulates partners of the BPEL composition – is quite complex. It simulates a complete Web service stack and can parse and handle the most important SOAP constructs. It contains a HTTP engine for receiving and sending SOAP messages, can process RPC/literal and document/literal styles and transparently handles callbacks using WS-Addressing. Other styles and SOAP processing options can be added by third-parties through extensions.

Test Results

Since BPELUnit uses a concrete BPEL server for execution, gathering runtime statistics is difficult. Up to now, BPELUnit only reports successful test cases, failures and errors. A failure represents an application-level defect. This normally indicates that an expected value is not received. In contrast, an error indicates a problem with the Web service stack: a server may not be responding, wrong error codes may have been sent etc.

BPELUnit itself does not offer a GUI or extensive output facilities. Instead, the test results are passed to front-ends, e.g. the Eclipse plug-in. The front-end processes and visualizes the test results.

6.6.2 Mocking Architecture

The main advantage of using BPELUnit – compared to other Web service testing tools – is its ability to emulate processes' partners. The real partners are replaced by simulated ones during run-time. The simulated partners are called stubs. At least one stub is needed per test, i.e. the partner stub. The partner stub is the partner initiating the BPEL process.

The behaviour of the stubs is configured in BPELUnit by the means of partner tracks. A partner track describes expected incoming messages and the corresponding reply messages to the process. The incoming messages can be checked by XPath statements for all relevant information, e.g. is a sent ID correct, is there certain number of products supplied etc. These checks are used by BPELUnit to evaluate whether the test was successful, i.e. if all checks were successful. Especially, the partner stub will check the final result of the BPEL process for an expected output.

Whenever a test is started, BPELUnit will start a thread for each mock. The thread is configured using the information supplied by the partner track definition. Afterwards, BPELUnit will open a port on which an own Web service stack listens. The Web service stack decodes the incoming message, and routes the incoming requests to the matching mock. The mock consequently processes the request by checking the incoming message for validity and the correct information as expected by the partner track. Afterwards, a reply message is sent back, which is again routed through BPELUnit. Within the partner track, the tester can give definitions to assemble parts of the reply message for copying dynamic elements, like dates and times into the message, which cannot be statically defined.

The mocks do not need to deal with SOAP details, because all the SOAP-related work is done by the framework itself. An example definition of a partner track which checks the incoming message looks like this ([12], p. 71):

```
 1 <sendReceive
 2     port="BookingProcessPort"
 3     operation="process"
 4     service="client:BookingProcess">
 5     <send>
 6        <data>
 7           <client:bookme>
 8              <client:employeeID>848</client:employeeID>
 9           </client:bookme>
10        </data>
11     </send>
12     <receive>
13        <condition>
14           <expression>
15              client:bookinganswer/client:booked/text()
16           </expression>
17           <value>'true'</value>
18        </condition>
19     </receive>
20 </sendReceive>
```

The client is a synchronous send and receive client, which checks whether a booking has completed successfully or not.

6.6.3 Extension of BPELUnit

BPELUnit itself is a basic implementation of a unit testing framework which handles test organization and execution well. However, the SOAP protocol and the BPEL application landscape are very complex and diverse. The SOAP protocol is very extensible, and there is no standard for accessing BPEL servers in order to deploy and undeploy processes to name two of the biggest problems.

BPELUnit supports SOAP over HTTP with literal messages for all mocks. If a process accesses other services, they cannot be mocked with BPELUnit in its current version. Besides being open source software, BPELUnit offers extension points for plugging in new protocols and header processors. Since BPELUnit itself calls processors after handling all incoming and outgoing

SOAP messages, new encodings and headers processors can be added independently of the BPELUnit source tree. For instance, the default BPELUnit distribution ships with WS-Addressing support, which is implemented as a header processor.

Another plug-in interface is offered for deployment and undeployment: Since all servers have their own way of handling deployment, it is necessary to separate these operations and make them extensible. New servers can be supported by BPELUnit by adding a corresponding plug-in. BPELUnit ships with support for ActiveBPEL, the Oracle BPEL Engine and – as a fall-back option – for manual deployment.

6.7 Example

Within this chapter the common example from the introduction is used. However, some additional technical properties will be presented at the beginning.

This example concentrates on a ticket reservation system and its associated services. The reservation system is developed and operated by a fictional, touristic company. This company is offering their services as Web services described in WSDL. For fulfilling their customers' requests, various databases of partners need to be queried: Different hotels and restaurants can be looked up and tickets can be ordered and reserved. Therefore, partner companies' services have to be integrated into the service composition.

A hotel is one of the touristic service provider's partners. It has developed a BPEL composition for fulfilling the reception of hotel reservations which includes the payment as well. The payment is realized by a Web service by a bank. The whole service architecture can be seen in Fig. 6.7.

From the point of view of the touristic service provider, the reservation services are atomic services. They can only see a black box which is outside their development organization and their control. For the hotel, however, the reservation service is a complex process using the bank's services as atomic services.

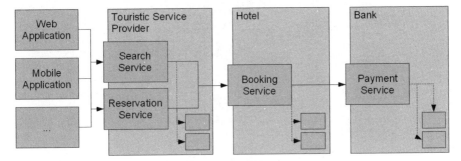

Fig. 6.7. Service architecture in the example

This scenario includes some problematic challenges for testing the corresponding compositions. Focusing on the touristic provider's process, it has no single reservation service: The Web service, which is actually called, depends on which hotel is to be booked. The provider itself has no own implementation of such a service and cannot randomly book and cancel hotel rooms for testing purposes. Therefore, the developers need to carefully unit test their process using stubs in order to minimize possible defects. For testing the whole system, organizational problems are dominant. However, the touristic provider has been able to get three hotels to offer them a test account which does not make effective bookings or cancellations. Therefore, the these parts of the system can be tested in integration tests thereby minimizing possible defects through misunderstood WSDL interfaces.

In Fig. 6.8 the touristic service provider's BPEL process is illustrated with a unit test: All hotels are queried in parallel and afterwards the results are merged. The best three results are returned. For simplicity, only a brief overview of the process is given. The unit test suite for this process simulates the hotels by returning a predefined set of possible booking options. Thereby, the correct merging of the results is validated. Moreover, service failures can be simulated by returning SOAP faults to the BPEL process to show correct behaviour in case of partner service failures. While the test could not find any errors in the merging part of the process, errors were not correctly caught in the BPEL process. This leads to termination of the whole process, instead of proceeding with only the available results. In this test, BPELUnit controls the whole execution and all mocks. The BPEL process is deployed onto the server and the test suite is run. There are no organizational borders conflicting with the test.

However, using unit tests alone, it is not possible to detect failures hidden in the communication between the BPEL process and a Web service. Web services are often created by exposing functionality written in traditional

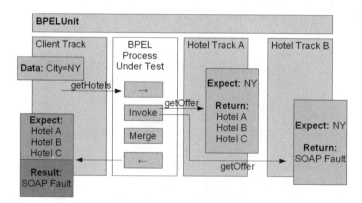

Fig. 6.8. Provider's unit test

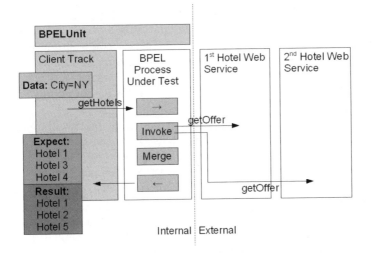

Fig. 6.9. Provider's integration test

languages. In most programming languages, indexes are counted from 0, while in XPath the first index is 1. What convention is used by a service is not stored in its WSDL description since it only defines that an integer is required. To counter such mistakes, BPELUnit can be used to do integration testing. In contrast to unit tests, no services are mocked. Instead, the original services are used. Since the touristic service provider is able to access some real services, this is possible. Such tests are consequently able to detect problems concerning the interfaces.

In the example's case, it is likely that a programmer, who misunderstood the index while writing the BPEL process, will consequently write a mock which waits for the wrong parameter. Therefore, the unit test is wrong in this regard and the error will not be spotted. However, using the test accounts during integration testing, it is possible to detect such failures as illustrated in Fig. 6.9. The BPELUnit test awaits the list of hotel offers. However, a wrong list is returned due to the wrong index. The testers can see this behaviour, report the bug and update the unit tests accordingly.

For integration tests, BPELUnit only controls the client track and the deployment of the BPEL process. However, the services used in this example are the real services. Therefore, this test spans multiple organizations.

6.8 Conclusions and Outlook

Testing service compositions, most notable such modelled in BPEL, is a relatively new aspect for quality assurance in software projects. Therefore, experiences and experience reports concerning testing are lacking. The first steps taken to better support the testing process is to try to improve tool support: This support must address the distributed nature of services and the necessary test set-up routines for deployment of all necessary compositions and stubs.

BPELUnit is the first version of such a unit testing framework supporting BPEL. It manages test cases and contains a stub engine, which can be parameterized by the test suites. The design is extensible for adding support of further BPEL engines and front-ends.

Next aim for the future is support for gathering metrics during test execution. Unfortunately, this is a tremendous effort due to missing standards for BPEL debugging and process introspection. However, adding generic interfaces which need to be implemented by the corresponding BPEL engine adapters is possible with support for one or two BPEL engines in the standard distribution.

While the stub facility of BPELUnit is very powerful, it cannot deal with dynamic service discovery. This type of discovery poses a significant challenge for all testing activities related to SOA. Since the service to be called is determined at run-time, it is not necessary to replace the service endpoint in the deployment. Therefore, other means must be found to redirect the service call to the stub service.

Another important aspect is the parallelization of tests: At least unit tests should be independent of each other, so their execution could be distributed to different test machines and be done in parallel. For other unit testing frameworks, research concerning distribution is available, for e.g. by [10] and [17], which should be adopted for BPELUnit or comparable frameworks as well.

Furthermore, testing habits and likely defects in BPEL compositions need to be empirically studied. Interesting questions would be, e.g., in which parts of a BPEL composition errors are likely to occur, by which rate certain tests can reduce defects in the software product concerning service compositions etc.

BPELUnit can serve as a stable foundation for all these research questions. Moreover, it can be used in a production environment for finding defects in developed BPEL compositions.

References

1. Alonso, Gustavo, Casati, Fabio, Kuno, Harumi, and Machiraju, Vijay (2003). *Web Services*. Springer, 1st edition.
2. Beck, Kent (2000). *Extreme Programming Explained*. Addison-Wesley.
3. Dijkstra, Edsger Wybe (1971). *Structured programming*, chapter Notes on structured programming, pages 1–82. Academic Press.
4. Flohr, Thomas and Schneider, Thorsten (2006). Lessons learned from an XP Experiment with Students: Test-First needs more teachings. In *Proceedings of the Profes 2006*.

5. George, Boby and Williams, Laurie (2003). A Structured Experiment of Test-Driven Developmen. *Information and Software technology*, 46(5):337–342.
6. java.net (2006). WSUnit - The Web Services Testing Tool. WWW: `https://wsunit.dev.java.net/`.
7. jmock.org (2006). jMock. WWW: `http://www.jmock.org/`.
8. JUnit.org (2006). JUnit. WWW: `http://www.junit.org`.
9. Juric, Matjaz B., Kezmah, Bostjan, Hericko, Marjan, Rozman, Ivan, and Vezocnik, Ivan (2004). Java RMI, RMI tunneling and Web services comparison and performance analysis. *SIGPLAN Not.*, 39(5):58–65.
10. Kapfhammer, Gregory M. (2001). Automatically and Transparently Distributing the Execution of Regression Test Suites. In *Proceedings of the 18th International Conference on Testing Computer Software*.
11. Li, Zhongjie, Sun, Wei, Jiang, Zhong Bo, and Zhang, Xin (2005). BPEL4WS Unit Testing: Framework and Implementation. In *ICWS '05: Proceedings of the IEEE International Conference on Web Services (ICWS'05)*, pages 103–110, Washington, DC, USA. IEEE Computer Society.
12. Mayer, Philip (2006). Design and Implementation of a Framework for Testing BPEL Compositions. Master's thesis, Gottfried Wilhelm Leibniz Unversität Hannover.
13. Mayer, Philip and Lübke, Daniel (2006). Towards a BPEL unit testing framework. In *TAV-WEB '06: Proceedings of the 2006 workshop on Testing, analysis, and verification of web services and applications*, pages 33–42, New York, NY, USA. ACM Press.
14. McConnell, Steve (2004). *Code Complete*. Microsoft Press, 2nd edition.
15. Myers, Glenford J. (1979). *The Art of Software Testing*. John Wiley & Sons.
16. Project, Cobertura (2006). Cobertura Homepage. WWW: `http://cobertura.sourceforge.net/`.
17. Safi, Bassim Aziz (2005). Distributed JUnit. Bachelor Thesis at University Hannover.
18. Zhu, Hong, Hall, Patrick A. V., and May, John H. R. (1997). Software unit test coverage and adequacy. *ACM Comput. Surv.*, 29(4):366–427.

A Model-Driven Approach to Discovery, Testing and Monitoring of Web Services

Marc Lohmann[1], Leonardo Mariani[2] and Reiko Heckel[3]

[1] University of Paderborn, Department of Computer Science Warburger Str. 100, 33098 Paderborn, Germany mlohmann@uni-paderborn.de
[2] Università degli Studi di Milano Bicocca – DISCo via Bicocca degli Arcimboldi, 8, 20126 Milano, Italy mariani@disco.unimib.it
[3] University of Leicester, Department of Computer Science University Road, LE1 7RH Leicester reiko@mcs.le.ac.uk

Abstract. Service-oriented computing is distinguished by its use of dynamic discovery and binding for the integration of services at runtime. This poses a challenge for testing, in particular, of the interaction between services.

We propose a model-driven solution to address this challenge. Service descriptions are promoted from largely syntactical to behavioural specifications of services in terms of contracts (pre-conditions and effects of operations), expressed in a visual UML-like notion. Through mappings to semantic web languages and the Java Modelling Language (JML) contracts support the automatic discovery of services as well as the derivation of test cases and their execution and monitoring.

We discuss an extended life cycle model for services based on the model-driven approach and illustrate its application using a model of a hotel reservation service.

7.1 Introduction

Service-oriented computing is becoming the leading paradigm for the integration of distributed application components over the Internet. Besides its implementation, the life cycle of a service includes the creation and publication of a service description to a registry. Clients will query the registry for service descriptions satisfying their requirements before selecting a description, binding to the corresponding service and using it.

Established technology for providing, querying and binding to services is largely based on syntactic information. From UDDI registries, e.g., services can only be retrieved by inspecting interface descriptions and associated keywords [50]. The lack of semantic information in service descriptions prevents reliable automatic integration of services. For instance, if an application interacting with a shopping cart assumes that the addItem(item,qt) operation adds qt to the quantity of the target item, interactions will fail with all carts that implement an `addItem(item,qt)` operation overwriting the quantity instead of increasing it [26]. To mitigate semantic problems, natural language specifications can be associated with interface descriptions. However, these descriptions cannot be automatically processed by clients and are often ambiguous and incomplete. For instance, according to [17], more than 80% of Web services have descriptions shorter than 50 words and more than 50% of service descriptions are even shorter than 20 words.

In addition to the danger of binding to incompatible services, problems can be caused by services which fail to correctly implement their specifications, i.e., their public service descriptions. A client application has only limited capacity to verify the quality of a remote Web service because it cannot access the service implementation. Moreover, owners of services can modify their implementations at any time without alerting existing clients. Hence, clients can neither rely on the quality of a service at the time of binding nor on its behavioural stability over time.

Several testing and analysis techniques for Web services and service-based applications have been developed [10], addressing the verification of functional and non-functional requirements, interoperability and regression, but they focus on the technical verification problem, failing to provide a sound embedding in the life-cycle of services. For example, many approaches focus on testing entire applications, which is obviously insufficient because it reveals faults of single services too late to be effectively fixed and does not consider dynamic changes.

In this chapter, we present a framework for developing high-quality service-based applications addressing both the verification problem, as well as its embedding in the service life-cycle. In line with the current best practice, this includes a model-driven approach for developing service specifications with automated mappings to languages for service description and matching, as well as monitoring at the implementation level. We focus on functional service specifications aimed at the interoperability of services.

Model-driven development provides the foundation for (formal) reasoning about the behaviour of services and their compositions. Models allow developers to focus on conceptual tasks and abstract from implementation details. Moreover, models are often represented with a high-level visual language that can be understood more intuitively than source code and formal textual descriptions and are effective for communication between developers [15].

We describe the data types visible at a service interface with a class diagram. We specify the behaviour of its operations by graph-transformation rules [13], describing the manipulation of object structures over the class diagrams. Graph transformation rules combine a number of advantages which make them particularly suitable for the high-level modelling of operations: (1) they have a formal semantics; (2) they address the transformation of structure and data, an aspect that would otherwise be specified textually in a programming- or logic-oriented style; (3) they form a natural complement to mainstream visual modelling techniques like state machines or sequence diagrams; and (4) they can easily be visualised themselves in a UML-like notation, supporting an intuitive level of understanding beyond the formal one [3].

Our approach aims to guarantee high-quality service-oriented applications by refining the classical life-cycle of service registration, discovery and usage as follows.

- Service registration: Only tested Web services should be allowed to participate in high-quality service-based applications. For this, we propose to extend the functionality of UDDI registries to automatically generate test cases that are executed when a Web service either adds or updates its behavioural description. Registration is allowed only if all test cases have been passed [26].
- Service discovery: Based on the extension of service descriptions to include behavioural specifications, service discovery can match descriptions against behavioural requirements [23]. For instance, a client can explicitly query for a cart that implements an addItem operation that overwrites the quantity of items already present in the cart.
- Service usage: Since clients can access services over a period of time, it is important that their behaviour remains consistent with their specifications. Service models are used to automatically generate monitors that are able to continuously verify the behaviour of Web service implementations [16].

In summary, our framework provides discovery mechanisms based on behavioural descriptions, supports continuous monitoring of web services at the provider and client sides and allows registration and composition of high-quality Web services only.

The rest of the chapter is organised as follows. Section 7.2 describes the life-cycle of high-quality service-based applications. Section 7.3 introduces graph-transformation as the formal language used to describe the behaviour of services, along with a running example used throughout the chapter to present our framework. Testing, discovery and monitoring techniques, which are the core of the approach, are presented in Sects. 7.4–7.6, respectively. Sects. 7.7 and 7.8 discuss empirical validation of our framework and related work, respectively. Finally, Sect. 7.9 outlines conclusions and future work.

7.2 Life-Cycle of High-Quality Service-Oriented Applications

High-quality service-oriented applications are systems obtained from *reliable composition* of *high-quality web services*. Reliable composition is achieved by automatic service discovery and binding based on the matching of behavioural

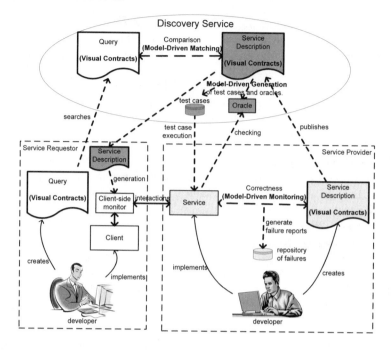

Fig. 7.1. The development process for high-quality service-based applications

specifications. High-quality services are tested before their registration and monitored throughout their life time.

Figure 7.1 shows the entities that participate in service development, publication and discovery of high-quality service-oriented applications. Different shades of grey are used to mark entities involved in different steps of the process. Items associated with *service development* are indicated in light grey, artefacts and activities related to *service registration* are shown with a dark grey background, and *service discovery* is indicated with a white background.

During *service development* software developers design and implement single services. The development methodology associated with our framework is based on the integrated use of UML diagrams to describe static aspects and graph transformations to describe dynamic properties of the service under development. The dynamic properties of a service are given in terms of pre- and post-conditions, both instances of the design class diagram as explained in Sect. 7.3. These visual descriptions are used both internally and externally.

Internal use consists of translating these visual descriptions into JML monitors that are embedded into the implementation.[4] External use consists in

---

[4] The Java Modelling Language (JML) [9, 33] is a behavioural specification language for Java classes and interfaces. JML assertions are based on Java expression and annotated to the Java source code. Thus, JML extends Java with concepts of Design by Contract following the example of Eiffel [37]. However, JML is more expressive than Eiffel, supporting constructs such as universal and existential

uploading these descriptions to the discovery service to support the generation of test cases and monitors required in the next phases. Violations detected by JML monitors are collected in a repository and examined by developers who use this information to fix bugs in the implementation.

The *translation process* from visual descriptions to JML monitors consists of two parts: first, Java class skeletons are generated from the design class diagrams; second, JML assertions are derived from graph transformation rules. The assertions allow us to validate the consistency of the models they are derived from with the manually produced code. The execution of such checks must be transparent in that, unless an assertion is violated, the behaviour of the original program remains unchanged. This is guaranteed since JML assertions are free of side-effects. (See Sect. 7.6 for details on the translation.)

Programmers use the generated Java fragments to fill in the missing behavioural code in order to build a complete and functional application according to the design models and visual contract of the system. They are not allowed to change the JML assertions, thus ensuring that they remain consistent with the visual contracts. If new requirements for the system demand new functionality, the functionality has to be specified using visual contracts first, in order to derive new assertions for implementation.

When behavioural code has been implemented, programmers use a JML compiler to build the executable binary code. This binary code includes the programmer's behavioural code and additional executable runtime checks that are generated from the JML assertions. The runtime checks verify if the manually coded behaviour of an operation fulfils its JML specification, i.e., pre- and post-conditions. Since the JML annotations are generated from the visual contracts, we indirectly verify that the behavioural code complies with the visual contract of the design model.

During *service registration* service developers publish specifications based on graph transformations to make services available to potential clients. When specifications are uploaded, discovery services automatically generate test cases and oracles, to verify that services satisfy their expectations. Test cases are executed against target services and oracles evaluate results. In some cases, services under test may need to implement special testing interfaces to let oracles inspect their internal states, to verify the correctness of the results. These interfaces implement a *get* operation that returns the current state of the web service, according to its behavioural descriptions. If necessary, these interfaces can include a *set* operation that assigns a given state to the target web service. Since both the signature of getter/setter methods and the structure of the web service state are known a priori, these interfaces can be automatically generated.

If a service does not pass all test cases, registries generate a report which is sent to service developers and they cancel service registration. Otherwise, if a

---

quantifications. Different tools are available to support, e.g., runtime assertion checking, testing, or static verification based on JML.

service passes all tests, registries complete registration and inform service developers that they can turn off any testing interface. This protocol guarantees that only high-quality Web services can register. If service providers modify the behaviour of their services, they must provide a new specification and repeat registration and testing. Service providers are discouraged to change the behaviour of services without publishing updated specifications because clients would discover services by referring to outdated specifications, and thus they would be unable to interact with these services. Moreover, client-side monitors can automatically detect anomalous behaviour to prevent clients from interacting with unsound implementations of a published specification.

During *service discovery* clients retrieve and bind to services. To this end, service requestors submit queries to discovery services. Discovery services automatically process requests and if any of the specifications satisfies the queries, references to the corresponding services are returned to clients. In our framework, both queries and specifications are visually expressed by graph transformations. Thus, developers use a coherent environment at both client and service provider sites.

While *using a service*, clients can download the service description (service specifications) and generate a client-side monitor to verify the correctness of its behaviour. A client-side monitor is similar to a client-side proxy, which can be generated from Web service engines like Apache Axis [1]. Additionally, the client-side monitor embeds JML assertions and checks if requests and results exchanged between clients and services satisfy expectations by wrapping the invocation of the service of the client.

Thanks to these refinements of the standard life cycle, clients have the guarantee of interacting with web services that have been verified against their requirements. Moreover, any deviations from the expected behaviour are revealed by client-side monitors.

The life-cycle of a web service described in this section allows the development of reliable web services. It helps developers of services to produce reliable services by generating test cases and JML assertions, which can be used to monitor the implementation at the provider side, e.g., during testing. During registration, automatic generation of test cases is able to detect and reject incorrect services. Client-side monitors help to ensure that the behaviour of a service remains consistent with its description.

Even if we only present how to generate Java and JML code from our models in this chapter, the overall framework does not mandate a specific programming language. The service descriptions exchanged between the service provider, service requester and the discovery service are not platform-specific, and the communication between them can also be based on platform independent XML-dialects like SOAP [39]. To be completely platform independent, we only need to adjust our code and test generators to support multiple programming languages. A translation of graph transformation rules to Microsoft's Spec# [4] (adds the idea of contracts to Microsoft's C# [32]) is also possible as shown in [44].

7.3 Web Service Specification

In this section, we describe the specification-related concepts underlying our modelling approach using the example of a hotel reservation system. This system is able to create a number of reservations for different hotels and manages them in a reservation list for each customer. For example, this allows John to organise a round trip, while visiting different hotels and celebrating the purchase of his new car. After John has finished planning his trip he can commit the reservation list. Later activities such as payment or check-in are not part of our example.

In our approach, a design model consists of a static and a functional view.

7.3.1 Modelling Static Aspects

UML class diagrams are used to represent the static aspects in our design model. Figure 7.2 shows the class diagram of our hotel reservation system. We use the stereotypes control, entity and boundary. Each of these stereotypes expresses a different role of a class in the implementation. Instances of control classes encapsulate the control flow related to a specific complex activity, coordinating simpler activities of other classes. Entity classes model long-lived or persistent information. Boundary classes are used to model non-persistent information that is exchanged between a system and its actors. The stereotype key indicates key attributes of a class. A key attribute is a

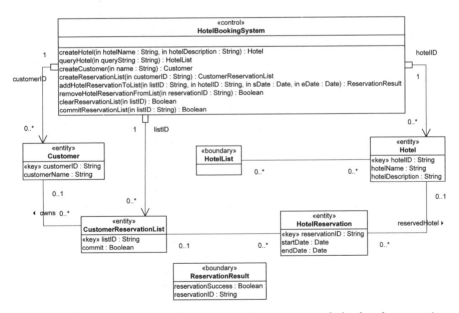

Fig. 7.2. Class diagram specifying the static structure of the hotel reservation system

unique identifier for a set of objects of the same type. A small rectangle associated with an association ending with a qualifier (e.g. hotelID) designates an attribute of the referenced class. In combination with the attributes, the qualifier allows us to get direct access to a specific object. For instance, the control class HotelBookingSystem is connected to the entity classes of the system via qualified associations.

7.3.2 Modelling Functional Aspects

Class diagrams are complemented by graph transformation rules that introduce a *functional view*, integrating static and dynamic aspects. They allow us to describe the pre-conditions and effects of individual operations, referring to the (conceptual) data state of the system. Graph transformation rules are formed over the classes of the design class diagram and are represented by a pair of UML object diagrams, specifying pre- and post-conditions. The use of graph transformations to specify the functional view of services is a key aspect of our approach because they enable specification of the service behaviour, automatic generation of test cases, automatic generation of monitors and specification of visual queries.

In particular, the functional view is used to (formally) match the behaviour required by the client and the behaviour offered by the server, at the discovery service side. When a client uploads a description of the required behaviour, the service discovery analyses all available specifications and responds with the list of all compatible services. The required behaviour is visually defined by the client as a set of graph transformation rules that represent the operations that must be implemented by returned services. The functional view of a service is also used during the registration phase to automatically generate test cases and oracles. Test cases are generated by the discovery service that executes them and rejects the requests for registration of services that do not pass all test cases. Finally, the modelling of the functional aspect is used both from the server and the client to automatically generate monitors that verify at runtime if the observed interactions satisfy expectations. Any violation is signalled to the client (server) that, in case of problems, can bind to another service (can search and repair the fault).

In the following, we will introduce graph transformation rules through a number of examples. The operation createReservationList of the control class HotelBookingSystem creates a new reservation list for an existing customer. Figure 7.3 shows a graph transformation rule that describes the behaviour of the operation. The rule is enclosed in a frame, containing a heading and a context area. The frame notation originates from UML 2.0, providing a portable context for a diagram. The heading is a string enclosed in a rectangle with a cutoff corner, placed in the upper left corner of the frame. The keyword gtr refers to the type of diagram, in this case a graph transformation rule. The keyword is followed by the name of the operation specified by the rule, in turn followed by a parameter list and a return parameter, if declared in

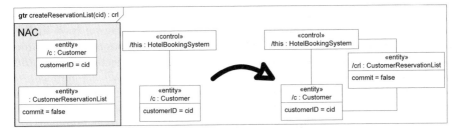

Fig. 7.3. Graph transformation rule for operation `createReservationList`

the class diagram. All parameters occur in the graph transformation rule. An extension of the UML 2.0 metamodel for graph transformation rules of this form can be found in [16].

The graph transformation rule itself is placed in the context area. It consists of two object diagrams, its left- and right-hand side, both typed over the design class diagram. The basic idea is to consider the left-hand side as a pattern, describing the objects, attributes and links that need to be present for the operation to be executable. Then, all items only present in the left-but not in the right-hand side of the rule are removed, and all present only in the right-hand side are newly created. Objects present in both sides are not affected by the rule, but required for its application. If there is only one object of a certain type, it can remain anonymous; if a distinction between different objects of the same type is necessary, then there must be an object identifier separated from the type by a colon.

We may extend the pre- or post-conditions of a rule by negative preconditions [20] or post-conditions. A negative condition is represented by a dark rectangle in the frame. If the dark rectangle is on the left of the precondition, it specifies object structures that are not allowed to be present before the operation is executed (negative pre-condition). If the dark rectangle is on the right of the post-condition, it specifies object structures that are not allowed to be present after the execution of the operation (negative postcondition). A detailed explanation of graph transformation rules can be found in [13].

The graph transformation rule as described in Fig. 7.3 expresses the fact that the operation `createReservationList` can be executed if the `HotelBookingSystem` object references an object of type `Customer`, which has an attribute `customerID` with the value `cid`. The concrete values are specified when the client calls the operation. The negative pre-condition additionally requires that the object `c:Customer` be not connected to an object of type `CustomerReservationList` that has the value `false` for the attribute `commit`. That means, the system only creates a new reservation list for an existing customer if there is no reservation list for the customer, which is not yet committed. As an effect, the operation creates a new object of type `CustomerReservationList` and two links between the objects of types

HotelBookingSystem and CustomerReservationList as well as Customer and CustomerReservationList. As indicated by the variables used in the heading, the object crl:CustomerReservationList becomes the return value of the operation createReservationList. The active object, executing the method, is designated by the variable this.

Figure 7.4 shows a functional specification of the operation addHotelReservationToList by two graph transformation rules. If the operation is successfully executed, it adds a new hotel reservation to the reservation list of the customer. If the operation is not successfully executed, it does nothing. The pre-conditions of both rules are identical. That means, from an external point the resulting behaviour is non-deterministic. A client does not know whether the hotel reservation system will create a new reservation or not. The reason is that the decision depends on the availability of the hotel, which is not known in advance. For a successful execution of the operation, the object this must know two different objects with the following characteristics: an object of type Hotel which has an attribute hotelID with the value hid, an object of type CustomerReservationList which has an attribute listID with the value lid and an attribute commit with the value false. If the requested hotel is available, the operation creates a new object HotelReservation and initialises its attributes startDate and endDate

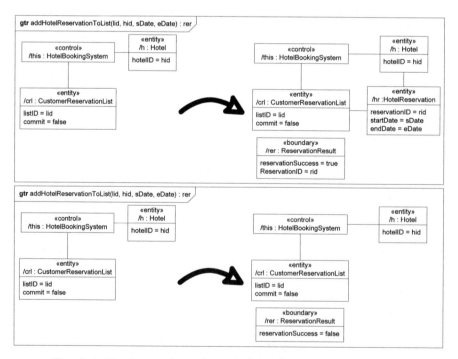

Fig. 7.4. Graph transformation rule for operation addHotelToList

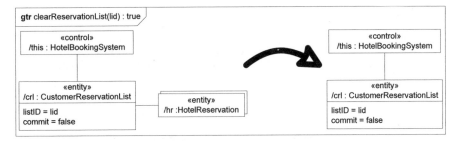

Fig. 7.5. Graph transformation rule for operation `clearReservationList`

according to the parameter values (see top rule in Fig. 7.4). This new object is linked to the objects `h:Hotel` and `crl:CustomerReservationList` identified in the pre-condition. Additionally, the object creates a new boundary object of type `ReservationList`, initialises its attributes and uses this object as return value. Generally, the boundary object is used to group different return values into one return object. If the requested hotel is not available, the service only creates a boundary object `rer:ReservationResult` and sets the value of its attribute to `false` (see bottom rule in Fig. 7.4). This allows to show the client that the reservation has not been successful.

Universally quantified operations, involving a set of objects whose cardinality is not known at design time, can be modelled using multi-objects. An example is shown in Fig. 7.5. This rule specifies an operation which removes all `HotelReservations`   from   an   existing,   not   committed `CustomerReservationList`. The multi-object `hr:HotelReservation` in the pre-condition indicates that the operation is executed if there is a set (which maybe empty) of objects of type `HotelReservation`. After the execution of the operation, all objects conforming to `hr:HotelReservation` (as well as the corresponding links) are deleted, i.e., the reservation list is cleared.

Figure 7.6 shows the remaining graph transformation rules for the operations of the hotel reservation system.

7.4 Web Service Registration

As outlined in Sect. 7.2, registration of web services includes a testing phase where registries automatically generate, execute and evaluate test cases. Only if all test cases are passed, the registration phase is successfully completed; otherwise, registration is aborted. In both cases, a report is sent to service owners.

Execution of test cases can require the implementation of ad hoc interfaces that are used by registries to set and reset the state of Web services, when normal interfaces do not support all necessary operations. In particular, test case execution usually requires a reset operation to clean the current state, a

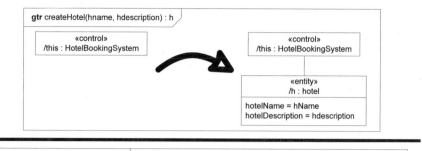

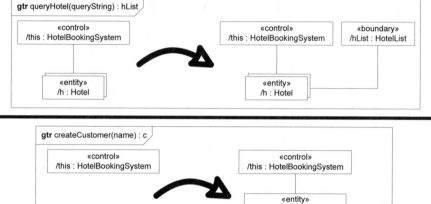

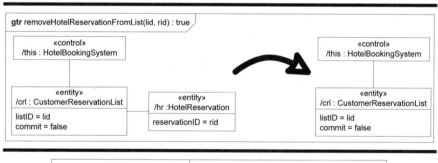

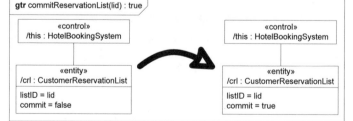

Fig. 7.6. Remaining graph transformation rule for operations of the hotel reservation system

creational interface to transform the target service into a given state (similarly to a setter method) and an inspection interface, to access the internal state of Web services (similarly to a getter method). Once testing has been passed, the testing interface can be disabled.

Automatic test case generation validates the behaviour of a given Web service by addressing two aspects: correctness of single operations, e.g., booking a hotel room, and correctness of multiple operations, e.g., fully managing a reservation list [26].

The registration phase also includes the generation of client-side monitors. The following sections present techniques for generation of test cases and monitors.

7.4.1 Test Cases for Single Operations

The result of an operation depends on both its inputs and the current state of the service. Admissible inputs are defined by operation signatures, which constrain each variable with a type, while states are defined by class diagrams limiting the types and relations of objects. This information is complemented by transformation rules that specify the pre-conditions and effects of the operations.

Testing single operations means executing them on samples from their domains to evaluate the general correctness of their behaviour. Since transformation rules provide information that allows the identification of different sets of "equivalent" inputs, we generate test cases by a domain-based strategy [54] known as partition testing. The rationale is that test cases can be suitably selected by dividing operations' domains into (possibly overlapping) subsets and choosing one or more elements from each subset [53]. Inputs from each domain should trigger sets of equivalents behaviours, according to Web service specifications.

Usually, input domains are identified by following fault-based guidelines, identifying small partitions, where several insidious faults can be present, and large partitions, where little assumptions about specific implementation threats can be made [53]. In case of operations specified by graph transformations, if op_i are the transformation rules that define the behaviour of an operation and the pre-condition of each rule is indicated with pre_i, we can identify the following domains:

- completeDomain: Each pre_i is a domain. Selecting at least one input from each pre_i guarantees the execution of all transformation rules.
- multiRules: Any $pre_i \cap pre_j \neq \varnothing$ is a domain. It represents the case of an input that can potentially trigger either of two rules. The choice is internal to the Web service, and can eventually be non-deterministic. The identification of the rule that must be triggered is a potential source of problems, coverage of these domains guarantees execution of all possible decision points.

- boundaryValues: Any pre_i can specify conditions on node attributes. Since many faults are likely to arise when attributes assume values at boundaries of their domain, a separate domain is represented for each input where at least one attribute assumes a boundary value.
- multiObjects: pre_i can contain multi-objects, which are satisfied by inputs with any cardinality of nodes. The operation must be able to suitably manage any input. We identified three domains that must be covered when a multi-object is part of a pre-condition: inputs with 0 elements, with 1 element and with more than 1 element.
- unspecified: Input values that do not satisfy any pre_i, but conform to the constraints represented by the operation signature. In these cases, a target Web service should respond by both signalling incorrectness of the input and leaving its state unchanged.

Note that domains are not disjoint because the same input can reveal a failure for multiple reasons.

Given an operation op and its rules op_i, we derive test cases by generating a set of triples (in, seq, out), where in is an input that belongs to one of the domains associated with op, seq consists of an invocation to op, and out is the expected result, which can be any $op_i(in)$, where in satisfies the pre-condition of op_i. Test cases must cover all domains. Moreover, different domains can be covered with different numbers of test cases, according to the tester's preference. For instance, we can cover the "completeDomain" with four test cases, and the "multiObjects" domain with one test case. Concrete attribute values are randomly generated taking into account constraints associated with rules. We only consider linear constraints; however, extensions to non-linear constraints can be incorporated as well [30]. Values from the *unspecified* domain are obtained by considering a transformation rule, and generating inputs that preserve the structure of the pre-condition of the rule, but includes attribute values that violate at least one constraint associated with the pre-condition.

For example, if we generate test cases for the rule `clearReservationList(lid)` shown in Fig. 7.5, we can identify the following domains:

- completeDomain: The operation is specified with one rule, thus the technique identifies only one domain that corresponds to the pre-condition of `clearReservationList(lid)`.
- multiRules: Since we have only one rule, there is no input that can potentially trigger multiple rules. Thus no domain is selected.
- boundaryValues: The rule includes only one unspecified attribute value, which is `listId`. The type of this attribute is `String`. Thus, two domains with `String`s of minimum and maximum length are considered (the maximum length can be either defined by the tester or inherited from the specification of the String type).

- multiObjects: The rule includes one multi-object. Thus the technique generates three domains: one with an empty set of `HotelReservation`, one with a single `HotelReservation` and one with multiple `HotelReservations`.
- unspecified: The only constraint about attribute values that can be violated is `commit=false`. Thus, the technique generates a domain with `commit=true`. This is an interesting test case because Web service developers may erroneously assume that the `clearReservationList` operation can be executed on commited reservation lists.

The exact number of test cases depends on the amount of samples that are extracted from each domain. For instance, if we extract 4 samples from *completedomain*, 1 sample from *boundaryValues*, 1 sample from *multiObjects* and 1 sample from *unspecified*, we obtain $4 \times 1 + 1 \times 2 + 1 \times 3 + 1 \times 1 = 10$ test cases.

7.4.2 Test Cases for Operation Sequences

To test the effect of sequences of operations, we analyse the relation between transformation rules. A sequence of rule applications leads to a sequence of transformations on the data state of the service. Typically, when state-dependent behaviour has to be tested, data-flow analysis is used to reveal state-dependent faults by exercising variable definitions and uses [19]. A similar idea can be applied to graph transformation rules.

In particular, given two transformation rules p_1 and p_2, p_1 may disable p_2 if it deletes or adds entities that are required or forbidden by p_2, respectively. In this case, we say that a conflict between p_1 and p_2 exists. Given two transformation rules p_1 and p_2, p_1 may cause p_2 if it deletes or adds state entities that are forbidden or required by p_2, respectively. In this case, we say that a dependency between p_1 and p_2 exists. For example, a dependency between rule `addReservationToList`, shown in Fig. 7.4, and rule `createReservationList`, shown in Fig. 7.3, exists. This is because the former rule can be applied only if the state includes a `CustomerReservationList` node, which can be created by the latter rule. Moreover, a conflict between rule `clearReservationList`, shown in Fig. 7.5, and rule `removeHotelReservationFromList`, shown in Fig. 7.6, exists. This is because the former rule deletes the `HotelReservation` node, which is required by the latter rule.

Our technique addresses testing of sequences of operations by covering dependencies and conflicts between rules. Sequences of operations that do not include any dependency or conflict are likely to be sequences of independent operations. Thus, they have been already covered by testing of the single operations.

To turn the test requirement to cover a sequence of two rules $\langle p_1, p_2 \rangle$ into an executable test case, we must solve a search problem. In particular, the pre-condition of rule p_1 may not be satisfied by the initial state of the target web service (this happens also for testing of single operations). Moreover, the state that results from the execution of rule p_1 may not allow the immediate execution of rule p_2. Thus, we need to identify two sequences of operations: seq_{pre}, which brings the Web service from the initial state to a state that satisfies the pre-condition of p_1, and seq_{betw}, which brings the web service from the state that results from the execution of p_1 to a state that satisfies the pre-condition of p_2. The sequence seq_{betw} should not modify the entities that are part of the conflict/dependency between p_1 and p_2, otherwise the dependency between the two transformations would be removed.

Conflicts and dependencies can automatically be identified by the AGG tool [51], while the search for sequences seq_{pre} and seq_{betw} can be supported by tools like PROGRESS [47] and GROOVE [46]. The existence of testing interfaces can simplify the solution to the search problem. Early experience presented in [26] shows that the problem is feasible at the level of complexity of several common Web service APIs.

For example, if we focus on rule createReservationList, shown in Fig. 7.3, we can automatically identify the following dependencies

- ⟨createCustomer, createReservationList⟩, because createCustomer creates the Customer node, which is required by the pre-condition of createReservationList.
- ⟨commitReservationList, createReservationList⟩, because commit-ReservationList modifies the value of the commit attribute from false to true, and the createReservationList rule forbids the presence of a CustomerReservationList with commit equals to false.

and conflicts:

- ⟨createReservationList, createReservationList⟩, because the first createReservationList creates a ReservationList with commit equals to false, which is forbidden by the second createReservationList.

Examples of concrete test cases that can be generated from the test requirements above are (attribute values are omitted):

- $TC1 =$ createCustomer; createReservationList
- $TC2 =$ createCustomer; createReservationList; commitReservationList; createReservationList
- $TC3 =$ createCustomer; createReservationList; createReservationList

7.4.3 Test Oracles for Services

Oracles evaluate the correctness of the test result by comparing the expected return values and post states with those produced by the test of the service. Graph transformation rules can be translated into JML assertions that verify consistency of runtime behaviour and specification. The mapping for generating JML assertions is presented in detail in Sect. 7.6.

Clients can use this technology to create client-side monitors. A client-side monitor is a stub with embedded assertions. In this case, JML assertions can only check data values sent and received by clients, and cannot inspect the web service state. Verification of internal behaviour of Web services is possible using server-side monitors. For example, a client-side monitor can verify that the `createCustomer` operation, shown in Fig. 7.6, returns a `customer` object with a name equal to the string passed as parameter, but cannot verify if the same object is part of the internal state of the web service.

All violations revealed by the client-side monitors are recorded, to be accessed by the developers of the service or prospective clients, to identify and fix problems, to adapt client applications or to select new web services.

7.5 Web Service Discovery

An important part of our approach, albeit not the focus of this book chapter, is the discovery of services based on their semantic descriptions. Current standards already enable much of the discovery process, but they concentrate largely on syntactic service descriptions. However, service requestors can be assumed to know what kind of service they need (i.e. its semantics), but not necessarily how the service is actually called (i.e. its syntax). Thus, a provider must be able to formulate a semantic request and a discovery service must be able to match a semantic service description to a corresponding request.

We will give only a brief overview of how our approach enables the semantic discovery of services. The interested reader is referred to previous publications on the discovery of services specified by graph transformation rules [23, 24].

In our approach, graph transformation rules serve as both description of an offered service and formulation of a request. From a provider's point of view, the left-hand side of the rule specifies the pre-condition of the provider's service (i.e. the situation that must be present or the information that must be available for the service to perform its task). The right-hand side of the rule depicts the post-condition (i.e. the situation after the successful execution of the web service). From a requester's point of view, the left-hand side of the rule represents the information the requester is willing to provide to the service, and the right-hand side of the rule represents the situation the requester wants to achieve by using the service.

Matching the rules of a provider with those of a requestor means deciding whether a service provider fulfils the demands of a service requestor and vice versa. Informally, a provider rule matches a requestor rule if (1) the requestor is willing to deliver the information needed by the provider and in turn (2) the provider guarantees to produce the results expected by the requestor.

We have formalized this informal matching concept using contravariant subgraph relations between the pre- and post-conditions of the rules of the service provider and the requestor [24]. In short, the requester is willing to deliver the information needed by the provider if the latter's pre-conditions is a subgraph of the requestor's pre-conditions. The provider produces the results expected by the requestor if the provider's post-condition is a subgraph of the requestor's post-condition. That means, the requestor is allowed to offer more information than needed by the provider and the provider can produce more results than needed by the requestor.

A prototypical implementation of our approach is available [23] using DAML+OIL [12] as semantic web language for representing specifications at the implementation level. Matching is based on the RDQL (RDF Data Query Language) [48] implementation of the semantic web tool Jena by HP [27]. RDQL is a query language for specifying graph patterns that are evaluated over a graph to yield a set of matches. A visual editor for graph transformation rules has been implemented, to support the creation of models [34, 16].

7.6 Web Service Monitoring

The loose coupling of services in a service-oriented application requires the verification that a service satisfies its description not only at the time of binding, but also that it continues to do so during its life time. We propose to use a monitoring approach to continuously verify services at runtime.

Monitors are derived from models, with class diagrams describing the structure and graph transformations describing the behaviour of services. In the following, we describe a translation of models into JML constructs to enable a *model-driven monitoring* [16, 25, 36].

7.6.1 Translation to JML

Class diagrams are used to generate static aspects of Java programs, like interfaces, classes, associations and signatures of operations. The transformation of graph transformations into JML constructs makes the graph transformations observable in the sense that they can be automatically evaluated for a given state of a system, where the state is given by object configurations. In the following, we will concentrate on the code generation for the service provider. The code generation for the client side monitors works similar and will not be discussed in detail in this book chapter. The requestor side monitors can be obtained by restricting the generation of JML assertion to the ones that include only references to parameters. Thus, any assertions with references to any other state variables will not part of the client-side monitor.

Translation of UML Class Diagrams to Java

Given a UML class diagram, we assume that each class is translated to a corresponding Java class. In the following, we will focus on the characteristics of such a translation that we need for explaining our mapping from graph transformation rules to JML.

All private or protected attributes of the UML class diagram are translated to private and protected Java class attributes with appropriate types and constraints, respectively. According to the Java coding style guides [45], we translate public attributes of UML classes to private Java class attributes that are accessible via appropriate `get`- and `set`-methods. Standard types may be slightly renamed according to the Java syntax. Attributes with multiplicity greater than one map to a reference attribute of some container type. Furthermore, each operation specified in the class diagram is translated to a method declaration in the corresponding Java class up to obvious syntactic modifications according to the Java syntax.

Associations are translated by adding an attribute with the name of the association to the respective classes. For handling, e.g., the association `owns` of Fig. 7.2, a private variable `owns` of type `Customer` is added to the class `CustomerReservationList`. Again, appropriate access methods are added to the Java class. Because the UML association `owns` is bidirectional, we additionally add an attribute named `revOwns` to the class `Customer`. For associations that have multiplicities with an upper bound bigger than one, we use classes implementing the standard Java interface `Collection`. A collection represents a group of objects. In particular, we use the class `TreeSet` as implementation of the sub-interface `Set` of `Collection`. A set differs from a collection in that it contains no duplicate elements. For qualified associations, we use the class `HashMap` implementing the standard Java interface `Map`. An object of type `Map` represents a mapping of keys to values. A map cannot contain duplicate keys; each key can map to at most one value. In addition, we provide access methods for adding and removing elements. Examples are the access methods `addCustomerReservationList` or `removeCustomerReservationList`. To check the containment of an element, we add operations like `hasCustomerReservationList`. In case of qualified attributes, we access elements via keys by adding additional methods like `getCustomerReservationListByID`. As described in [18], in order to guarantee the consistency of the pairs of references that implement an association, the respective access methods for reference attributes call each other.

Translation of Graph Transformation Rules to JML

For the transformation of graph transformation rules into JML, we assume a translation of design class diagrams to Java as described above. Listing 7.1 shows how a method is annotated with a JML specification. The behavioural information is specified in the Java comments. Due to their embedding into Java comments, the annotations are ignored by a normal Java compiler. The keywords `public normal_behavior` state that the specification is intended for clients, and that if the pre-condition is satisfied, a call must return normally, without throwing an exception. JML pre-conditions follow the keyword

```
1 public  class  A  {
2
3   ...
4
5   /*@  public  normal_behavior
6     @ requires JML–PRE;
7     @ ensures JML–POST;
8     @*/
9   public  Tr m(T1 v1,  ... Tn vn)  {...}
10
11  ...
12
13 }
```

Listing 7.1. Format for specifying pre- and post-conditions by JML

requires, and post-conditions follow the keyword ensures. Both JML-PRE and JML-POST are Boolean expressions. The pre-condition states what conditions must hold for the method arguments and other parts of the state of the systems. If the pre-condition is true, then the method must terminate in a state that satisfies the post-condition.

If a JML construct represents a visual contract, the JML's pre- and post-conditions must be interpretations of the graphical pre- and post-conditions. When a JML pre-condition (post-condition) is evaluated, figuratively an occurrence of the pattern that is specified by the pre-condition of the corresponding graph transformation rule has to be found in the current system data state. To find the pattern, a JML pre-condition (post-condition) applies a breadth-first search starting from the object this. The object this is the object that is executing the behaviour. If a JML pre-condition (post-condition) finds a correct pattern, it returns true, otherwise it returns false.

In Listing 7.2 the JML contract for verifying the visual contract of Fig. 7.3 is shown. Mainly, we test the pre- and post-conditions by nesting existence or universal quantifications that are supported by JML. Additionally, the negative application condition is nested into the pre-condition. The general syntax of JML's quantified expressions is given as (\forAll T x; r ; p) and (\exists T x; r; p). The forAll expression is true if every object x of type T that satisfies r also satisfies p. The exists expression is true if there exists at least one object x of type T that satisfies r also satisfies p.

Next, we explain the JML-contract of Listing 7.2 in more detail. The pre-condition including the negative application condition is tested in lines 2–11. Lines 3–5 check if the active object (object this of type HotelBookingSystem) knows an object of type Customer with the value cid (parameter of the operation createReservationList) for the attribute customerID.

In lines 6–11 the negative application condition is checked. It is checked whether the previously identified customer (c) references an object of type

```
1  /*@ public
2  normal_behavior
3    @ requires
4    @ (\exists Customer c;
5    @    this.getCustomer.values().contains(c);
6    @    c.getCustomerID().equals(cid) &&
7    @    !(
8    @      (\exists CustomerReservationList crlNAC;
9    @         c.owns.contains(crlNAC);
10   @         crlNAC.getCommit() == false
11   @      )
12   @    )
13   @ );
14   @
15   @ ensures (
16   @ (\exists Customer c;
17   @    this.getCustomer.values().contains(c);
18   @    c.getCustomerID().equals(cid) &&
19   @    (\exists CustomerReservationList crl;
20   @      this.customerReservationList.values().contains(crl);
21   @      crl.owns == c &&
22   @      crl.getCommit() == false &&
23   @      \result == crl
24   @    )
25   @ );
26   @*/
27  public CustomerReservationList createReservationList
28                                            (String cid);
```

Listing 7.2. JML contract of operation `createReservationList` of Fig. 7.3

`CustomerReservationList` with the value `false` for the attribute `commit`. If such an object is found, then lines 6–11 return `false` (see ! in line 7).

The post-condition is tested in lines 14–23. The objects of the post-condition are tested in the following order by the JML expression: `c:Customer` and `crl:CustomerReservationList`. Therefore, two JML-exists expressions are nested into each other. In line 22 whether the object `crl` is returned by the operation is tested. The JML-keyword `result` is used to denote the value returned by the method.

7.6.2 Runtime Behaviour

For enabling model-driven monitoring, we have bridged the gap between the model and the implementation level by the definition of a transformation of our visual contracts into JML assertions. On the implementation level we can take advantage of existing JML tools: The JML compiler generates assertion check methods from the JML pre- and post-conditions. The original, manual implemented methods are replaced by automatically generated *wrapper methods* and the original methods become a private method with a new name. The

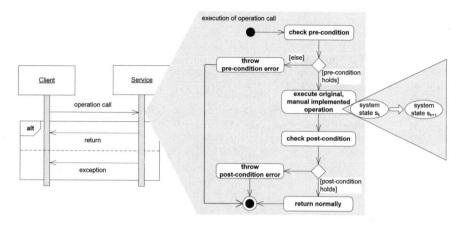

Fig. 7.7. Runtime behaviour of operation, model-driven monitoring approach

wrapper methods delegate client method calls to the original methods with appropriate assertions checks.

This leads to a runtime behaviour of an operation call as shown in Fig. 7.7. When a client calls an operation of a service, a pre-condition check method evaluates a method's pre-condition and throws a pre-condition violation exception if it does not hold. If the pre-condition holds, then the original operation is invoked. After the execution of the original operation, a post-condition check method evaluates the post-condition and throws a post-condition violation exception if it does not hold.

If an exception is thrown during the pre-condition test, then the client (routine's caller), although obligated by the contract to satisfy a certain requirement, does not satisfy it. This is a bug in the client itself; the routine is not involved. A violation of the post-condition means that the manual implemented operation was not able to fulfil its contract. In this case, the manual implementation contains a bug, the caller is innocent.

If the contracts are not violated at runtime, then automatic monitoring is transparent. The system state is only changed by the original operation. Our transformation of the visual contracts into JML ensures that the assertion checks generated by the JML compiler do not have any side effects on the system state. That is, except for time and space measurements, a correct implementation's behaviour is unchanged.

With the generated assertions, we can monitor the correctness of an implementation. If we want to take full advantage of our model-driven monitoring approach, a system needs to react adequately. As introduced before, an exception is thrown if a pre- or a post-condition is violated at runtime. The JML tools introduce the exception classes `JMLPreconditionError` and `JMLPostconditionError` to catch these exceptions. Listing 7.3 shows how to use these classes in an implementation. The operation at the beginning of the

```
1 try {
2    shop.cartAdd(item, cartId);
3 } catch (JMLPreconditionError e) {
4      System.out.println("Violation of precondition   "
5                              + e.getMessage());
6 } catch (JMLPostconditionError e) {
7    System.out.println("Violation of postcondition   "
8                              + e.getMessage());
9 } catch (Error e) {
10   System.out.println("Unidentified error!"
11                             + e.getMessage();
12 }
```

Listing 7.3. Exceptions handling at development time

```
1 Violation of pre-condition by method OnlineShop.cartAdd
2 regarding specifications at
3 File "de\upb\dbis\amazonmini\OnlineShop.refines-java",
4 line 34, character 18 when
5      'cid' is Cart_1
6      'item' is de.upb.dbis.amazonmini.Item@ecd7e
7      'this' is de.upb.dbis.amazonmini.OnlineShop@1d520c4
```

Listing 7.4. Example of an exception

try-catch block is an operation detailed by visual contracts on the design level. A programmer on the client side can now use these exception handling mechanisms to catch pre- and post-condition violations and implement an adequate reaction. Listing 7.4 shows the example of a message if a pre-condition is violated.

To summarise, with our model-driven monitoring approach we can build reliable (correct and robust) software systems. Correctness is the ability of a software system to behave according to its specification. Robustness is the ability to react to cases not included in the specification. At runtime, the generated JML assertions allow for the monitoring of the correctness. The generated exceptions allow a programmer to make a software system robust if it does not behave according to its specification.

7.7 Empirical Validation

The framework presented in this chapter has been used with several case studies: test case generation has been applied to publicly available web services and the monitoring technology has been used with web services provided by industrial partners. In the following, we summarize the results obtained so far. Details about these experiences are available in [26, 35, 14].

The technique for *automatic testing* has been applied to both a selection of web services available from www.xmethods.com and the Amazon web service. Since the GT-based specifications of these web services are not available, we manually specified the behaviour expected from these web services, and we used automatic testing to check if web service implementations conform with our expectations.

Testing showed that all web services, with the exception of the Kayak Paddle Guide web service, behave according to our expectations. The Kayak Paddle Guide web service returns the recommended length of a paddle given the height of the person who will use it. Testing revealed a fault that consists in suggesting a kayak of a maximum length, even if the input represents an incorrect height for a person.

Test case generation applied to the Amazon Web Service also revealed an incompatibility between its specification and the actual behavior of the web service. However, the incompatibility was due to our misinterpretation of the operation for adding items. Once the specification had been fixed, test cases did not identify any incompatibility.

This experience showed that the technique for test case generation scales well even with web services of non-trivial complexity, like the Amazon Web Service.

In an industrial case study [35, 14], we successfully applied graph transformations for specifying the interfaces of web services. In this case study, we used the web services of a business process for ordering new insurance contracts. We have been able to replace almost all previously created textual descriptions of web services by descriptions with graph transformations to allow for an efficient administration and monitoring of web services.

Moreover, we demonstrated the feasibility of the monitoring technology by implementing an in-house version of the Amazon Web service and generating its server-side monitors. The monitoring components worked fine and this experience demonstrated the feasibility of the technology.

7.8 Related Work

The vision of service-oriented architectures is that a program in need of some functionality (that it cannot provide itself) queries a central directory to obtain a list of service descriptions of potential suppliers of this functionality. The notion of service description is a central one in service-oriented architectures. A service description describes the functionality of a service. An important fact to note at this point is that a service requestor must know the *syntax* of a service to be able to call the service and additionally the service requestor must know the *semantics* of a service to be able to call the service correctly.

In this section, we will focus on the service descriptions, the usage of models and model-driven testing approaches in service-oriented architectures.

7.8.1 Service Descriptions

An interface definition is a technical description of the public interfaces of a web service. It specifies the format of the request and the response from the web service. The Web Service Description Language (WSDL) [11] proposed by the World Wide Web Consortium (W3C) is an XML (Extensible Markup Language) format for describing interfaces offered by a web service as a collection of operations. For each operation, its input and output parameters are described. The W3C refers to this kind of service description as the "documentation of the mechanics of the message exchange" [5, 7]. While these mechanics must be known to enable binding, a semantic description of services based on WSDL is not possible. WSDL only encodes the syntax of the web service invocation; it does not yield information on the service's semantics. Of course, human users might guess which service an operation (e.g. `orderBook(isbn:String)`) provides, but such explicit operation names are technically not required.

UDDI (Universal Description, Discovery, and Integration) [50], the protocol for publishing service descriptions, allows users to annotate their WSDL file with information about the service in the form of explanatory text and keywords. Using Keywords is one way of supplying semantics but not a reliable one, as there has to be a common agreement between requestors and providers about the meaning of the different keywords. The current state of web service technology is such that a developer solves these semantic problems by reading additional textual service descriptions in natural language.

Trying to describe a service with keywords also ignores the operational nature of services. When executing a service, one expects certain changes, i.e., the real world is altered in some significant way (e.g. an order is created, a payment is made or an appointment is fixed). Service descriptions should reflect this functional nature by providing a semantic description in the form of pre- and post-conditions (a style of description also known from contract-based programming) [38]. For a service-oriented architecture, this kind of semantic description can be found in [42, 49]. In both approaches the pre- and post-conditions are expressed in terms of specialised ontologies. While [42] shows the matching only for single input and output concepts, [49] combines a number of pre-defined terms to express the pre- and post-conditions (e.g. `CardCharged-TicketBooked-ReadyforPickup`). Using this style of description, it is possible to distinguish between rather similar services (e.g. booking a ticket, which is sent to the customer vs booking a ticket, which has to be picked up) without coining special phrases for each individual service in the ontology.

While this latter approach addresses human users, all previously mentioned solutions are directed towards machine-readable descriptions only. An important characteristic of our approach is its usability by mainstream software engineers.

7.8.2 Models

Models provide abstraction from the detailed problems of the implementation technologies and allow developers to focus on the conceptual tasks. In particular, visual structures can often be understood more intuitively than source code or formal textual descriptions. Thus, they are usually more effective for the communication between a service provider and a service requestor. Software engineers have long recognised this feature of visual languages and they make use of it. Especially, the diagrams of the industry standard Unified Modelling Language (UML) [41] have become very successful and accompanying software development tools are available. Further, models are an established part of modern software development processes. They are becoming more crucial with the advent of the Model Driven Architecture (MDA), since the MDA promotes generating implementation artefacts automatically from models, thus saving time and effort. Thus, a visual representation of pre- and post-conditions is a promising amalgamation that can be easily integrated into today's model-driven software development processes.

Since version 1.1, the UML standard comprises the Object Constraint Language (OCL) [40] as its formal annotation language for UML models. In contrast to the commonly used graphical diagrammatic UML sub-languages, OCL is a textual language. As a consequence, OCL expressions have a completely different notation for model elements than the diagrams of the UML. The types of constraints that can be expressed in OCL include invariants on classes and types as well as pre- and post-conditions of operations. However, OCL is of limited use even in organisations which employ UML diagrams. The limited readability of OCL and the difficulty of integrating a purely textual language like OCL with diagrams are important reasons for this situation.

Other proposals provide a visual counterpart of OCL by exploiting visualisations with set-theoretic semantics. Kent and Howse define a visual formalism for expressing constraints in object-oriented models. They first proposed constraint diagrams [31] that are based on Venn diagrams and visualised the set-theoretic semantics of OCL constraints. Later, Howse et al. advanced this approach towards Spider Diagrams [28] to support reasoning about diagrams. Visual OCL [8] is a graphical representation of OCL. Both proposals embed textual logic expressions in the diagrams, which leads to a hybrid notation of OCL constraints. In addition, the diagrams differ from the diagrams that are commonly used in organizations employing UML in software development and, thus, developers have to learn another visual language.

We rather prefer to represent practically relevant concepts of object constraints by using graph transformation rules. A graph transformation rule allows for the reuse of UML's object diagram notation. Thus, we have chosen a notation that is familiar to software developers and it easily integrates into today's software development processes.

7.8.3 Testing

There are several techniques for testing applications that include web services, see [10] for a survey on this topic. A few of these techniques investigated the development of enhanced UDDI servers that validate the quality of web services by executing test cases during the registration phase [6, 52]. In particular, Tsai et al. investigated the use of UDDI servers that execute test scripts developed by web service providers [52], and Bertolino et al. investigated the use of UDDI servers that generate test cases from Protocol State Machine diagrams [6]. The former technique focuses on validating a limited set of scenarios identified by testers at design-time, while the latter technique focuses on validating interaction protocols. These techniques follow a complemental point of view with respect to the one presented in this chapter, which focuses on validating if the effect of single invocations and invocation sequences modify the conceptual state of an external web service according to its specification. Moreover, existing techniques do not address the methodology aspect of the development.

We believe that high-quality applications can be obtained with thorough design and modelling of systems. UML is a well-known design language, and some of its diagrams, e.g., sequence diagrams and state charts, can be used for test case generation [43]. However, the generated test cases often fail to capture the concrete complexity of the exchanged parameters that are often restricted to few simple types, see for instance [22]. Moreover, due to the lack of a precise semantics, UML diagrams often need to be extended with some formalism that unambiguously defines the semantics of their elements.

Graph-transformations naturally integrate with UML diagrams, because they can be easily derived from UML design artefacts [3], they allow reasoning about behaviours of target applications and are suitable for test case generation. Moreover, graph transformations naturally address the complexity of both objects that can be exchanged between components and state objects.

A few approaches for test case generation from graph transformations exist [2, 55]. We advance these approaches in three ways: (1) we extend and apply domain-based testing and data-flow techniques to the case of graph transformations, (2) we generate executable test oracles from graph transformation rules and (3) we automatically test and validate web services. Finally, the idea of using registries which automatically test web services before registering seems to be original.

Automatic generation of assertions from models has been addressed in other works. For instance, different approaches show how to translate OCL constraints into assertions that are incorporated into Java code. Hamie [21] proposes a mapping of UML design class diagrams that are annotated with

OCL constraints to Java classes that are annotated with JML specifications. OCL is used to precisely describe the desired effects of the operations in terms of pre- and post-conditions. Invariants on the classes of a design model are also expressed using OCL. The Dresden OCL Toolkit [29] supports parsing, type checking and normalisation of OCL constraints. An application of the toolkit is a Java code generator that translates OCL constraints into Java code fragments that can compute the fulfilment of an OCL constraint. Even if different approaches facilitate the translation of OCL into executable contracts, OCL still lacks an easy-to-use representation.

7.9 Conclusions

Service-oriented applications are characterised by loosely coupled and dynamic interactions among participants. In particular, to obtain reliable and high-quality systems, service discovery, binding and integration must be extensively validated. Several approaches address quality problems in isolation, failing to provide a sound embedding of quality techniques into the life-cycle of services.

In contrast, our framework addresses coherent and model-driven development of high-quality service-based applications and its embedding into the service life-cycle. The resulting service-oriented architecture

- allows participation only of high-quality web services, i.e., web services that passed automatic testing;
- continuously monitors the behaviour of web services and instantaneously signals any violation of specifications;
- supports discovery based on behavioural descriptions rather than syntactical descriptions of interfaces;
- provides client-side monitoring facilities, which support clients in discovering integration problems and re-selecting new services if current services do not behave correctly.

We demonstrated the feasibility of our approach by applying the technologies that are part of the framework for high-quality service-based applications to several real web services.

References

1. Apache. Axis. http://ws.apache.org/axis/.
2. P. Baldan, B. König, and I. Stürmer. Generating test cases for code generators by unfolding graph transformation systems. In *proceedings of the 2nd International Conference on Graph Transformation*, Rome, Italy, 2004.
3. L. Baresi and R. Heckel. Tutorial introduction to graph transformation: a software engineering perspective. In *proceedings of the International Conference on Graph Transformation*, volume 1 of *LNCS*. Springer, 2002.

4. M. Barnett, K. R. M. Leino, and W. Schulte. The spec# programming system: An overview. In *CASSIS 2004*, volume 3362 of *LNCS*. Springer-Verlag, 2004.

5. B. Benatallah, M.-S. Hacid, C. Rey, and F. Toumani. Semantic reasoning for web services discovery. In *proceedings of the WWW 2003 Workshop on E-Services and the Semantic Web (ESSW' 03)*, 2003.

6. A. Bertolino, L. Frantzen, A. Polini, and J. Tretmans. *Architecting Systems with Trustworthy Components*, chapter Audition of Web Services for Testing Conformance to Open Specified Protocols. Number 3938 in Lectures Notes in Computer Science Series. Springer, 2006.

7. D. Booth, H. Haas, F. McCabe, E. Newcomer, C. Michael, C. Ferris, and D. Orchard. Web services architecture - W3C working group note 11 february 2004. Technical report, W3C, 2004.

8. P. Bottoni, M. Koch, F. Parisi-Presicce, and G. Taentzer. A visualization of OCL using collaborations. In M. Gogolla and C. Kobryn, editors, *proceedings of the 4th International Conference on The Unified Modeling Language, Modeling Languages, Concepts, and Tools*, volume 2185 of *Lecture Notes In Computer Science*, pages 257–271. Springer-Verlag, 2001.

9. L. Burdy, Y. Cheon, D. Cok, M. Ernst, J. Kiniry, G. T. Leavens, K. R. M. Leino, and E. Poll. An overview of JML tools and applications. *International Journal on Software Tools for Technology Transfer (STTT)*, February 2005.

10. G. Canfora and M. D. Penta. Testing services and service-centric systems: Challenges and opportunities. *IEEE IT Pro*, pages 10–17, March/April 2006.

11. R. Chinnici, J.-J. Moreau, A. Ryman, and S. Weerawarana. Web services description language (WSDL) version 2.0 part 1: Core language - W3C working draft 10 may 2005, May 2005.

12. D. Connolly, F. van Harmelen, I. Horrocks, D. L. McGuinness, P. F. Patel-Schneider, and L. A. Stein. DAML+OIL (march 2001) reference description - W3C note 18 december 2001, March 2001.

13. A. Corradini, U. Montanari, F. Rossi, H. Ehrig, R. Heckel, and M. Löwe. Chapter 3: Algebraic approaches to graph transformation - part I: Basic concepts and double pushout approach. In G. Rozenberg, editor, *Handbook of Graph Grammars of Computing by Graph Transformation*. World Scientific, 1997.

14. G. Engels, B. Güldali, O. Juwig, M. Lohmann, and J.-P. Richter. Industrielle Fallstudie: Einsatz visueller Kontrakte in serviceorientierten Architekturen. In B. Biel, M. Book, and V. Gruhn, editors, *Software Enginneering 2006, Fachtagung des GI Fachbereichs Softwaretechnik*, volume 79 of *Lecture Notes in Informatics*, pages 111–122. Köllen Druck+Verlag GmbH, 2006.

15. G. Engels, R. Heckel, G. Taentzer, and H. Ehrig. A view-oriented approach to system modelling based on graph transformation. In *proceedings of the 6th European Conference held jointly with the International Symposium on Foundations of Software Engineering*, pages 327–343. Springer-Verlag, 1997.

16. G. Engels, M. Lohmann, S. Sauer, and R. Heckel. Model-driven monitoring: An application of graph transformation for design by contract. In *proceedings of the Third International Conference on Graph Transformations (ICGT 2006)*, volume 4178 of *Lecture Notes in Computer Science*, pages 336–350. Springer, 2006.

17. J. Fan and S. Kambhampati. A snapshot of public web services. *SIGMOD Record*, 34(1):24–32, March 2005.

18. T. Fischer, J. Niere, L. Torunski, and A. Zündorf. Story diagrams: A new graph rewrite language based on the Unified Modeling Language. In H. Ehrig, G. Engels, H.-J. Kreowski, and G. Rozenberg, editors, *Selected papers from the 6th International Workshop on Theory and Application of Graph Transformations (TAGT)*, volume 1764 of *Lecture Notes In Computer Science*, pages 296–309. Springer Verlag, 1998.

19. P. Frankl and E. Weyuker. An applicable family of data flow testing criteria. *IEEE Transactions on Software Engineering*, 14(10):1483–1498, 1988.

20. A. Habel, R. Heckel, and G. Taentzer. Graph grammars with negative application conditions. *Fundamenta Informaticae*, 26(3,4):287–313, 1996.

21. A. Hamie. Translating the object constraint language into the java modeling language. In *proceedings of the 2004 ACM symposium on Applied computing*, pages 1531–1535. ACM Press, 2004.

22. J. Hartmann, C. Imoberdorf, and M. Meisinger. Uml-based integration testing. In *proceedings of the 2000 international symposium on Software testing and analysis (ISSTA)*, pages 60–70. ACM Press, 2000.

23. J. H. Hausmann, R. Heckel, and M. Lohmann. Model-based discovery of Web Services. In *proceedings of the International Conference on Web Services (ICWS)*, 2004.

24. J. H. Hausmann, R. Heckel, and M. Lohmann. Model-based development of web services descriptions enabling a precise matching concept. *International Journal of Web Services Research*, 2(2):67–84, April-June 2005.

25. R. Heckel and M. Lohmann. Model-driven development of reactive informations systems: From graph transformation rules to JML contracts. *International Journal on Software Tools for Technology Transfer (STTT)*, 2006.

26. R. Heckel and L. Mariani. Automatic conformance testing of web services. In *proceedings of the 8th International Conference on Fundamental Approaches to Software Engineering (FASE)*. Springer-Verlag, 2005.

27. Hewlett-Packard Development Company. Jena - a semantic web framework for Java. http://jena.sourceforge.net/.

28. J. Howse, F. Molina, J. Tayloy, S. Kent, and J. Gil. Spider diagrams: A diagrammatic reasoning system. *Journal of Visual Languages and Computing*, 12(3):299–324, June 2001.

29. H. Hussmann, B. Demuth, and F. Finger. Modular architecture for a toolset supporting OCL. *Science of Computer Programming*, 44:51–69, 2002.

30. B. Jeng and E. Weyuker. A simplified domain-testing strategy. *ACM Transactions on Software Engineering and Methodology*, 3:254–270, 1994.

31. S. Kent and J. Howse. Mixing visual and textual constraint languages. In R. France and B. Rumpe, editors, *proceedings of International Conference on The Unified Modeling Language (UML'99)*, volume 1723 of *Lecture Notes in Computer Science*, pages 384–398. Springer, 1999.

32. A. Kühnel. *Visual C# 2005*. Galileo Computing, 2006.

33. G. T. Leavens, A. L. Baker, and C. Ruby. Preliminary design of JML: A behavioral interface specification language for Java. Technical Report 98-06-rev27, Department of Computer Science, Iowa State University, February 2005.

34. M. Lohmann, G. Engels, and S. Sauer. Model-driven monitoring: Generating assertions from visual contracts. In *proceedings of the 21st IEEE International Conference on Automated Software Engineering (ASE'06)*, pages 355–356, September 2006.

35. M. Lohmann, J.-P. Richter, G. Engels, B. Güldali, O. Juwig, and S. Sauer. Abschlussbericht: Semantische Beschreibung von Enterprise Services - Eine industrielle Fallstudie. Technical Report 1, Software Quality Lab (s-lab), Unversity of Paderborn, May 2006.
36. M. Lohmann, S. Sauer, and G. Engels. Executable visual contracts. In M. Erwig and A. Schürr, editors, *proceedings of the 2005 IEEE Symposium on Visual Languages and Human-Centric Computing (VL/HCC'05)*, pages 63–70, 2005.
37. B. Meyer. Applying "Design by Contract". *IEEE Computer*, 25(10):40–51, 1992.
38. B. Meyer. *Object-Oriented Software Construction*. Prentice-Hall, Englewood Cliffs, second edition, 1997.
39. N. Mitra. SOAP version 1.2 part 0: Primer - W3C recommendation 24 june 2003, Juni 2003.
40. OMG (Object Management Group). UML 2.0 OCL final adopted specification, 2003.
41. OMG (Object Management Group). UML 2.0 superstructure specification - revised final adopted specification, 2004.
42. M. Paolucci, T. Kawmura, T. R. Payne, and K. Sycara. Semantic matching of web services capabilities. In I. Horrocks and J. A. Hendler, editors, *proceedings of the First International Semantic Web Conference on the Semantic Web*, volume Lecture Notes In Computer Science; Vol. 2342, pages 333–347, Sardinia, Italy, 2002. Springer-Verlag.
43. M. Pezzè and M. Young. *Software Test and Analysis: Process, Principles and Techniques*. John Wiley and Sons, 2007.
44. M. Raacke. Generierung von spec#-code aus visuellen kontrakten, October 2006. Bachelor Thesis at the University of Paderborn.
45. A. Reddy. Java coding style guide. Technical report, 2000.
46. A. Rensink. The GROOVE simulator: A tool for state space generation. In *2nd Intl. Workshop on Applications of Graph Transformations with Industrial Relevance*, volume 3062 of *LNCS*, pages 479–485. Springer, 2004.
47. A. Schürr, A. J. Winter, and A. Zündorf. The PROGRES approach: language and environment. In *Handbook of graph grammars and computing by graph transformation: vol.2: applications, languages, and tools*, pages 487–550. World Scientific, 1999.
48. A. Seaborne. RDQL - a query language for RDF - W3C member submission 9 january 2004. Technical report, W3C, 2004.
49. K. Sivashanmugam, K. Verma, A. Sheth, and J. Miller. Adding semantics to web services standards. In L.-J. Zhang, editor, *proceedings of the International Conference on Web Services, ICWS '03*, pages 395–401, Las Vegas, Nevada, USA, 2003. CSREA Press.
50. O. U. S. TC. UDDI version 3.0.2. OASIS standard, Organization for the Advancement of Structured Information Standards, 2004.
51. Technical University Berlin. The attributed graph grammar system (AGG). http://tfs.cs.tu-berlin.de/agg/.
52. W. Tsai, R. Paul, Z. Cao, L. Yu, A. Saimi, and B. Xiao. Verification of web services using an enhanced UDDI server. In *proceedings of the IEEE International Workshop on Object-oriented Real-time Dependable systems*, 2003.
53. E. Weyuker and B. Jeng. Analyzing partition testing strategies. *IEEE Transactions on Software Engineering*, 17:703–711, 1991.
54. L. White and E. Cohen. A domain strategy for computer program testing. *IEEE Transactions on Software Engineering*, 6:247–257, 1980.

55. J. Winkelmann, G. Taentzer, K. Ehrig, and J. Küster. Translation of restricted OCL constraints into graph constraints for generating meta model instances by graph grammars. In *proceedings of the International Workshop on the Graph Transformation and Visual Modeling Techniques*, Electronic Notes in Theoretical Computer Science, 2006.

8

Web Services Regression Testing

Massimiliano Di Penta, Marcello Bruno, Gianpiero Esposito,
Valentina Mazza and Gerardo Canfora

RCOST — Research Centre on Software Technology — University of Sannio
Palazzo ex Poste, Via Traiano 82100 Benevento, Italy
{dipenta, marcello.bruno, gianpiero.esposito}@unisannio.it,
{valentina.mazza, canfora}@unisannio.it

Abstract. Service-oriented Architectures (SOA) introduce a major shift of perspective in software engineering: in contrast to components, services are used instead of being physically integrated. This leaves the user with no control over changes that can happen in the service itself. When the service evolves, the user may not be aware of the changes, and this can entail unexpected system failures.

When a system integrator discovers a service and starts to use it, she/he may need to periodically re-test it to build confidence that (i) the service delivers over the time the desired functionality and (ii) at the same time it is able to meet Quality of Service requirements. Test cases can be used as a form of contract between a provider and the system integrators. This chapter describes an approach and a tool to allow users to run a test suite against a service to discover if functional and non-functional expectations are maintained over time.

8.1 Introduction

A challenging issue for the verification and validation of service-oriented systems is the lack of control a system integrator has over the services she/he is using. System integrators select services to be integrated in their systems based on a mixture of functional and non-functional requirements. An underlying assumption is that the service will maintain its functional and non-functional characteristics while being used. However, behind any service there is a software system that undergoes maintenance and evolution activities. These can be due to the addition of new features, the evolution of the existing ones, or corrective maintenance to cope with problems that arise during the service usage.

Whilst the service evolution strategy is out of the system integrators control, any changes to a service may have an impact on all the systems using it. This is a relevant difference with respect to component-based development:

when a component evolves, this does not affect systems that use previous versions of the component itself. Component-based systems physically integrate a copy of the component and, despite the improvements or bug fixing performed in the new component release, systems can continue to use an old version.

Several types of changes may entail that a service does not satisfy anymore the requirements of an integrator. When the evolution activity does not require modifying the service interface and/or specification—e.g., because the provider believes this is a *minor* update—the change remains hidden from whoever is using the service. In other words, the system continues to use the service without being aware that its behavior, in correspondence with some inputs, may be different from the one exhibited previously. Evolution cannot only alter the service functional behavior, but can also affect its Quality of Service (QoS). While the current version of a service meets integrator nonfunctional requirements, future versions may not. Finally, when the service is, on its own, a composition of other services, the scenario may be even more complex. As a matter of fact, changes are propagated between different system integrators, and it happens that the distance between the change and the actor affected by the change makes unlikely that, even if the change is advertised, the integrator will be able to get it and react accordingly. To summarize, functional or non-functional changes can violate the *assumptions* the integrator made when she/he discovered the service and negotiated the Service Level Agreement (SLA).

This chapter describes a regression testing strategy that can be used to test whether or not, during its lifetime, a service is compliant to the behavior specified by test cases and QoS assertions the integrator downloaded when she/he discovered the service and negotiated the SLA. Similarly to what made for components [1, 2], test cases are published together with the service interface as a part of its specification. In addition, they can be complemented by further test cases produced by the system integrator, as well as by monitoring data, to form a sort of *executable contract*, which may or may not be part of the legal contract. During the service lifetime, the integrator can run the test suite against the (possibly new versions of the) service. If some test cases or QoS assertions fail, the contract has been violated.

A relevant issue, that makes service testing different from component testing, is the cost of such a test. Test case execution requires service invocations, that are supposed to have a cost, and a massive testing can consume provider resources or even cause denial of service. Both provider and integrator, therefore, may want to limit actual service execution during testing. To this aim, this chapter explains how monitoring data can be used to reduce the number of service invocations when executing a test suite.

The proposed service regression testing approach is supported by a toolkit, described in the chapter. The toolkit comprises a *Testing Facet Generator*, that analyzes unit test suites (e.g., JUnit test suites) produced by the service developer/provider and generates XML-encoded test suites and QoS assertions that can be executed by service consumers, who do not have access to the service internal implementation but only to the service interface. Such test suites and QoS assertions will be one of the *facets* composing the whole service specification.[1] Another component of the toolkit, the *Test Suite Runner*, permits the downloading and the execution of the test suites against the service. Finally, the tool manages test logs and provides a capture/replay feature.

The chapter is organized as follows. Section 8.2 motivates the approach, describing the different service evolution scenarios that can result in a need for re-testing the service, discussing the different stakeholders that can be involved in service regression testing, and finally describing the running example used to describe the approach. Section 8.3 presents the regression testing approach through its different phases and the related tool support, also discussing issues and open problems. Section 8.4 presents case studies carried out to evaluate different aspects of the approach. After a discussion of the related literature in Sect. 8.5, Sect. 8.6 concludes the chapter.

8.2 Motivations and Testing Scenarios

This section motivates the need for service regression testing. It firstly describes how services can evolve and to what extent this can have an impact on systems using them. Then, it discusses the different perspectives from which a service can be tested and what makes service regression testing different from component regression testing. Finally, it presents some motivating examples that will be used to explain the testing approach.

8.2.1 Evolution Scenarios in SOA

Let us imagine that a system integrator has discovered the release r_n of a service and, after having negotiated the SLA with the service provider, starts to use it. At release r_{n+k} the service has evolved, and different scenarios may arise:

- Change in the service functional behavior: At release r_{n+k} the service may behave differently from release r_n. If the integrator negotiated the SLA at r_n, the new, unexpected behavior may cause failures in the system. This happens when the service, at release r_{n+k}, replies to a given set of inputs differently from release r_n, or it handles exceptions differently. For example, release r_{n+k} of a search hotel service may return an unbounded list of available hotels, while r_n only returned a single results.

---

[1] To enrich the service specification available within the WSDL interface, one could hyperlink other files, e.g., specifying the semantics, the QoS, or containing test cases.

- Change in the service non-functional behavior: This can be due to changes in the service implementation—which may or may not alter the service functional behavior—as well as to changes in the provider hardware, in the network configuration, or in any other part of the environment where the service is executed. For example, the *throughput* may decrease or the response time may increase, causing violations of the contract stipulated between the integrator and the provider.
- Change in the service composition/bindings: A service may, on its own, be composed of other services. It may happen that the composite service owner changes some bindings. For example, let us suppose that an image processing service (S_1) uses another service (S_2) for filtering the image. In particular, S_2 is able to ensure a given image resolution. It can happen that, since S_2 is not available anymore, S_1 re-binds its request to an equivalent image filtering service, S_2' which, however, is not able to ensure the same resolution anymore. As a result, S_1 users will obtain an image having a lower resolution without being aware of what actually happened behind S_1 interface.

The aforementioned scenarios may or may not be reflected in changes visible in the service interface/specification. If the interface does not change, the provider may decide to update the service without advertising the changes. In other cases, the interface update does not necessarily reflect changes made to the implementation. For example, the service interface indicates that a new release of the service has been deployed at a given date. However, since nothing has changed in the service specification nor in any operation input/output parameters, the integrators will continue to invoke the service without verifying whether the new release is still compliant with the assumption underlying their system. In summary, even if providers are encouraged to update service specifications/interfaces when the service evolves, there is no guarantee they will actually do it properly whenever needed.

This urges the need to provide system integrators with a way to test the service, either periodically or when they are aware that something has changed. This form of regression testing can be used to ensure that the functional and non-functional behavior is still compliant with the one observed when negotiating the SLA.

8.2.2 Service Testing Perspectives

Whilst the introduction motivates the need for service regression testing from a system integrator's point of view, there are different stakeholder interested to make sure that a service, during its lifetime, preserves its original behavior. Similarly to what Harrold *et al.* [3] defined for components, it is possible to foresee different service testing perspectives [4]:

1. Provider/developer perspective: The service developer would periodically check whether the service, after its maintenance/evolution, is still

compliant to the contract stipulated with the customers. To avoid affecting service performance, testing can be performed off-line, possibly on a separate instance (i.e., not the one deployed) of the service and on a separate machine. The cost of testing is therefore limited (no need for paying service invocation, no waste of resources). On the other hand, developer's inputs may not be representative of system integrator scenarios, and the non-functional testing does not necessarily reflect the environment where the service will be used.

2. System integrator's perspective: On his/her side, the system integrator may periodically want to re-test the service to ensure that its evolution, or even changes in the underlying software/hardware, does not alter the functional and non-functional behavior so to violate the assumptions she/he made when starting to use the service. Testing from this perspective is more realistic, since it better reflects integrator's scenarios and software/hardware configuration. On the other hand, as discussed in Sect. 8.3.5, testing from this side is a cost for the integrator and a waste of resources for the provider, raising the need for countermeasures.

3. Third-party/certifier perspective: A certifier has the responsibility of testing the service on behalf of another stakeholder, which can be either a service provider or one or more system integrators. The provider can rely on a certifier as a mean to guarantee the service reliability and performance to potential service users (e.g., integrators). Testing from this perspective has weaknesses for both the provider and the integrator perspective: the testing scenario and the configuration under which the service is tested may not fully reflect the environment where the service will actually work. As for system integrators, testing from this perspective has a cost and consumes provider's resources, although having a single certifier is certainly an improvement over having each integrator testing the service.

4. User perspective: As described by Canfora and Di Penta [4], the user might also be interested to have a mechanism which periodically re-tests the service his/her application is using. Let us imagine the onboard computer software installed in John's car. Such application communicates with some services (see Sect. 8.2.4) that, over the time, might vary their behavior, causing problems to the onboard computer software. For this reason, an automatic (the user is not a tester and would be unaware of such a detail) regression testing feature from the user side is highly desirable. The limitations and weaknesses are the same as for a service integrator.

8.2.3 What Makes Services Different from Components?

The above section explained the need for regression testing in service-oriented systems, while highlighting several commonalities with component-based software. In the authors' experience, the main differences with components, that need to properly adapt the approach, are, among others

- the lack of control the integrator/user has on the service evolution, and on the way the service, on its own, provides a piece of functionality by using other, dynamically bound, services;
- the testing cost, both for the tester and for the service provider;
- the key role played by the QoS: even if QoS is also relevant for component-based systems, in service-oriented computing it is used to determine binding choices and to assess whether a service provider is able to meet what stipulated with the service consumer in the SLA. Furthermore, the need for QoS testing is also due to the highly distributed nature of service-oriented systems that may cause huge variations in QoS values or even service unavailability.

8.2.4 Regression Testing Scenarios

To better explain the approach, let us consider the scenario described in the Chap. 1. When John searches for a restaurant in a given location, this search is made through a complex system that takes as inputs

1. the current latitude and longitude;
2. the maximum distance allowed;
3. the arrival date and hour;
4. the number of seats requested.

The system, among other services—e.g., services for computing the routing distance between two locations—accesses a third party service, *RestaurantService*, that provides five operations:

1. *getRestaurantID*, which, given the restaurant's name, the city name and the address returns the related ID composed of four decimal digits.
2. *getRestaurantInfo*, which returns an information record of the restaurant (i.e., address, location expressed in GPS coordinates, etc.).
3. *checkRestaurantAvailability*, which, given a list of restaurant IDs, the date and the number of seats requested, returns an array of availabilities.
4. *restaurantReservation*, which reserves a specified number of seats in the restaurant for a given date and hour.
5. *getRestaurantList*, which, given a city name, returns a list of up to three restaurants from that city.

Let us imagine now that the service undergoes a series of maintenance activities. Some of them have been inspired from maintenance/evolution activity actually carried out over the Amazon Web service and documented in its release notes[2]:

---

[2] http://developer.amazonwebservices.com/ecs/resources

1. The comma-separated list of restaurant IDs as parameter for the *checkRestaurantAvailability* operation is no longer supported. This means that, similar to the Amazon service, whilst the interface does not change, only a single ID is accepted.
2. The list returned by *getRestaurantList* is now unbounded, while in the previous release it contained at most three *restaurantInfo* objects.
3. The restaurant ID format changes, due to the increasing number of restaurants handled. The new ID is composed of five digits, rather than the original four digits.

8.3 The Approach

The previous section identified the need for a system integrator, as well as for other stakeholders, to perform service testing with the aim of ensuring that the service meets his/her functional and non-functional expectations. To this aim, it would be useful that the providers make available to the system integrator test cases she/he can use to regression test the service during its lifetime.

Since test suites are, very often, created during early stages of the software system development, it would be useful to reuse them to permit the testing of services that expose pieces of functionality of the system itself. However, since such test suites access system's internal resources not visible from outside, they must be adequately transformed so that they can be executed from the perspective of a service integrator, which has access only to the service interface.

8.3.1 Service regression testing process

Figure 8.1 describes a possible scenario for the test case publication and regression testing process. The scenario involves both a service provider (*Jim*) and two system integrators (*Alice* and *Jane*), and explains the capabilities of the proposed regression testing approach.

1. At time t_0 *Jim* deploys the *RestaurantService* service together with a test suite.
2. At time t_1 *Alice* discovers the service, negotiates the SLA and downloads the test suite; she can complement the test suite with her own test cases, perform a pre-execution of the test suite, and measure the service non-functional behavior. A SLA is agreed with the provider, and Alice stores both the test suite and the QoS assertions generated during the pre-execution.
3. Then, *Alice* regularly uses the service, until,
4. after a while, Jim updates the service. In the new version the *ID* return value for *getRestaurantID* is composed of five digits instead of four. Also,

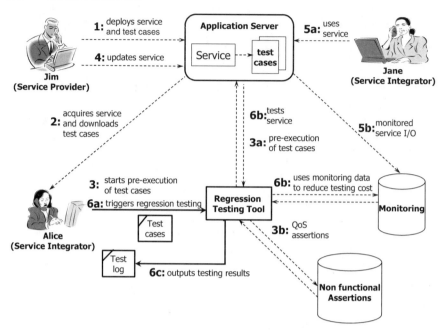

Fig. 8.1. Test generation and execution process

because of some changes in its configuration, the modified service is not able to answer in less than two seconds.

5. *Jane* regularly uses the new service with no problems. In fact, she uses a field that is large enough for visualizing a restaurant ID composed of five digits. Meanwhile, *Jane*'s interactions are monitored.

6. Since the service has changed, *Alice* decides to test it: data monitored from *Jane*'s executions can be used to reduce the number of service invocations during testing. A test log containing successes and failures for both functional test cases and QoS assertions is reported. For example, test cases expecting a restaurant ID composed of four digits will fail. The non-functional assertions that expect a response time less or equal than two seconds for *getRestaurantID* will also fail.

Test case publication and regression testing is supported by a toolkit, developed in Java, comprising two different tools:

1. The *Testing Facet Generator* that generates service test cases from test suites developed for the software system implementing the features exposed by the service. In the current implementation, the tool accepts JUnit[3] test suites, although it can be extended to accept unit test suites

---

[3] http://www.junit.org/

developed using different frameworks available for other programming languages (such as *SUnit* for Smalltalk or *PHPUnit* for PHP). JUnit supports the development of a unit test suite as a Java class, containing a series of methods that constitute the test cases. Each test case, in its turn, is composed of a sequence of assertions checking properties of the class under test.

2. The *Test Suite Runner* that permits the service consumer to
   - download the testing facet hyperlinked to the service;
   - generate QoS assertions by pre-executing the test suite;
   - execute the test suite and to produce the test log;
   - support capture/replay operations.

The toolkit relies on JavaCC[4] to perform Java source code analysis and transformation, on the Axis Web services framework[5] and on the Xerces[6] XML parser. The toolkit is freely available[7] and distributed under a BSD license.

The next subsections describe the different phases of the test case generation and execution process.

8.3.2 Testing facet generator

As shown in Fig. 8.2, the *Testing Facet Generator* produces a XML-encoded testing facet organized in two levels.

1. The **first level** contains
   - A *Facet Description*, providing general information such as the facet owner and creation date.
   - A *Test Specification Data*, containing information such as the type of assertions contained in the test suites (functional and/or non-functional), the number of test cases composing each test suite and the perspective from which QoS assertions were generated (i.e., provider or integrator).
   - *Links* to XML files containing the test suite itself and QoS assertions.
   - Some *Policies*, i.e., constraints that limit the number of operations that can be invoked during a test in a given period of time. For example, the facet in Fig. 8.2 defines the limitation of three operation invocations per day.
2. The **second level** comprises files containing XML-encoded test suites and QoS-assertions (the file `testRestaurant.xml` in our example).

---

[4] https://javacc.dev.java.net/
[5] http://xml.apache.org/axis/
[6] http://xml.apache.org/xerces2-j/
[7] http://www.rcost.unisannio.it/mdipenta/Testing.zip

```
<LanguageSpecificSpecification>
  <FacetType>Testing</FacetType>
  <ReferencedOntology></ReferencedOntology>
  <ReferencedSIM ></ReferencedSIM>
  <FacetSpecificationLanguage>XML</FacetSpecificationLanguage>
  <FacetSpecificationOwner>Sannio</FacetSpecificationOwner>
  <FacetSpecificationLastEdited>
        Mon Sep 04 12:17:16 CEST 2006
  </FacetSpecificationLastEdited>
  <FacetSpecificationData>
  <TestingSpec>
    <Perspective>Provider</Perspective>
    <Type>NonFunctionalANDFunctional</Type>
        <Description>This facet has been generated</Description>
    <TestSuite>
      <NumberOfTestCases>7</NumberOfTestCases>
      <NonFunctionalANDFunctional>
        <XMLlink>http://127.0.0.1:8080/XMLfile/testRestaurant.xml</XMLlink>
      </NonFunctionalANDFunctional>
      <TestPolicy>
        <NumberOfTestExecutions freq="daily">3</NumberOfTestExecutions>
        <ExceptionFacetViolationLink></ExceptionFacetViolationLink>
      </TestPolicy>
    </TestSuite>
  </TestingSpec>
  </FacetSpecificationData>
</LanguageSpecificSpecification>
```

Fig. 8.2. Structure of testing facet

Generating Service Test Cases from JUnit Test Suites

As mentioned before, the service test cases are obtained by analyzing and transforming test suites — implemented e.g., using JUnit — that the developer has produced for the system implementing the service's features. These test suites are very often available, and many software development methodologies, e.g., test-driven development, strongly encourage developers to produce them, even before implementing the system itself.

However, although these test suites are available, they cannot be directly used by a service integrator to test the service. This because assertions contained in the JUnit test cases can involve expressions composed of variables containing references to local objects and, in general, access to resources that are only visible outside the service interface. Instead, a test suite to be executed from a system integrator can only interact with the service operations. This requires that any expression part of a JUnit assertion, except invocations to service operations and Java static methods (e.g., methods of the Math class), needs to be evaluated and translated into a literal, by executing an instrumented version of the JUnit test class from the server-side. The obtained dynamic information is then complemented with test suite static analysis to generate service test cases. Such test cases, as any other piece of information describing the service, are XML-encoded and, to be executed, only require access to service operation, and not to any service internal resource.

The process of generating service test cases from JUnit test suites can be completely automatic, or user-guided. In the first case, the JUnit test suite is translated so that operation invocations are left symbolic, whilst other expressions are evaluated and translated into literals. In the second case, the

tool user can guide the transformation. The tool shows to the user the list
of test cases contained in the test suite (*Choose test cases* window in the
screenshot of Fig. 8.3). The user can select the JUnit test cases that should
be considered to generate service test cases. For the selected test cases, the
user can select (from the *Select analysis* window) two different options:

1. Default analysis: The tool automatically translates any expression, except
   service operation invocations, in literals and generates the service test
   suite;

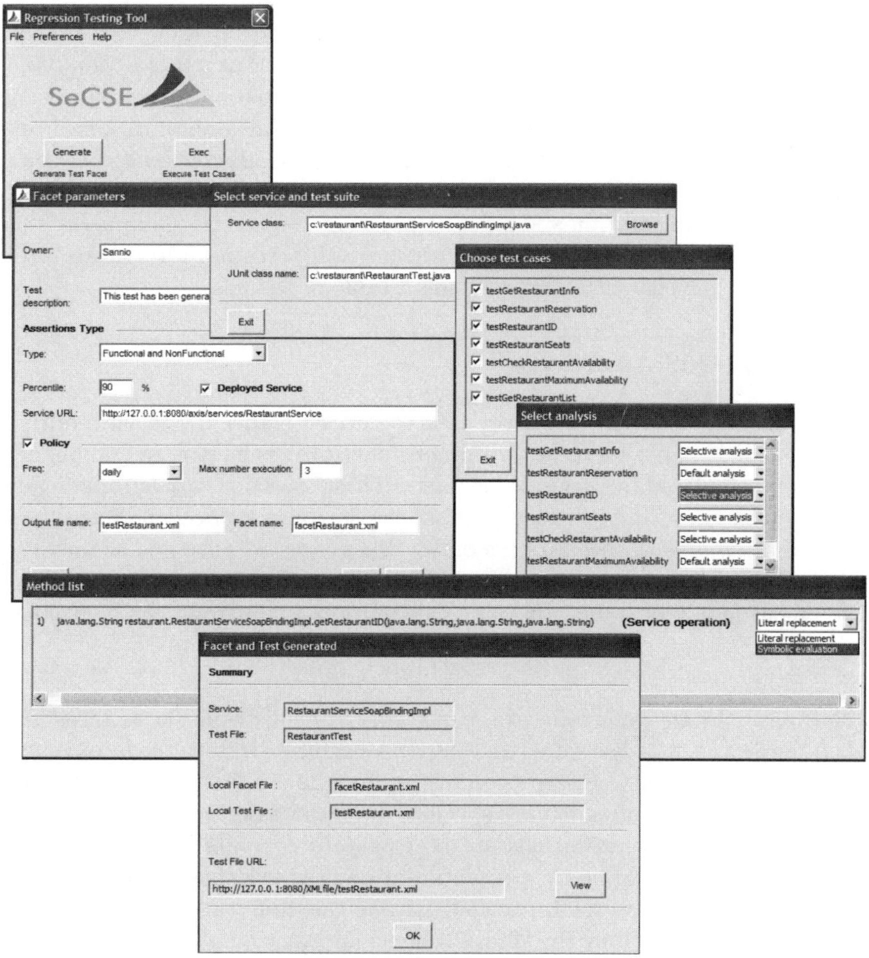

Fig. 8.3. Facet generation tool

2. Selective analysis: The user can select which method invocations, corresponding to service operations, should be evaluated and translated into literals, and which should be left symbolic in the testing facet.

Figure 8.4 shows an example of how a JUnit test case is mapped onto a XML-encoded service test suite. The first assertion checks whether the operation *getRestaurantID* returns a valid ID, i.e., a sequence of four digits. The upper part of the figure shows the JUnit test case, while the lower part shows how the two assertions are mapped onto the service test suite. Note that each functional assertion is followed by a QoS-assertion, which is checked against the QoS values monitored when executing the assertion. As shown, some assertion parameters appear as literals. For the first assertion, they were already literal in the JUnit test suite. However, it can happen that a literal value contained in the service test suite results from the evaluation of an expression contained in the JUnit test case. The service test suite also contains some symbolic parameters. These are Java static methods, e.g., *Pattern.matches*, that can be invoked from the regression testing tool without the need for accessing the service implementation and service operations, e.g., *getRestaurantID*. The second assertion checks whether the *restaurantReservation* returns an error output when someone attempts to book a table in the past.

Generating QoS Assertions

Assertions over QoS attributes are used to check whether the service, during its evolution, is able to preserve its non-functional behavior, in compliance with SLA stipulated by service consumers. These assertions are automatically generated by executing test cases against the deployed service, and measuring the QoS attributes by means of a monitor. Test cases are executed against the service for a large, specified number of times and QoS values (e.g., *response time*) measured. Given the QoS value distribution, a constraint can be fixed as

$$ResponseTime < p_i$$

where p_i is the i_{th} percentile of the *response time* distribution as measured when the service was discovered and the SLA negotiated. Both the facet generation tool and the service regression testing tool have a feature for generating the QoS assertions, after having specified how the assertion shall be generated, i.e., how many executions are necessary to compute the average QoS value and which would be the percentile to be used to define the boundary.

QoS assertions are XML-encoded within the test suite using a format similar to those defined by the WSLA schema [5]. An example of QoS assertion for the *getRestaurantID* operation is shown in Fig. 8.4. The example indicates that, when executing the *getRestaurantID* operation (part of the functional assertion), the response time must be less than 3949 ms, which is the 90 percentile of the response time distribution estimated when generating the

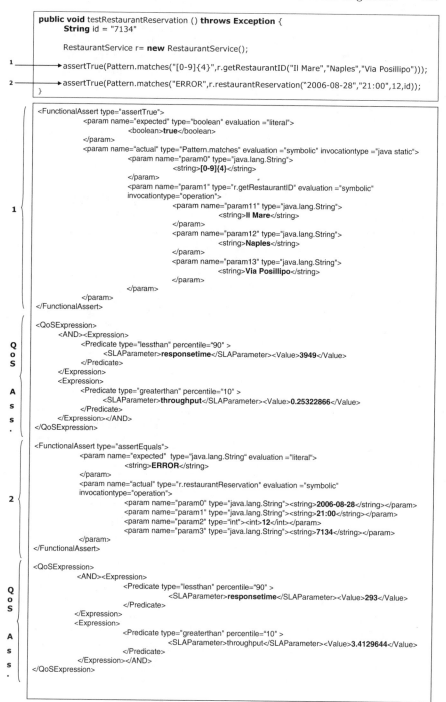

```
public void testRestaurantReservation () throws Exception {
    String id = "7134"

    RestaurantService r= new RestaurantService();

1   assertTrue(Pattern.matches("[0-9]{4}",r.getRestaurantID("Il Mare","Naples","Via Posillipo")));

2   assertTrue(Pattern.matches("ERROR",r.restaurantReservation("2006-08-28","21:00",12,id)));
}
```

```
1
<FunctionalAssert type="assertTrue">
        <param name="expected" type="boolean" evaluation ="literal">
                <boolean>true</boolean>
        </param>
        <param name="actual" type="Pattern.matches" evaluation ="symbolic" invocationtype ="java static">
                <param name="param0" type="java.lang.String">
                        <string>[0-9]{4}</string>
                </param>
                <param name="param1" type="r.getRestaurantID" evaluation ="symbolic"
                invocationtype="operation">
                        <param name="param11" type="java.lang.String">
                                <string>Il Mare</string>
                        </param>
                        <param name="param12" type="java.lang.String">
                                <string>Naples</string>
                        </param>
                        <param name="param13" type="java.lang.String">
                                <string>Via Posillipo</string>
                        </param>
                </param>
        </param>
</FunctionalAssert>
```

```
QoS Ass.
<QoSExpression>
    <AND><Expression>
        <Predicate type="lessthan" percentile="90" >
                <SLAParameter>responsetime</SLAParameter><Value>3949</Value>
        </Predicate>
    </Expression>
    <Expression>
        <Predicate type="greaterthan" percentile="10" >
                <SLAParameter>throughput</SLAParameter><Value>0.25322866</Value>
        </Predicate>
    </Expression></AND>
</QoSExpression>
```

```
2
<FunctionalAssert type="assertEquals">
        <param name="expected"  type="java.lang.String" evaluation ="literal">
                <string>ERROR</string>
        </param>
        <param name="actual" type="r.restaurantReservation" evaluation ="symbolic"
        invocationtype="operation">
                <param name="param0" type="java.lang.String"><string>2006-08-28</string></param>
                <param name="param1" type="java.lang.String"><string>21:00</string></param>
                <param name="param2" type="int"><int>12</int></param>
                <param name="param3" type="java.lang.String"><string>7134</string></param>
        </param>
</FunctionalAssert>
```

```
QoS Ass.
<QoSExpression>
    <AND><Expression>
                <Predicate type="lessthan" percentile="90" >
                        <SLAParameter>responsetime</SLAParameter><Value>293</Value>
                </Predicate>
    </Expression>
    <Expression>
                <Predicate type="greaterthan" percentile="10" >
                        <SLAParameter>throughput</SLAParameter><Value>3.4129644</Value>
                </Predicate>
    </Expression></AND>
</QoSExpression>
```

Fig. 8.4. Mapping of a JUnit test case onto a XML-encoded service test case

QoS assertion. While a SLA document expresses general QoS constraints[8] (e.g., *"Throughput > 1 Mbps"* or *"Average response time < 1 ms"*), QoS assertions indicate the expected service performance in correspondence with a given set of inputs (specified in the test case). For example, the assertion in figure indicates what is the maximum response time permitted when invoking the *getRestaurantID* operation.

As an alternative to using of QoS assertions, the service non-functional behavior can be checked against the SLA. However, while the assertions are used to check the QoS achieved for each test case, SLA can only be used to check aggregate QoS values (e.g., the average, the minimum, or the maximum against all test case executions).

An important issue to be discussed is who should generate QoS assertions. The provider can generate QoS assertions when deploying the service. These assertions will reflect the service QoS (e.g., response time or throughput) that only depends on the service behavior (e.g., an image compression service will respond slowly when the input is a large image) and on the provider's machine configuration. However, different integrators may experience response times having a large variability from those generated by the provider. To overcome this limitation, a system integrator can generate his/her own assertions, measuring the QoS expected in correspondence with the given inputs (specified by test cases) within a more realistic configuration.

8.3.3 Test Cases as a Contract

Test cases and QoS assertions constitute a kind of *executable contract* between the system integrator and the service provider. When executing the test cases, the integrator can observe the service's functional and non-functional behavior. If satisfied, she/he stipulates the contract. The provider, on his/her own, agrees to guarantee such a behavior over a specified period of time, regardless of any change that would be made to the service implementation in the future. If, during that period, the service evolves — i.e., a new release is deployed — deviations from the agreed behavior would cause a contract violation.

When a service has been found, the system integrator can download the test suite published as a part of the service specification. Since the system integrator may or may not trust the test suite deployed by the provider, she/he can complement it with further test cases, also to better reflect the intended service usage scenario. In a semi-structured environment — e.g., a service registry of a large organization — the system integrator can publish the new test suite, so that other integrators can reuse it. On the contrary, this may not be possible in an open environment, where the additional test suite is stored by the system integrator, and only serves to check whether future service releases still satisfy his/her requirements.

---

[8] That must hold for any service usage.

The decision on whether the integrator has to add further test cases may be based on the analysis of the provider's test suite (e.g., characterizing the range of inputs covered) and from the test strategy used by the provider to generate such a test suite — e.g., the functional coverage criterion used — also advertised in the testing facet. The trustability level of the provider's test suite can be assessed, for instance, by analyzing the domain in which the service inputs vary and the functional coverage criteria adopted.

8.3.4 Performing Service Regression Testing

Once the system integrator has downloaded the test suite and has generated the QoS assertions, she/he can use them to perform service regression testing. When regression testing starts, service operations contained in the test suite are invoked, and assertions are evaluated. A test log is generated, indicating, for each test case, (i) whether the test case has passed or failed and (ii) the differences between the expected and actual QoS values. Also in this case, the QoS monitoring is used to measure actual QoS values, thus permitting the evaluation of QoS assertions.

Figure 8.5 shows a screenshot of the *test suite runner*. After specifying the service URL and selecting a test facet from a local file or from a remote URL, it is possible to run the test cases against the service, selecting whether someone wants to perform only functional check, only non-functional, or both. Progress bars report the test cases that have been passed and failed, both for the functional and for the non-functional parts. Also, a progress bar indicates the percentage of operation invocations that were *avoided* because reuse was made through monitoring data. This would let the tester figuring out to which extent the use of monitoring data permits to reduce the service testing cost (further details will be provided in Sect. 8.3.5). After the execution has been completed, it is possible to analyze the test execution results from a XML-encoded log, or by browsing a table reporting summary results for each test case executed.

When Regression Testing Needs to be Performed

The lack of control system integrators have over services poses critical issues on when service regression testing should be performed.

- *Triggered by service versioning:* If the service specification provides information on when the service was changed, the integrator can check such an information and launch regression testing. For example, the WSDL can contain service versioning information, or the service deployment date. Nevertheless, this kind of information cannot be completely trusted: the service implementation can, in fact, change without the need for a service re-deployment.
- *Periodic re-testing:* The tool permits to automatically launch regression testing periodically.

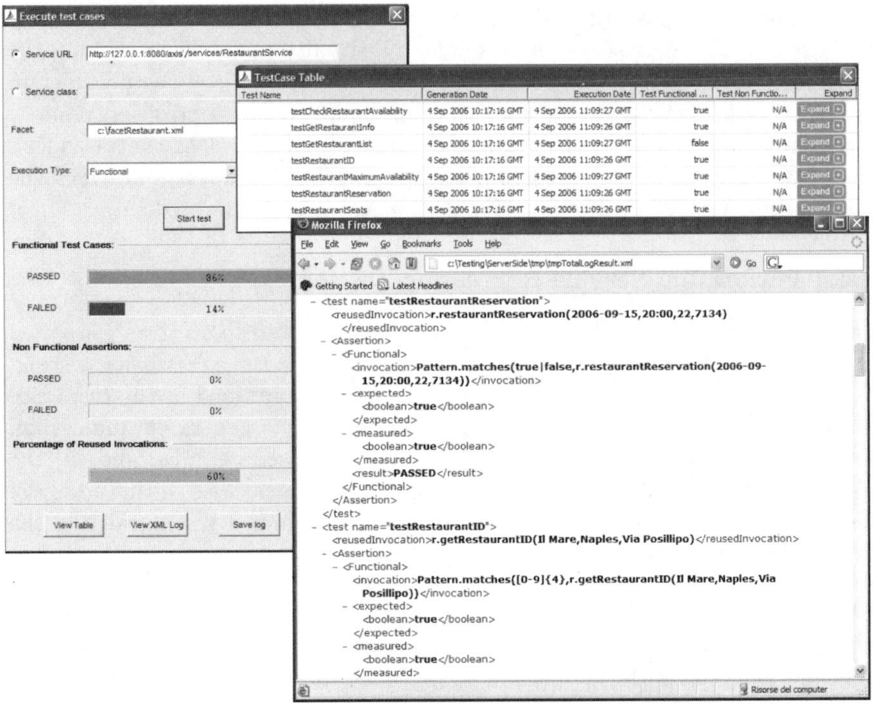

Fig. 8.5. Test suite runner

• *Whenever the service needs to be used:* This option is the most expensive; however, it may be required when high reliability is needed. In this case, the service should be re-tested before each execution. This, however, does not provide an absolute confidence on the fact that, if the test suite does not reveal any failure at time t_x, the same condition will be held at time $t_x + \delta$, where δ is the time interval between the testing and the subsequent service usage.

Finally, it is important to point out that service regression testing is not the only testing activity an integrator should perform. As discussed by Canfora and Di Penta [4], she/he should also perform integration testing between the system and the services being integrated.

8.3.5 Minimizing Service Invocations by Using Monitoring Data

A critical issue of service testing is cost. Test suite execution requires a number of service invocations that, in most cases, have a cost. In other words, the provider charges the service consumer when she/he invokes the service, even if the invocation is done for testing purposes. Also, a testing activity is generally undesired for a provider because it wastes resources reserved for production service usage. The number of service invocations needed for service regression testing should be, therefore, limited as much as possible. First, the test suite itself needs to be minimized. To this aim, whoever generates a service regression test suite — i.e., both the provider or the integrator — can use one of the several existing regression test suite reduction techniques (see Sect. 8.5). In addition, assuming that service executions are monitored, monitoring data can be used to mimic service behavior and, therefore, avoid (or at least reduce) service invocations during regression testing.

To explain how this can happen, let us recall the scenario explained in Sect. 8.3.1 and depicted in Fig. 8.1. After *Jim* has updated the service at time t_1, *Jane* uses it without experiencing any problem. After a while, *Alice* wants to use the service. She realizes that the service has changed (because, e.g., the versioning info is reported in the service interface) and decides to re-test it. When executing the test suite, some of the inputs can be part of *Jane*'s executions after t_1. For example, if *Alice*'s test suite contains an assertion to check that the *getRestaurantID* operation returns a correct restaurant ID, this result can be reused when *Jane*'s test suite is executed, thus avoiding to actually invoke the *getRestaurantID* operation. In other words, monitoring data can be used to mimic the service behavior.

For security reasons, however, testers should not be allowed to access monitoring data. This, in fact, could issue serious non-disclosure problems. Especially when services are used over the Internet, one would avoid to have other people looking at his/her own service invocation data. To overcome such a risk, in the proposed approach the (server side) monitor supports the possibility to check assertions sent by the client-side testing tool, as a way of mimicking the service behavior.

The usage of monitoring data to reduce the testing cost is feasible if the relationship between service I/O is deterministic, i.e., different service invocations with the same inputs always produce the same output. If this is not the case, it can be possible to overcome such a limitation by checking that the service output matches a pattern or belongs to a given domain, instead of performing an exact match.

A further possibility for reducing the testing cost is to provide the service with a testing interface. Such an interface uses monitoring data (if they are available) to answer a service request, otherwise it directly accesses the service. Whilst this solution still requires service invocation, it will certainly reduce the usage of server resources, due to the execution of the service implementation, on the provider side.

8.3.6 Capture/Replay

A useful feature that the proposed regression testing tool makes available is the possibility to perform capture/replay. Similar approaches have been used for GUI testing [6] and for Web application testing [7]. During the service usage, I/O data is *captured* and stored within a monitoring database. In our implementation, monitoring is performed by a plug-in installed behind the Axis application server, thus supported by the service provider. Nevertheless, alternative solutions, e.g., sniffing SOAP messages from client side, are also viable and have the advantage of being applicable for any service, even if the provider does not support monitoring.

When a service evolves, the tester can decide to re-test the service by *replaying* the inputs. Test case success or failure can be determined either by doing an exact match between previously monitored outputs and actual outputs or by performing a *weaker* check over the assertions, e.g., by checking that, in correspondence with a given input, the output still belongs to a given domain. The user can select the date interval from which captured data shall be taken. Then, when replay is being performed, the progress bar shows the percentage of test cases that failed. Finally, as for regression testing, it is possible to open a window where a detailed test log can be browsed.

8.3.7 Issues and Limitations

Service testing activities require to perform service invocation. In many cases, this can produce side effects, i.e., a change of state in the service environment. For example, testing a hotel booking service operation (like the *restaurantReservation* in our motivating example) can produce a series of unwanted room reservations, and it can be even worse when testing a book purchasing service. While a component can be tested in isolation, this is not possible for a service when the testing activity is carried out from the system integrator's perspective. In other words, the approach is perfectly viable for services that do not produce side effects in the real world. This is the case, e.g., of services performing computations, e.g., image compressing, DNA microarray processing, or any scientific calculus. For services producing side effects, the approach is still feasible from the provider's perspective, after having isolated the service from its environment (e.g., databases), or even from the integrator's side if the provider exports operations to allow integrators to test the service in isolation.

Despite the effort made to limit it, another important issue from integrator's perspective remains testing cost [4]. This is particularly true if the service has not got a fixed fee (e.g., a monthly usage fee) while the price depends on the actual number of invocations. From a different perspective, testing can have a high cost from the provider, when the service is highly resource-demanding.

The dependency of some service non-functional properties (e.g., response time) from the configuration where the service is used poses issues on the service non-functional testing. To this aim, the integrator can generate some non-functional assertion, by executing the test suite against the service and monitoring the QoS. However, monitoring data depends on the current configuration (server machine and load, network bandwidth and load, etc.). While averaging over several measures can mitigate the effect of network/server load at a given time, changes in network or machines may lead to completely different QoS values. Clearly, the way our toolkit computes QoS distribution estimates can be biased by network or server loads, although such an effect can be mitigated by sampling the response time over a large set of service executions. More sophisticated QoS estimation approaches are available in the literature, accounting for the server load [8], the HTTP protocol parameters [9] and, in general, to the network and server status [10, 11]. While such kind of QoS estimates are not implemented in our toolkit at the time of writing, their adoption would, in the future, make the QoS testing less dependent on the network/server configuration and load.

Moreover, in case the service to be tested is a composite service and dynamic binding mechanisms hold, it may still happen that the bindings at testing time are different from these that could be determined when using the service. As a consequence, the QoS testing may or may not be able to identify QoS constraint violations due to binding changes.

Finally, as also mentioned in Sect. 8.3.5, non-determinism can limit the possibility of using assertions to check service I/O. Many services do not always produce the same response when invoked different times using the same inputs. This is the case, e.g., of a service returning the temperature of a given city. However, this issue can be addressed by replacing a strong assertion — e.g., $temperature = 12.5^o\ C$ — with a weaker one, e.g., $-40^o\ C < temperature < 50^o\ C$.

8.4 Assessing the Approach

This section presents two studies that have been carried out to assess the usefulness of the approach. The first study aims to investigate to what extent a test suite can be used to check whether the evolution of service would have affected its functional and non-functional behavior. The second study shows how monitoring data has been used to reduce the number of service invocations — and therefore the testing cost — during regression testing.

8.4.1 Study I: Assessing the Service Compliance Across Releases

Due to the lack of availability of multiple releases of real services, we wrapped five releases of an open source system, i.e., *dnsjava*, as Web services. *dnsjava*[9] is a Domain Name System (DNS) client and server; in particular, we focused our attention on *dig* (domain information groper), a utility used to gather information from DNS servers. The service under test is not a real service;

---

[9] http://www.dnsjava.org/

however, it well reflects the evolution that any DNS existing service[10] could have undergone.

The Web service has five input parameters: the domain to be solved (mandatory), the server used to solve the domain, the query type, the query class, and an option switch. The service answers with two strings: the query sent to the DNS and the DNS answer. We carefully checked whether the response message contained values such as timestamps, increasing id, etc. that could have biased the result, i.e., causing a failure for any test case execution. Test case generation was based on equivalence classes for each input parameter. The number of test cases was large enough (1000) to cover any combination of the equivalence classes. Test cases were run against the five service releases.

Service outputs were checked by comparing the output of a reference release, corresponding to the service implementation running when the integrator started to use the service, with the output of future releases. The comparison has been performed using two types of checks:

1. a *strong check*, comparing both *dnsjava* response messages (i.e., the DNS query and answer). This is somewhat representative of a *stronger* functional-contract between the system integrator and the provider, which guarantees an exact match of the whole service response over a set of releases;

2. a *weak check*, comparing only the DNS answer, i.e., the information that often a user needs from a DNS client. This is somewhat representative of a *weaker* functional contract.

Finally, values of two QoS attributes—i.e., the response time and the throughput—were measured. To mitigate the randomness of these measures, the test case execution was repeated 10 times, and average values considered. The following subsections will discuss results related to functional and non-functional testing.

Functional Testing

Table 8.1 reports the percentage of test cases that failed when comparing different *dnsjava* releases, considering the *strong check* contract. Rows represent the releases when the integrator started to use the service, while columns represent the service evolution. It clearly appears that a large percentage of failures (corresponding to contract violations) is reported in correspondence with release 1.4. This is mostly explained by changes in the set of DNS types supported by *dnsjava*.

All the system integrators who started to use the service before release 1.4 could have reported problems in the service usage. Integrator-side testing

---

[10] Although many DNS services exist, the chapter does not provide any URL for them since they are fairly unstable and likely to change over the time.

Table 8.1. dnsjava: % of failed test cases

	strong check				weak check			
	1.3.0	**1.4.0**	**1.5.0**	**1.6.1**	**1.3.0**	**1.4.0**	**1.5.0**	**1.6.1**
1.2.0	3%	74%	74%	74%	1%	7%	7%	7%
1.3.0		74%	74%	74%		9%	9%	9%
1.4.0			0%	0%			0%	0%
1.5.0				0%				0%

would have been therefore effective to identify the change. If executed from the provider's perspective, testing would have suggested to advertise — e.g., updating the service description — the change made. *Vice versa*, integrators who started to use the service at release 1.4 experienced no problem when the service evolved toward releases 1.5 and 1.6.

Let us now consider the case in which the comparison is limited to the DNS answer (*weak check*). As shown in Table 8.1, in this case the percentage of violations in correspondence with release 1.4 is lower (it decreases from 74% to 7–9%). Such a large difference is due to the fact that only the DNS query (involved in the comparison only when using the *strong check* and not when using the *soft check*) reports DNS types: here the comparison of resolved IP addresses did not produce a large percentage of failures. Where present, failures are mainly due to the different way subsequent releases handle exceptions. While this happens in a few cases, it represents a situation to which both the provider and the system integrators should pay attention carefully.

Non-functional Testing

Figure. 8.6 reports average response time and throughput values measured over the different *dnsjava* releases. A response time increase (or a throughput decrease) may cause a violation in the SLA stipulated between the provider and the integrator. Basically, the figure indicates that

- except for release 1.6, the performance always improves;
- integrators who started to use the service at release 1.5 could have noticed a SLA violation, in case the provider guaranteed, for future releases, at least the same performances exhibited by release 1.5;
- integrators who started to use the service at release 1.4 could have noticed, in correspondence with release 1.6, a slight increase in the *response time*, even if a slight improvement in terms of *throughput*;
- finally, all the integrators who started to use the service before release 1.4 were fully satisfied.

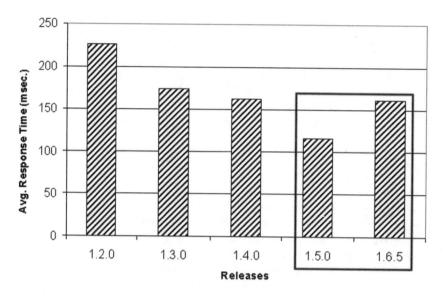

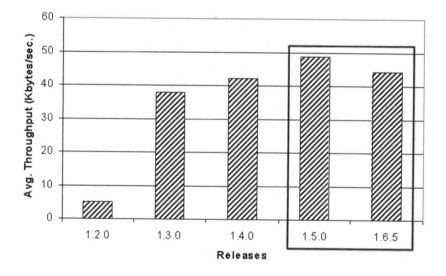

Fig. 8.6. dnsjava measured QoS over different releases

Overall, we noticed that the QoS always improved over its evolution, except for release 1.6.5, where developers decided to add new features at the cost of worsening the performances.

Table 8.2. Characteristics of the services under test

Operation	Inputs	Outputs	# of test Cases
HotelService			
getHotelInfo	HotelID, Arrival Date, # of Nights	# of Rooms Available	13
getHotelListByLocation	City, Location	List of Hotel IDs	
getHotelByLocation	City, Location	Hotel ID	
RestaurantService			
restaurantReservation	Restaurant ID, date, hour, # of seats	Reservation outcome	7
checkRestaurant-Availability	Restaurant ID, date, #of seats	Restaurant availabilities	
getRestaurantList	City, Location	List of Restaurant Info	
getRestaurantInfo	Restaurant ID	Info related to the specified restaurant	
getRestaurantID	restaurant name, city, address	the related ID	

8.4.2 Study II: Usage of Monitoring Data to Reduce Service Invocations During Regression Testing

The second study was performed with the aim of investigating the use of monitoring data to reduce the number of testing invocations. To this aim, we selected two services developed within our organizations and being used as a part of the *test-bed* for an integrated service marketplace developed within a large research project [12]. In particular, we considered a service for searching hotels *HotelService* and a service for searching restaurants *RestaurantService*, also used in Sect. 8.3 to explain the proposed approach and toolkit. Table 8.2 reports characteristics of these services in terms of operations provided and (JUnit) test cases developed for each service (each test case only contains a single service operation invocation).

As shown in Fig. 8.7, the two services underwent three evolution stages. As explained in Sect. 8.2, some of the evolution scenarios stem from the evolution of the Amazon Web service.

1. *Time t_0:* The two services are released.
2. *Time t_1:* The *HotelService* input parameter *location* becomes mandatory (while it was optional at time t_0). For *RestaurantService* the operation *getRestaurantList* now returns an unbounded list of Restaurant Info (at time t_0 the list contained three items at most).
3. *Time t_2:* For *RestaurantService* the maintenance activity impacted the *checkRestaurantAvailability* and *getRestaurantID* operations. In

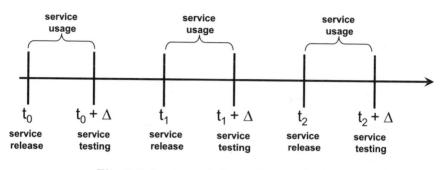

Fig. 8.7. Service evolution and usage timeline

particular, the *checkRestaurantAvailability* operation does not accept a comma-separated list of restaurant IDs anymore, but only a single ID. The *getRestaurantID* operation now returns a restaurant ID composed of five digits instead of four. Finally, the *HotelService* search criteria changed.

Services I/O were monitored. From the beginning of the analysis (t_0) to its completion ($t_2 + \Delta$) we monitored a total of 70 invocations for *HotelService* and 203 for *RestaurantService*. The time between the release time t_x and the testing time $t_x + \Delta$ was about five hours. During these time intervals, we monitored a number of invocations (Table 8.3) reusable to reduce service invocations when performing regression testing.

Figure. 8.8 reports the percentage of test cases that failed at time $t_0 + \Delta$, $t_1 + \Delta$, and $t_2 + \Delta$ respectively. No test case failed at time $t_0 + \Delta$. This is not surprising, since system integrators started to use the services and downloaded the test suites at that time. At time $t_1 + \Delta$, the change made to *HotelService* was not detected by any test case, because the *location* parameter was always specified for all test cases of the *HotelService* test suite. This was not the case of *RestaurantService*, where test runs were able to detect the change: the list returned by the operation *getRestaurantList* contains more elements than the three expected.

When running again the test suite at time $t_2 + \Delta$, it was able to identify the changes made to *HotelService*. In particular, the different outputs produced for the same query were captured when executing the test cases. For *RestaurantService*, the execution of the test suite discovered only the change related to *getRestaurantID* (five digits instead of four), while the change of implementation for *checkRestaurantAvailability* was not detected, since the test cases considered always contained a single ID, instead of a comma-separated list of IDs.

Table 8.3. Number of monitored messages for the services under test

Service	$[t_0, t_0 + \Delta]$	$[t_1, t_1 + \Delta]$	$[t_2, t_2 + \Delta]$
HotelService	11	8	18
RestaurantService	15	19	24

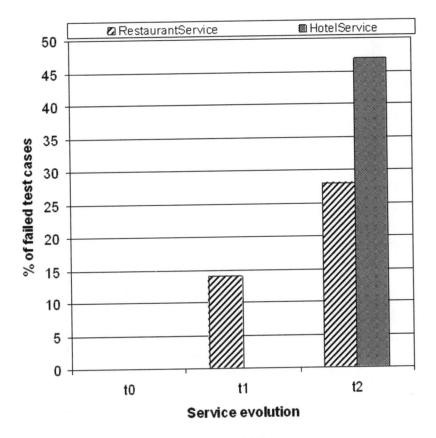

Fig. 8.8. Percentage of failed test cases

Figure. 8.9 shows how data from monitoring were used to reduce the number of operation invocations during the testing activity. Clearly, the percentage of the reused invocations (between 8% and 70% in our case studies) depends on the accesses made by external users during their normal usage of the services and, in particular, during the time interval $[t_x, t_x + \Delta]$ between a new release and the testing activity.

8.5 Related Work

The idea of complementing Web services with a support for testing comes from the testing of component-based systems. As described by Weyuker [2], Bertolino et al. [1], and Orso et al. [13, 14], components can be complemented with a high-level specification, a built-in test suite, and also a traceability map that relates specifications to component interfaces and test cases. Weyuker [2]

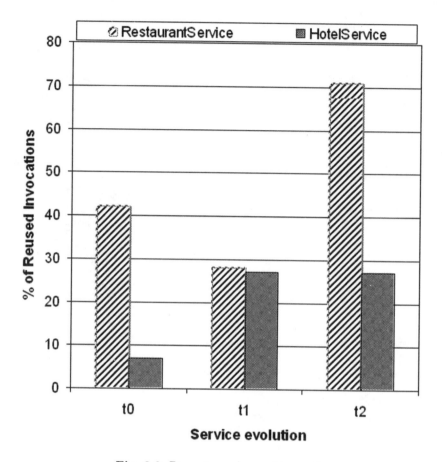

Fig. 8.9. Percentage of reused invocations

indicates that, especially for components developed outside the user organization, the provider might not be able to effectively perform component unit testing, because she/he is not aware of the target usage scenarios. As a consequence, the component integrator is required to perform a more careful re-test inside his/her own scenario. The aforementioned requirements are also true for services and, as discussed in Sect. 8.1 and in Sect. 8.2.3, the shift of perspective services enforces the need for testing during service evolution. In addition, while components are, very often, developed as independent assets for which unit test suites are available, services expose a limited view of complex software systems. However, test suites developed for such systems are not suitable to be executed by the system integrators.

The literature reports several approaches for regression testing. A comprehensive state of the art is presented by Harrold [15], explaining the different techniques and issues related to coverage identification, test-suite minimization and prioritization, testability, etc. Regression test selection [16, 17, 18] is an important aspect: it aims to reduce the cost of regression testing that largely affects the overall software maintenance cost [19]. Much in the same way, it is important to prioritize test cases that better contribute toward achieving a given goal, such as code coverage or the number of faults revealed [20, 21]. Cost-benefits models for regression testing have also been developed [22, 23, 24]. For services, the issue of cost reduction is particularly relevant, as discussed in Sects. 8.3.5 and 8.3.7. Nevertheless, the aforementioned white-box techniques cannot be applied for services, due to the unavailability of source code from the integrator's perspective.

While the research on service testing is at an initial stage, it is worth comparing a few approaches with ours. Tsai et al. [25] defined a scenario-based testing method and an extension to WSDL to test Web services. The Coyote tool [26] is an XML-based object-oriented testing framework to test Web services. It supports both test execution and test scenario management. The Coyote tool consists of two parts: a test master and a test engine. The test master produces testing scenarios from the WSDL specification. The test engine interacts with the Web service being tested and provides tracing information to the test master. Tsai et al. [27] also proposed to extend the UDDI registry with testing features: the UDDI server stores test scripts in addition to WSDL specifications.

Bertolino and Polini [28] proposed a framework to extend the UDDI registry to support Web service interoperability testing. With their approach, the registry changes its role from a passive role of a service directory toward an active role of an accredited testing organism.

The use of the above approaches and tools is limited to a closed environment, since the tools need to know the scenario in which the available Web services and the user applications are deployed. On the other hand, our tool is usable in a open environment, as it just requires that the provider releases the XML-encoded test suite together with the service. Even if the provider does not release a test suite, it is still possible for the system integrator to develop his/her own test suite and use it against the service.

Heckel and Mariani [29], use graph transformation systems to test single Web services. Like Tsai et al., their method assumes that the registry also stores additional information about the service. Service providers describe their services with an interface descriptor (i.e., WSDL) and some graph transformation rules that specify their behavior.

At the time of writing, some commercial tools supported Web service regression testing. Basically, they generate random test cases starting from input types defined in WSDL interfaces. Such an approach can lead to quite large and expensive test suites. In our case, we can either generate a test suite starting from unit test suites available for the software system which is behind the service interface, or use a capture/replay approach. Moreover, we try to reduce the testing cost further by using monitoring data to reduce the number of service invocations when executing the test. Finally, we combine the check of service functional and non-functional (QoS) properties.

In a companion paper [30] we introduced the idea of service testing as a contract and presented a preliminary description of the approach. This chapter thoroughly describes the service regression testing approach by means of a running example and provides details about the tool support. In addition, it outlines the main open issues for service regression testing and proposes the use of monitoring data to reduce the testing cost.

8.6 Concluding Remarks

The evolution of a service is out of control of whoever is using it: while being used, a service can change its behavior or its non-functional properties, and the integrator may not be aware of such a change. To this aim, regression testing, performed to ensure that an evolving service maintains the functional and QoS assumptions and expectations valid at the time of integration into a system, is a key issue to achieve highly reliable service-oriented systems.

This chapter discussed the idea of using test cases as an executable contract between the service provider and the system integrator. The provider deploys an XML-encoded test suite with the service, while the user can rely on such a test suite, properly complemented if necessary, to test the service during its evolution. The proposed approach is supported by a toolkit composed of (i) a tool that generates the XML-encoded test suite, which can be executed against the service, from JUnit test cases available from the system behind the service interface, and (ii) of a tool that allows the integrator to regression test the service.

Reducing the testing cost has always been an issue for any testing activity. This is particularly true when testing a service, since service invocations have a cost and consume provider's resources. This chapter proposes to exploit previously monitored I/O to reduce the number of service invocations due to the execution of test cases.

Service regression testing still presents a number of open issues. The testability of services that produce a side effect and the dependency of testing results, especially for non-functional testing, from the particular configuration and from factors such as the network workload, are just some of them. Work-in-progress is devoted to enhance the tool, further improving the mechanism for reducing invocations by using monitoring data and adopting more sophisticated mechanisms to model service QoS.

References

1. Bertolino, A., Marchetti, E., Polini, A.: Integration of "components" to test software components. ENTCS **82** (2003)
2. Weyuker, E.: Testing component-based software: A cautionary tale. IEEE Softw. **15** (1998) 54–59

3. Harrold, M.J., Liang, D., Sinha, S.: An approach to analyzing and testing component-based systems. In: First International ICSE Workshop on Testing Distributed Component-Based Systems, Los Angeles, CA (1999) 333–347
4. Canfora, G., Di Penta, M.: Testing services and service-centric systems: Challenges and opportunities. IT Professional **8** (2006) 10–17
5. Ludwig, H., Keller, A., Dan, A., King, R., Franck, R.: Web Service Level Agreement (WSLA) language specification (2005) *http://www.research.ibm.com/wsla/WSLASpecV1-20030128.pdf.*
6. Hicinbothom, J.H., Zachary, W.W.: A tool for automatically generating transcripts of human-computer interaction. In: Proceedings of the Human Factors and Ergonomics Society 37th Annual Meeting. (1993) 1042
7. Elbaum, S.G., Rothermel, G., Karre, S., Fisher, M.I.: Leveraging user-session data to support Web application testing. IEEE Trans. Software Eng. **31** (2005) 187–202
8. Zhang, L., Ardagna, D.: SLA based profit optimization in autonomic computing systems. In: Proceedings of the 2nd ACM International Conference on Service Oriented Computing (ICSOC 2004), ACM Press (2004)
9. Liu, H., Lin, X., Li, M.: Modeling response time of SOAP over HTTP. In: proceedings of the IEEE International Conference on Web Services (ICWS 2005), 11-15 July 2005, Orlando, FL, USA, IEEE Computer Society (2005) 673–679
10. Menasce, D.A.: Qos issues in web services. IEEE Internet Computing **06** (2002) 72–75
11. Menasce, D.A.: Response-time analysis of composite web services. IEEE Internet Computing **08** (2004) 90–92
12. Canfora, G., Corte, P., De Nigro, A., Desideri, D., Di Penta, M., Esposito, R., Falanga, A., Renna, G., Scognamiglio, R., Torelli, F., Villani, M.L., Zampognaro, P.: The C-Cube framework: Developing autonomic applications through web services. In: Proceedings of Design and Evolution of Autonomic Application Software (DEAS 2005), ACM Press (2005)
13. Orso, A., Harrold, M., Rosenblum, D., Rothermel, G., Soffa, M., Do, H.: Using component metacontent to support the regression testing of component-based software. In: Proceedings of IEEE International Conference on Software Maintenance. (2001) 716–725
14. Orso, A. Harrold, M., Rosenblum, D.: Component metadata for software engineering tasks. In: EDO2000. (2000) 129–144
15. Harrold, M.J.: Testing evolving software. J. Syst. Softw. **47** (1999) 173–181
16. Graves, T.L., Harrold, M.J., Kim, J.M., Porter, A., Rothermel, G.: An empirical study of regression test selection techniques. ACM Trans. Softw. Eng. Methodol. **10** (2001) 184–208
17. Harrold, M.J., Rosenblum, D., Rothermel, G., Weyuker, E.: Empirical studies of a prediction model for regression test selection. IEEE Trans. Softw. Eng. **27** (2001) 248–263
18. Rothermel, G., Harrold, M.J.: Empirical studies of a safe regression test selection technique. IEEE Trans. Softw. Eng. **24** (1998) 401–419
19. Leung, H.K.N., White, L.: Insights into regression testing. In: Proceedings of IEEE International Conference on Software Maintenance. (1989) 60–69
20. Elbaum, S., Malishevsky, A.G., Rothermel, G.: Test case prioritization: A family of empirical studies. IEEE Trans. Softw. Eng. **28** (2002) 159–182
21. Rothermel, G., Untch, R.J., Chu, C.: Prioritizing test cases for regression testing. IEEE Trans. Softw. Eng. **27** (2001) 929–948

22. Leung, H.K.N., White, L.: A cost model to compare regression testing strategies. In: Proceedings of IEEE International Conference on Software Maintenance. (1991) 201–208

23. Malishevsky, A., Rothermel, G., Elbaum, S.: Modeling the cost-benefits trade-offs for regression testing techniques. In: Proceedings of IEEE International Conference on Software Maintenance, IEEE Computer Society (2002) 204

24. Rosenblum, D.S., Weyuker, E.J.: Using coverage information to predict the cost-effectiveness of regression testing strategies. IEEE Trans. Softw. Eng. **23** (1997) 146–156

25. Tsai, W.T., Paul, R.J., Wang, Y., Fan, C., Wang, D.: Extending WSDL to facilitate Web services testing. In: 7th IEEE International Symposium on High-Assurance Systems Engineering (HASE 2002), 23-25 October 2002, Tokyo, Japan. (2002) 171–172

26. Tsai, W.T., Paul, R.J., Song, W., Cao, Z.: Coyote: An XML-based framework for Web services testing. In: 7th IEEE International Symposium on High-Assurance Systems Engineering (HASE 2002), 23-25 October 2002, Tokyo, Japan. (2002) 173–176

27. Tsai, W.T., Paul, R.J., Cao, Z., Yu, L., Saimi, A.: Verification of Web services using an enhanced UDDI server. (2003) 131–138

28. Bertolino, A., Polini, A.: The audition framework for testing Web services interoperability. In: EUROMICRO-SEAA, IEEE Computer Society (2005) 134–142

29. Heckel, R., Mariani, L.: Automatic conformance testing of Web services. In Cerioli, M., ed.: FASE. Volume 3442 of Lecture Notes in Computer Science., Springer (2005) 34–48

30. Bruno, M., Canfora, G., Di Penta, M., Esposito, G., Mazza, V.: Using test cases as contract to ensure service compliance across releases. In Benatallah, B., Casati, F., Traverso, P., eds.: ICSOC. Volume 3826 of Lecture Notes in Computer Science., Springer (2005) 87–100

Part III

Monitoring

9

Run-Time Monitoring in Service-Oriented Architectures

Carlo Ghezzi and Sam Guinea

Dipartimento di Elettronica e Informazione—Politecnico di Milano via Ponzio 34/5 – 20133 Milano (Italy) ghezzi|guinea@elet.polimi.it

Abstract. Modern software architectures are increasingly dynamic. Among them, Service-Oriented Architectures (SOAs) are becoming a dominant paradigm. SOAs allow components to be exported as services for external use. Service descriptions (which include functional and non-functional properties) are published by service providers and are later discovered by potential users. Service discovery is based on matching the published service descriptions with the required service specifications provided by the user. Once an external service is discovered, it may be bound and invoked remotely. New services may also be created by composing existing services.

To achieve full flexibility, the binding between a service request and a service provision may be set dynamically at run-time. Dynamic binding and decentralized management of external services by independent authorities, however, challenge our ability to perform verification and validation (V&V). Traditional V&V is a pre-deployment activity. In the new setting it extends to run-time and requires continuous monitoring of functional and non-functional attributes.

This chapter investigates continuous monitoring of SOAs, with particular emphasis on web services. It provides a classification scheme that can help understanding the different monitoring approaches a system designer can choose. It also analyzes the running example and discusses some of the functional and non-functional aspects one might be interested in monitoring in its context. The chapter then presents a short survey of the most important ongoing research in this field and concludes by discussing future research directions.

9.1 Introduction

Traditionally, software systems had a pre-defined, static, monolithic, and centralized architecture. This was largely due to the technology available at the time and to the need of making the resulting system more easily manageable and controllable. All the parts that composed a large application were under the control of a single organization, which was ultimately responsible for their design, development, verification, and deployment procedures. Software architectures have been constantly evolving toward increasing degrees of dynamism and decentralization, from statically bound compositions to dynamically composed federations of already deployed and running components.

To describe this evolution, and the requirements that drove it, it is important to provide an informal definition of some terms and concepts that will be used throughout this chapter. The term *component* denotes an identifiable piece of code implementing some useful function, which may become part of a larger system. The term *service* denotes a component that is deployed and run separately. *Composition* is the way a whole system is made up, by binding components together. The arrangement and relation between the bound components defines the system's *architecture*.

The evolution of software architectures has been dictated by the need for applications to evolve continuously as the environment in which they are embedded evolves. Continuous and rapid changes are requested from the real world, and reactions to change requests must be extremely fast. The traditional strategy to respond to change requests—which implies switching to off-line mode and re-designing, re-implementing, and re-deploying (parts of) the application—does not work in this new context. Rather, changes should be made dynamically at run-time.

Requirements for these new features arise in a large variety of application fields, from in-the-large web-based information systems to in-the-small embedded applications supporting ambient intelligence. Information systems need to evolve continuously to support dynamic federations of business organizations interacting through the web. In this setting, each organization exposes internal functions as new services that other members of the federation may use, and new bindings may be established between a service request and a service provision as the opportunistic goals of the federation change over time. In ambient intelligence settings, the requirements for dynamically composing services derive from the goal to support context-aware behaviors. In most practical cases, context is defined by the physical location, which may change because of mobility. For example, a print command issued by a mobile device should print a document from a closest printer, dynamically discovered in the surrounding physical environment. The concept of context, however, is more general. Suitable sensors, in general, may provide context information. For example, depending on where the service requester is located and on light conditions, the command to illuminate a room might imply sending signals to actuators to switch the light on or to open the window shades. Both cases are characterized by a novel distinctive feature: not only do the bindings among components of the application change dynamically, as the application is running, but the components that are available for composition do so as well.

The concept of service is the cornerstone of *service-oriented architectures* (SOAs). SOAs have been emerging as a most promising architectural paradigm which provides support to dynamically evolving software architectures, where both the components and their bindings may change dynamically. The style is characterized by the following features:

- Publication: Through publication, a service description is made available by a service provider in a standardized manner that potential clients may understand.
- Discovery: A service is searched based on the requested features it should offer, and by matching the request with the available published descriptions.
- Binding: Based on the search results, a binding is established between a service request and a service offer.

Since publication and discovery may be performed at run-time, bindings may also be established and modified dynamically. This high degree of dynamism, while providing great benefits in terms of flexibility, has a severe impact on the system's correctness and on the way verification can be performed. Traditionally, verification of correctness is performed statically, based on the known components that compose the application. After the application is deployed, no further verification is needed (nor possible). In the case of SOAs, however, an application is made out of parts (services) that are deployed and run independently, and may change unpredictably after deployment. Thus, correctness cannot be ascertained statically, but rather requires continuous verification that the service delivered complies with the request. In the case where serious problems are discovered, suitable recovery reactions at the architectural level should be put in place.

Many stakeholders are involved in service-oriented applications: clients, providers, and third-parties. Typically, they have different needs and different requirements. They have different business goals, and tend to state what they expect from a system differently, both in terms of functionalities and in terms of quality of service. Consequently, run-time monitoring has different objectives for each of them. In this chapter, we focus on the role of a service requester. This may be an end-user who acts as client, or a service provider who acts as a third-party by composing a new service out of existing services. Run-time monitoring, in this case, takes the requester's viewpoint: the service should deliver what it promised and should match the requester's expectations. If it does not, the system should take or initiate appropriate subsequent reactions, such as notifications, remedy, compensation, etc. This work focuses on monitoring; a study of reaction strategies falls beyond its scope. Also, we do not focus on the process that elicits business goals and derives run-time monitoring goals. Rather, we assume that such process is in place, and focus our attention on the monitoring process itself. Although our main focus is on requester-side monitoring, provider-side monitoring is also quite relevant. In this case, the objective is to monitor the quality of the delivered service and drive possible run-time optimizations, such as dynamic resource allocation in SOAs implemented on grid architectures [10]. We will only briefly touch on this point, which has received considerable attention in a number of industrial research approaches.

Although this chapter concentrates on service composition providers and their needs, most of what we present is general enough and easily extendible to cover the needs of different stakeholders [6]. Most of what we say here also holds for SOAs in general. However, we focus on web services and discuss solutions that hold in the case of the available web service technology.

The chapter is organized as follows. Since many different monitoring approaches exist, and since they all behave quite differently (i.e., each with its own strengths and weaknesses), Sect. 9.2 starts off by providing the reader with an overview of some key aspects that can be used to better understand and classify them. Section 9.3 continues by discussing the example introduced in the initial chapters of this book in the context of run-time monitoring. Section 9.4 introduces our own assertion-based approach to monitoring called "Dynamo," and its monitoring definition language called WSCoL (Web Service Constraint Language). Section 9.5 compares some of the other most prominent research and industrial monitoring approaches, while Sect. 9.6 concludes the chapter.

9.2 Run-Time Monitoring

The need to monitor SOAs at run-time has inspired a large number of research projects, both academic and industrial. The differences between these research proposals are manifold, and quite evident after an accurate analysis. This has led to an unfortunate situation in which the term "monitoring" is commonly used, but with many possible interpretations. Although their main goal—discovering potential critical problems in an executing system—remains the same, there are differences that concern important aspects, such as the goals of monitoring, the stakeholders who might be interested in them, the potential problems one might try to detect, etc.

A thorough understanding of these aspects that characterize SOA monitoring is important in order to classify the different monitoring approaches available in the literature, to evaluate them, and to choose the monitoring approach most suitable for the problem at hand.

Our presentation will concentrate on the following most significant aspects: the type of properties that can be monitored, the type of collaboration paradigm with which they can be coupled, the methods they use to collect data, their degree of invasiveness, and their timeliness in discovering anomalies. Even though the classification items are presented separately, they are heavily intertwined, and the choices made in the context of one dimension may influence the others. For example, the choice to monitor certain functional properties impacts the way run-time data are collected, which in turn has an impact on the degree of invasiveness of the approach.

9.2.1 Types of Properties

Monitoring approaches can be tailored to the verification of two main families of properties: functional and non-functional (or quality-of-service related) properties. When monitoring the former, we are interested in verifying whether a given service delivers the function we expect from it. This obviously requires that some specification of the expected behavior be available. Since the invocation of a service can be seen as a black box that, given certain inputs, produces certain outputs, most monitoring approaches tend to rely on procedural specifications expressed in terms of pre- and post-conditions.[1] The monitoring approaches, therefore, typically consist of mechanisms that produce suitable oracles for the service being monitored.

Since we focus on web services, most descriptions—such as those given using the WSDL standard[7]—only specify the syntactical aspects involved in invoking a web service. A number of special-purpose specification languages have been proposed to address this problem. Some of the proposals originated in the field of software engineering, such as our own language WSCoL, were built on the legacy of Design by Contract [22,23] and assertion languages for standard programming languages such as Anna [20] or APP [30]. Others originated in the field of Semantic Web, such as the current specification language candidates being considered in the context of OWL-S [29]. Their principal candidate is the Semantic Web Rule Language (SWRL) [11].

Regarding non-functional or "quality of service" related properties, monitoring focuses on those that can be measured in a quantitative way. This leaves out a number of relevant properties (such as usability or scalability) that are either qualitative (and subjective), or for which quantitative metrics do not exist. Some of the most common non-functional properties are as follows:

- *Availability*, which measures the readiness of a web service to be used by its clients. It also considers aspects such as how long a given service remains unavailable after occurrence of a failure.
- *Accessibility*, which considers the capability of the service provider's infrastructure to instantiate a service and guarantee provisioning even in the case of heavy traffic. In some way, it measures scalability of the provider's infrastructure.
- *Performance*, which is usually measured in terms of throughput and latency. The former defines the number of requests that can be addressed in a given time-frame. The latter defines the round-trip time of a request and its response.
- *Security*, which is perceived as an extremely important aspect due to the open environment (the Internet) in which service interactions occur. Its most important goals are to guarantee confidentiality, non-repudiation, and encryption.

---

[1] This works fairly easily for stateless services, which behave like functions. Stateful services require a way to model the hidden abstract state as well.

- *Reliability*, which measures the capability of a service to guarantee the promised or negotiated qualities of service.

9.2.2 Collaboration Paradigms

The true advantages of service-oriented architectures become evident when remote services are used cooperatively to achieve some overall business goals. Different existing collaboration paradigms exist, each presenting its own unique aspects. This leads to monitoring approaches that are tailored toward a specific style of collaboration.

Collaboration paradigms differ in the degree of coupling among the participating services and the degree with which business responsibility is distributed amongst them. A typical distinction is between *orchestration* and *choreography*. In the case of orchestration-based approaches, a single party is responsible for the correct evolution of the business process. The current state of the art in orchestration-based approaches is the Business Process Execution Language for Web Services (BPEL)[16], which became a de-facto standard in the last few years. BPEL is an executable workflow language that is processed by a suitable engine. Most current implementations are based on a centralized workflow engine (e.g., ActiveBPEL), although distributed BPEL engines have also been proposed [28]. The workflow engine is responsible for correctly executing the business process and invoking the required external services, as specified in the process. As we mentioned, the binding between an invocation of an external service and the actual service exported by a service provider can change dynamically at run-time. The monitoring approaches that are tailored to such a scenario are typically concerned with checking whether the external services behave as promised, and expected. That is, one needs to check that external services—when invoked—satisfy certain functional or non-functional requirements that allow the business process to achieve its goals.

At the other end of the spectrum, it is possible to envision paradigms in which services are individually responsible for the overall coordination effort and the correctness of different parts of the business process. This is the case of choreography-based approaches to collaboration. The current state of the art is the Web Service Choreography Description Language (WSCDL)[17]. WSCDL is a non-executable specification language that describes the messages exchanged among the different parties during a collaboration. It defines both the message formats and the order in which they must be sent. In a choreography, no central party is responsible for guiding the collaboration, but rather each partner must be (1) aware of the defined business-logic, (2) capable of correlating messages, and (3) capable of performing its role in the process. In such scenarios, it is important to monitor the functional and non-functional qualities of service invocations. It is also necessary to monitor the evolution of the business logic, by checking that the required messages are sent and received in the specified order. To achieve this goal, the monitor must be provided with a behavioral specification of the process being carried out, which can be derived from the specification of a choreography.

9.2.3 Collecting Monitoring Data

Data can be collected from different sources. At least four very prominent cases can be identified.

1. Collection of process state data: In orchestration-based systems, data may be collected through appropriate probes that are placed throughout the process. The properties that can be checked are those that predicate on process states. To make the approach less invasive, it is possible to limit the check of process states to the points where the workflow process interacts with the outside world, by capturing the data that flow in and out. In a centralized execution environment, this can be achieved quite simply by intercepting the incoming and outgoing messages. In a choreography, the probes must be set up in a distributed fashion.
2. Collection of data at the SOAP message level: In service collaborations, data can also be collected at the message level. This can be achieved through the use of appropriate probes that intercept all the SOAP messages entering or leaving the system on which a service is deployed. This is especially useful when we need to check the properties of a SOAP message header, or of a message's payload.
3. Collection of external data: Some monitoring approaches require additional data that must be collected externally. This happens when a certain property to monitor predicates on data that does not belong to the current business process. For example, it might be necessary to verify if the value of the interest rate, returned by a banking web service, satisfies the correctness requirement that it should not exceed a threshold defined by the National Bank. Since the threshold may change dynamically, it must be retrieved at run-time by invoking an appropriate external data source. Obviously, the monitoring framework must be aware of the existence of this data source in order to verify such a constraint.
4. Collection of low level events: Some monitoring approaches rely on data collection that is achieved at a lower level of abstraction, such as at the execution engine level. The events generated by the execution are collected and logged for on-the-fly or later analysis. For example, the ActiveBPEL execution engine[1] associates special states to the BPEL activities being executed. An invoke activity can be in an "inactive" state, a "ready to execute" state, or an "execute" state, and produces an event each time when there is a valid state transition. Data collection can be wired into the execution engine to capture these transitions, allowing analysis to predicate on the order in which they occur, when they occur, etc.

9.2.4 Degrees of Invasiveness

Existing monitoring approaches differ in the degree of invasiveness with respect to specification of the business logic and its execution.

Regarding specification—a typical design-time activity—in certain approaches the definition of the business logic and the monitoring activities are highly intertwined (e.g., through the use of annotations in the process definition). Other approaches keep the specification of the monitoring logic entirely separate from the business logic, thus encouraging a "separation of concerns" which allows designers to reason separately on the two problems.

Regarding execution, it is possible to distinguish between approaches in which the execution of the business and of the monitoring logic are highly intertwined, and approaches in which they execute independently.

An example of a highly invasive approach to monitoring is the use of pre- and post-conditions. Since they require process execution be blocked when the properties are checked, they have an adverse effect on performance. On the other hand, approaches that have a low degree of invasiveness usually take place externally to the process.

9.2.5 Timeliness in Discovering Undesirable Situations

A timely monitor detects an anomalous situation as soon as the data indicating the anomaly have been collected. In general, the distance between the two time points denotes the degree of timeliness of the monitoring approach, which can vary from early to late detection.

At one end of the spectrum, we can find approaches that adopt highly intrusive techniques, which aim at discovering erroneous situations as early as possible. These should be used in situations that are critical for the business process, such as cases in which we need to be sure that a message is transmitted in encrypted form, using the appropriate encryption algorithms. A possible way to ensure high degrees of timeliness is to express the properties in terms of assertions (e.g., pre- and post-conditions on service invocations) that block the business process while the run-time checking is being performed.

At the other end of the spectrum, we can find approaches that allow designers to do post-mortem analysis to discover erroneous situations. These approaches can be used to plan changes that may affect future executions, bindings, or versions of a business process. A possible implementation may be based on logging events and execution states for later analysis.

A special mention should also go to approaches that perform proactive monitoring. Thanks to the data collected both during previous executions of the business process and on-the-fly, these approaches try to identify situations in which it is progressively more and more likely that global process qualities (e.g., the overall response time) will not be maintained. However, since erroneous behaviors—especially those regarding non-functional qualities—can be transient, pro-active monitoring may lead to situations in which the monitoring signals a problem that actually does not manifest itself.

9.2.6 Abstraction Level of the Monitoring Language

The language used to specify the monitor depends on the expected end-user. Highly structured approaches provide a low-abstraction level and are heavily influenced by aspects such as the collaboration paradigm being used and its data formats. These must be considered tools for the designers responsible for delivering high quality and dependable processes.

On the other hand, it is also possible to envision approaches in which higher abstraction levels are used. These hide the intricacies of the business process' collaboration paradigm, and allow non-technical end-users to define functional and/or non-functional properties they consider important for their applications.

9.2.7 Other Aspects

Many other classification dimensions can be considered when analyzing existing monitoring approaches. An example is the degree of expressiveness provided by the monitoring specification language. Depending on the nature of the properties the approach is capable of verifying, we can find languages that require a more theoretical background, such as first-order logics or temporal logics, or that are closer to a more typical object-oriented system designer's background, such as OCL.

Another possible classification dimension is the degree of automation in the derivation of the monitoring directives. In fact, it is possible to envision approaches that require the designer to manually define the properties to be checked, and approaches in which the properties are automatically derived by the system, by formally reasoning on the requirements.

Monitoring approaches can also be classified based on the validation techniques they adopt. Some examples of techniques for verifying properties are assertion checking, trace analysis, model-checking, etc.

The approaches can also be classified based on their degree of adoptability. Some approaches, thanks to the adoption of standards, do not depend on the run-time infrastructure chosen by a service composition provider. Others, instead, from a technological and implementation standpoint, are tied to a certain proprietary run-time environment, and therefore cannot be easily configured to interoperate and integrate with different ones.

Finally, monitoring approaches can be classified based on the nature of their support infrastructure. It is possible to conceive monitoring infrastructures as centralized components that overlook service execution, or as distributed components that collaborate to check the functional and/or non-functional properties we need.

9.3 Case Study

The case study introduced in the initial chapters of this book provides informal common grounds for reasoning on the different facets of web services. To dwell deeper in the real intricacies of the monitoring problem, we need to further detail some key aspects of the proposed scenarios, such as their functional and non-functional requirements, the required collaboration paradigms, the underlying architecture, and its binding policies.

9.3.1 Functional Correctness of the Holiday Location-Finder Web Service

The process starts with John looking for suitable locations for his get-away weekend, locations that must satisfy certain requirements (they must be close to where he lives, by a lake, near the mountains, etc). Using his office computer, John interacts with a fairly simple orchestrated process that guides him in finding the location, booking the rooms in a hotel, etc.

Figure 9.1 specifies the interface of the holiday location-finder web service, using a stereotyped UML class diagram to avoid the low-level details of a WSDL XML interface. In this abstraction, web services are seen as boxes that only provide public methods. The input and output parameters for these methods are described through "dataType" stereotypes, which only contain public attributes.

Given a request that specifies the departure location (i.e., a location name and GPS coordinates), a maximum traveling distance the client is willing to go, and an articulate description (the format of which is omitted for simplicity)

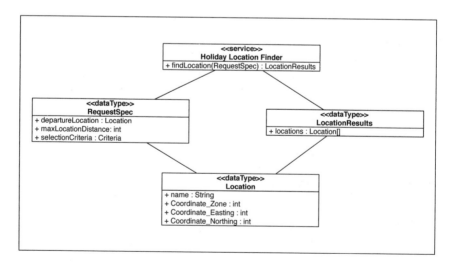

Fig. 9.1. The holiday location-finder web service

of key interests, such as proximity to a lake, mountains, etc., the web service responds with an array of possible holiday locations.

We assume that the external location-provider web service invoked by the workflow is used by John under a temporary trial license. Before subscribing a contract with the provider, John wishes to verify that the service delivers what it promises, and therefore he turns the monitor on. The monitor checks whether the returned locations satisfy all the user-defined selection criteria. To simplify our example, we will concentrate on verifying whether the locations are within the maximum distance specified in the request.

John decides to adopt an invasive monitoring approach, in which postconditions block the process while executing run-time checks. The postcondition that checks the validity of the service can be expressed as in Fig. 9.2.[2] However, an invasive monitoring approach based on a blocking postcondition is not the only possible solution. John could have instead adopted a solution that checks the property in a less timely fashion, using a less intrusive approach, and with a lower impact on the overall performance of the process.

9.3.2 Functional Correctness of the Map Web Service

The example scenario states that John and his wife decide to travel by car. The car is equipped with a haptic device to communicate with remote services for entertainment reasons (e.g., purchase a multimedia stream), or for gathering useful information from the environment. John decides to use his device to obtain a map illustrating how to reach the vacation resort. The device can show only certain image formats with a given resolution. Therefore, it is important that the map returned by the external service satisfies both requirements. Suppose that John's workflow has a pre-installed binding to a free-of-charge external service that does not always guarantee fulfillment of the requirement. It may, in fact, sometimes deliver maps whose format or resolution are invalid for the haptic device. The monitor is therefore turned on,

---

For all the returned locations l,
$(\text{RequestSpec.departureLocation.Coordinate\_Easting} - \text{l.Coordinate\_Easting})^2 +$
$(\text{RequestSpec.departureLocation.Coordinate\_Northing} - \text{l.Coordinate\_Northing})^2 <=$
$\text{RequestSpec.maxLocationDistance}^2$

Fig. 9.2. A functional property

---

[2] We assume that the monitoring language allows properties to be specified using universal quantifiers over the elements of a certain data set.

to allow for delivery of unacceptable maps to be trapped. A suitable reaction to a detected anomaly might consist of switching to another service provider who provides maps under payment.

In order to discover an image's format and resolution, special-purpose tools are needed. Since the delivery environment (i.e., the BPEL execution engine) does not possess the necessary tools for manipulating and/or aggregating the monitoring data, the monitor itself is responsible for retrieving the data it needs. Furthermore, John decides to adopt an invasive but timely monitoring policy, which prevents the haptic device from using a non-compliant image. As a non-compliant image is detected, the system starts a reaction strategy which tries to find a suitable substitute for the current map service. To achieve this goal, John decides to define the property in terms of a process-blocking post-condition.

9.3.3 Monitoring Security

In the example, John uses a service—provided by his bank—to pay for his reservations. John expects his banking services to provide standard encryption strategies and technologies capable of ensuring "safe transactions." Safe transactions prevent eavesdropping, message tampering, fake messages, etc. The main standards proposed for tackling these problems are WS-Security [2] and WS-Trust [15]. The former supports end-to-end security issues, such as origin authentication, integrity, and confidentiality, while the latter supports the creation of trust relationships between different parties.

In order to ensure end-to-end security, the monitor must have access to the SOAP messages flowing in and out of the execution engine. In fact, it is necessary to verify whether the messages carry the appropriate signature elements, and whether certain message parts are encrypted as specified. In practice, the messages should be intercepted after their preparation has been finalized by the sending party, but before they are sent out. Due to the importance security issues have, an intrusive and timely approach should be used, to prevent insecure messages from being sent out.

On the other hand, if the goal is to monitor the correct establishment of trust relationships, a slightly different approach should be used. Since WS-Trust embeds special tokens in messages using the WS-Security specification, it is important to verify their presence at the message level. However, WS-Trust also specifies multi-party protocols for obtaining the needed tokens, and these should be verified as well. Moreover, in these protocols, it is often the case that a number of intermediaries—already in a trust relationship—are used to help establish the new relationship (i.e., between John's system and the bank web service). These collaborations are typically choreographic in nature, especially when concepts such as trust federations are introduced. As a consequence, monitoring should also verify that the desired protocols perform as expected.

9.3.4 Monitoring Response Time

Web service response times are typically monitored by web service providers, who establish control policies on their assets and plan changes in their deployment strategies, should response time degrade over time (e.g., due to request overload). Examples of how a deployment strategy can be modified and improved are the migration to more capable servers or the deployment of new instances of the service.

However, clients are also directly interested in monitoring the response times of services they interact with. For example, in our scenario, John's haptic device could be interested in monitoring the time taken by his bank's web service to open a secure channel with the highway's tollgate payment service, pay the toll, and have the tollgate lift its bars. In this case, one might define a non-invasive approach that proceeds in parallel with the normal process execution. Through statistical analysis, the monitor may proactively discover non-functional problems before they actually occur. This would give the on-board computer the time to let John know if he should slow down, or avoid the automatic gates entirely and proceed to one where he can pay manually.

9.4 Dynamo

Dynamo (Dynamic Monitoring) is an approach and a toolset we developed to support service monitoring. Its conceptual roots originate from the software engineering community, and in particular can be traced back to assertion languages like Anna (Annotated Ada [20]), JML (Java Modeling Language [3]), and the notation added to the Eiffel language [22] to support "Design by Contract" [24]. These languages allow designers to add constraints to their programs in the form of assertions, typically pre-conditions, post-conditions, and invariants.

Dynamo provides a language called WSCoL [4]—similar to the light-weight version of JML—which allows designers to specify constraints on orchestrated collaborations. WSCoL is tailored toward the de-facto standard BPEL and supports the definition of pre- and post-conditions for activities that interact with external services (i.e., invoke, receive, reply, and pick). Dynamo monitors the evolving client-side state of the process and assumes that it can be modified erroneously only through external collaboration. That is, the approach trusts the internal business logic, but not the execution of the external services the process is bound to. This is the reason why post-conditions must be checked. On the other hand, pre-conditions may be useful in the debugging phase of a service composition to check that external services are invoked correctly. Dynamo also fosters separation of concerns since monitoring is defined as a cross-cutting concern. Designers can concentrate on the business logic and on the monitoring directives independently. Therefore, we can say the approach is non-invasive at the specification time.

To favor adoption of our monitoring approach, the BPEL execution environment was not changed: appropriate external services—called Monitoring Managers—are responsible for analyzing WSCoL constraints. The business logic is unaffected by the monitoring, but to allow the process to interact with the external monitors, additional BPEL code is added to the process at deployment time by means of static weaving. This leads to an intrusive approach (with regard to the execution of the system itself), which blocks the process execution to check pre- and post-conditons to discover erroneous situations in a timely fashion, i.e., as soon as they occur.

Dynamo explicitly supports—through the WSCoL specification language—two main kinds of data collection: (1) directly from the process and (2) from external data sources, if these are provided via web service interfaces.

Figure 9.3 summarizes the approach and gives a better idea of the static weaving that occurs at deployment time. The component responsible for weaving the code that ties the process to the external monitoring managers is called BPEL[2]. It takes as inputs both the non-monitored version of the business process—specified in terms of BPEL code—and an external *Monitoring Definition File*. This file contains both the WSCoL constraints to be checked and the "locations" within the process in which (i.e., the BPEL activities for which) the constraints should be verified. These locations are expressed using an XPATH [8] expression (since BPEL is an XML specification language) and a keyword indicating whether the condition is a pre-condition or a post-condition.

The monitored version of the process that is produced substitutes each BPEL invocation for which a pre-condition or a post-condition, or both, has been defined (see invocation of service B in Fig 9.3), with a call to the Monitoring Manager, which acts both as a proxy for the service invocation and as a gateway toward external components that can act as WSCoL constraint

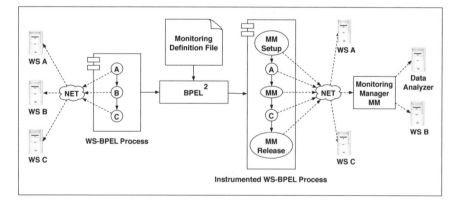

Fig. 9.3. An overview of Dynamo

analyzers. The weaving also adds some additional code at the beginning of the process and at the end, respectively responsible for the set up of the monitoring manager, and its release once the process execution terminates.

9.4.1 WSCoL

WSCoL, our monitoring language, allows the designer to do the following:

- Define and predicate on variables containing data originating both within the process and outside the process.
- Use pre-defined functions, e.g., string concatenation.
- Use the typical boolean operators such as && (and), || (or), ! (not), => (implies), and <=> (if and only if), the typical relational operators, such as <, >, ==, <=, and >=, and the typical mathematical operators such as +, −, *, and /.
- Predicate on sets of variables through the use of universal and existential quantifiers.

Since the web services invoked by a workflow may be considered as black boxes that expose public methods, which take an input and produce an output, there is no side effect on input variables. Assertion expressions may, therefore, refer to variables in the input message without distinguishing between the value prior to service invocation and the value afterward.

WSCoL will be introduced via examples, to describe properties that can be verified using Dynamo in the case study outlined in Sect. 9.3.

Internal Variables

It is common practice in BPEL to use one variable to contain the data that must be sent to a web service, and another variable to contain the data that the invocation returns to the process. These variables match the XSD types of the input and output messages of the web method being called, as defined in the service's WSDL description. WSCoL can refer to internal BPEL variables through use of a syntax which is somewhat similar to XPATH. The designer must specify the name of the variable, and the internal path from the root of the variable to the actual content he/she wants to refer to. The XPATH must point to a simple data type, since WSCoL does not allow the definition of relationships between complex data types.

In Sect. 9.3, to express the functional requirements of the "Holiday Location Finder" service, we need to refer to the maximum location distance. Figure 9.4 shows the structure of the internal BPEL variables "RequestSpec" and "LocationResults" used to call the "Holiday Location Finder Web Service" web method. To refer to the maximum location distance we can write:

```
($RequestSpec/maxLocationDistance)
```

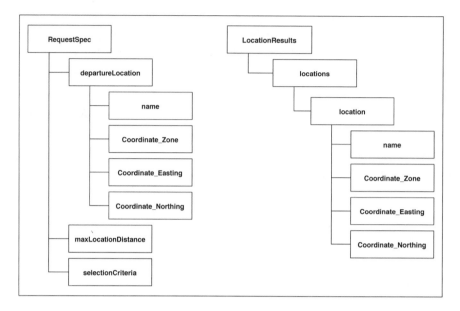

Fig. 9.4. The input and output messages for the Holiday Location Finder Web Service

The first part of the expression is introduced by a dollar sign and indicates the BPEL variable we are referring to (i.e., "RequestSpec") while the remaining part specifies how to obtain the "maxLocationDistance" value from the variable. In this case the XPATH expression matches a node containing a integer value (see Fig. 9.1), on which a function like "abs" can be used to evaluate the absolute value.

External Variables

WSCoL allows the designer to refer to external variables through the concept of external data collection. External variables can be simple data types such as strings, integers, longs, booleans, etc. WSCoL provides a number of functions for data collection, one for each simple data type that can be returned, and assumes the external data collectors being used can be queried through a web service interface.

In the example discussed in Sect. 9.3, we need to first discover the map's resolution (of which we only had a byte representation), and then compare it with the highest resolution accepted by the haptic device—say 300 by 200 pixels. To do so, we use a data collector (e.g., the "imageInfoService," whose return type is shown in Fig. 9.5), which provides the resolution of an image it is given as input.

The common signature for WSCoL's data collection functions is

```
(\return<X> (W, O, Ins, Out))
```

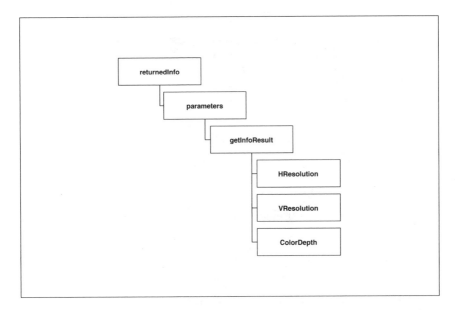

Fig. 9.5. Structure of the return type for "imageInfoService"'s "getInfo" web method

where

- X is the XSD type of the function's return value.
- W is the location of the WSDL specification for the data collector that is to be used.
- O is the name of the operation (web method) that is to be called on the data collector.
- *Ins* is a string concatenation of the input values that should be used when calling the data collector's web method.
- *Out* is an XPATH indicating how to obtain the correct return value within the complex data type returned by the data collector.

Figure 9.6 shows a post-condition that specifies the requested resolution (higher than 300 by 200 pixels) of the map returned by the service.

Quantifiers

WSCoL also offers designers the possibility to use universal and existential quantifiers. These are useful in cases in which we want to express constraints on sets of values.

Universal quantifiers indicate a constraint that must be true for each element in a given range. They follow a simple syntax:

```
(\forall $V in R; C)
```

```
(\returnInt('WSDL', 'getInfo', ($getRoute/parameters/getRouteResult),
'//parameters/getInfoResult/HResolution') <= 300 &&
(\returnInt('WSDL', 'getInfo', ($getRoute/parameters/getRouteResult),
'//parameters/getInfoResult/VResolution') <= 200
```

Fig. 9.6. The post-condition on the map web service

They indicate a constraint that must be true for each element in a given range. The meanings of the different parts are as follows:

- V *in* R defines the variable and the finite set in which the variable is considered. The set is defined using the syntax previously introduced for variables, where the XPATH expression returns a set of nodes, instead of a single node.
- C defines the constraint that must hold.

For example, the "findLocation" web method in the "Holiday Location Finder" web service returns an array of locations (see Fig. 9.4 for the structure of the returned data type). In Sect. 9.3 our post-condition for this method was that "all the returned locations should be within the maximum location distance specified in the request." The WSCoL constraint can be seen in Fig. 9.7.

Existential quantifiers follow a similarly simple, and equally intuitive, syntax:

$$(\verb|\exists $V in R; C|)$$

9.4.2 The Monitoring Manager

The internal architecture of the Dynamo monitoring manager is shown in Fig. 9.8. It follows a plug-in style, which allows it to interact with different kinds of data analyzers for different kinds of properties. In its current implementation, Dynamo uses the XlinkIt engine [27] as its external data analyzer. The following are the monitoring manager's principal components:

```
(\forall $l in ($LocationResults/locations/location/);
($l/Coordinate_zone)==($RequestSpec/departureLocation/Coordinate_Zone) &&
[($l/Coordinate_Easting) - ($Request/departureLocation/Coordinate_Easting)] ^2 +
[($l/Coordinate_Northing) - ($Request/departureLocation/Coordinate_Northing)] ^2 <=
($RequestSpec/maxLocationDistance)^2)
```

Fig. 9.7. The post-condition for the "findLocation" web method

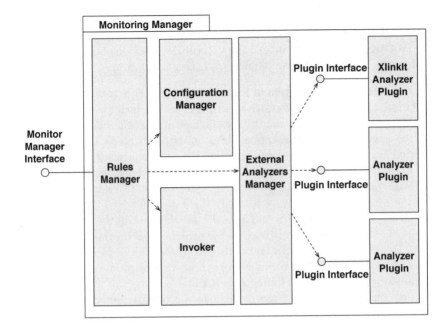

Fig. 9.8. The architecture of the monitoring manager

- *Rules manager*, which represents the interface through which the monitoring manager interacts with its clients. It is responsible for managing the monitoring manager's set up, for how the other internal components collaborate to achieve constraint verification, and for releasing the monitoring manager's resources, once the executing process no longer needs monitoring.
- *Configuration manager*, which contains all the information needed by the other components to verify the constraints. Every time weaving is performed, the BPEL^2 component adds a snippet of BPEL code at the beginning of the monitored process. This allows the configuration manager to be set up independently for each process to be monitored. In particular, the extra code sends the monitoring manager all the WSCoL assertions it will be asked to verify during the process execution, thereby reducing the amount of data that will be sent each time a constraint needs to be checked, by restricting it to information that can be obtained only at run-time.
- *External analyzers manager*, which allows different external data analyzers to be used by the monitor. This component is responsible for transforming the collected monitoring data and the WSCoL assertions into the specific formats that can be understood by the external data analyzers. In the case of XlinkIt, the data are transformed into XML data files, while the WSCoL rules are transformed into [25] rules.

- *Invoker*, which can invoke any external component, provided it has a WSDL interface. It is used for external data collection, to invoke external data analyzers, and to invoke the external web service being checked and for which the monitoring manager is acting as a proxy.

The collaboration diagram of Fig. 9.9 illustrates how run-time monitoring is achieved. The figure illustrates a simple case in which (1) the *Rules manager* checks whether a pre-condition is defined in the *Configuration manager* for the specific service invocation being monitored (steps 1–2), (2) discovers that a constraint exists and asks the *External analyzers manager* to use the appropriate analyzer plug-in to transform the monitoring data and the WSCoL constraint into suitable formats (steps 3–6), (3) asks the *Invoker* to call the external data analyzer to verify the constraint (steps 7–10), (4) finds out that the constraint holds and asks the *Invoker* to call the external service (steps 11–14), and finally gets back to the process with the data it is expecting (step 15). Although many interactions take place, the implementation is extensively configurable. All components can be kept local in order to minimize the amount of needed distributed interactions.

The actual cost of our approach in terms of distributed interactions is difficult to quantify. On the one hand, each call to an external service being monitored is substituted by a call to our *Monitoring manager* proxy. At that

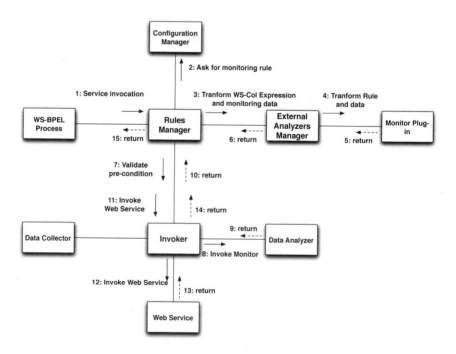

Fig. 9.9. Checking a pre-condition

point, two things can happen depending on whether a pre-condition has been defined or not. In the first case, if the pre-condition is verified correctly then the proxy will call the actual external service. In the second case, a post-condition must be present (if not the proxy would not have been called). In order to verify such a condition, the proxy must first call the actual external service. Therefore, in the worst case, from a performance standpoint, two service invocations are performed: one to the proxy and one to the service itself. Their payloads are similar, except that the call to the proxy contains the extra monitoring data collected from within the process in execution. The actual amount of extra data depends solely on the nature of the WSCoL expressions defining the pre- and/or post-condition being checked. External data collection, through which data are gathered from external sources that expose a web service interface, also affects performance. In fact, the occurrence of external variables in pre- or post-conditions implies extra remote invocations that must be performed at run-time.

Regardless of the actual number of service invocations being performed, however, the main performance bottleneck in the current version of Dynamo is due to the verification of the CLiX rules (after they have been translated from the original WSCoL rules) performed by XlinkIt, which uses XML files to perform its tasks. We are currently producing a pure WSCoL analyzer based on Java that will solve this problem by keeping the data in main memory, without leaning on filesystems and databases.

9.5 Other Monitoring Approaches

This section reviews a number of research and industrial monitoring approaches and discusses their properties in terms of the classification items presented earlier. For some of these approaches, more in-depth presentations can be found in the other chapters of this monograph. A summary of our comparative analysis of all the approaches is presented in Table 9.1.

9.5.1 Research Approaches

Requirements Monitoring

Spanoudakis and Mahbub [26] present an approach in which the requirements to monitor in a BPEL workflow are defined using event calculus, a first-order logic that incorporates predicates for expressing temporal features. An event interceptor component is needed to capture phenomena, such as operation invocations, return messages, etc. By tying the event interceptor to a centralized execution engine, with this approach it is not necessary to instrument the individual services in the collaboration.

Two kinds of requirements are considered: behavioral properties, automatically obtained from the BPEL collaboration specification, and behavioral assumptions that are manually specified. When events are collected at run-time, they are stored in an event database. The specified properties are then verified against the collected data, using variants of integrity-checking techniques in temporal databases.

This approach is meant to capture erroneous situations post-mortem. Even though the approach is tailored toward monitoring functional properties, non-functional properties can also be expressed and verified, such as properties regarding response times. Since events are collected in parallel with the process execution, a low degree of invasiveness is ensured.

For a deeper analysis of this approach, see Chap. 10.

Planning and Monitoring Service Requests

A significantly different approach is proposed by Lazovik et al. [18]. They present a planning architecture (with a specially tailored run-time environment) in which service requests are presented in a high-level language called XSRL (Xml Service Request Language). They adopt a proprietary orchestrated approach to collaboration, since they claim that current standards, like BPEL, do not have the necessary flexibility to satisfy user requirements that heavily depend on run-time context information.

The planing architecture is based on a continuous interleaving of planning steps and execution steps. Because BPEL lacks formal semantics, the authors decided to extrapolate state-transition systems from BPEL specifications and to enrich them with domain operators and constructs.

This framework is based on reactive monitoring. In particular, designers can define three kinds of properties: (1) Goals that must be true before transitioning to the next state (2) goals that must be true for the entire process execution, and (3) goals that must be true for the process execution and evolution sequence. The XSRL language also allows for the definition of constraints as boolean combinations of linear inequalities and boolean propositions. It provides sequencing operators such as "achieve-all," "before" and "then," "prefer" goal x "to" goal y, and "then." It also defines a number of operators that can be used on the propositions themselves, defining how these propositions should be satisfied such as "vital" and "optional."

The delivery platform continuously loops between execution and planning. In particular, the latter activity is achieved by taking into account context and the properties specified for the state-transition system. This makes it possible to discover, each time it is undertaken, whether a property has been violated by the previously executed step, or if execution is proceeding correctly.

9.5.2 Industrial Approaches

In the last few years, numerous industrial approaches to monitoring have been developed. With respect to research proposals, industrial approaches tend to be tailored on the requirements of service providers and concentrate on monitoring low-level events. Most of the monitoring approaches are part of a deployment environment, and consist of either ways to capture low-level information (such as response time and throughput) or exceptions that occur while trying to enforce certain non-functional properties (or policies). We will start by presenting examples of the latter, by looking at two industrial proposals: Cremona and Colombo. We will then conclude by investigating lower-level approaches such as GlassFish and IBM'sTivoli Composite Application Manager for SOAs.

Cremona

Cremona is a proposal from IBM, which is currently distributed within the Emerging Technologies Toolkit (ETTK) [19]. Cremona, which stands for "Creation and Monitoring of WS-Agreements," is a special-purpose library devised to help clients and providers in the negotiation and life-cycle management of WS-Agreements (i.e., their creation, termination, run-time monitoring, and re-negotiation).

A WS-Agreement is an XML binding between clients that require specific functional and/or non-functional properties be ensured at run-time and providers that promise them. The standard, proposed by the GRAAP(Grid Resource Allocation and Agreement Protocol) workgroup, provides XML syntactical templates for agreements—protocols that should be followed during the creation of an agreement—and a number of operations that can be used to manage them throughout their life-cycle.

Regarding the monitoring problem, the Cremona framework provides an "Agreement Provider" component, whose structure incorporates, among other things, a "Status Monitor." This component is specific to the system providing the service. By consulting the resources available on the system and the terms of an agreement, it helps decide whether a negotiation proposal should be accepted or refused. Once an agreement has been accepted by both parties (the client and the provider), its validity is checked at run-time by a "Compliance Monitor," a sophisticated system-specific component that can check for violations as they occur, predict violations that still have to occur, and take corrective actions. Since both monitoring components are system dependent, designers are guaranteed great flexibility in terms of the properties they can check.

Colombo

Colombo [9] is a lightweight middleware for service-oriented architectures proposed by IBM. It advocates that an optimized and native run-time environment, which does not build upon previously existing application servers, can provide greater performance, and guarantee simplified models for development and deployment. It supports the entire web service stack and, in particular, orchestrated collaborations defined using BPEL. It also supports declarative service descriptions, such as those expressed using WS-Policy [14].

Table 9.1. Comparing monitoring approaches

Approach Name	Types of Properties	Collaboration paradigm	Collecting monitoring data	Timeliness	Abstraction level	Validation technique	Monitoring goals
Dynamo	Mainly functional (and simple non-functional) properties	BPEL-based orchestrations	Collected by the process itself, or through external data sources	Blocking pre- and post-conditions	Programming level	Assertion-checking	Tools for composition providers who need to monitor the external services used
Requirements monitoring	Mainly functional (and simple non-functional) properties	BPEL-based orchestrations	An interceptor component listens for low-level engine events	Post-mortem	Low-level sequences of engine events	Variant of integrity checking in temporal deductive databases	Tools for composition providers who need to monitor the external services
Planning and monitoring Service Requests	Process and evolution sequence goals	Proprietary orchestration-based delivery framework	Collected within the proprietary framework	Errors discovered as soon as they occur	Requirements and specification level (market domain terminology)	Assertion-checking approach	Tools for composition providers who need to monitor process evolution
Cremona	Functional and non-functional, and properties of histories of interactions	No specific paradigm, but any interaction between a caller and the provider	Server-side regarding the interaction channel and the system's resources	Reactive approach	WS-Agreement templates with different property description languages.	Implementation-specific techniques	Tools for service providers who need to monitor agreements with their clients
Colombo	Mainly non-functional properties (WS-Policy)	Optimized middleware for SOA that supports BPEL	Through a pipe of dedicated policy-specific verifiers	Before a message leaves the system, or before the incoming message is processed.	Service, operation, or message level	Validation is policy dependent	Tools for service providers who need to monitor policy compliance of incoming and outgoing mesages
GlassFish	Mainly non-functional properties	Proprietary deployment infrastructure	Response times, throughputs, numbers of requests, and message tracing	No automatic analysis. Timeliness does not depend on the system	Three standard macro-degrees of monitoring	No automatic validation	Tools for service providers who need to monitor statistics of client-service interactions
IBM Tivoli Composite Application Manager	Mainly non-functional properties	Event-based system (integration bus)	Messages as they enter or leave the integration bus.	No automatic analysis. Timeliness does not depend on the system	WS-Policy for QoS	No automatic validation	Tools for service providers who can personalize monitoring on-top of the service bus structure

WS-Policy is a declarative language that aggregates quality-of-service assertions that are defined using domain-specific languages. Of the many domain-specific policy languages already defined or being defined, WS-Security and WS-Transactions are the most prominent. Policies are statements that can be attached to a service, to a single operation, or even to a single message type. Therefore, recalling the example of Sect. 9.3, Colombo could be used to monitor the messages being sent to the bank service and to check whether they satisfy the specified security policies (i.e., encryption, authentication, etc.). Colombo manages incoming and outgoing messages by passing them through two corresponding pipes of dedicated policy verifiers and enforcers (i.e., one for each kind of policy supported by the system), it can discover erroneous behavior in a timely fashion, but is intrusive in nature. It provides support for important issues, such as security.

9.5.3 Other Approaches

Many other industrial approaches to the monitoring of service-oriented systems exist. Most of them, however, tend to interpret monitoring at an even lower level of abstraction. In fact, they limit themselves to logging the messages being sent in and out of a system. They can be assimilated to mere data collectors, since there is seldom any automatic analysis of functional or non-functional properties, and data are interpreted manually.

GlassFish

GlassFish [12] is an open-source community implementation of a server for Java EE 5 applications. Regarding monitoring of deployed services, GlassFish provides a number of specific tools. Using technologies such as "J2EE Management" [13] and "Java Management Extensions" [21], GlassFish makes it possible to access information on resources and properties that are tied to the web services to be monitored. This information is given in the form of operational statistics (and in graphical form as well). The nature of the monitored aspects depends on the level of monitoring chosen for a given service. There are three possible levels: *low*, which monitors response times, throughput, and the total number of requests and faults; *medium*, which adds message tracing under the form of content visualization; and *off*, in which no data is collected. Captured information can also be automatically aggregated to obtain "minimum response times," "maximum response times," "average response times," etc.

Regarding the examples presented in Sect. 9.3, this approach could be helpful in monitoring response times. Analysis of the monitored data could then be achieved either manually, or automatically, possibly in conjunction with a more sophisticated monitoring approach, such as Dynamo. This could be the case of the examples presented in Sect. 9.3, in which John's haptic device needs to know how much time it usually takes to interact with the bank service, pay the toll, and open the toll bars.

IBM Tivoli Composite Application Manager for SOAs

Another similar approach is the IBMTivoli Composite Application Manager for SOAs [31]. This application manager uses an event-based collaboration paradigm, implemented through a special-purpose integration bus. Messages enter and leave the bus continuously, passing through special components called the "ServiceBusInbound" and the "ServiceBusOutbound," making it easy to monitor their behavior and, in particular, their performance. However, the application manager lacks the specially tailored tools present in other similar approaches.

9.6 Conclusions

In this chapter we argued that dynamic software architectures, like SoAs, require verification to extend to run-time. In fact, since both the components of an application and their interconnections may change after deployment, traditional pre-deployment verification is not enough to guarantee that the application will satisfy the required quality requirements. We discussed runtime monitoring as a possible solution to this problem, and we analyzed the possible dimensions that may characterize the monitoring activity. In particular, we zoomed into an approach to monitoring that we investigated in our research, based on assertions.

We believe that monitoring should also be the basis for architectural recovery. It should be possible to design SOAs that provide self-organized reactions, which may occur as deviations from the expected quality requirements detected by the monitor. This is still an open and challenging research direction in which we plan to invest our future efforts.

We are also considering a new version of the Dynamo framework that relies heavily on Aspect-oriented Programming technology. In particular, we are using AspectJ to enhance the ActiveBPEL engine [1] with Dynamo's monitoring capabilities. Such an approach is allowing us to treat business logic and monitoring as two completely cross-cutting concerns that are only intertwined at run-time. The original process is no longer modified at deployment-time and is directly deployed to the framework, regardless of the number of monitoring strategies defined by the different stakeholders. The approach also has another advantage. Since the actual service invocations are no longer performed by the Dynamo framework, which is only responsible for monitoring, but by the ActiveBPEL engine itself, all general-purpose policies supported by ActiveBPEL are a given. Such an approach also provides slightly better performance.

Finally, we have also been using WSCoL and slightly extended versions of Dynamo to enable the management of general policies such as those used within the WS-Policy spec [14]. Some initial results have been achieved [5], but the work is still ongoing.

References

1. ActiveBPEL The Open Source BPEL Engine, 2006.
2. B. Atkinson, G. Della-Libers, S. Hada, M. Hondo, P. Hallam-Baker, J. Klein, B. LaMacchia, P. Leach, J. Manferdelli, H. Maruyama, A. Nadalin, N. Nagaratnam, H. Prafullchandra, J. Shewchuk, and D. Simon. Web Services Security (WS-Security), 2002.
3. L. Burdy, Y. Cheon, D. R. Cok, M. D. Ernst, J. R. Kiniry, G. T. Leavens, K. R. M. Leino, and E. Poll. An Overview of JML Tools and Applications. *International Journal on Software Tools for Technology Transfer*, 7(3):212–232, 2005.
4. L. Baresi and S. Guinea. Towards Dynamic Monitoring of BPEL Processes. In B. Benatallah, F. Casati, and P. Traverso, editors, *ICSOC*, volume 3826 of *Lecture Notes in Computer Science*, pages 269–282. Springer, 2005.
5. L. Baresi, S. Guinea, and P. Plebani. WS-Policy for Service Monitoring. In C. Bussler and M. Shan, editors, *TES*, volume 3811 of *Lecture Notes in Computer Science*, pages 72–83. Springer, 2005.

6. L. Baresi, S. Guinea, and M. Plebani. Business Process Monitoring for Personal Dependability. In *Workshop SOAM 06 Modeling the SOA – Business Perspective and Model Mapping*, 2006.
7. E. Christensen, F. Curbera, G. Meredith, and S. Weerawarana. WSDL: Web Services Definition Language. W3C Technical Reports on WSDL, published online at http://www.w3.org/TR/wsdl/, 2004.
8. J. Clark and S. DeRose. Xml path language version 1.0, 1999.
9. F. Curbera, M. J. Duftler, R. Khalaf, W. A. Nagy, N. Mukhi, and S. Weerawarana. Colombo: Lightweight Middleware for Service-Oriented Computing. *IBM Syst. J.*, 44(4):799–820, 2005.
10. I. Foster and C. Kesselman. Scaling system-level science: Scientific exploration and it implications. *Computer*, 39(11):31–39, November 2006.
11. I. Horrocks, P.F. Patel-Schneider, H. Boley, S. Tabet, B. Grosof, and M. Dean. SWRL: A Semantic Web Rule Language Combining OWL and RuleML, 2004.
12. H. Hrasna. GlassFish Community Building an Open Source Java EE 5 Application Server, 2006.
13. H. Hrasna. JSR-000077 J2EETM Management, 2006.
14. IBM, BEA Systems, Microsoft, SAP AG, Sonic Software, and VeriSign. Web Services Policy Framework, 2006.
15. IBM, Microsoft, Layer 7 Technologies, Oblix, Verisign, Actional, Computer Associates, OpenNetwork Technologies, Ping Identity, Reactivity, and RSA Security. Web Services Trust Language, 2005.
16. IBM, BEA Systems, Microsoft, SAP AG, and Siebel Systems. Business Process Execution Language for Web Services 1.1, 2005.
17. N. Kavantzas, D. Burdett, and G. Ritzinger. Web Services Choreography Description Language Version 1.0, 2004.
18. A. Lazovik, M. Aiello, and M. P. Papazoglou. Associating Assertions with Business Processes and Monitoring their Execution. In *Proceedings of the 2nd International Conference on Service Oriented Computing*, pages 94–104. ACM, 2004.
19. H. Ludwig, A. Dan, and R. Kearney. Cremona: an Architecture and Library for Creation and Monitoring of WS-Agreements. In *Proceedings of the 2nd International Conference on Service Oriented Computing*, pages 65–74. ACM, 2004.
20. D. C. Luckham and F. W. von Henke. An overview of Anna, a specification language for Ada. *IEEE Software*, 2(2):9–22, March 1985.
21. E. McManus. JSR-000003 JavaTM Management Extensions, 2006.
22. B. Meyer. *Eiffel: The Language*. Prentice-Hall, 1992.
23. B. Meyer. *Object-Oriented Software Construction*. Prentice Hall, second edition, 1997.
24. B. Meyer. Design by Contract, Components and Debugging. *JOOP*, 11(8):75–79, 1999.
25. M. Marconi and C. Nentwich. CLiX ¡constraint language in xml/¿, 2004.
26. K. Mahbub and G. Spanoudakis. A Framework for Requirents Monitoring of Service Based Systems. In *Proceedings of the 2nd International Conference on Service Oriented Computing*, pages 84–93. ACM, 2004.
27. C. Nentwich, L. Capra, W. Emmerich, and A. Finkelstein. Xlinkit: a Consistency Checking and Smart Link Generation Service. *ACM Transactions on Internet Technology*, 2(2):151–185, 2002.
28. M. G. Nanda, S. Chandra, and V. Sarkar. Decentralizing Execution of Composite Web Services. In J. M. Vlissides and D. C. Schmidt, editors, *OOPSLA*, pages 170–187. ACM, 2004.

29. The OWL Services Coalition. OWL-S: Semantic Markup for Web Services, 2003.
30. D. S. Rosenblum. A Practical Approach to Programming with Assertions. *IEEE Trans. Software Eng.*, 21(1):19–31, 1995.
31. IBM Tivoli Composite Application Manager for SOA, 2006.

Monitoring *WS-Agreement*s: An Event Calculus–Based Approach

Khaled Mahbub and George Spanoudakis

Department of Computing, City University, London, EC1V 0HB
gespan|am697@soi.city.ac.uk

Abstract. In this chapter, we present a framework that we have developed to support the monitoring of service level agreements (SLAs). The agreements that can be monitored by this framework are expressed in an extension of *WS-Agreement* that we propose. The main characteristic of the proposed extension is that it uses an event calculus–based language, called *EC-Assertion*, for the specification of the service guarantee terms in a service level agreement that need to be monitored at runtime. The use of *EC-Assertion* for specifying service guarantee terms provides a well-defined semantics to the specification of such terms and a formal reasoning framework for assessing their satisfiability. The chapter describes also an implementation of the framework and the results of a set of experiments that we have conducted to evaluate it.

10.1 Introduction

The ability to set up and monitor service level agreements (SLAs) has been increasingly recognized as one of the essential preconditions for the deployment of web services [28]. Service level agreements are set through collaboration between service consumers and service producers in order to specify the terms under which a service that is offered to the former by the latter is to be deployed and the quality properties that it should satisfy under these terms. The ability to monitor the compliance of the provision of a service against a service level agreement at runtime is crucial from the point of view of both the service consumer and the service producer.

In the case of service consumers, monitoring service level agreements is necessary due to the need to check if the terms of an agreement are satisfied in a specific operational setting (i.e., the set of the running instances of the services involved in the agreement and the computational resources that these services are deployed on or they use to communicate), identify the consequences that the violation of certain terms in an agreement might have onto their systems, and request the application of any penalties that an agreement prescribes for the violated service provision terms.

For service providers, the monitoring of the provision of a service against the terms specified in an agreement is necessary in order not only to gather evidence regarding the provision, which may be necessary if a dispute with a service consumer arises over the provision, but also to identify problems with the delivery of the service and take action before an agreement is violated. For instance, if an agreement requires that on average a service should respond within N time units over a specific time period, monitoring the performance of the service may spot a performance deviation early enough to give the provider an opportunity to address the problem (by adding, for instance, an extra server at runtime or reducing the level of provision of the same service to other consumers who do not have strictprovision terms).

In this chapter, we describe a framework that we have developed to support the monitoring of functional and quality of service requirements which are specified as part of service level agreements. This framework can monitor the provision of services to service-based software systems (referred to as "SBS" systems, see Fig. 10.1). A for our framework is a system that deploys one or more external web services which are coordinated by a composition

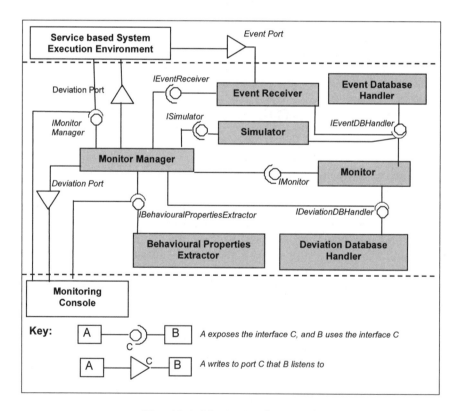

Fig. 10.1. Monitoring framework

process that is expressed in BPEL [1]. This composition process provides the required system functionality by calling operations in the external web services, receiving and processing the results that these services return, and accepting and/or responding to requests from them. It should be noted that the external services which are deployed by an SBS system may be interacting directly with third-party services without the intervention of this system. Such interactions are not taken into account during monitoring. Thus, all the external services of an SBS system are effectively treated as atomic services.

The service level agreements that can be monitored by the framework that we present in this chapter are expressed using an extension of *WS-Agreement* [2] that we have defined for this purpose. This extension supports the description of (a) the operational context of an agreement, (b) the policy for monitoring an agreement, and (c) the functional and quality requirements for the service which is regulated by the agreement and need to be monitored (i.e., the guarantee terms in the terminology of *WS-Agreement*). The extensions of *WS-Agreement* that we have introduced to support (a) and (b) have been directly integrated into the XML schema that defines this language. To support the specification of (c), we have developed a new language in which service guarantee terms are specified in terms of (i) events which signify the invocation of operations of a service by the composition process of an SBS system and returns from these executions, (ii) events which signify calls of operations of the composition process of an SBS system by external services and returns from these executions, and (iii) the effects that events of either of the above kinds have on the state of an SBS system or the services that it deploys (e.g., change of the values of system variables). This language has been defined by a separate XML schema and is called . *EC-Assertion*. It is based on (EC) [34] which is a first-order temporal logic language. Specifications of service guarantee terms in *EC-Assertion* can be developed independently of *WS-Agreement* and subsequently referred to by it.

The events which are used in the specification of the service description and guarantee terms in an agreement are restricted to those which can be observed during the execution of the composition process of an SBS system. This set of events is determined by a static analysis of the BPEL composition process of this system that is performed by our framework.

The choice of event calculus (EC) as the language for specifying the service guarantee terms in an agreement has been motivated by the need for (a) expressing the properties to be monitored in a formal language allowing the specification of temporal constraints and (b) being able to monitor an agreement using a well-defined reasoning process based on the inference rules of first-order logic (this criterion has also led to the choice of event calculus instead of another temporal logic language).

Our monitoring framework has been designed with the objective to support service level agreements. The term "non-intrusive monitoring" in this context signifies a form of monitoring that is carried out by a computational entity that is external to the system that is being monitored, is carried out in parallel with the operation of this system and does not intervene with this operation in any form. Given this definition, non-intrusive monitoring excludes approaches which perform monitoring by weaving code that implements the required checks inside the code of the system that is being monitored (e.g., monitoring oriented programming [10] or SBS monitoring by code weaved into BPEL processes [5]). It also excludes approaches which, despite deploying external entities in order to perform the required checks, require the instrumentation of the source code of the monitored system in order to generate the runtime information that is necessary for the checks (e.g., [19, 33]).

The framework that we present in this chapter is non-intrusive as it is based on events which are captured during the operation of an SBS system without the need to instrument its composition process or the code of the services that it deploys and is performed by a reasoning engine that is separate from the system that is being monitored and operates parallel with it. Furthermore, our framework can monitor different types of deviations from service guarantee terms including: (a) violations of terms by the recorded behavior of a system and (b) violations of service guarantee terms by the expected behavior of the system. These types of deviations were originally defined in [36] and are discussed in this chapter. Additional forms of violations that can be detected by the framework are described in [36].

The framework that we discuss in this chapter was originally developed to support the monitoring of functional service requirements outside the context of *WS-Agreement* and the main formal characteristics of the original form of the framework have been presented in [36]. Hence, in this chapter, our focus is to discuss how this framework can be used to support the monitoring of *WS-Agreement* and introduce the extensions to this standard that enable the use of our framework for this purpose. Furthermore, in this chapter, we present an extension of the specification language of the framework that is based on the use of internal and external operations in event calculus formulas which enable the specification and monitoring of wider range of quality of service requirements.

The rest of the chapter is structured as follows. In Sect. 10.2, we briefly introduce our monitoring framework. In Sect. 10.3, we describe the extensions that we have introduced to *WS-Agreement* in order to specify the service guarantee terms that can be monitored at runtime and policies for performing this monitoring. In Sect. 10.4 we describe the monitoring process that is realized by the framework. In Sect. 10.5, we discuss the prototype that we have developed to implement the framework. In Sect. 10.6, we present the results of an experimental evaluation of the framework. In Sect. 10.7, we review related work. Finally, in Sect. 10.8, we conclude with an overview of our approach and directions for future work.

10.2 Overview of Monitoring Framework

Our framework assumes that the deployment platform of a service-based system is an environment that executes the composition process of the system and can provide the events that will be used during monitoring (see the component *Service Based System Execution Environment* in Fig. 10.1). The framework itself consists of a *monitoring manager*, an *event receiver*, a *monitor*, an *event database*, a *deviation database*, and a *monitoring console*.

The *monitoring manager* is the component that has responsibility for initiating, coordinating, and reporting the results of the monitoring process. Once it receives a request for starting a monitoring activity as specified by the monitoring policy of an agreement, it checks whether it is possible to monitor the service guarantee terms of the agreement as specified in this policy (i.e., given the BPEL process of the SBS system that is identified in the policy and the event reporting capabilities indicated by the type of the execution environment of the SBS system). If the service guarantee terms can be monitored, it starts the event receiver to capture events from the SBS execution environment and passes to it the events that should be collected. It also sends to the monitor the formulas to be checked.

The *event receiver* polls the event port of the SBS execution environment at regular time intervals as specified in the monitoring policy in order to get the stream of events sent to this port. After receiving an event, the event receiver identifies its type and, if it is relevant to the service guarantee terms of the agreement being monitored, it records the event in the event database of the framework. All the events which are not relevant to monitoring are ignored.

The *monitor* retrieves the events which are recorded in the database during the operation of the SBS system in the order of their occurrence, derives (subject to the monitoring mode of an agreement) other possible events that may have happened without being recorded (based on assumptions set for an SBS system in an agreement and its behavioral properties), and checks if the recorded and derived events are compliant with the requirements being monitored. In cases where the recorded and derived events are not consistent with service guarantee terms in an agreement, the monitor records the deviation in a *deviation database*.

The *monitoring manager* polls the deviation database of the framework at regular time intervals to check if there have been any deviations detected with respect to a given monitoring policy and reports them to the port specified by the monitoring policy.

The *behavioral properties extractor* takes as input the BPEL process of the SBS system to be monitored and generates a specification of the behavioral properties of this system in event calculus. As a by-product of this extraction, it also identifies the primitive events which can be observed during the runtime operation of the SBS systems. These events are used by the monitoring manager to check whether the formulas specified in an agreement can be monitored at runtime. They are also used by the assumptions editor of the framework (see below) as primitive constructs for specifying the service guarantee terms that are to be monitored in cases where the service consumers and producers wish to specify these terms using the framework.

Finally, the framework incorporates a *monitoring console* that gives access to the monitoring service to human users. The console incorporates a terms editor that supports the specification of the service guarantee terms of an agreement in the high level syntax of our event calculus–based language, and a *deviation viewer* that displays the deviations from the monitored requirements. The terms editor provides a form-based interface that enables the user to select events extracted from the BPEL process of an SBS system and combine them in order to specify the formulas that define the service guarantee terms of an agreement.

10.3 Specification of Service Level Agreements

10.3.1 Overview of *WS-Agreement*

WS-Agreement is a standard developed by the Global Grid Form for specifying agreements between service providers and service consumers and a protocol for creating and monitoring such agreements at runtime [2]. The objective of a *WS-Agreement* specification is to define the guarantee terms that should be satisfied during the provision of a service. *WS-Agreement* is defined as an XML schema. An agreement drawn using *WS-Agreement* has two sections: the *Context* section and the *Terms* section.

The *Context* section specifies the consumer and the provider of the service that have created the agreement (i.e., the parties of the agreement) and other general properties of the agreement including, e.g., its duration and any links that it may have to other agreements.

The *Terms* section of a *WS-Agreement* specifies the service that the agreement is about and the objectives that the provision of this service should fulfill. This section is divided into two subsections: the *Service Description Terms* and *Service Guarantee Terms*. The service description terms constitute the basic building block of an agreement and define the functionalities of the service that is to be delivered under the agreement. An agreement may contain any number of service description terms. The guarantee terms specify assurances on service quality that need to be monitored and enforced during the provision of a service.

The agreement life cycle that is envisaged by *WS-Agreement* expects that an agreement initiator sends an agreement template to the service consumer. This template is defined by adding a new section to the agreement structure described above, called *Creation Constraints*. This new section contains constraints on possible values of terms for creating the agreement. The consumer fills in the template and sends it back to the initiator as an offer. Subsequently, the initiator notifies the consumer of the acceptance or rejection of the agreement depending on the availability of resources, the service costs, etc. The monitoring of an agreement that has been confirmed is expected to start when at least one of the services which are involved in the agreement is running.

10.3.2 Extensions of *WS-Agreement*

In its original form, *WS-Agreement* does not support the specification of policies determining the deployment context in which the provision of services will be monitored, and who will have responsibility for providing the information that will be necessary for assessing whether the guarantee terms of the agreement are satisfied. Also, it does not specify where the results of monitoring should be reported. This is problematic in cases where the agents who have responsibility for the monitoring of an agreement are expected to actively report deviations from it rather than waiting to be asked if deviations have occurred (i.e., notification of deviations in a push mode). Furthermore, *WS-Agreement* does not specify a language for defining the service description and service guarantee terms of an agreement or an operation protocol that would enable the monitoring of an agreement in the push mode described above. The choice of the language for the specification of the service description and service guarantee terms of an agreement is left to the concrete implementations of the standard as the language for the specification of these terms may need to vary for different domains. Our extensions to *WS-Agreement* address these limitations of the standard.

Specification of the Context of an Agreement

Our first extension to *WS-Agreement* is concerned with the specification of *policies* for monitoring an agreement. A policy, in our proposal, specifies the following:

- The composition process of the SBS system that deploys the services which are the subject of the agreement.
- The source of the runtime information which will enable the monitoring of the agreement.
- The way in which the monitoring of the agreement is to be performed including the mode, regularity, and timing of monitoring.
- The recipient of the results of the monitoring process.

To enable the specification of monitoring *policies*, we have extended *WS-Agreement* by a complex XML type, called *MonitoringPolicyType*. A graphical view of this type is shown in Fig. 10.2. According to *MonitoringPolicyType*, the description of the monitoring policy of an agreement includes the following elements:

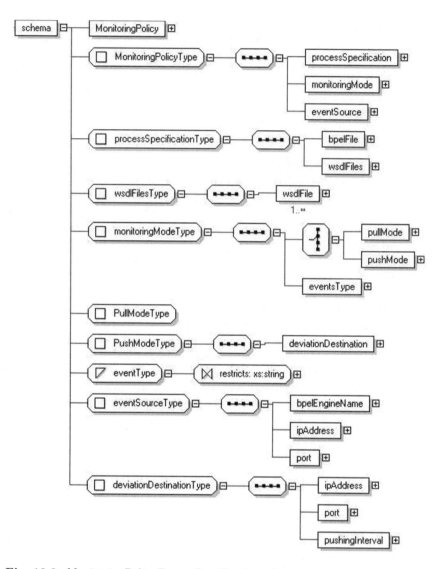

Fig. 10.2. *MonitoringPolicyType* – Specification of agreement monitoring policies

1. *processSpecificationType*. This element is used to identify the BPEL composition process of the SBS system that deploys the service(s) which the agreement is concerned with and the WSDL files of all the services that this process uses but are not regulated by the agreement (called third-party services in the following). The references to the WSDL specifications of third-party services in a monitoring policy is important as the behavior of these services may interfere with the service(s) regulated by

the agreement and, therefore, the guarantee terms in an agreement may need to be conditioned upon the satisfiability of conditions for third-party services. A *processSpecification* includes (a) an element called *bpelFile* that contains a reference to the BPEL file specifying the composition process in the context of which the agreement is to be monitored, and (b) an element called *wsdlFiles* that contains references to the list of the WSDL files that specify the services deployed by the composition process.

2. *monitoringModeType*. Elements of this type are used to specify the way of reporting the results of monitoring an agreement (i.e., the mode of reporting); the kind of events that are used to check whether the agreement's guarantee terms are satisfied; and the source of the events which are used to check an agreement. The results of monitoring may be reported in a *pullMode* or a *pushMode*. In the former mode, the client of the monitor has to check the status of the guarantee terms of the agreement. In the *pushMode*, the monitor reports the detected deviations to the client. When the *pushMode* is selected the destination where deviations should be reported (i.e., the *deviationDestination* element in Fig. 10.2) must also be specified. The specification of a deviation destination includes (a) an element called *ipAddress* that is of type string and is used to specify the IP address of the client where the deviation reports will be sent, (b) an element called port of type *int* which specifies the port in the client where the deviation reports should be sent, and (c) an element called *pushingInterval* of type *long* that defines the time interval between the generation of consecutive deviation reports. The type of the events used in monitoring is specified by the element *eventsType* that is of type *eventType*. Currently, our extension supports two types of events: recorded or derived events. Recorded events are events which are generated during the execution of the composition process of an SBS system. Derived events are events which are generated from recorded events.[1]

3. *eventSourceType*. An event source is described by (a) an element called *bpelEngineName* of type *string* which is used to specify the type of the BPEL engine, i.e., the execution environment of the service centric system, (b) an element called *ipAddress* of type *string* that is used to specify the IP address of the execution environment, and (c) an element called port of type *int* that specifies the port where the runtime events will be sent by the event source.

Overall, a monitoring policy is specified as part of the context of an agreement. The new definition of the context type in *WS-Agreement* that includes the element *monitoringPolicy* which allows the specification and attachment of a monitoring policy to the context of an agreement is shown in Fig. 10.3.

---

[1] In the monitoring framework that we have developed to support the runtime checking of WS-Agreements, derived events are generated by deduction (see Sect. 10.4.1).

Original Form of *WS-Agreement*	Extended Form of *WS-Agreement*

<xs:complexType name="AgreementContextType">
  <xs:sequence>
    <xs:element name="AgreementInitiator"
      type="xs:anyType" minOccurs="0"/>
    <xs:element name="AgreementProvider"
      type="xs:anyType" minOccurs="0"/>
    <xs:element
      name="AgreementInitiatorIsServiceConsumer"
      type="xs:boolean" default="true"
    minOccurs="0"/>
    <xs:element name="TerminationTime"
      type="xs:dateTime" minOccurs="0"/>
    <xs:element name="RelatedAgreements"
      type="wsag:RelatedAgreementListType"
      minOccurs="0"/>
    <xs:any namespace="##other"
          processContents="lax" minOccurs="0"
          maxOccurs="unbounded"/>
 	
  </xs:sequence>
  <xs:anyAttribute namespace="##other"/>
</xs:complexType>
	<xs:complexType name="AgreementContextType">
	  <xs:sequence>
	    <xs:element name="AgreementInitiator"
	      type="xs:anyType" minOccurs="0"/>
	    <xs:element name="AgreementProvider"
	      type="xs:anyType" minOccurs="0"/>
	    <xs:element
	      name="AgreementInitiatorIsServiceConsumer"
	      type="xs:boolean" default="true"
	    minOccurs="0"/>
	    <xs:element name="TerminationTime"
	      type="xs:dateTime" minOccurs="0"/>
	    <xs:element name="RelatedAgreements"
	      type="wsag:RelatedAgreementListType"
	      minOccurs="0"/>
	    <xs:any namespace="##other"
	          processContents="lax" minOccurs="0"
	          maxOccurs="unbounded"/>
	    **<xs:element name="monitoringPolicy"
	      type="MonitoringPolicyType
	      minOccurs="0" maxOccurs="1" />**
	  </xs:sequence>
	  <xs:anyAttribute namespace="##other"/>
	</xs:complexType>

Fig. 10.3. Extended definition of *AgreementContextType* in *WS-Agreement*

Specification of Service Description and Service Guarantee Terms

WS-Agreement defines a service guarantee term as a term that specifies "an assurance to the service consumer on the service quality and/or resource availability offered by the service provider" (see p. 16 in [2]). In our framework, this definition is refined to include *functional* and *quality of service (QoS) requirements* for the constituent services of an SBS system. Functional and QoS requirements may be associated with

- *qualifying conditions* conditions that must be met for a requirement to be satisfied and enforced if it is not (as defined in [2])
- *assumptions* specifying how the behavior of an SBS system and its constituent services affects the state of the system and therefore the satisfiability of the requirements.

At runtime, the monitor of a *WS-Agreement* checks whether the functional and QoS requirements that are defined as service guarantee terms in the agreement are satisfied. During monitoring, any assumptions that may have been specified for service guarantee terms are also used to generate additional information about the effect of the behavior of an SBS system and its constituent services. The identification of this effect is necessary as it may affect the satisfiability of the service guarantee terms.

Service guarantee terms along with their qualifying conditions and assumptions are specified in our framework using an XML schema that is based on event calculus, called *EC-Assertion*. In the following, we give an overview of event calculus and *EC-Assertion* how it is used in our monitoring framework to specify service guarantee terms, qualifying conditions, and assumptions for *WS-Agreements*.

10.3.3 Overview of Event Calculus

The event calculus (EC) is a first-order temporal formal language that can be used to specify properties of dynamic systems which change over time. Such properties are specified in terms of events and *fluents*.

An event in EC is something that occurs at a specific instance of time (e.g., invocation of an operation) and may change the state of a system. Fluents are conditions regarding the state of a system and are initiated and terminated by events. A fluent may, e.g., signify that a specific system variable has a particular value at a specific instance of time.

The occurrence of an event is represented by the predicate $Happens(e, t, \mathbb{R}(t_1, t_2))$. This predicate signifies that an instantaneous event e occurs at some time t within the time range $\mathbb{R}(t_1, t_2)$. The boundaries of $\mathbb{R}(t_1, t_2)$ can be specified by using either time constants or arithmetic expressions over the time variables of other predicates in an EC formula.

The initiation of a fluent is signified by the EC predicate $Initiates(e, f, t)$ whose meaning is that a fluent f starts to hold after the event e at time t. The termination of a fluent is signified by the EC predicate $Terminates(e, f, t)$ whose meaning is that a fluent f ceases to hold after the event e occurs at time t. An EC formula may also use the predicates $Initially(f)$ and $HoldsAt(f, t)$ to signify that a fluent f holds at the start of the operation of a system and that f holds at time t, respectively.

Special Types of Fluents and Events

EC-Assertion is based on event calculus but uses special types of events and fluents to specify service guarantee terms, and their qualifying conditions and assumptions. More specifically, the fluents in *EC-Assertion* have the form

$$valueOf(fluent\_expression, value\_expression) \qquad (10.1)$$

The meaning of the expression 10.1 is that the fluent signified by *fluent_expression* has the value *value_expression*. Furthermore, in this expression:

- *fluent_expression* denotes a typed SBS system variable or a list of such variables. *fluent_expression* may be an
  - *internal variable* that represents a variable of the composition process of an SBS system, or
  - *external variable* that is introduced by the creators of a service level agreement to represent the state of an SBS system at runtime.

If *fluent_expression* has the same name as a variable in the SBS system composition process then it denotes this variable, has the same name with it, and is treated as an internal variable. In all other cases, *fluent_expression* denotes an external variable and its type is determined by the type of *value_expression* as described below.

- *value_expression* is a term that either represents an EC variable or signifies a call to an operation that returns an object of some type. The operation called by *value_expression* may be an internal operation that is provided by the monitoring framework or an operation that is provided by an external web service. If *value_expression* signifies a call to an operation, it can take one of the following two forms:

  (i) $oc : S : O(\_O_{id}, \_P_1, ..., \_P_n)$ that signifies the invocation of an operation O in an external service S.

  (ii) $oc : self : O(\_O_{id}, \_P_1, ..., \_P_n)$ that signifies the invocation of the built-in operation O of the monitor.

  In these forms,

  – $\_O_{id}$ is a variable whose value identifies the exact instance of O's invocation within a monitoring session, and

  – $\_P_1, ..., \_P_n$ are variables that indicate the values of the input parameters of the operation O at the time of its invocation.

The internal operations which may be used in the specification of fluents are shown in Table 10.1. Note also that a fluent is valid if and only if the type of *fluent_expression* is more general than the type of *value_expression*. If *fluent_expression* is an external variable, the specification of its type is deduced from the type of *value_expression* in a fluent specification. In this case, if *fluent_expression* appears in different fluents that use different *value_expression* terms, the above type validity condition should be satisfied by the types of all the relevant *value_expression* terms. On the other hand, if *fluent_expression* is an internal variable, its type is determined by the specification of the variable in the composition process of the SBS system that it refers to.

The calls to external and internal operations in fluents allow us to deploy complex computations. As shown in Table 10.1, the internal operations of *EC-Assertion*, for instance, can perform various arithmetic operations over numbers and compute statistics of series of numerical values (e.g., compute the average, median, and standard deviation of a series of values), manage lists of primitive values and create new instances of object types which are supported by *EC-Assertion*.

These operations are necessary for checking QoS requirements within the reasoning process of the monitoring framework. The maintenance of lists of primitive data values, for instance, is useful for recording multi-valued fluents (e.g., recording the response times of a service operation). The operation *avg* for instance, which computes the average value of a list of real or integer number, can be used to compute the average response time of a service operation. During a monitoring session, when attempting to unify formulas which include

Table 10.1. Built-in operations for specification and computation of service guarantee terms

Operation	Description
add(n1:Real, n2:Real): Real	This operation returns n1+n2
sub(n1:Real, n2:Real): Real	This operation returns n1−n2
mul(n1:Real, n2:Real): Real	This operation returns n1* n2
div(n1:Real, n2:Real): Real	This operation returns n1/n2
append(a[]: list of <T>, e:T): list of <T> where T is Real, Int or String.	This operation appends e to a[].
del(a[]: list of <T>, e:T): list of <T> where T is Real, Int or String.	This operation deletes the first occurrence of e in a[].
delAll(a[]: list of <T>, e:T): list of <T> where T is Real, Int or String.	This operation deletes all occurrences of e in a[].
size(a[]: list of <T>): Int where T is Real, Int or String.	This operation returns the number of elements in a[].
max(a[]: list of <T>):<T> where T is Real, Int or String.	This operation returns the maximum value in a[].
min(a[]: list of <T>):<T> where T is Real, Int or String.	This operation returns the minimum value in a[].
sum(a[]: list of <T>):<T> where T is Real or Int.	This operation returns the sum of the values in a[].
avg(a[]: list of <T>): <T> where T is Real or Int.	This operation returns the average of the values in a[].
median(a[]: list of <T>):<T> where T is Real, Int or String.	This operation returns the arithmetic median of the values in a[].
mode(a[]: list of <T>): <T> where T is Real, Int or String.	This operation returns the most frequent element in a[].
new(type_name: String): ObjectIdentifier	This operation creates a new object instance of type T and returns an atom that is a unique object identifier for this object.

such calls, the EC variables which represent the operation parameters are unified first and then the monitor calls the relevant operation. If the operation returns successfully with a return value that is compliant with the type of *fluent_expression*, this value becomes the binding of the term *value_expression*. Otherwise, unification fails. In Sect. 10.4.3, we give examples of monitoring formulas that use built-in operations of the framework. (Table 10.1).

Events in our framework represent exchanges of messages between the composition process of an SBS system and the services coordinated by it. These messages either invoke operations or return results following the execution of an operation and – depending on their sender and receiver – they can be of one of the following types:

1. Service operation invocation events—These events signify the invocation of an operation in one of the partner services of an SBS system by its composition process and are represented by terms of the form

$$ic : S : O(\_O_{id}, \_P_1, ..., \_P_n) \qquad (10.2)$$

where O is the name of the invoked operation; S is the name of the service that provides O, $\_O_{id}$ is a variable identifying the exact instance of O's invocation within an execution of the SBS composition process, and

$_P_1, ..., _P_n$ are variables indicating the values of the input parameters of O at the time of its invocation.

2. Service operation reply events—These signify the return from the execution of an operation that has been invoked by the composition process of an SBS in one of its partner services and are represented by terms of the form

$$ir : S : O(\_O_{id}) \qquad (10.3)$$

where O, S, and $\_O_{id}$, are as defined in (1). Note that the values of the output parameters of such operations (if any) are represented by fluents which are initiated by the above event as discussed below.

3. SBS operation invocation events—These events signify the invocation of an operation in the composition process of an SBS by one of its partner services and are represented by terms of the form

$$rc : S : O(\_O_{id}) \qquad (10.4)$$

where S is the service that invokes O, and O, $\_Oid$ are as defined in (1). Note that the values of the input parameters of such operations (if any) are represented by fluents which are initiated by the above event as discussed below.

4. SBS operation reply events—These events signify the reply following the execution of an operation that was invoked by a partner service in the composition process of an SBS and are represented by terms of the form:

$$re : S : O(\_Oid, \_P1, ..., \_Pn) \qquad (10.5)$$

where S is the service that invoked O; $_P_1, ..., _P_n$ are variables that indicate the values of the output parameters of O at the time of its return, and O, $\_O_{id}$ are as defined in (1).

EC-Assertion uses another type of events which signify the assignment of a value to a variable used in the composition process of an SBS. These are called assignment events and are represented by terms of the form

$$as : aname(\_A_{id}) \qquad (10.6)$$

where *aname* is the name of the assignment in the composition process specification, and $\_A_{id}$ is a variable whose value identifies the exact instance of the assignment within an operational system session. An assignment event initiates a fluent that represents the value of the relevant variable.

In addition to the EC predicates and event/fluent denoting terms that were discussed above, formulas that express monitorable properties in *EC-Assertion* can use the predicates $<$ and $=$ to express time conditions (the predicate $t1 < t2$ is true if $t1$ is a time instance that occurred before $t2$, and the predicate $t1 = t2$ is true if $t1$ is a time instance that is equal to $t2$) and to compare values of different variables. Also, an EC formula that expresses a monitorable property must specify boundaries for the time ranges $\mathbb{R}(LB, UB)$ which appear in the *Happens* predicates.

If the variable t in such predicates is existentially quantified, at least one of LB and UB must be specified. These boundaries can be specified by using (i) constant time indicators or (ii) arithmetic expressions of time variables t' which appear in *Happens* predicates of the same formula provided that the latter variables are universally quantified, and that appears in their scope. If t is a universally quantified variable both LB and UB must be specified. *Happens* predicates with unrestricted universally quantified time variables take the form $Happens(e, t, \mathbb{R}(t, t))$. These predicates express instantaneous events. Furthermore, a formula is valid in our framework if the time variables of all the predicates, which include existentially quantified non-time variables, take values in time ranges with fixed boundaries. These restrictions guarantee the ability to check the satisfiability of formulas. Furthermore, a specification of requirements must also be compliant with the standard axioms of event calculus. These axioms are shown in Fig. 10.4.

The axiom *EC*1 in Fig. 10.4 states that a fluent f is clipped (i.e., ceases to hold) within the time range from $t1$ to $t2$, if an event e occurs at some time point t within this range and e terminates f. The axiom *EC*2 states that a fluent f is declipped (i.e., it comes into existence) at some time point within the time range from $t1$ to $t2$, if event e occurs at some time point t, between times $t1$ and $t2$ and fluent f starts to hold after event e at t. The axiom *EC*3 states that a fluent f holds at time t, if it is held at time 0 and has not been terminated between 0 and t. The axiom *EC*4 states that a fluent f holds at time $t2$, if an event e has occurred at some time point $t1$ before $t2$ which initiated f at $t1$ and f has not been clipped between $t1$ and $t2$. The axiom *EC*5 states that a fluent f does not hold at time $t2$, if there is an event e that occurred at some time point $t1$ before $t2$ which terminated fluent f and this fluent has not been declipped at any time point from $t1$ to $t2$. The axiom *EC*6 states that a fluent f holds at time $t2$, if it held at time $t1$ prior to $t2$ and has not been terminated between $t1$ and $t2$. The axiom *EC*7 states that a fluent f does not hold at time $t2$, if it did not hold at some time point $t1$ before $t2$

(EC1)	Clipped(t1,f,t2) $\Leftarrow$ ($\exists$e,t) Happens(e,t,$\mathfrak{R}$(t1,t2)) $\wedge$ Terminates(e,f,t)
(EC2)	Declipped(t1,f,t2) $\Leftarrow$ ($\exists$e,t) Happens(e,t,$\mathfrak{R}$(t1,t2)) $\wedge$ Initiates(e,f,t)
(EC3)	HoldsAt(f,t) $\Leftarrow$ Initially(f) $\wedge$ ¬Clipped(0,f,t)
(EC4)	HoldsAt(f,t2) $\Leftarrow$ ($\exists$e,t) Happens(e,t,$\mathfrak{R}$(t1,t2)) $\wedge$ Initiates(e,f,t) $\wedge$ ¬Clipped(t,f,t2)
(EC5)	¬HoldsAt(f,t2) $\Leftarrow$ ($\exists$e,t) Happens(e,t,$\mathfrak{R}$(t1,t2)) $\wedge$ Terminates(e,f,t) $\wedge$ ¬Declipped(t,f,t2)
(EC6)	HoldsAt(f,t2) $\Leftarrow$ HoldsAt(f, t1) $\wedge$ t1 < t2 $\wedge$ ¬Clipped(t1,f,t2)
(EC7)	¬HoldsAt(f,t2) $\Leftarrow$ ¬HoldsAt(f, t1) $\wedge$ (t1 < t2) $\wedge$ ¬Declipped(t1,f,t2)
(EC8)	Happens(e,t,$\mathfrak{R}$(t1,t2)) $\Rightarrow$ (t1 $\leq$ t2) $\wedge$ (t1 $\leq$ t) $\wedge$ (t $\leq$ t2)

Fig. 10.4. Axioms of Event Calculus

and f has not been declipped since then. Finally, the axiom $EC8$ states that the time range in a *Happens* predicate is inclusive of its boundaries.

Examples of Specification of Service Guarantee Terms

In the following, we present examples of functional and QoS guarantee terms that we can specify using *EC-Assertion*. Our examples are based on a simple SBS system, called *Quote Tracker Process (QTP)*, which we have implemented to test the monitoring framework (see [31] for a specification of the BPEL process and the services deployed by this system).

QTP allows a user to get a stock quote in US dollars given a stock symbol from New York Stock Exchange (NYSE) and convert it to some other currency. QTP uses a web service called Stock *Quote Service (SQS)* to get a quote for stocks traded in the New York Stock Exchange using a NYSE symbol. It also uses a second web service called *Currency Exchange Service* (CES) to get the currency exchange rate between US dollars and a target currency, and a third web service, called *Simple Calculator Service (SCS)*, to convert the quote into the target currency. QTP has been implemented as a BPEL process of QTP and uses the services *SQS* and *CES* of *XMethods*. In our implementation, *SCS* is a service that we have developed.

Fig. 10.5 shows specifications of functional and QoS properties for QTP in the high-level logical syntax of *EC-Assertion*.

The formula $F1$ in Fig. 10.5, for instance, specifies a functional requirement for the *CES* service. According to this requirement, any request for the exchange rate between two countries *_country1* and *_country2* that is sent to CES within a specific time period T should return the same exchange rate. This requirement is specified to ensure the consistency of the information returned by CES. The *EC-Assertion* formula specifies this requirement by stating that the results which are returned by any two invocations of the operation *getRate(_ID, _country2, _country1)* of the CES service that have happened within a time period $[t1, ..., t1 + T]$ must be the same. The invocations of the operation *getRate* in this case are represented by the predicates $Happens(ic : CES : getRate(\_ID1, \_country2, \_country1), t1, \mathbb{R}(t1, t1))$ and $Happens(ic : CES : getRate(\_ID2, \_country2, \_country1), t3, \mathbb{R}(t1, t1 + T))$ in the formula. The results of the invocations of *getRate* are represented by the initiation of the external fluent variables *Result1* and *Result2*. The assignment of values to these two fluent variables is expressed by the predicates

- $Initiates(ir : CES : getRate(_ID1), equalTo(Result1, \_result1), t2)$ and
- $Initiates(ir : CES : getRate(ID2), equalTo(Result2, \_result2), t4)$.

The formula $Q1$ in Fig. 10.5 expresses a quality requirement for the *CES* service of QTP. According to this requirement, the response time of the operation *getRate* of *CES* should be less than 100 milliseconds (ms). The response time in this formula is measured as the difference between the time of the receipt of the response of CES following the completion of the execution of $getRate$ (this is signified by the time variable $t2$ of the predicate $Happens(ir : CES : getRate(\_ID1), t2, \mathbb{R}(t1, t2))$ which represents the return of the operation in the formula) and the time when this operation was invoked in the service (this is signified by the time variable $t1$ of the predicate $Happens(ir : CES : getRate(\_ID1), t2, \mathbb{R}(t1, t2))$ which represents the call of the operation in the formula).

A second quality requirement is expressed by the formula $Q2$ in Fig. 10.5. The requirement that is expressed by this formula is that the average response time of all the invocations of operation $getQuote$ of the SQS service which take place in the time range $\mathbb{R}(T1, T2)$ should be less than 100ms. $Q2$ expresses this requirement by requiring the result of the calculation of the average of the values stored in the list $SQS\_get\_Quote\_RT[\,]$ to be less than 100ms. In $Q2$, $SQS\_get\_Quote\_RT[\,]$ is specified as an external fluent variable which is updated every time that there is an invocation of $getQuote$ followed by a return from the execution of this operation. In these cases, the response time of each invocation is appended to the list of values $SQS\_get\_Quote\_RT[\,]$. The update of the values of $SQS\_get\_Quote\_RT[\,]$ is specified by the assumption $A1$ which

```
(F1)   (∀_ID1,_country1,_country2: String) (∀ t1: Time)
       Happens(ic:CES:getRate(_ID1,_country2,_country1),t1, ℜ(t1,t1)) ∧ (∃t2:Time) ∧
       Happens(ir:CES:getRate(_ID1),t2, ℜ(t1,t2)) ∧
       Initiates(ir:CES:getRate(_ID1),valueOf(Result1,_result1),t2) ∧ (∃t3:Time) ∧
       Happens(ic:CES:getRate(_ID2, _country2, _country1),t3, ℜ(t1,t1+T)) ∧ (∃t4:Time) ∧
       Happens(ir:CES:getRate(_ID2),t4, ℜ(t3,t4)))
       Initiates(ir:CES:getRate(ID2),valueOf(Result2,_result2),t4) ⇒ _result1 = _result2
(Q1)   (∀_ID,_country1,_country2: String) (∃t1: Time)
       Happens(ic:CES:getRate(_ID,_country1,_country2),t1, ℜ(t1,t1)) ∧ (∃t2:Time) ∧
       Happens(ir:CES:getRate(_ID),t2, ℜ(t1,t2)) ⇒ oc:self:sub(t2,t1) < 100
(Q2)   (∀ t1: Time)  HoldsAt(valueOf(SQS_get_Quote_RT[],_resTime),t1) ⇒ oc:self:avg(_resTime]) < 100
(A1)   (∀ _ID, _symbol: String) (∃ t1: Time)
       Happens(ic:SQS:getQuote(_ID,_symbol),t1, ℜ(T1,T2)) ∧ (∃t2:Time)
       Happens(ir:SQS:getQuote(_ID),t2, ℜ(t1,t2)) ∧ HoldsAt(valueOf(SQS_get_Quote_RT[],_resTime),t2)
       ⇒
       Initiates(ir:SQS:getQuote(_ID), valueOf(SQS_get_Quote_RT[], oc:self:append(_resTime,
       oc:self:sub(t2, t1)), t2))
(Q3)   (∀ t1: Time) (t1 = T2+1) ∧
       HoldsAt(valueOf(getQuote_responses,_resNumber), t1) ∧
       HoldsAt(valueOf(getQuote_fails,_failsNumber), t1) ⇒
       oc:self:div(_resNumber, oc:self:add(_failsNumber,_resNumber)) > 0.999
(A2)   (∀ _ID, _symbol: String, t1: Time)
       Happens(ic:SQS:getQuote(_ID,_symbol),t1, ℜ(T1,T2)) ∧ (∃t2:Time)
       Happens(ir:SQS:getQuote(_ID),t2, ℜ(t1,t1+500)) ∧
       HoldsAt(valueOf(getQuote_responses,_resNumber),t2) ⇒
       Initiates(ir:SQS:getQuote(_ID), valueOf(getQuote_responses, oc:self:add(_resNumber, 1), t2))
(A3)   (∀ _ID, _symbol: String, t1: Time)
       Happens(ic:SQS:getQuote(_ID,_symbol),t1, ℜ(T1,T2)) ∧ ¬ (∃t2:Time)
       Happens(ir:SQS:getQuote(_ID),t2, ℜ(t1,t1+500)) ∧
       HoldsAt(valueOf(getQuote_fails,_failNumber),t2) ⇒
       Initiates(ir:SQS:getQuote(_ID), valueOf(getQuote_fails, oc:self:add(_failNumber, 1), t2))
```

Fig. 10.5. Functional and Quality of Service requirements for the CES and SQS services of QTP

appends each new response time of *getQuote* to the list of values already in $SQS\_get\_Quote\_RT[]$ (see the fluent initiation predicate $Initiates(ir : SQS : getQuote(\_ID), valueOf(SQS\_get\_Quote\_RT[], oc : self : append(\_resTime, oc : self : sub(t2, t1)), t2))$ in A1).

Formula $Q3$ in Fig. 10.5 expresses a second QoS requirement for the SQS service. According to this formula, the requirement that should be guaranteed for this service is that rate of responses which are received within 500ms after an invocation of the operation *getQuote* of SQS should exceed 99.9%. This requirement is expressed by $Q3$ as a condition over the values of the fluents *getQuote_responses* and *getQuote_fails*. These two fluents keep the counters of cases where *getQuote* produced a response within 500ms following its invocation and cases where it did not, respectively. The values of these two fluents are updated by deduction from the assumptions $A2$ and $A3$, respectively. More specifically, from $A2$ it can be deduced that the value of the fluent *getQuote_responses* should be increased by one every time that *getQuote* produces a response within 500 ms after its invocation. Similarly, from $A3$ it can be deduced that the value of the fluent *getQuote_fails* should be increased by one every time that *getQuote* does not produce a response within 500 ms from its invocation. $Q3$ uses the built-in operations of *EC-Assertion* to calculate the ratio of the values of these two fluents.

As noted earlier, the specification of the formulas in Fig. 10.5 is given in the high-level logic-based syntax of *EC-Assertion*. Our framework supports the transformation of the logic formulas which are specified in this logic-based syntax into an XML-based representation following the schema that defines *EC-Assertion*. This representation is generated by the editor of our framework from the specification of the formula in the high-level EC syntax automatically. Fig. 10.6 shows an extract of the representation of formula $Q2$ in *EC-Assertion*. The highlighted terms in the figure represent the specification of the two *Happens* predicate in the formula. The description of the full syntax of *EC-Assertion* is beyond the scope of this chapter. The specification of it, however, is available in [14] and a graphical representation of the XML schema that defines *EC-Assertion* is given in the appendix of this chapter.

Specification of Service Guarantee Terms

The specification of service guarantee terms using *EC-Assertion* is supported by a refinement of the definition of the sub-elements *QualifyingCondition* and *ServiceLevelObjective* in *WS-Agreement*.

The element *QualifyingCondition* in an agreement is used to specify a precondition that should be satisfied for the enforcement of a service guarantee term [2]. The element *ServiceLevelObjective* is used to specify a condition that must be met in order to satisfy a service guarantee. The type of both these elements in the original form of *WS-Agreement* is $xs : anyType$

```
<formula forChecking="true" formulaId="Q2">
 <quantification>
  <quantifier>existential</quantifier>
        <timeVariable> <varName>t1</varName> ... </timeVariable>
     </quantification>
 <quantification>
  <quantifier>existential</quantifier>
        <timeVariable> <varName>t2</varName> ... </timeVariable>
 </quantification>
 <body>
 <predicate negated="false" unconstrained="true">
    <happens>
        <ic_term>
        <operationName>GetRate</operationName> <partnerName>CES</partnerName>
        <id>_ID</id> <varName>_country1</varName> ...
        <varName>_country2</varName></varName>
        </ic_term>
        <timeVar> <varName>t1</varName> ... </timeVar>
        <fromTime> <time> <varName>t1</varName> ... </time> </fromTime>
        <toTime> <time> <varName>t1</varName> ...</time> </toTime>
    </happens>
 </predicate>
 <operator>and</operator>
 <predicate negated="false" unconstrained="false">
 <happens>
    <ir_term>
        <operationName>getRate</operationName> <partnerName>CES</partnerName>
        <id>_ID</id>
    </rc_term>
    <timeVar> <varName>t2</varName> ... </timeVar>
    <fromTime> <time> <varName>t1</varName> ... </time> </fromTime>
    <toTime> <time> <varName>t2</varName> ... </time> </toTime>
 </happens>
 </predicate>
 </body>
 <head>
 <relationalPredicate> <lessThan>
    <operand1> <operationCall> <name>sub</name> <partner>self</partner>
        <variable forMatching="false" ...> <varName>t2</varName> ... </variable>
        <variable forMatching="false" ...> <varName>t1</varName> ... </variable>
        </operationCall>
    </operand1>
    <operand2> <constant> <name>Vo</name> <value>1000</value> </constant>        </operand2>
 </lessThan> ...
 </relationalPredicate>
 </head>
 </formula>
```

Fig. 10.6. Extract of the representation of formula $Q2$ in *EC-Assertion*

(Fig. 10.7). In the extended form of *WS-Agreement*, the type of these elements is *ecQualifyingConditionType* and *ecServiceLevelObjectiveType*, respectively.

ecQualifyingCondition is used to specify the precondition of a service guarantee term. *ecQualifyingCondition* is defined as a type with a single subelement, called formula, of type ecFormula, i.e., the type of EC formulas in *EC-Assertion*.

ecServiceLevelObjectiveType is defined as a type with two sub-elements: one sub-element called *guaranteeFormula* defines the condition that must be met for the service guarantee term to be satisfied and the second sub-element called *assumption* specifies the effects of the behavior on an SBS and its

Extension for specifying *GuaranteeTerms*	
Original Form	**Extended Form**

`<xs:complexType name="GuaranteeTermType">`
  `<xs:complexContent>`
  ...
`<xs:element ref="wsag:QualifyingCondition"`
    `minOccurs="0"/>`
`<xs:element ref="wsag:ServiceLevelObjective"/>`
  ...
  `</xs:complexContent>`
...
`<xs:element name="GuaranteeTerm"`
    `type="wsag:GuaranteeTermType"/>`
`<xs:element name="QualifyingCondition"`
    `type="xs:anyType"/>`
`<xs:element name="ServiceLevelObjective"`
    `type="xs:anyType"/>`
  ...
	`<xs:complexType name="GuaranteeTermType">`
	  `<xs:complexContent>`
	  ...
	`<xs:element ref="wsag:QualifyingCondition"`
	    `minOccurs="0"/>`
	`<xs:element ref="wsag:ServiceLevelObjective"/>`
	  ...
	  `</xs:complexContent>`
	  ...
	
	`<xs:element name="GuaranteeTerm"`
	    `type="wsag:GuaranteeTermType"/>`
	`<xs:element name="QualifyingCondition"`
	    `type="xs:ecQualifyingConditionType"/>`
	`<xs:element name="ServiceLevelObjective"`
	    `type="xs:ecServiceLevelObjectiveType"/>`
	
	`<xs:complexType`
	    `name="xs:ecQualifyingConditionType">`
	    `<xs:sequence>`
	      `<xs:element name="formula"`
	        `type="ecas:ecFormula"`
	        `minOccurs="1"/>`
	    `</xs:sequence>`
	  `</xs:complexType>`
	
	`<xs:complexType`
	    `name="ecServiceLevelObjectiveType">`
	    `<xs:sequence>`
	      `<xs:element name="guaranteeFormula"`
	        `type="ecas:ecFormula" minOccurs="1"`
	        `maxOccurs="1"/>`
	      `<xs:element name="assumption"`
	        `type="ecas:ecFormula" minOccurs="0"`
	        `maxOccurs="unbounded"/>`
	    `</xs:sequence>`
	  `</xs:complexType>`

Fig. 10.7. Extensions in *WS-Agreement* for Specifying Service Guarantee Terms

constituent services which affect the satisfiability of a *guaranteeFormula*. The type of both these elements is *ecFormula*, as shown in Fig. 10.7.

10.4 Monitoring Service Level Agreements

10.4.1 Types of Agreement Deviations

A broad distinction that is made by our monitoring framework is related to the type of the events which are used in order to detect deviations from service level guarantee terms. These events may be of two types: (1) Events which have been captured during the operation of the system at runtime or (2) events which are generated from recorded events by deduction. The use of events of these two types also affects the characterisation of deviations from service level agreements in our framework. More specifically, if monitoring is based only on recorded events, it can detect only inconsistencies which are evidenced by violations of specific service guarantee terms by these recorded events. If, on the other hand, monitoring is based on both recorded and derived events, then the framework can also detect (a) inconsistencies which arise from the expected system behavior, (b) cases of unjustified system behavior, (c) possible inconsistencies evidenced from the expected system behavior, and (d) possible cases of unjustified system behavior.

In the following, we focus only on inconsistencies caused by recorded events and derived events. A description of the other types of inconsistencies that can be detected by our framework is beyond the scope of this chapter and may be found in [36].

10.4.2 Violations of Service Guarantee Terms by the Recorded Behavior of SBS Systems

The *recorded behavior* of an SBS system S at time T, $E_R(T)$, is defined as a set of event, and fluent initiation or termination literals of the forms: $Happens(e, t, \mathbb{R}(t,t))$, $Initiates(e, f, t)$, and $Terminates(e, f, t)$ which have been recorded during the operation of S and for which $0 \leq t \leq T$. A violation of a service guarantee term of the form $f : H \Rightarrow B$ is caused by the recorded behavior of a system at time T if the recorded behavior implies the negation of the term, that is if

$$\{E_R(T), EC_a\} \models \neg f$$

where

- $\models$ signifies logical entailment using also the principle of negation as failure, and
- EC_a are the axioms of event calculus.

Assuming the log of the runtime events of QTP shown in Fig. 10.8, the quality requirement $Q1$ that requires the response time of the operation *getRate* of the service CES to be less than 100ms is violated at time $T = 24657$. This is because at this time point an event signifying the response from the execution of this operation that was invoked at $T = 24500$ is received and the time difference between the invocation and the response of the operation is found to be 157ms (see the events L4 and L5 in the event log of Fig. 10.8 which represent the invocation and response of the operation *getRate*, respectively). The identification of the violation is identified since the events L4 and L5 imply the negation of Q1. This is because, following the unification of the variables $t2$ and $t1$ of $Q1$ with the values 24657 and 24500 respectively, the result of the execution of the built-in operation $oc : self : sub(24657, 24500)$ in the formula is not less than 100 as required by $Q1$.

Violations of Service Guarantee Terms by the Expected Behavior of SBS Systems

The second type of deviations that can be detected in our framework are violations of service guarantee terms by the expected behavior of an SBS system. The latter type of behavior includes the set of predicates that can be derived by deductive reasoning from the recorded behavior of a system using the formulas in the behavioral specification B_S of the system and the assumptions A_S that have been specified for it. As defined in [36], a service guarantee term of the form $f : C \Rightarrow A$ is violated with the expected behavior of a system at time T if

$$E_R(T), EC_a, dep(A_S \cup B_S, f) \models \!\!\!\!/ \; f$$

where $dep(A_S \cup B_S, f)$ is the set of formulas $g : B \Rightarrow H$ in the assumptions A_S defined for f and the service description terms of the SBS system (BS) which f depends on. In this definition, inter-formula dependencies are defined as follows. A formula f depends on a formula $g : B \Rightarrow H$ if the head H of g has a predicate L that unifies with some predicate K in the body C of f or with some predicate K in the body B'' of another formula g' that f depends on.

The runtime events of Fig. 10.8 and the events that can be derived from them given the assumptions of Fig. 10.5 and the axioms of event calculus violate the QoS requirement Q2 of QTP at $T = 26325$. This is because at this time point, the fluent vector variable $SQS\_get\_Quote\_RT[]$ has two values (50 and 200), the average value of which is not less than 100. The violation in this case is detected using the derived events and recorded events of QTP. More specifically the relevant derived events in this case are the events which update the value of the fluent (vector) variable $SQS\_get\_Quote\_RT[]$. These events are generated by deduction from the assumption A1. More specifically, following the events $L1$ and $L2$, $SQS\_get\_Quote\_RT[]$ is deduced by A1 to include the value 50 and following the events $L7$ and $L8$ the same fluent variable is deduced to include the value 200 too.

10.4.3 Monitoring Process

In the following, we describe the process by which our monitor checks for violations of service guarantee terms. At runtime, the monitor generates and maintains templates that represent different instantiations of the formulas

```
L1  :   Happens(ic:SQS:getQuote(ID1,SX),23100,ℜ(23100,23100))
L2  :   Happens(ir:SQS:getQuote(ID1),2315,ℜ(23150,23150))
L3  :   Initiates(ir:SQS:getQuote(ID1),valueOf(q,107),23150)
L4  :   Happens(ic:CES:getRate(ID2,US,UK),24500,R(24500, 24500))
L5  :   Happens(ir:CES:getRate(ID2),24657,R(24657, 24657))
L6  :   Initiates(ir:CES:getRate(ID2),  valueOf(rate,1.77),24657)
L7  :   Happens(ic:SQS:getQuote(ID3,SY),26125,ℜ(26125,26125))
L8  :   Happens(ir:SQS:getQuote(ID3),26325,ℜ(26325,26325))
L9  :   Initiates(ir:SQS:getQuote(ID3),valueOf(q,54),26325)
L10 :   Happens(ic:CES:getRate(ID4,US,UK),27555,R(27555, 27555))
L11 :   Happens(ir:CES:getRate(ID4),28000,R(28000, 28000))
L12 :   Initiates(ir:CES:getRate(ID4),  valueOf(rate,1.77),28000)
```

Fig. 10.8. Runtime events of QTP

that specify the service guarantee terms of an agreement which should be monitored. A template for a formula f stores the following:

- The identifier (Id) of f.
- A list of pairs (i, p) where i indicates a formula that depends on f, and p indicates the predicate that creates the dependency.
- The variable binding (VB) computed for the template (i.e., the set of value bindings of the variables of the formula represented by the template).
- For each predicate p in f
  - The *quantifier* of its time variable (Q) and its signature (SG).
  - The boundaries (LB, UB) of the time range within which p should occur.
  - The *truth value* (TV) of p. TV is defined to be UN if the truth value of the predicate is not known yet, T if the predicate is known to be true, and F if the predicate is known to be false.
  - The *source* (SC) of the evidence for the truth value of p. The value of SC is UN if the truth value has not been established yet, RE if the truth value of the predicate has been established by a recorded event, DE if the truth value of the predicate has been established by a derived event, and NF if the truth value of the predicate has been established by the principle of negation as failure.
  - A *time stamp* (TS) indicating the time in which the truth value of p was established.

The monitor creates two sets of templates for each formula: a set of *deviation templates* which are used to check for violations of the formula, and a set of *derivation templates* which are used to derive predicates from the formula.[2]

Both types of templates are updated by recorded and derived events. Recorded events are captured by the event receiver and stored in the event database of the framework (see Fig. 10.1). These events are processed by the monitor in the exact order of their occurrence and used to update the truth values of predicates in templates. When a new event is taken from the event database, the monitor checks it against all the different templates to establish if the event could be unified with a predicate in the template. In cases where the event can be unified with a predicate in a template and the truth value of the predicate has not been set yet, the template is updated. The form of the update depends on whether the predicate has an existentially or a universally quantified time variable.

More specifically, the truth value of a predicate with an existentially quantified time variable—i.e. a predicate of the form $(\exists t)p(x, t)$ where t is in the range $\mathbb{R}(t1, t2)$—is set to $T(true)$ as soon as the first event e that can be unified with p occurs between $t1$ and $t2$. If no such event occurs at the distinguishable time points within $\mathbb{R}(t1, t2)$, the truth value of p is set to $F(false)$.

---

[2] Derivation templates are not generated if the mode of monitoring in a monitoring policy is set to recorded events only (see Sect. 10.3).

The absence of events unifiable with p is confirmed as soon as the first event that cannot be unified with p occurs after $t2$. The truth value of a predicate of the form $(\exists p)(x, t)$ is established in the opposite way: as soon as an event e that can be unified with p occurs between $t1$ and $t2$, the truth value of p is set to $F(false)$ and if no such events occur at the distinguishable time points between $t1$ and $t2$, the truth value of p is set to $T(true)$.

The truth value of a predicate with a universally quantified time variable— i.e., a predicate of the form $(\forall t)p(x, t)$ where t must be in the range $\mathbb{R}(t1, t2)$— is set to $F(false)$ as soon as an event which is not unifiable with p occurs between $t1$ and $t2$, and to $T(true)$ if all the events that occur at the distinguishable time points between $t1$ and $t2$ can be unified with p. The truth value of predicates of the form $(\forall t)p(x, t)$, where t must be in the range $\mathbb{R}(t1, t2)$, is set to $T(true)$ as soon as the first event that is not unifiable with p occurs within the time range $\mathbb{R}(t1, t2)$ and $F(false)$ if all the events at the distinguishable time points between $t1$ and $t2$ can be unified with p. The truth value of predicates of the form $(\forall t)p(x, t)$, where t is unconstrained (i.e., it is defined to be in a range of the form $\mathbb{R}(t, t)$), is set to $T(true)$ as soon as an event that can be unified with the predicate is encountered.

As an example of this process, consider the check of the satisfiability of the formula $Q1$ in Sect. 10.3. Initially, the template of this formula will have the form shown in Fig. 10.9.

Then, when the event $L4$ in the even log of Fig. 10.8 occurs, the monitor detects that it can be unified with the first predicate in the template (i.e., the predicate $Happens(ic : CES : getRate(\_ID, \_country1, \_country2),$ $t1, \mathbb{R}(t1, t1)))$ and creates a new instance of the template in which the event is unified with the predicate. Following the unification, in the new template instance, which is shown in Fig. 10.10, the truth value of the predicate $Happens(ic : CES : getRate(\_ID, \_country1, \_country2), t1, \mathbb{R}(t1, t1))$ is set to T. This is because the time variable $t1$ of the predicate is universally quantified and unconstrained. Also, the source (SC) of this truth value is set to RE (as the value was set due to a recorded event), the timestamp at which the truth value of the predicate was determined is set to 24500 (i.e., the timestamp of the event that was unified with the predicate) and the lower (LB) and upper (UB) time boundaries of the time variable

Template-1							
ID	Q1						
DP							
VB	(_ID,?) (_country1,?) (_country2,?) (1, ?) (t2, ?)						
P	Q	SG	TS	LB	UB	TV	SC
1	∀	Happens(ic:CES:getRate(_ID,_country1,_country2),t1, ℜ(t1,t1))	t1	t1	t1	UN	UN
2	∃	Happens(ir:CES:getRate(_ID),t2, ℜ(t1,t2))	t2	t1	t2	UN	UN
3		oc:self:sub(t2,t1) < 100	?	–	–	UN	UN

Fig. 10.9. Template for formula $Q1$

Template-2							
ID	Q1						
DP							
VB	(_ID, ID2) (_country1,US) (_country2, UK) (t1, 24500) (t2, ?)						
P	**Q**	**SG**	**TS**	**LB**	**UB**	**TV**	**SC**
1	∀	**Happens**(ic:CES:getRate(_ID,_country1,_countr y2),t1, ℜ(t1,t1))	24500	24500	24500	T	RE
2	∃	**Happens**(ir:CES:getRate(_ID),t2, ℜ(t1,t2))	t2	24500	t2	UN	UN
3		oc:self:sub(t2,t1) < 100	?	–	–	UN	UN

Fig. 10.10. Template for formula $Q1$ updated due to the event $L4$

of the predicate are both set to 24500. The update of the template due to the event $L4$ also changes the variable binding of the template. More specifically, the variables $\_ID$, $\_country1$, $\_country2$, and $\_t1$ of the predicate $Happens(ic : CES : getRate(\_ID, \_country1, \_country2), t1, \mathbb{R}(t1, t1))$ are bound to the values ID2, US, UK, and 23500, respectively. Note also that the lower boundary (LB) of $t2$ which is the time variable of the second predicate in the template has been updated so as to be equal to the value bound to $t1$ (i.e., 24500). As a result of the update of the lower bound of $t2$, the truth value of the second predicate in the template will subsequently be updated only by events that happen after $t = 24500$.

When the event $L5$ in the event log of Fig. 10.8 occurs the template of Fig. 10.10 will be updated again. This is because $L5$ can be unified with the second predicate in the template, i.e., the predicate $Happens(ir : CES : getRate(\_ID), t2, \mathbb{R}(t1, t2))$, and has taken place within the time boundaries of this predicate (i.e., after 24500). The result of this update is shown in Fig. 10.11. As shown in this figure, the truth value of the predicate $Happens(ir : CES : getRate(\_ID), t2, \mathbb{R}(t1, t2))$ is set to T, its timestamp is set to 24657, and the source of the truth value of the predicate is set to RE as the event that led to the update was again a recorded event. At this point, the truth value of the only remaining predicate in the template (i.e., the predicate $oc : self : sub(t2, t1) < 100$) can also be computed. This is because $oc : self : sub(t2, t1) < 100$ is not a predicate with a time variable and all

Template-3							
ID	Q1						
DP							
VB	(_ID, ID2) (_country1,US) (_country2, UK) (t1, 24500) (t2, 24657)						
P	**Q**	**SG**	**TS**	**LB**	**UB**	**TV**	**SC**
1	∀	**Happens**(ic:CES:getRate(_ID,_country1,_countr y2),t1, ℜ(t1,t1))	24500	24500	24500	T	RE
2	∃	**Happens**(ir:CES:getRate(_ID),t2, ℜ(t1,t2))	24657	24500	24657	T	RE
3		oc:self:sub(t2,t1) < 100	–	–	–	UN	UN

Fig. 10.11. Template for formula $Q1$ updated due to the events $L4$ and $L5$

its variables ($t1$ and $t2$) are bound to specific values in the current variable binding of the template.

As the predicate $oc : self : sub(t2, t1) < 100$ refers to an operation (i.e., $oc : self : sub(t2, t1)$), to establish its truth value the monitor must execute this operation. In this case, the monitor will call the operation $oc : self : sub$ using as parameters the values of the variables $t2$ and $t1$ and will substitute the result of this call (i.e., 257) for the operation in the predicate "$<$". Following the substitution, the predicate "$<$" becomes "$257 < 100$" and consequently its truth value is evaluated to F.

When the truth values of all predicates in a template have been determined, a check for possible formula violations is performed. This check is carried out according to the following rules:

- If the truth value all the predicates in the template is T, the instance of the formula represented by the template is satisfied.
- If the truth value of all the predicates in the body of the template is T and the truth value of at least one predicate in the head is F and there is no predicate in the template whose source is a derived event (i.e., DE), the instance of the formula represented by the template is inconsistent with the recorded behavior of the system.
- If the truth value of all the predicates in the body of the template is $True$ and the truth value of at least one predicate in the head of the template is $False$ and the source of at least one predicate in the template is a derived event, the formula is inconsistent with the expected behavior of the system.

The template checking process will be triggered following the update of the truth value of the predicate $oc : self : sub(t2, t1) < 100$ in the template of Fig. 10.11. This process will establish that the specific instance of the formula $Q1$ that is expressed by the template has been violated and since the events that have been taken into account in order to establish the truth values of the predicates in the formula are all recorded events, the detected violation is classified as a violation due to recorded behavior.

The monitor also generates derived events by deduction from event derivation templates. More specifically, if in an event derivation template the truth-value of all the predicates in the body of the template is T and there is a predicate p in the head of the template that has an unknown truth value but whose variables are bound to specific values in the variable binding of the template, the truth value of p is set to T and the monitor generates a derived event as a copy of the bound form of p.

Derived events are used to update derivation templates in order to derive further events and to detect deviations. In the update process for derived events, the truth value of a predicate of the form $(\exists t)p(x, t)(\neg(\exists t)p(x, t))$, where t is in the range $\mathbb{R}(t1, t2)$ in a template, is set to $T(F)$ if there is a not-negated derived event e that can be unified with p and the range $\mathbb{R}(t1', t2')$ of e is within $\mathbb{R}(t1, t2)$. The truth value of a predicate of the form $(\forall t)p(x, t)$

(where t is in the range $\mathbb{R}(t1, t2)$) with a yet unknown truth value is set to T if there is a derived event e that can be unified with p and the range $\mathbb{R}(t1, t2)$ is within the range $\mathbb{R}(t1', t2')$ of e. The truth value of a predicate in a template of the form $\neg(\forall t)p(x, t)$ (where t is in the range $\mathbb{R}(t1, t2)$) with a yet unknown truth value is set to T if there is a derived negated event e that can be unified with p and the range $\mathbb{R}(t1', t2')$ of e is within the range $\mathbb{R}(t1, t2)$.

According to this process, the derivation template *Template-4* shown in Fig. 10.12 will be created from formula $A1$ at $T = 23150$. This template will be created from an uninstantiated template of $A1$ following the events $L1$ and $L2$ in Fig. 10.8. More specifically, the truth value of the predicate $Happens(ic : SQS : getQuote(\_ID, \_symbol), t1, \mathbb{R}(T1, T2))$ in *Template-4* will be set to T due to the event $L1$ and the truth value of the predicate $Happens(ir : SQS : getQuote(\_ID), t2, \mathbb{R}(t1, t2))$ will be set to T due the event $L2$ at $t = 23150$. At this time point, the truth value of the predicate $HoldsAt(valueOf(SQS\_get\_Quote\_RT[], \_resTime), t2)$ in the template can also be derived from axiom $EC3$ of event calculus and the predicate $Initially(valueOf(SQS\_get\_Quote\_RT[], []))$ which represents the initial set of the response times of the operation get_Quote. Thus, since all the predicates in the body of the template *Template-4* are true, the monitor will use *Template-4* to deduce the truth value of the predicate $Initiates(ir : SQS : getQuote(\_ID), valueOf(SQS\_get\_Quote\_RT[], oc : self : append(\_resTime, oc : self : sub(t2, t1)), t2))$ in the head of the template at $T = 23150$ deriving the following bounded form of this predicate: $Initiates(ir : SQS : getQuote(\_ID), valueOf(SQS\_get\_Quote\_RT[], [50]), 23-150))$. This bounded form is derived by first evaluating the term $oc : self : sub(23150, 23100)$, substituting its result (i.e., the value 50) into the term $oc : self : append(\_resTime, oc : self : sub(t2, t1))$ and finally evaluating the latter term. The result of the latter evaluation is the list of values: [50]. This list is substituted for the term $oc : self : append(\_resTime, oc : self : sub(t2, t1))$ in the predicate.

Template-4							
ID	A1						
DP	Q2						
VB	(ID, ID1) (symbol, SX) (resTime, [])						
P	Q	SG	TS	LB	UB	TV	SC
1	∀	Happens(ic:SQS:getQuote(_ID,_symbol),t1, ℜ(T1,T2))	23100	23100	23100	T	RE
2	∃	Happens(ir:SQS:getQuote(_ID),t2, ℜ(t1,t2))	23150	23150	23150	T	RE
3	∃	HoldsAt(valueOf(SQS_get_Quote_RT[],_resTime) , t2)	23150	23150	23150	T	DE
4	∃	Initiates(ir:SQS:getQuote(_ID), valueOf(SQS_get_Quote_RT[], oc:self:append(_resTime, oc:self:sub(t2, t1)), t2))	23150	23150	23150	UN	UN

Fig. 10.12. Template for formula $A1$

Template-5							
ID	Q2						
DP							
VB	(resTime, [50])						
P	Q	SG	TS	LB	UB	TV	SC
1	∀	HoldsAt(valueOf(SQS_get_Quote_RT[], resTime),t1)	23150	23150	23150	T	DE
2		oc:self:avg(_resTime]) < 100	23150	23150	23150	T	DE

Fig. 10.13. Template for formula $Q2$

Subsequently, from the derived predicate $Initiates(ir : SQS : getQuote(\_ID), valueOf(SQS\_get\_Quote\_RT[], [50]), 23150))$ and the axiom $EC3$ of event calculus the predicate $HoldsAt(valueOf(SQS\_get\_Quote\_RT[], [50]), 23150)$ can also be derived. The latter predicate can then be used to update a deviation template for the formula $Q2$. The template that results from this update and the evaluation of the predicate $oc : self : avg(\_resTime]) < 100$ in the formula is shown in Fig. 10.13. Thus, at $T = 23150$ the formula $Q2$ is satisfied.

10.5 Implementation

Our framework has been implemented by a prototype written in Java$^T M$. This prototype realizes the architecture of the framework that we discussed in Sect. 10.2 and can monitor SBS systems whose composition process is specified in BPEL. In the prototype, we have used the *bpws4j* BPEL process execution engine [6]. This engine uses *log4j* [26] to generate logs of the events during the execution of the composition process of an SBS. This event log is fed into our framework in order to provide the runtime information that is necessary for monitoring. The output of *log4j* is analyzed by the event receiver of the prototype in order to extract the events which are taken into account during the monitoring process.

Figure 10.14 shows a snapshot of the monitoring console of the prototype. This snapshot was taken during a session of monitoring an implementation of the SBS system that we described in Sect. 10.3. The upper left panel of the monitoring console shows the formulas that express the service guarantee terms in a *WS-Agreement* for this system. Using the console, the user of our framework can select one or more of the formulas in an agreement to monitor. Once selected, a formula appears in the lower left panel of the console. In Fig. 10.14, the formula $Q1$ has been selected for monitoring and its EC specification is shown in the lower left panel. When monitoring is activated, the cases which violate and satisfy the selected formulas are shown in the monitoring console (see upper right panel of the console in Fig. 10.14). The user can select any of these cases in order to see the exact instantiation of the formula (template) that underpins the case. This instantiation includes

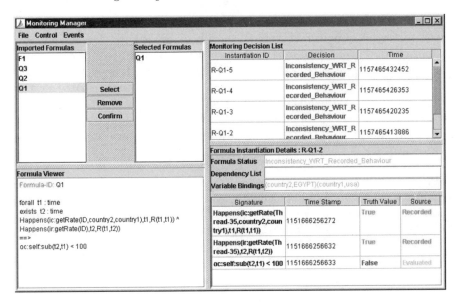

Fig. 10.14. Snapshot of Monitoring

the events that have been unified with the different predicates in the formula, the source, and timestamp of each of these events and the truth values of the predicates that the events have been unified with.

Figure 10.14 shows four violations of the formula $Q1$ which, as discussed in Sect. 10.3, requires that the response time of the operation *getRate* of the service Currency Exchange Service should always be less than 100ms. These violations are identified as *R-Q1-5*, *R-Q1-4*, *R-Q1-3*, and *R-Q1-2* in Fig. 10.5. The user can select any of these violations to see the details of the events that have caused it. The violation selected in the figure corresponds to the instance *R-Q1-2* of the formula. As shown in the lower right panel of the figure, this violation has occurred since there was a call of the operation *getRate* (i.e., the event $ic : getRate(Thread - 35, country2, country1), tR(t, t))$ at T=1151666256272 and the response to this call (i.e., the event $ir : getRate(Thread - 35), tR(t, t))$ occurred $T = 1151666256272$. Following the unification of these two events with the *Happens* predicates in the body of $Q1$, the monitor executed the operation $oc : self.sub(t2, t1)$ in the head of the formula and as the result of this operation was 360 ms the truth value of the "$<$" predicate in the head of $Q1$ was evaluated to F and the whole formula instance was violated.

The current implementation of the framework does not support the checking of past EC formulas (a past EC formula is a formula in which a predicate p that has a time variable which is constrained by the time variable of an unconstrained predicate q^3 must occur before q). It also assumes that all the non-time variables in formulas are universally quantified and does not support the invocation of external operations in order to perform complex computations during the reasoning process (only invocations of built-in operations are supported by the current implementation). Furthermore, based on our implementation, we found that the impact of generating the events used for monitoring onto the performance of the monitored system was about 18% (i.e., the extra time that it takes from the BPEL engine to create an event log). Currently, we are developing event captors which instead of using *log4j* to generate events capture SOAP messages which are sent to and from the BPEL execution engine and transform these messages into EC events before sending them to the monitor. The impact of this alternative event capturing solution on both the performance of the SBS system that is being monitored and the monitoring process itself is to be evaluated.

10.6 Evaluation

10.6.1 Experimental Set Up

To evaluate the monitoring framework, we have carried out a series of experiments. The objectives of these experiments were as follows:

1. To measure the efficiency of monitoring in terms of the average time that it takes to detect a formula violation from the time that it occurred.
2. To establish whether performance is affected by the frequency and type of the events which are taken into account and the size of the domains of the non-time variables used in the formulas.

In our experiments, we used an implementation of a *Car Rental System* (CRS) that is described in [12]. This system acts as a broker to car rental companies enabling the hire of cars from different car parks. The system has been implemented by a BPEL composition process that coordinates interactions with different web services including (a) services which provide access to information about the car fleet of different companies and the availability of cars at different car parks and can make car rental reservations and (b) services which operate as drivers of sensors installed at different car parks, tracking car entries and departures.

Our experiments were based on simulations of the BPEL process of CRS. In these simulations, we initially extracted the set of all the possible distinct execution paths of the BPEL process of CRS and expressed them as formulas in *EC-Assertion*. Then we generated different execution paths of the process by selecting different formulas from the extracted formulas set and generating

---

[3] A predicate p is constrained (unconstrained) if the range of its time variable is (not) defined in terms of the values of other time variables.

randomly events from each selected formula. The random generation of events from a formula was controlled by the following parameters:

1. The size of the domain of the non-time variables in the formula (i.e., the number of the distinct possible values of each variable).
2. The distribution of the values of the constrained time variables within the formula.
3. The distribution of the time that elapses between the initial events of each consecutively selected formulas or, equivalently, the distribution of the values of the unconstrained time variables in the formulas.

Our experimental design covered two different factors that could affect the performance of the monitoring process, namely:

- The *frequency of events*—To explore this factor, we ran simulations of high and moderate event frequency. These two categories of event frequency were controlled by the distribution of the time between the starting events of two consecutively selected formulas in the simulations. In high event frequency (HEF) simulations, the difference between the timestamps of the starting events of two consecutively selected formulas had a *normal distribution* with an average of 3 seconds and a standard deviation of 0.8 seconds. In moderate event frequency (MEF) simulations, the difference between the timestamps of the starting events of two consecutively selected formulas had a *normal distribution* with an average of 10 seconds and a standard deviation of 0.8 seconds. In both simulation categories, the timestamps of the constrained predicates in the formulas were distributed according to the uniform distribution within the range defined by their boundaries. Based on these parameters, in HEF simulations we generated 30,000 events per hour on average and in MEF simulations we generated 9,000 events per hour on average.
- The *size of the domain*—To explore this factor, we ran simulations using large and small domain sizes denoted as LD and SD, respectively. In our case study, we had three different domains for non-time variables, namely customers, cars, and car parks. In LD simulations, we used sets of 200 customers, 80 cars, and 12 car parks. In SD simulations, we used sets of 50 customers, 20 cars, and 3 car parks (i.e., domains whose size was 1/4 of the size of the respective LD domain).

In total, we performed four different experiments in which we monitored four functional requirements for CRS with an average of seven predicates per formula. The experiments were categorized with respect to the previous two differentiation factors as shown in Table 10.2. In each of these experiments, we generated 30,000 events using the simulator of our framework (see Fig. 10.1) and the parameter values that were described above and fed them into the monitor which carried out the monitoring process. The number of events that were used in our experiments corresponded to about 1 hour of operation of

Table 10.2. Classification of experiments

	MEF	HEF
DL	Exp 1	Exp 3
DS	Exp 2	Exp 4

CRS in the case of HEF experiments and 3.3 hours of operation in the case of MEF experiments.

In each experiment, we computed the in making a decision about possible violations of a formula, called d-delay. *d-delay* was measured as:

$$d - delay = \sum_{j=1,...,N} d_j/N$$

In this formula, N is the number of the formula templates for which a decision was made during the experiment and d_j is the delay in making the decision for a formula template j. d_j was computed as

$$d_j = T_E^{F_j} - max_{i \in F_j}(t_i^{e(d)}) \ if \ T_E^{F_j} - max_{i \in F_j}(t_i^{e(d)}) \geq 0 \qquad (10.7)$$

$$d_j = T_E^{F_j} - max_{i \in F_j}(t_i^M) \ if \ T_E^{F_j} - max_{i \in F_j}(t_i^{e(d)}) < 0 \qquad (10.8)$$

where

- t_i^e is the time of occurrence of an event i as generated by the simulator
- T_s^m is the starting time of the monitor
- T_c^m is the current time of the monitor
- $t_i^{e(d)}$ is the time of recording an event i in the monitor's database; $t_i^{e(d)}$ is computed by the formula $t_i^{e(d)} = (t_i^e - t_0^e) + T_s^m$ where t_0^e is the time of the first event that is generated by the simulator. $t_i^{e(d)}$ is the relative time of the occurrence of the event i after the occurrence of the first event that is processed with the monitor and which is assumed to coincide with the starting time of the monitoring process (i.e., T_s^m)
- t_i^M is the time when the monitor retrieves an event i from its database to process it
- $T_S^{F_j}$ is the starting time of the decision procedure that the monitor executes in order to check for violations after the truth values of the predicates in the template j for a formula F have been established
- $T_E^{F_j}$ is the completion time of the decision procedure that the monitor executes in order to check for violations after the truth values of the predicates in the template j for a formula F have been established
- i ranges over the events used to establish the truth values of the predicates in a template F_j.

Formula 10.7 above is used to compute the delay in making a decision about a template in cases where the monitor starts checking this template after the occurrence of all the events that were used to instantiate and set the truth values of the predicates in the template. Formula 10.8 is used in cases where the monitor is capable of checking a template before the last event that was used to instantiate one of its predicates really occurred (this case was only possible due to the use of simulations in which the time of the real occurrence of an event could be after its generation by the simulator and its transmission to the monitor).

Furthermore, for each of the four experiments we produced two sets of results. The first set recorded the average delay in monitoring sessions using only the events generated by the simulator (i.e., recorded events). The second set included the average delay in monitoring sessions using both events generated by the simulator and additional events that were derived from them using the monitored requirement formulas and assumptions (i.e., both recorded and derived events).

10.6.2 Results

Tables 10.3 and 10.4 show the average *d-delay* in making decisions about the satisfiability of monitored formulas that was measured in our experiments. The average delay measures in Table 10.3 refer to monitoring sessions where only the recorded events (i.e., the events generated by the simulator) were taken into account. The average delay measures in Table 10.4 refer to monitoring sessions where both the recorded events and events that could be derived from them and assumptions by deduction were taken into account. The measures appearing in both tables are in seconds.

The experimental results shown in Tables 10.3 and 10.4 demonstrate that the frequency of events had a significant impact on the performance

Table 10.3. *d-delay* with recorded events

	Exp 1	Exp 2	Exp 3	Exp 4
# Events	Avg *d-delay*	Avg *d-delay*	Avg *d-delay*	Avg *d-delay*
2500	0.06	0.62	0.03	0.04
5000	0.14	0.13	15.34	15.21
7500	0.21	0.20	185.95	210.22
10000	0.28	0.28	535.56	585.42
12500	0.36	0.36	1184.38	1195.02
15000	0.43	0.43	1896.70	2010.52
17500	105.56	66.29	2781.94	3034.48
20000	620.06	531.39	4121.51	4086.69
22500	1598.23	1397.85	5476.30	5590.25
25000	2993.66	2666.99	7003.27	7137.67
27500	4643.43	4343.57	9055.78	8838.63
30000	6493.96	6150.47	10671.60	11148.4

Table 10.4. *d-delay* with mixed (recorded and derived) events

	Exp 1	Exp 2	Exp 3	Exp 4
# Events	Avg *d-delay*	Avg *d-delay*	Avg *d-delay*	Avg *d-delay*
2500	49.47	44.70	61.04	68.90
5000	190.65	166.84	451.17	442.47
7500	380.23	342.41	1310.37	1380.84
10000	628.59	569.36	2650.79	2789.45
12500	1059.32	989.13	4420.99	4675.73
15000	1845.82	1744.56	6592.42	6971.83
17500	3205.74	3059.82	9435.23	9970.17
20000	5130.91	4926.66	12992.60	13366.00
22500	7624.29	7266.17	17063.41	17619.07
25000	10607.41	10134.35	21539.77	22325.48
27500	13976.86	13524.91	26647.47	27339.53
30000	17923.68	17452.27	31843.39	33171.97

of the monitor. The average decision delay increased linearly up to a certain number of events and then it increased exponentially. In high event frequency experiments, the exponential rise occurred earlier than in the moderate event frequency (MEF) experiments. More specifically in MEF experiments where only recorded events were used (i.e., *Exp1* and *Exp2*), the exponential rise of *d-delay* started in the range of 17,500–20,000 events as shown in Table 10.3 (i.e., the equivalent of about 1.9 hours of operation of CRS), whereas in the recorded event HEF-experiments (i.e., *Exp3* and *Exp4*) the exponential rise of *d-delay* started in the range of 5,000–7,500 events (i.e., after about 0.2 hours of operation of CRS). The same phenomenon was observed for the experiments where we used both recorded and derived events as shown in Table 10.4.

Our experiments also showed that the size of the domains of the non-time variables had no significant effect on the performance of the monitor. This is evident from comparing the *d-delay* between *Exp1* and *Exp2* and between *Exp3* and *Exp4* both in the case of experiments where only recorded events were used (see Table 10.3) and in the case of experiments where both recorded and derived events were used (see Table 10.4). The reason for the absence of any effect of this factor is likely to have been due to the fact that in our experiments the monitored formulas had predicates which had a small number of shared variables. Thus, increments in the size of the domains of these variables did not lead to a combinatorial proliferation in the number of the templates (instances) of the formulas during the monitoring process.

Our experiments also demonstrated that the use of mixed events had a significant effect on *d-delay*. Table 10.5 shows the ratio of the average *d-delay* of mixed events over the average *d-delay* of recorded only events that was measured in different experiments after processing 10,000, 20,000, and 30,000 events. In both MEF and HEF experiments, this ratio decreased as more events were being processed going down to less than 3 at 30,000 events. This

Table 10.5. Mixed vs recorded events *d-delay* ratio

# Events	Exp 1	Exp 2	Exp 3	Exp 4
10,000	2197.85	2033.42	4.95	4.76
20,000	8.27	9.27	3.15	3.27
30,000	2.76	2.84	2.98	2.98

was due to the fact that at 30,000 events the monitor had been saturated with events and substantial delays were being observed for recorded events alone anyway. At the initial states of monitoring (10,000 events), however, the use of mixed events (i.e., deduction in the monitoring process) caused a substantial difference in *d-delay* which in the case of HEF experiments was almost 5-fold and in the case of MEF experiments (*Exp*1 and *Exp*2) reached a ratio of more than 2,000. The reason for the latter ratio was that monitoring based on recorded events only in the case of MEP experiments was very efficient up to 10,000 events (*d-delay* in this case was less than 0.3 seconds). These results clearly demonstrate, as expected, that the use of deduction affects substantially the efficiency and, therefore, the applicability of the monitoring process.

Also, our experimental results have demonstrated that the average delay in the detection of a formula deviation was substantial after some time. This confirmed the results of a smaller scale experimentation that have been reported in [29, 36]. The observed decision delays suggest that monitoring can be deployed only for certain types of properties where the timeliness in the detection of a deviation is not critical for a system (e.g., monitoring of long-term performance properties of a system) and exclude time critical properties (e.g., safety).

10.7 Related Work

The importance of being able to specify and monitor agreements between providers and consumers of web services setting the objectives that the services should satisfy and the penalties that may arise when they fail to do so is widely recognized in industry and academia [2, 5, 23]. As a result of this recognition, several standards and approaches have emerged, in addition to *WS-Agreement* that we overviewed in Sect. 10.3.1.

WSLA (Web Service Level Agreement) is another framework that can be used to specify a service level agreement between a service provider and service consumer and the obligations of the two parties [23, 28]. This framework provides an XML-based language for specifying quality objectives only (e.g., service performance and throughput) without covering functional requirements. A web service level agreement is agreed and signed by both parties (known as signatory parties) through negotiation. Signatory parties may monitor directly the agreement or employ one or more third parties (known as *supporting parties*) to monitor it. The *WS-Agreement*-based framework that we have described in this chapter provides support for the specification of the entire range of quality properties that can be specified in *WSLA*.

WS-Policy is a W3C standard that provides an XML-based language for expressing the capabilities, requirements, and general characteristics of entities in an SBS system [3]. *WS-Policy* focuses on the provision of operators for combining assertions that specify the above characteristics into policies and the specification of qualifiers indicating the circumstances under which an assertion has to be met. However, it does not provide the equivalent of a full logic–based language that would be required in order to express arbitrary logical conditions regarding the capabilities and requirements of services in a service-based system and does not support the specification of assertions that should hold over specific periods of time. Thus, it does not have the expressive power that is necessary in order to express the entire range of service guarantee terms that might be required as part of a *WS-Agreement*. It would not, for instance, be possible to express the functional requirement F1 in Fig. 10.5 using *WS-Policy*.

Baresi et al. [5] have developed a monitoring tool that supports the monitoring of assertions inserted into the composition process of an SBS system. This work also assumes composition processes specified in BPEL. An assertion is checked by a call to an external service and the execution of the composition process waits until the monitor returns the result of the check. Then, the execution of the composition process may continue or be aborted with the raise of an exception depending on whether the assertion has been violated. The main difference between the work of Baresi et al. and our framework is that the latter cannot perform preventive monitoring in which the violation of a certain property can block the execution of a system operation as [5]. However, our approach is not intrusive to the normal operation of an SBS system and, therefore, the monitoring that it can perform does not affect the performance of the monitored system. Furthermore, our approach makes it possible to monitor more than one service guarantee terms not in isolation (as in [5]) but jointly and complex service guarantee terms which involve conditions over time.

Baresi et al. [4] have also used the *WS-Policy* framework to support the monitoring of security properties for BPEL processes. In this approach the constraints to be monitored are expressed in *WS-Policy* and *WS-PolicyAttachment* is used to attach the policy to a particular context of the BPEL process. Monitoring is performed using the approach described in [5], i.e., given the specification of the constraints to be monitored in *WS-Policy* and *WS-PolicyAttachment*, a process weaver instruments the BPEL process to make it invoke an external service at runtime that checks the relevant constraints.

Another approach for monitoring SBS systems has been developed by Robinson [33]. In this approach, requirements are expressed in KAOS and analyzed to identify obstacles for them (i.e., conditions under which the requirements can be violated). Obstacles are identified by negating a requirement formula R and then identifying all the primitive events that can imply $\neg R$ through a regressive analysis of formulas that $\neg R$ depends on. If an obstacle is observable (i.e., it corresponds to a pattern of events that can be observed at runtime), it is assigned to an agent for monitoring it. At runtime, an event adaptor translates web service requests and replies expressed as SOAP messages into events and a broadcaster forwards these events to the obstacle monitoring agents, which are registered as event listeners to the broadcaster.

Farrell et al. [17] have developed an ontology to capture aspects of service level agreements agreed between service provider and consumer. This work is concerned with the monitoring of properties related to computational resources used by services such as computational power, storage, and network bandwidth. A service level agreement in this approach is specified in terms of an ontology that includes (i) contract management norms defining the effects of contract events on the contract state, (ii) obligation norms that define the actions a party has to perform in case of violation/fulfillment of contract management norms, and (iii) privilege norms that define non-contractual actions that the parties of an agreement are permitted to perform. Contracts in [17] are specified in an XML-based language called CTXML that has a semantics grounded on event calculus. Their framework is supported by a query execution engine that checks whether a CTXML contract is satisfied at runtime. The contract deviations that can be detected in the framework of Farrell et al. are similar to the inconsistencies caused by the recorded behavior of a system in our framework.

Ludwig et al. [28] have developed architecture for a middleware that can be used to create and monitor *WS-Agreements*, called *Cremona*. *Cremona* has a Java library that implements the protocol for creating service level agreements as defined by *WS-Agreement*. It also proposes the use of monitors that can check the status of the service guarantee terms in an agreement. These monitors are seen in [28] as domain-specific components that can gather primitive information from the systems that provide and/or use a service and use it to evaluate the status of service guarantee terms. As no further information is available to us regarding the implementation of such monitors, we are unable to compare them with the monitoring framework described in this chapter.

Runtime requirements monitoring has been the focus of different strands of requirements engineering research since the late 1990s. Most of the existing techniques (e.g., [19]) express requirements in the KAOS framework [13] as high-level goals that must be achieved by a system. These goals are mapped onto events that must be monitored at runtime. Typically, the existing approaches assume that the events to be monitored are generated by special statements, which must be inserted in the code of a system for this purpose (i.e., *instrumentation*) [32]. Note, however, that instrumentation cannot be always applied to SBS systems since typically SBS system providers are not the owners of the services deployed by the system.

The acquisition of information about the environment of a system during monitoring is even more difficult and most of the approaches do not address this problem. As a solution to this problem, which is prominent in highly dynamic settings (e.g., in mobile computing), Capra et al. [9] have suggested the use of reflective middleware. Such middleware could maintain metadata about an application and its execution context and give dynamic access to this information upon request. In this approach, applications can influence the middleware behavior by changing their own profile based on the reflected information provided by the middleware. The reflective approach is also used in the monitoring framework proposed in [11, 15, 20].

Recently, there has also been work that is concerned with the runtime verification of program behavior [7, 8, 22, 24]. Work in this area focuses on the development of framework for emitting and tracing program events during the execution of a program and verifying them at runtime against properties specified in some formal language, typically a variant of temporal logic. Events normally correspond to change values of program variables at the start or end of method executions. Work in this area focuses on the runtime verification of Java programs and the deployed runtime events are generated either by instrumentation [22, 24] or by using Java debugger interface [7, 8]. These approaches are more close to debugging or perpetual testing of Java programs rather than monitoring high-level user requirements.

10.8 Conclusions and Directions for Future Work

In this chapter, we presented a framework that we have developed to support the monitoring of service level agreements. The agreements that can be monitored are expressed in an extension of *WS-Agreement* that we have described in this chapter. The main characteristic of this extension is that it uses an event calculus–based language, called *EC-Assertion*, for the specification of the service guarantee terms that constitute the core of a service level agreement and specify the conditions regulating the provision of services that should be monitored at runtime. The use of *EC-Assertion* for specifying service guarantee terms provides a well-defined semantics to the specification of such terms and a formal reasoning framework for assessing their satisfiability.

EC-Assertion enables the specification of complex service guarantee terms using full first-order logic formulas as well as conditions about time which are necessary for the specification of not only behavioral but also quality of service guarantees. It also enables the use of well-understood reasoning procedures for the assessment of the satisfiability of service level agreements by our framework. In addition to these characteristics, it should be noted that *EC-Assertion* defines special events and operations which can be used in event calculus formulas to enable the specification of complex service guarantee terms. The use of internal and external operations in formulas enables the delegation of computations of complex data functions which are often required for the specification of service guarantee terms to computational entities outside the main reasoning engine which checks the satisfiability of the terms.

The monitoring framework that supports the proposed extension of *WS-Agreement* has been evaluated in a series of experiments that we reported in this chapter. These experiments have shown that the adoption of non intrusive monitoring approach of our framework introduces some delay in the detection of the deviations for an agreement but does not affect the performance of the system which is being monitored significantly.

Beyond performance, it should be noted that, although our framework is expressive enough to support a wide spectrum of monitorable service guarantee terms, we appreciate that the use of *EC-Assertion* for the specification of such terms may be difficult for users who are not familiar with formal languages. To address this point, we are investigating the development of patterns that specify generic service guarantee terms in *EC-Assertion* and an editor to support the automatic generation of instances of these patterns for specific SBS systems. An initial set of such patterns which specify generic security properties, including confidentiality, integrity, and availability properties, in *EC-Assertion* has been developed by Spanoudakis et al. [35]. The extension of this set is the subject of the ongoing work.

Further ongoing work on the framework focuses on its further experimental evaluation and the introduction of capabilities for probabilistic reasoning as part of the monitoring process.

References

1. Andrews T. et al.: Business Process Execution Language for Web Services, v1.1. http://www-106.ibm.com/developerworks/library/ws-bpel
2. Andrieux A. et al.: Web Services Agreement Specification. Global Grid Forum, May 2004, available from: http://www.gridforum.org/Meetings/GGF11/Documents/draft-ggf-graap-agreement.pdf
3. Bajaj S. et al.: Web Services Policy Framework. Sep 2004, available from: ftp://www6.software.ibm.com/software/developer/library/ws-policy.pdf
4. Baresi L, Guinea S, and Plebani P.: WS-Policy for Service Monitoring. 6th VLDB Workshop on Technologies for E-Services (TES-05), Trondheim, Norway, September 2–3, 2005
5. Baresi L., Ghezzi C., and Guinea S.: Smart Monitors for Composed Services. Proc. of 2nd Int. Conf. on Service Oriented Computing, New York, 2004
6. BPWS4J: http://alphaworks.ibm.com/tech/bpws4j
7. Brorkens M. and Moller M.: Dynamic Event Generation for Runtime Checking using the JDI. In Klaus Havelund and Grigore Rosu (Eds.), Proceedings of the Federated Logic Conference Satellite Workshops, Runtime Verification. Electronic Notes in Theoretical Computer Science 70.4, Copenhagen, July 2002.
8. Brorkens M., and Moller M.: Jassda Trace Assertions, Runtime Checking the Dynamic of Java Programs. In: Ina Schieferdecker, Hartmut Konig and Adam Wolisz (Eds.), Trends in Testing Communicating Systems, International Conference on Testing of Communicating Systems, Berlin, March 2002, pp. 39–48.

9. Capra L., Emmerich W., and Mascolo C.: Reflective middleware solutions for context-aware applications. LNCS 2192, 2001
10. Chen F. and Rosu G.: Java-MOP: A Monitoring Oriented Programming Environment for Java. Proceedings of the 11th International Conference on Tools and Algorithms for the construction and analysis of systems, 2005
11. Clarke L. and Osterweil L.:   Continuous Self-Evaluation for the Self-Improvement of Software. Springer Verlag Lecture Notes in Computer Science #1936, Proceedings of the 1st International Workshop on Self-Adaptive Software (IWSAS 2000), pp 27–29, April 2000, Oxford, England.
12. CRS Case Study: Available from: www.soi.city.ac.uk/~am697/monitoring/case_studies/CRS_Case_Study.html
13. Dardenne A., van Lamsweerde A., and Fickas S.: Goal-Directed Requirements Acquisition. Science of Computer Programming, 20, pp. 3–50, 1993.
14. EC-Assertion: http://www.soi.city.ac.uk/~gespan/EC-assertion.xsd
15. Efstratiou C., Friday A., Davies N., and Cheverst K.: Utilising the event calculus for policy driven adaptation on mobile systems. In Jorge Lobo Bret J. Michael and Naranker Duray, editors, 3rd International Workshop on Policies for Distributed Systems and Networks, pages 13–24, Monterey, Ca., U.S., 2002. IEEE Computer Society.
16. Emerging Technology Toolkit: http://www.alphaworks.ibm.com/tech/ettk
17. Farrell A, Sergot M., Salle M., and Bartolini C.: Using the event calculus for performance monitoring of Service Level Agreements in Utility Computing. In Proc. Workshop on Contract Languages and Architectures (CoALa2004), 8th International IEEE Enterprise Distributed Object Computing Conference, Monterey, September 2004.
18. Feather M. and Fickas S.: Requirements Monitoring in Dynamic Environments. Proceedings of IEEE International Conference on Requirements Engineering, 1995
19. Feather M.S., Fickas S., Van Lamsweerde A., and Ponsard C.: Reconciling System Requirements and Runtime Behaviour. Proc. of 9th Int. Work. on Software Specification & Design, 1998.
20. Finkelstein A. and Savigni A.: A Framework for Requirements Engineering for Context-Aware Services. In Proc. of 1st Int. Workshop From Software Requirements to Architectures (STRAW 01), Toronto, Canada, May 2001.
21. Firesmith D.: Engineering Security Requirements. Journal of Object Technology, 2(1), 53–68, Jan-Feb 2003
22. Kannan S., Kim M., Lee I., Sokolsky O., and Viswanathan M.: Runtime Monitoring and Steering based on Formal Specifications. Workshop on Modeling Software System Structures in a fastly moving scenario, June 2000.
23. Keller A. and Ludwig H.: The WSLA Framework: Specifying and Monitoring Service Level Agreements for Web Services. Technical Report RC22456 (W0205-171), IBM Research Division, T.J. Watson Research Center, May 2002.
24. Kim M., Kannan S., Lee I., Sokolsky O., and Viswanathan M.: Java-MaC: a Runtime Assurance Tool for Java Programs. In Klaus Havelund and Grigore Rosu, editors, Electronic Notes in Theoretical Computer Science, Vol. 55. Elsevier Science Publishers, 2001.
25. Lloyd J.W.: Logic for Learning: Learning Comprehensible Theories from Structured Data. Springer Verlag, ISBN 3-540-42027-4, 2003.
26. Log4j: http://logging.apache.org/log4j/docs/, September 2003

27. Ludwig H., Dan A., and Kearney R.: Cremona: An Architecture and Library for Creation and Monitoring of WS-Agreements. Proceedings of the 2nd International Conference on Service Oriented Computing, November 2004, New York
28. Ludwig H., Keller A., Dan A., King R.P., and Franck R.: Web Service Level Agreement (WSLA) Language Specification, Version 1.0. IBM Corporation (January 2003), http://www.research.ibm.com/wsla
29. Mahbub K. and Spanoudakis G.: Run-time Monitoring of Requirements for Systems Composed of Web-Services: Initial Implementation and Evaluation Experience. 3rd International IEEE Conference on Web Services (ICWS 2005), July 2005
30. OWL-S: http://www.daml.org/services/owl-s/
31. QTP: http://www.soi.city.ac.uk/~am697/QTP_Case_Study.html
32. Robinson W.: Monitoring Software Requirements using Instrumented Code. In Proc. of the Hawaii Int. Conf. on Systems Sciences, 2002.
33. Robinson W.N.: Monitoring Web Service Requirements. Proc. of 12th Int. Conf. on Requirements Engineering, 2003
34. Shanahan M.: The event calculus explained. In Artificial Intelligence Today, 409–430, Springer, 1999
35. Spanoudakis G., Kloukinas C., and Androutsopoulos K.: Towards Security Monitoring Patterns. 22nd Annual ACM Symposium on Applied Computing, Technical Track on Software Verification, March 2007
36. Spanoudakis G. and Mahbub K.: Non Intrusive Monitoring of Service Based Systems. International Journal of Cooperative Information Systems, 15(3): 325–358, 2006

A Graphical Representation of EC-Assertion

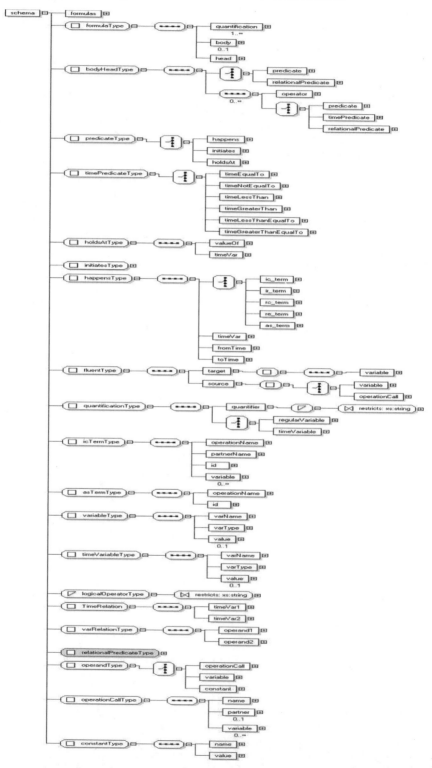

Assumption-Based Composition and Monitoring of Web Services

Marco Pistore and Paolo Traverso

ITC-IRST
Via Sommarive 18, Povo, 38050 Trento, Italy
[pistore,traverso]@itc.it

Abstract. We propose an approach to the automated synthesis and the run-time monitoring of web service compositions. Automated synthesis, given a set of existing component services that are modeled in the BPEL language, and given a composition requirement, generates a new BPEL process that, once deployed, interacts with the components to satisfy the requirement. The composition requirement expresses assumptions under which component services are supposed to participate in the composition, as well as conditions that the composition is expected to guarantee. Run-time monitoring matches the actual behaviors of the service compositions against the assumptions expressed in the composition requirement, and reports violations. We describe the implementation of the proposed approach, which exploits efficient synthesis techniques, and discuss its scalability and practical applicability.

11.1 Introduction

Service composition is one of the key ideas underlying web services and service-oriented applications: composed services perform new functionalities by interacting with component services that are available on the web. The automated synthesis of composed services is one of the key tasks that can significantly support the design and development of service-oriented applications. Given a set of component services and a description of the interaction protocols that one has to follow in order to exploit them (e.g., in BPEL [3]), and given a composition requirement, the problem is to automatically synthesize a composed service that, once deployed, interacts with the components to satisfy the requirements.

Beyond composition requirements and component descriptions, in real life scenarios, key elements of the problem are the so-called *choreographic assumptions*, i.e., assumptions under which the component services are supposed to participate in the composition. Such assumptions may not be necessarily encoded in the descriptions of each component service. For instance, an assumption between an on-line shop and an electronic payment service can represent the agreement that the bank will always accept to process a request for a money transfer, even if the interaction protocol may allow for a refusal of the request from the bank. Similarly, a reasonable agreement may be that it is always possible to cancel an order before paying for it, even if the interface description of the service may allow for a refusal of cancellations even before paying. Together with the description of the interactions with the available components, the choreographic assumptions constitute, therefore, the environment in which the composed service has to operate. As a consequence, the automated synthesis task should take them into account.

Beyond influencing the synthesis at design time, assumptions should also be monitored at run-time. Run-time monitoring should match the actual behaviors of service compositions against the assumptions, and report violations. This is a compelling requirement in service-oriented applications, which are most often developed by composing services that are made available by third parties, and which are autonomously developed and managed. Moreover, monitors are also needed to detect those problems that can emerge only at run-time. This is the case, for instance, of situations that, even if admissible in general at design time, must be promptly revealed when they happen, e.g., the fact that a bank refuses to transfer money to a partner on-line shop, even if this was part of an agreement.

While there have been several works on the automated synthesis of web services, see, e.g., [33, 27, 12, 41, 37], and several works on monitoring web services, see, e.g., [5, 30], much less emphasis has been devoted to the problem of the "assumption-based synthesis and monitoring of web services," i,e., to the problem of automatically generating composed services by possibly taking into account assumptions at design time, which are then monitored at run-time.

In this chapter, we address this problem: given a formal composition requirement, given a set of component service descriptions in BPEL, and given a set of choreographic assumptions expressed in temporal logic, we synthesize automatically an executable BPEL process that, once deployed, satisfies the composition requirement, as well as a set of Java monitors that report at run-time possible assumption violations. The automated generation of the composed BPEL process takes into account the choreographic assumptions during the synthesis, by discarding behaviors that violate them during the search for a solution. We synthesize a composed service that is not supposed to work and to satisfy the requirements in the case some assumptions are violated. A first advantage of this assumption-based synthesis is that the search for a solution may be simpler and scale up to more complex problems than the previous approach, since assumptions can be used to prune the search space (see, e.g., [2]). But, more important, this approach is mandatory in the case the composition only exists under the choreographic assumptions. This means that the assumptions are so crucial that, if they are violated, the composition does not make sense. In these cases, assumption-based synthesis and monitoring is the only viable solution.

The chapter is structured as follows. We start with a motivating example (Sect. 11.2) and with a conceptual architecture for automated composition and monitoring (Sect. 11.3). The next two sections describe our approach to assumption-based synthesis (Sect. 11.4) and monitoring (Sect. 11.5). We conclude with an evaluation of the approach (Sect. 11.6) and an analysis of related works (Sect. 11.7).

11.2 Motivating Example

As motivating example, we consider a virtual travel agency (VTA) that offers a transportation and accommodation service to clients, by interacting with three external services: one for booking flights, another for booking hotel rooms, and a third one for managing the payment (Fig. 11.1). When the agency receives a request from a client for a travel to a given location and period of time, it contacts the flight service. If available flights are found, the flight service returns an offer including the cost. Similarly, the agency contacts the hotel service and asks for a hotel room for the period of permanence in the desired location. If flight and hotel are both available, then the agency prepares and sends to the client an aggregated offer, which includes travel and accommodation, and sends it to the client. If the client decides to accept the offer, then she/he sends payment information (e.g., the credit card number) to the agency, which starts the payment procedure interacting with the payment service. Eventually, the flight and hotel services will receive a confirmation of the payment, and will emit electronic tickets that the agency will forward to the client.

In this chapter, we assume that BPEL [17] is used to describe the behavior of the involved services. BPEL provides an operational description of the (stateful) behavior of web services on top of the service interfaces defined in their WSDL specifications. A BPEL description identifies the partners of a service, its internal variables, and the operations that are triggered upon the invocation of the service by some of the partners. Operations include assigning variables, invoking other services and receiving responses, forking

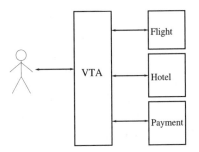

Fig. 11.1. The virtual travel agency example

parallel threads of execution, and non-deterministically picking one amongst different courses of actions. Standard imperative constructs such as if-then-else, case choices, and loops, are also supported.

BPEL can describe a web service at two different levels of abstraction. An *executable BPEL* model describes the actual behavior of a participant in a business process in terms of the internal activities and of the interactions undertaken with the partners. In an *abstract BPEL* model, instead, only the interface behavior of a service is described. That is, only the flow of messages exchanged with the other parties is defined, without revealing internal behaviors.

In this example, flight, hotel, and payment services are the external services. We assume, therefore, that their abstract BPEL specifications are available and can be downloaded from the web. These specifications describe the interaction protocols that the agency is expected to respect when interacting with the external services. In Fig. 11.2 we see the graphical descriptions of the BPEL processes for the flight, the hotel, and the payment service. We also assume that the protocol that the VTA follows in the interactions with the client is given as an abstract BPEL specification, which we also represent in Fig. 11.2. This protocol has to be considered an additional input to the composition, as it defines the interactions with the fourth partner of the VTA, namely its user. Notice that, in Fig. 11.2, transitions whose labels start with a "?" correspond to inputs received by the service, while labels starting with a "!" denote outputs of the service. Labels starting neither with "?" nor with "!" are *internal* actions of the protocol and correspond, for instance, to decisions or other private computations.

When automated web service composition techniques like those described in [41] are applied in this framework, the executable BPEL process of the VTA is generated automatically starting from the abstract BPEL specifications of the component services and from a composition requirement that specifies the goal of the composite process. In our example, the composition requirement specifies that the goal of the agency is to "sell holiday packages," i.e., to find a suitable flight and a suitable hotel for the client, and to manage the payment procedure. Achieving this goal means leading the interaction protocols with flight, hotel, payment service, and client to the successful final states (the states marked with SUCC in Fig. 11.2). However, there are cases in which the goal "sell holiday packages" cannot be achieved by the VTA: it might be that there are no flights or rooms available, the client may not accept the offer, the payment procedure may fail, etc. In all these cases, the VTA should at least guarantee that there are "no pending commitments" at the end of the execution: i.e., the VTA has to avoid the cases where a flight or a room are booked, if the client has not accepted or is not able to pay for them. If one of the interaction protocol fails, then we have to guarantee that all of them terminate in failure states (i.e., final states not marked with SUCC). The composition requirement for the VTA is hence something like "do whatever

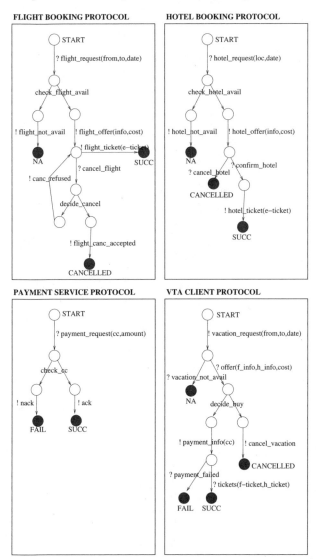

Fig. 11.2. Abstract BPEL protocols

possible to 'sell holiday packages,' but if something goes wrong guarantee that there are 'no pending commitments'."

In Fig. 11.3 we report a possible executable BPEL process that implements the VTA and satisfies the composition requirement just described. One can notice that the BPEL process behaves as an orchestrator that interacts with the flight, the hotel, the payment services, and the user according to the

VTA COMPOSITE SERVICE

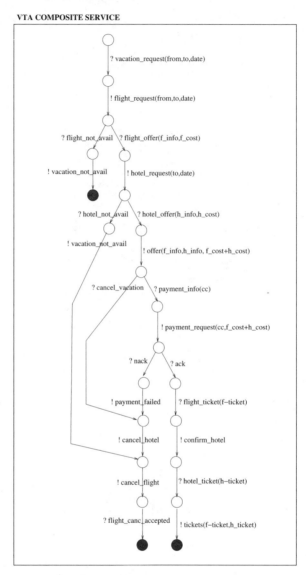

Fig. 11.3. Composite BPEL process for the VTA

protocols in Fig. 11.2, and directs and interleaves these interaction is a suitable way, in order to guarantee the achievement of the composition requirement.

In many cases, it is necessary or convenient to restrict the behaviors of the external services (hotel, flight, payment) with additional assumptions on their behaviors which are not implied by the abstract BPEL specifications. This is the case also for our scenario. Indeed, consider the behavior of the Flight service in case of a cancellation request: the BPEL specification simply specifies that the request can be accepted or refused by the service. However, we may know, for instance from a service level agreement, that the flight cancellation is granted whenever the payment of the requested flight has not yet been done. We remark that the composition reported in Fig. 11.3 is based on this assumption: when a `cancel_flight` is issued by the VTA, the only expected outcome is an approval of the cancellation. More in general, without this assumption, it would not be possible for the VTA to achieve its composition requirement: indeed, if a flight offer has been obtained, but the user is not interested in the package returned by the VTA, then it would be impossible for the VTA to guarantee the possibility of canceling it, as requested by the "avoid pending commitments" requirement.

Besides being used to restrict the possible behaviors of the component services, our framework exploits these assumptions at run-time. *Assumption monitors*, which can be automatically generated from the specification of the assumptions, are executed in parallel with the composed BPEL process so as to check if the assumptions are respected during execution. Indeed, if the flight service violates our assumption, and refuses to cancel a flight even before the payment, the violation has to be detected and reported, since it will prevent the VTA from achieving its goal.

Monitoring is not limited to those assumptions that we use to restrict the valid behaviors at composition time. Indeed, it may be useful to have monitors also for additional assumptions that we did not exploit for generating the composition. Consider, for instance, the assumptions that rooms are guaranteed to be available if the request is done sufficiently in advance, or that flight availability is guaranteed for VIP clients, or also that the payment procedure will always succeed for "gold" credit cards, etc. These assumptions do not need to be exploited to obtain a correct composition. Still, it is important for the VTA to monitor them, since their violation may lead to loose clients.

Finally, an implicit assumption of the VTA on the component processes is that they respect the flow of interactions described in their abstract BPEL specification. This violation can happen, for instance, due to evolutions in the implementations of the external services, or also due to malicious external parties. In our framework, *domain monitors*, which detect violations of the specified protocols in the actual interactions with external services, can be automatically generated from the abstract BPEL specifications.

11.3 The Framework

Figure 11.4 depicts the design-time and run-time environments in our framework.

11.3.1 Design-Time Environment

The *Design-Time Environment* has two main components, a Composer and a Monitor Generator. The *Composer* can be used to automatically generate

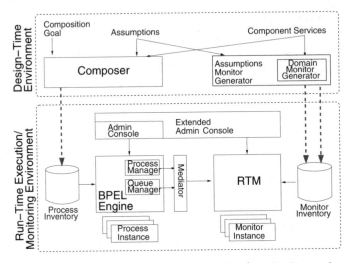

Fig. 11.4. Design-time and run-time execution/monitoring environments

the executable BPEL processes implementing the composed service. It takes in as input the component services and a composition goal. The component services are abstract BPEL specifications that are available on the web, and they can be seen as the environment the composed service has to interact with. The composition goal specifies requirements on the composed service. The composer can also take advantage of assumptions about the behavior of component services, in order to prune the search for a composed service. The composition task performed by the Composer is further analyzed in Sect. 11.4.

The second component of the Design-Time Environment is the *Monitor Generator*, which is composed of a core component, the *Domain Monitor Generator*, and the *Assumption Monitor Generator*, which is built upon the generator of domain monitors. The algorithms run by these modules are described in detail in Sect. 11.5.

11.3.2 Run-Time Environment

The *Run-Time Execution/Monitoring Environment* runs in parallel executable BPEL processes (for instance, the composite services generated at design time) and Java monitors (also possibly generated by the monitor generator). In our approach, monitors observe BPEL process behaviors by intercepting the input/output messages that are received/sent by the processes, and signal some misbehavior or, more in general, some situation or event of interest. In Fig. 11.4, the components on the left-hand side constitute the BPEL process execution environment, while the monitor run-time environment consists of the components on the right-hand side. For the *BPEL process execution environment*, we have chosen a standard engine for executing BPEL processes.

Among the existing BPEL engines, we chose Active BPEL [1] for our experiments, since it is available as open source, and since it implements a modular architecture that is easy to extend. From a high-level point of view, the Active BPEL run-time environment can be seen as composed of four parts. A *Process Inventory* contains all the BPEL processes deployed on the engine. A set of *Process Instances* consists of the instances of BPEL processes that are currently in execution. The *BPEL Engine* is the most complex part of the run-time environment, and consists of different modules (including the Process Manager, the Queue Manager, the Process Logger, and the Alarm Manager), which are responsible for the different aspects of the execution of the BPEL processes. The Process Manager creates and terminates process instances, and the Queue Manager is responsible for dispatching incoming and outgoing messages. The *Admin Console* provides web pages for checking and controlling the status of the engine and of the process instances.

The *Run-Time Monitoring Environment* is composed of four parts (see Fig. 11.4). The *Monitor Inventory* and the *Monitor Instances* are the counterparts of the corresponding components of the BPEL engine: the former contains all the monitor classes deployed in the engine, while the latter is the set of instances of these classes that are currently in execution. Each monitor class is associated to a specific BPEL process, while each monitor instance is associated to a specific process instance. Each monitor class is a Java class that implements the methods described in Fig. 11.5. The *Run-Time Monitor (RTM)* is responsible to support the life-cycle (creation and termination) and the evolution of the monitor instances. The *Mediator* allows the RTM to interact with the Queue Manager and the Process Logger of the BPEL engine and to intercept input/output messages as well as other relevant events such as the creation and termination of process instances. The *Extended Admin Console* is an extension of the Active BPEL Admin Console that presents,

---

- `init()`: init method, executed when an instance of the monitor is created
- `evolve(BpelMsg message)`: handles a message, updating the state of the monitor instance
- `terminate()`: handles the notification of a process termination event
- `isValid()`: returns true if the monitor instance is in a valid state (i.e., no misbehavior has been detected)
- `getErrorString()`: returns an error string if the monitor instance is in an invalid state
- `getProcessName()`: returns the name of the BPEL process associated to the monitor
- `getPropertyName()`: returns the (short) property name of the monitor
- `getPropertyDescription()`: returns the description of the property checked by the monitor

---

Fig. 11.5. Methods of a monitor Java class

along with other information on the BPEL processes, the information on the status of the corresponding monitors.

The monitor life-cycle is influenced by three relevant events: the process instance creation, the input/output of messages, and the termination of the process instance. When the RTM receives a message for the Mediator, it tries to find a match with the already instantiated monitors. If a match is found, the message is dispatched to all the matching monitor instances through method `evolve`. If no match is found, then a new process instance has been created in the BPEL engine, and hence a set of monitor instances specific for that process instance is created by the RTM and initialized through the method `init`. For each message, the Mediator provides also information on the process instance receiving/sending the message, as well as on the BPEL process corresponding to the instance. The information on the BPEL process is used to select the relevant set of monitors to be instantiated for that process. The process termination is captured via a *termination event*, the event is dispatched, through the invocation of method `terminate`, to all the monitor instances associated to the process instance.

11.4 Assumption-Based Composition of Web Services

In this section we describe the theory underlying the assumption-based Composer of Fig. 11.4 exploiting a general framework for the automated composition of web services.

11.4.1 An Automated Composition Framework

The work in [41] (see also [42, 37]) presents a formal framework for the automated composition of web services which is based on planning techniques: component services define the planning domain, composition requirements are formalized as a planning goal, and planning algorithms are used to generate the composite service. The framework of [41] differs from other planning frameworks since it assumes an asynchronous, message-based interaction between the domain (encoding the component services) and the plan (encoding the composite service). We now recall the most relevant features of the framework defined in [41].

The planning domain is modeled as a *state transition system* (STS from now on) which describes dynamic systems that can be in one of their possible *states* (some of which are marked as *initial states*) and can evolve to new states as a result of performing some *actions*. Actions are distinguished in *input actions*, which represent the reception of messages, *output actions*, which represent messages sent to external services, and a special action τ called *internal action*. The action τ is used to represent internal evolutions that are not visible to external services, i.e., the fact that the state of the system can evolve without producing any output, and independently from the reception of inputs. A *transition relation* describes how the state can evolve on the basis of inputs, outputs, or of the internal action τ. Finally, a *labeling function* associates to each state the set of properties $\mathcal{P}rop$ that hold in the state. These properties will be used to define the composition requirements.

Definition 1 *[State transition system (STS)]* A state transition system Σ is a tuple $\langle \mathcal{S}, \mathcal{S}^0, \mathcal{I}, \mathcal{O}, \mathcal{R}, \mathcal{L} \rangle$ where

- $\mathcal{S}$ *is the finite set of states*
- $\mathcal{S}^0 \subseteq \mathcal{S}$ *is the set of initial states*
- $\mathcal{I}$ *is the finite set of input actions*
- $\mathcal{O}$ *is the finite set of output actions*
- $\mathcal{R} \subseteq \mathcal{S} \times (\mathcal{I} \cup \mathcal{O} \cup \{\tau\}) \times \mathcal{S}$ *is the transition relation*
- $\mathcal{L} : \mathcal{S} \rightarrow 2^{\mathcal{P}rop}$ *is the labeling function.*

A state s is said to be final *if there is no transition starting from s (i.e., $\forall a \in (\mathcal{I} \cup \mathcal{O} \cup \{\tau\}), \forall s' \in \mathcal{S}.(s, a, s') \notin \mathcal{R})$.*

The automated synthesis problem consists in generating a state transition system Σ_c that, once connected to Σ, satisfies the composition requirement ρ. We now recall the definition of the state transition system describing the behavior of Σ when connected to Σ_c.

Definition 2 (controlled system) *Let $\Sigma = \langle \mathcal{S}, \mathcal{S}^0, \mathcal{I}, \mathcal{O}, \mathcal{R}, \mathcal{L} \rangle$ and $\Sigma_c = \langle \mathcal{S}_c, \mathcal{S}_c^0, \mathcal{O}, \mathcal{I}, \mathcal{R}_c, \mathcal{L}_\emptyset \rangle$ be two state transition systems, where $\mathcal{L}_\emptyset(s_c) = \emptyset$ for all $s_c \in \mathcal{S}_c$. The STS $\Sigma_c \triangleright \Sigma$, describing the behaviors of system Σ when controlled by Σ_c, is defined as*

$$\Sigma_c \triangleright \Sigma = \langle \mathcal{S}_c \times \mathcal{S}, \mathcal{S}_c^0 \times \mathcal{S}^0, \mathcal{I}, \mathcal{O}, \mathcal{R}_c \triangleright \mathcal{R}, \mathcal{L} \rangle$$

where

- $\langle (s_c, s), \tau, (s_c', s) \rangle \in (\mathcal{R}_c \triangleright \mathcal{R})$ *if* $\langle s_c, \tau, s_c' \rangle \in \mathcal{R}_c$
- $\langle (s_c, s), \tau, (s_c, s') \rangle \in (\mathcal{R}_c \triangleright \mathcal{R})$ *if* $\langle s, \tau, s' \rangle \in \mathcal{R}$
- $\langle (s_c, s), a, (s_c', s') \rangle \in (\mathcal{R}_c \triangleright \mathcal{R})$*, with $a \neq \tau$, if* $\langle s_c, a, s_c' \rangle \in \mathcal{R}_c$ *and* $\langle s, a, s' \rangle \in \mathcal{R}$.

Notice that we require that the inputs of Σ_c coincide with the outputs of Σ and vice versa. Notice also that, although the systems are connected so that the output of one is associated to the input of the other, the resulting transitions in $\mathcal{R}_c \triangleright \mathcal{R}$ are labeled by input/output actions. This allows us to distinguish the transitions that correspond to τ actions of Σ_c or Σ from those deriving from communications between Σ_c and Σ. Finally, notice that we assume that the plan has no labels associated to the states.

In an automated synthesis problem, we need to generate a Σ_c that guarantees the satisfaction of a composition requirement ρ. This is formalized by requiring that the controlled system $\Sigma_c \triangleright \Sigma$ must satisfy the goal ρ, written as $\Sigma_c \triangleright \Sigma \models \rho$. In [41], ρ is formalized using EAGLE, a requirement language which allows to specify conditions of different strengths (like **"try"** and **"do"**), and preferences among different (e.g., primary and secondary) requirements. EaGLE operators are similar to CTL [24] operators, but their semantics, formally defined in [21], takes into account the notion of preference and the handling of failure when subgoals cannot be achieved.

For example, the EaGLE formalization of the composition requirement for the VTA example discussed in Sect. 11.2 is the following:

TryReach

    c.SUCC ∧ f.SUCC ∧ h.SUCC ∧ p.SUCC

Fail DoReach

    (c.NA ∨ c.FAIL ∨ c.CANCELLED) ∧

    (f.NA ∨ f.CANCELLED ∨ f.START) ∧

    (h.NA ∨ h.CANCELLED ∨ h.START) ∧

    (p.FAIL ∨ p.START)

Where c is the client, f the flight, h the hotel, and p the payment services and propositions like c.SUCC correspond to require that the client has reached the state marked with SUCC according to the interaction protocols in Fig. 11.2.[1] The goal is of the form "**TryReach** c **Fail DoReach** d." **TryReach** c requires a service that tries to reach condition c, in our case the condition "sell holiday packages." During the execution of the service, a state may be reached from which it is not possible to reach c, e.g., since the product is not available. When such a state is reached, the requirement **TryReach** c fails and the recovery condition **DoReach** d, in our case "no pending commitments" is considered.

The definition of whether ρ is satisfied, which we omit for lack of space, is defined on top of the executions that $\Sigma_c \triangleright \Sigma$ can perform. Given this, we can characterize formally an automated synthesis problem.

Definition 3 *[Automated Synthesis] Let Σ be a state transition system, and let ρ be an EaGLE formula defining a composition requirement. The automated synthesis problem for Σ and ρ is the problem of finding a state transition system Σ_c such that*

$$\Sigma_c \triangleright \Sigma \models \rho.$$

The work in [41] shows how to adapt to this task the "Planning as Model Checking" approach, which is able to deal with large non-deterministic domains and with requirements expressed in EaGLE. It exploits powerful BDD-based techniques [16] developed for Symbolic Model Checking [17] to efficiently explore domain Σ during the construction of Σ_c.

---

[1] Note that in the "no pending commitments" part of the composition goal we allow the flight, the hotel, and the payment services to "terminate" in the START state. This permits to skip calling some of the services (e.g., the payment service) in case of failures in previous services (e.g., no flight is available).

11.4.2 BPEL Processes and Assumptions as STSs

The domain for the composition task corresponds to the BPEL specifications of the component services *and* to the assumptions that we decide to enforce in the composition and that, as a consequence, restricts the valid behaviors of the BPEL components. We now show that BPEL processes and assumptions can all be mapped to STSs.

In [41], we have defined a translation that associates a state transition system to each component service, starting from its BPEL specification. We omit the formal definition of the translation, which can be found at http://www.astroproject.org.[2] Intuitively, input actions of the STS represent messages received from the component services, output actions are messages sent to the component services, internal actions model assignments and other operations which do not involve communications, and the transition relation models the evolution of the service.

For what concerns the assumptions, we allow the user to specify them in Linear Temporal Logic (LTL [24]).

Definition 4 (LTL) *Let $\mathcal{P}rop$ be a property set and $p \in \mathcal{P}rop$. LTL properties on $\mathcal{P}rop$ are defined as follows:*

$$\phi ::= \text{true} \mid p \mid \neg\phi \mid \phi \wedge \phi \mid \mathbf{X}\,\phi \mid \mathbf{F}\,\phi \mid \mathbf{G}\,\phi \mid \phi_1\;\mathbf{U}\;\phi_2 \mid \phi_1\;\mathbf{W}\;\phi_2.$$

Intuitively, the temporal operators above can be read as follows:

- $\mathbf{X}\,\phi$ means "ϕ will be true in the next state."
- $\mathbf{F}\,\phi$ means "ϕ will be true eventually in the future."
- $\mathbf{G}\,\phi$ means "ϕ will be true for all the future states."
- $\phi_1\mathbf{U}\,\phi_2$ means "ϕ_2 will be eventually true, and ϕ_1 will be true till that moment."
- $\phi_1\mathbf{W}\,\phi_2$ means "ϕ_1 will be true till ϕ_2 becomes true or the history terminates."

In our context, the properties $p \in \mathcal{P}rop$ are atoms of the form s.q, where s is the name of one of the component services and q is either an input/output operation or one of the properties labeling the states of (STS modeling) s.

For example, the assumption that it is possible to cancel a flight until we start the payment process can be formalized as the following LTL formula:

---

[2] For the moment, the translation is restricted to a significant subset of the BPEL languages. More precisely, we support all BPEL *basic* and *structured activities*, like **invoke**, **receive**, **sequence**, **switch**, **while**, **pick**, and **flow**. Moreover, we support restricted forms of **assignments** and **correlations**. The considered subset does not deal at the moment with important BPEL constructs like **scopes**, **fault**, **event**, and **compensation handlers**; while these constructs are often required in *executable* BPEL implementation, we found the considered subset expressive enough for describing the *abstract* BPEL interface of complex services in real applications domains.

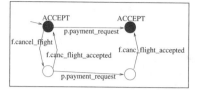

Fig. 11.6. Example of STS corresponding to an assumption

(f.cancel_flight ⇒ F f.canc_flight_accepted)) W p.payment_request.

It says that, until a payment request received by the payment service p (output payment_request in the protocol of Fig. 11.2), if a flight cancellation request is sent to the flight booking service f (message cancel_flight according to the interaction protocol of the flight), then an acknowledgement of the cancellation will eventually be received (message canc_flight_accepted). Alternatively, the same assumption can be written exploiting the labeling of the states of flight and payment service:

G ((f.cancel_flight ∧ p.START) ⇒ F (f.CANCELLED)).

It says that, if a flight cancellation request (message cancel_flight) is received when the payment procedure is still in its initial state (state labeled with START in the protocol of the payment service), then the state where the flight has been cancelled will eventually be reached (state labeled CANCELLED of the interaction protocol of the flight).

Standard techniques [24] can be used to translate the LTL specification of an assumption into an STS.[3] For instance, Fig. 11.6 reports the graphical description of the STS corresponding to property

(f.cancel_flight ⇒ F f.canc_flight_accepted)) W p.payment_request.

We remark that, despite the simplicity of this STS, its role is fundamental in order to guarantee the feasibility of the composition.

11.4.3 Generating the Composed BPEL Process

We are ready to show how we can perform assumption-based composition within the automated composition framework presented in Sect. 11.4.1. Given n component services $W_1, ..., W_n$ and m assumptions $A_1, ..., A_m$ that we want to enforce, we encode each component service W_i as a STS Σ_{W_i} and each assumption A_i as a STS Σ_{A_i}. The planning domain Σ for the automated

---

[3] Notice that we are interested in finite executions of the web services, hence we have to interpret the LTL assumptions on finite words. We can hence avoid the difficulties in modeling acceptance conditions that arise when interpreting LTL on infinite executions/words.

composition problem is the synchronized product of all these STSs. Formally, $\Sigma = \Sigma_{W_1} \parallel ... \parallel \Sigma_{W_n} \parallel \Sigma_{A_1} \parallel ... \parallel \Sigma_{A_m}$.

The planning goal is obtained from the formalization ρ of the composition termination requirements expressed in EAGLE. This formula has to be enriched to capture the fact that we require the conditions expressed in goal ρ to be satisfied only for those executions that satisfy the enforced assumptions, i.e., for those executions that terminate in a state where all the automata Σ_{A_i} are in accepting states (e.g., the states marked as **ACCEPT** in the STS of Fig. 11.6). Consider, for instance, the requirement $\rho = $ **TryReach** c **Fail DoReach** d, and let us assume that property a expresses the condition that all the automata Σ_{A_i} are in accepting states. Then the modified goal is

$$\rho_a = \textbf{TryReach } (a \Rightarrow c) \textbf{ Fail DoReach } (a \Rightarrow d).$$

Given the domain Σ and the planning goal ρ_c, we can apply the approach presented in [41] to generate a controller Σ_c, which is such that $\Sigma_c \triangleright \Sigma \models \rho_a$. Once the state transition system Σ_c has been generated, it is translated into the executable BPEL implementation of the composite service. This translation is conceptually simple, but particular care has been put in its implementation (see **http://www.astroproject.org**) in order to guarantee that the generated BPEL is of good quality, e.g., it is emitted as a structured program that can be inspected and modified if needed.

11.5 Automatic Generation of Monitors

In this section we describe how monitors can be automatically generated from the BPEL description of the component services and from the assumptions specifying the properties to be monitored. As discussed in Sect. 11.2, we distinguish two kinds of monitors: *domain monitors*, which are responsible to check whether the component services respect the protocols described in their abstract BPEL specification, and *assumption monitors*, which check whether the component services satisfy additional assumptions on their behavior.

11.5.1 Domain Monitors

Monitors can only observe messages that are exchanged among processes. As a consequence, they cannot know exactly the internal state reached by the evolution of a monitored external service. Non-observable behaviors of a service (such as assign activities occurring in its abstract BPEL) are modeled by τ-transitions, i.e., transitions from state to state that do not have any associated input/output. From the point of view of the monitor, this kind of evolutions of external services cannot be observed, and states involved in such transitions are indistinguishable. Such sets of states are called *belief*

procedure build-mon()
   $\mathcal{MS} = \mathcal{MT} = \mathcal{MF} = \emptyset$
   $ms_0 = \{\tau\text{-closure}(s_0) : s_0 \in \mathcal{S}_0\}$
   build-mon-aux(ms_0)

procedure build-mon-aux(B:Belief)
   if $B \notin \mathcal{MS}$ **then**
      $\mathcal{MS} = \mathcal{MS} \cup \{B\}$
      if $\exists s \in B.\ s$ is final **then**
         $\mathcal{MF} = \mathcal{MF} \cup \{B\}$
      end if
      for all $m \in (\mathcal{I} \cup \mathcal{O})$ **do**
         $B' = Evolve(B, m)$
         if $B' \neq \emptyset$ **then**
            build-mon-aux(B')
            $\mathcal{MT} = \mathcal{MT} \cup \{< B, m, B' >\}$
         end if
      end for
   end if

Fig. 11.7. The domain monitor generation algorithm

states, or simply *beliefs* [15]. We denote with τ-closure(s) the set of the states reachable from s through a sequence of τ-transitions. The evolution of an external service, as perceived by a monitor, is modeled by the evolution from belief states to belief states.

Definition 5 (belief evolution) *Let $B \subseteq \mathcal{S}$ be a belief on some STS $\Sigma = \langle \mathcal{S}, \mathcal{S}^0, \mathcal{I}, \mathcal{O}, \mathcal{R}, \mathcal{L} \rangle$. We define the evolution of B on message $m \in (\mathcal{I} \cup \mathcal{O})$ as the belief $Evolve(B, m)$, where*

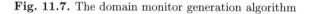

$$Evolve(B, m) = \{s' : \exists s \in B. \exists s'' \in \mathcal{S}. \langle s, m, s'' \rangle \in \mathcal{R} \wedge s' \in \tau\text{-}closure(s'')\}.$$

The generation of a domain monitor for an external abstract BPEL process is based on the idea of beliefs and belief evolutions. The domain monitor generation algorithm (Fig. 11.7) incrementally generates the set $\mathcal{MS}$ of beliefs starting from the initial belief ms_0, by grouping together indistinguishable states of the STS. The beliefs in $\mathcal{MS}$ are linked together with (non τ) transitions $\mathcal{MT} \subseteq \mathcal{MS} \times (\mathcal{I} \cup \mathcal{O}) \times \mathcal{MS}$, as described by function $Evolve$. Beliefs that contain at least one state that is final for the STS are considered possible final states also for the domain monitor, and are stored in $\mathcal{MF}$.

Once the algorithm in Fig. 11.7 has been executed, the Java code implementing the domain monitor can be easily generated. A skeleton of this Java code, parametric with respect to the set of beliefs $\mathcal{MS}$, initial and final beliefs ms_0 and $\mathcal{MF}$, and the belief transitions $\mathcal{MT}$, is reported in Fig. 11.8.

In the Java code, the belief states in $\mathcal{MS}$ are used to trace the current status of the evolution of the monitored BPEL process, using ms_0 as initial state and the transitions in $\mathcal{MT}$ to let the status of the monitor evolve whenever a message is received. The final beliefs $\mathcal{MF}$ are exploited when a termination event is received: indeed, if the process instance terminates and the monitor is a belief that is not final, then a premature termination of the process instance has occurred.

We remark that one can interpret the algorithm in Fig. 11.7 as a transformation of the STS in input, which is non-deterministic and contains τ transitions, into a new STS that is deterministic and is fully observable (i.e., that does not contain τ transitions). Actually, the algorithm is an adaptation of the standard power-set construction for transforming non-deterministic finite automata into deterministic ones.

11.5.2 Assumption Monitors

The algorithm for the generation of assumption monitors takes as input the (STSs corresponding to the) abstract BPEL processes of the external services plus an assumption to be monitored. As already discussed in Sect. 11.4.2, we express assumptions in LTL [24], using as propositional atoms the input/output messages of the component services as well as the properties labeling the states of the STSs modeling these services.

To build an assumption monitor, the corresponding LTL formula is mapped onto an STS, which is then emitted as Java code.

The evolution of the assumption monitor depends on the input/output messages received by the composite services, which are directly observable by the monitor. However, it also depends on the evolution of the truth values of those basic propositions labeling the states of the components STSs which appear in the LTL formula. These truth values are computed by tracing the evolution of the beliefs of the component services relevant to the formula, similarly to what is described in Fig. 11.8 for the domain monitor. However, it is possible in this case to simplify the "domain" monitor, by pruning out parts of the protocol that are not relevant to tracing the evolution of the basic propositions which appear in the formula. This prune is obtained by applying a reduction algorithm inspired by the classical minimization algorithm for finite state automata (Fig. 11.9). This algorithm builds a partition Π of the belief states of the domain monitor, so that beliefs in the same class are considered equivalent for monitoring the basic propositions $P_1, \ldots, P_n$ we are interested in. The initial partition consists of different classes corresponding to different truth values of the basic propositions. This partition is then iteratively refined by splitting a class into two parts, until a fixed point is reached. The splitting of class C into the two classes $\mathrm{split}(C, m, C')$ and $C \setminus \mathrm{split}(C, m, C')$ is performed whenever there are some beliefs in C from which class C' is reached performing message m, while for other beliefs in C a class different from C' is reached performing x (see procedures "split" and "splittable" in Fig. 11.9). When a stable partition is reached, the reduced monitor is obtained by merging beliefs in the same class of the partition.

```
public class Monitor implements IMonitor {
    private enum MS { ... } // monitor states
    private MS _bs;    // current monitor state
    private boolean is_valid = true;
    public void init() { _bs = ms0; }
    public boolean isValid() {
        return is_valid;
    }
    private boolean isFinal() {
        return (_bs in MF);
    }
    public void terminate()
    {
        is_valid= is_valid && isFinal() ;
    }
    public String getErrorString()
    {
        if(!isValid()){
            return "Protocol violation";
        } else {
            return "No error";
        }
    }
    public void evolve(BpelMsg msg)
    {
        if (is_valid){
            if (exists <_bs,msg,next> in MT){
                _bs = next;
            } else {
                is_valid = false;
            }
        }
    }
    public Monitor() { init(); }
    public String getProcessName() { ... }
    public String getPropertyName() { ... }
    public String getPropertyDescription() { ... }
}
```

Fig. 11.8. Skeleton of the domain monitor

procedure reduce-monitor($P_1, \ldots, P_n$)
  /* Building the initial partition */
  for all $PS \subseteq \{P_1, \ldots, P_n\}$ **do**
    $C = \{B \in \mathcal{MS} : \forall i = 1, \ldots, n. \ (B \models P_i \ \Leftrightarrow \ P_i \in PS)\}$
    if $C \neq \emptyset$ **then** $\Pi = \Pi \cup \{C\}$ **end if**
  end for
  /* Refining the partition */
  while $\exists C, C' \in \Pi. \ C \neq C' \wedge \exists m \in (\mathcal{I} \cup \mathcal{O}).$ splittable(C, m, C') **do**
    $\Pi = \Pi \smallsetminus \{C\} \cup \{\text{split}(C, m, C'), C \smallsetminus \text{split}(C, m, C')\}$
  end while
  return Π

procedure split(C, m, C')
  return $\{B \in C : \exists B' \in C'. \ < B, m, B' > \in \mathcal{MT}\}$

procedure splittable(C, m, C')
  return $\emptyset \neq \text{split}(C, m, C') \neq C$

Fig. 11.9. The assumption monitor reduction algorithm

11.6 Experimental Evaluation

The performance of the automated composition task have been tested experimentally, see, e.g., [41, 37, 42] in the case without assumptions. We have also used the automated composition techniques on some real applications in the field of e-government, telcos, and on-line banking. The experiments and the applications have shown the feasibility and the scalability of the approach. We have shown that the automated composition task takes a rather low amount of time, and it is surely much faster than manual development of executable BPEL composite processes. Moreover, the automatically generated BPEL is of good quality. In some cases, we have asked experienced programmers to develop manually the BPEL processes and we have compared the automatically generated and the hand-written solutions. We have discovered that the solutions often implement the same strategy and have a similar structure. The main differences are mainly due to possible different styles of programming, and the automatically generated code is reasonable and rather easy to read and understand.

In this chapter, we report the performance of the automated construction of monitors, as well as the overhead caused by the execution of monitors at run-time. All experiments have been run on a 3 GHz Pentium 4 PC machine, equipped with 1 GB memory, and running a Linux 2.6.7 operating system.

In order to test the performance of the monitor generation, we have performed two sets of experiments. In the first set, we test the automatic generation of domain monitors w.r.t. the complexity of the planning domain. We report the results of the automatic generation w.r.t. the number of activities of an abstract BPEL process in input to the monitor generation (Fig. 11.10). The input BPEL is a generalized version of the hotel service which can perform different kinds of reservations one after the other, thus increasing its number of activities. We start the experiments from six activities, corresponding to the

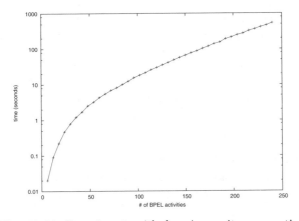

Fig. 11.10. Experiments with domain monitor generation

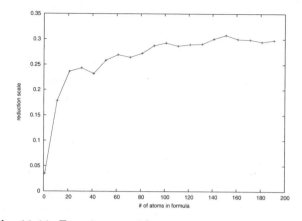

Fig. 11.11. Experiments with assumption monitor reduction

activities of a very simple hotel service, and we scale up to 240, corresponding to a service dealing with about 40 different kinds of reservations. On the vertical axis, we report the monitor generation time in seconds. As expected, the time for monitor construction increases regularly with the number of activities. The monitor generation however manages to deal with rather complex BPEL specifications in a rather short time. The case of 100 activities takes 10 seconds, and we manage to automatically generate monitors for BPEL specifications with about 250 activities in 1000 seconds. In our example, BPEL with 100 activities generate a monitor with more than 300 beliefs, while 250 activities correspond to about 1000 beliefs.

In Fig. 11.11 we report the results of our second set of experiments. Given a service, we test the monitor reduction algorithm performance. In the horizontal axis, we have the number of propositions in a set of randomly generated assumption formulas of increasing complexity. The number of atoms in the formula is indeed the parameter that can affect monitor reduction. In the vertical axis, we report the average gain ratio in number of beliefs obtained by performing the monitor reduction (a value of 0.25 means that the size of the reduced automaton is 25% of the original). The reduction is significant. Notice also that, as the number of atomic propositions in the formula grows, the gain ratio stabilizes somewhere around 0.30. This corresponds to the fact that about 70% of the states in the monitor are useful only for protocol monitoring, but do not give any information for the monitoring of the specific formula.

Figure 11.12 reports instead an experimental evaluation of the overhead that can be caused by executing monitors in parallel to BPEL processes. We measure the overhead at increasing number of monitors that check at run-time a process: the number of monitors per process is reported on the horizontal axis. The overhead is the time to run the processes without any monitor divided by the time to run the processes with their monitors. Fig. 11.12 reports

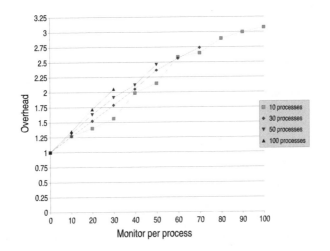

Fig. 11.12. Experiments with monitor generation

four curves that measure the overhead with a different number of process instances: 10, 30, 50, and 100. Notice that the overhead, even for a very high number of monitors per process, is acceptable, and the decrease in performances is not high. Consider the case of 10 process instances. We have 25% overhead with 10 monitors for each instance. The execution with 40 running monitors per process instances takes just twice the time required for running processes without monitors. It is about three times with 100 monitors per process instances (for a total of 1000 monitors running on the run-time environment). Moreover, the overhead does not increase significantly by increasing the number of process instances. In the case of more than 10 process instances, the fact that results are not reported after a given number of monitors is due to the fact that, in the setting we used for the experiments, the memory is exhausted if more than 3000 monitor instances are running at the same time. We are working to a more efficient implementation of the run-time monitoring environment that solves this problem.

Overall, the experiments show that monitor generation can be done efficiently also for complex component services and properties. Moreover, they show that run-time checking does not reduce significantly performances, and that this fact is independent of the load of the BPEL execution engine.

In conclusion, it turns out that both automated composition and run-time monotoring manage to deal in practice with cases of a certain complexity, have the potentiality to scale up to real applications, and can reduce significantly the effort in the development process. We leave for the future an extensive user evaluation dedicated to test the acceptance of the technology from the point of view of the developers.

11.7 Conclusions and Related Work

As far as we know, the contribution described in this chapter presents several elements of novelty. The work provides a uniform framework that integrates the automatic generation of composed BPEL processes with the automated generation of monitors. Moreover, the approaches to both composition and monitoring present elements of novelty by themselves, as discussed in the next two subsections.

11.7.1 Automated Composition of Web Services

In this chapter, we address the problem of automated composition in a *mediator-based architecture* where, given a set of component services (defined in our case as abstract BPEL processes), and a composition requirement, we synthesize one new web service that acts as a mediator and implements the composition by interacting with the component services. A different problem is that of the automated composition in a *peer-to-peer architecture*, where, given n component services and a composition requirement, the task is to generate n distributed new executable BPEL processes, one for each component, that interact with their own component and with the other new BPEL processes that are generated. The extension of our approach to a peer-to-peer automated composition is under study and development.

As far as we know, no other approaches provide the capability of taking into account assumptions in the automated composition of web services. In the following, we consider other approaches that have some relations with our underlying technique for automated composition without assumptions.

Automata-Based Approaches

The approach presented in this chapter is based on the idea that published abstract BPEL processes and composed executable BPEL processes can be given semantics and can be translated to state transition systems.

In [9, 7, 8, 10], the authors describe web services in terms of their interactions, e.g., with state machines. They do not provide an automated composition technique like the one described in this chapter.

In [27], a formal framework is defined for composing e-services from behavioral descriptions given in terms of automata. This approach considers a problem that is fundamentally different from ours, since the e-composition problem is seen as the problem of coordinating the executions of a given set of available services, and not as the problem of generating a new composite web service that interacts with the available ones. Solutions to the former problem can be used to deduce restrictions on an existing (composition automaton representing the) composed service. We generate (the automaton corresponding to) the BPEL composed service, thus addressing directly the problem of reducing time, effort, and errors in the development of composite web services.

In [11, 12], decision procedures for satisfiability are used to address the problem of coordinating component services that are described as finite state machines. The model used in [11, 12] is based on a finite alphabet of activity names, and transitions labeled with activity names specify the process flow of component services, while input and output messages are not modeled. In the initial works, the model is limited to deterministic state transition systems, while in [12], the framework is extended to non-deterministic finite state transition systems, corresponding to a "devilish" form of non-determinism. In this setting, the so-called "realizability" problem, i.e., the problem of determining the existence of a composition, can be solved as a satisfiability problem in propositional dynamic logic. The work studies the complexity of this reduction. Similarly to the work in [27], in these works the e-service composition problem is reduced to selecting among the activities that the component services should perform, a problem that is fundamentally different from the one addressed in this chapter, both in a mediator-based and in a peer-to-peer architecture.

More in general, our work shares some ideas with work on the automata-based synthesis of controllers (see, e.g., [43, 50]). Indeed, the composite service can be seen as a module that controls an environment which consists of the component services. However, the work on the synthesis of controllers is based on rather different technical assumptions on the interaction with the environment (BPEL interactions are asynchronous), and on a different language for expressing requirements, which cannot distinguish among primary and secondary requirements. Finally, this work has never been extended or applied to deal with the problem of the synthesis of web services, and in particular of BPEL processes.

Semantic Web Services

The semantic web community has used automated planning techniques to address the problem of the automated discovery and composition of semantic web services, e.g., based on OWL-S [19] or WSMO [26] descriptions of input/outputs and of preconditions/postconditions (see, e.g., [33, 32]). Two general remarks are in order. First, while here we do not address the problem of discovery (we assume the n component services are given), we tackle a form of automated composition that is more complex than the one considered by the semantic community, where usually services are atomic and compositions are simply sequences of service invocations. In our problem, services do not correspond to actions in the planning domain. Second, while here we do not address the problem of the automated composition of web services with semantic annotations, the approach can be extended to semantic web services along the lines of the work presented in [49, 38]. In [40], semantic annotations are kept separated from process descriptions, thus allowing for a practical and incremental approach to the use of semantics.

There is a large amount of literature addressing the problem of automated composition of semantic web services. However, most of the approaches address composition at the functional level (see, e.g. [35, 20]), and much less emphasis has been devoted to the problem of process-level composition. In [33], web service composition is achieved with user defined re-usable, customizable, high-level procedures expressed in Golog. The approach is orthogonal to ours: Golog programs can express programming control constructs for the generic composition of web service, while we automatically generate plans that encode web service composition through programming control constructs. In [32], Golog programs are used to encode complex actions that can represent DAML-S process models. However, the planning problem is reduced to classical planning and sequential plans are generated for reachability goals. In [34], the authors propose an approach to the simulation, verification, and automated composition of web services based on a translation of DAML-S to situation calculus and Petri Nets, so that it is possible to reason about, analyze, prove properties of, and automatically compose web services. However, the automated composition is again limited to sequential composition of atomic services for reachability goals, and does not consider the general case of possible interleavings among processes and of extended business goals. Moreover, Petri Nets are a rather expressive formalism, but algorithms that analyze them have less chances to scale up to complex problems compared to symbolic model-checking techniques.

The work in [31] is close in spirit to the general objective of [49, 38, 40] to bridge the gap between the semantic web framework and the process modeling and execution languages proposed by industrial coalitions. However, [31] focuses on a different problem, i.e., that of extending BPEL with semantic web technology to facilitate web service interoperation, while the problem of automated composition is not addressed.

Planning for Web Services

Different automated planning techniques have been proposed to tackle the problem of service composition, see, e.g., [51, 22, 47]. However, none of these can deal with the problem that we address in this chapter, where the planning domain is non-deterministic, partially observable, and asynchronous, and goals are not limited to reachability conditions.

Other planning techniques have been applied to related but somehow orthogonal problems in the field of web services. The interactive composition of information-gathering services has been tackled in [48] by using CSP techniques. In [28] an interleaved approach of planning and execution is used; planning techniques are exploited to provide viable plans for the execution of the composition, given a specific query of the user; if these plans turn out to violate some user constraints at run-time, then a re-planning task is started. Works in the field of Data and Computational Grids are more and more moving toward the problem of composing complex workflows by means of planning and scheduling techniques [14].

Planning for the automated discovery and composition of semantic web services, e.g., based on OWL-S, is used in [33, 32, 34]. These works do not take into account behavioral descriptions of web service, like our approach does with BPEL.

Our work is based on the idea of and extends the technique called "planning via symbolic model checking" [18, 13, 21, 2, 39], a framework that differentiates from classical planning techniques since it can deal with planning in non-deterministic domains, with partial observability, and with goals that can express requirements with temporal and preference conditions. A detailed discussion on how the planning via symbolic model checking approach must be extended to deal with asynchronous domains that are constructed from BPEL processes can be found in [41]. In [37], the approach is extended to deal with large and possibly infinite ranges of data values that are exchanged among services.

11.7.2 Run-Time Monitoring of Web Services

Run-time monitoring has been extensively studied in different areas of computer science, such as distributed systems, requirement engineering, programming languages, and aspect-oriented development, see, e.g., [23, 25, 36, 46]. There have been several proposals that deal with different aspects of the monitoring of web services and distributed business processes, see, e.g., [45, 44, 4, 5, 29, 30]. A different but related topic is that of monitoring service level agreements (SLAs), i.e., contracts on services between parties that are signed to guarantee some quality of service, satisfy expectations, control costs, and resources. Monitoring SLAs means monitoring their compliance and reacting properly if compliance is not satisfied. An extension of our framework to the monitoring of SLAs is in our plans for future work.

Considering the problem of monitoring BPEL processes, an obvious alternative to our approach would be to code manually monitors in BPEL. The developer should embed special-purpose controls in the BPEL process implementing the business logic. However, this approach has several drawbacks. It does not allow for a clear separation of the business logic from the monitor, it does not allow for implementing monitors that capture misbehaviors caused by BPEL execution engines, and finally but perhaps more importantly, this task is time-consuming, error prone, requires programming effort, and does not allow for an independent maintenance of the monitor functionality w.r.t. the application layer. Similar problems exist in different frameworks based on BPEL, see, e.g., BPELJ [6]. BPELJ allows the programmer to embed monitors as Java code into BPEL processes.

The works closest to ours are those described in [4, 5] and in [29, 30]. We refer to them as *assertion-based monitoring* and *requirement-based monitoring*.

Assertion-Based monitoring

In [4], monitors are specified as assertions that annotate the BPEL code. Assertions can be specified either in the C# programming language or as pre- or post-conditions expressed in the CLIX constraint language. Annotated BPEL processes are then automatically translated to "monitored processes," i.e., BPEL processes that interleave the business processes with the monitor functionalities. This approach allows for monitoring time-outs, runtime errors, as well as functional properties.

In [5], Baresi and Guinea extend the work presented in [4] with the ability to perform "dynamic monitoring," i.e., the ability to specify monitoring rules that are dynamically selected at run-time, thus providing a capability to dynamically activate/deactivate monitors, as well as to dynamically set the degree of monitoring at run-time. Monitoring rules abstract web services into UML classes that are used to specify constraints on the execution of BPEL processes. In [5], assertions are specified in WS-COL (Web Service Constraint Language), a special purpose language that extends JML (Java Modeling Language) with constructs to gather data from external sources. Monitoring rules are defined with parameters that specify the degree of monitoring that has to be performed at run-time. The user can instantiate dynamically these parameters at run-time, changing in this way the amount of monitoring that is performed.

On the one hand, the approach described in [4, 5] provides some advantages w.r.t. ours. First, monitors are themselves services implemented in BPEL. As a consequence, they can run on standard BPEL engines without requiring any modification. A further challenge could also be the possibility to apply composition techniques developed for the BPEL business logic to the monitoring task. Second, annotations of BPEL processes with assertions constitute an easy and intuitive way to specify monitor tasks. Finally, the approach is extend to dynamic monitoring, a feature that is not provided in our framework.

On the other hand, we allow for the monitoring of properties that depend on the whole history of the execution path. These kinds of monitors would be hard to express as assertions. Moreover, we allow for a clearer separation of the business logic from the monitoring task than in [4, 5], since we generate an executable monitor that is fully distinguished from the executable BPEL that runs the business logic. Finally, our monitors can capture misbehaviors generated by the internal mechanisms of the BPEL execution engine. For instance, since there is no way to guarantee that a message is sent to a process instance only when the instance is ready to consume it, in BPEL, messages can be consumed in a different order from how they are received: indeed a process may receive a message that it is not able to accept at the moment, which can be followed by another message that can instead be consumed. The first message can be consumed later on by the process, or may never be consumed. This phenomenon, that we call *message overpass*, cannot be captured by monitors based on assertions that annotate the BPEL code.

Requirement-Based monitoring

In the work described in [29, 30], Mahbub and Spanoudakis share with us the idea to have a monitor that is clearly separated from the BPEL processes. Another similarity is that the framework allows for specifying requirements that represent either behavioral properties or assumptions to be monitored.

The framework allows for extracting automatically the behavioral properties from the abstract BPEL specification of component services. Requirements to be monitored are expressed in event-calculus, and the specified events are observed at run-time and stored in a database. An algorithm based on integrity constraint checking is then used to analyze the database and perform a run-time checking of the specified behavioral properties and assumptions.

The technical setting of this work is very different from ours. It is based on event calculus rather than linear temporal logic and on constraint checking rather than model checking.

References

1. ActiveBPEL. The Open Source BPEL Engine - http://www.activebpel.org.
2. A. Albore and P. Bertoli. Generating Safe Assumption-Based Plans for Partially Observable, Nondeterministic Domains. In *Proc. AAAI*, 2004.
3. T. Andrews, F. Curbera, H. Dolakia, J. Goland, J. Klein, F. Leymann, K. Liu, D. Roller, D. Smith, S. Thatte, I. Trickovic, and S. Weeravarana. Business Process Execution Language for Web Services (version 1.1), 2003.
4. L. Baresi, C. Ghezzi, and S. Guinea. Smart Monitors for Composed Services. In *Proc. of Int. Conf. on Service-Oriented Computing*, 2004.
5. L. Baresi and S. Guinea. Towards dynamic monitoring of WS-BPEL Processes. In *Proc. of Int. Conf. on Service-Oriented Computing*, 2005.
6. BEA and IBM. BPELJ: BPEL for Java - http://www-106.ibm.com/developerworks /webservices/library/ws-bpel.
7. B. Benatallah, F. Casati, H. Skogsrud, and F. Toumani. Abstracting and Enforcing Web Service Protocols. *Int. Journal of Cooperative Information Systems*, 2004.
8. B. Benatallah, F. Casati, and F. Toumani. Analysis and Management of Web Services Protocols. In *ER*, 2004.
9. B. Benatallah, F. Casati, and F. Toumani. Representing, analysing and managing web service protocols. *Data Knowl. Eng.*, 58(3), 2006.
10. B. Benatallah, F. Casati, F. Toumani, and R. Hamadi. Conceptual Modeling of Web Service Conversations. In *CAiSE*, 2003.
11. D. Berardi, D. Calvanese, G. De Giacomo, M. Lenzerini, and M. Mecella. Automatic composition of E-Services that export their behaviour. In *Proc. ICSOC'03*, 2003.
12. D. Berardi, D. Calvanese, G. De Giacomo, and M. Mecella. Composition of Services with Nondeterministic Behaviours. In B. Benatallah, F. Casati, and P. Traverso, editors, *Proceedings of the Third International Conference on Service-Oriented Computing (ICSOC'05). Lecture Notes in Computer Science LNCS 3826*. Springer, 2005.

13. P. Bertoli, A. Cimatti, M. Roveri, and P. Traverso. Planning in Nondeterministic Domains under Partial Observability via Symbolic Model Checking. In *Proc. IJCAI'01*, 2001.
14. Jim Blythe, Ewa Deelman, and Yolanda Gil. Planning for Workflow Construction and Maintenance on the Grid. In *Proceedings of ICAPS'03 Workshop on Planning for Web Services*, Trento, Italy, June 2003.
15. B. Bonet and H. Geffner. Planning with Incomplete Information as Heuristic Search in Belief Space. In *Proc. AIPS'00*, 2000.
16. R. E. Bryant. Symbolic boolean manipulation with ordered binary-decision diagrams. *ACM Computing Survey*, 24(3):293–318, 1992.
17. A. Cimatti, E. M. Clarke, E. Giunchiglia, F. Giunchiglia, M. Pistore, M. Roveri, R. Sebastiani, and A. Tacchella. NuSMV 2: An OpenSource Tool for Symbolic Model Checking. In *CAV*, 2002.
18. A. Cimatti, M. Pistore, M. Roveri, and P. Traverso. Weak, Strong, and Strong Cyclic Planning via Symbolic Model Checking. *Artificial Intelligence*, 147(1-2):35–84, 2003.
19. The OWL Services Coalition. OWL-S: Semantic Markup for Web Services. In *Technical White paper (OWL-S version 1.0)*, 2003.
20. I. Constantinescu, B. Faltings, and W. Binder. Typed Based Service Composition. In *Proc. WWW2004*, 2004.
21. U. Dal Lago, M. Pistore, and P. Traverso. Planning with a Language for Extended Goals. In *Proc. AAAI'02*, 2002.
22. D. Mc Dermott. The Planning Domain Definition Language Manual. Technical Report 1165, Yale Computer Science University, 1998. CVC Report 98-003.
23. A. Dingwall-Smith and A. Finkelstein. From Requirements to Monitors by way of Aspects. In *Int. Conf. on Aspect-Oriented Software Development*, 2002.
24. E. A. Emerson. Temporal and modal logic. In J. van Leeuwen, editor, *Handbook of Theoretical Computer Science, Volume B: Formal Models and Semantics*. Elsevier, 1990.
25. M. Feather and S. Fickas. Requirements Monitoring in Dynamic Environment. In *Int. Conf. on Requirements Engineering*, 1995.
26. The Web Service Modeling Framework. SDK WSMO working group - http://www.wsmo.org/.
27. R. Hull, M. Benedikt, V. Christophides, and J. Su. E-Services: A Look Behind the Curtain. In *Proc. PODS'03*, 2003.
28. A. Lazovik, M. Aiello, and Papazoglou M. Planning and Monitoring the Execution of Web Service Requests. In *Proc. of the 1st International Conference on Service-Oriented Computing (ICSOC'03)*, 2003.
29. K. Mahbub and G. Spanoudakis. A Framework for Requirements Monitoring of Service Based Systems. In *Int. Conf. on Service-Oriented Computing (ICSOC)*, 2004.
30. K. Mahbub and G. Spanoudakis. Run-Time Monitoring of Requirements for Systems Composed of Web-Services: Initial Implementation and Evaluation Experience. In *Int. Conf. on Web Services (ICWS)*, 2005.
31. D. Mandell and S. McIlraith. Adapting BPEL4WS for the Semantic Web: The Bottom-Up Approach to Web Service Interoperation. In *Proc. of 2nd International Semantic Web Conference (ISWC03)*, 2003.
32. S. McIlraith and R. Fadel. Planning with Complex Actions. In *Proc. NMR'02*, 2002.

33. S. McIlraith and S. Son. Adapting Golog for composition of semantic web Services. In *Proc. KR'02*, 2002.
34. S. Narayanan and S. McIlraith. Simulation, Verification and Automated Composition of Web Services. In *Proc. WWW2002*, 2002.
35. M. Paolucci, K. Sycara, and T. Kawamura. Delivering Semantic Web Services. In *Proc. WWW2003*, 2002.
36. D.K. Peters. Deriving Real-Time Monitors for System Requirements Documentation. In *Int. Symp. on Requirements Engineering - Doctoral Symposium*, 1997.
37. M. Pistore, A. Marconi, P. Bertoli, and P. Traverso. Automated Composition of Web Services by Planning at the Knowledge Level. In *Proc. Int. Joint Conf. on Artificial Intelligence (IJCAI)*, 2005.
38. M. Pistore, P. Roberti, and P. Traverso. Process-level compositions of executable web services: on-the-fly versus once-for-all compositions. In *Proc. ESWC'05*, 2005.
39. M. Pistore, D. Shaparau, and P. Traverso. Contingent Planning with Goal Preferences. In *Proc. AAAI'06*, 2006.
40. M. Pistore, L. Spalazzi, and P. Traverso. A Minimalist Approach to Semantic Annotations for Web Processes Compositions. In *Proc. ESWC'06*, 2006.
41. M. Pistore, P. Traverso, and P. Bertoli. Automated Composition of Web Services by Planning in Asynchronous Domains. In *Proc. Int. Conf. on Automated Planning and Scheduling (ICAPS)*, 2005.
42. M. Pistore, P. Traverso, P. Bertoli, and A. Marconi. Automated Synthesis of Composite BPEL4WS Web Services. In *IEEE Int. Conf. on Web Services (ICWS)*, 2005.
43. A. Pnueli and R. Rosner. On the synthesis of an asynchronous reactive module. In *Proc. ICALP'89*, 1989.
44. W. Robinson. Monitoring Web Service Requirements. In *IEEE Int. Conference on Requirement Engineering*, 2003.
45. A. Sahai, V. Machiraju, A. van Morsel, and F. Casati. Automated SLA Monitoring for Web Services. In *Int. Workshop on Distributed Systems: Operations and Management*, 2002.
46. K. Sen, A. Vardhan, G. Agha, and G. Rosu. Efficient Decentralized Monitoring of Safety in Distributed Systems. In *Proc. of ICSE*, 2004.
47. M. Sheshagiri, M. desJardins, and T. Finin. A Planner for Composing Services Described in DAML-S. In *Proc. AAMAS'03*, 2003.
48. Snehal Thakkar, Craig Knoblock, and Jose Luis Ambite. A View Integration Approach to Dynamic Composition of Web Services. In *Proceedings of ICAPS'03 Workshop on Planning for Web Services*, Trento, Italy, June 2003.
49. P. Traverso and M. Pistore. Automated Composition of Semantic Web Services into Executable Processes. In *Proc. Int. Semantic Web Conference (ISWC)*, 2004.
50. M. Y. Vardi. An automata-theoretic approach to fair realizability and synthesis. In *Proc. CAV'95*, 1995.
51. D. Wu, B. Parsia, E. Sirin, J. Hendler, and D. Nau. Automating DAML-S Web Services Composition using SHOP2. In *Proc. ISWC'03*, 2003.

Part IV

Reliability, Security, and Trust

Reliability Modeling and Analysis of Service-Oriented Architectures

Vittorio Cortellessa[1] and Vincenzo Grassi[2]

[1] Universita' dell'Aquila, `cortelle@di.univaq.it`
[2] Universita' di Roma Torvergata, `vgrassi@info.uniroma2.it`

Abstract. Service selection and composition are central activities in service-oriented computing, and the prediction of the QoS attributes of a Service-Oriented Architecture (SOAs) plays a key role to appropriately drive these activities. Software composition driven by QoS criteria (e.g., optimization of performance, maximization of reliability) has been mostly studied in the Component-Based Software Engineering domain, whereas methodological approaches are not well established in the service-oriented area. Indeed, prediction methodologies for service-oriented systems should be supported by automated and efficient tools to remain compliant with the requirement that most of the activities connected with service discovery and composition must be performed automatically. Moreover, the adopted implementation should respect the autonomy and independence of each provider of the services we want to include in our analysis. In this chapter we focus on the modeling and analysis of the *reliability* attribute in Service-Oriented Architectures, with particular emphasis on two aspects of this problem: (i) the mathematical foundations of reliability modeling of a Service-Oriented Architecture as a function of the reliability characteristics of its basic elements and (ii) the automatization of service composition driven by reliability criteria.

12.1 Introduction

Designing and building software systems by composition is one of the distinguishing features of the component-based and service-oriented approaches. Several methodologies and techniques have been proposed to drive the assembly of software systems from pre-existing components/services [16]. In particular, in the domain of software services, the automation of service discovery, selection and composition plays a key role to fully enable a service-oriented vision.

However, current proposals for the automated assembly of service-oriented systems are mostly based on criteria related to functional features, such as the minimal distance between the descriptions of required and offered services, despite the high relevance that QoS attributes (such as performance and availability) may have in this type of systems.

In a *service market* vision, the delivered QoS plays an important role in determining the success of a service provider [6]. In this respect, an important issue is how to assess the QoS delivered by a service, for instance its performance or dependability characteristics. Delivering QoS on the Internet is by itself a critical and significant challenge, because of its dynamic and unpredictable nature. Assessing the delivered QoS of Service-Oriented Architectures (SOAs) is even more challenging, given the emphasis on dynamically binding service requests with the available services and resources in a given context.

QoS attributes are undeniably harder to take into account with respect to functional ones also because they relate to factors that rarely enter the software development process, such as the operational profile. Approaches have been introduced for service selection and assembly that also consider QoS attributes, but the selection is based, in best cases, on intelligent agents, in most other cases on empirical estimations and/or on the developers' experience, thus lacking model-based automated support [20]. It is also true that special skills are often required to model QoS attributes of software systems, due to the mathematical aspects and modeling intricacies that must be often faced in this domain.

In the context of SOA-based applications, the QoS assessment involves both *monitoring* the actual QoS experienced by a client, and *predicting* the QoS that could be experienced in some context. In particular, QoS prediction may play a crucial role either to drive the selection of services to be assembled to fulfill a given request, or to foresee potential QoS problems caused by changes in the application environment and to support corrective actions (e.g., re-binding to a different service provider). In other words, the ability of predicting QoS would allow to answer crucial questions on SOA, such as "What the reliability of my service-oriented architecture would be if I select this given set of services?" or "How would the performance of my architecture be affected from replacing a certain service with another one?"

A real breakthrough in this area would therefore be brought from the introduction of modeling techniques that allow to predict QoS properties of an SOA on the basis of features of the services involved, thus in practice extending the mechanisms successfully applied to functional aspects.

Modeling the overall QoS of an SOA-based application on the basis of properties of the component services may require very different efforts, depending on the QoS property we are interested in. In this respect, an interesting classification of QoS properties has been presented in [10] in the field of component-based software systems. Most of the ideas presented in [10] can be applied to the SOA domain.

However, a main issue for the QoS analysis of SOA is the parameter estimation. The properties of basic services are not easily made available from service providers. Thus, monitoring/estimation techniques are needed to "populate"

QoS models with values of basic service characteristics (such as the probability of failure). In Sect. 12.3.2 we shortly discuss this aspect.

In this chapter we focus on the modeling and the analysis of the *reliability* property of SOA, with a special emphasis on two aspects of this problem: (i) the mathematical foundations of reliability modeling of a service-oriented architecture as a function of the reliability characteristics of its basic elements and (ii) the automatization of service composition activity driven by reliability criteria.

According to the classification in [10], based on the capability of assembling a system-level model starting from characteristics of basic elements (such as components or services), the reliability is defined as an *usage-dependent attribute*, i.e., an attribute which is determined by the system usage profile. This means, in the SOA domain, that the service developers and assemblers must predict as far as possible the use of the service in different systems, which may not yet exist. A second problem is the transfer of the usage profile from the assembly (or from the system) to the service. Even if the usage profile on the assembly level is specified, the usage profile for the services is not easily determined especially when the assembly is not known.

The chapter is structured as follows: in Sect. 12.2 we shortly introduce the basic concepts of reliability theory; in Sect. 12.3 we discuss specific issues of reliability in SOA and review related work; in Sect. 12.4 we introduce a model for reliability of SOA along with an algorithm for its evaluation, then in Sect. 12.5 we propose an implementation of this algorithm complying with the SOA principles of decentralization and autonomy; in Sect. 12.6 we use the example described in the Introduction of this book to present an application of our reliability model, and finally in Sect. 12.7 we provide some conclusions.

12.2 Software Reliability Basics

Reliability is a specific aspect of the broader concept of dependability [3]. Other dependability aspects are, e.g., availability and safety. Reliability specifically refers to the continuity of the service delivered by a system. In this respect, two basic definitions of reliability can be found in the literature: (i) the probability that the system performs its required functions under stated conditions for a specified period of time [19] and (ii) the probability that the system successfully completes its task when it is invoked (also known as "reliability on demand") [12].

The definition in (i) refers in particular to "never ending" systems that must operate correctly over all the duration time of a given mission (e.g., the on-board flight control system of an airplane that should not fail during the enitre duration of a flight). The definition in (ii) refers to systems offering services that, once invoked, must be successfully completed.

Both definitions can be applied to systems at whatever level of granularity (e.g., a distributed software system, a software component, a software service, etc.), whose correctness can be unambiguously specified. A correct behavior is intended here as a "failure-free" one, where the system produces the expected output for each input following the system specifications.[3]

However, "failure-free" only refers to what can be observed at the system output level. A system may in fact experience a certain degree of incorrectness without showing any failure. This assertion is easily understandable on the basis of three fundamental reliability concepts: *fault*, *error*, and *failure*. A fault is a wrong statement introduced somewhere in the software.[4] An error is an unexpected state in which a system may enter upon executing a fault (e.g., an internal variable assumes an unexpected value). A failure occurs when an error propagates up to the system output (e.g., an output variable assumes an unexpected value).

The presence of a fault in a system does not necessarily imply that the system eventually experiences an error. In fact, a wrong statement might not be executed, even in a very long interval of time, due to the structure of the code and the sequence of inputs given. And, even if executed, the wrong statement could not originate any unexpected value of the internal variables.[5] Moreover, a system in an erroneous state does not necessarily manifest a failure, because the error may be masked from the operations that are executed between the erroneous state and the output production.

Failures can be classified with respect to different attributes. With respect to the way a failure manifests itself, they can be partitioned as follows:

- *Regular failure*—A failure that manifests itself as an unexpected value of any system output.
- *Crash failure*—A failure that immediately brings the system to stop its elaboration; systems that only account for this type of failure are also known as *fail-and-stop* systems.
- *Looping failure*—A failure that prevents the system to produce any (correct or incorrect) output; this type of failure is particularly problematic because it may take some time to assess that the system has failed under such a failure.

With respect to their severity, failures can be partitioned as follows:

- *Repairable failure*—A failure that can be somehow repaired without restarting the whole system.
- *Unrepairable failure*—A failure that requires the system to be restarted to restore its correct behavior.

---

[3] We assume readers are familiar with basics of reliability theory; however, we redirect those interested to details on this topic to [19].

[4] For sake of tractability, we consider in this chapter only software faults, even though the reliability of SOAs may be affected by hardware faults as well.

[5] For example, both statements $y = x * 2$ and $y = x^2$ produce the result $y = 4$ when $x = 2$.

Each reliability model undergoes several hypotheses on the types of failures that the modeled system can experience. Obviously, the less restrictive the hypotheses are the more complicated is the model formulation. Note, however, that the attributes specified above are not independent of each other, e.g., a crash failure cannot be repairable.

12.3 Specific Reliability Issues in SOA

Reliability models of modular software systems aim at formulating the reliability of the whole system as a function of the reliabilities of the basic elements. This idea is behind models for object-oriented, component-based, service-based systems and, in general, any system that can be viewed as an assembly of basic elements.

In this section we discuss specific issues for the modeling and estimation of the service reliability in SOA-based systems.

First of all, we note that the definition (ii) of reliability on demand given in Sect. 12.2 appears more suitable than definition (i) within the SOA domain, since it finely matches with the expectation and the degree of trustworthiness a user may have about a service. On the basis of this definition of reliability, in the following subsections we discuss, respectively, of

- the additional information that must be provided to support reliability analysis of SOAs;
- the estimation of this information in an SOA environment;
- the viewpoint that can be assumed in the SOA reliability analysis (i.e., client vs provider viewpoint);
- the failure model that we adopt in the modeling of SOA reliability.

In the last subsection of this section, we review existing work that is related to this chapter topic. Given the lack of specific reliability models for service-based systems, we take a wider view on software systems that are built by assembling basic elements, such as components.

12.3.1 Information to Support SOA Reliability Analysis

In an SOA environment, services are expected to publish information needed to correctly invoke them over the network. This information, expressed by a suitable language like WSDL [30], includes the name of the provided operations, and the name and type of their input and output parameters. To support predictive analysis of some QoS attribute like the service reliability, each service must also publish QoS-related information.

This raises the question about which information should be published to better support QoS predictive analysis. In this perspective, it is important to note that a basic principle of the SOA paradigm is that each composition of services may become itself a service that can be recursively used to build other services. As a consequence, it is useful to distinguish two kinds of service:

1. *Atomic service* that does not require any other service or resource to carry out its own task; this includes, e.g., not only the services offered by basic processing and communication resources, but also "self-contained" software services strictly tied to a particular computing environment and that cannot be re-deployed;
2. *Composite service*, realized as a composition of other selected services that it requires to carry out its own tasks; the glue logic of this composition may be expressed using workflow description languages like BPEL [31].

From the reliability prediction viewpoint (but the same consideration holds for other QoS attributes), the basic difference between these two kinds of services is that the provider of an atomic service can publish complete reliability information that can be directly used by the clients to figure out the service reliability, while the provider of a composite service is only aware of reliability information concerning the part of the service implementation which is under his/her direct control (we call it as the *service internal segment*). This information must be combined with the reliabilities of the other (dynamically) selected services to get the overall service reliability.

In order to properly combine these reliabilities, attention must be paid to give the right weight to the reliability of each single service: a rarely invoked service has obviously a smaller impact on the reliability of the invoking service than a frequently used one. Hence, besides knowing which services are required by a composite service, we must also take into account how they are used (i.e., we must know the service operational profile).

Therefore, to support the reliability prediction of a service composition, we need the following information on each service[6]:

- *Internal reliability* (both atomic and composite services), i.e., a reliability measure that expresses the probability of successfully completing some task considering only the internal segment of the service; in the case of an atomic service it corresponds to the actual service reliability, whereas in the case of a composite service it must be suitably combined with the reliabilities of the invoked services;
- *Service usage profile* (composite services only), i.e., a description of the pattern of external service requests expressed in a stochastic form (also known as operational profile); e.g., if a certain service may invoke two alternative services for completing its task (depending on the user inputs) then the probability of each service invocation is an element of the service usage profile.

---

[6] In Sect. 12.5 we present an architecture in which providers have three alternative approaches to disclose this information.

12.3.2 Estimation of Additional Information

In an ideal scenario, the internal reliability of a service shall be associated to the service description at the time the provider publishes the service on a registry. On the contrary, the service usage profile is a very domain-dependent information, therefore it cannot be a priori estimated.

However, in a more realistic scenario, the information described in Sect. 12.3.1 can be estimated by monitoring the service activity.

In particular, with regard to the service usage profile, the structure of the composite service workflow (expressed with a service composition language like BPEL) provides information about the possible invocation patterns of external services. To estimate the probability of different patterns, we must basically monitor the relative frequencies of the different branches at each workflow branching point, and collect such data over an adequate number of different invocations of the composite service.

On the other hand, the internal reliability can be estimated as the ratio between the number of service invocations and the number of failures that occur. We point out that, in the case of a composite service, the failures that should be recorded at a composite service site are those generated by the internal segment of the service. Collecting failure statistics about the used external services could not be significant, as at different time instants we could bind to different implementations of the same abstract service and, given the autonomy principle of the SOA environment, we are not generally aware of these changes.

However, methods for the estimation of the probability of failure of software components and the usage profile (in component-based systems) have been reviewed in [12], and are extensively discussed in [11].

12.3.3 Client vs Provider Viewpoint of Reliability

We may adopt two different perspectives in the assessment of the reliability of a service in an SOA framework, depending on whether we look at services from the client or provider viewpoint. This is generally not an issue in traditional distributed systems, where the network and other environment components are under the control of a single organization. On the contrary, in an SOA environment, the reliability information published by a service provider is likely to concern only what can be observed at the service site and does not include information about the reliability of the network infrastructure used to access the service, which is generally out of the provider control. On the other hand, from the perspective of the client of a service, this information must be integrated into the overall reliability assessment procedure, as the used network infrastructure may greatly affect the reliability perceived by the user. Neglecting this information could lead to poor predictions about the overall reliability of a service. We point out, however, that all the above considerations can be extended to other QoS attributes.

In some cases, a reference to the network used to access a remote service could be explicitly expressed in the workflow of a composite service, e.g., when the latter explicitly intends to use networking functionalities offered through some service-oriented interface (like in OSA/Parlay [29]) by a network service provider. This could facilitate the inclusion of network reliability information in the overall reliability model, assuming that a network service publishes its reliability information like any other service. If the network services needed to access remote services are not explicitly mentioned in a composite service workflow, their use should be made explicit at the reliability modeling level. However, the assignment of a meaningful reliability value to the network services could be more problematic in this case, as it could not be clear at the composite service level which kind of network is going to be used (possibly some kind of "best effort" network).

However, if the provider does not publish any data about the service reliability then the client can refer to trusted third-parties to collect this information [5].

12.3.4 Failure Models for SOA

As reported in Sect. 12.2, failures can be classified as regular, crash, and looping failures according to the way they manifest themselves, while they can be classified as repairable or non-repairable failures according to their severity.

Crash failures are the simplest ones to model from the reliability viewpoint, as they lead to the complete system failure as soon as they occur. In this respect, it is worth noting that it has been argued, based on an analysis of existing systems, that components and services for Internet-based systems should be designed to be "crash-only" [7].

On the other hand, regular failures causes the generation of incorrect output values. As discussed in Sect. 12.2, the incorrect output generated by an inner service invoked within the workflow of a composite service does not generally imply the overall failure of the composite service itself. This is due to the possibility that the inner service failure does not propagate up to the composite service outputs because some other service on the path to the output is able to mask the error. Hence, to include regular failures in the reliability analysis of SOA-based systems would require to take into account the *error maskability* factor, i.e., the capability for a service to map an incorrect input to a correct output. This factor can be ignored by assuming that any regular failure occurring in an inner service always propagates to the composite service outputs. This simplifies the analysis but could lead to overly pessimistic estimations of the overall reliability.

With regard to the failure repairability we note that, given the definition of reliability on demand that we have adopted, repairable failures are not actually a concern. Indeed, a repairable failure does not prevent, by definition, the correct termination of a service, and hence does not affect its reliability on demand. Nevertheless, it may affect other quality attributes like the service performance (because the repair leads to a "degraded" mode of operation) or availability (because of service interruption during the repair).

Finally, we point out that many existing reliability analysis methodologies for service- or component-based systems rely on the assumption of independence among the system components. When applying these methodologies in an SOA framework we must be careful about the validity of such an assumption. Indeed, it may happen that originally independent services are assembled in such a way that they exploit some common service, so becoming no longer independent. However, considering the impact of service sharing on reliability is not an easy task.

12.3.5 Related Work

The scientific literature has produced several interesting approaches to the modeling of reliability in modular software systems based on characteristics of modular units. Most of them can be somehow adapted to the case of service-based systems, but the adaptation may bring to loose peculiarities of SOA like the ones discussed in the previous subsections. Due to the lack of specific approaches for SOA, in this subsection we briefly present the major contributions in the wider field of modular software systems.

Hence, the originality of this chapter with respect to the existing work is to build a reliability model for SOA that takes into account the specifics of service-based systems.

A thorough review of reliability modeling in the field of software architectures can be found in [12], where architectural models are partitioned as follows: (i) *path-based models*, where the reliability of an assembly of components is calculated starting from the reliability of architectural paths; (ii) *state-based models*, where the reliability is calculated starting from the reliability of system states and from the transition probabilities among states.[7]

One of the main differences between these two types of models emerges when the control flow graph of the application contains loops. State-based models analytically account for the infinite number of paths that might exist due to loops. Path-based models require instead an explicit enumeration of the considered paths; hence, to avoid an infinite enumeration, the number of paths must be somehow restricted, e.g., to the ones observed experimentally during the testing phase or by limiting the depth traversal of each path. In this respect, the methodology we propose in Sect. 12.4 adopts a state-based model.

As said in Sect. 12.3.4, the impact of service sharing on SOA reliability may be consistent, even though modeling this aspect is not an easy task. In fact, it

---

[7] Quite often state transitions are triggered by the control flow between system components.

falls under the more general problem of modeling error propagation in modular software systems [1]. Most of the existing models do not consider the impact of error propagation on the estimation of the system reliability due to the extremely high complexity of finding closed-form formulations to the problem.

Models for the reliability estimation of a component-based system embedding the error propagation and the error maskability factors have been recently presented in [14] and [22], which are based on quite different failure models. In [14] it is assumed that an error arising within a component does not cause an immediate failure, but it can rather propagate to other components up to the system output, unless it is masked before reaching the output. On the other hand, in [22] it is assumed that each error arising within a component immediately causes a system failure and, at the same time, it can also propagate to other components affecting their failure probability. This latter failure model, based on the contemporary assumption of immediate failure and propagation to other components, deserves in our opinion further investigation about its significance.

Quite interesting work has been done in other topics somehow related to the SOA reliability. In particular, we provide several seminal references for readers interested to the following topics: ontologies for QoS [21, 23, 27], representing QoS in UML [28], monitoring QoS in SOA [4], and Service Level Agreement in SOA [17, 18].

12.4 A Model for Predicting the Reliability of SOAs

Any reliability prediction methodology for SOA-based applications must be compliant with the specific constraints and requirements of this environment. In particular, this means that prediction methodologies must be implemented by automated and efficient tools to remain compliant with the requirement that most of the activities connected with service discovery and composition must be performed automatically. Moreover, the implementation of a methodology should meet the openness and distribution characteristics of SOAs. This implies that it should respect the autonomy of each provider of the services involved in the reliability prediction.

In order to address these automation and efficiency issues, in this section we tackle them by proposing an algorithmic reliability analysis methodology. Assuming that, in general, an offered service is built as a composition of other services, the methodology is based on the service assembly structure and exploits reliability information published by each assembled service in its description. In Sect. 12.5, we propose an architecture for the implementation of this methodology that supports different degrees of autonomy among the providers of the services involved in a composition. In this methodology, we take into account all the SOA specific issues outlined in Sect. 12.3.

The failure model we adopt is the "fail-stop with no repair" model. Hence, we only consider crash failures that occurs within a service component and lead to the service interruption. The methodology can be applied as well to regular failures that does not cause service interruption, under the hypothesis that each error generated by a service always propagates up to the system output.

We do not consider repairs because, as discussed in Sect. 12.3, they are basically not relevant in the reliability on demand analysis. However, this model does not imply that we are assuming repairs never occur within the system. Simply, we are restricting our attention to those failures that cannot be repaired, as our focus is on the system reliability.

A key element of this methodology is the definition of a suitable model for the information associated with each service that concerns its internal reliability, and, in case of a composite service, the pattern of requests addressed to other services. We use a unique model to represent both these types of information, and assume that the QoS-related information of a service is published by means of an instance of this model.

12.4.1 A Model Based on Internal Reliability and Service Usage Profile

The model is based on a probabilistic flow graph, where each node of the graph models a "stage" of the service execution that must be completed before a transition to the next node can take place. Each stage may include the request for one or more external services. The flow graph includes two special nodes, a *Start* node that represents its entry point and an *End* node with no outgoing transitions, representing the successful completion of the service. This flow graph can be considered as a representation "distilled" from some description of the service workflow (e.g., expressed using a language like BPEL), and enriched with statistical information needed to support reliability prediction.

Transitions from node to node of the flow graph follow the Markov property, where $p(i, j)$ denotes the probability that stage j is selected after the completion of stage i. This kind of transition rule basically models (in a probabilistic way) a sequential flow of control. We introduce other kinds of control flows in our model by allowing more than one external service request to be specified within each node. In this case, before a transition to the next stage can take place, the service requests associated with node i must be completed according to a specified completion model. In the current version of our methodology, we consider two possible completion models:

1. *AND* model – all the service requests included in node i must be completed to enable a transition to the next stage.
2. *OR* model – at least one of the service requests included in node i must be completed to enable a transition to the next stage.

The *AND* model allows to represent a request for the parallel execution of a set of services, as expressed, e.g., "by the flow" control construct of BPEL (corresponding to a *fork-join* execution pattern) [31]. The *OR* model allows to represent a race among different service requests, as expressed, e.g., "by the pick" control construct of BPEL (where one out of several activities is non-deterministically selected) [31]. It can also be used to model the presence of fault-tolerance features, where different instances of a service are tried until at least one of them succeeds. We are planning to include in our methodology other completion models (e.g., "k out of n").

Besides the pattern of requests addressed to other services, we also embed in this flow graph information about the internal reliability of a service, by associating with each node i of the graph a failure probability $intf(i)$, that represents the probability of a failure occurrence during the execution of that stage. This probability concerns only the internal segment of the service described by the flow graph. In general, $intf(i)$ may be expressed as a real valued function of suitable parameters (e.g., the probability of a failure occurrence when a processing service is invoked may depend on the number of operations to be processed). The *Start* and *End* nodes have zero failure probability, as they do not correspond to any real activity.

This flow graph can be used to model information on the reliability of atomic as well as composite services. As the example in Fig. 12.1a shows, an atomic service can be modeled by a flow graph consisting of only one node (besides the Start and End nodes), which does not contain any request for external services. Thus, the single node of this graph only reports an $intf$ value. In particular, the flow graph in Fig. 12.1a models the reliability characteristics of a computing resource that offers a processing service. Figure 12.1b depicts an example of flow graph for a composite service that includes

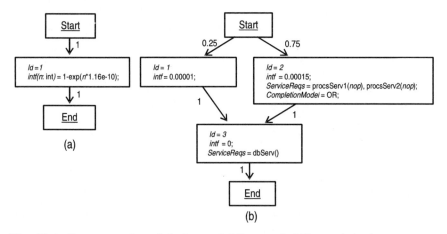

Fig. 12.1. Representation of the internal failure probability and service usage profile of a service by a probabilistic flow graph: (**a**) flow graph of an atomic service (processing service with exponential failure rate depending on the number n of operations to be processed), (**b**) flow graph of a composite service (at node 2, *nop* is the number of operations whose execution is requested to the two processing services)

requests for external services. It consists of two alternative stages 1 and 2, followed by a final stage 3. At stage 1, no external service is requested: this stage may model the execution of "locally implemented" operations, and the corresponding value of $intf(1)$ models their failure probability (i.e., 0.00001). On the other hand, at stage 2 two external processing services are requested, with an *OR* completion model. This stage may model the request for the remote execution of some code provided by the service, where the value $intf(2)$ models the intrinsic failure probability of that code (i.e., 0.00015) that must be combined with the failure probabilities of the selected processing services to get the overall reliability. The *OR* completion model of this stage models the use of a fault-tolerant approach in its design, since it is sufficient that only one of the two service requests succeeds to make the invoking service able to continue its execution. Finally, stage 3 models the request for another external service (i.e., a database service in this example).

12.4.2 An Algorithm for Model Evaluation

Given this model, we can now present our evaluation methodology, where we adopt a client-side perspective which means, as discussed in Sect. 12.3, that we include in the reliability evaluation of a service also the reliability of the network used by the client to access the service.

For this purpose, let us introduce the following notation:

- $Rel_{cli}(S)$ – the probability that a service S is able to complete its task, as seen by a client invoking S.
- $Rel_{pro}(S)$ – the probability that a service S is able to complete its task, as seen by the provider of S.
- $Rel_{net}(S)$ – the reliability of the network used to access a service S, when it is invoked by a client.
- $P_{fail}(i)$ – the probability of a failure occurrence before the completion of stage i of a given service.
- $p_S^*(Start, End)$ – probability of reaching, in any number of steps, the *End* state of the flow graph associated with S, starting from its *Start* state.[8]

Given this notation, the client-side reliability of a service S can be expressed as follows, once its provider-side reliability and the reliability of the network used to access S are known:

$$Rel_{cli}(S) = Rel_{net}(S) \cdot Rel_{pro}(S) \qquad (12.1)$$

Using the flow graph model defined above, we can calculate $Rel_{pro}(S)$ in (12.1) as follows:

$$Rel_{pro}(S) = p_S^*(Start, End) \qquad (12.2)$$

---

[8] We remind that, under the fail-and-stop assumption, reaching the *End* node means that there have been no failures in the execution path.

$p_S^*(Start, End)$ can be calculated by standard results from the Markov processes theory [24]. However, to get a meaningful result, we must elaborate transition probabilities on the flow graph before calculating $p_S^*(Start, End)$. Indeed, each transition probability $p(i, j)$ associated with an outgoing arc from a node i is an information about how frequently a stage j is executed after a stage i. For reliability prediction purposes, this information must be weighed by the probability $(1 - P_{fail}(i))$ that no failure occurs before the completion of stage i. Hence, to calculate expression (12.2), we must first calculate $P_{fail}(i)$ for each stage i of the flow graph of S.

The calculation of $P_{fail}(i)$ is immediate when i does not contain any request for external services. This is the case of a single-stage flow graph associated with an atomic service, whose $Rel_{pro}(S)$ (given by (12.2)) can be immediately calculated. In all other cases we enter a recursive process, as to calculate $P_{fail}(i)$ we must first calculate the reliability of all the services S_k requested by S at stage i. In this respect, we point out that S is the "client" of the services S_k. Hence, the reliability of the generic S_k to be used in the evaluation of $P_{fail}(i)$ is $Rel_{cli}(S_k)$, which can be calculated using expressions (12.1) and (12.2).

Once the $Rel_{cli}(S_k)$ reliabilities are known, we can combine them with $intf(i)$, according to the completion model of i, to calculate the overall $P_{fail}(i)$. By adapting the results that we have presented in [13], $P_{fail}(i)$ can be expressed as follows for the OR completion model:

$$P_{fail}(i) = \tag{12.3}$$
$$= 1 - (1 - intf(i))(1 - \prod_{S_k}(1 - Rel_{cli}(S_k)))$$
$$= 1 - (1 - intf(i))(1 - \prod_{S_k}(1 - Rel_{net}(S_k) \cdot Rel_{pro}(S_k)))$$
$$= 1 - (1 - intf(i))(1 - \prod_{S_k}(1 - Rel_{net}(S_k) \cdot p_{S_k}^*(Start, End)))$$

For AND completion model we instead have

$$P_{fail}(i) = \tag{12.4}$$
$$= 1 - (1 - intf(i))\prod_{S_k} Rel_{cli}(S_k)$$
$$= 1 - (1 - intf(i))\prod_{S_k} Rel_{net}(S_k) \cdot Rel_{pro}(S_k)$$
$$= 1 - (1 - intf(i))\prod_{S_k} Rel_{net}(S_k) \cdot p_{S_k}^*(Start, End)$$

Expressions (12.3) and (12.4) hold under the assumption that all the S_k's requested at stage i are independent. As pointed out in Sect. 12.3, this assumption could not hold in an SOA environment. However, taking into account all the possible inter-dependencies is really challenging. In [13] we have analyzed a restricted dependency scenario, where all the service requests at stage i are actually invocations of the same service S' offered by a single resource. This scenario occurs, e.g., when we allocate n software components to the same processing resource, thus requesting the same processing service offered by that resource. Under this scenario, we have shown in [13] that expression (12.4) still holds, with $\prod_{S_k} Rel_{net}(S_k) \cdot p^*_{S_k}(Start, End) = (Rel_{net}(S') \cdot p^*_{S'}(Start, End))^n$, where n is the number of invocations of S'. On the contrary, expression (12.3) is no longer valid, and must be substituted by the following expression:

$$P_{fail}(i) = 1 - (1 - intf(i))Rel_{net}(S') \cdot p^*_{S'}(Start, End) \qquad (12.5)$$

The intuition behind (12.5) follows from the stopping failure and no repair assumptions. If all the S_k's invocations are actually invocations of the same service, then its failure prevents the possibility of trying other alternatives. Hence, the "OR-reliability" of n invocations of S' is equal to the simple reliability of S'. Using (12.3) instead of (12.5) when this scenario occurs would lead to an underestimation of the service reliability.

The recursive Algorithm 1 summarizes all the operations described above. Given the flow graph $fg(S)$ associated with a service S, the algorithm returns the provider-side reliability of S.

Algorithm 1 Model evaluation algorithm: **double** Rel-pro-Alg$(fg(S))$

1: **for** each node i in $fg(S)$ (except the *Start* and *End* nodes) **do**
2:     **if**(i does not include any request for external services)
3:     **then** $P_{fail}(i) = intf(i)$
4:     **else**
5:         **for** each S_k requested in i **do**
6:             net_k = reliability of the network used to invoke S_k
7:             get $fg(S_k)$
8:             $r_k = net_k \cdot$ Rel-pro-Alg$(fg(S))$ //recursive step
9:         **endfor**
10:         **case** *CompletionModel:*
11:             OR : $P_{fail}(i) = 1 - (1 - intf(i))(1 - \prod_k(1 - r_k))$ // expression (12.3)
12:             AND : $P_{fail}(i) = 1 - (1 - intf(i))\prod_k r_k$ // expression (12.4)
13:         **endcase**
14:     **endif**
15:     **for** each outgoing transition from i to j with probability $p(i,j)$ **do**
16:         replace $p(i,j)$ with $(1 - P_{fail}(i)) \cdot p(i,j)$
17:     **endfor**
18: **endfor**
19: **return** absorption probability in the *End* node of the discrete time Markov process described by $fg(S)$, calculated using standard Markov process solution techniques

---

Step 11 of this algorithm relies on the independence assumption discussed above. If this assumption does not hold and the conditions of the "single service sharing" scenario occurs, then step 11 must be modified according to expression (12.5). Step 8 is the recursive step. The recursive call returns the provider-side reliability of S_k. To turn it into the client-side reliability (as it is perceived at the S site), this reliability must be multiplied by the reliability of the network used to access S_k. The bottom of the recursion is reached when S is an atomic service. In this case, steps 5–13 are skipped, and the calculation of step 19 is greatly simplified as $fg(S)$ consists of only one node, plus the *Start* and *End* nodes.

12.5 Analyzing Reliability in the SOA Framework

In this section we discuss issues concerning the implementation, in an SOA environment, of the methodology presented in Sect. 12.4.

The methodology relies on the assumption that each provider of a composite service collects and publishes information concerning the service internal structure that consists of (i) the external services it exploits, (ii) how they are glued together, and (iii) how frequently they are invoked. In Sect. 12.4 we have presented a data structure (i.e., a flow graph) which able to represent all this information. We remark here that the construction of such a data structure can be completely automated. Indeed, with regard to the flow graph structure (i.e., nodes and edges that connect them), it can be easily extracted from the executable workflow description of a composite service. For example, if the workflow is expressed in BPEL, which is an XML-based language, we can use XML navigation libraries, like JDom [32], to implement this algorithm. With regard to the flow graph parameters (i.e., branching probabilities and internal failure probability at each node), they can be estimated through monitoring activities, as discussed in Sect. 12.3.2.

However, according to the decentralization and autonomy principles of the SOA paradigm, the provider of a composite service (which could be in turn required to build a new composition) might want to adopt different transparency policies in revealing this information and in selecting the services his/her own service requires. In the following we present an architecture that implements the methodology described above, still remaining compliant with the SOA autonomy and decentralization principles.[9] For this purpose, we identify three possible policies that cover the spectrum of different autonomy degrees (from high to low):

1. No transparency—The provider reveals only information about the overall (possibly parametric) service reliability. This policy implies that it is up to the provider to select the services to be assembled when the service is invoked, and to calculate the resulting reliability. A provider adopting

---

[9] The content of this section is based on results presented in [15].

this policy wants to maintain full autonomy in the selection of services required by his/her service, without disclosing any information about its architecture.

2. Partial transparency—The provider reveals both the service internal reliability and its usage profile of other external services, but autonomously decides the external services to select. This policy implies that it is up to the provider to select the services to be assembled, while it is up to the invoker of the composite service to calculate its overall reliability. A provider adopting this policy wants to maintain full autonomy in the selection of services required by his/her service, but does not want to bear the burden of evaluating the resulting overall reliability (maybe because he/she selects services according to different criteria than reliability).

3. Total transparency—The provider reveals both the internal reliability and the usage profile of the service, indicating only the kind of services that should be selected, without actually selecting them. This policy implies that it is totally up to the user of the composite service to select the services to be assembled and to calculate the resulting reliability. A provider adopting this policy actually provides only a service template consisting of some glue logic that connects services to be selected, and does not want to bear the burden of both selecting those services and evaluating the resulting reliability.

Figure 12.2 illustrates the SOA compliant architecture in which we propose to implement the reliability prediction methodology of Sect. 12.4. The building blocks of this architecture are

- an implementation of the *Rel-pro-Alg()* (which, in an SOA environment, could be itself defined as a particular type of service, called *RelServ* in Fig. 12.2);
- an operation *GetFlowGraph(S)* that returns the flow graph describing the behavior of a service *S*. Note that this operation could be included within the ones offered in a Web accessible *S* interface; it is the responsibility of the *S* provider to build and parameterize the flow graph, using his/her knowledge of the *S* structure and the results of monitoring the *S* execution.

A client of a service *S* who wants to get a prediction about the service reliability must first call the *GetFlowGraph(S)* operation, and then invoke the *RelServ* service, passing to it the obtained flow graph as a parameter. The result returned by *RelServ* must then be combined with the reliability of the network the client uses to access *S*, according to expression (12.1).

In this architecture, the fulfillment of the three different policies listed above is guaranteed by the implementation of the *GetFlowGraph(S)* operation (which is under the control of the *S* provider) as follows:

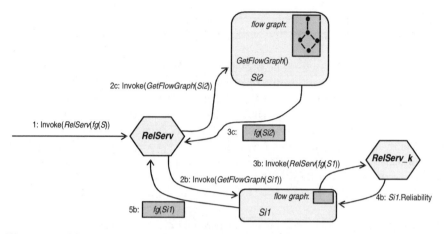

Fig. 12.2. The *RelServ* service architecture. The path (2b, 3b, 4b, 5b) describes the distributed part of this architecture (scenario *b*): the request from *RelServ* to get the flow graph of *Si1* causes the invocation of another instance of the reliability prediction service (*RelServ_k*); the flow graph returned to *RelServ* is actually the "collapsed" version of the "true" flow graph, so that *RelServ* gets no knowledge about *Si1* except for its overall reliability. The path (2c, 3c) describes the internally recursive realization of *RelServ* (scenario *c*): the reliability of *Si2* is recursively calculated by *RelServ* itself, since only the usage profile of *Si2* is returned to *RelServ*; in this way, *RelServ* gets knowledge about the internal realization of *Si2*

a) *S* is an atomic service – *GetFlowGraph(S)* returns the (single node) flow graph associated with *S*;

b) *S* is a composite service whose provider adopts a "no transparency" policy – *GetFlowGraph(S)* builds and returns a flow graph consisting of a single stage that expresses the overall reliability of S; this "collapsed" flow graph is built by "privately" invoking a (possibly different) instance of *RelServ* (i.e., *RelServ_k* in Fig. 12.2). In this way, the invoker of *GetFlow-Graph(S)* gets only information about the overall *S* reliability;

c) *S* is a composite service whose provider adopts a "partial or total transparency" policy – *GetFlowGraph(S)* returns the "true" flow graph describing the internal structure of *S*. In this way, the invoker of *GetFlowGraph(S)* gets information about the internal reliability and usage profile of *S*.

We point out that the flow graph $fg(S)$, that *RelServ* receives as input to calculate the reliability of a service *S*, must explicitly specify the services that *S* invokes during its execution. This information is necessary to contact these services and get the corresponding reliability information (i.e., step 7 of the Algorithm 1). These services are determined by means of a suitable selection procedure. If the provider of *S* adopts a "no transparency" or "partial transparency" policy, then this selection is carried out by the provider. Otherwise, it must be carried out by the one that is requesting the evaluation of the *S* reliability. In both cases, this procedure must in general be carried out each time we want to evaluate the reliability of S. Indeed, given the dynamic nature of an SOA environment, the same *abstract service* (i.e., the type of inner service required at a certain stage of execution of a composite service) could be bound to different *concrete services* (i.e., Internet accessible implementations of an abstract service). This is due to the possibility that either previously accessible concrete services could be no longer available, or new concrete services could have emerged. A discussion on how to set up a service selection procedure is beyond the scope of this chapter, and a quite rich literature exists about this topic [2, 8, 9, 25, 26]. We only remark that the reliability analysis methodology presented here can be used to support such a selection procedure, by comparing the reliability of different available concrete services.

Given this implementation of the *GetFlowGraph(S)* operation, we get a mixed recursive/distributed implementation of the recursive algorithm *Rel-pro-Alg()* of Sect. 12.4. The distributed implementation occurs when *RelServ* executes step 6 of *Rel-pro-Alg()* under the scenario *b* described above, since this in general involves a call, on behalf of *GetFlowGraph()*, to a different *RelServ* instance. The true recursion occurs when step 6 is executed under scenario *c*; in this case *RelServ* must first solve the Markov processes associated with the services invoked by S, before solving the Markov process associated with S.

Finally, it is worth noting that, in this architecture, if a single-node flow graph is received as a result of a *GetFlowGraph(S)* call, then there is no need to be aware whether this is occurring under scenario *a* or *b*. Hence, besides allowing a service provider to select the preferred autonomy level, this architecture allows also to not revealing the autonomy policy that has been actually selected, thus preserving the "privacy" of each provider.

12.6 A Case Study

In this section we apply our modeling framework to a slightly modified and simplified version of the scenario outlined in the introductive chapter of this book. In particular, we consider the "travel planning" part of this scenario.

We assume that John, to plan his trip, invokes an Internet accessible *Trip-Planner* service. This service allows John to specify his preferences and constraints about the trip, and supports him in an interactive way in the selection and booking of everything he could need during this trip.

Figure 12.3 shows a possible workflow of this service. As shown, *Trip-Planner* invokes several other services to carry out its task. Given the user preferences and constraints, it first invokes a specialized *HotelSelection* service that returns a possible list of hotels for the site of interest, with their corresponding features. Looking at these features, John selects an hotel. As the information provided by *HotelSelection* could not be up to date, *Trip-Planner* checks (by contacting the *HotelInfo* service of that hotel) whether

TripPlanner(preferences, constraints) (*S1*):

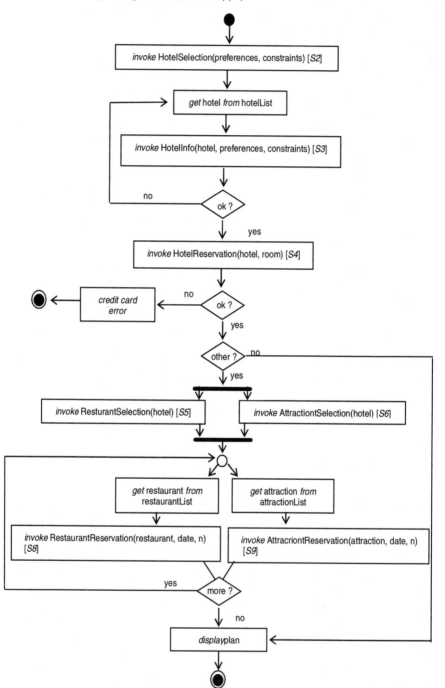

Fig. 12.3. A workflow for the *TripPlanner* service

the listed features are really present (e.g., the swimming pool, even if present, could be closed). When a selection has been finalized, *TripPlanner* invokes the *HotelReservation* service of the selected hotel to make a reservation, providing the John's credit card number. *HotelReservation*, in turn, invokes the *CreditCardManager* service of the credit card company to check whether the card is valid. In the positive case, the booking is completed and *TripPlanner* asks John whether he wants to reserve some attractions or restaurants in the site he is going to visit. Also in this case, *TripPlanner* relies on two specialized services (i.e., *RestaurantSelection* and *AttractionSelection*) to get a list of possible attractions and restaurants close to the hotel that has been selected. Given these lists, John selects one or more attractions or restaurants. After that, *TripPlanner* displays the complete trip plan.

Figure 12.4 depicts the workflows of other services invoked in the *Trip-Planner* scenario. *TripPlanner* is in fact a composite service that exploits other services. One of the invoked services (i.e., *HotelReservation*) is, in turn, a composite service, as it invokes another service to carry out its task.

To predict the reliability of a given composition of such services, the provider of each of such services has to "distill" from its workflow the flow graph described in Sect. 12.4, parameterizing it with suitable transition probabilities and failure probabilities (possibly estimated through a monitoring activity).

Figure 12.5 depicts possible flow graphs associated with some of the services included in our scenario. For example, we can see that most (except the last one) of the stages in *TripPlanner* flow graph have an internal failure probability equal to zero. This means that the reliability of this service will mostly depend on the reliability of the services it invokes and of the network it uses to contact them. For example, we could assume that John starts his session with *TripPlanner* while he stays at work (thus using a reliable wired

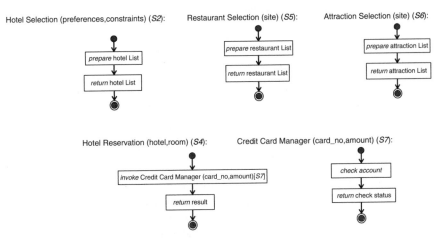

Fig. 12.4. Workflows of services invoked from *TripPlanner*

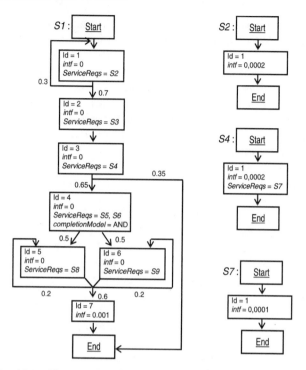

Fig. 12.5. Flowgraphs of services in the *TripPlanner* scenario

Internet connection), but he completes the last part of the session (attraction and restaurants reservation) while he is going back home using public transportation (thus using a less reliable wireless connection).

Given this scenario, the Algorithm 1 can be executed on the flow graphs shown in Fig. 12.5 to retrieve at what extent the reliability of the wireless network affects the overall reliability of the system.

12.7 Conclusions

In this chapter, we have introduced the problem of modeling and analyzing reliability of Service-Oriented Architectures. We have raised the main issues related to this problem that fall, on one hand, in the general problem of composing QoS attributes in modular software systems and, on the other end, in the specific constraints and requirements of the SOA environment such as automation support and provider autonomy.

Upon introducing very basic reliability concepts, we have presented a model for SOA reliability and an algorithm to evaluate our model. Finally, we have described a service implementation of our methodology.

We have tried to open a window on the actual possibility of pursuing model-based automated prediction of QoS attributes in SOAs. In fact we retain that these practices have not yet entered the development and assembly process mostly for lack of automated supports, and we hope that the research community will spend more efforts in future in this direction, because very good results can be at hand in the next few years in the field of model-based QoS in SOAs.

References

1. H. Ammar , D. Nassar, W. Abdelmoez, M. Shereshevsky, A. Mili, "A Framework for Experimental Error Propagation Analysis of Software Architecture Specifications", Proc. of International Symposium on Software Reliability Engineering (ISSRE'02), 2002.
2. Ardagna, D., Pernici, B., "Global and Local QoS Guarantee in Web Service Selection", Proc. of Business Process Management Workshop, 2005.
3. A. Avizienis, J.C. Laprie, B. Randell, C. Landwehr, "Basic Concepts and Taxonomy of Dependable and Secure Computing", IEEE Trans. on Dependable and Secure Computing, Vol.1, no.1, January-March 2004, pp. 11–33.
4. L. Baresi, C. Ghezzi, S, Guinea, "Smart monitors for composed services", Proc. of 2nd International Conference on Service Oriented Computing (ICSOC'04), 2004.
5. B. Bhusha, J. Hall, P. Kurtansky, B. Stiller, "Operations Support System for End-to-End QoS Reporting and SLA Violation Monitoring in Mobile Services Environment", Quality of Service in the Emerging Networking Panorama, LNCS 3266, 2004.
6. R. Buyya, D. Abramson, J. Giddy, H. Stockinger, "Economic models for resource management and scheduling in Grid computing", Concurrency and Computation: Practice and Experience, Vol. 14, 2002, pp. 1507–1542.
7. G. Candea, A. Fox, "Crash-only software", Proc. of the 9th Workshop on Hot Topics in Operating Systems, 2003.
8. Canfora, G., Di Penta, M., Esposito, R., Villani, M. L., "An Approach for QoS-aware Service Composition Based on Genetic Algorithms", Proc. of Genetic and Computation Conference, 2005.
9. F. Casati, M. Castellanos, U. Dayal, M.C. Shan, "Probabilistic, Context-sensitive, and Goal-oriented Service Selection", Proc. of 2nd International Conference on Service Oriented Computing (ICSOC'04), 2004.
10. I. Crnkovic, M. Larsson, O. Preiss, "Concerning Predictability in Dependable Component-Based Systems: Classification of Quality Attributes", Proc. of Workshop on Architecting Dependable Systems (WADS'04), 2004.
11. S. Gokhale, W.E. Wong, J.R. Horgan, K. Trivedi, An analytical approach to architecture-based software performance and reliability prediction, Performance Evaluation, n.58 (2004), pp. 391–412.
12. K. Goseva-Popstojanova, A.P. Mathur, K.S. Trivedi, "Architecture-based approach to reliability assessment of software systems", Performance Evaluation, no. 45 (2001), pp. 179–204.
13. V. Grassi, "Architecture-based Reliability Prediction for Service-oriented Computing", Architecting Dependable Systems III (R. de Lemos, A. Romanovsky, C. Gacek Eds.), LNCS 3549, Springer-Verlag, 2005, pp. 279–299.

14. V. Grassi, V. Cortellessa, "Embedding error propagation in reliability modeling of component-based software systems", Proc. of International Conference on Quality of Software Architectures (NetObjectDays'05), 2005.
15. Grassi, V., Patella, S., "Reliability Prediction for Service-Oriented Computing Environments", IEEE Internet Computing, Volume 10, Issue 3 (2006), pp. 43–49.
16. Inverardi, P., Scriboni, S., "Connectors Synthesis for Deadlock-Free Component-Based Architectures", Proc. of Automated Software Engineering Conference (ASEÃ01), 2001.
17. H. Ludwig, A. Keller, A. Dan, R. Franck, and R.P. King, "Web Service Level Agreement (WSLA) Language Specification", IBM Corporation, July 2002.
18. Ludwig, H., Dan, A., Kearney, R. Cremona, "An Architecture and Library for Creation and Monitoring of WS-Agreements", Proc. of 2nd international conference on service oriented computing (ICSOC'04), 2004.
19. M.R. Lyu (Editor), "Handbook of Software Reliability Engineering", IEEE Computer Society Press, 1996.
20. Maximilien, E.M., Singh, M.P., "Toward Autonomic Web Services Trust and Selection", Proc. of International Conference on Service Oriented Computing (ICSOC'04), 2004.
21. I.V. Papaioannou, D.T. Tsesmetzis, I.G. Roussaki, M.E. Anagnostou, "A QoS Ontology Language for Web-Services", Proc. of the 20th International Conference on Advanced Information Networking and Applications (AINA'06), Vol. 1, 2006.
22. P. Popic, D. Desovski, W. Abdelmoez, B. Cukic, "Error propagation in the reliability analysis of component based systems", Proc. of International Symposium on Software Reliability Engineering (ISSREÃ05), 2005.
23. M. Tian, A. Gramm, T. Naumowicz, H. Ritter, J. Schiller, "A Concept for QoS Integration in Web Services", Proc. of the 4th International Conference on Web Information Systems Engineering Workshops (WISEWÃ03), 2003.
24. H.C. Tijms, "Stochastic models: an algorithmic approach", John Wiley and Sons, 1994.
25. Yu, T. and Lin, K. J., "Service Selection Algorithms for Web Services with End-to-End QoS Constraints", Journal of Information Systems and E-Business Management, vol.3, no.2, July 2005.
26. Zeng, L., Benatallah, B., Ngu, A.H.H., Dumas, M., Kalagnanam, J., Chang, H., "QoS-Aware Middleware for Web Services Composition", IEEE Trans. Software Engineering, vol.30, no.5, August 2004.
27. C. Zhou, L.T. Chia, B.S. Lee, "DAML-QoS Ontology for Web Services", Proc. of IEEE International Conference on Web Services, 2004.
28. "UML Profile for Modeling Quality of Service and Fault Tolerance Characteristics and Mechanisms", OMG Adopted Specification, ptc/2004-06-01, 2004.
29. "Parlay Web Services Overview", The Parlay Group: Web Services Working Group, Version 1.0, Oct. 2002, on line at: www.parlay.org.
30. "Web Services Description Language 1.1", W3C Note, March 2001, http://www.w3.org/TR/wsdl.
31. "Business Process Execution Language for Web Services 1.1", http://www-128.ibm.com/developerworks/library/specification/ws-bpel/.
32. www.jdom.org

Vulnerability Analysis of Web-Based Applications

Marco Cova, Viktoria Felmetsger and Giovanni Vigna

Reliable Software Group, Department of Computer Science, University of California, Santa Barbara
[marco,rusvika,vigna]@cs.ucsb.edu

Abstract. In the last few years, the popularity of web-based applications has grown tremendously. A number of factors have led an increasing number of organizations and individuals to rely on web-based applications to provide access to a variety of services. Today, web-based applications are routinely used in security-critical environments, such as medical, financial, and military systems.

Web-based systems are a composition of infrastructure components, such as web servers and databases, and of application-specific code, such as HTML-embedded scripts and server-side CGI programs. While the infrastructure components are usually developed by experienced programmers with solid security skills, the application-specific code is often developed under strict time constraints by programmers with little security training. As a result, vulnerable web-based applications are deployed and made available to the whole Internet, creating easily exploitable entry points for the compromise of entire networks.

To ameliorate these security problems, it is necessary to develop tools and techniques to improve the security of web-based applications. The most effective approach would be to provide secure mechanisms that can be used by well-trained developers. Unfortunately, this is not always possible, and a second line of defense is represented by auditing the application code for possible security problems. This activity, often referred to as *web vulnerability analysis*, allows one to identify security problems in web-based applications at early stages of development and deployment.

Recently, a number of methodologies and tools have been proposed to support the assessment of the security of web-based applications. In this chapter, we survey the current approaches to web vulnerability analysis and we propose a classification along two characterizing axes: detection model and analysis technique. We also present the most common attacks against web-based applications and discuss the effectiveness of certain analysis techniques in identifying specific classes of flaws.

13.1 Introduction

The World Wide Web started in the mid-1990s as a system to support hyper-textual access to static information and has since then evolved into a full-fledged platform for the development of distributed applications. This has been made possible by the introduction of a number of mechanisms that can be used to trigger the execution of code on both the client and the server side. These mechanisms are the basis to implement web-based applications.

As the use of web applications for critical services has increased, the number and sophistication of attacks against web application has grown as well. A series of characteristics of web-based applications make them a valuable target for an attacker. First, web applications are often designed to be widely accessible. Indeed, by design, they are almost always reachable through firewalls and a significant part of their functionality is available to anonymous users. Because of this, they are considered the most effective entry point for the compromise of computer networks. Second, web-based applications often interface with back-end components, such as mainframes and product databases, that might contain sensitive data, such as credit card information. Therefore, they become an attractive target for attackers who aim at gaining a financial profit. Third, the technology used to implement, test, and interact with web-based applications is inexpensive, well known, and widely available. Therefore, attackers can easily develop tools that expose and automatically exploit vulnerabilities.

Other factors contribute to make web applications a preferred target for attackers. For example, some of the most popular languages used to develop web-based applications are currently easy enough to allow novices to start writing their own applications, but, at the same time, they do not provide a comprehensive, easy-to-use set of mechanisms that support the development of secure applications. This problem is particularly difficult to solve. In fact, while the infrastructure components, such as web servers and browsers, are usually developed by experienced programmers with solid security skills and reviewed by a large developer team, the application-specific code is often developed under strict time constraints by few programmers with little security training. As a consequence, vulnerable code is made available on the web.

This trend is confirmed by various statistics. In the first semester of 2005, Symantec cataloged 1,100 new vulnerabilities, which represent well over half of all new vulnerabilities, as affecting web-based applications. This is a 59% increase over the previous semester, and a 109% increase over the same period of the previous year [33].

An analysis of the reported vulnerabilities shows various types of problems. Web applications can be affected by flaws that are not web specific and that have been commonly found also in traditional applications. Examples of such problems include broken authentication and authorization management, where account credentials and session tokens are not properly protected; improper handling of errors or exceptional conditions, which leads to the leaking of confidential information or to unexpected system behavior.

In addition to these well-known security problems, web-based applications are affected by a number of vulnerabilities that are specific of the web environment. Some vulnerabilities are due to architectural choices, such as the use of relational databases as back-ends for long-term storage, which lead to vulnerabilities such as SQL injections [1, 30] and permanent Cross Site Scripting (XSS) [14]. Other causes of web-based vulnerabilities are the incorrect handling of trust relations between clients and servers, which might lead to XSS, and inconsistencies in web protocols implementations, which lead to request smuggling [20] and response splitting [15]. Another source of security problems are the unforeseen consequences of the use of special features provided by the languages used to implement web-based applications, such as the use of the `register_globals` option in the PHP language. In this chapter, we will focus on vulnerabilities that are specific to the web environment.

Clearly, the abundance of vulnerabilities in web-based applications and their increasing popularity make a strong case for the need of techniques and tools for their security assessment. A number of approaches to secure web-based applications have been proposed in the recent past by both industry and academia. While most of these techniques reuse well-known ideas from the past, these ideas have to be extended to take into account the novel aspects of web-based application security. These approaches can be classified on the basis of when they can be applied in the life-cycle of a web-based application.

At the coding phase, new programming languages have been adopted that, among other things, take away from the programmer the burden of performing error-prone tasks and, in addition, eliminate the ability to perform insecure operations commonly found in traditional languages, such as memory management and pointer arithmetic.

New testing tools and methodologies have been proposed that aim at identifying and removing flaws by exercising an instance of an application with unexpected, random, or faulty input. Testing-time approaches are appealing because, in general, they can be performed even on applications whose source code is not available. In addition, they are usually independent of the internals of the application under testing, and, therefore, they are reusable on different applications. Finally, they are characterized by the absence of false positives, i.e., flaws found through testing correspond to actual bugs in the application code. The main disadvantage of these testing approaches is their lack of completeness, i.e., in general, they cannot guarantee to expose all vulnerabilities in a program.

Code reviews and security audits are part of the quality assurance phase. In particular, vulnerability analysis is the process of examining different characteristics of an application in order to evaluate whether there exists a sequence of events that are capable of driving the application into an insecure state. Thus, vulnerability analysis supports the identification and fixing of errors. In its simplest form, the analysis is performed by manually auditing the source code of an application. However, a number of more sophisticated and automatic approaches have been proposed in the last few years.

Finally, at deployment and operation time, an application can be protected through the use of web application firewalls. These applications examine the requests directed to a web server and determine if a request is to be considered an attack or not. The focus of web application firewalls is on preventing attacks directed against a web-based application rather than identifying and fixing its errors. These security mechanisms usually do not require the understanding of an application's internals or its modification.

This chapter reviews and discusses a number of techniques that can be used to perform the vulnerability analysis of web-based applications. Before delving into the details of these techniques, Sect. 13.2 presents the existing mechanisms for the execution of code in web-based applications. Then, Sect. 13.3 discusses the type of attacks that are common of web-based application. Finally, Sect. 13.4 provides a survey of the techniques used to perform vulnerability analysis of web-based applications.

13.2 Technologies

The technologies used to implement web-based applications have rapidly evolved since the appearance of the first simple mechanisms to create dynamic web pages. In this section, we will briefly present the most important steps in this evolution.

13.2.1 Common Gateway Interface

One of the first mechanisms that enabled the generation of dynamic content was the Common Gateway Interface (CGI) [23]. The CGI standard defines a mechanism that a server can use to interact with external applications. The CGI standard specifies the rules of this interaction but does not dictate the use of any particular technology for the implementation of the external applications. Therefore, CGI programs can be written virtually in any programming language and executed by virtually all web servers.

The original goal of the CGI invocation mechanism was to provide web-based access to legacy applications. In this case, a CGI program acts as a *gateway* between the web server and the legacy application, e.g., a database. More precisely, the life-cycle of a CGI-based program is as follows. Whenever a request references a CGI program, the server creates a new process to execute the specified application. Then, the web server passes to the program the data associated with the user request. The CGI program executes and produces data, which is passed back to the server. The server, in turn, passes the data to the client. When the CGI program exits, the request is completed.

The CGI specification defines different ways for a web server to communicate with a CGI program. At every request, the web server sets a number of environment variables that contain information about both the server (e.g., server name and version, or CGI specification supported) and the request (e.g., request method, request content type, and length). The request itself is passed to the CGI program through its standard input (if the request is issued using the POST HTTP method) or through an environment variable (if the request is issued using the GET HTTP method). When the CGI program has finished serving the request, it sends back the results to the server through its standard output. The output can either consist of a document generated by the program or one or more directives to the server for retrieving the output.

The example in Fig. 13.1 shows a CGI program written in Perl. The program allows users to authenticate with the application to access services offered only to authenticated users. Users are expected to send their credentials as two request parameters, namely **username** and **password**. The program uses two Perl modules, **CGI** and **CGI::Session**, which provide a number of library functions to ease the tasks of parameter decoding and session management. The credential parameters are extracted from the request and validated through the **validate** function (which, e.g., could lookup a database of registered users). If the credentials are found to be valid, a new session is started and a welcome message is shown to the user. Otherwise, the program returns to the user an error message. Note that this is just one of the components of a web-based application. For example, there might be other components that will provide access to information or services.

Developing web-based applications using the CGI mechanism to invoke server-side components has some advantages. First, as noted before, the CGI mechanism is language independent, i.e., each CGI-based component of the

```
1 #!/usr/bin/perl -w
2 use CGI;
3 use CGI::Session;
4
5 $cgi = new CGI;
6
7 my $user = $cgi->param("username");
8 my $pass = $cgi->param("password");
9
10 if (validate($user, $pass) == 1) {
11     my $session = new CGI::Session("driver:File",
12         undef, {Directory=>"/tmp"});
13     $cookie = $cgi->cookie(CGISESSID => $session->id);
14     print $cgi->header(-cookie=>$cookie);
15     print $cgi->start_html("Login");
16     print "Welcome!";
17 } else {
18     print $cgi->header;
19     print $cgi->start_html("Login");
20     print "Invalid username or password!";
21 }
22
23 print $cgi->end_html;
```

Fig. 13.1. A sample CGI program

application can be implemented using a different language. Second, CGI programs run in separate processes so problems in one program do not affect other components of the web applications or the web server.

The main disadvantage of using the CGI mechanism is that it requires that a new process be created and executed for each request, with significant impact on the performance and scalability of the web-based application. On many systems (notably UNIX), the creation of a new process is a costly operation. Furthermore, the use of a separate process for each request poses a limit to the maximum number of requests that can be satisfied at the same time, which is bounded by the maximum number of processes allowed by the OS. In addition, CGI programs run in a separate address space than the web server, and, therefore, they can only have a limited interaction with it. In particular, they cannot take advantage of its services (e.g., logging) leading to a duplication of functionalities between the server and the CGI programs.

In an attempt to overcome some of these problems, several extensions to the original CGI standard have been proposed. For example, the FastCGI mechanism creates a pool of resident processes that handle multiple requests without exit and need to be restarted [3]. Also, the FastCGI mechanism allows the web server and the external program to communicate through Unix-domain or TCP sockets rather than pipes, allowing developers to create more sophisticated architectures where server-side components are not required to run on the same host as the web server.

A different approach to overcome these limits consists in leveraging various functionalities of the server that are exposed through vendor-specific APIs. The most notable examples are the ISAPI extensions for Microsoft IIS and the API provided by Apache. External programs that use these server-specific APIs generally have low initialization cost and can perform more general functionalities than CGI-based programs. For example, they can rely on the web server to enforce access control or even hook into the server's request handling process.

However, server-specific APIs lack some of the benefits provided by the CGI mechanism. Writing a program that relies on server-specific APIs is generally more complex than writing a CGI program, because it requires some knowledge of the server's inner workings. In addition, the APIs are typically language specific (i.e., they have C or C++ bindings) and vendor specific, and, thus, not portable.

13.2.2 Embedded Web Application Frameworks

Today, the most common approach to web-based application implementation is a middle way between the original CGI mechanism and the use of server-specific APIs. More precisely, the web server is provided with extensions that implement frameworks for the development of web-based applications. At a minimum, these frameworks include an interpreter or compiler for the language used to encode the application's components and define rules that govern the interaction between the server and the application's components.

Frameworks vary greatly in the support provided to the application developer. At their most basic level, they simply parse request parameters and make them available to the application. Some frameworks also offer mechanisms to deal with HTTP-specific characteristics, e.g., cookies, authentication mechanisms, and connection handling. Most frameworks generally support other commonly used features, such as access to back-end databases and sessions. More sophisticated environments are designed to support large-scale enterprise applications and include support for features such as transactions and complex authorization mechanisms.

Web application frameworks are available for a variety of programming languages. Most frameworks are built around scripting languages, such as PHP, Perl, and Pyhton. These high-level languages, which are generally interpreted, provide support for object-oriented programming and are loosely typed. These characteristics simplify the development of small components, which is a perfect match for web-based applications. In fact, these applications are usually characterized by a number of small server-side components that perform relatively simple tasks. Other significant choices are Java, used in the J2EE platform, and the languages compatible with the ASP.NET environment, such as Visual Basic, C#, and JScript.

The example in Fig. 13.2 shows a PHP-based version of the login example shown in the Sect. 13.2.1. In PHP, the parameters of requests issued through the HTTP GET method are available in the predefined $_GET array. Also, PHP provides native support for sessions, and, therefore, it is extremely easy to keep

```
1  <?php
2
3  $username = $_GET["username"];
4  $password = $_GET["password"];
5
6  if (validate($username, $password)) {
7      session_start();
8      $_SESSION["user"] = $username;
9  ?>
10     <p>Welcome!</p>
11 <?php
12 } else {
13 ?>
14     <p>Invalid username or password!</p>
15 <?php
16 }
17 ?>
```

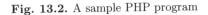

Fig. 13.2. A sample PHP program

```
 1 <%
 2 String username = request.getParameter ("username");
 3 String password = request.getParameter ("password");
 4
 5 if (validate(username, password)) {
 6     session.setAttribute ("user", username);
 7 %>
 8     <p>Welcome!</p>
 9 <%
10 } else {
11 %>
12     <p>Invalid username or password!</p>
13 <%
14 }
15 %>
```

Fig. 13.3. A sample JSP program

track of a user across different requests. In the example, users credentials are first checked using the `validate` function. If the validation is successful, a new session is started and a welcome message is printed; otherwise, an error message is sent back to the user. Note that in a PHP program it is possible to interleave PHP and HTML code.

Figure. 13.3 shows a similar program written using the JavaServer Pages (JSP) framework [32]. In both examples, the code of the `validate` function has been omitted for the sake of clarity.

13.3 Attacks

Web-based applications have fallen prey to a variety of different attacks that violate different security properties that should be enforced by the application. Note that here we are not concerned with attacks that might involve the infrastructure (e.g., in terms of web server and databases) or the operation of the network (e.g., in terms of routers and firewalls). Instead, we focus on attacks that try to induce a web-based application to behave in unforeseen (and unwanted) ways to disclose sensitive information or execute commands on behalf of the attacker.

Many web-based applications offer services that are available only to registered users, e.g., "premium" functionalities or personalized content. These services require that some *authentication* mechanism be in place to establish the identity of users. Errors in authentication code or logic can be exploited to bypass authentication or lock out legitimate users. For example, user credentials transferred in the clear to the application can be stolen by eavesdropping the network connection and weak authentication mechanisms can be broken by brute force or dictionary attacks [6].

Once a user has been authenticated, the application has to enforce the policy that establishes which resources are available to the user. Broken *authorization* can lead to elevation of privileges, disclosure of confidential data, and data tempering. Authorization mechanisms are particularly critical when web-based applications handle sensitive data, such as financial or health information.

Web-based applications tend to be large, heterogeneous, complex pieces of software, whose *configuration* is far from being trivial. Configuration problems may affect both the infrastructure (e.g., the account under which the web server runs or the configuration of a back-end database) and the web application itself (e.g., where the application stores its temporary files). Configuration errors can allow an attacker to bypass otherwise-effective authentication and authorization mechanisms. For example, improper configuration has been exploited to gain unauthorized access to administrative functionalities or retrieve sensitive information, such as secrets stored as plain-text in configuration files, such as database server passwords.

Attacks that exploit poorly designed authentication, faulty authorization, or configuration mechanisms are the cause of serious compromises. However, currently, most of attacks against web applications can be ascribed to one class of vulnerabilities: *improper input validation*. Most web application developers assume that they might receive from their users incorrect input, as a result either of an error or of malicious intent. Input validation is a defensive programming technique that makes sure that all user input is in the expected format and does not contain dangerous content. While simple in principle, performing correct and complete validation of all input data is a time-consuming task that requires notable expertise. Therefore, this type of flaw is all too common in current web-based applications.

The remaining of this section explores different types of attacks that take advantage of incorrect or missing input validation.

13.3.1 Interpreter Injection

Many dynamic languages include functions to dynamically compose and interpret code. For example, the PHP language provides the `eval` function, which accepts a string as a parameter and evaluates it as PHP code. If unchecked user input is used to compose the string to be evaluated, the application is vulnerable to arbitrary code execution.

For example, consider the following simple example of interpreter injection that was present in *Double Choco Latte* (version 0.9.4.3 and earlier), a PHP web-based application that provides basic project management functionality [2]. The attack URL is of the form

```
http://[target]/[dcl-directory]/
    main.php?menuAction=htmlTickets.show;system(id);ob_start
```

The parts of the request URL containing the strings `menuAction=html-Tickets.show` and `ob_start` are required to avoid errors. The arbitrary code is the part between these two string and, in the example above, corresponds to the part containing `system(id)`.

The vulnerability is contained in the following code snippet:

```
1 if ($g_oSec ->ValidateMenuAction () == true)
2 {
3       list ($class , $method) = explode ("." , $menuAction );
4       $obj = CreateObject ('dcl.' . $class );
5       eval ("\$obj ->$method ();");
6 }
7 else
8 {
9       commonHeader ();
10      PrintPermissionDenied ();
11 }
```

As can be seen from the code above, the `class` and `method` variables, obtained from the user's controlled `menuAction` variable, are never validated. Therefore, it is possible to insert a command to be executed in the string that represents the variable's value. After requesting the attack URL, the `eval` call becomes

```
eval("$obj->show;system(id);ob_start();");
```

Thus, in addition to execute the `show` method on the `obj` object, the interpreter will also execute the command specified by the attacker. In this example, the `id` UNIX command will be executed and the information about the user ID under which the command is executed will be printed. Of course, arbitrary (and more malicious) commands can be executed by exploiting this flaw.

One difficulty in preventing interpreter injection attacks is that popular languages offer many attack vectors. In PHP, `eval` and `preg_replace` can be used to interpret PHP code. In addition, the functions `system`, `passthru`, backticks, and `shell_exec` pass a command to the system shell. Finally, `exec`, `pcntl_exec`, `popen`, and `proc_open` can be used to execute external programs.

Some languages offer natively *sanitization* primitives that ensure that malicious user input is properly removed before use. For example, in PHP, `escapeshellarg` and `escapeshellcmd` can be used to escape quotes or other special characters that might be inserted to trick an application into executing arbitrary commands. However, programmers must be aware of the problem, choose the proper sanitization function, and remember to invoke it on all possible code paths that lead to an invocation of a dangerous function. This requires substantial expertise, and might be foiled by subsequent reorganizations of the code.

13.3.2 Filename Injection

Most languages used in the development of web-based applications allow programmers to dynamically include files to either interpret their content or present them to the user. This feature is used, e.g., to modularize an application by separating common functions into different files or to generate different page content depending on user's preferences, e.g., for internationalization purposes. If the choice of the file to be included can be manipulated by the user, a number of unintended consequences can follow. To worsen the situation, some languages, most notably PHP, even supports the inclusion of files from remote sites.

The following snippet of code illustrates a filename injection vulnerability in *txtForum*, an application to build forums [11]. In *txtForum*, pages are divided into parts, e.g., header, footer, forum view, etc., and can be customized by using different "skins," which are different combination of colors, fonts, and other presentation parameters. For example, the code that defines the header is the following:

```
1 DEFINE("SKIN","$skin");
2 ...
3 function
4 t_header($h_title,$pre_skin='',$admin_bgcolor='') {
5     ...
6     include(SKIN.'/header.tpl');
7 }
```

During execution, each page is composed by simply invoking the functions that are responsible for creating the various parts, e.g., t_header("page title"). Unfortunately, the skin variable can be controlled by an attacker, who can set it to cause the inclusion and evaluation of arbitrary content. Because PHP allows for the inclusion of remote files, the code to be added to the application can be hosted on a site under the attacker's control. For example, requesting the login.php page and passing the parameter skin with value http://[attacker-site] leads to the execution of the code at http://[attacker-site]/header.tpl.

For this type of problem, PHP does not offer any sanitization methods natively. Therefore, appropriate, ad hoc checks must be put in place by the developers.

13.3.3 Cross-Site Scripting

In Cross-site Scripting (XSS) attack, an attacker forces a client, typically a web browser, to execute attacker-supplied executable code, typically JavaScript code, which runs in the context of a trusted web site [14].

This attack allows the perpetrator to bypass the *same-origin* policy enforced by browsers when executing client-side code, typically JavaScript. The same-origin policy states that scripts or documents loaded from one site cannot get or set the properties of documents from different sites (i.e., from different "origins"). This prevents, for instance, a malicious web application from stealing sensitive information, such as cookies containing authentication information, associated with other applications running on different sites.

However, the same-origin policy can be circumvented, under certain conditions, when an application does not perform correct input validation. In these cases, the vulnerable application can be tricked into storing malicious code from an attacker and then presenting that malicious code to users, so it will be executed under the assumption that it originates from the vulnerable application rather than from the attacker.

There exist different forms of XSS attacks, depending on how malicious code is submitted to the vulnerable application and later echoed from the application to its users. In *non-persistent* (or *reflected*) attacks, the user is lured into visiting a specially crafted link that points to the vulnerable application and embeds the malicious code (e.g., as the value of a parameter or the name of a resource). When the link is activated the vulnerable web application immediately reflects the code to the user (e.g., as part of an error message). The code is then executed in the context of the vulnerable site and has access to all the information associated with the attacked application, such as authentication cookie or session information.

In *persistent* (or *stored*) attacks, the malicious code is first stored by the vulnerable application, and then, at a later time, it is presented to its users. In this case, the security of a user is compromised each time he/she visits a page whose content is determined using the stored malicious code. Typical examples of vulnerable applications include guestbook applications or blog systems. If they allow users to submit entries containing scripting code, then they are vulnerable to persistent XSS attacks.

A third form of XSS attacks, called *DOM-based*, is also possible. In this case, the vulnerable application presents to the users an HTML page that uses data from parts of its Document Object Model (DOM) in insecure ways [16]. The DOM is a data structure that allows client-side scripting code to dynamically access and modify the content, structure, and style of HTML documents. Some of its properties are populated by the browser on the basis of the request parameters, rather than on the characteristics of the document itself. For example, the `document.URL` and `document.location` properties are set to the URL of the document by the browser. If an HTML page contains code that dynamically changes the appearance of the page using the content of `document.URL` (e.g., to show to the user the URL associated with the page), it is possible to use a maliciously crafted URL to execute malicious scripting code.

An example of code vulnerable to non-persistent XSS attacks could be found in the application *PHP Advanced Transfer Manager* (version 1.30 and earlier) [28]. The vulnerability is contained in the following snippet of code.

```
1 $font = $_GET['font'];
2 ...
3 echo "<font face=\"$font\" color=\"$normalfontcolor\"
4          size=\"1\">\n";
```

The variable $font is under the control of the attacker because it is extracted from the request parameters and it is used to create the web page returned to the user, without any sanitizing check. To exploit this vulnerability, an attacker might request the following URL:

```
http://[target]/[path]/viewers/txt.php?font=
  \%22\%3E\%3Cscript\%3Ealert(document.cookie)\%3C/script\%3E
```

As a consequence, the vulnerable application will generate the following web page:

```
<font face=""><script>alert(document.cookie)</script>
```

When interpreted by the browser, the scripting code will be executed and it will show in a pop-up window the cookies associated with the current page. Clearly, a real attack would, for instance, send the cookies to the attacker.

13.3.4 SQL Injection

A web-based application has an SQL injection vulnerability when it uses unsanitized user data to compose queries that are later passed to a relational database for evaluation [1, 30]. This can lead to arbitrary queries being executed on the database with the privileges of the vulnerable application.

For example, consider the following code snippet:

```
1 $activate = $_GET["activate"];
2 $result = dbquery("SELECT * FROM new_users " .
3                    "WHERE user_code='$activate'");
4 if ($result) {
5    ...
6 }
```

The dbquery function is used to perform a query to a back-end database and return the results to the application. The query is dynamically composed by collating a static string with a user-provided parameter. In this case, the activate variable is set to the content of the homonymous request parameter. The intended use of the variable is to contain the user's personal code to dynamically compose the page's content. However, if an attacker submits a request where the activate parameter is set to the string ' OR 1=1 -- the query will return the content of the entire new_users table. If the result of the query is later used as the page content, this will expose personal information. Other attacks, such as the deletion of database tables or the addition of new users, are also possible.

13.3.5 Session Hijacking

Most web applications use HTTP as their communication protocol [5]. HTTP is a stateless protocol, i.e., there is no built-in mechanism that allows an application to maintain state throughout a series of requests issued by the same user. However, virtually all non-trivial applications need a way to correlate the current request with the history of previous requests, i.e., they need a "session" view of their interaction with users. In e-commerce sites, e.g., a user adds to a cart items he/she intends to buy and later proceeds to the checkout. Even though these operations are performed in separated requests, the application has to keep the state of the user's cart through all requests, so that the cart can be displayed to the user at checkout-time.

Consequently, a number of mechanisms have been introduced to provide applications with the abstraction of sessions. Some languages provide session-like mechanisms at the language level, others rely on special libraries. In other cases, session management has to be implemented at the application level.

The session state can be maintained in different ways. It can be encoded in a document transmitted to the user in a way that will guarantee that the information is sent back as part of later requests. For example, HTML hidden form fields can be used for this purpose. These fields are not showed to the user, but when the user submits the form, the hidden variables are sent back to the application as part of the form's data. In our e-commerce example, the application might keep the current sub-total of the transaction in a hidden field. When the user chooses the shipping method, the field is returned to the application and used to calculate the final total cost.

The state can be kept in cookies sent to a user's browser and automatically resent by the browser to the application at subsequent visits. Cookies might contain the items currently inserted in a user's cart. The application, during checkout, looks up the price of each item and presents the total cost to the user.

All the methods mentioned above require the client to cooperate with the application to store the session state. A different approach consists in storing the state of all sessions on the server. Therefore, each user is assigned a unique session ID, and this is the only information that is sent back and forth between the application and the user, e.g., by means of a cookie, or of a similar mechanism that rewrites all the URLs in the page adding the session identifier as a parameter. As a consequence, every future request will include the session identifier as a parameter. Then, whenever the user submits a request to the site, e.g., to add an item to the cart, the application receives the session ID, looks up the associated session in its repository, and updates the session's data according to the request.

A number of attacks have been designed against session state management mechanisms. Approaches that require clients to keep the state assume that the client will not change the session state, e.g., by modifying the hidden field (or the cookie) and storing the current sub-total to lower the price of an item. Countermeasures include the use of cryptographic techniques to sign parameters and cookies to make them tamper-resistant.

A more general attack is *session fixation*. Session fixation forces a user's session ID to an explicit value of the attacker's choice [17]. The attack requires three steps. First, the attacker sets up a session with the target application and obtains a session ID. Then, the attacker lures the victim into accessing the target application using the fixed session ID. Finally, the attacker waits until the victim has successfully performed all the required authentication and authorization operations and then impersonates the victim by using the fixed session ID. Depending on the characteristics of the target web applications, different methods can be used to fix the session ID. In the simplest case, an attacker can simply lure the users into selecting a link that contains a request to the application with a parameter that specifies the session ID, such as `<a href="http://[target]/login.php?sessionid=1234">`.

13.3.6 Response Splitting

HTTP response splitting is an attack in which the attacker is able to set the value of an HTTP header field such that the resulting response stream is interpreted by the attack target as two responses rather than one [15]. Response splitting is an instance of a more general category of attacks that takes advantage of discrepancies in parsing when two or more devices or entities process the data flow between a server and a client.

To perform response splitting the attacker must be able to inject data containing the header termination characters and the beginning of a second header. This is usually possible when user's data is used (unsanitized) to determine the value of an HTTP header. These conditions are commonly met in situations where web applications need to redirect users, e.g., after the login process. The redirection, in fact, is generally performed by sending to the user a response with appropriately set `Location` or `Refresh` headers.

The following example shows part of a JSP page that is vulnerable to response splitting attack:

```
1 <%
2 response.sendRedirect ("/by_lang.jsp?lang=" +
3     request.getParameter ("lang"));
4 %>
```

When the page is invoked, the request parameter `lang` is used to determine the redirect target. In the normal case, the user will pass a string representing the preferred language, say en_US. In this case, the JSP application generates a response containing the header

`Location: http://vulnerable.com/by\_lang.jsp?lang=en\_US.`

However, consider the case where an attacker submits a request where `lang` is set to the following string:

```
dummy%0d%0a
Content-Length:%200
%0d%0a%0d%0a
HTTP/1.1%20200%20OK%0d%0a
Content-Type:%20text/html%0d%0a
Content-Length:%2019%0d%0a%0d%0a
<html>New document</html>
```

The generated response will now contain multiple copies of the headers Content-Length and Content-Type, namely those injected by the attacker and the ones inserted by the application. As a consequence, depending on implementation details, intermediate servers and clients may interpret the response as containing two documents: the original one and the document forged by the attacker.

Use cases of the attack most often mention web cache poisoning. In fact, if a caching proxy server interprets the response stream as containing two documents and associates the second one, forged by the attacker, with the original request, then an attacker would be able to insert in the cache of the proxy a page of his/her choice in association to a URL in the vulnerable application.

Recently, support to contrast response splitting has been introduced in some languages, most notably PHP. In the remaining cases, the programmer is responsible to properly sanitize data used to construct response headers.

13.4 Vulnerability Analysis

The term *vulnerability analysis* refers to the process of assessing the security of an application through auditing of either the application's code or the application's behavior for possible security problems. In this section, we survey current approaches to vulnerability analysis of web-based applications and classify them along two characterizing axes: *detection model* and *analysis technique*. We show how existing vulnerability analysis techniques are extended to address the specific characteristics of web application security, in terms of both technologies (as seen in Sect. 13.2) and types of attacks (as shown in Sect. 13.3).

The identification of vulnerabilities in web applications can be performed following one of two orthogonal detection approaches: the *negative* (or vulnerability based) approach and the *positive* (or behavior based) approach.

In the negative approach, the analysis process first builds abstract models of known vulnerabilities (e.g., by encoding expert knowledge) and then matches the models against web-based applications, to identify instances of the modeled vulnerabilities. In the positive approach, the analysis process first builds models of the "normal," or expected, behavior of an application (e.g., using machine-learning techniques) and then uses these models to analyze the application behavior to identify any abnormality that might be caused by a security violation.

Regardless of whether a positive or negative detection approach is followed, there are two fundamental analysis techniques that can be used to analyze the security of web applications: *static analysis* and *dynamic analysis*.

Static analysis provides a set of pre-execution techniques for predicting dynamic properties of the analyzed program. One of the main advantages of static analysis is that it does not require the application to be deployed and executed. Since static analysis can take into account all possible inputs to the application by leveraging data abstraction techniques, it has the potential to be sound, i.e., it will not produce any false negatives. In addition, static analysis techniques have no impact on the performance of the actual application because they are applied before execution. Unfortunately, a number of fundamental static analysis problems, such as *may alias* and *must alias*, are either undecidable or uncomputable. Consequently, the results obtained via static analysis are usually only a safe and computable approximation of actual application behavior. As a result, static analysis techniques usually are not complete and suffer from false positives, i.e., these techniques often flag as vulnerable parts of an application that do not contain flaws.

Dynamic analysis, on the other hand, consists of a series of checks to detect vulnerabilities and prevent attacks at run-time. Since the analysis is done on a "live" application, it is less prone to false positives. However, it can suffer from false negatives, since only a subset of possible input values is usually processed by the application and not all vulnerable execution paths are exercised.

In practice, hybrid approaches, which mix both static and dynamic techniques, are frequently used to combine the strengths and minimize the limitations of the two approaches. Since many of the approaches described hereinafter are hybrid, in the context of this chapter, we will use the term *static techniques* to signify that the detection of vulnerabilities/attacks is done based on some information derived at pre-execution time and the term *dynamic techniques* when the detection is done based on dynamically acquired data. We will use the *positive* vs *negative* approach dichotomy as our main taxonomy when describing current research in security analysis of web-based applications.

This section is structured as follows. Sects. 13.4.1 and 13.4.2 discuss negative and positive approaches, respectively. Each section is further divided into subsections covering static and dynamic techniques. Sect. 13.4.3 summarizes the challenges in the security analysis of web-based applications and proposes directions for future work.

13.4.1 Negative Approaches

In the context of the vulnerability analysis of web-based applications, we define as the *negative approaches* those approaches that use characteristics of known security vulnerabilities and their underlying causes to find security flaws in web-based applications. More specifically, known vulnerabilities are first modeled, often implicitly, and then applications are checked for instances of such models. For example, one model for the *SQL Injection* vulnerability in PHP applications can be defined as "untrusted user input containing SQL commands is passed to an SQL database through a call to mysql_query()."

The vast majority of negative approaches to web vulnerability analysis are based on the assumption that web-specific vulnerabilities are the result of insecure data flow in applications. That is, most models attempt to identify when untrusted user input propagates to security-critical functions without being properly checked and sanitized.

As a result, the analysis is often approached as a *taint propagation* problem. In taint-based analysis, data originated from the user input is marked as tainted and its propagation throughout the program is traced (either statically or dynamically) to check whether it can reach security-critical program points.

When taint propagation analysis is used, models of known vulnerabilities are often built implicitly and are simply expressed in the form of the analysis performed. For example, the models are often expressed by specifying the following two classes of objects:

1. A set of possible sources of untrusted input (such as variables or function calls).
2. A set of functions, often called *sinks*, whose input parameters have to be checked for malicious values.

To track the flow of data from sources in (1) to sinks in (2), the type system of the given language is extended with at least two new types: tainted and untainted. In addition, the analysis has to provide a mechanism to represent transitions from tainted to untainted, and vice versa. Usually, such transitions are identified using a set of technique-specific heuristics. For example, tainted data can become untainted if it is passed to some known sanitization routine. However, modeling sanitization is a very complex task, and, therefore, some approaches simply extend the language with additional type operations, such as untaint() and require programmers to explicitly execute these operations to untaint the data.

In the following two subsections, we explore in greater details how negative approaches are applied, both statically and dynamically, to the vulnerability analysis of web-based applications.

Static Techniques

All of the works described in this section use standard *static analysis* techniques to identify vulnerabilities in web-based applications. Despite the fact that many of the static analysis problems have been proven to be undecidable, or at least uncomputable, this type of analysis is still an attractive approach for a number of reasons. In particular, static analysis can be applied to applications before the deployment phase, and, unlike dynamic analysis, static analysis usually does not require modification of the deployment environment, which might introduce overhead and also pose a threat to the stability of the application. Therefore, static analysis is especially suitable for the web applications domain, where the deployment of vulnerable applications or the execution in an unstable environment can result in a substantial business cost.

As a result, there is much recent work that explores the application of static analysis techniques to the domain of web-based applications. The current focus of the researchers in this field is mostly on the analysis of applications written in PHP [10, 12, 13, 37] and Java [9, 21]. This phenomenon can be explained by the growing popularity of both languages. For example, the popularity of PHP has grown tremendously over the last five years, making PHP one of the most commonly used languages on the Web. According to the Netcraft Survey [24], about 21,000,000 sites were using PHP in March of 2006 compared to about 1,500,000 sites in March of 2000. In the monthly Security Space Reports [29], PHP has constantly been rated as the most popular Apache module over the last years. In the Programming Community Index report published monthly by TIOBE Sofware [34], Java and PHP are consistently rated in the top five most popular programming languages around the world.

A tool named WebSSARI [10] is one of the first works that applies taint propagation analysis to finding security vulnerabilities in PHP. WebSSARI targets three specific types of vulnerabilities: cross-site scripting, SQL injection, and general script injection. The tool uses flow-sensitive, intra-procedural analysis based on a lattice model and typestate. In particular, the PHP language is extended with two *type-qualifiers*, namely `tainted` and `untainted`, and the tool keeps track of the type-state of variables. The tool uses three user-provided files, called *prelude files*: a file with pre-conditions to all sensitive functions (i.e., the sinks), a file with post-conditions for known sanitization functions, and a file specifying all possible sources of untrusted input. In order to untaint the tainted data, the data has to be processed by a sanitization routine or cast to a safe type. When the tool determines that tainted data reaches sensitive functions, it automatically inserts *run-time guards*, or sanitization routines.

The WebSSARI tool is not publicly available and the chapter does not provide enough implementation details to draw definitive conclusions about the tool's behavior. However, from the information available, one can deduce that WebSSARI has at least the following weaknesses. First of all, the analysis performed seems to be intra-procedural only. Secondly, to remain sound, all dynamic variables, arrays, and other complex data structures, which are commonly used in scripting languages, are considered tainted. This should greatly reduce the precision of the analysis. Also, WebSSARI provides only a limited support for identifying and modeling sanitization routines: sanitization done through the use of regular expressions is not supported.

A more recent work by Xie and Aiken [37] uses intra-block, intra-procedural, and inter-procedural analysis to find SQL injection vulnerabilities in PHP code. This approach uses *symbolic execution* to model the effect of statements inside the basic blocks of intra-procedural Control Flow Graphs (CFGs). The resulting *block summary* is then used for intra-procedural analysis, where a standard reachability analysis is used to obtain a *function summary*. Along with other information, each block summary contains a set of locations that were untainted in the given block. The block summaries are composed to generate the function summary, which contains the pre- and post-conditions of the function. The pre-conditions for the function contain a derived set of memory locations that have to be sanitized before function invocation, while the post-conditions contain the set of parameters and global variables that are sanitized inside the function. To model the effects of sanitization routines, the approach uses a programmer-provided set of possible sanitization routines, considers certain forms of casting as a sanitization process, and, in addition, it keeps a database of sanitizing regular expressions, whose effects are specified by the programmer.

The approach proposed by Xie and Aiken has a number of advantages when compared to WebSSARI. First of all, it is able to give a more precise analysis due to the use of inter-procedural analysis. Secondly, their analysis technique is able to derive pre-conditions for some functions automatically. Also, the Xie and Aiken approach provides support for arrays, commonly used data structures in PHP, in the presence of simple aliases. However, they only simulate a subset of PHP constructs that they believe is relevant to SQL injection vulnerabilities. In addition, there seems to be no support for the object-oriented features of PHP, and the modeling of the effects of many sanitization routines still depends on manual specification.

One of the most recent works on applying taint-propagation analysis for security assessment of applications written in Java is the work by Livshits and Lam [21]. They apply a scalable and precise points-to analysis to discover a number of web-specific vulnerabilities, such as SQL injection, cross-site scripting, and HTTP response splitting. The proposed approach uses a context-sensitive (but flow insensitive) Java points-to analysis based on Binary Decision Diagrams (BDDs) developed by Whaley and Lam [36]. The analysis is performed on the byte-code–level image of the program and a Program Query Language (PQL) is used to describe the vulnerabilities to be identified.

The main problem with the Livshits and Lam's approach is the fact that each vulnerability that can be detected by their tool has to be manually described in PQL. Therefore, previously unknown vulnerabilities cannot be detected and the detection of known vulnerabilities is only as good as their specification.

Even though static analysis has a number of desirable characteristics that make it suitable for web vulnerability analysis, it also has a number of both inherent and domain-specific challenges that have to be met to be able to apply it to real-world applications in an effective way. First of all, static analysis heavily depends on language-specific parsers that are built based on a language grammar. While this is not generally a problem for general-purpose languages, such as Java and C, grammars for some scripting languages, like PHP, might not be explicitly defined or might need some workarounds to be able to generate valid parsers.

More importantly, many web applications are written in dynamic scripting languages that facilitate the use of complex data structures, such as arrays and hash structures using non-literal indices. Moreover, the problems associated with alias analysis and the analysis of object-oriented code are exacerbated in scripting languages, which provide support for dynamic typing, dynamic code inclusion, arbitrary code evaluation (e.g., `eval()` in PHP), and dynamic variable naming (e.g., $$ in PHP). Some of these challenges are described in greater details in the recent research work of Jovanovic et al. who developed a static analysis tool for PHP, called Pixy [12], and implemented new precise alias analysis algorithms [13] targeting the specifics of the PHP language.

Other solutions and workarounds to these challenges include different techniques, such as abstraction of language features or simplification of the analysis, and result in different levels of precision of the analysis. For example, the WebSSARI tool chooses to ignore all complex language structures by simply considering them tainted. The tool proposed by Xie and Aiken models only a subset of PHP language that is believed to be relevant to the targeted class of vulnerabilities. Lam and Livshits, on the other hand, apply scalable points-to analysis to the full Java language, but choose to abstract away from flow sensitivity.

Precise evaluation of sanitization routines becomes even more difficult for applications written in scripting languages. Dynamic languages features stimulate programmers to extensively use regular expression and dynamic-type casting to sanitize user data. Unfortunately, it is not possible to simply consider the process of matching a regular expression against tainted data as a form of sanitization, if the analysis has to be sound. To increase the precision of the analysis, it is necessary to provide a more detailed characterization of the filtering performed by the regular expression matching process.

One of the main drawbacks of static analysis in general is its susceptibility to false positives caused by inevitable analysis imprecisions. Researches only started exploring the benefits of applying traditional static analysis techniques, such as symbolic execution and points-to analysis, to the domain of web-based applications. However, the first efforts in this direction clearly show that web-based applications have their domain-specific additional complexities, which require novel static analysis techniques.

Dynamic Techniques

The dynamic negative approach technique is also based on taint analysis. As for the static case, untrusted sources, sensitive sinks, and the ways in which tainting propagates need to be modeled. However, instead of running the analysis on the source code of an application, either the interpreter or the program itself are first extended/instrumented to collect the right information and then the tainted data is tracked and analyzed as the application executes.

Perl's *Taint mode* [27] is one of the best-known example of dynamic taint propagation mechanism. When the Perl interpreter is invoked with the -T option, it makes sure that no data obtained from the outside environment (such as user input, environment variables, calls to specific functions, etc.) can be used in security critical functions (commands that invoke sub-shell, modify files, etc.). Even though this mode can be considered too conservative because it can taint data that might not be tainted in reality,[1] it is a valuable security protection against several of the attacks described in Sect. 13.3.

Unsurprisingly, approaches similar to Perl taint mode have been applied to other languages as well. For example, Nguyen-Tuong et al. [25] propose modification of the PHP interpreter to dynamically track tainted data in PHP programs. Haldar et al. [8] apply a similar approach to the Java Virtual Machine (JVM).

The approach followed by Nguyen-Tuong et al. modifies the standard PHP interpreter to identify data originated from untrusted sources in order to prevent command injection and cross-site scripting attacks. In the modified interpreter, strings are tainted at the granularity of the single character and tainting is propagated across assignments, compositions, and function calls. Also, the source of taintedness, such as the parameters of a GET method and the cookies associated with a request, is kept associated with each tainted string. Such precision comes at a price, and even though the authors report a low average overhead, the overhead of run-time taint tracking sometimes reaches 77%. Besides the possible high overhead, the proposed solution has the additional disadvantage that the only way to untaint a tainted string is to explicitly call a newly defined `untaint` routine, which requires manual modification of legacy code. In addition, deciding when and where to untaint a string is an error-prone activity that requires security expertise.

The approach proposed by Haldar et al. implements a taint propagation framework for an arbitrary JVM by using Java bytecode instrumentation. In the framework, system classes like `java.lang.String` and `java.lang.-StringBuffer` are instrumented to propagate taintedness. This instrumentation has to be done off-line because no modification of system classes is allowed at run- or load-time by the JVM. All other classes are instrumented at loading time. Tainted data can be untainted by passing the data to one of the methods of the `java.lang.String` class that performs some kind of checking or matching operations.

The dynamic approach to the taint propagation problem has some advantages over static analysis. First of all, a modified interpreter can be transparently applied to all deployed applications. Even more important, no complex

---

[1] For example, Perl considers any sub-expression of tainted expressions to be tainted as well.

analysis framework for features such as alias analysis is required, because all the required information is available as the result of program execution.

However, there are some inherent disadvantages of this approach as well. As noted earlier, the analysis is only performed on executed paths and does not give any guarantee about paths not covered during a given execution. This is not a problem if the modified interpreter is used in production versions of the application, but provides no guarantees of security if the dynamic analysis framework is used in test versions only.

Another problem associated with the use of dynamic techniques is the possible impact on application functionality. More precisely, dynamic checks might result in the termination or blocking of a dangerous statement, which, in turn, might have the side-effect of halting the application or blocking it in the middle of a transaction. Also, any error in the modifications performed on the interpreter or in the instrumentation code can have an impact on application stability and might not be acceptable in some production systems.

More importantly, despite the fact that dynamic analysis has the potential of being more precise, it can still suffer from both false positives and false negatives. If taint propagation is done in an overly conservative way, safe data can still be considered tainted and lead to a high false positive rate. Imprecisions in the modeling of untainting operations, on the other hand, can lead to false negatives. Unfortunately, in either case, the increased precision comes at the price of increased overhead and worse run-time performance.

Summary

As we have shown, many known classes of web-specific vulnerabilities are the result of improper or insufficient input validation and can be tackled as a taint propagation problem. Taint propagation analysis can be done either statically or dynamically, and, depending on the approach taken, it has both strengths and weaknesses. In particular, if it is done statically, the precision of the analysis highly depends on the ability of dealing with the complexities of dynamic features. Precise evaluation of sanitization routines is especially important, and none of the current approaches is able to deal with this aspect effectively. If taint propagation analysis is done dynamically, on the other hand, issues of analysis completeness, application stability, and performance arise.

Regardless of the approach taken, taint propagation analysis depends on the correct identification of the sets of untrusted sources and sensitive sinks. Any error in identifying these sets can lead to incorrect results. Currently, there is no known fully automated way to derive these sets, and at least some sources and sinks have to be specified manually. The other challenge, which is common to all taint propagation based approaches, is how to safely untaint previously tainted data to decrease the number of false positives. In many cases, this becomes a problem of precise sanitization identification, evaluation, or modeling.

However, taint propagation analysis is not the only possible negative approach to vulnerability analysis of web-based applications. For example, Minamide [22] proposes another approach to static detection of cross-site scripting attacks in PHP applications. The PHP string analyzer developed by Minamide approximates the output of PHP applications and constructs a context-free grammar for the output language. This grammar is then statically checked against user-provided description of unsafe strings.

For example, a user can describe the cross-site scripting vulnerability as the regular expression ".*<script>.*." In this case, if the `script` tag is contained in the output language of an application, the application will be marked as vulnerable to cross-site scripting. As originally presented by Minamide, this approach cannot be applied to check for cross-site scripting vulnerabilities in real-world applications, because of its high false-positive rate. For example, all applications that are designed to generate JavaScript code would be considered vulnerable. Since cross-site scripting is in the class of vulnerabilities caused by improper handling of user input, some mechanism to identify user input in program-produced output is needed.

In general, negative approaches rely on the knowledge of causes and manifestations of different types of vulnerabilities. Their main disadvantage is that the analyzers developed for a particular set of vulnerabilities might not be able to recognize previously unknown classes of vulnerabilities. Nonetheless, currently, this is the most adopted approach because many vulnerabilities, both known and newly discovered, are caused by the same type of problems, such as insufficient input validation. As a result, the same analysis techniques can be effectively applied to detect a wide range of vulnerabilities.

13.4.2 Positive Approaches

In the *positive approaches* to the identification of vulnerabilities in web-based applications, the analysis is based on inferred or derived models of the "normal" application behavior. These models are then used, usually at run-time, to verify if the dynamic application behavior conforms to the established models, in the assumption that (1) deviations are manifestations of attacks or vulnerabilities and (2) attacks create an anomalous manifestation.

Models are built either statically, using some form of analysis done at preexecution time, or dynamically, as a result of analysis of dynamic application behavior. Detection of attacks (or vulnerabilities) is almost always done at run-time, and, thus, most approaches are not purely static or dynamic in the traditional sense, but should be considered hybrid. In the context of this section, we will classify the approaches as *static* if models are built prior to program execution, and as *dynamic* otherwise.

Static Techniques

Static models of expected application behavior are usually derived either automatically, by means of traditional static analysis techniques, or analytically, by deducing a set of rules that must hold during program execution. Usually, models are not concerned with all aspects of application behavior, but instead they focus on specific application properties that are relative to specific types of attacks/vulnerabilities.

A good example of the static, positive approach is the work of Halfond and Orso, whose tool is called AMNESIA [9]. AMNESIA is particularly concerned with detecting and preventing SQL injection attacks for Java-based applications. During the static analysis part, the tool builds a conservative model of expected SQL queries. Then, at run-time, dynamically generated queries are checked against the derived model to identify instances that violate the intended structure of a query. AMNESIA uses the Java String Analysis (JSA) [4], a static analysis technique, to build an automata-based model of the set of legitimate strings that a program can produce at given points in the code. AMNESIA also leverages the approach proposed by Gould et al. [7] to statically check type correctness of dynamically generated SQL queries.

More precisely, Halfond and Orso define an SQL injection as the attack in which the logic or semantics of a legitimate SQL statement is changed due to malicious injection of new SQL keywords or operators. Thus, to detect such attacks, the semantics of dynamically generated queries must be checked against a derived model that represents the intended semantics of the query.

AMNESIA builds a Non-Deterministic Finite Automata (NDFA) model of possible string expressions for each program point where SQL queries are generated. The derived character-level NDFA is then simplified through string abstraction. The resulting model represents the structure of the legitimate SQL query and consists of SQL tokens intermixed with a place holder, which is used to denote any string other than SQL tokens. To detect SQL injection attacks at run-time, the web-based application is instrumented with calls to a monitor that checks if the queries generated at run-time respect the abstract query structure derived statically.

The approach proposed by Halfond and Orso is based on the following two assumptions. First of all, they assume that the source code of the program contains enough information to build models of legitimate queries. It can be argued that this is usually the case with most applications. The second assumption, stated also by the authors, is that the SQL injection attack must violate the derived model in order to be detected. This is generally a safe assumption given that models are able to distinguish between SQL tokens and other strings. However, AMNESIA will generate false positives if an application allows user input to contain SQL keywords. The authors argue that this does not represent a real problem because usually only database-administration tools perform such queries.

The work by Su and Wassermann [31] is another example of positive approach that targets *injection attacks*, such as XSS, XPath injection, and shell injection attacks. However, the current implementation, called *SqlCheck* is designed to detect SQL injection attacks only. The approach works by tracking substrings from user input through program execution. The tracking is implemented by augmenting the string with special characters, which mark the start and the end of each substring. Then, dynamically generated queries are intercepted and checked by a modified SQL parser. Using the meta-information provided by the substring markers, the parser is able to determine if the query syntax is modified by the substring derived from user input, and, in that case, it blocks the query.

Unlike in AMNESIA, in *SqlCheck* the model of application-specific legitimate SQL queries is built somewhat implicitly at pre-execution time and is expressed in the form of an *augmented grammar*. The observation made by the authors is that any non-malicious SQL query should have a node whose descendants comprise the entire input substring. These syntactically correct queries are modeled by introducing additional rules into the augmented SQL grammar. For example, if characters ≪ and ≫ are used to mark the start and the end of user input strings and the augmented SQL grammar has a production rule `value ::= ≪id≫`, then an entire user input substring covered by the subtree of the `value` node is considered non-malicious even if it contains SQL keywords. Thus, SQL grammar productions are used to implicitly specify which non-terminals are allowed to be roots of user input substrings.

The approach proposed by Su and Wassermann has one advantage over other approaches that have been shown so far. Since it works with the output language grammar (i.e., the SQL grammar), it does not require any analysis of the application source code, and, therefore, the tool can be potentially applied to applications written in different languages. However, the approach requires that the application code marks user input with meta-characters, which have to be inserted into the application either manually by the programmers or automatically as a result of some form of static analysis. In addition, from the published research, it is not clear whether or not the augmented SQL grammar has to be redefined for each tested application based on knowledge of the type of queries generated by that application.

One disadvantage that both the approaches described above have in common is the fact that detection of attacks or vulnerabilities can only be done at run-time. As a result, any error in model construction can result in undesired side effects, such as undetected application compromises or the blocking of valid queries.

To the best of our knowledge, in the web applications domain, the positive approach so far has only been applied to the detection of SQL injection attacks. However, this approach has the potential of being applied to a wider range of attacks resulting from insecure input handling by an application, such as cross-site scripting and interpreter injection attacks. More important, unlike the taint propagation analysis approaches described in Sect. 13.4.1, positive approaches have the potential for being used to detect attacks that exploit logical errors in applications, such as attacks exploring insufficient authentication, authorization, and session management mechanisms.

Dynamic Techniques

Positive approaches based on dynamic information build models of expected behavior of an application by analyzing the application's execution profiles associated with attack-free input. In other words, the application's behavior is monitored during normal operation, and then the profiles are derived on the basis of the collected meta-information such as log files or system call traces. After the models have been established, the run-time behavior of an application is compared to the established models, to identify discrepancies that might represent evidence of malicious activity.

Traditionally, this approach has been applied to the area of learning-based anomaly detection systems. An example of the application of this approach to web-based application is represented by the work of Kruegel and Vigna [18]. In this case, an anomaly detection system utilizes a number of statistical models to identify anomalous events in a set of web requests that use parameters to pass values to the server-side components of a web-based application.

The anomaly detection system operates on the URLs extracted from successful web requests. The set of URLs is further partitioned into subsets corresponding to each component of the web-based application (e.g., each PHP file). The anomaly detector processes each subset of queries independently, associating models with each of the parameters used to pass input values to a specific component of the web-based application.

The anomaly detection models are a set of procedures used to evaluate a certain feature of a request parameter, and operate in one of two modes, learning or detection. In the learning phase, models build a profile of the "normal" characteristics of a given feature of a parameter (e.g., the normal length of values for a parameter), setting a dynamic detection threshold for the parameter. During the detection phase, models return an anomaly score for each observed example of a parameter value. This is simply a probability on the interval $[0, 1]$ indicating how probable the observed value is in relation to the established profile for that parameter (note that a score close to zero indicates a highly anomalous value). For example, there are models that characterize the normal length and the expected character distribution of string parameters, models that derive the structure of path-like parameters, and models that infer if a parameter takes only a value out of a limited set of constants [19].

Since there are generally multiple models associated with each parameter passed to a web application, a final anomaly score for an observed parameter value during the detection phase is calculated as 1 minus the weighted sum of the individual model scores. If the weighted anomaly score is greater than the detection threshold determined during the learning phase for that parameter, the anomaly detector considers the entire request anomalous and raises an alert.

The advantage of this approach is that, in principle, it does not require any human interaction. The system is able to automatically learn the profiles that describe the normal usage of an application and then it is able to determine abnormal use of a server-side component. In addition, by following a positive approach, this technique is able to detect both known and unknown attacks. Finally, by operating on the requests sent to the server, this approach is completely language independent and therefore can be applied, without modification, to web-based application developed with any technology.

The main disadvantage of this approach is shared by all the anomaly detection systems. These systems rely on two assumptions, namely that an anomaly is evidence of malicious behavior and that malicious behavior will generate an anomaly. Neither assumption is always valid. When the first assumption is violated, the system generates a false positive, i.e., a normal request is blocked or identified as malicious. When the second assumption is violated, the system generates a false negative, i.e., it fails to detect an attack.

Summary

Positive approaches have the advantage that, by specifying the normal, expected state of a web-based application, they can usually detect an attack whether it is part of the threat model or not. On the other hand, the concept of normality is difficult to define for certain classes of applications, and the creation of models that correctly characterize the behavior of an application still requires the use of ad hoc heuristics and manual work. Therefore, web vulnerability analysis systems based on the positive approach are not as popular as the ones based on the negative approach.

Another problem of these systems is that they are in general vulnerable to mimicry attacks [35]. These are attacks where a vulnerability is exploited in a way that makes its manifestation similar to what is considered to be normal usage in order to avoid detection. To counter these attacks, the models should be tightly "fit" to the application. Unfortunately, tighter models are more prone to produce false positives, and determining the right detection threshold to optimize detection and minimize errors still requires manual intervention and substantial expertise.

Finally, all known positive approaches require some form of run-time monitoring of the application behavior and, therefore, are likely to introduce some form of overhead.

13.4.3 Challenges and Solutions

Web-based applications are complex systems, and while in the previous sections we have shown a number of approaches that attempt to make this class of applications more secure, there are still a number of open problems, which will likely be the focus of research in the next few years.

A first general consideration is that there is no approach or technique that can be considered "the silver bullet," under all conditions and cases. One challenge is, thus, that of combining the strengths from the various techniques and approaches that we have described so far.

Another general consideration is that there is already a corpus of work on vulnerability analysis techniques for traditional applications that can be extended to web-based applications. While some of the existing techniques can be applied to the web domain with little effort, some characteristics of web-based applications make the adaptation process difficult. For example, web-based applications implement shared, persistent state in a number of ways, such as cookies, back-end databases, etc. Modeling this state is not trivial when applying "traditional" vulnerability analysis techniques that were mostly developed for the analysis of structured languages such as C and C++.

In addition, some web-based applications have a complex interaction model and are assembled as a composition of various, heterogeneous modules, written in different languages. One challenge is thus to develop analysis techniques that are able to take into account the interaction between all the different technologies used in a web-based application. Consider, e.g., a web-based application, in which a module, written in PHP, stores a value obtained from a user in a back-end database. This value is then retrieved by a module written in Python and used, without any sanitization, to perform a sensitive operation. In this case, the vulnerability analysis process should be able to analyze PHP, Python, and SQL code to identify the path that can bring the user-defined value to be used in a sensitive operation. Unfortunately, currently there are no techniques that are able to perform this type of analysis.

Another group of challenges is specific to the different techniques and approaches. For example, in the case of static analysis, it is necessary to include new techniques to perform more precise analysis in the context of dynamic languages. These new techniques should support object-oriented code, dynamic features of languages (e.g., $$ in PHP), complex data structures, etc.

Another major challenge is represented by the correct modeling of sanitization. So far, the only way to characterize sanitization in an application has been through simple heuristics. For example, if tainted data is passed to string manipulation functions or to functions that return an integer value, the data is considered "safe." This approach is too naïve and it might lead to attacks that are able to exploit "blind spots" in the sanitization routines. Therefore, it is important to provide techniques and tools to better model sanitization operations and to assess whether a sanitization operation is appropriate for the task at hand (e.g., the sanitization necessary to prevent SQL injection is different from the sanitization required to avoid XSS attacks.)

Another set of challenges is represented by novel, web-specific attack techniques. In fact, while vulnerabilities caused by improper input validation are starting to be well known, well studied, and effectively detected, new vulnerabilities begin to surface. For example, attacks that tend to violate the intended logic of a web application cannot be easily expressed in terms of tainting. Consider, e.g., a web-based application that implements an e-commerce site. A login process allows a registered user to access a catalog with links to sensitive documents. The developer assumed that the only way to access these documents is through the catalog page, which is presented to the user after the login process. Unfortunately, there is no automatic mechanism that prevents a de-registered user to simply provide the address of a sensitive document and completely bypass the authentication procedure. In this case, the attacker has not violated the logic of a web-application component. It has simply violated the implicit workflow of the application. Modeling and protecting from this types of attacks is still an open problem.

Finally, a set of challenges in the field is posed by the need to compare results between different approaches. Currently, there is no standard, accepted dataset usable as base-line for evaluation. While there exists some effort to build "standard" applications with known sets of vulnerabilities (e.g., Web-Goat [26]), there is still no consensus inside the security community on which applications to use for testing and how. As a consequence, every tool is evaluated on a different set of applications and a fair comparison of different approaches is not possible.

As web-based applications will become the prevalent way to provide services and distribute information on the Internet, the challenges described above will have to be addressed to support the development of secure applications based on web technologies.

References

1. C. Anley. Advanced SQL Injection in SQL Server Applications. Technical report, Next Generation Security Software, Ltd, 2002.
2. J. Bercegay. Double Choco Latte Vulnerabilities. http://www.gulftech.org/?node=research&article_id=00066-04082005, April 2005.
3. M. Brown. FastCGI Specification. Technical report, Open Market, Inc., 1996.
4. A. Christensen, A. Møller, and M. Schwartzbach. Precise Analysis of String Expressions. In *Proceedings of the 10th International Static Analysis Symposium (SAS'03)*, pp. 1–18, May 2003.
5. R. Fielding, J. Gettys, J. Mogul, H. Frystyk, L. Masinter, P. Leach, and T. Berners-Lee. Hypertext Transfer Protocol – HTTP/1.1. RFC 2616 (Draft Standard), June 1999. Updated by RFC 2817.
6. K. Fu, E. Sit, K. Smith, and N. Feamster. Dos and Don'ts of Client Authentication on the Web. In *Proceedings of the USENIX Security Symposium*, Washington, DC, August 2001.
7. C. Gould, Z. Su, and P. Devanbu. Static Checking of Dynamically Generated Queries in Database Applications. In *Proceedings of the 26th International Conference of Software Engineering (ICSE'04)*, pages 645–654, September 2004.
8. V. Haldar, D. Chandra, and M. Franz. Dynamic Taint Propagation for Java. In *Proceedings of the 21st Annual Computer Security Applications Conference (ACSAC'05)*, pages 303–311, December 2005.
9. W. Halfond and A. Orso. AMNESIA: Analysis and Monitoring for NEutralizing SQL-Injection Attacks. In *Proceedings of the International Conference on Automated Software Engineering (ASE'05)*, pp. 174–183, November 2005.

10. Y.-W. Huang, F. Yu, C. Hang, C.-H. Tsai, D. Lee, and S.-Y. Kuo. Securing Web Application Code by Static Analysis and Runtime Protection. In *Proceedings of the 12th International World Wide Web Conference (WWW'04)*, pp. 40–52, May 2004.

11. N. Jovanovic. txtForum: Script Injection Vulnerability. `http://www.seclab.tuwien.ac.at/advisories/TUVSA-0603-004.txt`, March 2006.

12. N. Jovanovic, C. Kruegel, and E. Kirda. Pixy: A Static Analysis Tool for Detecting Web Application Vulnerabilities. In *Proceedings of the IEEE Symposium on Security and Privacy*, May 2006.

13. N. Jovanovic, C. Kruegel, and E. Kirda. Precise Alias Analysis for Static Detection of Web Application Vulnerabilities. In *Proceedings of the ACM SIGPLAN Workshop on Programming Languages and Analysis for Security (PLAS'06)*, June 2006.

14. A. Klein. Cross Site Scripting Explained. Technical report, Sanctum Inc., 2002.

15. A. Klein. "Divide and Conquer". HTTP Response Splitting, Web Cache Poisoning Attacks, and Related Topics. Technical report, Sanctum, Inc., 2004.

16. A. Klein. DOM Based Cross Site Scripting or XSS of the Third Kind. Technical report, Web Application Security Consortium, 2005.

17. M. Kolšek. Session Fixation Vulnerability in Web-based Applications. Technical report, ACROS Security, 2002.

18. C. Kruegel and G. Vigna. Anomaly Detection of Web-based Attacks. In *Proceedings of the 10th ACM Conference on Computer and Communication Security (CCS'03)*, pp. 251–261, October 2003.

19. C. Kruegel, G. Vigna, and W. Robertson. A Multi-model Approach to the Detection of Web-based Attacks. *Computer Networks*, 48(5):717–738, August 2005.

20. C. Linhart, A. Klein, R. Heled, and S. Orrin. HTTP Request Smuggling. Technical report, Watchfire Corporation, 2005.

21. V. Livshits and M. Lam. Finding Security Vulnerabilities in Java Applications with Static Analysis. In *Proceedings of the 14th USENIX Security Symposium (USENIX'05)*, pp. 271–286, August 2005.

22. Y. Minamide. Static Approximation of Dynamically Generated Web Pages. In *Proceedings of the 14th International World Wide Web Conference (WWW'05)*, pp. 432–441, May 2005.

23. NCSA Software Development Group. The Common Gateway Interface. `http://hoohoo.ncsa.uiuc.edu/cgi/`.

24. Netcraft. PHP Usage Stats. `http://www.php.net/usage.php`, April 2006.

25. A. Nguyen-Tuong, S. Guarnieri, D. Greene, and D. Evans. Automatically Hardening Web Applications Using Precise Tainting. In *Proceedings of the 20th International Information Security Conference (SEC'05)*, pp. 372–382, May 2005.

26. OWASP. WebGoat. `http://wwwo.wasp.org/software/webgoat.html`, 2006.

27. Perl. Perl security. `http://perldoc.perl.org/perlsec.html`.

28. rgod. PHP Advanced Transfer Manager v1.30 underlying system disclosure / remote command execution / cross site scripting. `http://retrogod.altervista.org/phpatm130.html`, 2005.

29. Security Space. Apache Module Report. `http://www.securityspace.com/s_survey/data/man.200603/apachemods.html`, April 2006.

30. K. Spett. Blind SQL Injection. Technical report, SPI Dynamics, 2003.

31. Z. Su and G. Wassermann. The Essence of Command Injection Attacks in Web Applications. In *Proceedings of the 33rd Annual Symposium on Principles of Programming Languages (POPL'06)*, pp. 372–382, 2006.
32. Sun. JavaServer Pages. `http://java.sun.com/products/jsp/`.
33. Symantec Inc. Symantec Internet Security Threat Report: Vol. VIII. Technical report, Symantec Inc., September 2005.
34. TIOBE Software. TIOBE Programming Community Index for April 2006. `http://www.tiobe.com/index.htm?tiobe_index`, April 2006.
35. D. Wagner and P. Soto. Mimicry Attacks on Host-Based Intrusion Detection Systems. In *Proceedings of the ACM Conference on Computer and Communications Security*, pp. 255–264, Washington DC, November 2002.
36. J. Whaley and M. Lam. Cloning-Based Context-Sensitive Pointer Alias Analysis Using Binary Decision Diagrams. In *Proceedings of the Conference on Programming Language Design and Implementation (PLDI'04)*, pp. 131–144, June 2004.
37. Y. Xie and A. Aiken. Static Detection of Security Vulnerabilities in Scripting Languages. In *Proceedings of the 15th USENIX Security Symposium (USENIX'06)*, August 2006.

Challenges of Testing Web Services
and Security in SOA Implementations

Abbie Barbir[1], Chris Hobbs[1], Elisa Bertino[2], Frederick Hirsch[3]
and Lorenzo Martino[4]

[1] Nortel, 3500 Carling Avenue, Ottawa, Canada {abbieb,cwlh}@nortel.com
[2] Department of Computer Science and CERIAS, Purdue University, West
Lafayette, Indiana, USA bertino@cerias.purdue.edu
[3] Nokia, 5 Wayside Rd, Burlington, Mass., USA frederick.hirsch@nokia.com
[4] Department of Computer Technology and Cyber Center, Purdue University,
West Lafayette, Indiana, USA lmartino@purdue.edu

Abstract. The World Wide Web is evolving into a medium providing a wide array
of e-commerce, business-to-business, business-to-consumer, and other information-
based services. In Service Oriented Architecture (SOA) technology, Web Services are
emerging as the enabling technology that bridges decoupled systems across various
platforms, programming languages, and applications.

The benefits of Web Services and SOA come at the expense of introducing new
level of complexity to the environments where these services are deployed. This
complexity is compounded by the freedom to compose Web Services to address
requirements such as quality of service (QoS), availability, security, reliability, and
cost. The complexity of composing services compounds the task of securing, testing,
and managing the quality of the deployed services.

This chapter identifies the main security requirements for Web Services and describes how such security requirements are addressed by standards for Web Services
security recently developed or under development by various standardizations bodies. Standards are reviewed according to a conceptual framework that groups them
by the main functionalities they provide.

Testing composite services in SOA environment is a discipline at an early stage
of study. The chapter provides a brief overview of testing challenges that face early
implementers of composite services in SOA taking into consideration Web Services
security. The importance of Web Services Management systems in Web Services deployment is discussed. A step toward a fault model for Web Services is provided. The
chapter investigates the use of crash-only software development techniques for enhancing the availability of Web Services. The chapter discusses security mechanisms
from the point of view of interoperability of deployed services. The work discusses
the concepts and strategies as developed by the WS-I Basic Security profile for
enhancing the interoperability of secure Web Services.

14.1 Introduction

The use of Web Services in IT is becoming more relevant as the key technology for enabling the foundation of a loosely coupled, language-neutral, platform-independent way to link applications across multiple organizations. Despite the heterogeneity of the underlying platforms, Web Services enhance interoperability and are thus able to support business applications composed of chains of Web Services. Interoperability among heterogeneous systems is a key promise of Web Service technology and therefore notions such as Web Service composition and technologies like workflow systems are being investigated and developed. Interoperability and security play an important role in positioning Web Services as the industry choice for realizing Service Oriented Architectures (SOAs) [27].

The use of Web Services in loosely coupled service environments enables enterprises quickly to adapt to changing business demands. However, the benefits of Web Services and SOA come at the expense of introducing new complexity to the environments where these services are deployed (see, for instance, [31] and [47]). In this new programming paradigm, services are used as part of a business process. The solution implements a workflow composed of many services that are combined to achieve the required business objective. The complexity is compounded with the ability to compose services whereby services can be interchangeable based on various factors such as QoS, availability, security, reliability, and cost. This complexity compounds the task of securing, testing, and managing [35] the quality of the deployed services.

In the SOA environment, testing Web Services requires an end-to-end approach including service integration points and the connected systems themselves. The set of connected systems includes services, web applications, security gateways, legacy systems, and back-end systems. Web Service(s) consumers and providers should be able to measure the service levels of the invoked services [35].

Service Level Agreement (SLA) is a term widely used in the industry to express contracts between service consumers and service providers [35]. A Service Level Agreement defines the quality of service, how quality is measured, and what happens if the service quality is not met. In today's environment, SLAs are implicit and in most cases negotiated in advance. However, the same concept can be extended and used as means to express the performance of a Web Service throughout the whole integration chain. Consumers of Web Services can generate tests against the exposed services and compare the results with the SLAs. Service providers can publish test suits for their services that can be used by the consumers to test the compliance to the published SLA. However, service management and diagnosis require the knowledge and view of the end-to-end service. This constraint entails the sharing of management across the administrative domain in order to provide an end-to-end view [14, 35].

Web Service must protect its own resources against unauthorized access. This in turn requires suitable means for identification, whereby the recipient of a message must be able to identify the sender; authentication, whereby the recipient of a message needs to verify the claimed identity of the sender; authorization, whereby the recipient of a message applies access control policies to determine whether the sender has the right to use the required Web Services and the protected resources.

In a Web Service environment it is, however, not enough to protect the service providers, it is also important to protect the parties requiring services. Because a key component of the Web Service architectures is represented by the discovery of services, it is crucial to ensure that all information used by parties to this purpose be authentic and correct. Also, we need approaches by which a service provider can prove its identity to the party requiring the service in order to avoid attacks, such as phishing attacks. Within this context, the goal of securing Web Services can be decomposed into three broad subsidiary goals:

1. Providing mechanisms and tools for securing the integrity and confidentiality of messages as well as the guarantee of message delivery.
2. Ensuring that the service acts only on message requests that comply with the policies associated with the services.
3. Ensuring that all information required by a party in order to discover and use services is correct and authentic.

The overall goal of Web Services security standards is to make interoperable different security infrastructures and to reduce the cost of security management. To achieve this goal, Web Services security standards have to provide a common framework, and common protocols, for the exchange of security information between/among Web Services that, once implemented and deployed,

- can accommodate such existing heterogeneous mechanisms, i.e. different encryption algorithms, different access control mechanisms, etc.
- can be extended so as to cope with new requirements and/or available security technologies.

Ensuring the integrity, confidentiality, and security of Web Services through the application of a complete security model is essential for the wide adoption of this technology in SOAs. Security should be a testable property of a published service SLA. Testing Web Services for vulnerabilities is a difficult task [31] complicated by current trends in service collaboration that includes federation. The OASIS WS-Security versions (WSS) 1.0 and 1.1 [12, 13, 14, 15, 16, 17, 18] use SOAP extensibility facilities to provide security functions for SOAP messages. The WS-Security specifications secure the SOAP foundation layer by leveraging core technologies such as XML Signature [20], XML Encryption [21], XML Canonicalization [28], and SSL/TLS [30] as well as standards for conveying key and other information, such as SAML [16] and X509 [15] certificates. The WS-Security (WSS) specification provides a flexible framework for securing SOAP messages. For this reason, it is difficult for various implementations of WS-Security to interoperate unless similar choices have been made. Lack of interoperability at the SOAP and SOAP message security layer adds complexity for security testing of Web Services implementations.

This work is organized as follows. Section 14.2 discusses Web Services security challenges. Section 14.3 develops a Web Services security standards framework. Section 14.4 discusses the complexities of testing Web Services. This section provides a brief overview of current testing strategies and discusses the role of Web Services middleware in real-life deployments. Additionally, this section identifies Web Services interaction stake holders, their testing perspectives, and their testing levels.

Section 14.5 addresses Web Services security interoperability as an enhancement for testability. The section discusses the Basic Security Profile (BSP) usage scenarios, BSP strength of requirements, BSP conformance and BSP testability. This section provides an example of BSP profiling and takes a close look at BSP security considerations.

Section 14.6 considers strategies for testing Web Services security with a focus on developing a Web Services security fault model. The section provides an overview of testing strategies for Web Services security that includes general testability guidelines. A case study for securing an application is also provided. Section 14.7 investigates the use of crash-only software for enhancing the availability of and reducing testing complexities for composite Web Services. Section 14.8 provides research proposals and discusses open research issues. Section 14.9 concludes the discussion of this work and provides guidelines for future research.

14.2 Web Services Security Challenges

The discussion in the previous sections highlights the difficulties of testing Web Services. The complexities increase when security is taken into consideration, especially when application security applied at the server is not enough. A multilayer service and resource protection strategy is required, including the application of security techniques for Web Services description, discovery, and messaging.

The main features that make Web Services attractive to enterprises, such as accessibility to data, dynamic application connections, platform independence, and open run-time environment, are at odds with traditional security approaches. Security can be a key inhibitor to the wide adoption of Web Services [22]; there is need to develop a Web security vulnerabilities framework reflecting the service deployment environment. Understanding these vulnerabilities would help developers choose the right testing tools to detect faults in the services.

14.2.1 Web Services Threats

This section provides a brief description of the most common threats facing the security of Web Services. For a more complete analysis of these challenges, the reader is referred to [10], where Web Services threats and possible counter measures are discussed in more detail.

1. Message alteration: In this threat, message information is altered by inserting, removing, or modifying information created by the originator of the information and mistaken by the receiver for the originator's intention. This type of attack is easily performed due to the use of intermediaries and transformation mechanisms in Web Services.
2. Confidentiality: This type of threat makes information within the message visible to unauthorized participants.
3. Falsified messages: This threat occurs when an attacker constructs counterfeit messages and sends them to a receiver who believes them to have originated from a party other than the sender.
4. Man in the middle: The term "man in the middle" is applied to a wide variety of attacks that have little in common except for their topology. In our context, this type of attack occurs when a third party poses as the other participant to the real sender and receiver in order to fool both participants (e.g. the attacker is able to downgrade the level of cryptography used to secure the message). Designers have to examine their developed applications on a case-by-case basis for susceptibility to anything a third party might do.
5. Principal spoofing: A message is sent which appears to be from another principal (e.g., Alice sends a message which appears as if it is from Bob).
6. Forged claims: A message is sent in which the security claims are forged in an effort to gain access to otherwise unauthorized information (e.g., a security token which was not really issued by the specified authority).
7. Replay of message parts: A message is sent which includes portions of another message in an effort to gain access to unauthorized information or to cause the receiver to take some action (e.g., a security token from another message is added). This technique can be applied in a wide variety of situations. All designs must be carefully inspected from the perspective of what could an attacker do by replaying messages or parts of messages.
8. Replay: A whole message is resent by an attacker.
9. Denial of service: This is a form of an amplifier attack where the attacker does a small amount of work forcing the system under attack to do a large amount of work. This can cause the attacked system to provide a degraded service or even fail completely.

14.2.2 End-to-End Security Requirements for Web Services

For Web Services Security, the objective is to create an environment where message-level transactions and business processes can be conducted securely in an end-to-end fashion. The requirements for providing end-to-end security for Web Services are as follows:

- Mutual authentication: Mutual authentication of a service provider and a service invoker to verify their identities enables them to interact with confidence. This also includes data origin authentication whereby the receiver can be sure that the data came from the sender without modification.
- Authorization to access resources: Authorization mechanisms control invoker access to appropriate system resources, controlling access to systems and their components. Authentication may be necessary to perform authorization.
- Data integrity and confidentiality: Ensure that information has not been modified during transmission and is only accessible by the intended parties. Encryption technology and digital signature techniques can be used for this purpose.
- End-to-end integrity and confidentiality of messages: Ensure the integrity and confidentiality of messages even in the presence of intermediaries.
- Integrity of transactions and communications: Ensure that the business process was done properly and the flow of operations was executed in a correct manner.
- Audit records and mechanisms: Enable dispute resolution and system verification. Records are necessary to enable a resolution if a party to a transaction denies the occurrence of the transaction, or if other disputes arise; also to trace user access, behavior, and to enable system integrity verification.
- Distributed enforcement of security policy: Enable implementers to define a security policy and enforce it across various platforms with varying privileges.

14.2.3 Role of Cryptography

Cryptography [10] can play an important role in mitigating some of the threats to Web Services. For example, symmetric cryptography in the form of encryption can be used to provide confidentiality for messages. Asymmetric cryptography, on the other hand, can be used to enable authentication, confidentiality, and dispute resolution. This can be achieved through the appropriate use of public and private keys. Here, it is assumed the original sender and the receiver (including intermediaries if they are on the trust path) have access to the appropriate public keys through some mechanism. In this regard, dispute resolution can be enabled when the sender encrypts a message using its private key since it is harder for the sender to deny the sending of the message.

Confidentiality can be achieved when the original sender encrypts a message using the receiver public key, requiring the receiver private key for decryption. In a typical deployment, asymmetric cryptography is used as a mechanism for exchanging session keys to be subsequently used in symmetric cryptography. This technique is more efficient since symmetric cryptography is usually faster to execute than asymmetric cryptography.

Asymmetric cryptography can provide authentication. In this case the sender digitally signs a message using its private key. The receiver then verifies the signature and the authenticity of the sender certificate to confirm that the sender is the party that actually sent the message.

Asymmetric cryptography can be used to provide message integrity whereby a message is first digitally signed by the original requestor private key and is then encrypted using the ultimate receiver public key. Upon receiving the message, the receiver first decrypts the message with its corresponding private key and then decrypts the message with the sender public key. Integrity is verified when the process executes without any errors.

14.2.4 Transport Layer Security

This subsection addresses using Transport layer [10] to secure SOAP messages that are sent from a sender to a receiver. This approach is limited when there are intermediaries; since termination of transport layer security at an endpoint may allow that intermediary to modify or examine messages. For HTTP-based bindings of SOAP, TLS/SSL provides point-to-point security (Fig. 14.1). For Web Services, however, there is a need for end-to-end security, which becomes an important distinction when one or more intermediaries exist between the original service requester and the service provider. In this case the use of Transport layer TLS/SSL has significant limitations. Transport layer security mechanisms may be used to secure messages between two adjacent SOAP nodes and message layer security mechanisms should be used (possibly in conjunction with TLS/SSL) in the presence of intermediaries or when data origin authentication is required.

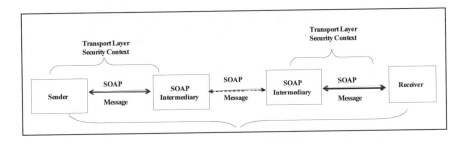

Fig. 14.1. Transport and message level Security

14.2.5 Message Level Security

The SOAP specifications [23, 24] do not specify how to deal with security-related issues such as authentication, integrity, and confidentiality. However, they provide an extensibility model that can be used to build extensions to the original SOAP standard. The OASIS WS-Security versions (WSS) 1.0 and 1.1[12, 13, 14, 15, 16, 17, 18] use these extensibility facilities to add security functions to SOAP. WS-Security specifications secure the SOAP foundation layer by leveraging core technologies such as XML Signature[20], XML Encryption [21], XML Canonicalization [28], and SSL/TLS. The WS-Security specification adds security to SOAP messages by specifying how the header part of the message can carry security information in conjunction with rules on how to apply security technologies.

The OASIS WSS 1.0 standard [12] provides the underlying foundation for SOAP message level security. It defines mechanisms for identifying the origin of a message and verifying tampering through the use of signatures. It provides mechanisms for message confidentiality by ensuring that only the intended recipient is able to see the message through the use of encryption. WSS 1.0 introduces a security header in a SOAP message and three key elements:

1. Tokens: SOAP messages can contain security tokens with authentication information. The standard defines Username tokens, X.509 Tokens, and SAML tokens, among others. These tokens can be part of security headers and can vouch for security claims to a recipient.
2. Signature elements: Security headers can contain Signature elements that contain an XML Signature used to sign any part of the message. The recipient can use the signature to verify that the request of the sender has not been changed and that the message really originated from the sender.
3. Encryption elements: Some parts of the SOAP message can be encrypted to protect sensitive information from unauthorized entities.

WS-Security defines a security header for SOAP messages as a mechanism for conveying security information with and about a SOAP message. This header is, by design, extensible to support many types of security information. The security header may contain security tokens, references to security tokens found elsewhere, timestamps, nonce, signatures, encrypted keys, and encrypted data. Each security header is targeted to a specific SOAP actor. A SOAP message may contain multiple security headers; however, each must be targeted to a different SOAP actor. Each security header may contain multiple security tokens, security token references, nonce, signatures, encrypted keys, and encrypted data; however, the BSP recommends that there may be at most one timestamp in a message.

The WS-Security standard describes the processing rules for using and processing XML Signature [20] and XML Encryption [21] in the context of a SOAP message; however, these rules do not apply to using these standards directly in application data. These WS-Security rules must be followed when using any type of security token. The specification does not dictate if and how claim confirmation must be done; however, it does define how signatures may be used and associated with security tokens (by referencing the security tokens from the signature) as a form of claim confirmation.

WS-Security 1.1 enhances WSS 1.0 with additional mechanisms to convey token information (e.g., sending Thumbprint of an X.509 certificate, or a SHA1 hash of an Encrypted key). WSS1.1 also introduces the concept of SignatureConfirmation that enables a communication sender to confirm that the received message was generated in response to a message it initiated in its unaltered form. In this technique, the recipient sends back the signature values received from sender in SignatureConfirmation element. This technique helps to prevent certain forms of reply and message alteration attacks. WS-Security 1.1 has become an OASIS standard as of February 1, 2006. WSS1.1 also introduces a mechanism to encrypt SOAP headers.

WS-Security provides mechanisms to send security tokens as part of a message, message integrity, and message confidentiality. Developers can use the specification in conjunction with other Web Service extensions and higher-level application specific protocols to accommodate a wide variety of security models and security technologies. It does not specify how a security context or authentication mechanisms are established. Furthermore, key derivation, advertisement and exchange of security policy, trust establishment, and non-repudiation are out of scope of the specification.

14.3 Web Services Security Standard Framework

In this section we present first the different notions of standards. We then present the conceptual framework for Web Services security standards, and, for each level of this framework, we survey existing and proposed standards, their specific purpose, and their current status.

14.3.1 The Concept of Standard

The concept of "standard" covers different notions, ranging from a public specification issued by a set of companies, to a de jure standard issued by a recognized standardization body. These different notions can provide to the potential users useful indications about the maturity, the stability, and the level of endorsement of a given standard. A de facto standard is a technology that is used by a vast majority of the users of a function. Such function may, e.g., be provided in a product from a single supplier that dominates the market; or it may be a patented technology that is used in a range of products under license. A de facto standard may be endorsed by a standardization initiative, and eventually become a consortium recommendation, or a de jure standard. The relevant requirements are that it is widely used, meets the needs for functionality, and supports interoperability.

A de jure standard is usually defined by entities with a legal status in international or national law such the International Organization for Standardization (ISO). Consortium recommendations on the other hand are a technology agreed on and recommended by groups of companies in order to fulfill some functionality. The Organization for the Advancement of Structured Information Standards (OASIS), the World Wide Web Consortium (W3C), and the Internet Engineering Task Force (IETF) are examples of examples of such consortia.

De facto standards, eventually promoted to the de jure standard by a subsequent endorsement by a standardization body, offer a higher guarantee of support for interoperability. Conversely, de jure standards or consortia recommendations do not guarantee per se that a standard will be widely endorsed nor the market availability of really interoperable implementations by multiple vendors. Moreover, the definition of a standard and its issuance by a standardization body or by a consortium is a long-lasting process, subject to formalized organizational procedures.

14.3.2 Framework for Web Services Security Standards

Web Services security standards address a variety of aspects, ranging from the message-level security to the identity management. In order to provide a structured and engineered approach to the development of the standards, an overall conceptual reference framework was needed. Such a reference framework is crucial in organizing the standards according to layers and in promoting the reuse of already developed specification.

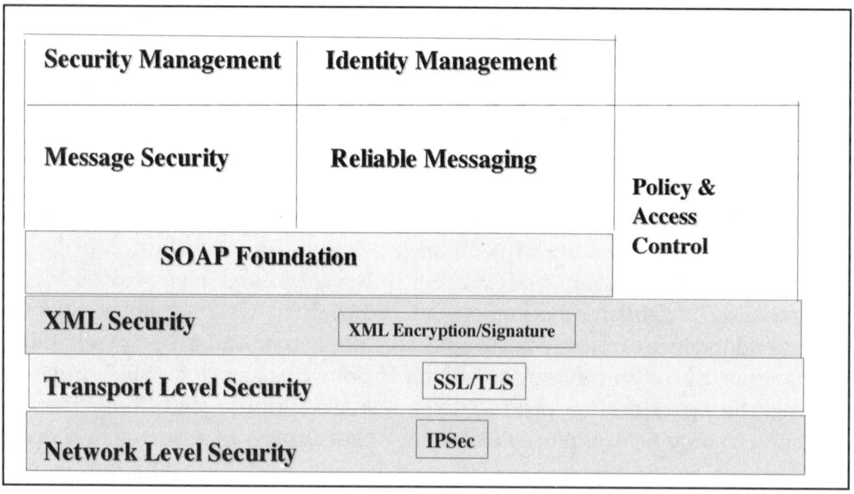

Fig. 14.2. Refined classification of standards

In this work, we adopt the following classification, as shown by Fig. 14.2. This classification has been adopted in order to take into account in the discussion the standards below the SOAP layer and most importantly, to group the standards by their main intended purpose rather than adopting a "stack" view that emphasizes mainly how each specification is built on top of the other ones. In particular, we deemed useful to separate message-level security specifications (the two groups labeled Message Security and Reliable Messaging) from the specifications addressing Policy and Access Control, Security Management, and Identity Management issues.

14.4 Complexities of Testing Web Services

Currently, Web Services are generally managed using tools supplied by platform vendors [34]. This makes testing a vendor-dependent activity. Service management includes configuration, accounting, QoS, policy and fault identification, containment, and repair. Passive or active testing mechanisms are widely used as tools for fault detection. Active testing techniques require the generation and the application of test cases in order to detect faults [31, 32, 33, 34, 35]. Passive testing techniques use observers to track the interaction between the entities being tested. Observers can be inserted directly on-line in the data flow or can be off-line and with access to log files.

Current proposed Web Services strategies are either based on active testing techniques [34] or require Web Services to participate in their management through the support of a management interface to active testers [34]. These solutions assume that a Web Service will participate in its management by providing specific interfaces that are based on active testers. Requiring Web Services to provide their own management interfaces adds complexity to Web Services architecture and may impact performance. In addition, there are security risks associated with these interfaces.

14.4.1 Brief Overview of Current Testing Strategies

The advent of Web Services and their role in realizing SOA are changing the Internet to a platform of application collaboration and integration. This will change the traditional design, build, test, launch, and retire software life cycle. The change will be more profound once companies start to realize the importance of orchestrating loosely coupled services into coarse-grained business services as a way of quickly developing business solutions.

As enterprises adopt SOA principles, the traditional test after development approach to software testing will no longer work. Instead, software projects in enterprises will be based on agile approaches [48]. Accordingly, software development will require developers to work closely with their clients to identify their needs. Developers will produce code that is tested and evaluated by the customers and the process is repeated until the project is done. This approach requires a change in the way test code is developed and will result in developing the test code as part of the software development process [48].

In the Web Services world, dynamic binding allows developers to define service centric systems as a workflow of invocations to abstract interfaces. The interfaces are then bound to concrete services before or during workflow execution. Testing techniques that require the pre-identification of system components cannot be used to test these workflows [47]. The ability to use dynamic bindings in a workflow raises the need to test a composite service partner link for all possible endpoints [47]. The problem can be very complex since the endpoint can be dynamically generated or unknown at testing time [47].

Currently, Web Services testing is a discipline at its early stages of study by the academic and industrial communities [38]. Some approaches in the R&D community [42, 43] have suggested the possibility of augmenting the functionality of a Universal Description, Discovery and Integration (UDDI) service broker with logic to permit a testing step before a service is registered. The aim of the testing step is to ensure that the logic of the registered service is error free. This approach focuses on requiring Web Services to include well-defined test suites that can be run by the enhanced UDDI, or the inclusion of Graph Transformation Rules that allow the automatic derivation of meaningful test cases that can be used to evaluate the behavior of the service when invoked. This approach require that Web Services providers implement interfaces that increase the service testability by bringing the service into a known state from which a specified sequence of tests can be performed.

A modification of this approach is presented in [38]. In their work, the authors propose a UDDI extension mechanism to verify that a Web Service can correctly cooperate with other services. This is done by checking that a correct sequence of invocations to the service results in a correct interaction of the service with services from other providers. The proposed framework extends the UDDI registry role from a passive service directory to an accredited testing entity that performs service validation before registering a service.

Mei et al. in [46] propose a framework to automate the testing process of Web Services. This framework is designed to generate test data according to the description of Web Services in an extended version of Web Services Description Language (WSDL). The work extends WSDL with contract information, including pre-conditions and post-conditions. From the basic information and the contract information, test data for a Web Service can be generated. Relational expressions appearing in the pre-conditions are used to partition the range of each input parameter into several sub-ranges. For each parameter, the technique randomly selects a value from a sub-range together with the boundary values between sub-ranges. The different combinations of the values for the parameters become the initial generated test data which is used for the automatic execution of the Web Service under test. For composed Web Services, the framework can intercept and record the inputs from each

Web Service to be used for future regression test. The framework specifies two ways to acquire test data. The first way is to use a test data generator; the second way is to record the runtime information while executing an application that invokes the service under test.

Benharref et al. [34] proposes architecture based on passive testing techniques (using observers) for detecting faults in Web Services. The observers are designed as Web Services that makes them platform independent. Their architecture enables the testing of deployed Web Services by independent third parties.

Tsai et al. [38] proposes an XML-based, object-oriented framework to test Web Services. The framework supports test execution and test scenario management, consisting of a test master and a test engine. The test master enables developers to identify test scenarios, perform dependency, completeness and consistency analysis. The test engine interacts with the Web Services under test and provides tracing information. XML perturbation testing techniques, such as discussed in [43, 44, 45], can also be conducted in the framework of Tsai as given in [38].

Testing strategies are even more complex when Web Services security is also taken into consideration. Security challenges when testing Web Services and the need for interoperability at the SOAP message security level are addressed in a subsequent section.

14.4.2 Web Services Middleware

Web Services Middleware [37], also known as Web Services Management (WSM), is a distributed infrastructure that acts like enforcement points. WSM can be either a gateway that handles traffic for multiple Web Services or agents co-resident on systems running a given Web Service.

The presence of the WSM infrastructure [37] is often transparent to a given Web Service and to any software invoking that service. In actual deployment scenarios, a WSM would appear like a standard service consumer to a Web Service and a Web Service to the consuming application. The WSM uses standard Web Services technology to communicate with the Web Service and the software consuming that service.

WSM infrastructure addresses key areas that are related to Web Services; in particular, security, system management, and service virtualization. Interoperability of Web Services at the WSDL, SOAP, and SOAP message–level security can also be addressed in the WSM.

Figure 14.3 provides an overview of Web Services Management framework's functional components. Components can communicate with each other. For clarity, the communication lines are omitted from Fig. 14.3. Not all components need to be present in WSM infrastructure. The following components are included in Fig. 14.3:

- Access control component enforces access control policies that may include the capability to authenticate and authorize Web Services' clients.

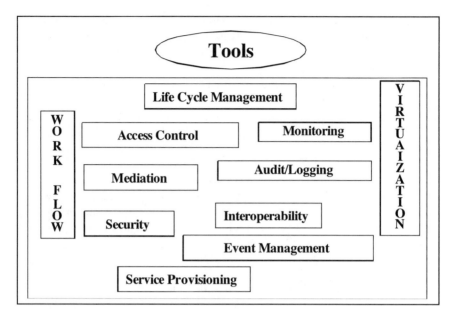

Fig. 14.3. WSM architecture

- Audit/logging logs requests, responses, various events, and session information.
- Event management handles events that are related to Web Services. For example, alerts can be sent based on pre-set conditions.
- Interoperability component is responsible for insuring interoperability that may include many layers such as the WSDL, SOAP, and SOAP message security layer.
- Life cycle manger manages the development, deployment, registering, and testing stages of services.
- Mediation component enables Web Services federation through the enforcement of federation policies.
- Monitoring component monitors events from all deployed Web Services.
- Security component is a Policy Enforcement Point (PEP). It addresses security-related issues across services that may include secure communication channels, authentication, authorization, privacy, trust, integrity, confidentiality, federation, delegation, and auditing.
- Workflow manager creates, tests, and manages the logical flows of Web Services.
- Service provisioning defines system behavior policies and the interactions of the Web Services. It can be used to specify how Web Services clients can subscribe to a given service. It can also be used to specify the rules for client authentication and authorization before they can access Web Services.

- Virtualization component creates and manages virtual endpoints for Web Services. These endpoints can be dynamically associated with physical endpoints to manage fail-over, provide load balancing, and concurrently manage multiple versions or invocations of a Web Service.

The tools are presented as separate components to emphasize the need not to be locked into vendor-specific tool set that can lead to limited testing functionality of the WSM infrastructure. Selecting the right tools is critical for the task of testing Web Services. It is important to note that Web Services impose specialized testing challenges for test tools. These tools need to be able to emulate realistic usage scenarios. They should enable developers to create the ability to rapidly test Web Services for functionality, performance, reliability, scalability, and security. Since service re-use and service availability are essential to achieving robust SOA implementations, automated regression testing is necessary in order to guarantee secure, reliable, and complaint services.

The use of an agile software development methodology requires the testing process to be capable of detecting errors early in the development cycle. This requires the flexibility to address known usage scenarios as well as unanticipated use cases. Most errors are caused when a system component is used in an unexpected manner. Improperly tested code, executed in a way that the developer did not intend, is often the primary culprit for security vulnerability.

The WSM framework allows developers to perform fault management, configuration, accounting, performance, and security aspects of service management. Fault management includes fault detection, localization, and repair. Passive or active testing techniques can be used for fault detection. Active testing is based on the generation and the application of specific test cases while passive testers just observe the interaction between a tested system and its clients. The introduction of WSM into a corporation's infrastructure allows developers to concentrate on developing the services while letting the WSM handle non-application, context-specific security needs, manageability, and other aspects of the service. Developers need to note that Web Services' gateway solutions usually do not have access to application context. Developers still need to perform tests that check the content of XML messages since attackers can embed malicious content in the XML documents that pass straight through the WSM software to the service interface of the application.

The use of a WSM framework allows practical implementations of Web Services where providers can develop Web Services Service Level Agreements (WSLAs) that the clients can use as contracts when invoking the services. In traditional terminology, SLAs represent a formal contract between a service provider and a client guaranteeing quantifiable network performance at defined levels. These types of SLAs are network centric and generally deal with packet flows across a network. At the Web Services level, a WSLA is more concerned with message flows that span the end-to-end business transaction. These are both depicted in Fig. 14.4. WSLAs can be used to provide QoS that is based on the contract they have agreed upon when they subscribed

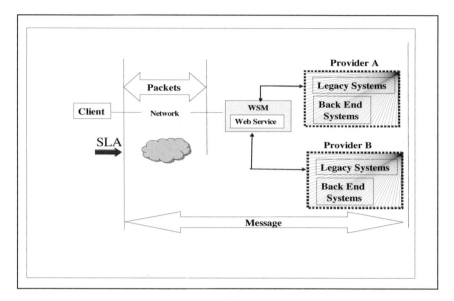

Fig. 14.4. Client's view of SLA testing for Web Services

to services. Clients can develop testing strategies that stress the WSLA to ensure that the service provider has met the contracted QoS commitment.

Stress testing WSLA requires interoperability of the Web Services at the WSDL, UDDI, SOAP, and SOAP message–level security. The Basic Profile (BP) [11] from the Web Services Interoperability Organization (WS-I) provides a profile for enhancing interoperability at the SOAP level. In addition, WS-I has developed the Basic Security Profile (BSP) [11] for enhancing interoperability at the SOAP message–level security. In a subsequent section, we will take a closer look at the BSP.

14.4.3 Stake Holders Testing Perspectives and Levels

Many players can get involved when a Web Services consumer invokes a Web Service. The stakeholders are the end-user or client, service developer, service provider, service integrator, and service broker (certifier) [47]. Testing scope, strategies, techniques, and perspective will vary based on the stakeholder. Each stakeholder must deal with different requirements and issues [47].

The client or end-user expects any application to perform in a satisfactory manner. An important aim of the service provider is to provide reliable services; the service provider will focus on functional testing in order to ensure the minimum number of failures. The service provider cannot anticipate the details of how the service will be combined with all other services. Hence, although the service developer can perform some non-functional testing of the developed services, these tests are limited since the service developer lacks exposure to the infrastructure of the end-to-end message flow. In general, the service developer will focus on performing service functional testing that can be based on common techniques that are used in component or subsystem testing [47]. The provider will need to perform tests on the WSDL, UDDI, and SOAP layers. Tests based on mutation strategies [44, 45, 46, 47] are important for the service developer in order to detect faults. The developer will need to perform regression testing if any of the components of the service change. The developer may need to provide an interface to the service to allow the service provider, integrator, or certifier to test the service in an SLA scenario.

The main focus of the service provider is to ensure that the service meets the claims as stated by the service developer. The aim is to be sure it can meet the requirements of a WSLA. The service provider can use the same testing techniques as the service developer. However, load testing the service may also be an option in order to gain confidence in its WSLA conformance. From the service provider point of view, non-functional testing of the service has limited value since it does not include the end customer infrastructure.

The role of service integrator is to test its services that can be used in a composite fashion by consumers in order to ensure that the original design (functional and nonfunctional) objectives are met at invocation time [47]. Dynamic binding adds complexity to the service integrator testing scope, strategies, and capabilities. At runtime, dynamic binding adds uncertainty since the bound service can be one of many possible services. From the point of view of a service workflow, the service integrator has no control over the service in use, since it can change over its deployed lifetime. To increase confidence in the testing process, the service integrator will need to invoke the service in order to gain insight on how it will behave in the real world. Testing from this perspective will result in additional costs to the service integrator. The use of service emulators and stubs can reduce this cost, but do not fully replace the need for the actual invocation of the services under test. The service integrator may invoke more sophisticated test generation strategies. Pre-conditions, post-conditions, and genetic algorithm testing ([43, 44, 45, 46, 47]) can be used to create test oracles. Stress testing WSLA (at least with focus on the infrastructure components or sub-systems that the integrator can control) should be performed in order to get better understanding of whether the service will meet the QoS requirements of the contract.

The service certifier can be used by the service developer, provider, or integrator to help test and find faults. The service certifier can also be the service broker. The service certifier can play an important role in reducing the number of players involved in testing a service and as a result can reduce the overall cost of testing. However, the service certifier still lacks visibility of how the service will be composed with other services and lacks access to the infrastructure of the end-to-end message flow. The service certifier may invoke more sophisticated test generation strategies on the service. Pre-conditions, post-conditions, and genetic algorithm [47] testing can be used to create test oracles for a given service. Due to dynamic binding and the lack of visibility of network and infrastructure factors that can affect the performance of a service, the service certifier may not be able to guarantee the QoS claims of a WSLA.

14.5 Interoperability as an Enhancement for Testability

The framework for security standard development postulates a layered approach, such that every upper layer standard can re-use and extend the specification of lower-layer standards. However, the specifications of the standard at a given layer (e.g., WS-Policy) are sometimes developed by a standardization body different from that specifying the standard at the other layer (e.g., SAML). Thus, the two involved standard specifications are not always synchronized. Such situation requires an activity of verification and alignment of the specifications, which involves further iterations within each standardization body.

Due to the role played by SOAP messages and by SOAP message security, interoperability of different WS-Security implementation is crucial. For this reason, WS-I has developed the Basic Security Profile (BSP) [11] to provide clarifications and constraints in order to enhance the interoperability of WS-Security implementations. The BSP extends the profiles created by the WS-I SOAP Basic Profile (BP) [11] by adding interoperability guidelines for security. BSP 1.0 profiles WSS 1.0 and is available on the WS-I public site. BSP 1.1 profiles WSS 1.1 and should be available to the public in the near future. In this chapter, we use the term BSP to mean both BSP 1.0 and 1.1

SOAP messages are composed of XML elements. Using WS-Security techniques, these elements may be signed, encrypted, or signed and encrypted. The elements can be referenced from other elements. Each element within a SOAP message may be processed by an intermediary that can add more data and sign and encrypt the incremental data and/or the combined data. For example, in an order processing chain of events, one intermediary can assign an order number and sign the associated element. Another intermediary can check credit worthiness of the consumer and either signs only the credit data or the whole order data, and so forth.

14.5.1 BSP Usage Scenarios

The BSP adds security to the following three basic Message Exchange Patterns (MEPs) that were adapted from the scenarios defined for the Basic Profile [11]:

1. One-way: A SOAP message is sent, potentially through intermediaries, to a SOAP receiver. No response message is returned (Fig. 14.5).

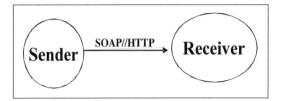

Fig. 14.5. One-way SOAP message

2. Synchronous request/response: A SOAP message (the request) is sent, potentially through intermediaries, to an ultimate SOAP receiver. A SOAP message (the response) is sent by the request's ultimate SOAP receiver through the reverse path followed by the request to the request's initial SOAP sender (Fig. 14.6).
3. Basic callback: A SOAP message (the request) is sent, potentially through intermediaries, to an ultimate SOAP receiver, and an acknowledgment message is returned in the manner of synchronous request/response. The request contains information that indicates an endpoint for a SOAP node, where the response should be sent. The request's ultimate SOAP receiver sends the response to that SOAP node, which returns an acknowledgment message in the manner of synchronous request/response (Fig. 14.7).

14.5.2 BSP Strength of Requirements

The BSP focuses on improving interoperability by strengthening requirements when possible and constraining flexibility and extensibility when appropriate. The BSP limits the set of common functionality that vendors must implement and thus enhances the chances for interoperability. This in return reduces the complexities for the testing of Web Services security.

The guiding principles enumerated in the BSP declare that there is no guarantee interoperability, that the profile should "do no harm," that it makes testable statements when possible, and focus on interoperability. The BSP committee worked so that enhancing interoperability does not create new security threats.

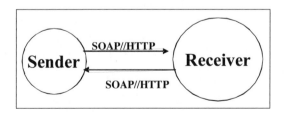

Fig. 14.6. Synchronous request/response

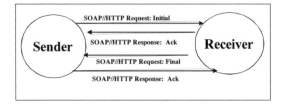

Fig. 14.7. Basic callback

It is not the intent of the profile to define security best practices. However, when multiple options exist, the profile considers known security weaknesses and makes choices that reduce the risks and reduces choice thus enhancing interoperability. The Profile speaks to interoperability at the Web Services layer only; it assumes that interoperability of lower-layer protocols (e.g., TCP, HTTP) and technologies (e.g., encryption and signature algorithms) are adequate and well understood. The Basic Security Profile restates selected requirements from the WS-Security Errata rather than including the entire Errata by reference, preferring interoperability over strict conformance.

The profile includes requirement statements about two kinds of artifacts: SECURE_ENVELOPE and SECURE_MESSAGE. A SECURE_ENVELOPE is a SOAP envelope that has been subjected to integrity and/or confidentiality protection. A SECURE_MESSAGE expands the scope of the SECURE_ENVELOPE to include protocol elements transmitted with the SECURE_ENVELOPE that have been subjected to integrity and/or confidentiality protection (an example is SOAP messages with attachments).

14.5.3 BSP Conformance

In order to conform to the BSP, any artifact that contains a construct that is addressed in the profile must conform to any statements that constrain its use. Conformant receivers are not required to accept all possible conformant messages. Conformance applies to deployed instances of services. Since major portions of the BSP may or may not apply in certain circumstances, individual URIs may be used to indicate conformance to parts of the BSP including the core profile or additional sections of the BSP for Username token, X.509 token, and SOAP messages with attachments.

The BSP includes statements that are interoperability requirements as well as statements that are security considerations. The normative requirement statements are identified by numbers prefixed with the letter 'R', e.g., Raaaa where aaaa is the statement number. These statements contain one requirement level keyword (i.e., "MUST") and one conformance target. Examples of BSP conformance targets include the following:

SECURE_ENVELOPE: A SOAP envelope that contains sub-elements that have been subjected to integrity and/or confidentiality protection.

A message is considered conformant when all of its contained artifacts are conformant with all statements in the BSP that are related to them. Use of artifacts for which there are no statements in the Basic Security Profile does not affect conformance.

SECURE_MESSAGE: Protocol elements that have WS-Security applied to them. Protocol elements include a primary SOAP envelope and optionally associated SOAP attachments.

SENDER: Software that generates a message according to the protocol(s) associated with it. A sender is considered conformant when all of the messages it produces are conformant and its behavior is conformant with all statements related to SENDER in BSP.

RECEIVER: Software that consumes a message according to the protocol(s) associated with it. A receiver is considered conformant when it is capable of consuming conformant messages containing the artifacts that it supports and its behavior is conformant with all statements related to RECEIVER in the BSP.

In BSP, certain statements are considered clarifying statements. The intent of these statements is to eliminate confusion about the intended interpretation of a requirement from an underlying specification. Clarifying requirements are identified by adding a suffix of a superscript letter 'C', i.e. RxxxxC, where xxxx is the requirement number. Additional consideration statements are also identified by numbers prefixed by the letter 'C', i.e. Cyyyy, where yyyy is the statement number. These statements are non-normative and are used to provide clarification in order to eliminate confusion.

14.5.4 BSP Testability

The security consideration statements provide guidance that is not strictly interoperability related but are testable best practices for security. It was considered valuable to include these statements so that testing tool designers can have the option of flagging potentially insecure practices. It is not feasible to provide a comprehensive list of security considerations and not all security considerations can easily be converted into testable statements. A complete security analysis must be conducted on specific solutions based on the BSP and underlying standards, based on a risk analysis of the application using BSP technologies.

Even a fully standard compliant application may not interoperate with another when the set of functionality supported is disjoint. For example, while a sender may encrypt using one of three specific algorithms prescribed by the BSP, a receiver may expect a different one of the three. Certain agreements must be made using mechanisms currently out of scope for the profile.

14.5.5 Example of BSP Profiling

This section provides an example of BSP profiling with respect to SOAP Message Security. BSP allows limited flexibility and extensibility in the application of security to messages. Since no security policy description language or negotiation mechanism is within the scope of the profile, BSP expects that the sender and receiver can agree out of band over which mechanisms and choices should be used for message exchanges including which security tokens can be used. The next sections provide selected examples of the profiling in the BSP. The reader can check [11] for the complete profile.

WSS 1.1 allows a Binary Security Token for the option of specifying its Value Type, but requires that it specifies its encoding type. Base64Binary is the only acceptable value. The Profile restricts the Value Type to one of those specified by a security token profile and requires its specification. Note that this token profile need not be one of the OASIS WSS profiles, although that is preferred when possible. The listing below provides an example of the profiled usage of Binary Security Token.

```
Correct:

<wsse:BinarySecurityToken wsu:Id='SomeCert'
    ValueType="http://docs.oasis-open.org/wss/2004/01/oasis-
    200401-wss-x509-token-profile-1.0#X509v3"
    EncodingType="http://docs.oasis-open.org/wss/2004/01/
    oasis-200401-wss-soap-message-security-1.0#Base64
    Binary">
lui+Jy4WYKGJW5xM3aHnLxOpGVIpzSg4V486hHFe7sHET/uxxVBovT7JV
1A2RnWSWkXm9jAEdsm/...
</wsse:BinarySecurityToken>
```

14.5.6 BSP Security Considerations

This section lists a number of security considerations as specified by the BSP that should be taken into account when using one or more of the technologies discussed in this section.

Use of the SOAPAction in protected messages can result in security risks. The SOAPAction header can expose sensitive information about a SOAP message such as the URI of the service, or the context of the transaction. If the SOAPAction header is used for routing messages, there is a possibility that an attacker can modify the header value to direct the message to a different receiver. This can defeat a replay detection mechanism based on the assumption that the message would always be routed to the same place.

Additional risks can occur if multiple intermediaries are present. For example, one intermediary can be designed to select the set of its processing steps based on the value of SOAPAction or application/soap+xml. A second intermediary (such as a security gateway) can base its processing on the message content (which could be secured through XML signatures). An attacker can manage to trick the security gateway by allowing illegal operations by modifications in HTTP headers. To remedy the situation, the BSP requires that SOAPAction attribute of a `soapbind:operation` element to either be omitted or have as its value an empty string.

BSP uses time-based mechanisms to prevent replay attacks. These mechanisms will be ineffective unless the system clocks of the various network nodes are synchronized. The BSP assumes that time synchronization is performed.

For messages that are signed using a Security Token that binds a public verification key with other claims, and if specific processing is performed based on those claims, the BSP requires that the Security Token itself be part of the signature computation. This can be achieved by putting child `ds:Reference` element whose URI attribute contains a shorthand XPointer reference to the `wsse:SecurityTokenReference` that specifies the Security Token into the `ds:SignedInfo` element of a signature. If a `ds:SignedInfo` contains one or more `ds:Reference` children whose URI attribute contains a shorthand XPointer reference to a `wsse:SecurityTokenReference` that uses a potentially ambiguous mechanism to refer to the Security Token (e.g., KeyIdentifier) then it is recommended that the content of the Security Token be signed either directly or using the Security Token Dereferencing Transform. This approach can help to protect against post-signature substitution of the Security Token with one that binds the same key to different claims.

When a key is provided in band within a Security Token or for the purpose of specifying a key to be used by another node for encrypting information to be sent in a subsequent message, the profile recommends that the sender of the key cryptographically bind the key to the message in which it is transmitted. This can be done either by using the key to perform a Signature or HMAC over critical elements of the message body or by including the key under a signature covering critical elements of the message body that uses some other key. If a key is sent in a message that the receiver is expected to encrypt data in some future message, there is a risk that an attacker could substitute some other key and thereby be able to read unauthorized data. This is true even if the key is contained in a signed certificate, but is not bound to the current message in some way. If the future encryption key is used to sign the initial request, the receiver can determine by verifying the signature that the key is the one intended. Readers can consult [11] for more detailed security risk analysis.

14.6 Strategies for Testing Web Services Security

Testing developed and deployed secure Web Services applications is a challenge. Security is an ongoing process as opposed to a one-time development task. Developers should start with the security of the application in mind from the origin concept of the service and during the development, deployment, and maintenance phases.

The major concerns in testing the security of Web Services are the lack of security testing standards and specifications. For a given service at the functional level, input manipulation, information disclosure, and DoS constitute the most common vulnerabilities against a service [45]. Testing strategies should emphasize testing for these vulnerabilities. Common defense techniques involve the use of strategies based on integrity and confidentiality to counter these threats.

The WSM framework allows developers to perform fault detection, configuration testing of security aspects of Web Service. Passive or active testing techniques can be used for fault detection. As stated before, the incorporation of WSM into Web Services infrastructure allows developers to concentrate on developing the services while letting the WSM handle the non-application specific context security tasks, manageability, and other aspects of the services.

The following sections provide an approach for testing security for Web Services. In this approach, the WSM plays an integral part, where layer separation between the service and its security is established.

14.6.1 Web Services Security Fault Model

Effective testing of Web Services security requires the development of a fault model covering all interaction aspects of the service and spanning all the Web Services layers that include UDDI, WSDL, and SOAP. The fault model should encompass the entire group of stakeholders as discussed in Section 14.2. The fault model is assumed to be part of the security component of the WSM. In effect, the model builds on the generic fault model for Web Services security as proposed in [45].

The fault model [45] must address threats to the UDDI that includes information disclosure, availability, DoS attacks, and unauthorized access. Attackers could use UDDI's published WSDL to obtain information about Web Services and use the information to carry out the attack [45]. Attackers could use scanning and parameter mutation techniques to search for unpublished backdoor capabilities of the services in order to gain unauthorized access to resources and data. Buffer overflow and other types of attacks can also be used.

The fault model should consider the effect of intermediaries on a client's messages. The presence of intermediaries introduces threats to these messages. For example, an attacker may take over an intermediary and launch man-in-the-middle attacks. The attacker may redirect the messages to a different destination causing the equivalent of a DoS attack on the service [45].

At the service provider, integrator or certifier level, the fault model takes into consideration that Web Services could spread over multiple tiers [45]. Services on these tiers could be exposed as Web Services. Exposed Web Services could interact with infrastructure components that include mail servers, application servers, file systems, and various databases [45]. Web Services security may be affected if any of these infrastructure components are compromised. The advent of Web Services has the effect of forcing developers to re-think which components of a system should be trusted or which components should be considered vulnerable.

In this work, XML firewalls are viewed as an integral component of the Web Services fault model. The XML firewall can perform deep inspection of the messages with the ability to inspect data for XML conformance and exploits. XML firewalls can protect against attacks that do not require application context. In Fig. 14.8, the extended model from [45] is depicted.

14.6.2 General Testability Guidelines

An application or service may consist of a single functional component or multiple sets of local or networked components. Security is a multifaceted process consisting of mechanisms that cover network security elements, application level security systems, authentication systems, and cryptography systems. In a layered security approach, these mechanisms are developed independently at different OSI layers and are expected to be combined together to secure the deployed services in a useful manner.

For all phases of the application development life-cycle, it is important to identify security-related threats and vulnerabilities. This requires that developers embrace the use of systematic security design methodologies with well thought-out implementation processes.

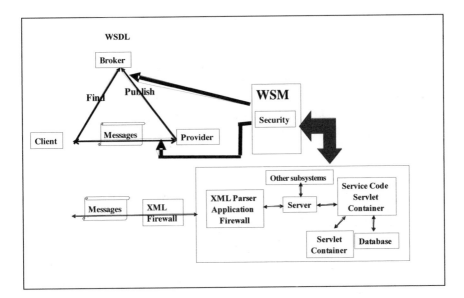

Fig. 14.8. Fault model

Architects should ensure that all aspects of application security are considered at early design stage in a structured manner. Best practices for applying security should be put in place before starting an application design process. It is important to be proactive in checking and verifying the security design for risks, tradeoffs, security policies, and defensive strategies ahead of the completion of the application design phase. During the deployment and production phases, it is good practice to adopt reactive security measures to ensure service stability and recovery in the event of a security breach.

Organizations can minimize the effort of testing for security of the developed applications by following strategies that reduce the factors that need to be tested. A crude but effective approach for minimizing the scope of testing is to pursue some of the following steps:

1. Create a set of use case scenarios that can accommodate the majority of services to be exposed as Web Services.
2. Determine the security boundaries of these services. Identify which services are internal and which are external.
3. Determine the overall security requirements of the service, including threats, risks, and vulnerabilities (internal and external).
4. Determine the set of messages to be exchanged by each service.
5. Determine the security requirements of each message. This can vary, depending on whether the message is internal or external.
6. Determine the resources that are required or can be accessed by each service and the type of access mechanism allowed.
7. Take a close look at the organization current network infrastructure and determine what is currently available to support the security requirements for these services. It is preferable to try to re-use existing security infrastructure (such as LDAP directories or PKI systems [10]) to support the security requirements of the services.
8. Determine if any specific applications must be either developed in house, out-sourced, or purchased to fulfill the security needs or other functionality of the new Web Services.
9. Determine the impact of the new services on the management, auditing, and logging facilities in the network and the applications.
10. Take a close look at the organization's security policy and integrate the new requirements to it.
11. Build the new services using secure code practices and standard-based technologies. Developers need to be conservative in the use of features in this step. Developers need to identify the minimum set of capabilities that would be specified to meet the security requirements so far identified. Minimizing the extent of supported services from SOAP message security reduces the testing scope and reduces overall vulnerabilities.

Developers can generate test suits for testing the new security mechanisms for the developed services. If the use case scenarios were broadly chosen then they should be able to incorporate new services where developers can re-use the test patterns. However, developers need to understand that using regular Web testing tools is not appropriate for testing Web Services. Web Services testing requires understanding of the unique security issues related to them, including XML, SOAP, WSDLs, and other WS standards.

14.6.3 Testing Strategies for Web Services Security

Testing strategies should conduct forcing errors tests to ensure that the error messages that are returned by the service do not reveal information about the service [45]. Testing for man-in-the-middle attacks should be used in the event that intermediaries are expected to be in the data path. Data origin authentication techniques can be used to remedy this threat. Authentication bypass tests should be conducted to ensure that only authorized requests are processed by the service.

At the UDDI, testing should be constructed that includes WSDL scanning and parameter tampering to detect vulnerabilities in the exposed service. Mutation tests techniques can be used to test for parameter tampering. Buffer overflow tests can also be used in this step. Tests should also include sanity checks on the UDDI to ensure that hackers cannot access services that should not be made public. These tests are similar to file or directory traversal attacks in web applications [45]. WSDL scanning tests must be conducted to ensure that hackers cannot access unpublished transactional methods by playing on variations of the published ones. It is really a bad practice when developers provide unpublished methods as a backdoor technique for invoking the service by insiders. This practice leaves the service vulnerable to the persistent attacker.

The above-mentioned testing steps need to be repeated if configuration of the system or the security mechanism is changed. For this reason, tests should be repeated if the system configuration is changed [45]. Testing cannot guarantee an error-prone implementation. Testing is used to increase the level of confidence that the service will operate according to its design objectives. Test oracles should be saved and used in regression testing for the modified service.

14.6.4 Testing Strategies for Web Services Application Data

This section addresses functional testing strategies for Web Services security from the developer's point of view, with a focus on testing security related to message data passed to applications. The testing strategy aims at addressing the vulnerabilities as specified by the fault model of the previous section. The aim is to perform tests that involve application context–type attacks. Some examples of these types of attacks are given next, from [45].

1. Cross-site scripting: In this type of attack, the hacker embeds a script into an XML document. The aim here is that the script will be stored (for example, in a database) and then served to an unsuspecting client

Web browser. The script can then execute in the client's browser and can perform tasks on the behalf of the attacker. For example, the script can steal sensitive information such as credit card numbers or passwords from the unsuspecting client. Variation on this type of attack occurs when a hacker embeds in an XML document a script, such as a shell script. The attacker hopes that the script will be executed on the targeted system. If the code executes, the attacker can perform unauthorized operation on the compromised system. Possible counter measures include proper data parsing and validation and to scan for all possible attack patterns and the use of application layer countermeasures, such as Web application firewalls.

2. XPath exploits: This is a form of XML injection attack. In this type of attack, a hacker aiming for illegally accessing data from a database injects malicious input into an XML document. The attacker aims to get the data to be part of a dynamically created XPath query against an XML document in a native XML database. An example of malicious input for XPath exploits is OR 1=1. This expression, when executed in the content of an XML document will always be true and can return data to the attacker. Possible counter measures include proper data parsing and validation and to scan for all possible attack patterns and the use of application layer countermeasures, such as Web application firewalls.

3. SQL injection exploits: In this attack, a hacker injects malicious input disguised as data into an application via an XML document or Web form, with the hope that the input will end up in a WHERE clause of a SQL query that is executed against a backend database. The hackers hope to gain access to data in an unauthorized fashion. The main vulnerability that enables Web Service enabled databases to be attacked in this fashion is the insecure practice of configuring the backend systems to accept and execute valid SQL queries received from any user with the necessary access privileges. Possible counter measures include proper data parsing and validation and to scan for all possible attack patterns and the use of application layer countermeasures, such as Web application firewalls.

4. Buffer overflow exploits: These exploits are targeted atWeb Service components that store input data in memory. These attacks succeed when the Web Service component does not adequately check the size to ensure that it is not larger than the allocated memory buffer that will receive it. Possible counter measures include the use of programming languages that perform input validation such as JAVA. The employment of appropriate memory management techniques that protect memory segments that are allocated for code form data overwrite can also be used as a counter measure to this threat.

Developing remedies for the above threats requires the practice of safe coding technique and the training of the developers in safe code practice. In some cases, there will be a need to have the code inspected by independent security professionals to ensure that the code can pass tests performed to detect these threats. Buffer overflow attacks usually target endpoints [45]. Tests must be conducted to ensure that the endpoint is capable of filtering out large data loads. Hence, testing with large data load must be conducted by developers to gain confidence that the service will survive such attacks.

Mutation-based test techniques can play an important role in detecting vulnerabilities in the code for threats 1 to 3. Mutation test strategies change, or mutate, inputs to the Web Service under test. By applying these changes to input messages, testers can check whether these mutations produce observable effects on the service outputs. Based on the observed behavior, faults in the service can be detected and the offending code can be fixed. The test oracles must be saved and then used to perform regression testing when any modifications have been performed on the service. Testing for script injection exploits may require the identification of the operating system commands in the language that is used to implement the system. These commands can then be imbedded in the validation tests.

14.6.5 Securing an Application: Case Study

To illustrate some of the points of the above-stated approach, consider a fictitious book selling company that has stores nation wide. The company has two warehouses for storing book supplies. For a given book, the company will contact the supplier to re-order copies if a minimum threshold is reached. For the purpose of this example,the company deals with only one supplier. The company needs to develop a web application based on a Web Service to be used by the store employees to query the warehouses for the availability of a given book. The company will use a Web Service to re-order a book once the threshold is met. This example is based on the same concepts of use-case scenarios developed in WS-I to illustrate usage of the BSP profile [11].

Case Study Functional Overview

An employee uses a web-based application that invokes a Web Service to interact with the retailer application. For simplicity, the retailer service manages stock in the two warehouses (Fig. 14.9). If Warehouse A cannot fulfill an order, the retailer service checks Warehouse B. When a warehouse's inventory of a book falls below a defined threshold, the retailer service orders more books from the supplier. The example consists of the following:

1. Client Web Service: A web-based application that provides a user interface. The web client application invokes the client Web Service to get catalogue information and submit an order for a book to the retail service. It also sends to the Retail service a one-way store update statement frequently.

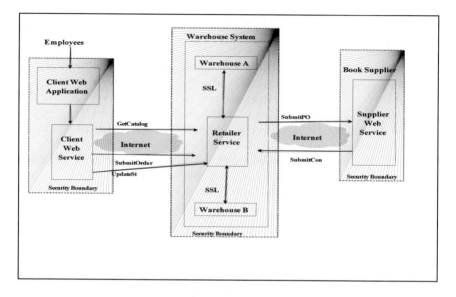

Fig. 14.9. Book service functional overview

2. Retailer service: A service invoking a Web Service that interacts with the warehouse to determine the availability of book and the time to order based on a given threshold.
3. Supplier service: An application that invokes a Web Service for accepting purchase orders and provides callback functionality when the order is fulfilled or an error occurs.
4. At a store, employees use the Web Client Application to view and place orders for available books. A standard web browser that supports SSL is used. Employees are authenticated using a user ID and password. The system does not have certificates that could be used for authentication.

The company has existing X.509 certificate security capabilities. The company uses the Internet for connecting the stores to the retail application and to communicate with the supplier. The company has a dedicated communication service with the warehouses and uses SSL for extra security. The company would like to use SOAP message layer security for securing the interactions.

SOAP Messages Usage Patterns

The use case scenario employs three usage patterns as follows:

1. One-way: Request messages are sent to a Web Service that does not issue a corresponding response. For example, the store update message that is sent to the retail service is a one-way exchange.

2. Synchronous request/response: A SOAP request elicits a SOAP response.

3. Basic callback: A set of paired request/response messages to enable asynchronous operation. The interchange between a retail service and the supplier requires a callback pattern since the supplier cannot instantly respond to the retail service request. The conventions used for callbacks can vary. In this fictitious example, the following sequence of events takes place:

- In an initial synchronous exchange, the retail service sends a purchase order. The supplier validates the order and sends back an acknowledgment.
- In a follow-up exchange between the supplier and the retail callback service, the supplier ships the goods and sends a shipping notice to the retail service. The retail service then sends back an acknowledgment.

Security Requirements

For each of the systems and operations of the use case scenario, the security requirements are specified for message integrity, authentication, and confidentiality.

Message integrity. Message integrity is needed to ensure that messages have not been altered in transit. For simplicity, attachments are not considered. In order to support verification of message integrity, messages are signed. In order to improve on processing speed, digest values are first calculated, and then these values are signed. Developers need to determine which elements of the messages need a signature. For the case under consideration, some or all of the following parts may need to be signed:

- UsernameToken: The `wsse:UsernameToken` element in the WS Security header containing the identity of the user who originally made the purchase request.
- Timestamp: The `wsu:Timestamp` element added to the message when it was created as defined in [12].
- Any custom SOAP headers such as a Start header that contains a conversation ID element and a callback location element. The conversation ID is provided by the Retailer to the Supplier so that the Supplier can include it in the Callback header responses asynchronously.
- The Callback custom header which keeps the conversation ID apart from the Start header.
- SOAP Body: The part of the SOAP message (e.g., soap:Body) that contains the exchanged document (such as a purchase order).

Message integrity is implemented by creating a digital signature using the sender's private key over the elements that need to be signed. To protect against dictionary attacks on plain text signature, the signature is encrypted, meaning that a `xenc:EncryptedData` element replaces this `ds:Signature` element in the message. Note that only the children of each element are used by the signing algorithm. The element itself is not signed.

Authentication. Authentication is performed to allow the receiver to establish the message origin. It is a good practice for the recipient of a message to authenticate the sender of a message. This is done by first checking that the signed data in the message has been signed using the public certificate whose private key was used to sign the message for message integrity purposes and then checking the credentials in that public certificate to determine the identity of the sender. If the sender includes a `wsse:BinarySecurityToken` in the `wsse:Security` header, the token contains the X.509 signing certificate.

The recipient should verify that it can trust the certificate issuer, and may also need to compare the data in the content of the message that identifies the sender, either in the SOAP header or in the payload, with the identity as stated in the public certificate.

The identity of the original user may also be included, in a UsernameToken. If the username token is not used for authentication, a password is not required.

Confidentiality. Confidentiality is required to conceal sensitive information in messages. Not all parts of messages are necessarily sensitive, and in some cases a message may not be considered sensitive at all, and thus there may be no need for confidentiality. In this example, parts of the message that are considered sensitive include the following:

- The SOAP Body since it could contain information such as order data, which could aid competitors.
- The Signature element since in some cases the body of the message can contain predictable variations, making it subject to guessing or dictionary-based attacks. Encrypting the signature can prevent such attacks.
- Custom headers such as the Start Header since it include the location of the callback service.

Confidentiality is implemented by first deriving the `xenc:EncryptedData` elements with the appropriate encryption algorithm and using the appropriate public key. The `xenc:EncryptedKey` element is encrypted using a chosen encryption algorithm. The `xenc:EncryptedKey` element will contain a security token reference to the public key information of the X.509 certificate used for encrypting, along with DataReferences to the `xenc:EncryptedData` elements. In this scenario the certificate itself is not included since it is assumed to be already public. For the Soap Body and the Start Header elements, only the children of the elements are encrypted. For the Signature element, the whole element is encrypted.

14.7 Crash-Only Web Services Design

In an SOA [53] environment, new Web Services are typically built by orchestrating underlying services. In mission-critical applications, it is necessary for both the underlying services and the composite service to advertise their failure models. In general, failure models are complex and difficult to combine but this section argues that the "crash-only software" architecture [49, 50, 51] provides not only a simplifying coherence for designers, but also a paradigm whose characteristics align particularly well with those of Web Services.

Within a Service-Oriented Architecture (SOA), new services are typically created by orchestrating underlying services. Figure. 14.10 illustrates a particularly simple case when two underlying services, X and Y, are orchestrated in some way to produce a new service, Z. In the general case, X and Y will not be owned by the developer of Z, being services exposed by other service providers.

To determine Z's characteristics, so that WSLA guarantees can be offered to customers, it is necessary to combine the characteristics of X and Y with those of the additional logic provided by Z. To enable this, the characteristics of X and Y must be known and although the SOA specifications make provision for X and Y to advertise their interface syntax, their behavior and their contracts, no formal method has been proposed for defining many of the behavioral characteristics. For example, the performance, scaling, management, security, privacy, availability, reliability, and many other models of X and Y need to be known by the developer of Z in order to determine the service-level agreements for the corresponding characteristics of Z. As a simple example, consider privacy: X, Y, and Z may be implemented in different countries with differing laws regarding privacy and security of data. For the developer of Z, to ensure that the service complies with the local regulations and to be able to offer reassurances to customers of Z about the privacy of their data, the privacy policies of X and Y need to be available.

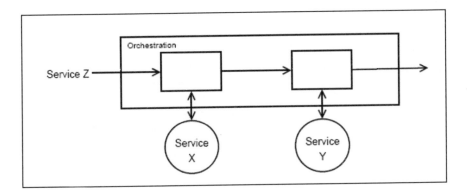

Fig. 14.10. Service orchestration

Each of the models listed above, and others, are needed but this section addresses one particular model: the failure model. If the failure model of Z is to be understood, the failure modes of X and Y have to be known. It may be, e.g., that X supports a transactional model and rolls back its input following a failure, guaranteeing that it returns to a sane state, putting the responsibility for re-submission of inputs onto the consumer (Z). Y, on the other hand, may buffer information and the precise state of an interaction may be difficult to determine when a failure occurs.

To permit Z to determine necessary actions following the failure of X or Y and to allow it to make claims about its own failure modes, a failure ontology is required that could capture X's and Y's (and Z's) failure semantics. This section argues that the technique of "crash-only software" [50] is particularly suited to the loosely coupled environment of SOAs, providing particularly simple behavior that can be described and advertised in a formal manner. It is unrealistic to expect all services to comply with this failure paradigm but this work proposes that it forms the basis of the failure semantics for Web Services.

14.7.1 Crash-Only Software

Studies (dating back to 1986 see [52]) support the view that failures in deployed software are mainly caused by Heisenbugs [52], bugs caused by subtle timing interactions between threads and tasks which are impervious to conventional debugging, being non-reproducible and sensitive to tracing and other observation. Reproducible bugs, the so-called "Bohrbugs," are easier to detect and fix during development and can largely be removed before shipment of a final product.

It must be accepted that, in any software-based system, if Heisenbugs exist then failures will occur. When they do, telecommunications and other high-availability systems have been built to detect the failure, save state, shut down the offending task and any other affected components (defined by some form of failure tree) down gracefully, take whatever recovery action is required and then restart the affected components.

The technique of crash-only argues that this is not only unnecessary but, in many cases, counter-productive. Consumers of the services, it is argued, must anticipate that their provider will, from time to time, crash cleanly without the opportunity for sophisticated failure handling (perhaps because of a power failure to the computer running the provider). Consumers must therefore already have the capability of handling such a crash. If this is the case, then consumers can always crash the component whenever any failure occurs.

This crash-only semantic has several advantages:

- It defines simpler macroscopic behavior with fewer externally visible states.
- It reduces the outage time of the provider by removing all shutting-down time.

- It simplifies the failure model significantly by reducing the size of the recovery state table. In particular, crashing can be invoked from outside the software of the provider. Recovery from a failed state is notoriously difficult and the crash-only paradigm coerces the system into a known state without attempting recovery, reducing substantially the complexity of the provider code.
- It simplifies testing by reducing the failure combinations that have to be verified.

If software is to crash cleanly more often, then it should also be written in such a way as to reload quickly [51].

14.7.2 Crash-Only Software and Web Services

Candea in [50] lists the properties required of a crash-only system and these can be abstracted remarkably well to match those of Web Services as described in [53]:

- Components have externally enforced boundaries. This is an implementation recommendation but one supported by the virtual machine concept used on many Web Service systems.
- All interactions between components have a timeout. This is implicit in any loosely coupled Web Services interaction.
- All resources are leased to the service rather than being permanently allocated. This is an implementation recommendation but clearly one which it is useful to follow in any implementation, particularly a Web Services one.
- Requests are entirely self-describing. For crash-only services, this requires that the request carries information about idempotency and time-to-live. The work in [50] maps this request to a REST[1]-like [54] environment but the comments are equally applicable to a true SOAP-defined Web Service.
- All important non-volatile state is managed by dedicated state stores.

In Section 14.2 of this chapter, in effect, the WSM performs runtime governance. The WSM is enabled in an SOA environment by having access to the service description of the invoked service and being in a position to intercept and decode all incoming requests.

Deliberately induced crashes are a useful technique for software rejuvenation (see [55]) and this requires detection of periods of low usage of the service. Runtime governance is an obvious candidate for recognizing such periods and causing the restarts.

The description of crash-only software in [50] assumes, when recast using SOA terminology, that the providers (X and Y in Fig.14.10) will exhibit crash-only failure behavior but that consumers, having failed to obtain timely

---

[1] Representational State Transfer.

or correct service, can initiate the crash. This is acceptable only when the consumer and provider, although loosely coupled, are within one trust domain. This is clearly not generally the situation with Web Services.

One common function of the WSM software layer is the monitoring of response times from the service to ensure that the consumer is getting the level of service paid for. This provides the perfect location for invocation of the power-off switch provided by crash-only software that switch is external to the service, relying in no way on continued correct operation of the service code, and its operation is idempotent, ensuring that the decision to kill the server does not require knowledge of internal state.

Crash-only design principles can be used as a starting point in the design of Web Services (we term them crash-only Web Services). In this aspect, the service can be designed in such a fashion that the state of the service that identifies critical information is always stored in the system even in the event of a crash. The same crash-only design principles are extended at the service level whereby, e.g., in business process interaction, information such as the status of an order is stored in a non-volatile state [50]. Tree techniques as defined in [49] and [50] can be used to identify the data components from a service that should be stored and be available when the service is crashed.

The use of crash-only systems combined with crash-only Web Services in combination with a reliable SOAP stack can enhance on the availability of a Web Service and reduces the complexity of its testing. Crash-only Web Services can be re-started quickly and with a known state. In [56] a SOAP reliable transport protocol is described (WSRM). The protocol allows a reliability agent to acknowledge the receipt of SOAP messages to the Web Services consumer. Reliability in WSRM is used to ensure that the messages are delivered to the targeted server (application server). The reliability agent can be implemented at the Web Services end point in Fig. 14.11.

For systems with hardware redundancy, by using crash-only techniques, SOAP WSRM can be extended in order to produce an always available Web Service (although at reduced WSLA if and when a service is forced to crash) from the provider's and consumer's point of view. The architecture is depicted in Fig. 14.11. Here, the components of the system are designed using crash-only, which means that re-booting is fast and reliable. The Web Services end point is used as the gateway between the Web Services consumer and provider. At runtime, the system stores all of its important data innonvolatile states. The WSRM agent acknowledges the receipt of the SOAP messages to the consumer only after a confirmation is received from the system that the important data is safely stored in the system. The recovery agent monitors the operation of the Web Services. If the agent determines that the Web Service is misbehaving (due to fault in the code or any other reason, actually the cause need not be known or investigated), then the agent will instruct the stall proxy to delay the acknowledgment of the SOAP messages to the consumer. The stall proxy will basically ensure that the session is

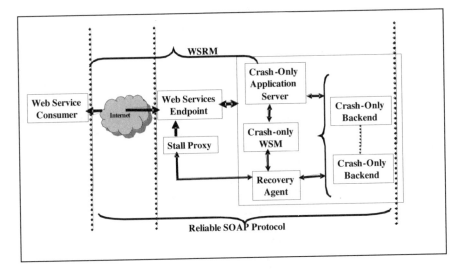

Fig. 14.11. Architecture of crash-only reliable Web Services

kept alive. The system is re-started (multiple sub-component reboots may be needed see [49] and [50] for details). When the system is back up again, the WSRM agent can request the transmission of the last set of lost messages from the consumer.

The above approach provides for the capability of extending the SOAP WSRM protocol to enhance on the availability and reliability at the service level. Testing scope is also minimized.

14.8 Research Proposals and Open Research Issues

Despite such intense research and development efforts, current Web Service technology does not yet provide the flexibility needed to "tailor" a Web Service according to preferences of the requesting clients. At the same time, Web Service providers demand enhanced adaptation capabilities in order to adapt the provisioning of a Web Service to dynamic changes of the Web Service environment according to their own policies. Altogether, these two requirements call for policy-driven access controls model and mechanisms, extended with negotiation capabilities. Models and languages to specify access and management control policies have been widely investigated in the area of distributed systems [3].

Standardization bodies have also proposed policy-driven standard access control models [1]. The main goals of such models are to separate the access control mechanism from the applications and to make the access control mechanism itself easily configurable according to different, easily deployable access control policies. The characteristics of open web environments, in which the interacting parties are mostly unknown to each other, have lead to the development of the trust negotiation approach as a suitable access control model for this environment [4, 5].

Trust negotiation itself has been extended with adaptive access control, in order to adapt the system to dynamically changing security conditions. Automated negotiation is also being actively investigated in different application domains, such as e-business. However, a common key requirement that has been highlighted is the need of a flexible negotiation approach that enables the system to dynamically adapt to changing conditions. In addition, the integration of trust negotiation techniques with Semantic Web technologies, such as semantic annotations and rule-oriented access control policies, has been proposed. In such approaches, the resource under the control of the access control policy is an item on the Semantic Web, with its salient properties represented as RDF properties. RDF metadata, managed as facts in logic programming, are associated with a resource and are used to determine which policies are applicable to the resource. When extending a Web Service with negotiation capabilities, the invocation of a Web Service has to be managed as the last step of a conversation between the client and the Web Service itself. The rules for such a conversation are defined by the negotiation protocol itself. Such a negotiation protocol should be described and made publicly available in a similar way as a Web Service operation is publicly described through WSDL declarations. An XML-based, machine-processable negotiation protocol description allows an electronic agent to automatically generate the messages needed to interact with the Web Service.

The client and the Web Service must be equipped with a negotiation engine that evaluates the incoming messages, takes decisions, and generates the outgoing messages according to the agreed upon protocol. The models already proposed for peer-to-peer negotiations assume that both parties are equipped with the same negotiation engine that implements the mutually understood negotiation protocol. This assumption might not, however, be realistic and may prevent the wide adoption of negotiation-enhanced, access-control model and mechanisms.

In the remainder of this section, we present a short overview of a system, addressing those requirements, and then we discuss open research issues.

14.8.1 Ws-AC1: An Adaptive Access Control System for Web Services

In order to address the adaptation and negotiation requirements, we propose the use of a system that supports Web Service access control model and an associated negotiation protocol as given in [6]. The proposed model, referred to as Web Service Access Control Version 1 (Ws-AC1, for short) is based on a declarative and highly expressive access control policy language.

Such language allows one to specify authorizations containing conditions and constraints not only against the Web Service parameters but also against the identity attributes of the party requesting the service and context parameters that can be bound, e.g., to a monitor of the Web Service operating environment. An additional distinguishing feature of Ws-AC1 is the range of object-protection granularity it supports. Under Ws-AC1 the Web Service security administrator can specify several access control policies for the same service, each one characterized by different constraints for the service parameters, or can specify a single policy that applies to all the services in a set. In order to support such granularity, we introduce the notion of service class to group Web Services. To the best of our knowledge, Ws-AC1 is the first access-control model developed specifically for Web Services characterized by articulated negotiation capabilities. A model like Ws-AC1 has important applications, especially when dealing with privacy of identity information of users and with dynamic application environments. In order to represent the negotiation protocol, an extension to the Web Services Description Language standard has also been developed.

The main reason of that choice is that, although the Web Services Choreography Description Language (WS-CDL) is the emerging standard for representing Web Services interactions, WS-CDL is oriented to support a more complex composition of Web Services in the context of a business process involving multiple parties.

Ws-AC1 is an implementation-independent, attribute-based, access-control model for Web Services, providing mechanisms for negotiation of service parameters. InWs-AC1 the requesting agents (also referred to as subjects) are entities (human being or software agents). Subjects are identified by means of identity attributes qualifying them, such as name, birth date, credit card number, and passport number.Identity attributes are disclosed within access requests invoking the desired service. Access requests to a Web Service (also referred to as provider agent) are evaluated with respect to access control policies. Note that in its initial definition,Ws-AC1 does not distinguish between the Web Service and the different operations it provides, i.e., it assumes that a Web Service provides just a single operation. Such a model can be applied to the various operations provided by a Web Service without any extension. Access control policies are defined in terms of the identity attributes of the requesting agent and the set of allowed service parameters values. Both identity attributes and service parameters are further differentiated in mandatory and optional ones. For privacy and security purposes, access control policies are not published along with the service description but are internal to the Ws-AC1 system. Ws-AC1 also allows one to specify multiple policies at different levels of granularity. It is possible to associate fine-grained policies with a specific service as well with several services. To this end, it is possible to group different services in one or more classes and to specify policies referring to a specific service class, thus reducing the number of policies that need to be specified by a policy administrator. A policy for a class of services is then applied to all the services of that class, unless policies associated with the specific service(s) are defined.

Moreover, in order to adapt the provision of the service to dynamically changing conditions, the Ws-AC1 policy language allows one to specify constraints, dynamically evaluated, over a set of environment variables, referred to as context, as well as over service parameters. The context is associated with a specific service implementation and it might consist of monitored system variables, such as the system load. The access control process of Ws-AC1 is organized into two main sequential phases. The first phase deals with the identification of the subject requesting the service. The second phase, executed only if the identification succeeds, verifies the service parameters specified by the requesting agent against the authorized service parameters.

The identification phase is adaptive, in that the provider agent might eventually require the requesting agent to submit additional identity attributes in addition to those originally submitted. Such an approach allows the provider agent to adapt the service provisioning to dynamic situations;for example, after a security attack, the provider agent might require additional identity attributes to the requesting agents. In addition, to enhance the flexibility of access control, the service parameter verification phase can trigger a negotiation process. The purpose of this process is to drive the requesting agent toward the specification of an access request compliant with the service specification and policies. The negotiation consists in an exchange of messages between the two negotiating entities in order to limit, fix, or propose the authorized parameters the requesting agent may use. The negotiation of service parameters allows the provider agent to tailor the service provisioning to the requesting agent preferences or, at the opposite, to enforce its own preferred service provisioning conditions.

14.8.2 Open Research Issues

Even though Ws-Ac1 provides an initial solution to the problem of adaptive access control mechanisms for Web Services, many issues need to be investigated. A first issue is related to the development of models and mechanisms supporting a comprehensive characterization of Web Services that we refer to as Web Service profiles. Such a characterization should be far more expressive than conventional approaches, like those based on UDDI registries or OWL. The use of such profiles would allow one to specify more expressive policies, taking into account various features on Web Services, and to better support adaptation.

The second issue is related to taking into account the conversational nature of Web Services, according to which interacting with real world Web Services involves generally a sequence of invocations of several of their operations, referred to as conversation. Most proposed approaches, like Ws-AC1, assume a single-operation model where operations are independent from each other.

Access control is either enforced at the level of the entire Web Service or at the level of single operations. In the first approach, the Web Service could ask, in advance, the client to provide all the credentials associated with all operations of that Web Service. This approach guarantees that a subject will always arrive at the end of whichever conversation. However, it has the drawback that the subject will become aware of all policies on the base of which access control is enforced. In several cases, policies need to be maintained confidentially and disclosed only upon some initial verification of the identity of the client has been made. Another drawback is that the client may have to submit more credentials than needed. An alternative strategy is to require only the credentials associated with the next operation that the client wants to perform. This strategy has the advantage of asking from the subject only the credentials necessary to gain access to the requested operation. However, the subject is continuously solicited to provide credentials for each transition. In addition, after several steps, the client may reach a state where it cannot progress because of the lack of credentials. It is thus important to devise strategies to balance the confidentiality of the policies with the maximization of the service completion. A preliminary approach to such strategies has been recently developed [2]; the approach is based on the notion of k-trustworthiness where k can be seen as the level of trust that a Web Service has on a client at any point of their interaction. The greater the level of trust associated with a client, the greater is the amount of information about access control policies that can be disclosed to this client, thus allowing the client to determine early in the conversation process if it has all necessary credentials to satisfy the access control policies. Such approach needs, however, to be extended by integrating it with an exception-based mechanism tailored to support access control enforcement. In particular, in a step-by-step approach, whenever a client cannot complete a conversation because of the lack of authorization, some alternative actions and operations are taken by the Web Service.

A typical action would be to suspend the execution of the conversation, ask the user to acquire the missing credentials, and then resume the execution of the conversation; such a process would require investigating a number of issues, such as determining the state information that need to be maintained, and whether revalidation of previous authorizations is needed when resuming the execution.

A different action would be to determine whether alternative operations can be performed to replace the operation that the user cannot execute because of the missing authorization. We would like to develop a language according to which one can express the proper handling of error situations arising from the lack of authorization.

The third issue is related to security in the context of composite services; in such a case, a client may be willing to share its credentials or other sensitive information with a service but not with other services that can be invoked by the initial service. To handle such requirement, different solutions may be adopted, such as declaring the possible services that may be invoked by the initial service or associating privacy policies with the service description, so that a client can specify its own privacy preferences. Other relevant issues concern workflow systems. Such systems represent an important technology supporting the deployment of business processes consisting of several Web Services and their security is thus crucial. Even though some initial solutions have been proposed, such as the extension of the WS-BPEL [9] standards with role-based access control [7], more comprehensive solutions are required, supporting adaptive access control and sophisticated access-control constraints.

Finally, the problem of secure access to all information needed to use services, such as information stored by UDDI registries, needs to be addressed. To date, solutions have been developed to address the problem of integrity through the use of authenticated data structures [8]. However, work is needed to address the problem of suitable access control techniques to assure the confidentiality and privacy of such information in order to support its selective sharing among multiple parties.

14.9 Conclusion

Testing Web Services and security in an SOA environment is a discipline that is still in its infancy. Experience gained from Web Development can be used as a guiding principle for the development of testing strategies in the SOA world at large. There are still many open areas that still need to be worked on. For example, there are no standard mechanisms to share management information between the various service providers. Faults in the Web Services stack are more centered toward the SOAP message level. Current standards are not designed with fault management in mind. Regression tests need enhancement, coverage, and speed improvement to be able to cope with the testing scope of composite services.

References

1. OASIS eXtensible Access Control Markup Language 2 (XACML) Version 2.0 OASIS Standard, 1 Feb 2005.
2. M. Mecella, M. Ouzzani, F. Paci, E. Bertino. Access Control Enforcement for Conversational-based Services. *Proceedings of 2006 WWW Conference*, Edimburgh, Scotland, May 23-26, 2006.
3. N. Damianou ,N. Dulay, E. Lupu and M. Sloman. The Ponder Policy Specification Language. *Proceedings of the 2nd IEEE International Workshop on Policies for Distributed Systems and Networks*, 2001.
4. T. Yu, M. Winslett, K. Seamons. Supporting Structured Credentials and Sensitive Policies through Interoperable Strategies for Automated Trust Negotiation. *ACM Transactions on Information and System Security*, Vol. 6, No. 1, February 2003.
5. E. Bertino, E. Ferrari, A.C. Squicciarini. X -TNL: An XML-based Language for Trust Negotiations. *Proceedings of the 4th IEEE International Workshop on Policies for Distributed Systems and Networks*, 2003.

6. E.Bertino, A.C. Squicciarini, L.Martino, F. Paci. An Adaptive Access Control Model for Web Services. *International Journal of Web Service Research*, (3), 27-60 July-September 2006.

7. E.Bertino, B.Carminati, E.Ferrari. Merkle Tree Authentication in UDDI Registries. *International Journal of Web Service Research*, 1(2): 37-57(2004).

8. E.Bertino, J.Crampton, F.Paci. Access Control and Authorization Constraints for WS-BPEL. Submitted for publication.

9. OASIS Web Services Business Process Execution Language Version 2.0. Committee Specification, 31 January 2007

10. Schwarz, J, Bret Hartman B., Nadalin A, Kaler C., F. Hirsch, and Morrison S, , Security Challenges, Threats and Countermeasures Version 1.0, WS-I, May, 2005, http://www.ws-i.org/Profiles/BasicSecurity/SecurityChallenges-1.0.pdf

11. Barbir, A. Gudgin M and McIntosh M., , Basic Security Profile Version 1.0, WS-I, May 2005, http://www.ws-i.org/Profiles/BasicSecurityProfile-1.0-2004-05-12.html

12. Nadalin, A., Kaler C., Hallam-Naker, P., Monzillo R., Web Services Security: SOAP Message Security 1.0, (WS-Security 2004), OASIS, March 2004, http://docs.oasis-open.org/wss/2004/01/oasis-200401-wss-soap-message-security-1.0.pdf

13. Web Services Security: SOAP Message Security 1.1, (WS-Security 2004), OASIS, February 2006, http://www.oasis-open.org/committees/download.php /16790/wss-v1.1-spec-os-SOAPMessageSecurity.pdf

14. Nadalin, A., Kaler C., Hallam-Naker, P., Monzillo R.,, Web Services Security: UsernameToken Profile 1.1,OASIS, February 2006, http://www.oasis-open.org/committees/download.php/16782/wss-v1.1-spec-os-Username Token-Profile.pdf

15. Nadalin, A., Kaler C., Hallam-Naker, P., Monzillo R., Web Services Security: X.509 Certificate Token Profile 1.1, OASIS, February 2006, http://www.oasis-open. org/committees/download. php/16785/wss-v1.1-spec-os-x509TokenProfile.pdf

16. Monzillo R., Kaler C., Nadalin A., Hallam-Naker, P.,,, Web Services Security: SAML Token Profile 1.1, OASIS, February 2006, http://www.oasis-open. org/committees/download.php/16768/wss-v1.1-spec-os-SAMLTokenProfile.pdf

17. Nadalin, A., Kaler C., Hallam-Naker, P., Monzillo R.,,, Web Services Security: Kerberos Token Profile 1.1, OASIS, February 2006, http://www.oasis-open.org/committees/download.php/16788/wss-v1.1-spec-os-KerberosTokenProfile.pdf

18. Monzillo R., Kaler C., Nadalin A., Hallam-Naker, P., Web Services Security: Rights Expression Language (REL) Token Profile 1.1, OASIS, February 2006, http://www.oasis-open.org/committees/download.php/16687/oasis-wss-rel-token-profile-1.1.pdf

19. Hirsch, F., Web Services Security: SOAP Messages with Attachments (SwA) Profile 1.1, OASIS, February 2006, http://www.oasis-open.org/committees/download.php/16672/wss-v1.1-spec-os-SwAProfile.pdf

20. Signature Syntax and Processing, W3C Recommendation February 2002, http://www.w3.org/TR/xmldsig-core/

21. XML Encryption Syntax and Processing, W3C Recommendation December 2002, http://www.w3.org/TR/xmlenc-core/

22. Nortel Unified Security Framework for corporate and government security, Nortel, http://www.nortel.com/solutions/security/collateral/nn104120-051705.pdf

23. SOAP Version 1.2 Part 1: Messaging Framework, W3C, June 2003, http://www.w3.org/TR/soap12-part1/
24. Simple Object Access Protocol (SOAP) 1.1, W3C Note, May 2000, http://www.w3.org/TR/2000/NOTE-SOAP-20000508/
25. Rescorla E., HTTP Over TLS, RFC 2818, May 2000.
26. Web Services Description Language (WSDL) 1.1, W3C Note 15 March 2001, http://www.w3.org/TR/wsdl
27. Bloomberg, J., Schmelzer, R, Service Orient or Be Doomed!: How Service Orientation Will Change Your Business, SBN: 0-471-79224-1, Wiley, May 2006.
28. Boyer, J., Exclusive XML Canonicalization Version 1.0, W3C, July 2002, http://www.w3.org/TR/xml-exc-c14n/
29. Bray, T., Extensible Markup Language (XML) 1.0 (Third Edition), W3C, February 2004, http://www.w3.org/TR/REC-xml/
30. The Transport Layer Security (TLS) Protocol,Version 1.1, RFC 4346, April 2006.
31. Demchenko, Y.,, Web Services and Grid Security Vulnerabilities and Threats Analysis and Model, Grid Computing Workshop, 2005.
32. Nakamura, Y., Model-Driven Security Based on a Web Services Security Architecture, Proceedings of the 2005 IEEE International Conference on Services Computing (SCC'05), 2005.
33. Tarhini et al., Regression Testing Web Services-based Applications, Computer Systems and Applications, March 8, Page(s):163 - 170, 2006.
34. Benharref A. et al, A Web Service Based-Architecture for Detecting Faults in Web Services, IFIP/IEEE International Symposium on Integrated Network Management 2005.
35. Bhoj, P. , Management of new Federated Services, Integrated Network Management V., 1997.
36. Weiping He, Recovery in Web Service Applications, Proceedings of the 2004 IEEE International Conference on e-Technology, e-Commerce and e-Service (EEE'04), 2004.
37. Papazoglou, M. and Heuvel, W., Web Services Management: A Survey, IEEE Internet Computing, November 2005.
38. Bertolino A. and Polini A., The Audition Framework for Testing Web Services Interoperability, Proceedings of the 2005 31st EUROMICRO Conference on Software Engineering and Advanced Applications (EUROMICRO-SEAA'05), 2005. 30. Karjoth, G., Service-oriented Assurance: Comprehensive Security by Explicit Assurances, Publications of the Network Security and Cryptography Group, 2005.
39. Tsai, W., Ray Paul R., Weiwei S. and Cao Z.,, Coyote: An XML-Based Framework for Web Services Testing, 7th IEEE International Symposium on High Assurance Systems Engineering (HASE'02), 2002.
40. Yuan Rao, Y., Feng, O, Han, J., and Li, Z.,, SX-RSRPM: A Security Integrated Model For Web Services, Proceedings of the Third International Conference on Machine Learning and Cybernetics, Shanghai, 26-29 August 2004.
41. Bruno, M., Gerardo, C., and Di Penta, M., Using Test Cases as Contract to Ensure Service Compliance across Releases, Proc. 3rd Int'l Conf. Service Oriented Computing (ICSOC 2005), LNCS 3826, Springer, 2005, pp. 87-100.
42. Tsai, W., Paul, R, Cao, Z., L. Yu, L., A. Saimi, A. and B. Xiao, B., . Verification of Web Services using an enhanced UDDI server. In Proc. of WORDS 2003, pages 131-138, Jan., 15-17 2003. Guadalajara, Mexico.

43. Tsai, W., Paul R., Wei S. and Cao Z. Scenario-based Web Service testing with distributed agents. IEICE Transaction on Information and System, E86-D(10):2130-2144, 2003.

44. Xu, W., Offutt, J., Juan Luo, J., Testing Web Services by XML Perturbation, Proceedings of the 16th IEEE International Symposium on Software Reliability Engineering (ISSRE'05), 2005.

45. Yu, W., Supthaweesuk, P., and Aravind, D. Trustworthy Web Services Based on Testing, Proceedings of the 2005 IEEE International Workshop on Service-Oriented System Engineering (SOSE'05), 2005.

46. Mei H. and Zhang L., A Framework for Testing Web Services and Its Supporting Tool, Proceedings of the 2005 IEEE International Workshop on Service-Oriented System Engineering (SOSE'05), 2005.

47. Canfora G. and Di Penta M., Testing Services and Service-Centric Systems: Challenges and Opportunities, IT Pro Published by the IEEE Computer Society, April 2006.

48. Zapthink, www.zapthink.org

49. Fox A. and D. Patterson D., When does fast recovery trump high reliability? In 2nd Workshop on Evaluating and Architecting Systems for Dependability (EASY), 2002.

50. Candea G. and A. Fox A., Crash-only software. In 9th Workshop on Hot Topics in Operating Systems, 2003.

51. Candea G. Et, Microreboot-a technique for cheap recovery. In Proceedings of the 6th Symposium on Operating Systems Design and Implementation, 2004.

52. Gray J., Why do computers stop and what can be done about it? In 5th Symposium on Reliability in Distributed Systems, 1986.

53. OASIS SOA Reference Model TC. Reference model for service-oriented architecture 1.0. Technical report, OASIS, 2006.

54. Fielding, R., Architectural Styles and the Design of Network-based Software Architectures. Ph.D. Dissertation. University Of California, Irvine, 2000.

55. K. Vaidyanathan, K. et al., Analysis and implementation of software rejuvenation in cluster systems. In SIGMETRICS '01: Proceedings of the 2001 ACM SIGMETRICS international conference on Measurement and modeling of computer systems, pages 62-71, New York, NY, USA, 2001. ACM Press.

56. OASIS (www.oasis-open.org) Web Services Reliable Exchange Technical Committe (WS-SX). 49. W3C (www.w3.org) WS-Policy WG.

57. IBM; The Enterprise Privacy Authorization Language (EPAL 1.1) - Reader's Guide to the Documentation.

58. OASIS eXtensible Access Control Markup Language 2 (XACML) Version 2.0 OASIS Standard, 1 Feb 2005.

59. T. Yu, M. Winslett, K. Seamons. Supporting Structured Credentials and Sensitive Policies through Interoperable Strategies for Automated Trust Negotiation. ACM Transactions on Information and System Security, Vol. 6, No. 1, February 2003.

60. OASIS (www.oasis-open.org) WS-BPEL TC.

61. Mecella, M., Ouzzani, M., Paci, F., Bertino, E. Access Control Enforcement for Conversation-based Web Services. Proceedings of the 2006 WWW Conference, Edinburgh, Scotland, May 23-26, 2006.

62. Bertino, E., Crampton J.,, and Paci F. Access Control and Authorization Constraints for WS-BPEL. Submitted for publication.

63. Bertino, E., B. Carminat, and E. Ferrari, E. Merkle Tree Authentication in UDDI Registries. International Journal of Web Service Research, 1(2): 37-57 (2004).
64. Liberty Alliance Project - Introduction to the Liberty Alliance Identity Architecture Revision 1.0 March, 2003

15

ws-Attestation: Enabling Trusted Computing on Web Services

Sachiko Yoshihama[1], Tim Ebringer[2], Megumi Nakamura[1], Seiji Munetoh[1], Takuya Mishina[1] and Hiroshi Maruyama[1]

[1] IBM Tokyo Research Laboratory, 1623-14, Shimotsuruma, Yamato-shi, Kanagawa, Japan
   {*sachikoy, nakamegu, munetoh, tmishina, maruyama*} *@jp.ibm.com*
[2] CA Labs, 658 Church St., Richmond, Victoria, Australia
   tim.ebringer@ca.com

Abstract. This chapter proposes ws-Attestation, an attestation architecture based upon a Web Services framework. The increasing prevalence of security breaches caused by malicious software shows that the conventional identity-based trust model is insufficient as a protection mechanism. It is unfortunately common for a computing platform in the care of a trustworthy owner to behave maliciously.[3]

Specifications created by the Trusted Computing Group (TCG) [27, 26] introduced the concept of platform integrity attestation, by which a computing platform can prove its current configuration state to a remote verifier in a reliable manner. ws-Attestation allows Web Services providers and consumers to leverage this technology in order to make better informed business decisions based on the security of the other party.

Current TCG specifications define only a primitive attestation mechanism that has several shortcomings for use in real-world scenarios: attestation information is coarse grained; dynamic system states are not captured; integrity metrics are difficult to validate; platform state as of an attestation is not well bound to the platform state as of interaction and platform configuration information is not protected from attackers. We aim to provide a software-oriented, dynamic, and fine-grained attestation mechanism which leverages TCG and ws-Security technologies to increase trust and confidence in integrity reporting. In addition, the architecture allows binding of attestation with application context, privacy protection, and infrastructural support for attestation validation.

15.1 Introduction

The current and planned Web Services Specifications describe a set of functionality for providing distributed services in a heterogeneous computing environment. A service describes its functional interface in WSDL (Web Services

---

[3] Zombie computers used to send spam being a common example.

Description Language) [20] and advertises itself through a centralized UDDI registry [28] or ad hoc metadata exchange [11]. The messages sent between services are in SOAP envelopes [19] and transported over various protocols, the most common of which is HTTP.

In order to secure interactions between Web services, various Web Services Specifications are defined or being defined as proposed in the Web Services Security Roadmap [13]. These specifications are defined as building blocks allowing various specifications integrated together to enable security, reliable messages, policy, and transactions [12].

At the simplest level the messages can be protected against malicious parties who would eavesdrop on sensitive data or alter messages. The WS-Security specification [30] defines mechanisms for protecting message integrity and confidentiality. WS-Trust [5] defines a generic framework for exchanging security tokens between endpoints to establish trust. WS-SecureConversation Language [4] utilizes WS-Trust and enables secure interaction context that will last for a series of message exchanges. The WS-PolicyFramework [2] and the WS-SecurityPolicy Language [10] defines syntax and vocabularies for exchanging security policies between endpoints. WS-Federation Language [9] allows federating identities between multiple parties.

In the WS-Security framework, a trust relationship is established based on the identity of each entity who is participating in a transaction. For example, the sender of a message is identified by a digital signature, which is authenticated by the receiver using an X.509 certificate. The receiver checks the trustworthiness of the certificate and a trust decision is made, depending on the authenticity of the signature and the trust relationship to the Certification Authority (CA) who issued the certificate.

In the business world, an entity utilizes fine-grained information to decide whether another entity is trustworthy enough to make a deal. For example, a customer may be interested in whether a service provider has ability to perform a certain service, with certain quality and quantity, by a certain deadline. A customer may also be interested in whether the service provider is honest, abides by the law, respects the privacy policy, has a good reputation, etc. On the other hand, a service provider is generally interested in the customer's financial credibility and his/her eligibility for receiving the service (e.g., does the customer have a license for buying controlled materials).

In addition, when the transaction takes place on the Internet, it is also important to verify that a computer platform, acting on behalf of a service provider or a requester, does not betray the service requester or provider's will. For example, if a user trusts an on-line shopping service and submits his credit card number—even if the service provider company is actually honest and trustworthy—the server platform might be infected with a Trojan horse that surreptitiously sends the credit card number to a malicious remote attacker. In another case, the server software might have a vulnerability that would be attacked by an attacker, allowing the attacker to obtain the super user privilege and steal customer information and credit card numbers. Therefore, it is important to make sure that the service is running on a trustworthy platform; i.e., it is running on the hardware that it claims to be, and that the OS and software are not infected by malicious software and has no known vulnerabilities.

Remote attestation is one of the key functionalities of Trusted Computing which allows a remote challenger to verify not only the identity of the other party but also the integrity of the platform that represents the party. The platform integrity information allows the challenger to verify the configuration and the state of the system (e.g., what OS is running, which security patches are applied, what security policies are being observed or whether it is infected with viruses). It allows intelligent decisions to be made as to whether a service which runs on a trusted platform is fit to use. Conversely, the service provider may choose whether to accept a service request from a requester based on the trustworthiness of the requester. The trusted computing allows establishing a trust relationship among potentially distrusted distributed parties, thus enabling new types of secure interaction.

There are several issues that need to be considered when enabling Trusted Computing on Web Services. First, it is obviously dangerous for a platform to advertise its precise configuration, because such information is very useful for an attacker in choosing the most effective attack technique. Therefore, it is important that access to the precise configuration information is only seen by authorized parties. For distrusted parties, the platform needs to prove only its security properties without revealing configuration details. Second, exchanging and validating a platform attestation can be a relatively heavy process and it is important to adjust balance between fine granularity and effectiveness. Third, the architecture has to support validation of complicated computer platform that consists of various components.

This chapter proposes WS-Attestation, attestation architecture built on top of the Web Services framework. WS-Attestation provides a software-oriented, dynamic, and fine-grained attestation mechanism which leverages TCG and WS-Security technologies to increase trust and confidence in integrity reporting. In addition, the architecture allows binding of attestation with application context, as well as infrastructural support for attestation validation.

The following sections are structured as follows. Sect. 15.2 discusses an overview of the trusted computing technology. Sect. 15.3 discusses design principles. Sect. 15.4 discusses WS-Attestation architecture of attestation support for Web Services framework. Sect. 15.5 and 15.6 discusses the WS-Attestation profile and token exchange model respectively. Sect. 15.7 describes prototype implementation. Sect. 15.8 shows observations on the architecture. Sect. 15.9 discusses related work. Sect. 15.10 concludes this chapter.

15.2 Trusted Computing Technology

The Trusted Computing Group (TCG) [27, 26] defines a set of industry standard specifications for hardware and software for enabling trusted computing among wide variety of computing platforms, such as PCs, servers, mobile phones, etc. The center of the TCG technology is a security module called the Trusted Platform Module (TPM) which is usually implemented as a tamper-resistant hardware module. In addition to serving as a cryptographic co-processor and a protected storage for secrets and keys, the TPM is used to *measure* and *report* platform integrity in a manner that cannot be compromised even by either platform owners or the software running on it. In this section, we review mechanisms of platform integrity measurement and platform integrity reporting (i.e., attestation) in more detail.

15.2.1 Platform Integrity Measurement

Platform integrity measurement consists of multiple phases of measuring and storing integrity of hardware and software components that constitute a platform. Integrity measurement can be categorized into two types: (1) TCG trusted bootstrap and (2) other integrity measurement built on top of trusted bootstrap.

TCG defines the trusted bootstrap process [27, 26] that comprises an iterative process of "measurement" (cryptographic hashing), loading, and execution of software components. When the system is powered-on, the immutable initial bootstrap code (such as BIOS boot block) measures next component and stores the measurement in the TPM before transferring control to the next component. In subsequent steps, each software component recursively measures next component and records the measurements in the TPM, until the operating system is loaded. The BIOS boot block and TPM are called Core Root of Trust for Measurement (CRTM), because they need to be trusted in order to trust measurement in trusted bootstrap.

Each measurement is taken as a SHA-1 (Secure Hash Algorithm 1) value of the binary image of a component, and stored into Platform Configuration Registers (PCRs). PCRs are special purpose registers within the TPM which record integrity measurements, and are protected from an arbitrary modification.[4]

The specification requires 16 PCRs at minimum on a TPM, but each PCR can store fingerprint of multiple components using a hash-chain mechanism. That is, a PCR supports only the extend operation to update its value; i.e.,

---

[4] TPM Specification 1.2 supports a new operation to reset the PCRs to 0, in order to allow a virtualized operating system to leverage TCG capabilities without a hard reset.

when recording a measurement value v into a PCR, the value v is extended into the PCR, which results in a SHA-1 hash over concatenation of the current PCR value and the value v.

$$\text{PCR}_i^n = \text{SHA-1}(\text{PCR}_{i-1}^n || v)$$

where the initial PCR value after power-on is $\text{PCR}_0^n = 0$, n denotes the index of the PCR register ($0 \leq n < 16$), and $||$ denotes a concatenation.

After the OS is loaded and initialized in a trusted bootstrap process, the PCRs will contain some predictable values, provided that the PLATForm runs a known set of components that are intact. If any bits of measured components are modified from the original, the PCR value will be different, and such modification can be detected. The PCR values form a fingerprint of the exact software stack on a particular platform. Note that trusted bootstrap is different from secure bootstrap, in the sense that the system continues the bootstrap process even if there has been unauthorized modification of the components that are loaded, though this modification is recorded. In contrast, secure bootstrap terminates the bootstrap process when unauthorized code is detected.

Trusted bootstrap provides a basis for platform integrity measurement, but it does not prove all aspects of trustworthiness of a system. Various modules and application software which are loaded after the bootstrap process contribute to the trustworthiness of a platform. Similarly, even identical OS kernels can have different level of security if they have different configuration settings,[5] thus such configuration information needs to be measured. Measurement by TPM can be further extended into modules, applications, and configurations as follows:

- Run-time measurement at OS: While the system is running, various behavior, such as module loading or application execution, are monitored and measured by the operating system and recorded into PCRs. Integrity Measurement Architecture [24] realizes such measurement on the Linux kernel, and enhances the role of the TPM to measure not only the static state of a system but also the dynamic state.
- Run-time measurement at middleware: Various forms of middleware constitute today's computing systems. However, it is not practical to extend OS to measure integrity of data that are used by middleware, because it requires rebuilding the OS each time to support new middleware or data. It is preferable that each middleware layer measures data that is loaded or used by itself. An example of the measurement at middleware is a Java^{TM} Virtual Machine (JVM) that measures integrity of Java class files when each class is loaded.

---

[5] For example, the Security Hardened Linux kernel supports an option noenforce which disables its mandatory access controls.

- Measurement by agents: SHA-1 has its limitations when used as an integrity metric for policy or configuration files as any semantically meaningless change (such as insertion of a white-space character or re-ordering configuration properties in a text-based configuration file) will change the PCR values, resulting in unnecessary complexity when validating PCR values. A solution is to allow a software agent to measure policy and configuration files. Such an agent might be a local daemon which reads system configuration files, and composes a structured message, in canonical form, that describes the properties of the configuration (e.g., network settings, minimum password length, etc.). Similar to the middleware-level measurement, the chain of trust from the root-of-trust to agents must be maintained.

Care needs to be taken, though, that a chain of trust needs to be maintained from the CRTM to the component being measured. That is, in the case of measurement at middleware, (1) the integrity of the base code up to OS is measured in the trusted bootstrap sequence, (2) the integrity of a middleware is measured by OS, (3) and finally, the integrity of a file being loaded by the middleware is measured by the middleware. The record of measurements (stored in TPM) must prove that each component is measured by a component that is already measured, and the measurement record is not forgeable. Similarly, integrity of measurement agents need to be assured by OS (or any middleware which integrity is measured by OS) for such agent to be trustworthy.

15.2.2 Platform Integrity Reporting

Platform Integrity Reporting, or attestation, is the mechanism defined in the TCG specification to report integrity measurements stored in the PCRs. In the attestation process, the TPM signs the PCR values and an external 160-bit challenge (such as a nonce from a challenger to avoid replay attacks) using an RSA private key, the confidentiality of which is protected by the TPM. The attestation is an atomic, protected operation and the attestation signature cannot be forged by malicious software. Therefore, if the TPM is properly designed and implemented to adhere to the TCG specifications and the platform, including the initial bootstrap code, is properly integrated with the TPM, a remote verifier can have confidence in the integrity measurement reported by TPM.

Note that the platform may also send additional information in an attestation, and prove authenticity of such information using an attestation signature. For example, the list of modules and applications loaded on a platform is useful information to validate the state of a platform and can be included as part of the attestation process. In addition, an attestation signature over the PCRs which record the hash values of loaded modules and applications can prove which components have been actually measured and loaded, thus the challenger can verify authenticity of the modules listed by the PCR value.

15.3 Design Principles

This section discusses principles that are taken into account in the design of the attestation support in Web Services.

15.3.1 Fine Granular, Dynamic, Verifiable, and Efficient Attestation

Although TCG provides a hardware-based root of trust, platform integrity measurement, and reporting, it conveys little information compared with the complex state of a running system. In ws-Attestation, we aim to complement TCG attestation with fine granularity, dynamicity, and verifiability.

- Fine granularity: Trusted bootstrap, as defined in TCG, is designed to measure binary images of executables and components (e.g., BIOS configurations) during the bootstrap sequence. However, today's computing systems are complicated and include properties that cannot be meaningfully measured from their binary image. For example, behavior of Linux systems can significantly differ because of parameters specified in configuration files, even if they run on an identical OS kernel and the executable image is the same. It is not practical to measure configuration files with SHA-1 hash values; as most of the Linux configuration files are text based, the system administrator can easily break the integrity of a configuration files by adding a white-space or a blank line, even though the semantics of the configuration file is unchanged. Therefore, it is desirable that attestation can provide not only binary measurements but also semantic information, e.g., platform configuration retrieved by a software-based attestation agent.
- Dynamicity: Trusted bootstrap measures integrity of executable components up to the operating system. However, various executables and data loaded on the operating system and on the application layer affect behavior of a running system [24]. It is desirable that the ws-Attestation supports rich semantic attestation information whilst leveraging the root-of-trust mechanism defined in the TCG specification.
- Verifiability: TPM stores a measurement of components in PCRs in the form of composite hash values. Each composite hash value represents a list of components that are measured and "extended" into a PCR. Since the PCR extension mechanism allows one PCR to record a list of measurements, each PCR is used to measure many components; e.g., TCG defines minimum 16 PCRs for PC platforms, and 8 of them are reserved for measuring BIOS, while the other 8 are used for measuring the OS and the application layer. As the number of components measured by a PCR becomes bigger, and as the number of possible revisions of each component becomes bigger, the number of permutations that constitute a PCR value becomes factorial. It becomes very difficult for a verifier to validate the platform integrity from a PCR value.

- Efficiency: As the information conveyed and validated in the attestation process becomes more detailed, the attestation process can become overly expensive. On the other hand, it is not possible to simply separate attestation from the application context, because an entity sending an application message may not be in the same state as what was attested, thus may not be trusted anymore. It is desirable to increase efficiency while maintaining a cryptographic binding between attestation and application context.

15.3.2 Attestation Supporting Infrastructure

As a large number of vulnerabilities are found everyday [3], software vendors release security patches frequently. A typical security patch consists of multiple files that replace vulnerable components on the system. Each patch may fix one or more vulnerabilities. Thus, it becomes increasingly difficult to make educated decisions as to whether vulnerability is present in a particular file. A well-organized infrastructural support is, therefore, essential to enable validation measurement of each component on the system. Finally, each entity requesting attestation may not be capable of validating attestation information. We assume presence of trusted third-party validation services that validate attestation on behalf of requesters. We aim at defining communication models between the attestation requester, responder, and the validation service.

15.3.3 Privacy Protection

There are two types of privacy that need to be considered in attestation: identity and integrity of the platform being attested.

1. Identity privacy: It is one of the key objectives of TCG-defined attestation to protect the privacy of the platform identity while establishing trust. TCG defines two mechanisms for identity privacy: the Privacy-CA and Direct Anonymous Attestation (DAA). Since current TCG specifications already address identity privacy issues, we do not focus on the identity privacy in this chapter.
2. Integrity privacy: The most unique aspect of attestation is that it proves not only the identity of the platform but also the integrity and state of the platform. Although it is useful information for a legitimate verifier to judge trustworthiness of a platform, it can also become a source of vulnerability if distrusted parties are allowed to perform an attestation. By investigating the OS and application versions, an attacker can quickly deduce the most effective attack technique. Therefore, it is important, especially in cross-organizational transactions, that a platform can prove its trustworthiness to anonymous challengers without disclosing its configuration details. This is addressed in Sect. 15.6.3.

15.4 WS-Attestation Architecture

In order for WS-Attestation to be widely adopted and interoperable, it is important that WS-Attestation matches the model and framework of the existing WS-Security standards. Therefore, rather than invent a new protocol for attestation, we leverage existing Web Services standards and define a profile for supporting attestation on top of these standards.

Figure 15.1 shows architecture of attestation support on Web Services. The attestation requester is an entity who initiates attestation request. The validation service is a trusted third-party authority that validates (or sometimes performs) attestation on behalf of the requester. The validation service refers to the integrity database for validating integrity of each component measurement. The Privacy CA or the DAA issuer is responsible for certification of Attestation Identity Keys (AIKs) generated on attested platforms.

- Attested Platform (AP): The platform being attested implements various forms of integrity measurements and is capable of responding to an attestation request. It is also assumed that the attested platform implements appropriate security mechanisms and policies that is to be required by the attestation requester, and presence of such implementation can be measured

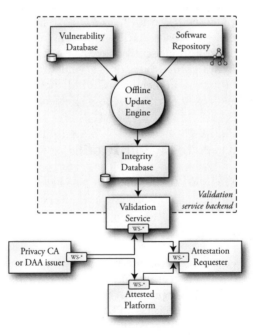

Fig. 15.1. WS-Attestation architecture and data flow. (Note WS-* denotes WS standards)

and reported in the attestation process. Typically, an attested platform is an entity which provides services through a Web service interface.

- Attestation Requester (AR): A party who is interested in platform integrity of the attested platform. An attestation requester may not be capable of validating integrity measurement by itself, and relies on a validation service to make judgments. Typically, an attested platform is an entity who is attempting to use a service provided by AP.
- Validation Service (VS): A trusted third-party service which issue attestation credentials each of which asserts a set of security properties that represents the state of a platform. Typically, VS verifies integrity measurements of an AP, derives a set of properties, and issues an attestation credential that asserts the properties. The VS needs to be trusted by both AP and the AR, in a sense that (1) AP has to trust VS that VS does not disclose configuration information of AP and (2) AR has to trust VS that VS correctly performs validation based on the criteria that is understood by both AR and VS.
- Integrity Database: It is a repository of black-list and white-list of metrics of known components and used by VS in validating the platform integrity measurements. The Integrity Database leverages external information sources, such as software repository and vulnerability database, to consolidate various information sources into a representation useful for VS.
- Identity Credential Issuer (Privacy CA or DAA Issuer): Identity credential issuer certifies identity of each AP by issuing a credential (e.g., an X.509 certificate) on an attestation identity key (AIK) of AP. In TCG specifications, it is important to prove that AP is a genuine trusted platform, which has a genuine TPM and implements CRTM, because trust on integrity measurement builds on the trust on the implementation of the platform.

15.5 ws-Security Attestation Profile

This section defines detailed ws-Attestation protocol as a profile on existing ws-Security standards.

15.5.1 Attestation Signature

ws-Security defines a flexible framework for protecting message integrity and confidentiality using various cryptographic algorithms. We define a new signature algorithm profile that represents TCG attestation signature.

The TCG attestation signature is an RSA signature value generated by an AIK over the concatenation of the target data and PCR values. The signature operation is an atomic operation performed by the TPM. The values in the PCRs and the use of the AIK are also protected by the TPM. Therefore, a TCG attestation signature proves that the signed PCR values are not compromised and represents the state of the attested platform at the time of signing. The signature value is considered a special form of the RSA signature. In order to handle the attestation signature in WS-Security as an XML digital signature, we define a new signature method that is identified by the URI and specified in the algorithm attribute of the SignatureMethod element of the XML digital signature.

In order to verify an attestation signature, the verifier needs to be informed of the TPM_QUOTE_INFO structure that is being signed. The TPM_QUOTE_INFO includes a 160-bit challenge and a composite hash of selected PCR values. In the proposed signature method, this structure is concatenated to the signature value that is included in the SignatureValue element as

$$\mathrm{TPM\_QUOTE\_INFO} || [\mathrm{TPM\_QUOTE\_INFO}]_{\mathrm{AIK}}$$

where $||$ denotes bitwise concatenation and $[x]_K$ denotes a signature over x with the key K).

In the XML Digital Signature, which defines extensible XML schema, it is also possible to add the TPM_QUOTE_INFO structure as a separate XML element. However, adding this structure to the signed value has two advantages. First, the same signature method can be used in protocols other than WS-Security where messages have no or little extensibility to include an additional element of information. Secondly, a provider-model crypto API such as Java Cryptographic Extension (JCE) supports different crypto algorithms under the same generic API. Such generic API cannot be extended to add an extra parameter without losing advantage of plugability. By including the TPM_QUOTE_INFO in the signature value, the crypto provider can receive the necessary information for verification of an attestation signature through a generic API.

15.5.2 Platform Measurement Description

The Platform Measurement Description (PMD) is structured data that describes the state of the platform in a fine-grained and semantic manner. A PMD includes the log of measurements which are recorded during the trusted bootstrap and run-time, and describes the components that have been measured by PCRs. Such a log allows the verifier to validate the integrity of each component running on the system. The verifier can also verify that the hash of all components in the log matches the PCR values in the attestation signature. Since the PCR values in the attestation signature are not forged, provided that the TPM is genuine and not in direct contact with an attacker who performs hardware-level attacks, we can use these values to verify integrity of the PMD in such a way that malicious software cannot cause false-positive validation.

In addition, a PMD may include non-TPM measurements such as semantic configuration parameters and properties of the platform which are tested or read by an *attestation agent* running on the platform. The integrity of such agent can be measured and reported in TPM-based measurement, providing a chain from the root-of-trust (CRTM) to the software-based measurements.

15.5.3 Attestation Credentials

As PMDs become richer, validating the PMD at each transaction may become a bottleneck. To make attestation more efficient, we propose the notion of attestation credentials. An attestation credential has properties that are asserted by an authority, and may have expiration period. A typical attestation credential is issued by a trusted authority that asserts some properties (e.g., `hasKnownVulnerability='false'` or the level of trustworthiness such as `trustLevel` $= \{1, \ldots, N\}$) regarding an attested platform. An attestation credential may bind a particular set of PCR values to the properties. Upon a challenge by an attestation requester, the attested platform may present the attestation credential along with the attestation signature signed over the challenge. (See Sect. 15.6 for more details) By verifying the challenge, the PCR values and attestation credentials, the attestation requester can verify, without knowing the details of measurement description, that the attested platform's current state is represented by the PCR values in the attestation signature, and the PCR values represent the properties that are asserted in the attestation credential. The attestation credential also protects integrity privacy of the attested platform from potentially distrusted attestation requesters, especially by utilizing PCR obfuscation technique described in Sect. 15.6.3.

An attestation credential can be represented in various forms; e.g., an X.509 attribute certificate and a SAML Assertion are well-standardized formats for this purpose.

15.6 ws-Attestation Token Exchange Model

In ws-Attestation, we propose exchanging attestation information in the form of security tokens, based on ws-Trust, a standard token exchange protocol [5]. By transforming attestation information into security tokens and exchanging them, we can communicate the state of the platform integrity efficiently, rather than performing the PMD-based attestation process for each message.

This section describes how we map attestation token exchange into ws-Trust, and then review logical token exchange patterns with observation on pros and cons of each pattern. Next, we propose a method to protect platform integrity privacy from misuse, and show an example message exchange scenario that integrates all proposed technology elements. Finally, we discuss advantages and disadvantages of several different mechanisms that bind attestation and messaging context.

15.6.1 Mapping to ws-Trust

Rather than defining a proprietary protocol for attestation, we leverage ws-Trust [5]. In a ws-Trust message, a requester may request a particular type of a security token, with an optional challenge. Upon a successful response, the responder returns the requested security token. The challenge in the request should be returned back to the requester with a responder's signature over it, thus proving that the response is fresh and is not replayed from past records.

ws-Trust defines generic framework for exchanging security tokens on Web services. The basic message structures in ws-Trust are `RequestSecurityToken` and `RequestSecrityTokenResponse`, which represent token request and response respectively. The basic structure of these messages are as follows:

```
RequestSecurityToken:          TokenType [, Supporting]
                               [, SignChallenge]
RequestSecurityTokenResponse:  TokenType, RequestedSecurityToken
                               [, SignChallengeResponse]
```

(Note that ws-Trust supports more flexible message structure, but we discuss only minimal elements that are relevant to our proposal, for the sake of simplicity.)

Here, the `TokenType` in `RequestSecurityToken` message specifies URI that represents particular token type, which the requester demands. An optional Supporting element provides a security token and provides additional claim information. An optional `SignChallenge` element contains a value, for which requester demands the responder to return a signature.

The `TokenType` in the `RequestSecurityTokenResponse` message is the type of actual returning token. The `RequestedSecurityToken` element contains the returning token, and `SignChallengeResponse` contains the responder's signature over the challenge.

In ws-Attestation we have three kinds of token request/response interactions that are illustrated below in an informal syntax:

1. Requesting full attestation information in PMD. This implies that an entity (i.e., usually an attestation requester) may ask for a PMD from an attested platform.

```
RequestSecurityToken:          TokenType=PMD_TokenType,
                               SignChallenge=nonce
RequestSecurityTokenResponse:  TokenType=PMD_TokenType,
                               RequestedSecurityToken=PMD,
                               SignChallengeResponse=[nonce]Sig
```

2. Requesting issuance of an attestation credential by presenting a PMD. This implies that an entity (i.e., an attested platform or attestation requester) may request a validation service to evaluate a PMD and to issue an attestation credential which represents the result of validation.

```
RequestSecurityToken:          TokenType=AC_TokenType,
                               Supporting=PMD
RequestSecurityTokenResponse:  TokenType=AC_TokenType,
                               RequestedSecurityToken
                                 =AttestationCredential
```

3. Requesting an attestation credential. This implies that an attestation requester may request for an attestation credential to the attested platform.

```
RequestSecurityToken:          TokenType=AC\_TokenType,
                               SignChallenge=nonce
RequestSecurityTokenResponse:  TokenType=AC_TokenType,
                               RequestedSecurityToken
                                 =AttestationCredential,
                               SignChallengeResponse=[nonce]Sig
```

Note that the responder in each interaction may be a trusted party itself, or a validation service which issues attestation credential for the attested platform.

In the following subsection, we illustrate four communication patterns using WS-Trust messages above.

15.6.2 Attestation Token Exchange Patterns

An attestation requester (AR), an attested platform (AP), and a verification service (VS) play central roles in an attestation, especially in verification of integrity of the attested platform. This section discusses four attestation models each of which is built on a different trust model and has advantages and disadvantages.

Direct Attestation

Figure 15.2a shows the Direct Attestation Model in which an attestation requester challenges the attested platform, which then returns the measurements back to the requester. The attestation requester validates information by itself, which has the advantage of not requiring that any other party need be trusted. This model has two notable disadvantages. (1) The attestation requester has to be capable of validating the attestation response and (2) the attested platform has to disclose all of its integrity information to the requester, which violates its integrity privacy to potentially distrusted attestation requesters.

Attestation with Pulled Validation

The second model (Fig. 15.2b) is similar to the direct attestation, except that the attestation requester consults the validation service to validate the PMD, and does not have to be capable of validating attestation. Integrity privacy of the attested platform is not protected in this model. An additional disadvantage is that this model may suffer from the performance bottleneck of the validation service, because for every attestation the validation service needs to be contacted.

Attestation with Pushed Validation

In the attestation with pushed validation model (Fig. 15.2c), the attested platform pushes the attestation to the validation service, to request an attestation credential. Upon a challenge from the attestation requester, the attested platform sends the attestation credential along with the attestation signature over the challenge, thus allowing the attestation requester to verify that the attested platform has the properties asserted in the credential. The advantages of this model are that (1) the attested platform does not have to disclose integrity information to the attestation requester; (2) the attestation requester does not have to be capable of validating attestations, (3) the performance bottleneck at the validation service is of less concern, because once an attestation credential is issued by the validation service, the attested platform can re-use the credential for subsequent transactions. Finally, the attested platform can choose which validation service to disclose its integrity information to, thus helping maintain the privacy of platform.

Delegated Attestation

In the delegated attestation model (Fig. 15.2d), the attestation requester requests a validation service to perform attestation on behalf of the requester, and then sends only the validation result in the form of a credential. The advantages of this model are that (1) the integrity privacy of the attested platform is protected; (2) the attestation requester does not have to be capable of validating attestation.

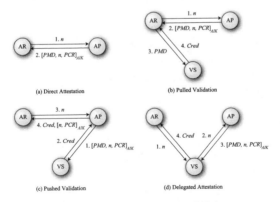

Fig. 15.2. Attestation Model

15.6.3 Privacy Protection—PCR Obfuscation

As we discussed in Sect. 15.3.3, attestation must address two types of privacy issue: identity and integrity. This chapter focuses on privacy of integrity information. One problem with attestation is that it provides detailed configuration information useful to an attacker, since they may use this to choose which attack tools will be effective against the platform, or when a platform has changed its configuration. The solution is to extend each PCR register with a random value at random times, yet at the same time recording these random values in the log. The resulting PCR value is unpredictable; provides no information about configuration details to the attacker. However, using the log of all PCR measurements, a legitimate verifier can still verify integrity of all other components.

In attestation models with a third-party validation service, the validation service may issue a credential to the measurement log including random extensions, and the credential asserts that some properties are true only when the attested platform has a particular set of PCR values. The attestation requester who receives the credential and the current PCR values cannot derive detailed configuration information from PCR values, but can verify that the current PCR values prove the properties asserted in the attestation credential.

Random extension of PCRs may be performed any number of times, provided the log of the extensions is maintained. Especially important is that the extension is performed more frequently than release of security patches components that run on the system. If a patch that fixes vulnerability is released, by observing PCRs before and after the patch release, an attacker can infer whether the patch is applied to the platform and will be able to make an educated decision on attack tactics.

15.6.4 Binding to Secure Conversational Context

Several approaches are possible to bind the state of an attested platform to an application context.

First, the attestation requester and the attested platform may establish a secure communication channel before attestation. WS-SecureConversation [4] defines a key exchange protocol to exchange a shared secret, which enables the binding between attestation and subsequent transactions by adding Hashed Message-Authentication Code (HMAC) to the messages. Care needs to be taken to protect the shared secret from being bound to distrusted attested platforms, not only must the attestation requester discard the shared secret when the attestation fails, but the attested platform must also discard the shared secret when its state changes. When the application is terminated, or the system is rebooted, the attested platform must exchange a new shared secret and start the attestation process again; it must be verified before a key exchange that the attested platform and its applications are implemented to relinquish shared secrets at termination. However, if the state of the attested platform changes without terminating the application, e.g., as a result of additional kernel module being loaded, this change is difficult to detect at the application layer. To prevent the use of a shared secret in a context that is not expected, the secret should expire and be renewed in a short window of time. This has the obvious side-effect of reducing performance.

Second, the attested platform can sign each application message with the attestation signature. The PCR composite hash value included in the attestation signature proves the state of the attested platform at the time of signing, and therefore that the properties asserted in the credential are still in effect. The freshness of the attestation signature has to be verifiable; e.g., by having a signature over the timestamp and the application message body. If the attestation signature is performed on a SOAP response message, the entire application protocol should include a challenge-and-response scheme. Although performing attestation signature on each message requires extra processing power on each party, this mechanism allows verifying the latest state of the attested platform without the need to maintain shared secret keys between peers. An attestation credential should be sent to the attestation requester when it needs a new credential for verifying the attestation signature, but the credential can be re-used until it expires or is revoked. An attestation credential may be valid even for multiple attested platforms as long as they have identical integrity measurements.

15.6.5 Example: Pushed Validation with PCR Obfuscation

WS-* specifications are defined to be building blocks that can be composed together to meet specific requirements. Likewise, WS-Attestation profile is intended to be a flexible set of building blocks. However, in order to illustrate its usage, we review an example scenario with one particular combination of the profile and a model.

In this scenario, the attested platform (AP) wants to prove its platform integrity to the attestation requester (AR), but does not trust AR in a sense that AR might misuse AP's configuration details. On the other hand, the AR requires verifying platform integrity of AP on each message exchange, to make sure that the state of AP has not been changed into unexpected state as of the time of message exchange. Presumably, attestation and validation are heavy processes and should be performed as few as possible.

In order to meet these requirements, we employ the following steps as shown in Fig. 15.3. (Note that for the sake of simplicity, we use only one PCR in this example while actual attestation may deal with multiple PCRs.)

1. In the integrity measurement phase, AP uses PCR obfuscation technique to randomize the values in PCR. After trusted bootstrap finishes, the original PCR value is PCR_i, where i is the number of components that have been measured by the PCR. An attacker may infer exact platform configuration from PCR_i. Then AP extends PCR_i with a random value

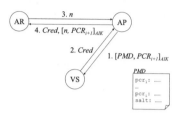

Fig. 15.3. Pushed validation with PCR obfuscation

salt, and also records the salt value into the measurement log. Resulting PCR_{i+1} is randomized and no detailed configuration can be inferred
from it.

2. AP requests VS to issue an attestation credential for the PMD (including
   the measurement log) of the AP. AP's intention is to present the attestation credential to any party to prove its security properties, without
   showing detailed configuration information.

3. When VS receives a PMD from AP, it first verifies integrity and trustworthiness of each component in the measurement log. The random value
   extended into PCR will be ignored in this phase, as it is marked as salt
   in PMD. Second, VS verifies that the hash chain derived from the measurement log, including the salt, matches the PCR value PCR_{i+1} in the
   attestation signature; i.e., the measurement log is not altered. Third, VS
   validates any additional properties measured by agents and recorded into
   PMD. Finally, VS generates an attestation credential which asserts validation result as particular security properties, and those properties are
   to be associated with particular set of PCR values, and then sends the
   credential back to AP. Note that the PCR value in the attestation credential is obfuscated with salt, thus nobody can infer the precise platform
   configuration from this value.

4. AP sends the attestation credential to AR to present its security properties and the PCR values that the properties are associated with. When
   sending application level messages, AP signs each message with the attestation signature with PCR_{i+1}, to prove the PCR values as of the
   signature.

5. Upon reception of each application level message, AR verifies the signature as if it is an ordinary digital signature over the message (which might
   also include a challenge from the AR), with the specific attestation signature algorithm as defined in this chapter. Then AR verifies that PCR_{i+1}

in the signature matches the PCR values in the attestation credentials, thus the security properties asserted in the credential is still effective as of the message generation.

15.7 Prototype

Figure 15.4 shows the architecture of the attested platform.

The integrity of the Linux OS is measured by the modified boot loader, and loadable modules and executables are measured by IMA [24]. The measurements (SHA1 hash values of files) are stored in PCRs as well as in the kernel-held store measurement log (SML).

Linux Intrusion Detection System (LIDS) [16] is used to improve the OS level security. LIDS consists of a kernel patch and administration tools which enhances the OS security by enforcing Mandatory Access Control (MAC) policies on operating system resources.

The prototype service is implemented in Java, and runs on the OSGi (Open Service Gateway initiative) [18] platform, which is an open-standard framework for Java-based applications and services. We extended IBM Service Management Framework (SMF) [14], one of the OSGi implementations, to measure each bundle JAR file when it is loaded and record the measurement into PCR and the log.

We also extended the ws-OSGi, a light-weight SOAP/ws-Security engine for OSGi platforms, to support the attestation signature and tokens described in Sect. 15.3. The attestation signature and verification operation are implemented as a crypto provider of Java Cryptography Extension (JCE) [15] and communicates with TPM via TCG Software Stack (TSS) [25]. The WS-Security engine can switch between an ordinary RSA signatures and the attestation signature simply by specifying the signature algorithm and the key storage as a set of options.

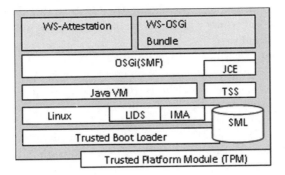

Fig. 15.4. Prototype attested platform

The attestation requester and the validation service are also implemented as services on the OSGi platform and communicate each other using the ws-Trust protocol. PMDs returned by the attested platform consists of stored measurement log in the XML format, while an attestation credentials are implemented as a SAML attribute assertion signed by the validation service. See the appendix for sample SOAP messages.

15.7.1 Validation Service and Integrity Database

The validation service implements a Web services interface which receives PMD and returns an attestation credential that contains the validation result of the PMD.

Our validation service prototype provides a database which is used for making informed decisions as to the integrity and quality of each component represented by an integrity metrics. This allows attestation verifiers to query the integrity and vulnerability of each measured component.

Many operating systems support mechanisms to distribute software components and patches in precompiled packages. For instance, RedHat's Package Manager (RPM) is the standard way of distributing and deploying components of RedHat's Linux distribution. When a different version is distributed, the executable images in the package almost always have a new hash value. Thus, the exact version of an RPM package can often be deduced from the hash values of its executable files.

A relatively recent endeavor in platform security is the Online Vulnerability and Assessment Language (OVAL) [17], sponsored by MITRE and supported by various operating system vendors, including RedHat [21]. OVAL is a language for expressing the preconditions necessary for a vulnerability to exist. Although the exact semantics differ depending on the operating system platform, the RedHat variant references particular RPM packages.

A hash database of RPM packages was built by simply unpackaging RPMs and generating hash values of all ELF executables. By parsing OVAL vulnerability descriptions and correlating these with RPM package versions, we would be able to deduce which executable hash values would indicate the presence of vulnerabilities.

We found that a verifier with a database like the one could verify the RPM-providence of all the executable images loaded. Furthermore, by cross-referencing with OVAL vulnerabilities, they could determine the presence of vulnerabilities, merely from the hash values.

The integrity database prototype is built on DB2 and queried by the validation service by SQL over JDBC. The integrity database currently supports RPM packages only; data entries are generated from RPM package repository for RedHat Enterprise Linux 3 (REL3) and OVAL repository for this OS, thus capable of validating integrity of REL3 systems (Fig. 15.5).

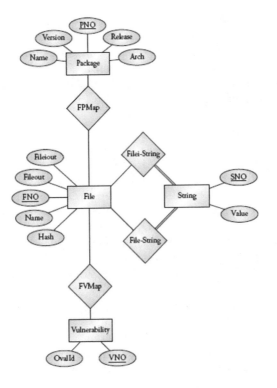

Fig. 15.5. Integrity database ER diagram

15.8 Discussion

In this section, we discuss how Ws-Attestation contributes in achieving our design objectives.

15.8.1 Performance of Attestation

We refer to an attestation with full PMD a "full attestation" and an attestation with an attestation token a "token-based attestation." Our proposal assumes that full attestation is required to fine granular validation of precise state of the attested platform, but it is expensive in terms of computational cost. So light-weight token-based attestations can replace full attestation in each application message. Therefore, performance difference between a full attestation and a token-based attestation signifies the performance improvement achieved by this proposal.

Time required for full attestation is $T_{f_a} = msg_{comp} + pmd_{comp} + as_{gen} + tr + ps + as_{ver} + pmd_{ver}$, where msg_{comp} and pmd_{comp} are the time required for composition of SOAP message and PMD respectively, as_{gen} is time required for generating an attestation signature, tr is time required for transmission, ps is time required for message parsing, as_{ver} is time required for verifying attestation signature, and pmd_{ver} is time required for validating PMD.

Time required for token-based attestation is $T_{t_a} = msg_{comp} + at_{comp} + as_{gen} + tr + ps + as_{ver} + at_{ver}$, where at_{comp} is the time required for composition of an attestation token, and at_{ver} is the time required for verifying an attestation token.

Therefore, performance difference between a full attestation and a token-based attestation is $(pmd_{comp} - at_{comp}) + (pmd_{ver} - at_{ver})$. The performance difference between pmd_{comp} and at_{comp} usually depends on how much overhead it costs to collect information for PMD. Since a PMD consists of measurement log and other information, it requires access to stored measurement log in files and BIOS memory. Caching or precollection mechanisms may be used to optimize composition of PMD. On the other hand, composition of an attestation token does not require much processing, since the same attestation token can be reused for every transaction.

Verification of a PMD takes significantly more time than verification of an attestation token, as it requires accessing validation database for looking up semantics of measurement hash values. In our first prototype, verification of a PMD with approximately 100 hash values took more than a minute, because of the overhead of the 100 database queries. This was significantly reduced by using stored procedure to look up all hash values in one query. Still, access to database takes about a second in our environment. Validation of an attestation token is quicker, as it does not require any network access but just parsing the token and checking the properties stored in it. Therefore, we can safely say that the token-based attestation is quicker than the full attestation.

Although it can provide fine-granularity, token-based attestation does not provide much of performance benefit compared to the binary attestation of TCG, since most performance overhead is caused by the generation of an attestation signature, which is a 2048 bits RSA signature generated by TPM. Additional performance improvement, in a long-running transaction, can be achieved by adopting WS-SecureConversation [4] to bind the attestation token into the secure messaging context using a light-weight symmetric key signature algorithm (such as HMAC).

15.8.2 Vulnerability Detection

The architecture combining TCG trusted boot, IMA, allows measuring all native applications running on the platform. In addition, supporting measurement at the OSGi framework allows each JAR file to be measured when being loaded. Therefore, proposed scheme allows fine-grained and dynamic measurement of the platform integrity, which enables detection of vulnerabilities or malicious software in timely manner. If malicious code runs after an attestation credential is obtained, the presence of the malicious code can be detected from the latest PCR value included in the attestation signature. In addition, the platform measurement description (PMD) in our architecture can be easily extended to include any finer-granular information measured by software agents. Examples of non-TPM measurement include the Java security policy, or system properties such as the minimum length and the maximum lifetime of the administrator's password.

However, still some problems exist in the current proposal.

First, it provides weak binding between integrity measurements and an entity involved in a transaction. For example, when an attestation proves that the platform runs a genuine application and a (potentially) malicious application, it is difficult to assure which application is the originator of the messages. This leads to the "all-or-nothing" policy, in which all applications cannot be trusted when there is any potentially malicious components present on the same platform. Strong isolation of execution environment for each application and binding between attestation and the execution environment would be required to prevent such overly strict policy.

Second, the current architecture only deals with the trustworthiness of known components that are either in a black-list or in a white-list. However, in reality, many Web services are running custom-made applications which potentially have unknown vulnerabilities. One of the potential solutions for this problem is to have a distributed trusted computing base (TCB) among services. That is, all services run a common middleware (or one of a few common middleware) as a distributed TCG, which can confine application behavior with a given policy. Through integrity attestation, each service proves not only integrity of the TCB but also which policy is being enforced. Trusted Virtual Domains [7, 29] envisions such an architecture for establishing trust-based distributed coalition.

15.8.3 Attestation Supporting Infrastructure

The current prototype uses OVAL database as the source of vulnerability information. An OVAL document consists of a set of tests for detecting vulnerabilities. An OVAL document consists of two type of tests: to cheek whether particular components exist on the platform and to find the configuration parameters of the platform. Combination of these two types of tests enables to make intelligent decision on vulnerability presence. We utilize OVAL only as a source of the vulnerability information, thus the information about configuration parameters is not utilized. This introduces false-positives, since some vulnerability may exist only when a particular version of the component runs with particular configuration parameters. The other problem of OVAL is that although it is a comprehensive vulnerability database which is based on unique numbering of vulnerability in Common Vulnerabilities and Exposures (CVE), the support of operating systems is limited. OVAL scheme consists of two parts: the core scheme which is generic among all platforms and platform specific schemas. At the time of writing this chapter, schemas for Cisco IOS,

UNIX, HP-UX, Debian Linux, Red Hat Linux, Apple Macintosh, Sun Solaris, and Microsoft Windows were released. However, vulnerability definition of only three platforms, i.e., Windows, Red Hat Linux and Sun Solaris, were released. Since timely update of maintenance of vulnerability information requires contribution of OS vendors, we still need to wait for emergence of the eco-system for the supporting infrastructure to mature.

15.9 Related Work

Related work includes previous efforts to secure Web services interactions and establish trust relationship between parties measuring, reporting, and verifying system integrity.

As discussed earlier, various WS-* specifications have been defined or being defined [13] for protecting interaction on Web services and communicating trust models. However, current specifications are concerned only with identity-based trust model and do not deal with platform integrity–based trust. WS-Attestation leverages flexible WS-Trust framework to communicate platform integrity metrics and assertions in an effective manner.

WS-Policy [2] is a generic framework for expressing policies of web services, and WS-SecurityPolicy[10] defines a set of vocabulary for expressing policies on how to protect Web services messages. They are concerned with messaging level security, but new set of vocabulary can be defined in future for expressing requirements on state of the platform which behaves on behalf of the service provider and the requester.

The AEGIS system [1] provides secure bootstrapping architecture on PC system that maintains integrity chain from the lowest trustable layer of a system. Secure bootstrap is different from trusted bootstrap in a sense that its objective is not to allow remote verification of the system integrity; in the secure bootstrapping, the system aborts bootstrap process upon integrity check failure.

Sailer et al. leverages TCG in Integrity Measurement Architecture (IMA) [24], to enhance the role of the TPM to measure not only static state of a system but also dynamic state. IMA is implemented as a Linux Security Module to measure each executable, library, or kernel module upon loading and record the SHA1 hash values into TPM and the log. As mentioned earlier, we leverage TCG and IMA to build Linux-based attested platforms.

The work of Sailer [23] utilizes the integrity measurements and attestation to protect remote access points and to enforce corporate security policies on remote clients in a seamless and scalable manner. Cisco and IBM have announced an enterprise network security solution based on their current products: Cisco's Network Admission Control (NAC) protects the network infrastructure by enforcing security policy compliance on all devices seeking to access network computing resources. The integrated security solution leverages IBM Tivoli Compliance Manager (TSCM) which inspects device configurations, thus denies network access to the devices that are not compliant to the corporate security policies. The compliance checks are based on software agents (e.g., whether anti-virus software is up to date, or the OS is running the latest software patches), but NAC's extensible architecture would allow incorporating further attestation mechanisms in the future.

Terra [6] realizes isolated trusted platforms on top of a virtual machine monitor, and allows attestation by a binary image of each virtual machine, e.g., virtual disks, virtual BIOS, PROM, and VM descriptions.

Recent efforts on mitigating drawbacks of TCG attestation include a proposal [8], which leverages language-based security and virtual machines to enable semantic attestation, e.g., attestation of dynamic, arbitrary, and system properties as well as behavior of the portable code.

Property-based attestation [22] proposes an attestation model with a trusted third party that translates low-level integrity information into a set of properties.

This chapter leverages prior work and defines substantial mapping to the ws-Security framework. Our contribution includes (1) extension of integrity measurement architecture [24] into upper layers, especially Java applications, (2) definition of ws-Attestation profile that works on top of existing ws-Security standards with the ability to attest fine-grained system configuration while protecting integrity privacy, and (3) a proposal for attestation supporting infrastructure.

15.10 Conclusion and Future Direction

This chapter presents our proposal on ws-Security support for attestation. Although attestation is a generic technique to allow remote verification of platform integrity, our proposal is based on TCG, which was the most promising and available technology at time of writing. This chapter shows a set of profiles that seamlessly works on existing ws-Security standards. On top of the ws-Trust protocol, attestation information can be exchanged as two forms of tokens; i.e., the platform measurement description that conveys fine granular and semantic information, and the attestation credential that binds low-level integrity measurement to high-level property assertion. Using these tokens, the attested platform can prove its properties to requesters with little performance overhead. We also take privacy protection into account, so that the configuration privacy of the attested platform is protected from potentially distrusted challengers and allows only high-level properties to be reported. The integrity database, which incorporates information on binary measurements and vulnerabilities of deployed package software, provides base for efficient, accurate, and fine-granular attestation validation.

References

1. W.A. Arbaugh, J. Farber, and J.M. Smith. A secure and reliable bootstrap architecture. In *IEEE Computer Society Conference on Security and Privacy*, pp. 65–71, 1997.
2. BM, BEA Systems, Microsoft, SAP AG, Sonic Software, and VeriSign. Web services policy framework (ws-policy), Sep 2004.
3. Cert/cc statistics 1988-2005. Accessed 2005. http://www.cert.org/stats/cert_stats.html.
4. IBM et al. Web services secure conversation language (ws-secureconversation), Feb 2005.
5. IBM et al. Web services trust language (ws-trust), Feb 2005.
6. T. Garfinkel, B. Pfaff, J. Chow, M. Rosenblum, and D. Boneh. Terra: A virtual machine-based platform for trusted computing. In *19th ACM Symposium on Operating Systems Principles*, 2003.
7. John L. Griffin, Trent Jaeger, Ronald Perez, Reiner Sailer, Leendert van Doorn, and Ramon Caceres. Trusted virtual domains: Toward secure distributed services. In *Workshop on Hot Topics in System Dependability*, 2005.
8. V. Haldar, D. Chandra, and M. Franz. Semantic remote attestation — a virtual machine directed approach to trusted computing. In *3rd Virtual Machine Research and Technology Symposium*, May 2004.
9. IBM. Web services federation language (ws-federation), Jul 2003.
10. IBM, Microsoft, RSA Security, and VeriSign. Web services security policy language (ws-securitypolicy).
11. IBM, BEA Systems, Microsoft, SAP AG, Computer Associates, Sun Microsystems, and webMethods. Web services metadata exchange (ws-metadataexchange), Sep 2004. http://www-128.ibm.com/developerworks/library/specification/ws-mex/.
12. IBM, BEA Systems, Microsoft, Arjuna, and Hitachi. Web services transactions specifications, Nov 2004.
13. Microsoft IBM. Security in a web services world: A proposed architecture and roadmap, Apr 2002. http://www-128.ibm.com/developerworks/library/specification/ws-secmap/.
14. Ibm service management framework. http://www-306.ibm.com/software/wireless/smf/.
15. Java cryptography extension (jce). http://java.sun.com/products/jce/.
16. Linux intrusion detection system (lids). http://www.lids.org/.
17. Open vulnerability and assessment language. http://oval.mitre.org/.
18. OSGi alliance. http://www.osgi.org/.
19. W3C Recommendation. Soap version 1.2, Jun 2004. http://www.w3.org/TR/soap/.
20. W3C Candidate Recommendation. Web services description language (wsdl) version 2.0 part 0: Primer, Mar 2006. http://www.w3.org/TR/2006/CR-wsdl20-primer-20060327/.
21. Redhat enterprise linux. http://www.redhat.com/.
22. A. Sadeghi and C. Stüble. Property-based attestation for computing platforms: Caring about properties, not mechanisms. In *2004 Workshop on New Security Paradigms (NSPW 2004)*, pages 67–77, 2004.

23. R. Sailer, T. Jaeger, X. Zhang, and L. Van Doorn. Attestation-based policy enforcement for remote access. In *11th ACM Conference on Computer and Communications Security*, pages 308–317, Oct 2004.

24. R. Sailer, X. Zhang, T. Jaeger, and L. van Doorn. Design and implementation of a tcg-based integrity measurement architecture. In *13th USENIX Security Symposium*, pages 223–238, Aug 2004.

25. Tcg software stack specification version 1.2. `http://www.trustedcomputing.org/specs/TSS`.

26. Tcg specification architecture overview, revision 1.2. Trusted Computing Group, Apr 2004. Available at `https://www.trustedcomputinggroup.org/groups/TCG_1_0_Architecture_Overview.pdf`.

27. Trusted computing platform alliance main specification, version 1.1b. Trusted Computing Group, Feb 2002. `https://www.trustedcomputinggroup.org/specs/TPM`.

28. Uddi spec technical committee draft, version 3.02, Oct 2004. `http://www.oasis-open.org/`.

29. Yuji Watanabe, Sachiko Yoshihama, Takuya Mishina, Michiharu Kudo, , and Hiroshi Maruyama. Bridging the gap between inter-communication boundary and inside trusted components. In *11th European Symposium on Research in Computer Security(ESORICS 2006)*, LNCS. Springer, 2006.

30. Web service security: Soap messaging security 1.0 (ws-security 2004). OASIS Standard 200401, Mar 2004.

Appendix

```
1   <S:Envelope xmlns:S="..." xmlns="../secext" xmlns:wsu="../utility"
2       xmlns:wst="...">
3       <S:Header>
4           <wss:Security>
5               <wsse:BinarySecurityToken wsu:Id="targetAIK"
6                   ValueType="...X509v3">
7                   <!--... Binary encoded certificate of the AIK ... -->
8               </wsse:BinarySecurityToken>
9               <tcg:AttestationToken Id="myMeasurement">
10                  <tcg:Measurement ValueType="tcg:PCRComposite"
11                      Encoding="xsd:hexBinary">
12                      00020A010000003C770FDFE8CD1CA4AEE432B818DBE...
13                  </tcg:Measurement>
14                  <wsse:SecurityTokenReference>
15                      <wsse:Reference URI="#targetAIK" />
16                  </wsse:SecurityTokenReference>
17              </tcg:AttestationToken>
18              <ds:Signature>
19                  <ds:SignedInfo>
20                      <ds:CanonicalizationMethod
21                          Algorithm="http://www.w3.org/2001/10/xml-exc-c14n#" />
22                      <ds:SignatureMethod
23                          Algorithm="http://trustedcomputinggroup.org/2005/03/
24                          rsa_pcr" />
25                      <ds:Reference URI="#body">
26                          <ds:Transforms>
27                              <ds:Transform
28                                  Algorithm="http://www.w3.org/2001/10/xml-
```

```
29                          exc - c14n #"  />
30              </ds:Transforms>
31              <ds:DigestMethod
32                  Algorithm="http://www.w3.org/2000/09/xmldsig
33                  #sha1"  />
34              <ds:DigestValue>
35                  LyLsF094hPi4wPU ...
36              </ds:DigestValue>
37          </ds:Reference>
38      </ds:SignedInfo>
39      <ds:SignatureValue>MC0CFFrVLtRlk=...</ds:SignatureValue>
40      <ds:KeyInfo>
41          <wsse:SecurityTokenReference>
42              <wsse:Reference URI="#myMeasurement" />
43          </wsse:SecurityTokenReference>
44      </ds:KeyInfo>
45      </ds:Signature>
46      </wss:Security>
47      <!-- ... -->
48  </S:Header>
49  <S:Body>
50      <wst:RequestSecurityToken>
51          <wst:TokenType>saml:Assertion</wst:TokenType>
52          <wst:SignChallenge>
53              <wst:Challenge>Huehf...</wst:Challenge>
54          </wst:SignChallenge>
55          <wst:Supporting>
56              <xxx:PlatformMeasurementDescription>
57                  <!-- platform measurement description -->
58              </xxx:PlatformMeasurementDescription>
59          </wst:Supporting>
60      </wst:RequestSecurityToken>
61  </S:Body>
62 </S:Envelope>
```

Listing 15.1. Message requesting for an Attestation Credential

```
1  <S:Envelope xmlns:S="..." xmlns=".../secext" xmlns:wsu=".../utility"
2      Xmlns:wst="...">
3      <S:Header>
4          <wss:Security>
5              <wsse:BinarySecurityToken wsu:Id="vpKey"
6                  ValueType="...X509v3">
7                  ... Binary encoded certificate of the Verification
8                  Services Key
9              </wsse:BinarySecurityToken>
10             <ds:Signature>
11                 <ds:SignedInfo>
12                     <ds:CanonicalizationMethod
13                         Algorithm="http://www.w3.org/2001/10/xml-exc-
14                         c14n#"  />
15                     <ds:SignatureMethod
16                         Algorithm="http://www.w3.org/2000/09/xmldsig#
17                         rsa-sha1"  />
18                     <ds:Reference URI="#body">
19                         <ds:Transforms>
20                             <ds:Transform
21                                 Algorithm="http://www.w3.org/2001/10/xml-exc-
22                                 c14n#"  />
23                         </ds:Transforms>
24                         <ds:DigestMethod
25                             Algorithm="http://www.w3.org/2000/09/xmldsig#
```

```
26                          sha1" />
27                        <ds:DigestValue>
28                            LyLsF094hPi4wPU ...
29                        </ds:DigestValue>
30                      </ds:Reference>
31                    </ds:SignedInfo>
32                    <ds:SignatureValue>MC0CFFrVLtRlk=...</ds:SignatureValue>
33                    <ds:KeyInfo>
34                        <wsse:SecurityTokenReference>
35                            <wsse:Reference URI="#vpKey" />
36                        </wsse:SecurityTokenReference>
37                    </ds:KeyInfo>
38                </ds:Signature>
39          </wss:Security>
40      </S:Header>
41      <S:Body>
42          <wst:RequestSecurityTokenResponse>
43              <wst:TokenType>saml:Assertion</wst:TokenType>
44              <wst:SignChallengeResponse>
45                  <wst:Challenge>Huehf...</wst:Challenge>
46              </wst:SignChallengeResponse>
47              <wst:RequestedSecurityToken>
48                  <saml:Assertion saml:AssertionID="..." saml:Issuer="..."
49                      saml:IssueInstant="...">
50                      <saml:AttributeStatement>
51                          <saml:Attribute saml:AttributeName="trusted">
52                              <saml:AttributeValue>
53                                  true
54                              </saml:AttributeValue>
55                          </saml:Attribute>
56                          <saml:Attribute saml:AttributeName="pcr">
57                              <saml:AttributeValue>
58                                  00020A010000003C770FDFE8CD1CA4AEE432B818DBE
59                              </saml:AttributeValue>
60                          </saml:Attribute>
61                      </saml:AttributeStatement>
62                  </saml:Assertion>
63              </wst:RequestedSecurityToken>
64          </wst:RequestSecurityTokenResponse>
65      </S:Body>
66  </S:Envelope>
```

Listing 15.2. Response message for returning a SAML assertion as an Attestation Credential

Index

Printing: Krips bv, Meppel
Binding: Stürtz, Würzburg